MOON

D0485890

Montréal & Québec City

SACHA JACKSON

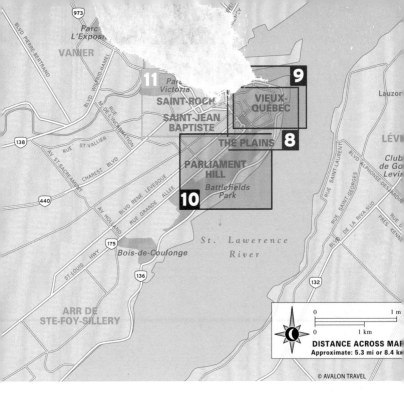

Québec City Maps

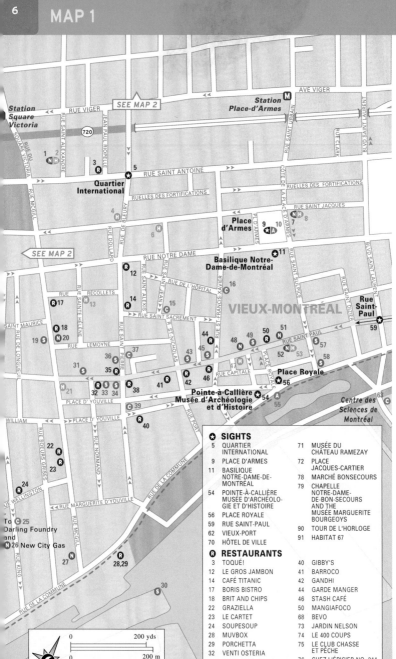

AVE VIGER

Station Square Victoria

RUE VIGER

SEE MAP 2

Station Place-d'Armes M

RUE SAINT URBAIN

RUE CLARK

BLVD SAINT LAURENT

RUE SAINT ALEXANDRE

RUE DU SQUARE VICTORIA

JEAN PAUL RIOPELLE

720

1 N

3 R

5 RUE SAINT ANTOINE

Quartier International

RUELLES DES FORTIFICATIONS

RUE MCGILL

RUE DE BLEURY

RUE SAINT JACQUES

CÔTE DE LA PLACE D'ARMES

RUELLES DES FORTIFICATIONS

4

6

Place d'Armes

9 10

7 N

8

SEE MAP 2

RUE DOLLARD

RUE NOTRE DAME

PLACE D'ARMES

Basilique Notre-Dame-de-Montréal

11

RUE SAINT SULPICE

BLVD SAINT LAURENT

12 R

RUE SAINT JEAN

RUE SAINT ALEXIS

RUE DE L'HÔPITAL

16

Rue Saint-Paul

RUE RÉCOLLETS

17 R

13

14 R

15

RUE SAINT SACREMENT

RUE ST-FRANÇOIS-XAVIER

VIEUX-MONTRÉAL

RUE SAINT DIZIER

SAINT MAURICE

RUE SAINTE HÉLÈNE

18 R

20 N

RUE ST-NICOLAS

RUE SAINT PIERRE

RUE LEMOYNE

44

48 49

50 51

52 N 53

57

59

RUE SAINT PAUL

19

36 37

43 45

46

41

42

55

56

58

Place Royale

31

35

38

32 33 34

39

40

PLACE D'YOUVILLE

PLACE D'YOUVILLE

Pointe-à-Callière Musée d'Archéologie et d'Histoire 54

RUE DU PORT

Centre des Sciences de Montréal

63

WILLIAM

RUE SŒURS GRISES

RUE NORMAND

22

23

24

RUE WELLINGTON

RUE MARGUERITE D'YOUVILLE

RUE DE LA COMMUNE

To 25 Darling Foundry and N 26 New City Gas

RUE MCGILL

RUE KING

27

28,29

30

RUE DE LA COMMUNE

⊕ SIGHTS

5	QUARTIER INTERNATIONAL	71	MUSÉE DU CHÂTEAU RAMEZAY
9	PLACE D'ARMES	72	PLACE JACQUES-CARTIER
11	BASILIQUE NOTRE-DAME-DE-MONTRÉAL	78	MARCHÉ BONSECOURS
54	POINTE-À-CALLIÈRE MUSÉE D'ARCHÉOLOGIE ET D'HISTOIRE	79	CHAPELLE NOTRE-DAME-DE-BON-SECOURS AND THE MUSÉE MARGUERITE BOURGEOYS
56	PLACE ROYALE	90	TOUR DE L'HORLOGE
59	RUE SAINT-PAUL	91	HABITAT 67
62	VIEUX-PORT		
70	HÔTEL DE VILLE		

® RESTAURANTS

3	TOQUÉ!	40	GIBBY'S
12	LE GROS JAMBON	41	BARROCO
14	CAFÉ TITANIC	42	GANDHI
17	BORIS BISTRO	44	GARDE MANGER
18	BRIT AND CHIPS	46	STASH CAFÉ
22	GRAZIELLA	50	MANGIAFOCO
23	LE CARTET	68	BEVO
24	SOUPESOUP	73	JARDIN NELSON
28	MUVBOX	74	LE 400 COUPS
29	PORCHETTA	75	LE CLUB CHASSE ET PÊCHE
32	VENTI OSTERIA	76	CHEZ L'ÉPICIER NO. 311
35	OLIVE & GOURMANDO	77	LE BREMNER
38	LE MARCHÉ DE LA VILLETTE		

0		200 yds
0		200 m

DISTANCE ACROSS MAP
Approximate: 1 mi or 1.6 km

NIGHTLIFE
1 WUNDERBAR
7 TERRASSE PLACE D'ARMES
20 LE CONFESSIONAL
26 NEW CITY GAS
27 LES SOEURS GRISES
48 DOLCETTO
51 LE PHILÉMON BAR
52 VERSES SKY
60 LE VELVET SPEAKEASY
64 TAVERNE GASPAR
66 LES DEUX PIERROTS
67 PUB ST-PAUL
87 TERRASSES BONSECOURS

ARTS AND CULTURE
15 DHC/ART
16 CENTAUR THEATRE
25 DARLING FOUNDRY
37 PHI CENTRE
39 CENTRE D'HISTOIRE DE MONTRÉAL
63 CENTRE DES SCIENCES DE MONTRÉAL AND IMAX TELUS THEATRE
81 SIR GEORGE-ÉTIENNE CARTIER NATIONAL HISTORIC SITE OF CANADA
83 JACQUES-CARTIER PIER
84 CIRQUE DU SOLEIL
89 CIRQUE ÉLOIZE

SPORTS AND ACTIVITIES
10 CALÈCHES–PLACE D'ARMES
55 LACHINE CANAL BIKE PATH
61 ÇA ROULE MONTRÉAL
69 CALÈCHES–PLACE JACQUES-CARTIER
85 LE BATEAU-MOUCHE
86 BONSECOURS BASIN
88 SAUTE MOUTONS

SHOPS
19 CLUSIER HABILLEUR
30 BOTA BOTA
31 CAHIER D'EXERCICES
33 MICHEL BRISSON
34 ESPACE PEPIN
36 ZONE ORANGE
43 REBORN
45 U&I
49 ROLAND DUBUC JOAILLIER
57 SSENSE
58 SCANDINAVE LES BAINS VIEUX-MONTRÉAL

HOTELS
2 W HOTEL
4 HÔTEL LE ST-JAMES
6 LHOTEL MONTRÉAL
8 PLACE D'ARMES HÔTEL AND SUITES
13 HÔTEL GAULT
21 HÔTEL ST-PAUL
47 LE PETIT HÔTEL
53 HÔTEL NELLIGAN
65 AUBERGE DU VIEUX-PORT
80 PIERRE DU CALVET
82 L'HÔTEL CHAMPS-DE-MARS

SIGHTS

1	GRAND SÉMINAIRE DE MONTRÉAL	22	MUSÉE MCCORD
11	CENTRE CANADIEN D'ARCHITECTURE	52	DORCHESTER SQUARE
15	MUSÉE DES BEAUX-ARTS DE MONTRÉAL	54	CATHÉDRALE MARIE-REINE-DU-MONDE
21	MCGILL UNIVERSITY	56	PLACE VILLE-MARIE
		61	CENTRE BELL

DISTANCE ACROSS MAP
Approximate: 1.4 mi or 2.2 km

0 — 200 yds
0 — 200 m

RESTAURANTS

4	QING HUA DUMPLING	50	QUEUE DE CHEVAL
6	AVESTA	51	EUROPEA
9	KAZU	68	TUCK SHOP
10	LE PARIS	70	PIZZERIA GEPPETTO
24	BURRITOVILLE	71	LIVERPOOL HOUSE
25	BOUSTAN	72	BURGUNDY LION
26	CAFÉ NESPRESSO	73	JOE BEEF
28	M:BRGR	78	LE BOUCAN
32	CAFÉ MYRIADE	80	BONNY'S
33	GARAGE BEIRUT	81	NORA GRAY
42	DUNN'S FAMOUS DELI	82	GRIFFINTOWN CAFÉ

NIGHTLIFE

34	NEWTOWN	48	BRUTOPIA
43	DOMINION SQUARE TAVERN	49	LE CINQ
47	HURLEY'S IRISH PUB	57	ALTITUDE 737
		65	LE BAR SOLEIL

ARTS AND CULTURE

5	CINEPLEX ODEON	41	CINEMA BANQUE SCOTIA
12	CANADIAN GUILD OF CRAFTS	66	PARISIAN LAUNDRY
20	REDPATH MUSEUM OF NATURAL HISTORY	76	CORONA THEATRE

SPORTS AND ACTIVITIES

38	YMCA	62	MONTRÉAL CANADIENS
44	MANSFIELD ATHLETIC CLUB	64	LE ATRIUM 1000

To **C** 20
Redpath Museum
of Natural History

21

**McGill
University**

To **C** 22
Musée McCord →

**Musée des Beaux-
Arts de Montréal**

SEE MAP 3

RUE SHERBROOKE OUEST

BLVD DE MAISONNEUVE OUEST

**Station
Peel**

To **S** 46
Centre Eaton →

RUE SAINTE CATHERINE OUEST ▶▶

PL DOMINION

CENTRE-VILLE

**Dorchester
Square**

**Place
Ville-Marie**

BLVD RENÉ LÉVESQUE OUEST

AVÉ OVERDALE ▶▶

**Station
Lucien l'Allier**

Place
du
Canada

**Cathédrale Marie
Reine-du-Monde**

RUE BELMO

AVÉ DES CANADIENS DE MONTRÉAL ▶▶

Centre Bell

**Station
Bonaventure**

SEE MAP 1

RUE SAINT ANTOINE OUEST

RUE TORRANCE

RUE SAINT JACQUES OUEST ▶▶

RUE NOTRE DAME OUEST

RUE BARRÉ

S SHOPS

8	MEDIAPHILE	39	LES COURS MONT ROYAL
13	MONA MOORE	40	RUE SAINTE-CATHERINE
14	LES CRÉATEURS		
16	HOLT RENFREW	45	LA MAISON SIMONS
17	TIFFANY & CO.	46	CENTRE EATON
23	PARAGRAPHE	58	MURALE
27	MARIE SAINT PIERRE	67	HARRICANA
29	BLEU COMME LE CIEL	69	RETRO-VILLE
30	CHEAP THRILLS	74	GRAND CENTRAL
35	LA MAISON OGILVY	75	BEIGE
36	STUDIO BEAUTÉ DU MONDE	77	RUE NOTRE-DAME WEST
37	BROWNS	79	L'ECUYER ANTIQUES

H HOTELS

2	CHÂTEAU VERSAILLES	53	L'HÔTEL LE CRYSTAL
3	LE MÉRIDIEN VERSAILLES	55	FAIRMONT QUEEN ELIZABETH
4	L'HÔTEL DU FORT	59	L'HÔTEL ESPRESSO
18	RITZ-CARLTON	60	LE PETIT PRINCE
19	SOFITEL MONTRÉAL	63	MARRIOTT CHÂTEAU CHAMPLAIN
21	HÔTEL LE GERMAIN		

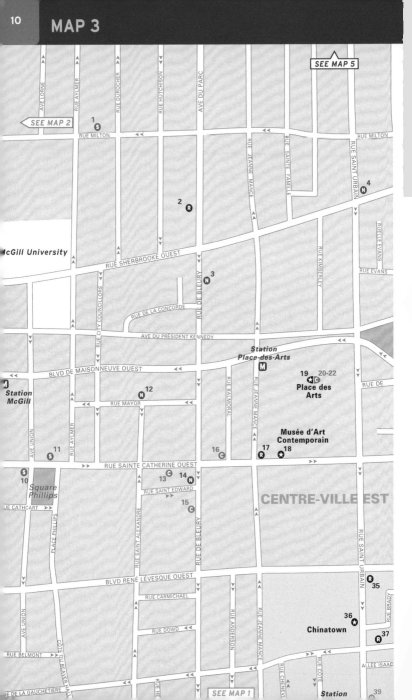

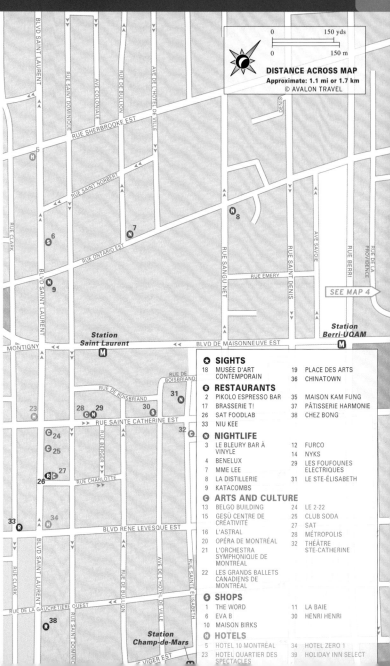

DISTANCE ACROSS MAP
Approximate: 1.1 mi or 1.7 km
© AVALON TRAVEL

SEE MAP 4

Station
Saint Laurent

Station
Berri-UQAM

Station
Champ-de-Mars

☉ SIGHTS
18	MUSÉE D'ART CONTEMPORAIN	19	PLACE DES ARTS
		36	CHINATOWN

☉ RESTAURANTS
2	PIKOLO ESPRESSO BAR	35	MAISON KAM FUNG
17	BRASSERIE T!	37	PÂTISSERIE HARMONIE
26	SAT FOODLAB	38	CHEZ BONG
33	NIU KEE		

☉ NIGHTLIFE
3	LE BLEURY BAR À VINYLE	12	FURCO
4	BENELUX	14	NYKS
7	MME LEE	29	LES FOUFOUNES ÉLECTRIQUES
8	LA DISTILLERIE	31	LE STE-ÉLISABETH
9	KATACOMBS		

☉ ARTS AND CULTURE
13	BELGO BUILDING	24	LE 2-22
15	GESÙ CENTRE DE CRÉATIVITÉ	25	CLUB SODA
16	L'ASTRAL	27	SAT
20	OPÉRA DE MONTRÉAL	28	MÉTROPOLIS
21	L'ORCHESTRA SYMPHONIQUE DE MONTRÉAL	32	THÉÂTRE STE-CATHERINE
22	LES GRANDS BALLETS CANADIENS DE MONTRÉAL		

☉ SHOPS
1	THE WORD	11	LA BAIE
6	EVA B	30	HENRI HENRI
10	MAISON BIRKS		

☉ HOTELS
5	HOTEL 10 MONTRÉAL	34	HOTEL ZERO 1
23	HOTEL QUARTIER DES SPECTACLES	39	HOLIDAY INN SELECT

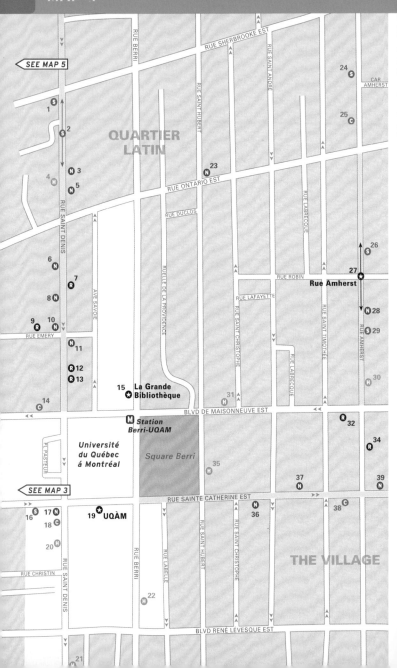

SEE MAP 5

RUE BERRI

RUE SHERBROOKE EST

RUE SAINT ANDRÉ

24 S

CAR AMHERST

25 C

RUE SAINT HUBERT

QUARTIER LATIN

1 S

2 S

3 N

4 H

5 N

23 N

RUE ONTARIO EST

RUE DUCLOS

RUE LABRECQUE

RUE SAINT DENIS

RUELLE DE LA PROVIDENCE

AVE SAVOIE

6 N

7 R

8 N

9 R

10 N

RUE EMERY

11 N

12 R

13 R

14 C

RUE ROBIN

RUE LAFAYETTE

RUE SAINT CHRISTOPHE

RUE LABRECQUE

RUE SAINT TIMOTHÉE

RUE AMHERST

26 S

27 ✪ **Rue Amherst**

28 N

29 S

30 R

15 ✪ **La Grande Bibliothèque**

31 H

BLVD DE MAISONNEUVE EST

Ⓜ **Station Berri-UQAM**

32 R

34 R

Université du Québec á Montréal

Square Berri

PL PASTEUR

35 H

37 N

39 N

SEE MAP 3

RUE SAINTE CATHERINE EST

38 C

16 S

17 N

18 C

19 ✪ **UQÀM**

20 H

36 N

RUE SAINT HUBERT

RUE SAINT CHRISTOPHE

THE VILLAGE

RUE SAINT DENIS

RUE BERRI

RUE LABELLE

RUE CHRISTIN

22 H

21 N

BLVD RENÉ LÉVESQUE EST

SIGHTS
- 15 LA GRANDE BIBLIOTHÈQUE
- 19 UQÀM
- 27 RUE AMHERST
- 44 RUE SAINTE-CATHERINE EST
- 50 ÉGLISE ST-PIERRE-APÔTRE

RESTAURANTS
- 7 MÂCHE
- 9 CAMELLIA SINENSIS
- 12 JULIETTE ET CHOCOLAT
- 13 LA BRIOCHE LYONNAISE
- 32 O'THYME
- 34 PORQUOI PAS ESPRESSO BAR
- 41 AUTOUR D'UN PAIN
- 45 LE MIE MATINALE
- 48 AU PETIT EXTRA
- 49 MEZCLA
- 51 KITCHENETTE

NIGHTLIFE
- 3 L'AMÈRE À BOIRE
- 5 CAFÉ CHAOS
- 6 L'ABSYNTHE
- 8 LE SAINT-SULPICE
- 10 LES TROIS BRASSEURS
- 11 AMBASSADE BORIS
- 17 LA MOUCHE
- 23 LE CHEVAL BLANC
- 28 GOTHA
- 36 STEREO
- 37 CIRCUS
- 39 CABARET CHEZ MADO
- 40 CLUB UNITY
- 42 CLUB DATE PIANO BAR
- 46 LE DRUGSTORE
- 47 SKY PUB CLUB

ARTS AND CULTURE
- 14 CINÉMATHÈQUE QUÉBÉCOISE
- 18 TELUS THEATRE
- 25 ÉCO MUSÉE DU FIER MONDE
- 38 L'OLYMPIA
- 43 LE NATIONAL

SHOPS
- 1 ATOM HEART
- 2 RUE SAINT-DENIS
- 16 DESERRE
- 24 SPOUTNIK BOUTIQUE
- 26 CITÉ DÉCO
- 29 SECONDE CHANCE

HOTELS
- 4 AUBERGE HOTEL LE JARDIN D'ANTOINE
- 20 L'HÔTEL ST-DENIS
- 21 CELEBRITIES LOVELY HOTEL
- 22 L'HÔTEL LORD BERRI
- 30 LA LOGGIA
- 31 AUBERGE HOTEL LE POMEROL
- 33 SIR MONTCALM
- 35 L'HÔTEL GOUVERNEUR PLACE DUPUIS

0   100 yds
0   100 m

DISTANCE ACROSS MAP
Approximate: .9 mi or 1.5 km

SEE MAP 6

RUE MARMETTE
RUE ELMIRE
RUE DEMERS
RUE VILLENEUVE OUEST
RUE VILLENEUVE EST

DISTANCE ACROSS MAP
Approximate: 2.6 mi or 4.2 km

0   200 yds
0   200 m

Parc
Jeanne-
Mance

AVE DU MONT ROYAL OUEST

RUE CERAT
RUE VARENNES

PLATEAU
MONT-ROYAL

Drolet

RUE MARIE ANNE EST

CAR
VALLIERES

RUE RACHEL OUEST

The Main

AVE DULUTH OUEST

RUE BAGG

RUE NAPOLEON

R SAINT CUTHBERT

Musée des
Hospitalières
de l'Hôtel-Dieu

Rue
Saint-Denis

RUE ROY EST

AVE DES PINS EST

AVE DES PINS OUEST

McGill
Health
Center

RUE GUILBAULT
RUE GUILBAULT

Par de
Bullion

Carré
Saint-Louis

RUE PRINCE ARTHUR EST

RUE
LAVERS

RUE DU SQ SAINT LOUIS
RUE DU SQ SAINT LOUIS

RUE
MALINES

RUE
RIGAUD

RUE PRINCE ARTHUR OUEST

RUE MILTON

RUE SHERBROOKE EST

SEE MAP 3

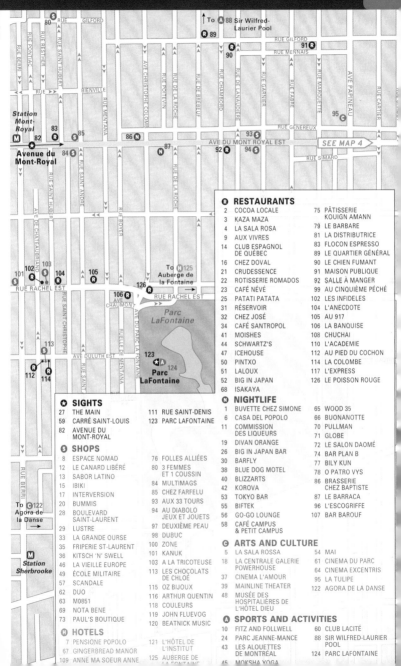

RUE GILFORD

To Ⓐ88 Sir Wilfred-Laurier Pool

Ⓡ89

Ⓡ90

91Ⓡ

RUE MENNAIS

RUE GILFORD

95Ⓖ

Station Mont-Royal
Ⓜ 82
83Ⓡ
Ⓢ85
86Ⓝ

93Ⓢ

Avenue du Mont-Royal
84Ⓢ
87
AVE DU MONT ROYAL EST
92Ⓡ
94Ⓢ
SEE MAP 4

RUE SIMARD

101Ⓢ
102Ⓡ
103
104Ⓡ
105Ⓡ
RUE RACHEL EST
106Ⓡ

To Ⓗ125 Auberge de la Fontaine
126Ⓡ
RUE RACHEL EST

Parc LaFontaine

113
112Ⓡ
114Ⓡ

123
124Ⓐ
Parc LaFontaine

Ⓡ RESTAURANTS

2 COCOA LOCALE
3 KAZA MAZA
4 LA SALA ROSA
9 AUX VIVRES
14 CLUB ESPAGNOL DE QUÉBEC
16 CHEZ DOVAL
21 CRUDESSENCE
22 ROTISSERIE ROMADOS
23 CAFÉ NÉVÉ
25 PATATI PATATA
31 RÉSERVOIR
32 CHEZ JOSÉ
34 CAFÉ SANTROPOL
41 MOISHES
44 SCHWARTZ'S
47 ICEHOUSE
50 PINTXO
51 LALOUX
52 BIG IN JAPAN
68 ISAKAYA

75 PÂTISSERIE KOUIGN AMANN
79 LE BARBARE
81 LA DISTRIBUTRICE
83 FLOCON ESPRESSO
89 LE QUARTIER GÉNÉRAL
90 LE CHIEN FUMANT
91 MAISON PUBLIQUE
92 SALLE À MANGER
99 AU CINQUIÈME PÉCHÉ
102 LES INFIDELES
104 L'ANECDOTE
105 AU 917
106 LA BANQUISE
108 CHUCHAI
110 L'ACADEMIE
112 AU PIED DU COCHON
114 LA COLOMBE
117 L'EXPRESS
126 LE POISSON ROUGE

Ⓝ NIGHTLIFE

1 BUVETTE CHEZ SIMONE
6 CASA DEL POPOLO
11 COMMISSION DES LIQUEURS
19 DIVAN ORANGE
26 BIG IN JAPAN BAR
30 BARFLY
38 BLUE DOG MOTEL
40 BLIZZARTS
42 KOROVA
53 TOKYO BAR
55 BIFTEK
56 GO-GO LOUNGE
58 CAFÉ CAMPUS & PETIT CAMPUS

65 WOOD 35
66 BUONANOTTE
71 PULLMAN
71 GLOBE
72 LE SALON DAOMÉ
74 BAR PLAN B
77 BILY KUN
O PATRO VYS
86 BRASSERIE CHEZ BAPTISTE
87 LE BARRACA
96 L'ESCOGRIFFE
107 BAR BAROUF

Ⓞ SIGHTS

27 THE MAIN
59 CARRÉ SAINT-LOUIS
82 AVENUE DU MONT-ROYAL

111 RUE SAINT-DENIS
123 PARC LAFONTAINE

Ⓢ SHOPS

8 ESPACE NOMAD
12 LE CANARD LIBÉRÉ
13 SABOR LATINO
17 INTERVERSION
20 BUMMIS
28 BOULEVARD SAINT-LAURENT
29 LUSTRE
33 LA GRANDE OURSE
35 FRIPERIE ST-LAURENT
36 KITSCH 'N' SWELL
46 LA VIEILLE EUROPE
49 ÉCOLE MILITAIRE
57 SCANDALE
62 DUO
63 M0851
69 NOTA BENE
73 PAUL'S BOUTIQUE

76 FOLLES ALLIÉES
80 3 FEMMES ET 1 COUSSIN
84 MULTIMAGS
85 CHEZ FARFELU
94 AUX 33 TOURS
94 AU DIABOLO JEUX ET JOUETS
97 DEUXIÈME PEAU
98 DUBUC
100 ZONE
101 KANUK
103 A LA TRICOTEUSE
113 LES CHOCOLATS DE CHLOÉ
115 OZ BIJOUX
116 ARTHUR QUENTIN
118 COULEURS
119 JOHN FLUEVOG
120 BEATNICK MUSIC

121 L'HÔTEL DE L'INSTITUT
125 AUBERGE DE LA FONTAINE

Ⓗ HOTELS

7 PENSIONE POPOLO
67 GINGERBREAD MANOR
109 ANNE MA SOEUR ANNE

Ⓒ ARTS AND CULTURE

5 LA SALA ROSSA
18 LA CENTRALE GALERIE POWERHOUSE
37 CINEMA L'AMOUR
39 MAINLINE THEATER
48 MUSÉE DES HOSPITALIERES DE L'HÔTEL DIEU

54 MAI
61 CINEMA DU PARC
64 CINEMA EXCENTRIS
95 LA TULIPE
122 AGORA DE LA DANSE

Ⓐ SPORTS AND ACTIVITIES

10 FITZ AND FOLLWELL
24 PARC JEANNE-MANCE
43 LES ALOUETTES DE MONTRÉAL
45 MOKSHA YOGA

60 CLUB LACITÉ
88 SIR WILFRED-LAURIER POOL
124 PARC LAFONTAINE

0 300 yds
0 300 m

DISTANCE ACROSS MAP
Approximate: 2.2 mi or 3.6 km

RUE DE CASTELNAU OUEST

M Station de Castelnau

RUE JEAN TALON OUEST

M Station Acadie

PETITE ITALIE

Parc Martel

RUE BEAUBIEN OUEST

RUE BEAUBIEN EST

AVE VAN HORNE

M Station Outremont

AVE BERNARD

MILE END

Parc St Viateur

Parc Outremont

Church of Saint-Michael and Saint-Anthony

RUE BERNARD OUEST

AVE SAINT VIATEUR OUEST

RUE GROLL

AVE FAIRMOUNT OUEST

Parc de St Michel

AVE LAURIER OUEST

⊕ SIGHTS

6 MARCHÉ JEAN-TALON
13 CHIESA DELLA MADONNA DELLA DIFESA
52 CHURCH OF SAINT-MICHAEL AND SAINT-ANTHONY

⊕ RESTAURANTS

3 KITCHEN GALERIE
4 LE PETIT ALEP
7 DÉPANNEUR LE PICK-UP
9 CAFÉ ITALIA
10 LUCCA
12 PIZZERIA NAPOLETANA
14 BOTTEGA PIZZERIA
17 DINETTE TRIPLE CROWN
20 VIEUX VÉLO
27 LE BILBOQUET
28 LE PETIT ITALIEN
29 CAFÉ SOUVENIR
37 LA LUMIÈRE DU MILE END
45 CAVA
48 CLUB SOCIAL
49 LES DEUX SINGES DE MONTARVIE
51 CAFÉ OLIMPICO
53 LE PANTHÈRE VERTE
55 COMPTOIR 21
57 LE CAGIBI
61 MAÏS
67 LAWRENCE
68 CAFÉ SARDINE
69 BOULANGERIE GUILLAUME
70 MILOS
72 LA CROISSANTERIE FIGARO
74 WILENSKY'S LIGHT LUNCH
77 HÔTEL HERMAN
81 LEMÉAC
91 CHEZ CLAUDETTE

⊕ NIGHTLIFE

2 IL MOTORE
16 ALEXANDRAPLATZ BAR
21 VICES ET VERSA
21 NOTRE DAMES DES QUILLES
32 HELM
41 WHISKY CAFÉ
42 ROYAL PHOENIX BAR
56 BAR WAVERLY
62 SPARROW
65 BU
71 5296 PARC
89 BALDWIN BARMACIE
90 DIEU DU CIEL

⊕ ARTS AND CULTURE

1 BATTAT CONTEMPORARY
23 GALERIE YVES LAROCHE
31 THEATRE OUTREMONT
33 RIALTO THEATRE
60 GALERIE SIMON BLAIS
73 ARTICULE

⊕ SPORTS AND ACTIVITIES

59 NAADA YOGA
76 LE YETI

⊕ SHOPS

5 FROMAGERIE HAMEL
8 MILANO
11 QUINCAILLERIE DANTE
15 SAVON POPULAIRE
18 LA (FOUND)ERIE
22 LA GUILDE CULINAIRE
24 BELLE ET REBELLE
25 EFFILOCHÉ
26 LOZEAU
30 AUX PLAISIRS DU BACCHUS
34 DRAWN & QUARTERLY
35 PHONOPOLIS
36 ARTERIE
38 MAISON MONTURES
39 LOCAL 23
40 BODYBAG BY JUDE
43 ATELIER B.
44 STYLE LABO
46 S.W. WELCH
47 BOUTIQUE OXFORD
50 GENEVIEVE GADBOIS
54 THE ANNEX
58 MONASTIRAKI
63 CITIZEN VINTAGE
66 CO
75 AU PAPIER JAPONAIS
78 JAMAIS ASSEZ
79 BOUTIQUE UNICORN
80 GENERAL 54
82 GOURMET LAURIER
83 BILLIE
84 LYLA
85 LISE WATIER INSTITUT
86 LA CANADIENNE
87 BOUTIQUE CITROUILLE
88 LES TOUILLEURS

SEE MAP 5

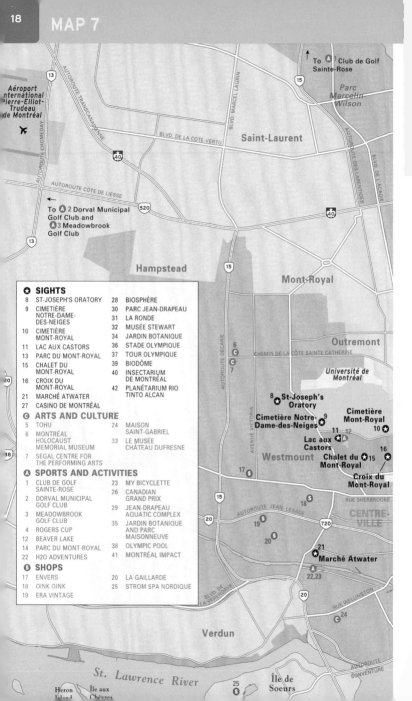

Aéroport
international
Pierre-Elliot-
Trudeau
de Montréal

To ⓐ 1 Club de Golf
Sainte-Rose

Parc
Marcelin
Wilson

Saint-Laurent

To ⓐ 2 Dorval Municipal
Golf Club and
ⓐ 3 Meadowbrook
Golf Club

Hampstead

Mont-Royal

Outremont

Université de
Montréal

CHEMIN DE LA CÔTE SAINTE CATHERINE

⁸ St-Joseph's
Oratory

Cimetière Notre-
Dame-des-Neiges

Cimetière
Mont-Royal

Lac aux
Castors

Westmount   Chalet du
Mont-Royal

Croix du
Mont-Royal

RUE SHERBROOKE

CENTRE-
VILLE

AUTOROUTE JEAN LESAGE

Marché Atwater

Verdun

St. Lawrence River

Île de
Soeurs

Heron
Island

Île aux
Chèvres

⚪ SIGHTS

8	ST-JOSEPH'S ORATORY	28	BIOSPHÈRE
9	CIMETIÈRE NOTRE-DAME-DES-NEIGES	30	PARC JEAN-DRAPEAU
		31	LA RONDE
10	CIMETIÈRE MONT-ROYAL	32	MUSÉE STEWART
11	LAC AUX CASTORS	34	JARDIN BOTANIQUE
13	PARC DU MONT-ROYAL	36	STADE OLYMPIQUE
15	CHALET DU MONT-ROYAL	37	TOUR OLYMPIQUE
		39	BIODÔME
16	CROIX DU MONT-ROYAL	40	INSECTARIUM DE MONTRÉAL
21	MARCHÉ ATWATER	42	PLANÉTARIUM RIO TINTO ALCAN
27	CASINO DE MONTRÉAL		

ⓒ ARTS AND CULTURE

5	TOHU	24	MAISON SAINT-GABRIEL
6	MONTRÉAL HOLOCAUST MEMORIAL MUSEUM	33	LE MUSÉE CHÂTEAU DUFRESNE
7	SEGAL CENTRE FOR THE PERFORMING ARTS		

ⓐ SPORTS AND ACTIVITIES

1	CLUB DE GOLF SAINTE-ROSE	23	MY BICYCLETTE
2	DORVAL MUNICIPAL GOLF CLUB	26	CANADIAN GRAND PRIX
3	MEADOWBROOK GOLF CLUB	29	JEAN-DRAPEAU AQUATIC COMPLEX
4	ROGERS CUP	35	JARDIN BOTANIQUE AND PARC MAISONNEUVE
12	BEAVER LAKE		
14	PARC DU MONT-ROYAL	38	OLYMPIC POOL
22	H2O ADVENTURES	41	MONTRÉAL IMPACT

ⓢ SHOPS

17	ENVERS	20	LA GAILLARDE
18	OINK OINK	25	STROM SPA NORDIQUE
19	ERA VINTAGE		

Contents

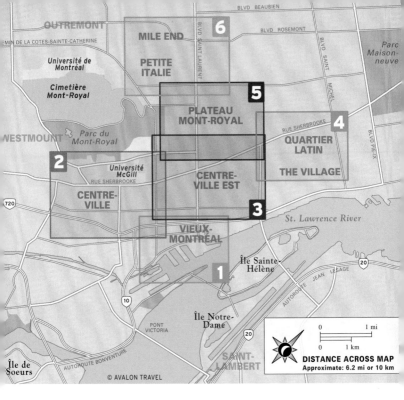

Montréal Maps

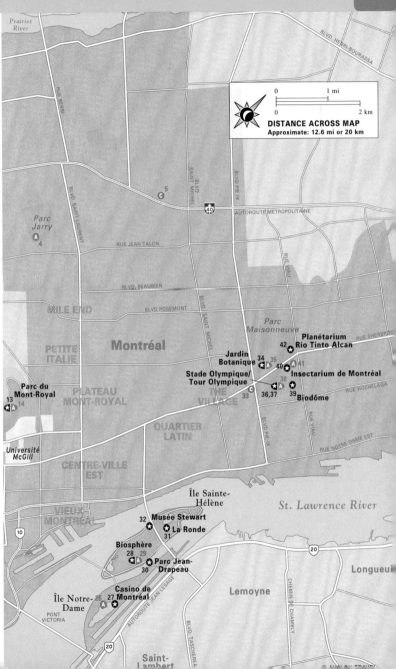

Prairies River

BLVD HENRI-BOURASSA

RUE BERRI

BLVD SAINT MICHEL

BLVD PIE-IX

G 5

40

AUTOROUTE MÉTROPOLITAINE

Parc Jarry

A 4

RUE JEAN TALON

RUE VIAU

BLVD SAINT LAURENT

BLVD BEAUBIEN

MILE END

BLVD ROSEMONT

Parc Maisonneuve

RUE SHERBROOKE

PETITE ITALIE

Montréal

Planétarium Rio Tinto Alcan

42

Jardin Botanique 34 35

Insectarium de Montréal

40 41

Stade Olympique/ Tour Olympique

38

RUE HOCHELAGA

Parc du Mont-Royal

13 A 14

PLATEAU MONT-ROYAL

THE VILLAGE

G

33 36,37 39

Biodôme

RUE VIAU

QUARTIER LATIN

BLVD PIE-IX

Université McGill

RUE NOTRE-DAME EST

CENTRE-VILLE EST

Île Sainte-Hélène

St. Lawrence River

VIEUX MONTRÉAL

10

32 Musée Stewart

La Ronde

31

20

Longueui

Biosphère

28 29

30 Parc Jean-Drapeau

Lemoyne

CHEMIN DE CHAMBLY

Casino de Montréal

Île Notre-26 27 Dame

PONT VICTORIA

AUTOROUTE JEAN LESAGE

20

BLVD TASCHEREAU

Saint-Lambert

DISTANCE ACROSS MAP
Approximate: 12.6 mi or 20 km

0   1 mi
0   2 km

SIGHTS

35	PARC DE L'ARTILLERIE
37	LES FORTIFICATIONS
51	SÉMINAIRE DE QUÉBEC
52	MUSÉE DE L'AMÉRIQUE FRANCOPHONE
53	BASILIQUE-CATHÉDRALE NOTRE-DAME-DE-QUÉBEC
67	PLACE D'ARMES
69	TERRASSE DUFFERIN
70	CHÂTEAU FRONTENAC
80	MUSÉE DES URSULINES
83	PARC DU CAVALIER-DU-MOULIN
88	LA CITADELLE

RESTAURANTS

2	CHEZ TEMPOREL
6	LES FRÈRES DE LA CÔTE
8	CHEZ ASHTON
10	CASSE-CRÊPE BRETON
11	CHEZ BOULAY BISTRO BORÉAL
14	CAFÉ-BOULANGERIE PAILLARD
18	LE PATRIARCHE
19	LES TROIS GARÇONS
22	CHEZ SOI LA CHINE
26	LE PETIT COIN LATIN
30	CHEZ L'AUTRE
31	IL TEATRO
42	LE SAINT-AMOUR
45	APSARA
55	LE CAFÉ BUADE
60	LE PAIN BÉNI
62	LA CRÉMAILLÈRE
71	LE CHAMPLAIN
72	LE CAFÉ DE LA TERRASSE
77	AUX ANCIENS CANADIENS
79	CONTI CAFFE
81	LE CONTINENTAL

NIGHTLIFE

3	L'OSTRADAMUS
4	PUB ST-PATRICK
12	LES YEUX BLEUS
17	PUB ST-ALEXANDRE
25	BAR STE-ANGÈLE
27	LE SAPRISTI
65	LE CHARLES BAILLAIRGÉ JAZZ BAR
73	ST-LAURENT BAR AND LOUNGE

ARTS AND CULTURE

1	MUSÉE BON PASTEUR
32	LE CAPITOLE
34	PALAIS MONTCALM
39	MORRIN CENTRE
56	QUÉBEC EXPERIENCE
68	MUSÉE DU FORT
78	GALERIE D'ART BROUSSEAU AND BROUSSEAU

SPORTS AND ACTIVITIES

29	PATINOIRE DE LA PLACE D'YOUVILLE
36	GOLF TOURISTIQUE DE QUÉBEC
41	PARC DE L'ESPLANADE
63	CROISIÈRE DUFOUR
86	GLISSADES DE LA TERRASSE DUFFERIN

SHOPS

5	MAGASIN GÉNÉRAL P.L. BLOUIN
7	BOUTIUQE & SPA SIGNÉ PREVONIA
13	CONFISERIE C'EST SI BON
15	LIBRAIRIE PANTOUTE
16	ARCHAMBAULT
20	BOUTIQUE CANADEAU
21	MAISON DE LA PRESSE INTERNATIONALE
23	LES DÉLICES DE L'ÉRABLE
24	BOUTIQUE L'ÉCHELLE
28	PREMIÈRE ISSUE
46	BIBI ET COMPAGNIE
47	ZIMMERMANN
48	BOUTIQUE ARTISANS CANADA
49	LA MAISON SIMONS
50	BOUTIQUE CLAUDE BERRY
54	LA BOUTIQUE DE NOËL
57	LA MAISON DARLINGTON
58	BOUTIQUE LE SACHEM
66	ARTISANS DE LA CATHÉDRALE
74	PAYOT INSTITUTE
76	LAMBERT & CO.
82	GALERIE D'ART LES TROIS COLOMBES

HOTELS

9	HÔTEL MANOIR VICTORIA
33	LE CAPITOLE DE QUÉBEC
38	AUBERGE INTERNATIONALE DE QUÉBEC
40	HÔTEL LE CHAMPLAIN
43	CHEZ HUBERT
44	HÔTEL LE CLOS SAINT-LOUIS
59	HÔTEL STE-ANNE
61	AUBERGE PLACE D'ARMES
64	HÔTEL CLARENDON
75	FAIRMONT LE CHÂTEAU FRONTENAC
84	LA MARQUISE DE BASSANO
85	HÔTEL CHÂTEAU BELLEVUE
87	HÔTEL CAP DIAMANT

RUE SAINT PAUL

RUELLE DES BAINS

RUE SAINT-VALLIER EST

CÔTE DINAN

RUE DES

RUE SAINT-NICOLAS

RUELLE DU RO

RUE DES VAISSEAUX DU ROI

Hôtel-Dieu de Québec

CÔTE DE LA POTASSE

RUE DE L'ARSENAL

SEE MAP 11

Parc de l'Artillerie

35

36

Les Fortifications

37

RUE MCMAHON

CÔTE DU PALAIS

RUE SAINT-JEAN

RUE SAINT-STANISLAS

RUE ELGIN

RUE MCWILLIAM

RUE STE-ANGÈLE

RUE D'AUTEUIL

RUE DAUPHINE

RUE SAINTE-ANNE

RUE SAINTE-URSULE

RUELLE PANET

RUE DAUPHINE

city wall

Parc de l'Esplanade

AVE HONORÉ MERCIER

GRANDE ALLÉE EST

Parlement du Québec

SEE MAP 10

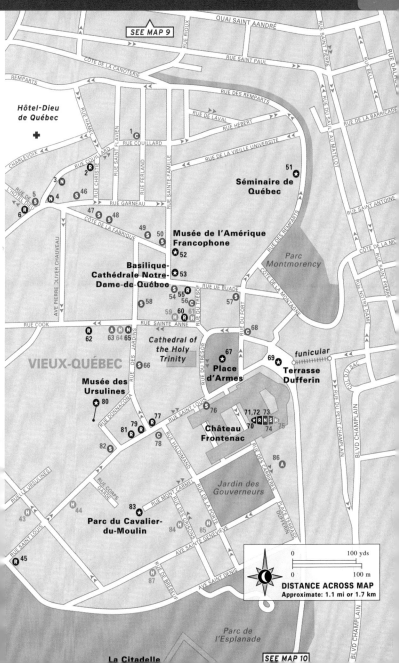

SEE MAP 9

QUAI SAINT AANDRÉ

RUE SAINT PAUL

CÔTE DE LA CANOTERIE

REMPARTS

RUE DES REMPARTS

Hôtel-Dieu
de Québec

RUE DE LAVAL

RUE HÉBERT

RUE DE LA VIEILLE UNIVERSITÉ

1 ⓒ

RUE COUILLARD

51 ✪

**Séminaire de
Québec**

RUE SAINT ANTOINE

R 2

3 ⓝ
5
ⓝ 4 ⓢ 46

RUE GARNEAU

47 ⓢ 48

CÔTE DE LA FABRIQUE

49
ⓢ 50

**Musée de l'Amérique
Francophone**

✪ 52

Parc
Montmorency

CÔTE DE LA M

**Basilique-
Cathédrale Notre-
Dame-de-Québec**

✪ 53

RUE DE BUADE

54 55
56 58

57 ⓢ

59 60 61
ⓝ

RUE SAINTE ANNE

68 ⓒ

62
63 64 65

ⓝ 66

*Cathedral of
the Holy
Trinity*

67 ✪

**Place
d'Armes**

69 ○ funicular

**Terrasse
Dufferin**

VIEUX-QUÉBEC

**Musée des
Ursulines**

✪ 80

77
79 81 ⓡ

76

71,72 73
70 ⓡⓝⓢⓡ
74

**Château
Frontenac**

82 ⓢ

ⓒ
78

86 ⓐ

43

ⓗ 44

83 ✪

**Parc du Cavalier-
du-Moulin**

*Jardin des
Gouverneurs*

84

85 ⓗ

ⓡ 45

87 ⓗ

BLVD CHAMPLAIN

Parc de
l'Esplanade

SEE MAP 10

La Citadelle

0		100 yds

0		100 m

DISTANCE ACROSS MAP
Approximate: 1.1 mi or 1.7 km

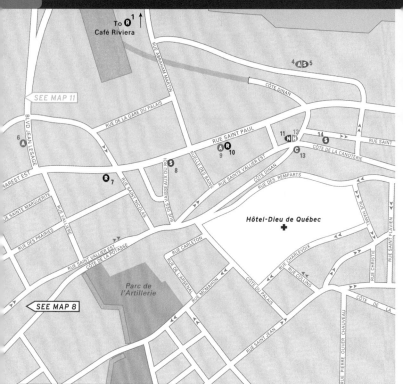

To **R** 1
Café Riviera

4 **A** **S** 5

SEE MAP 11

RUE DE LA GARE DU PALAIS

RUE SAINT PAUL

A **R**
9 10

11 12 **N** **H**

14 **S**

CÔTE DE LA CANOTERIE

RUE SAINT

CÔTE DINAN

C
13

S
8

R 7

Hôtel-Dieu de Québec
✚

RUE DES REMPARTS

CÔTE DE LA POTASSE

RUE CARLETON

Parc de
l'Artillerie

CÔTE DU PALAIS

RUE COLLINS

SEE MAP 8

RUE SAINT-JEAN

RUE COOK

RUE PIERRE OLIVER CHAUVEAU

⊛ SIGHTS

17	VIEUX-PORT DE QUÉBEC	47	PLACE ROYALE
29	MUSÉE DE LA CIVILISATION	48	ÉGLISE NOTRE-DAME-DES-VICTOIRES
33	RUE SOUS-LE-CAP	53	FUNICULAIRE DU VIEUX-QUÉBEC
45	LA FRESQUE DES QUÉBÉCOIS	65	QUARTIER DU PETIT-CHAMPLAIN

ⓝ RESTAURANTS

1	CAFÉ RIVIERA	28	CAFÉ DU MONDE
7	BRYND SMOKED MEAT	34	L'ÉCHAUDÉ
10	LA PIZZ	35	CAFÉ BISTRO DU CAP
15	LA CABANE LOBSTER SHACK	39	PANACHE
18	LES CAFÉS DU SOLEIL	40	TOAST!
20	BUFFET DE L'ANTIQUAIRE	43	RESTAURANT L'INITIALE
23	SSS	54	MARIE-CLARISSE
25	LE QUAI 19	57	LAPIN SAUTÉ
26	LAURIE RAPHAËL	63	LE COCHON DINGUE

ⓝ NIGHTLIFE

11	TAVERNE BELLEY	51	LE PAPE-GEORGES
44	L'ONCLE ANTOINE		

ⓒ ARTS AND CULTURE

2	MUSÉE NAVAL DE QUÉBEC	32	ATELIER GUY LÉVESQUE
13	GALERIE MADELEINE LACERTE	42	GALERIES D'ART BEAUCHAMP AND BEAUCHAMP
27	L'AGORA DU VIEUX-PORT	59	MAISON CHEVALIER
30	LA CASERNE DALHOUSIE	64	LE THÉÂTRE DU PETIT CHAMPLAIN

Ⓐ SPORTS AND ACTIVITIES

3	CROISIÈRES COUDRIER	9	CYCLO SERVICES
4	ÉCOLOCYCLO	49	CROISIÈRE AML
6	PLANÈTE FITNESS GYM	70	CORRIDOR DU LITTORAL

Ⓢ SHOPS

5	LE MARCHÉ DU VIEUX PORT	55	POT EN CIEL
8	FOURRURES RICHARD ROBITAILLE	56	PAULINE PELLETIER
14	MACHIN CHOUETTE	58	PONT BRIAND JOALLIER
16	MAISON DAMBOURGÈS	60	LE CAPITAINE D'ABORD
19	RUE SAINT-PAUL	61	OCLAN
21	BOUTIQUE AUX MÉMOIRES ANTIQUITÉS	62	O PETITES DOUCEURS DU QUARTIER
22	ANTIQUITÉS BOLDUC	66	QUARTIER DU PETIT-CHAMPLAIN
46	BOUTIQUE DES MÉTIERS D'ART	67	MADAME GIGI CONFISERIE
50	ATELIER LA POMME	68	SOIERIE HUO
52	LA FUDGERIE	69	LA PETITE CABANE À SUCRE DE QUÉBEC

Ⓗ HOTELS

12	HÔTEL BELLEY	37	HÔTEL 71
24	HÔTEL PORT-ROYAL	38	AUBERGE SAINT-ANTOINE
31	HÔTEL LE GERMAIN-DOMINION	41	HÔTEL LE PRIORI
36	AUBERGE SAINT PIERRE		

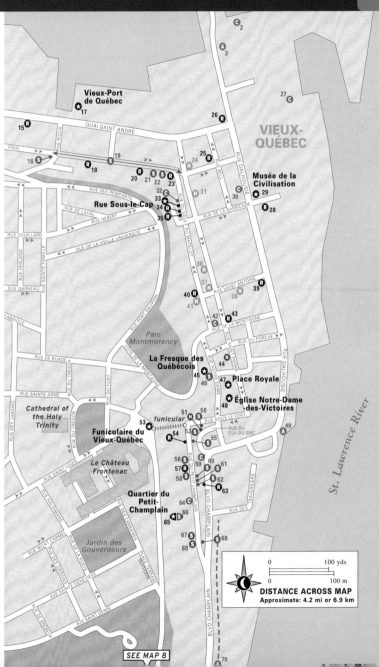

Vieux-Port de Québec 17

VIEUX-QUÉBEC

15 R
QUAI SAINT ANDRÉ
PAUL
16 S
RUE RIOUX
19
18 R
20 21 R 22 S S R 23
24 H
25 R
26 R
RUE BELL
RUE DALHOUSIE

Musée de la Civilisation 29
30 C
28 R

RUE DES REMPARTS
RUE DE LAVAL
RUE HÉBERT
31
32 C
33 C
Rue Sous-le-Cap 34 C
35 C
RUE DU SAULT AU MATELOT
RUE DE LA BARRICADE

RUE COUILLARD
RUE DE LA VIEILLE UNIVERSITÉ
RUE SAINTE FAMILLE
RUE FERLAND
RUE GARNEAU

36
37 H
RUE SAINT ANTOINE
38
39 R
40 R H
41
42 S
43 R
RUE DE LA MONTAGNE

FABRIQUE
Parc Montmorency
CÔTE DE LA MONTAGNE
RUE DU PORCHE
RUE SAINT PIERRE
RUE DALHOUSIE

RUE DE BUADE
RUE SAINTE ANNE
RUE DU TRÉSOR
RUE DU FORT

La Fresque des Québécois
44
45 S
46
47 Place Royale
48 C Église Notre-Dame-des-Victoires

RUE DES JARDINS
Cathedral of the Holy Trinity

RUE NOTRE DAME

funicular
51
53
54
52 S
55 S
59
RUE SOUS LE FORT
RUE DU CUL DE SAC
50
49 A

Funiculaire du Vieux-Québec

Le Château Frontenac

RUE SAINT LOUIS
RUE HALDIMAND
RUE DES CARRIÈRES

56 S
57 R
58 S
60
61 R
62 R
63 R
RUE DU PETIT CHAMPLAIN

Quartier du Petit-Champlain
64 S
65 S
66
RUE DES TRAVERSIERS

Jardin des Gouverneurs
RUE MONT CARMEL
RUE DES CARRIÈRES
PLACE FERLAND
DUFFERIN

67 S
69 S
68 R
BLVD CHAMPLAIN

St. Laurent River / St. Laurence River

AVE SAINTE GENEVIÈVE
RUE SAINT DENIS
RUE DE BRÉSOLY

0   100 yds
0   100 m
DISTANCE ACROSS MAP
Approximate: 4.2 mi or 6.9 km

2 C
3 A
27 C

BLVD CHAMPLAIN
70

SEE MAP 8

SIGHTS
1 FONTAINE DE TOURNY
2 HÔTEL DU PARLEMENT
3 OBSERVATOIRE DE LA CAPITALE
4 PARC DES PLAINES D'ABRAHAM
6 MANÈGE MILITAIRE
8 LA GRANDE-ALLÉE
18 TOUR MARTELLO 1
19 TOUR MARTELLO 2
46 MUSÉE NATIONAL DES BEAUX-ARTS DU QUÉBEC

RESTAURANTS
11 CASA CALZONE
13 LE COSMOS
14 VOO DOO GRILL
21 SEBZ THÉS AND LOUNGE
25 BÜGEL FABRIQUE DES BAGELS
26 MILANO PIZZA
30 MORENA
32 CAFÉ KRIEGHOFF
35 BISTRO B
36 GLACIER ABERDEEN
38 MÉTROPOLITAN EDDIE SUSHI BAR
39 GRAFFITI
40 LE FASTOCHE
47 RESTAURANT DU MUSÉE DES BEAUX-ARTS

NIGHTLIFE
9 LES VOÛTES NAPOLÉON
10 L'INOX
12 LE DAGOBERT
15 LE MAURICE
16 SOCIÉTÉ CIGARE
17 LE CHARLOTTE ULTRA LOUNGE
31 LE JULES ET JIM
33 PUB GALWAY
34 RIDEAU ROUGE
42 BLAXTON PUB AND GRILL

ARTS AND CULTURE
20 GRAND THÉATRE DE QUÉBEC
29 CINÉMA
43 MAISON HENRY-STUART

SPORTS AND ACTIVITIES
5 PARC DES PLAINES D'ABRAHAM
23 ASHTANGA YOGA QUÉBEC
44 PARC DU MUSÉE
45 PISCINE PARC DU MUSÉE

SHOPS
22 IZBA SPA
24 KETTO
27 URBAIN PRÊT-À-PORTER
28 ZONE
37 SILLONS LE DISQUAIRE
41 LES HALLES DU PETIT QUARTIER

HOTELS
7 HÔTEL CHÂTEAU LAURIER

SEE MAP 11

Parc de l'Amérique Française

RUE CRÉMAZIE EST
RUE LOCKWELL
BLVD RENÉ LÉVESQUE EST
RUE SAINT-AMABLE
AVE TURNBULL
RUE SAINT FOY
CHEMIN SAINT FOY
RUE SHERBROOKE
FRANCISCAINS
RUE DE CANDIAC
RUE DUMONT
AVE CARTIER
RUE SAINT LAURENT
RUE DE MAISONNEUVE
AVE LOUIS SAINT LAURENT
PÈRE MARQUETTE
RUE CRÉMAZIE OUEST
BLVD RENÉ LÉVESQUE OUEST
AVE DE SALABERRY
AVE DU PARC
AVE DES ÉRABLES
AVE BOURLAMAQUE
RUE FRASER
RUE ABERDEEN
AVE CARTIER
AVE WILFRID
AVE SCOTT
AVE BRIAND
RUE DE BERNIÈRES
RUE SAUNDERS
LA GRANDE ALLÉE OUEST
AVE WOLFE
AVE GEORGE VI

Parc des Champs-de-Bataille

Musée National des Beaux-Arts du Québec

© AVALON TRAVEL

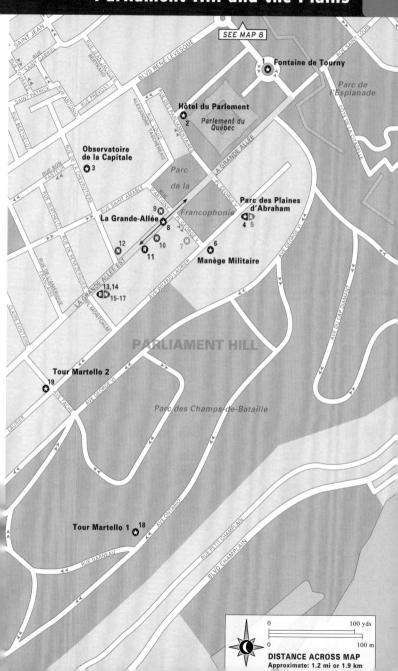

SEE MAP 8

1 Fontaine de Tourny

Parc de l'Esplanade

Hôtel du Parlement
2
Parlement du Québec

Observatoire de la Capitale
3

Parc de la Francophonie

La Grande Allée

Parc des Plaines d'Abraham
4 5

9
La Grande-Allée
8
12
10
11

6
Manège Militaire

PARLIAMENT HILL

13,14
15-17

Tour Martello 2
19

Parc des Champs-de-Bataille

Tour Martello 1
18

0   100 yds
0   100 m

DISTANCE ACROSS MAP
Approximate: 1.2 mi or 1.9 km

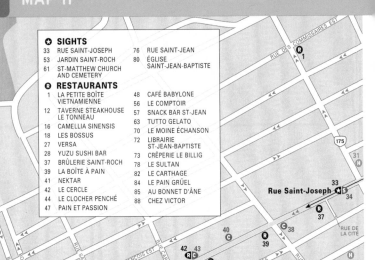

SIGHTS

33 RUE SAINT-JOSEPH
53 JARDIN SAINT-ROCH
61 ST-MATTHEW CHURCH AND CEMETERY
76 RUE SAINT-JEAN
80 ÉGLISE SAINT-JEAN-BAPTISTE

RESTAURANTS

1 LA PETITE BOÎTE VIETNAMIENNE
12 TAVERNE STEAKHOUSE LE TONNEAU
16 CAMELLIA SINENSIS
18 LES BOSSUS
27 VERSA
28 YUZU SUSHI BAR
37 BRÛLERIE SAINT-ROCH
39 LA BOÎTE À PAIN
41 NEKTAR
42 LE CERCLE
44 LE CLOCHER PENCHÉ
47 PAIN ET PASSION
48 CAFÉ BABYLONE
56 LE COMPTOIR
57 SNACK BAR ST-JEAN
63 TUTTO GELATO
70 LE MOINE ÉCHANSON
72 LIBRAIRIE ST-JEAN-BAPTISTE
73 CRÊPERIE LE BILLIG
78 LE SULTAN
82 LE CARTHAGE
84 LE PAIN GRÜEL
85 AU BONNET D'ÂNE
88 CHEZ VICTOR

Rue Saint-Joseph

RUE DE LA CITÉ

To Taverne Jos Dion

NIGHTLIFE

4 LA BARBERIE
7 MO
17 LE LARGO
26 LE BOUDOIR
46 TAVERNE JOS DION
49 LA CUISINE
50 LES SALONS D'EDGAR
51 SCANNER
58 LA NINKASI
64 PUB NELLIGAN'S
65 LE DRAGUE
66 BAR LE ST-MATTHEW
68 LE TEMPS PARTIEL
74 FOU-BAR
79 LE SACRILÈGE

ARTS AND CULTURE

2 LE LIEU
3 MORGAN BRIDGE
11 GALERIE D'ART FACTORY
35 CENTRE MATERIA
38 THÉÂTRE LA BORDÉE
40 IMPÉRIAL DE QUÉBEC
43 LE CERCLE
54 MÉDUSE

HOTELS

31 HÔTEL PUR
36 AUBERGE L'AUTRE JARDIN
52 AUBERGE LE VINCENT
67 AUBERGE J.A. MOISAN
81 LE CHÂTEAU DU FAUBOURG
87 CHÂTEAU DES TOURELLES

SHOPS

5 LE KNOCK-OUT
6 DÉJA VU
8 CHAMPAGNE LE MAÎTRE CONFISEUR
9 TOHU BOHU
10 SWELL & GINGER
13 FANAMANGA
14 LIBRAIRIE PHYLACTÈRE
15 LA QUINTESSENS
19 LALIBERTÉ
20 BENJO
21 SIGNATURES QUÉBÉÇOISES
22 MADEMOISELLE B
23 PHILIPPE DUBUC
24 FLIRT
25 COSMÉTIQUES BLOOMI
29 BALTHAZAR
30 KITSCH
32 MOUNTAIN EQUIPMENT CO-OP
34 RUE SAINT-JOSEPH
45 BOUTIQUE LUCIA F.
55 ESTHER P
59 JUPON PRESSÉ
60 POINT D'EXCLAMATION
62 SCHÜZ
69 CHOCO-MUSÉE ERICO
71 EPICERIE EUROPÉENNE
75 LOBO LAVIDA
77 RUE SAINT-JEAN
83 ROSE BOUTON
86 CD MÉLOMANE

SEE MAP 10

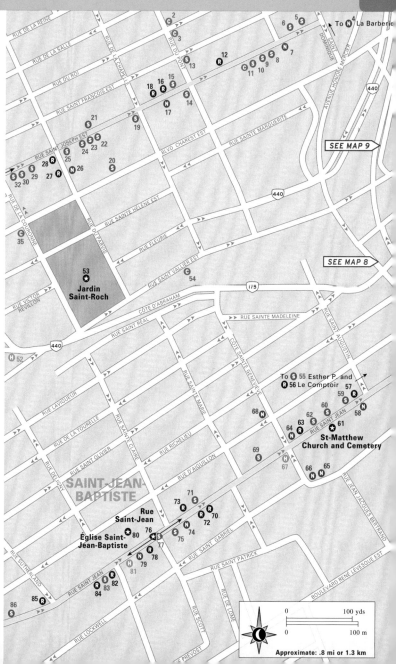

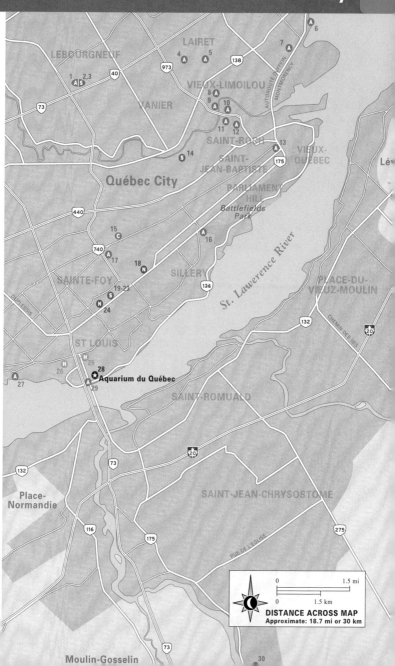

LEBOURGNEUF

LAIRET

VIEUX-LIMOILOU

VANIER

SAINT-ROCH

VIEUX-QUÉBEC

Québec City

Lé

SAINT-JEAN-BAPTISTE

PARLIAMENT HILL

Battlefields Park

St. Lawrence River

SAINTE-FOY

SILLERY

PLACE-DU-VIEUX-MOULIN

ST LOUIS

Aquarium du Québec

SAINT-ROMUALD

Place-Normandie

SAINT-JEAN-CHRYSOSTOME

Moulin-Gosselin

DISTANCE ACROSS MAP
Approximate: 18.7 mi or 30 km

0   1.5 mi
0   1.5 km

30

DISCOVER

Montréal & Québec City

The province of Québec is a place all its own: It's a country within a country with its own traditions, architecture, and language. Its two major cities, Montréal and Québec City, illustrate the diverse character of the province.

Montréal has been shaped by Franco-Anglo tensions and an ever-changing wave of immigrants. Because of this, the city is unbelievably diverse and dynamic. Known for its laissez-faire and hedonistic attitude, the city is one of the most artistic and culturally rich places in the country—and can throw a hell of a good party. From the vine-covered alleys to the corkscrew staircases, Montréal should be discovered by foot or bike. Take your time exploring its nooks and crannies, stopping for a coffee in a cozy café or a drink in one of its historic taverns along the way.

Perched on a cliff above the St-Lawrence River, Québec City is the soul of the province: the first city to be founded in Canada, the seat of the Québec government, and the self-proclaimed "Capitale Nationale." You can still walk the narrow, cobblestone streets of Vieux-Port or pose next to one of the many cannons that line the city's walls. But a youthful revolution in the old working-class neighborhoods is bringing a daring new quality of art and culture to this historic city.

In both cities, the historic landmarks and 17th-century architecture are captivating. But what will impress you the most is the infectious energy that people exude here. Temperatures drop below freezing in winter but bars and restaurants are still packed, with windows steaming with that unmistakable joie de vivre.

Planning Your Trip

Where to Go

Montréal

VIEUX-MONTRÉAL

You'll be captivated by the heart of the city's historical district, with cobblestone streets, early-New France architecture, regal Beaux-Arts buildings, and the grandeur of the Basilique Notre-Dame-de-Montréal. It's here that you'll also find some of the city's trendier restaurants, shops, and hotels. In the south end, a gradual slope leads to the converted warehouses and green spaces of the Vieux-Port and the St-Lawrence River.

CENTRE-VILLE

The downtown core is the city's main commercial district. Rue Ste-Catherine is lined with everything from historical department stores to trendy boutiques, while rue Crescent is popular for clubbing. South of the shopping area is the Centre Bell, home of the popular hockey team Montréal Canadiens, and to the north, the Musée des Beaux-Arts de Montréal sits among other stately Belle Époque buildings. In cold weather, enjoy the shelter of the Underground City.

CENTRE-VILLE EST

The main cultural district known as the Quartier des Spectacles is home to the Belgo Building, an arts hub, and the Place des Arts, where you can catch the symphony, ballet, and opera and check out the Musée d'Art Contemporain next door. In summer, the streets are taken over by the Festival International de Jazz and the Just for

the St-Lawrence River

Marché Jean-Talon in Montréal's Petite Italie has thrived since the days of the Great Depression.

Laughs festival. South of the cultural district is Chinatown, the place to find the best dim sum in the city.

QUARTIER LATIN AND THE VILLAGE

Centered around UQÀM, this is the stomping ground of Francophone university students. The city's main library, La Grande Bibliothèque, is a masterful piece of contemporary architecture, and lively and boisterous bars and restaurants can be found on rue St-Denis. To the east is the Village, Montréal's gay neighborhood, a mecca for late-night partying, karaoke bars, and antiques shopping on rue Amherst.

PLATEAU MONT-ROYAL

This charming artistic enclave features tree-lined streets, cozy neighborhood bistros, and 100-year-old townhouses. The best restaurants in the city are located here, and the bars that line the historic Main have secured Montréal's place as a nightlife destination, while the bars, cafés, and boutiques on rue St-Denis are a quintessential part of the Francophone community.

MILE END AND PETITE ITALIE

Populated by hipsters and artists, the Mile End is also home to a large Orthodox Jewish population. This mix of cultures is part of the neighborhood's DNA, as witnessed in the Italian cafés, Greek restaurants, and famous bagel shops, which mix well with the chic stores on avenue Laurier and rue Bernard in Outremont. North of Mile End is Little Italy, with its pre-fascism Mussolini fresco at Chiesa della Madonna della Difesa and the sprawling farmers market Marché Jean-Talon.

the entrance into Vieux-Québec's Upper Town

GREATER MONTRÉAL

Parc du Mont-Royal is a haven for recreation, and it provides the best views of the city. To the east of the park are the buildings for the 1976 Olympics, including the breathtaking Stade Olympique. Île Sainte-Hélène and Île Notre-Dame make up Parc Jean-Drapeau, a great place for biking, outdoor concerts, and exploring the Biosphère.

EXCURSIONS FROM MONTRÉAL

Montréalers typically head north into the Laurentian Mountains for skiing and staying in cottages and south to the Cantons de l'Est for the picturesque villages and antiquing—though a bit of each can be done in both.

Québec City

VIEUX-QUÉBEC'S UPPER TOWN

Les Fortifications surround Vieux-Québec's Upper Town, a 400-year-old neighborhood where the history of the winding streets and original architecture remains safe from the ravages of time. Protected by these walls is the Château Frontenac, Québec City's most famous sight, and the Séminaire de Québec, one of the city's oldest sights.

VIEUX-QUÉBEC'S LOWER TOWN

The stone Norman-style buildings and cobblestone streets of Place Royale mark the country's birthplace. History is unavoidable here, from the narrow lanes of Quartier du Petit-Champlain to the historic Vieux-Port, with its converted warehouses, antiques shops, and trendy hotels.

PARLIAMENT HILL AND THE PLAINS

Outside of the walls are the Plains of Abraham and Battlefield Park, the site of France's historic defeat by the British. The seat of the provincial government is to its north, housed in Hôtel du Parlement. Running alongside the government building are the nightclubs and bars of La Grande-Allée, the city's nightlife destination. Also in the Plains is Musée National des Beaux-Arts du Québec, which holds the largest existing collection of Québec art.

SAINT-JEAN-BAPTISTE AND SAINT-ROCH

Once working-class neighborhoods, Saint-Jean-Baptiste and Saint-Roch are now trendy, bohemian neighborhoods, home to the city's coolest kids, and the area where you'll find the best bars, browse independent boutiques, and catch the latest bands. It's also a major arts hub, and the contemporary arts complex Méduse is located here.

GREATER QUÉBEC CITY

In the areas surrounding the center of the city, find kid-friendly destinations like the Aquarium du Québec and the beautiful, sprawling gardens of Parc du Bois-de-Coulonge. The slopes of Mont-Sainte-Anne are fun for the whole family.

EXCURSIONS FROM QUÉBEC CITY

Just a half-hour drive from the city are the picturesque towns of Île d'Orléans and Côte-de-Beaupré, while an hour north, the Charlevoix region has some of the most spectacular scenery in the region.

When to Go

Though summer is the busiest time to visit, it's also the best time to explore the cities' neighborhoods, and you'll get to experience fun summer festivals like Montréal's Festival International de Jazz and Quebec's Festival d'Été.

It's no surprise that prices drop considerably October-April, so if you can handle a bit of cold, your pocketbook will thank you. Plus, the cold isn't so bad when it's hockey season and 98 percent of the people—and you—are crowded into bars watching the game. Quebéc City winters can be particularly freezing, but December-March is an ideal time to visit if you love skiing or other winter recreational activities. October is particularly pretty thanks to the changing fall foliage, and even February has a couple of bright spots with Montréal en Lumière's all-night art party and the Carnaval de Québec's unadulterated celebration of snow.

Before You Go

Passports and Visas

All visitors must have a valid passport or other accepted secure documents to enter the country; even those entering from the United States by road or train must have these documents.

Citizens of the United States, Australia, New Zealand, Israel, Japan, and most Western European countries don't need visas to enter Canada for stays up to 180 days. U.S. permanent residents are also exempt.

Nationals from South Africa, China, and about 150 other countries must apply for a temporary resident visa (TRV) in their home country. Full details can be found at Citizen and Immigration Canada. Single-entry visitor visas are valid for six months and cost $75, while multiple-entry visas cost $150 and last for two years, as long as a single stay doesn't last for longer than six months. A separate visa is required if you intend to work in Canada.

Transportation

Visitors arriving by air will arrive at Montréal's Pierre Trudeau International Airport, the main hub for both national and international air travel to the province. It's about 21 kilometers from downtown, and shuttles and public transport are available. Direct flights are also available to Quebéc City's Aéroport International Jean-Lesage de Québec. It's about 15 kilometers from Quebéc City's downtown, but there are no shuttles to downtown from this airport.

If you're arriving by train you'll arrive at Montréal's Gare Centrale in the downtown core, or Québec City's Gare du Palais near the Vieux-Port.

Those arriving by bus in Québec City will also arrive at the Gare du Palais. In Montréal, buses arrive at the main bus terminal, Gare d'Autocars, in the Quartier Latin.

The Montréal public transit system is run by STM, and it includes both the Métro (subway) and buses. Pay-as-you-go public bike rentals, otherwise known as Bixis, are available between April and November, and navigating the city's streets by car is fairly simple, though parking can be a pain and expensive.

Québec City's transit system is limited to buses, but they are fast and efficient in getting you up those steep hills. Taxis are useful when the winter hits, though they can be hard to flag down, depending on the area. Although driving the city streets is straightforward enough, if you're not used to ice and snow, it's better to leave it to the pros.

The Best of Montréal and Québec City

Ten days is the perfect length of time to visit both Montréal and Québec City, allowing you to dedicate enough time to experience Montréal's legendary nightlife and Québec City's historic center, with a few side trips.

Day 1

Arrive in Montréal and head to your hotel in Vieux-Montréal. Drop your bags and head out to grab a coffee and a light bite at Olive & Gourmando. Then stroll down rue St-Paul, the oldest street in the city, and do a little browsing.

Head to the Pointe-à-Callière Musée d'Archéologie et d'Histoire to brush up on your Québec history. Kitty-corner to the museum is Place Royale, the first public square in Ville-Marie. Walk down to the Vieux-Port and stroll along the waterside promenade and check out Habitat 67 and Chapelle Notre-Dame-de-Bon-Secours, the oldest church in the city.

In the late afternoon head out onto Jacques-Cartier Quay to Terrasses Bonsecours for a drink on the patio and a great view of the skyline as the sun begins to dip down. Head past the artists and street vendors on Place Jacques-Cartier and up to Basilique Notre-Dame-de-Montréal for the nightly light show.

Try local French favorite Le Club Chasse et Pêche for dinner. After the meal, head to Place d'Armes Hôtel and Suites for a nightcap and a view of the city's twinkling lights at rooftop bar La Terrasse Place d'Armes. If you're not ready to head back to your hotel, there's

Cyclists, rollerbladers, and pedestrians take to the Lachine Canal in Montréal.

Musée d'Art Contemporain.

always a chance to make a few late-night dance moves at dance club Wunderbar.

Day 2

After breakfast at Le Cartet, rent a Bixi from the closest stand and head down to the river and along the Lachine Canal. Hook a right and cross the bridge at Marché Atwater; leave the bike there and head along rue Notre-Dame West to dig for treasures in the numerous antiques shops. Stop for lunch at Burgundy Lion for their classic fish and chips before hopping back on a bike or walking up to the Centre Canadien d'Architecture.

From there head along rue Ste-Catherine for some retail therapy, making sure to stop into classic Montréal department stores Holt Renfrew and La Maison Ogilvy, as well as Marie Saint Pierre, the eponymous boutique of designer Marie Saint Pierre. Grab dinner at the Dominion Square Tavern and sip on a Canuck cocktail.

Catch a dance production at the Place des Arts or see an old art house film or foreign flick at the Cinémathèque Québécoise, before walking back to your hotel through Chinatown and picking up a slice of Japanese cheesecake at Pâtisserie Harmonie.

Day 3

Take the Métro to rue Sherbrooke and walk north on rue St-Denis, taking as many side streets as possible to explore the neighborhood's true character. Grab breakfast at French bistro L'Express and keep your eyes peeled for the cobblestone avenue Duluth and, farther north, avenue Marie Anne, Leonard Cohen's old haunt. Explore a bit of the French side of avenue Mont-Royal before heading back west.

Take advantage of one of the best lunch deals in the city at Au Cinquième Péché and then head for boulevard St-Laurent. Browse the shops and take in the street's history as you head south. Stop in at Kitsch 'n' Swell and La Centrale Galerie Powerhouse. Have a microbrew at Réservoir and get a thick, smoked-meat sandwich at Schwartz's. Catch an up-and-coming band or dance the night away to the city's most eclectic DJs at Casa del Popolo.

Day 4

Go for breakfast at Le Gros Jambon before heading to the latest exhibit at the Musée d'Art Contemporain. Then lunch at Brasserie T! next door. Hop on bus 80 up avenue du Parc, getting off at the George-Étienne Cartier statue, and follow the signs to the top of Mont-Royal for a spectacular view of the city. Take your time coming back down, and head north on avenue du Parc toward Mile End.

Browse the chic boutiques on avenue Laurier, then make your way to St-Viateur Bagel Shop and eat your hot-from-the-oven treat with a coffee from Café Olimpico. Check out the vintage stores on rue St-Viateur and avenue Bernard. Comic fans should hit up Drawn & Quarterly.

Walk north into Petite Italie on St-Laurent and pop into Café Italia for a shot of espresso, then over to Marché Jean-Talon for some local Québec goods. Keep dinner simple but chic at Bottega Pizzeria and then hop a cab (or take a stroll) to Bar Waverly for a little nightlife.

Day 5

Head to the Village, get goodies to go from Le Mie Matinale, and make your way to the Pont Jacques-Cartier. Built over the St-Lawrence River, the bridge has spectacular panoramic views of the city, and it's a unique way to get to Parc Jean-Drapeau. Once on the island, you can head off for a day of rides at La Ronde or just ogle the awe-inspiring wonder that is Buckminster Fuller's Biosphère.

Have a picnic on the shores of the river, wander the gardens, then hop the Métro back for an unparalleled dining experience at Toqué! and an evening performance at Cirque du Soleil.

Day 6

Throw your hiking boots in a bag and leave Montréal on the first bus to Mont-Tremblant National Park for a day in the rugged out-doors. At the largest and oldest park in the province, you can hike, swim, canoe, and kayak here to your heart's content. For something a little less taxing, head to Mont-Tremblant Resort for some alpine luging and pedal-boating. Spend the night in Mont-Tremblant's Auberge la Porte Rouge and have dinner at Seb l'Artisan Culinaire.

Québec City's Musée de la Civilisation

The Escalier du Casse-Cou connects Québec City's Upper and Lower Town.

Day 7

Get up early for the drive to Québec City. Check into your hotel in Vieux-Québec's Upper Town then head directly to Café-Boulangerie Paillard for some fresh croissants. Browse the shops and historic buildings on Côte de la Fabrique until it brings you to Terrasse Dufferin in the shadow of Château Frontenac. Snack on a beaver tail pastry as you stroll the promenade and look out over the St-Lawrence, then head into the chateau for a guided tour.

Tour the historic Citadelle and then wander through the winding streets and alleys of Upper Town.

For dinner, take your pick of the restaurants along rue St-Louis or splurge at Le Patriarche. After dinner, walk along Les Fortifications and finish the night at a *boîte à chansons,* such as Le Pape-Georges, or with a nightcap at the cozy Bar Ste-Angèle.

Day 8

After breakfast at Crêperie le Billig take the Escalier du Casse-Cou or ride the Funiculaire du Vieux-Québec down to one of the oldest streets in North America, rue du Petit-Champlain. Browse the independent boutiques and follow the cobblestone lanes that will eventually lead you to Place Royale. Take a peek at La Fresque des Québécois and see if you can point out the famous characters. Whether you fail the test or not, head to the Musée de la Civilisation and brush up on your history.

After visiting the museum, head west along rue St-Paul to browse antique stores. Or skip the stores and take the well-hidden rue Sous-le-Cap until it brings you to Galerie Madeleine Lacerte. Check out the latest exhibit and then cross the street for a drink at Taverne Belley and watch the locals playing petanque.

Get Outside

No matter where you are in the province or how low the temperature drops, you're never far from serious outdoor fun.

Montréal

- **Parc du Mont-Royal** is the ideal place to jog, walk, or bike in the warmer months. Come winter, you can snowshoe up that same incline or cross-country ski along the mountain's 20 kilometers of trails. Once you get to the top, enjoy skating at **Beaver Lake.** If you want to relive your childhood, join others who toboggan down the eastern face of the mountain when the snow is flying.

- Biking is the best way to explore the city and get your daily dose of exercise. There are 350 kilometers of bike paths for you to explore. The bike rental program **Bixi** makes it simple.

- **The Lachine Canal** is great for cycling in summer and an ideal spot to cross-country ski come winter. It's also one of the few places in the city where you can rent a kayak or rowboat.

- On Montréal's south shore you'll find **Mont Sutton** and Mont Bromont, home to the ski hill **Ski Bromont.** Both hills are ideal for skiing in the winter and hiking in the summer.

- **Mont-Tremblant National Park** to the north of the city is great for skiing, hiking, mountain climbing, canoeing, and kayaking.

- **Oka National Park** has a beach and is ideal for water sports and swimming when it's warm out. There are also a number of hiking trails that can be used for snowshoeing come winter.

- **Parc Jean-Drapeau,** on an island south of the city, offers an Olympic-sized outdoor pool, tons of biking paths, and even a beach where you can bathe in the St-Lawrence.

- **Parc LaFontaine** on the Plateau is ideal for running or walking in the summer, while during the winter it becomes the ultimate place to lace up your skates.

Québec City

- **Baie de Beauport,** just outside of the city, is a great place to canoe, kayak, sail, or play beach volleyball.

- **Parc des Plaines d'Abraham** is the place in the city to run, walk, bike or even swim. Come winter you can cross-country ski, ice skate, or snowshoe.

- A 20-minute drive out of the city will bring you to the bird-watching and hiking heaven that is **Cap-Tourmente.**

- **Corridor du Littoral** follows the coast of the river and is ideal for experienced (or determined) cyclists.

- **Domaine Maizerets** is great for biking, skating, cross-country skiing, snowshoeing, and tobogganing.

- Some of the best skiing in the country is just an hour's drive away at **Le Massif.**

- Ski station **Mont-Sainte-Anne** is busiest throughout winter, but in summer, the area offers camping and mountain biking trails.

- **Parc de la Plage Jacques-Cartier,** just outside of the city, offers boating, mountain climbing, and 2.5 kilometers of hiking trails.

- **Parc du Bois-de-Coulonge,** which is easily accessible from downtown, offers cycling, a number of walking trails, and lawn bowling in summer.

- **Parc Linéaire de la Rivière St-Charles,** with 32 kilometers of trails to choose from, offers opportunities for biking, rollerblading, snowshoeing, cross-country skiing, and even ice-skating.

Québec City as viewed from the Citadelle

On your way to Saint-Roch, stop to admire the graffiti murals on the highway overpass, then head for a bistro dinner at Les Bossus. Cap the night off with a show at Le Cercle and a bit of dancing at La Cuisine.

Day 9

Have a hearty breakfast at Le Petit Coin Latin, then head to the Fontaine de Tourny and take a trip around the statues at the Hôtel du Parlement. Stroll the rolling hills of the Parc des Plaines d'Abraham and make a stop at Tours Martellos. Continue through the park all the way to the Musée National des Beaux-Arts du Québec. After seeing the latest exhibit, grab launch at Morena on avenue Cartier.

Follow Cartier south, down the sloping hill, and take a right on rue St-Jean, where you can spend the rest of the afternoon popping in and out of stores and drinking coffee at the many cafés. Don't miss Auberge J.A. Moisan, the oldest grocery store in North America, or the quiet shade of St-Matthew Church and Cemetery.

While you've got the European vibe going why not continue with a French wine and regional cuisine at Le Moine Échanson. After your meal, head over to La Grande-Allée for a taste of sophisticated nightlife at Le Charlotte Ultra Lounge.

Day 10

Head down to Cyclo Services and rent bikes for the day. Pack your bags with sandwiches and goodies from the Marché du Vieux-Port and then take the Corridor du Littoral heading west. Ride about three kilometers and make a stop at the historic park Domaine Maizerets. After a wander among the ancient trees and lily-pad ponds, get back on your bike and ride another nine kilometers to the impressive park Chute Montmorency.

Leave your bike and follow the path closest to the falls and cool off in the mist. If you have any energy left, climb the stairs to the top for a view of the falls and mythic Île d'Orléans.

After you've taken in the view, go for a well-earned dinner at L'Aventure, then get back on your bikes and return to the city. Once there, leave the bikes at the rental place and head for a late-night stroll around the Vieux-Port, grabbing a treat at Le Marché du Vieux Port along the way.

Head back to your hotel for a good night's rest and an early drive back to Montréal in the morning before heading home.

Romantic Weekend Getaways

For a short, romantic getaway, Montréal offers the perfect balance of sightseeing and nightlife. Whether it's a moonlit walk along the Vieux-Port or a dinner at one of the city's best restaurants, couples can't help but be intoxicated by the city's French charm.

Québec City meanwhile is considered one of the most romantic cities in North America. The winding cobblestone streets, classic New France architecture, and overall charming ambience have a tendency to bring out the amorous side in visitors. But nothing seems forced about it—instead, it carries its romantic status quite naturally.

Montréal

DAY 1

After you check into the sumptuous Pierre du Calvet, stroll through Vieux-Montréal. Go for lunch at Les 400 Coups, then take in the latest exhibit at DHC/ART and check out some local talent at Marché Bonsecours. In the Vieux-Port, climb the steps to the top of the Tour de l'Horloge for a magnificent view of the river and skyline.

As the stars start to come out, grab a pre-dinner drink at Le Philémon Bar before your reservations at the cozy and inviting Le Bremner. Head back to your hotel or hire a *calèche* to take you for a horse-drawn carriage tour, and take in the scenery as you snuggle up.

DAY 2

It's off to the Plateau for brunch at Le Chien Fumant. Afterwards, hop on the Métro and head out to Jardin Botanique, Montréal's botanical gardens, and explore the 30 different gardens and get an up-close look at the Stade Olympique. Head back toward the city

Montréal on the Cheap

The popular Casa del Popolo is a café, bar, and live music venue.

Montréalers are all about having the highest standard of living on the smallest possible budget. That's part of what makes Montréal such an attractive city in the first place. Sure, you can still enjoy exclusive shops and four-star restaurants, but you don't need a bank loan to do it. Here are a few tips to get the most from your travel budget.

Restaurants

When downtown, Asian eateries are often a budget-friendly choice. Try **Qing Hua Dumpling** and **Kazu.**

Dining alfresco is a Montreal tradition. **Dinette Triple Crown** makes it easy by supplying you with a picnic basket filled with a tablecloth, cutlery, extra hot sauce, and your order of southern favorites like fried chicken and grits. All you have to do is cart it over to the adjacent park. Farther south on the Main, the mini-burgers and fries at **Patati Patata** are the ultimate takeout, especially for an alfresco dinner at Parc Jeanne-Mance.

A number of upscale restaurants offer affordable lunchtime meals. Some of the best include **Toqué!, Kitchenette,** and **Graziella.**

Diners in the know bring their own bottle to **La Colombe** and **Le Quartier Général.**

The king of upscale late-night dinners is the classic French bistro **Leméac,** where they serve a table d'hôte special for $22 after 10pm.

Vegans and vegetarians should head to the Mile End for some of the best and most affordable vegetarian food in the city. Top spots include **Le Cagibi, La Lumière du Mile End, Le Panthère Verte,** and **Dépanneur le Pick-Up.**

Nightlife

Most bars have nightly music and impromptu dancing for the price of a drink. Check the listings at **Bar Plan B, Korova, Casa del Popolo, L'Escogriffe,** and **Brutopia.**

Museums and Galleries

Most of the city's independent galleries are free and host weekly or monthly vernissages (exhibition openings) with complimentary drinks. Top spots include **Belgo Building, DHC/ART,** and **Parisian Laundry.**

At the **Musée des Beaux-Arts de Montréal** many exhibits can be viewed free of charge, and the museum offers half-price admission on Wednesday nights.

Admission is free on Wednesday nights after 5pm at **Musée d'Art Contemporain.**

Hotels

Vieux-Montréal is the ideal place to stay, but the prices can be polarizing. If you're on a budget, try the welcoming hostel **Auberge Alternative de Vieux-Montréal,** which offers private rooms, or the affordable and charming bed-and-breakfast **Le Petit Prince.**

Move away from the tourist areas and stay in the residential neighborhood Plateau Mont-Royal at a bed-and-breakfast like **Gingerbread Manor** or **Pensione Popolo.**

on a Bixi and stop off in Parc LaFontaine to leave the bikes and pick up some chocolate at Les Chocolats de Chloé.

Continue along Duluth to grab a quick bite at Chez José for lunch before browsing the shops along St-Laurent. Don't forget to check out the urban chic selection at Boutique Unicorn or the effortlessly cool designer pieces at Les Étoffes, then step into Bu for an early evening drink.

Take a mini-tour of the Mile End and then make your way south on Park avenue and nab a cozy table for two at Buvette Chez Simone. When dinner's over, stay for a drink and the heady nightlife or stroll under the stars to Big in Japan Bar and finish the night off with one of their killer cocktails.

DAY 3

Grab croissants from Boulangerie Guillaume, a latte from Café Sardine next door, and leave the city behind for a day in the country; take Route 20 out to the Eastern Townships and follow La Route des Vins (The Wine Route). Stop in for a tasting at Vignoble Les Pervenches, then head to the town of Knowlton to check out the quaint English-influenced architecture and antiques shops.

Continue on the Route des Vins to Domaine Vitis for a sip of their ice wine. Keep on the trail and head a bit farther south for a final tasting at Vignoble d'Orpailleur. From there it's a short drive through the country to the town of Sutton, where you can get a bit of fresh air during a walk on Mount Sutton before settling in for a rustic French meal at Auberge des Appalaches. After dinner drive back into the city or hang out in the country and book a room above the restaurant.

Parc LaFontaine is a bit of greenery in the middle of Montréal.

Québec City

DAY 1

Check into your suite at the plush Auberge Saint-Antoine and then go exploring along the cobblestone streets of Quartier du Petit-Champlain. Stop for a coffee or a cool drink on the corner terrace of Lapin Sauté and be charmed by the traditional music of street performers. Head to Place Royale and check out the small but beautiful chapel in Église Notre-Dame-des-Victoires.

Browse antiques and galleries on rue St-Pierre and rue St-Paul. Stroll among the boats and quays of the Vieux-Port, then head to Quai Chouinard and board the *Louis Jolliet.*

Enjoy views of Chute Montmorency, Île d'Orléans, and the illuminated city on this four-hour boat cruise as you dine on a five-course meal.

DAY 2

Breakfast at Panache and then take the Funiculaire du Vieux-Québec to Terrasse Dufferin. Snap the requisite shots of Château Frontenac before taking the stairs at the far end to the Parc des Plaines d'Abraham. Stroll through the park to the Musée National des Beaux-Arts du Québec. After browsing the largest existing collection of Québec art, pick up some gourmet treats at Les Halles du Petit Quartier on Cartier, then grab a cab to Parc du Bois-de-Coulonge. Picnic overlooking the St-Lawrence River, then wander the grounds, and don't miss the arboretum close to the shore.

Hail a cab back to Upper Town and shop the independent boutiques along rue St-Jean. Freshen up back at the hotel and cab it to your reservation in the glass dining room at Le Saint-Amour. After dinner, take a moonlight tour through the streets in a caléche

Église Notre-Dame-des-Victoires, on Place Royale in Québec City

a quaint staircase in the historic Quartier du Petit Champlain

Winter Pursuits and Cold Comforts

Château Frontenac

Life in Montréal and Québec City completely changes once winter hits. And though it might seem like the perfect season to hibernate, the mounting snow is no excuse to stay indoors. Whether you're in the city or the country, there's a variety of things to do when the mercury drops.

Montréal

- Enjoy shopping and exploring the linked walkways in Montréal's **Underground City.** Running 32 kilometers, its size and diversity make it more than just a shopper's paradise.

- Winter means hockey and cheering on the **Canadiens.** Grab tickets to a game at the **Bell Centre** or head to a local bar to catch the game.

- Ice-skating is the ultimate Canadian pastime, and the open-air rink in **Parc LaFontaine** is large enough to accommodate hockey players, wannabe figure skating stars, and those just finding their skating legs.

- There are few things in the world as decadent as real hot chocolate. Warm up and indulge in a cup of the good stuff at **Juliette et Chocolat.**

- "If you can't beat 'em join 'em" is the Montréaler's attitude to winter, and most of them join by hopping on toboggans and sliding down **Mont-Royal** to avenue du Parc.

- See a different side of the city and **cross-country ski** along the historic **Lachine Canal.** The old, converted warehouses and views of the downtown skyline will give you a whole new perspective.

Québec City

- Drive an hour north to **Le Massif,** the highest ski mountain in the province. The ski runs offer 49 different trails and have the most breathtaking views of the St-Lawrence River.

- Bundle up and head to **Château Frontenac** for some serious winter sledding down the **Glissades de la Terrasse Dufferin.**

- The sweet treat known as *tire sur la neige* (maple syrup frozen on snow) can be found at just about every corner come winter.

- A typical après-ski meal of **raclette** is the perfect end-of-the-day fare. It can be procured in the cozy confines of restaurant **Le Petit Coin Latin.**

- **Carnaval de Québec,** which takes place between the end of January and early February, is two weeks of mostly free outdoor fun, from dog-sled races and ice-canoeing to outdoor dance parties and snow sculpture competitions.

(horse-drawn carriage), stopping to admire the view at the Parc du Cavalier-du-Moulin. Then grab a cozy nook at Pub St-Alexandre for a nightcap.

DAY 3

Rise early and drive to the base of the Chute Montmorency, about 20 minutes outside of Québec City, where you'll board the train Le Massif for a leisurely trip up-river. Take in the stunning views of the Charlevoix region and the St-Lawrence from this luxury locomotive. Disembark at Baie-Saint-Paul, check out the modern and ecofriendly hotel La Ferme before exploring the town's cultural heritage at the many galleries and artisanal shops. If all that walking makes you thirsty, grab a local microbrew at Le Saint-Pub.

Hop back on the train heading a farther 40 minutes north to the majestic Fairmont le Manoir Richelieu in La Malbaie for an overnight stay. Located on the banks of the river, it's one of the prettiest spots in the region and a perfect place to kick back for the night. When you're settled in your room, relax next to the outdoor pool and get a massage at the in-house spa.

In the evening have dinner at Vices Versa, and get a taste of the local cuisine.

MONTRÉAL

Sights

With historic roots and a thoroughly modern outlook, Montréal is one of the most distinctive cities in North America. Old Montréal, Notre-Dame Basilica, the Olympic Stadium, Buckminster Fuller's Biosphère, even its legendary Underground City are all part of what makes the city unique. Home to both French- and English-speakers, it also has a large immigrant community; these cultures have inspired and left their marks on the various neighborhoods, and their history is reflected in the sights.

Montréal may have the second-largest population in Canada, but geographically it is tiny, making it ideal to navigate by foot, bike, or Métro (the subway system). Many of the sights, like the Musée d'Art Contemporain, Chinatown, and Basilique Notre-Dame-de-Montréal, are concentrated in the downtown and Vieux-Montréal areas, so even when temperatures drop, it's easy to walk from one to the next.

Spend a day wandering the historic Vieux-Montréal (Old Montréal), brush up on your Canadian history at Pointe-à-Callière Musée d'Archéologie et d'Histoire, then stroll along the waterfront and stop in at the Chapelle Notre-Dame-de-Bon-Secours. While you're there take a peek at Hôtel de Ville (city hall) and catch an evening light show at Notre-Dame Basilica. If you're not worn out yet, an after-dark calèche ride is a romantic way to end the day.

In the western part of downtown you'll find the Centre Canadien d'Architecture (Canadian Centre for Architecture); check out the post-modernist facade and then head over to see the latest exhibit

Look for ★ to find
recommended sights.

Highlights

★ **Most Beautiful Church:** The iconic **Basilique Notre-Dame-de-Montréal** has the most stunning interior decoration (page 53).

★ **Best History Museum:** Learn about Montréal's history at **Pointe-à-Callière Musée d'Archéologie et d'Histoire,** the site where the city was officially established (page 61).

★ **Best Contemporary Art Museum: Musée d'Art Contemporain** features the work of some of the world's most well known contemporary artists (page 73).

★ **Best Street Party:** Closed to traffic for most of the summer, **rue Ste-Catherine Est** is the spot for festivals, food trucks, and fun all summer long (page 76).

★ **Best Public Market:** Marché Jean-**Talon** is a year-round farmers market that offers some of the most diverse and delicious food in the city (page 82).

★ **Best Architecture:** Buckminster Fuller's geodesic dome, the **Biosphère,** hovers in the distance like a great architectural puzzle (page 83).

★ **Best Views:** Parc du Mont-Royal offers amazing vantage points to the city and tons of places to stop and admire the view (page 88).

★ **Most Miraculous Sight:** Built to honor Brother André Bessette and his chosen saint, **St-Joseph's Oratory** is a place of pilgrimage for those seeking healing (page 89).

★ **Most Spectacular Botanical Garden:** Wander for hours through 20 different gardens at **Jardin Botanique** (page 91).

★ **Most Iconic Sight:** Built for the 1976 Olympics, the **Stade Olympique** has since become an internationally recognized building (page 92).

at the Musée des Beaux-Arts on rue Sherbrooke, which is famous for its stately buildings. From there it's an easy walk to the Musée McCord, or if you're all museumed out, take a tour of McGill University. Afterwards, walk through the campus and head up avenue du Parc to Mont-Royal; it's only a few hundred steps up to a beautiful night view of the city.

Ride the Métro to Marché Jean-Talon and from there make your way through Little Italy to see a fresco of Italian dictator Benito Mussolini at the Chiesa della Madonna della Difesa. Continue south and grab a bagel and a coffee with the locals in Mile End, then keep heading south along St-Laurent to take in the history of one of the city's most famous streets.

Sights that are farther away, like the Stade Olympique (Olympic Stadium) and the Jardin Botanique (Botanical Gardens), are easily accessible by Métro. Plan to dedicate a day to exploring the area, especially if you have kids in tow, since the Biodôme (animals!) and Insectarium de Montréal (insects!) are all found in the same Olympic grounds.

Marché Atwater southwest of downtown is best explored on bike—or cross-country skis in the winter—since it backs directly onto the Lachine canal. Make a morning out of it and head to rue Notre-Dame for breakfast and antiquing, then grab lunch from the market and follow the canal back downtown. Watch a Canadiens game at the Centre Bell or visit the Hall of Fame. Montréal may just be an island, but its varied sights pack a punch.

Vieux-Montréal   Map 1

Old Montréal is the city's historic center and remains one of its most charming neighborhoods. It's here that you'll find the Basilique Notre-Dame-de-Montréal and rue St-Paul, the oldest street in the city. As you stroll through the area, it's difficult not to swoon at the cobblestone streets, narrow, tin-roofed boutiques, and converted warehouses. All this history, however, means that when you buy anything here, whether it's a lunchtime snack or a drink at a bar, you're paying, in part, for the ambience.

★ Basilique Notre-Dame-de-Montréal

Presiding over Place d'Armes, the Basilique Notre-Dame-de-Montréal is in the heart of Old Montréal. It's here that thousands of fans lined the streets to celebrate Celine Dion's wedding and paid their respects to the funeral processions of former prime minister Pierre Elliot Trudeau and hockey legend Maurice Richard. The basilica is not only in the heart of historic Montréal—in many ways it represents the heart of the city.

As you approach the basilica you get a feel for its grandness; its bell towers rise high, and on the building's facade are three statues looking out over the growing metropolis: Virgin Mary (representing Montréal), St-John the Baptist (representing Québec), and St-Joseph (representing Canada).

Completed in 1830, the Gothic Revival church, the first of its kind in Canada, is set back from the site of the original Notre-Dame parish church, a baroque-style chapel built by the Roman Catholic Sulpician Order in 1672. By 1800, the original chapel was too small to accommodate the population and plans were underway for the basilica. It was designed by James O'Donnell, an Irish-American Protestant who eventually converted to Catholicism and is buried in the crypt.

Specially ordered and designed by Father Olivier Maurault to celebrate the church's centennial in 1929, the stained-glass windows are entirely unconventional. Depicting the religious and social life of the early Ville-Marie settlement, they show the city's strong ties to the Catholic religion. The deep blue and gold of the ceiling is both particularly striking and unusual. The basilica was viewed as too grandiose for such common events as weddings and funerals, so a second, smaller chapel, Notre-Dame du Sacré-Coeur, was completed in 1891—only to be destroyed by arson nearly 100 years later in 1978. The restoration that took place shortly after drew inspiration from original drawings, but the vault and altar were given a new, modern twist.

Today, the basilica is a site for many high-profile events. Daily mass continues to be held in French at the basilica, and a 20-minute tour is free with entry. "Let There Be Light," a light show telling the story of the building, plays nightly Tuesdays-Saturdays. If you're interested in classical and religious music, the basilica plays host to concerts throughout the year.

MAP 1: 110 rue Notre-Dame W., 514/842-2925, www.basiliquenddm.org; Mon.-Fri. 8:30am-4:30pm, Sat. 8am-4pm, Sun. 12:30pm-4pm; tours daily on the hour and half hour Mon.-Fri. 9am-4pm, Sat. 9am-3:30pm, Sun. 12:30pm-3:30pm; $5 adults, $4 children, children 6 and under free

Chapelle Notre-Dame-de-Bon-Secours and the Musée Marguerite Bourgeoys

Marguerite Bourgeoys was 33 years old when she arrived in Montréal in 1653, recruited by Paul de Chomedey de Maisonneuve, founder of Montréal, to teach school and religion classes. By 1658, she had traded her skills teaching, mending, and sewing in return for a stone chapel, the first of its kind in the colonial outpost and the only one dedicated to the Virgin Mary, Our Lady of Perpetual Help. It's over the ruins of this original church that the existing Chapelle Notre-Dame-de-Bon-Secours was built in 1771.

Look Up: Architectural Montréal

Old Montreal's historic buildings and areas from Expo 67 and the 1976 Olympics stand out as some of the best architecture in the city, but there are a number of other buildings worth a look.

- **Aldred Building:** Completed in 1931 in the art deco style, this stands as an ode to the architectural style that once dominated the cityscape (507 Place d'Armes).

- **Château Apartments:** Passing this aptly named 14-story apartment block gives you a glimpse of why this section downtown was referred to as the "Golden Mile." Built in 1925, it was home to author Mordecai Richler until his death in 2001 (1321 rue Sherbrooke W.).

- **École de Musique Schulich:** McGill University's latest addition is sleek, with black cladding and dark windows. It also has an acoustically perfect auditorium (555 rue Sherbrooke W.).

- **Gare Windsor:** Headquarters of the Canadian Pacific Railway, this Romanesque Revival building was completed in 1889, and you can still visit its old arrival terminal (1100 ave. des Canadiens-de-Montréal).

- **Guaranteed Pure Milk Bottle:** This 10-meter high water tower/milk bottle has always stood out among the downtown skyline. Built in 1930, it's such a part of Montréal culture that even T-shirts are emblazoned with its image (1025 Lucien L'Allier).

- **Habitat 67:** Architect Moshe Safdie was only 24 years old when his master's thesis for McGill University was chosen to be constructed as part of Expo 67. An architectural marvel, Habitat 67 is loosely based on the idea of a kibbutz; 158 interlocking concrete forms are the basis of the experimental housing complex—a must-see (2600 ave. Pierre-Dupuy).

- **The Linton:** The largest apartment of its kind when it was built in 1906-07, this Beaux-Arts building still retains much of its charm and grandeur (1509 rue Sherbrooke W.).

- **L'ITQ:** L'Institut de Tourisme et D'Hotellierie du Québec was once a mass of brown, corrugated siding but is now a glamorous glass building with lots of light and glimmer (3535 rue St-Denis).

- **Palais des Congrès:** Mario Saia's kaleidoscopic extension has put a new, colorful twist on what could have been another concrete slab (159 rue St-Antoine W.).

- **Sun Life Building:** This 24-story office building was an imposing figure when it was completed in 1931 and it continues to stand its ground as one of the most impressive sites on the Montréal skyline (1155 Metcalfe).

- **Tour de la Bourse:** Erected in 1964, this is the home of the Montréal stock exchange and an example of the international style (800 Place Victoria).

- **Université de Montréal:** The main building, designed by Ernest Cormier, was finished in 1943 and is situated on the northern slope of Mont-Royal (2900 blvd. Edouard-Monpetit).

- **Westmount Square:** Designed by Mies van de Rohe, this is one of the preeminent examples of international style in the city (1 Square Westmount).

With its soft pastels and trompe l'oeil effect, the arched vault of the chapel, an 1886 addition, gives the space a distinctly feminine feel, one that's juxtaposed by a number of ex-votos (a votive offering to a saint) of ships that hang above the pews. Dating back to 1872, the ex-votos give thanks to Mary for a safe passage, a tradition that continues to this day as every September 21 descendants of those who sailed on these ships return to the chapel to pay thanks. Given that the chapel went through a number of different incarnations, the final effect is an eclectic mishmash. One permanent fixture, however, is a wooden statuette of Notre-Dame-de-Bon-Secours, brought from France by Marguerite Bourgeoys in 1672, which miraculously survived the fire of 1754. The chapel also includes artwork by Québécois painters Théophile Hamel and Ozias Leduc.

From the chapel, climb the 69 steps up to the tower and the remaining 23 to the belvedere for two great views of the Old Port (Vieux-Port). Then head down to the crypt. Once used as a school rec room, it now houses treasures that the museum uncovered while excavating the original site of the chapel, which was discovered in 1996.

Much smaller than the chapel, the Marguerite Bourgeoys Museum is housed on the third floor of what was once an adjacent schoolhouse. Famous for founding the Sisters of the Congregation of Notre Dame, Bourgeoys's order still exists today, and the nuns have made a charming history of her life in doll form. Tours of varied length and focus are available, designed to suit visitors' interests and time constraints.

MAP 1: 400 rue St-Paul E., 514/282-8670, www.marguerite-bourgeoys.com; Mar.-Apr. Tues.-Sun. 11am-3:30pm, May-Canadian Thanksgiving Tues.-Sun. 10am-5:30pm, Canadian Thanksgiving-mid-Jan. Tues.-Sun. 11am-3:30pm; $10 adults, $7 seniors and students, $5 children

Habitat 67

Architect Moshe Safdie was only 24 years old when his master's thesis for McGill University was chosen to be constructed as part of Expo 67. An architectural marvel, Habitat 67 sits on a thin peninsula in the St-Lawrence just south of the Old Port. Loosely based on the idea of a kibbutz, 158 interlocking concrete forms are the basis of the experimental housing complex, which was supposed to reflect cities of the future, a time when the population would outgrow urban space. Contrary to the original aim of affordable housing, it's one of the most sought-after addresses in Montréal today and is home to the city's affluent and cultured elite. This is a private residence, so tours are not possible, but it deserves to be viewed nonetheless.

MAP 1: 2600 ave. Pierre-Dupuy, www.habitat67.com; free

Hôtel de Ville (City Hall) overlooks the port and takes its place alongside other important administrative buildings, including the provincial courts. Its green copper roof and stoic facade lend it an air of old-world nostalgia, but even after 130 years it retains a youthful vitality as the city's political hub. Housing the offices of the mayor and city councilors, it remains the site of countless protests and speeches. In 1967, French president Charles de Gaulle stood on the balcony and shouted to a frenzied crowd, "Vive le Québec libre!" (Long live a free Québec!), further fanning the flames of bilingual unrest and leaving an indelible mark on the province's conscience.

Built in 1872-1878, the original building was gutted by a fire in 1922. The roof collapsed, the interior was destroyed, and the city's records turned to ash. With only the exterior wall left standing, architect Louis Parant rebuilt from the inside out, reinforcing the building with a self-supporting steel structure from behind the ruins. Taking inspiration from the city hall of Tours in France, he remodeled the roof in a Beaux-Arts style, swapping its slate-tiled roof for the existing copper one.

Inside, you're greeted by the Hall of Honour, an open space full of marble and gold embellishments. Just off the hall is the council room, adorned with five stained-glass windows by John Patrick O'Shea. Installed in 1926, they depict the fundamental aspects of the city: religion, agriculture, the port, commerce, and finance. Open to visitors year-round, the hall plays host to a number of exhibits. Free, hour-long tours are offered throughout the day, though certain areas, such as the protocol room and the mayor's office, are off-limits.

Behind city hall is a wide swath of land known as the Champ-de-Mars. Used for military maneuvers and parades, it was once the site of Montréal's fortifications, which protected the city from invasion. Buried under a municipal parking lot for most of the last century, it was returned to its former incarnation in the 1980s, and remnants of the original city walls are now integrated into the landscape of the park.

MAP 1: 275 rue Notre-Dame E., 514/872-0077, www.ville.montreal.qc.ca; Mon.-Fri. 8am-5pm; tours daily 10am-4pm; free

Marché Bonsecours

When the city of Montréal decided to build a structure to house an indoor market in the 19th century, the site on which Marché Bonsecours now sits was an ideal choice. Since the early days of Nouvelle France, many prominent Montréalers made their home on the site, including François Bigot, last Intendant of Nouvelle France, and John Molson, founder of the popular Canadian brewery.

Guided City Tours

A great way to discover the city is through a mix of social and historical contexts. **L'Autre Montréal** (3680 Jeanne-Mance #331, 514/521-7802, ext. 226, www.autremontreal.com, $15-25 adult) offers guided tours with a focus on history, architecture, urban planning, and sociology and gives you a great vision of the city's unique culture and community. Some of the more interesting tours include a tour of Montréal's back alleys and a look at the various immigrant communities. Tours of smaller neighborhoods not included in this book are also available and a great way to see places off the beaten path.

Les Fantômes du Vieux-Montréal (469 rue St-François-Xavier, 514/844-4021, www.fantommontreal.com, May-Oct., $22 adults, $19 students, $13 children) is not for the easily scared. On this ghost tour of Old Montréal, guides in period costume tell you all about the hangings, sorcery, tortures, and spooky sightings that make up the city's past. They also have specialized tours come Halloween.

Fitz and Folwell (115 ave. Mont-Royal W., 514/840-0739, www.fitzand-follwell.co, $39-120), which offers both bike and snow shoe tours come winter, offers three distinct walking tours, one of which centers around the Montréal of writer Mordecai Richler. The other two tours feature the Underground City (perfect for -40° weather) and a food tour of the Main. All tours include lunch and range in price, so reserve and budget accordingly.

Guidatour (360 rue St-François-Xavier, 514/844-4021, www.guidatour.qc.ca, May-Oct., $18 adults, $16 students, $9 children) runs walking tours of Old Montréal, offering amusing anecdotes and snippets of history as you wander the cobblestone streets. Guides are bilingual and tours depart from the gift shop at Basilique Notre-Dame-de-Montréal.

Héritage Montréal (100 rue Sherbrooke E., 514/286-2662, www.heritagemontreal.qc.ca, May-Oct. Sat.-Sun., cost varies) is a nonprofit organization that takes visitors on various tours that explore the architectural, social, or historical evolution of the city's neighborhoods. Departure points vary depending on the week and the tour, and reservations are recommended.

Charles Dickens and his group of amateur actors performed on this very site during its incarnation as the Théâtre Royal, whose ruins are buried underneath the existing structure's foundations.

Designed by architect William Footner in 1844, the building was inaugurated with its first public market in January 1847 and remained the city's main agricultural market for over a century. With its tin-plated dome and neoclassical style it's considered one of the 10 major achievements in the history of Canadian architecture.

From 1852 to 1878 it served as city hall and as such demanded specialized banquet and dining halls to accommodate the social demands of the city. The spirit of a public market remains, with exclusive boutiques selling everything from authentic Canadian crafts to jewelry, leather, and hand-blown glass, all designed and made in Québec. Cafés and restaurants line the facade of the building, and it still hosts a number of events.

Musée du Château Ramezay

When the governor of Montréal, Claude de Ramezay, started work on his house in 1704, Montréal was a mere colonial outpost, home to approximately 1,500 inhabitants and barely 200 buildings. He chose a plot of land at the edge of the fortified city (it now sits across the street from city hall). He was obsessed with having a home that matched his perceived importance and he paid for the construction of the property out of his own pocket, promptly going into debt, though not before becoming the envy of the city's residents. The house has gone through many incarnations in its 300-year history, including head offices for the French West India Company (1745-1764), the base for American Revolutionaries including Benjamin Franklin (1775-1776), and a university (1884-1889).

Little of the original structure remains inside the house, though, so if you're expecting a trip back in time, you'll be a tad disappointed. Though multimedia displays take you through the building's evolution, the real focus is on the history and progression of the city itself. One of the highlights includes the Salle de Nantes, a dark-wood-paneled room from 1725 that is thought to have been carved by Germain Boffrand, chief architect to Louis XIV and Louis XV. The room was part of the French pavilion at the 1967 Expo and was donated to the museum shortly after. Of the entire house, the basement feels the most preserved, with vaulted ceilings and authentic fireplaces that still smell of freshly burned wood. It's also where the life of Montréal's 18th-century inhabitants is depicted, with recreations of one-room homes, mannequins in traditional dress, examples of farming material, and a room dedicated to the furniture found in homes during the period. From May to October, the museum also boasts an outdoor café that looks out over the house's gardens and that is, in a genius move, catered by the renowned restaurant Le Club Chasse et Pêche.

MAP 1: 280 rue Notre-Dame E., 514/861-3708, www.chateauramezay.qc.ca; June-Canadian Thanksgiving daily 10am-6pm; Canadian Thanksgiving-May Tues.-Sun. 10am-4:30pm; $10 adults, $9 seniors, $8 students, $5 children

Place d'Armes

As early as 1720, citizens of the Ville-Marie settlement would gather on this site to watch military maneuvers on the Place d'Armes, a French name for the area where a city's defenders would congregate. After the Notre-Dame church was demolished and replaced by the

SIGHTS
VIEUX-MONTRÉAL

basilica, Place d'Armes became a public square, the site of hay and wood markets and, later, of a Victorian garden and tramway hub.

The site's real significance, however, comes not so much from the spot itself as from what surrounds it. Located in the heart of historic Montréal, it's bordered on all sides by structures that define Montréal's diverse heritage. Directly to the right of Notre-Dame Basilica is the Séminaire de Saint-Sulpice, the city's oldest building. It was constructed in a U-shape by the Sulpician priests in 1684. The building's clock, built in 1701, is the oldest of its kind in North America, and the gardens are said to be among the oldest on the continent. It's still owned and run by the same church order that founded it, the Compagnie des Prêtres de Saint-Sulpice.

Erected in 1888, the New York Life building on the northeast corner of the square became the city's first skyscraper, a whole eight floors up and furnished with an elevator. Kitty-corner to New York Life, the Royal Trust Building and the Duluth Building (to the left of the basilica) are two early-20th-century skyscrapers. They represent a distinct architectural shift around the square, one that is cemented with the arrival of the art deco Aldred Building in 1931. A glass and steel structure, now known as the National Bank Tower, completed the square's architectural timeline in 1968.

The newly refurbished square features the de Maisonneuve monument depicting the founders of Montréal: Paul de Chomedey de Maisonneuve, Charles Lemoyne, Lambert Closse, Jeanne Mance, and an Iroquois warrior. The square has been made more pedestrian friendly, surrounded by cobblestone streets and fitted with sprawling benches that are perfect for a rest.

MAP 1: Corner of rue St-Jacques W. and Côte-de-la-Place d'Armes

Place Jacques-Cartier

Lined with restaurants, inns, and cafés and populated by street artists and seasonal fruit stalls, Place Jacques-Cartier, sloping down toward the St-Lawrence River, remains true to its roots as a natural meeting place. An archaeological dig in 1991 uncovered remains of a First Nations campsite in this exact spot. By the early 1800s, it had become the site of the New Marketplace, surrounded by wooden stalls, inns, and stores. With the creation of Marché Bonsecours, the "New Marketplace" was no longer needed, but it remained the market's outdoor extension and started its transformation into a center for hotels and restaurants.

At the north end of the square you'll find Nelson's Column, erected in 1809. The second monument to be built in the city—the first was a bust of King George III, which stood for five years before it was mutilated in 1775—and the first monument in the British Empire to be dedicated to the admiral famous for defeating Napoleon during the Seven Years' War. As in Nelson's Column in London's Trafalgar Square (which was built 31 years after its Montréal counterpart), Nelson faces away from the banks of the river, allegedly to combat his seasickness. The monument was highly controversial, and in 1930 Montréal's Francophone population erected a statue in honor of French naval officer Jean Vauquelin, who fought against the British before being subsequently captured and released. Waging an eternal personal battle, their statues now stare at each other from across rue Notre-Dame.

MAP 1: Between rue Notre-Dame E., rue de la Commune E., and Place Jacques-Cartier

Place Royale

This flat square of concrete tiles might not be much to look at, but it represents one of the most important places in all of Old Montréal. From the early days of the Ville-Marie settlement this was the spot where inhabitants would gather to hear royal orders and decrees read out. Between 1642 and 1676, this was the location of the annual fur-trading fairs where the First Nations would bring their pelts to be traded for various goods from the French.

The most important event to have taken place on this spot, however, is the signing of the Great Peace Treaty of Montréal in 1701 between the French, their native allies, and the Five Nations Iroquois, ending nearly a century of war.

MAP 1: Corner of rue de la Commune and Place Royale

★ Pointe-à-Callière Musée d'Archéologie et d'Histoire

It was on this site on May 17, 1642, that Montréal was established. Founding members of the colony—Paul de Chomedey de Maisonneuve, Jeanne Mance, and Father Vimont—were on hand to mark the occasion at what was then a small point of land that jutted out into the St-Lawrence and St-Pierre Rivers. By 1688 the site was home to Louis Hector de Callière, third governor of Montréal and the museum's namesake. When the settlement began to build fortifications in 1716, the point fell outside of those boundaries, making it an invaluable archaeological site. Dedicated to the various people—native, French, and English—that make up the city's past, Pointe-à-Callière is Canada's only sizable archaeology museum and the quintessential museum on Montréal.

Opened in 1992 as part of the celebrations for the city's 350th anniversary, the museum's architecture is distinctly contemporary, standing out in the historic port and disguising the rich history that sits within and beneath its walls. Don't be fooled by the modern reception area: Historic artifacts and archaeological finds confront you at every turn throughout the six distinct buildings, which include Montréal's first custom house (Ancienne-Douane Building) and first electrically operated wastewater pumping system (Youville

Pumping Station). The most fascinating exhibit, however, remains the museum's own archaeological site.

Below the ground level of the main Éperon building, you'll discover traces of Montréal's (then Ville-Marie) first Catholic cemetery. Burial plots of both French colonists and First Nations show the unique reality of the early days of the settlement, when French and First Nations were encouraged to live and mix harmoniously.

Montréal's oldest collector sewer is also on display here: Completed in 1838, it canalized the St-Pierre River underground into one of the first sewer pipes, one that remained in use until 1989.

The number of yearly visitors to the museum has hit the 350,000 mark, so you can almost always expect to find a crowd, especially during the high season of June through August.

MAP 1: 350 Place Royale, 514/872-9150, www.pacmusee.qc.ca; Tues.-Fri. 10am-5pm, Sat.-Sun. 11am-5pm; tours Mon.-Fri. 12:30pm, 2:30pm, 3:30pm, and 4:30pm and Sat.-Sun. 12:30pm, 2:30pm, and 3:30pm; $20 adults, $16 seniors, $12 students 18-30, $9.50 students 13-17, $7 children

Quartier International

Linking Old Montréal and downtown, the newly designated Quartier International is the result of one of the city's most extensive redevelopment projects. Inaugurated in 2004, the centerpiece of the area is Place Jean-Paul-Riopelle, a fountain and public square flanked on one side by the newly developed Palais des Congrès (Montréal's convention center). On the other side, you'll find the sleek glass headquarters of Caisse de Dépôts et Placements du Québec, new home of Montréal's renowned restaurant Toqué!

Riopelle, who died in 2002, was a seminal Québécois artist and member of the Automatistes movement, whose work was influenced by surrealism and is similar to abstract-expressionism. The fountain at the center of the square incorporates his 1969 sculpture *La Joute,* a tribute to the hockey heroes of his youth, which originally stood in the Parc Olympique, the complex that includes the Stade Olympique.

MAP 1: Corner of rue St-Jacques and rue de Bleury

Rue Saint-Paul

Winding and narrow rue St-Paul is the oldest street in Montréal. Designed by priest, historian, and urban planner François Dollier de Casson, creator of the majority of the street layout of what is now Old Montréal, rue St-Paul was originally paved in 1672 under the direction of city founder Paul de Chomedey de Maisonneuve, whose home, conveniently enough, was also on the same road. Linking Fort Ville-Marie with the Hôtel Dieu (the hospital), the settlement's main thoroughfare remained a vital part of the historic center until the 20th century.

clockwise from top left: Place d'Armes in Vieux-Montréal; Basilique Notre-Dame-de-Montréal in the heart of Vieux-Montréal; the Casino de Montréal, Île Notre-Dame, Greater Montréal

Many of the buildings that line the street date back to the 19th century. They now house some of the city's most modern and contemporary stores and restaurants. Between June and September, it is partially closed to traffic.

MAP 1: Between rue McGill and rue Berri

Tour de l'Horloge

Jutting out into the St-Lawrence, the Montréal Clock Tower marks the entry to the Port of Montréal. Built in 1919-1922 in the Beaux-Arts style, the 45-meter-high tower commemorates the merchant navy seamen who lost their lives in World War I and World War II. It is fitted with a clock face, a replica of the one that sits atop Big Ben in London, that looks out over four directions of the port and was built in England by Gillett and Johnson. It also served as a lighthouse, guiding ships into shore. Climb up the tower's 192 steps and look out over the St-Lawrence for an unparalleled view.

MAP 1: Clock Tower Quay; www.oldportofmontreal.com, May 6-Sept. 8 daily 10am-7pm; free

Vieux-Port

For centuries after the first explorers arrived, Montréal was the final destination of hundreds of thousands of immigrants who made their way for the first time onto Canadian shores. Until 1948, when a series of locks finally connected the St-Lawrence with the Great Lakes, Montréal was the disembarkation point for both trans-Atlantic ships and trains from all over North America. Between 1896 and 1930, Montréal was the major distribution point for merchandise both into and out of the country. At the west end of the Old Port, soil no. 5, which closed for good in 1995, is one of its grandest monuments.

The sheds, grain elevators, and quays that line the port are relics from its heyday, but a major revamp in the 1980s transformed the port into today's booming district. Converted warehouses are now quay-side restaurants, cafés, and boutiques. You'll find a labyrinth in shed 16, the Montréal Science Center and IMAX on King Edward Pier, and Cirque du Soleil one pier over.

Rue de la Commune and a thin park is the only thing separating Vieux-Montreal from the Vieux-Port. The park runs the entire length of the Old Port Promenade, offering tourists and locals an ideal spot to relax and catch a cool breeze off the water. Yu can dock your boat in the many marinas, take a boat cruise on the St-Lawrence, or rent a pedal boat for a trip around the Bonsecours basin.

MAP 1: Old Port Promenade, between rue McGill and rue Amherst

Cathédrale Marie-Reine-du-Monde

After St. James Cathedral burnt down in 1852, Ignace Bourget, the first bishop of Montréal, decided he wanted to recreate a smaller version of Rome's St-Peter's Basilica. After drawing up the plans, architect Victor Bourgeau quit, saying he could not replicate St-Peter's on a smaller scale. The project went ahead without him (though he subsequently returned), and the first cornerstone for the existing church was laid in 1870. It opened to the public in 1894 and became a cathedral in 1919. Bourget got his wish, though he wasn't around to see it; the sizable church is a perfect replica, right down to the red copper baldachin that was hand-carved in Rome.

Unsurprisingly, the cathedral appears older than its years; behind the facade, the limestone on the outer part of the nave of the church looks distinctly aged. In a delightfully modern move, however, the wrought iron and glass front doors open automatically, sweeping out and ushering you into the narrow narthex. Columns with gilded crowns and the otherwise modest ceiling moldings inlayed with gold support the high, arched ceilings of the nave. Hues of soft green and blush decorate the cathedral, giving it a gentle and slightly feminine touch. Rising 80 meters in height, the cupola is surrounded with stained-glass windows. Similar to Notre-Dame Basilica, the cathedral's main works of art are dedicated to the city's devout Catholics and include depictions of Marguerite Bourgeoys teaching native children and Grey Nun founder Marguerite d'Youville aiding the sick. Bourget's remains are buried beneath one of the pillars, but there is a mortuary chapel in his honor; the floor and walls are covered in Italian marble, and his tomb takes center stage.

Like St-Peter's, the cathedral has 13 statues that adorn the facade, but breaking with tradition they do not represent Jesus and the 12 apostles. Instead they represent the patron saints of parishes that offered them to the diocese and include Saint Hyacinth, Saint Francis of Assisi, and Saint John the Baptist.

MAP 2: 1085 rue de la Cathédrale, 514/866-1661, www.cathedralecatholiquedemontreal.org; Mon.-Sat. 7am-7pm, Sun. 9am-6pm; free

Centre Bell

Even those who know little about Montréal have probably heard of the city's passionate relationship with their beloved Montréal Canadiens. Partially hidden on the southern edge of downtown, the enormous red-brick and concrete Centre Bell (Bell Center) building is not the most inspired of sports arenas—at least not from the outside. Home of the Canadiens since 1996, it replaced the history-laden Montréal Forum (now a movie theater) and seats 21,273 fans, alternately olé-ing and booing.

Originally called the Molson Centre—the arena changed hands and names in 2002, though Molson still owns the team—it is the largest hockey arena in North America. The interior is exclusively dedicated to Canadiens history and features team photographs and bronze busts of many players. History is present outside the arena with statues honoring the team's four greatest players: Howie Morenz, Guy Lafleur, Maurice "Rocket" Richard, and Jean Béliveau.

Below street level you'll find the Montréal Canadiens Hall of Fame, inaugurated as part of the centennial celebrations. It features memorabilia from throughout the team's 100-year-old history, including Jacques Laplant's original goalie mask, which was the first of its kind in 1959. You can also visit a replica of the 1976-1977 Canadiens dressing room (luckily without the smell), and interactive features invite you to play the hockey journalist—a favorite pastime of many Montréalers. Proceeds from the Hall of Fame go toward helping retired players, many of whom did not profit from the game as much as the owners.

When not packing the house with hockey fans, the center hosts stars of a different kind; entertainers like U2, Celine Dion, Lady Gaga, and Justin Timberlake have performed here.

MAP 2: 1909 ave. des Canadiens-de-Montréal, 514/932-2582, www.centrebell.ca; Tues.-Sat. 10am-6pm, Sun. noon-5pm; tours daily 11:15am and 2:45pm; $11 adults, $8 seniors and children

Centre Canadien d'Architecture

Unique in aim and design, the Centre Canadien d'Architecture (CCA) is the only cultural institution of its kind in Canada. Founded in 1979 by architect Phyllis Lambert, the aim of the institution is to expand the public's awareness of the role architecture plays in our lives, and to act as a research center for scholars.

Lambert, who convinced her father, Samuel Bronfman, to hire Mies van de Rohe to design the famous Seagram's building in New York, later studied architecture at the Illinois Institute of Technology before going on to design Montréal's Saidye Bronfman Centre for the Arts, which is named after her mother. It was Lambert's vast collection of architectural drawings, photographs, and books that became the founding objects of the center's research collection.

Designing the museum to incorporate a Victorian mansion, the 1872 Shaughnessy House, Lambert stayed true to her vision of modern architecture, one that focused on both preservation and progress. Built in 1985-1989 by Montréal-born Peter Rose (Lambert was a consulting architect), the CCA is a perfect example of post-modern architecture. The new wings of the center attach themselves seamlessly to the existing structure, and elements such as the color of limestone, the bay windows, and the windows' placement mimic those of the mansion, preserving and simultaneously mixing the two distinct styles.

From the entrance, however, none of this is visible. Instead you have a view of a thoroughly modern building; it's not until you're inside and past the entrance stairs that you really understand the extent that these two visions have been fused. The fully restored Victorian Devencore Conservatory is one of the museum's highlights and offers a glimpse of the home's past glory.

The center houses exhibits each year that examine the effects of modern living on our surroundings, our environment, and ourselves. It also hosts interesting talks throughout the year as well as family-friendly workshops.

Across the busy boulevard René-Lévesque and just above the highway, you'll find the institute's unconventional garden. Designed by artist and architect Melvin Charney, its use of concrete and unique statues is a comment on the city's architectural and cultural history, and most importantly it offers a great view of the CCA's post-modern facade.

MAP 2: 1920 rue Baile, 514/939-7026, www.cca.qc.ca; Wed.-Sun. 11am-6pm, Thurs. 11am-9pm; $10 adults, $7 seniors, students and children free

Dorchester Square

Inaugurated in 1878, Dorchester Square became a central meeting point and a prestigious address for a number of large companies. The largest was Sun Life Insurance, whose Sun Life Building continues to preside over the east side of the square. Completed in 1931, after 24 years of on and off construction, its architectural presence is rivaled only by the Dominion Square Building at the north end. Designed as both a shopping arcade and an office tower, Dominion Square Building opened in 1930 and now houses the offices of the Montréal *Gazette,* the city's English-language newspaper and one of Canada's oldest.

The square's four monuments honoring the Boer War, Canadian prime minister Sir Wilfrid Laurier, Scottish poet Robert Burns, and Queen Victoria were refurbished and have kept their positions on the square's pathways, which form a five point equilateral cross.

Though it is now surrounded by some of the more interesting architecture in the downtown area, between 1799 and 1854 the square was the site of a Catholic cemetery, an ideal burial spot at the end of the 18th century when it would have been situated in open countryside. And it is the final resting place of many victims of the 1832 cholera epidemic. During the renovations, archaeologists examined the remains before exhuming the bodies and moving them to Notre-Dame-des-Neiges Cemetery on Mont-Royal. To honor those who were laid to rest in this spot, 60 crosses have been installed in the brickwork of the walkways.

Across the street you'll find Place du Canada, inaugurated at the same time. It too was the site of cemeteries until the late 1800s. Today, it's one of a few green spaces in the downtown core and home of the Macdonald Monument, honoring Canada's first prime minister, John A. Macdonald. It was here in 1995 that 100,000 Canadian citizens gathered as part of the Unity Rally to protest Québec's referendum and persuade the province to vote against separating from the rest of Canada.

MAP 2: Blvd. René-Lévesque W. and rue Peel

Grand Séminaire de Montréal

Barricaded by two stone turrets and a high stone wall, the Grand Séminaire de Montréal is well hidden from the busy stretch of Sherbrooke. Built in 1840 as a place to train priests, it is the second seminary to be built in the city—the first is next door to Notre-Dame Basilica—and stands on the same site as the Fort de la Montagne.

Constructed in 1685, the purpose of the fort was to help ward off attacks from the native population; today only the turrets and fieldstone walls remain and are some of the oldest structures in Montréal. Along with the towers, the priests built a series of canals that run along Mont-Royal. The first of these was built in 1675 and remains in use today. The seminary also houses a Romanesque chapel, which boasts hand-carved oak stalls and is one of the best examples of the Beaux-Arts style in the city.

Now the home of a private college, it continues to educate future priests.

MAP 2: 2065 rue Sherbrooke W., 514/935-1162, www.gsdm.qc.ca; tours July-Aug. Tues.-Sat. 1pm and 3pm; free

McGill University

Built on the southern slope of Mont-Royal on ground that was once owned by James McGill, McGill University is one of the oldest universities in Canada, predating confederation by 46 years.

Born in Glasgow, McGill immigrated to Canada, where he became a successful merchant. Upon his death in 1813 he donated his Burnside summer estate to the Royal Institution for the Advancement of Learning, and by 1829, classes were being held in his former home. McGill University granted its first medical degree in 1833; the medical faculty remained the school's only faculty until the addition of the faculty of arts in 1843.

Between 1880 and 1920 the university experienced a huge

amount of expansion, thanks in large part to the financial backing of the city's wealthiest men—William Molson (beer), Sir Peter Redpath (sugar), Lord Strathcona (Hudson's Bay Company), and Sir William Macdonald (tobacco). Much of the architecture from this time still exists today, including the Arts Building, which sits as the focal point of the university's campus looking north from rue Sherbrooke. The Roddick Gates, which so nicely frame the entrance, are themselves a gift, donated by Lady Amy Redpath Roddick in memory of her doctor husband in 1924.

The campus with its sprawling tree-lined lawns is an ideal place to take a rest from the downtown, and it also offers an ideal shortcut to the Plateau Mont-Royal, which is reached by wandering through McGill Ghetto, a nice quiet neighborhood full of gorgeous townhouses and university students.

Historical tours covering the rise and development of the university and campus are provided to the general public but require an email request (welcome@mcgill.ca) at least a week in advance, or you can download your own self-guided tour on the website. Visitors can pass through the campus any time of day, but the Welcome Center, which offers tours, is only open Monday-Friday 9am-5:30pm.

MAP 2: 845 rue Sherbrooke W., www.mcgill.ca; free

Musée des Beaux-Arts de Montréal

Framed in white marble, Musée des Beaux-Arts' Jean-Noël Desmarais Pavilion stands out among the limestone and columns of rue Sherbrooke's Golden Square Mile. Designed by Moshe Safdie of Expo 67 fame, and inaugurated in 1991, the modern building stands in contrast to the museum's original Beaux-Arts structure by William Sutherland Maxwell, which sits across the street.

In 1860 a group of art-loving Montréalers convened to create the Art Association of Montréal, with the aim of spreading knowledge of the arts with exhibitions and art classes. Little was done, however, until 1879, when the association finally got its first building, at the time the only one in the country specifically designed to exhibit and house works of art. By 1909, the association was financially stable enough to live up to its aspirations and it built the Beaux-Arts building, which still exists today.

The pavilions (which are connected through underground walkways), with their distinct designs, speak volumes about the museum's collections and exhibitions. The modern Jean-Noël Desmarais Pavilion is filled with light, the space open and the floors a beautiful black slate. The majority of the museum's permanent collection is found here and includes religious pieces, works by First Nations peoples, and a number of recent acquisitions, contemporary pieces by young Canadian and international artists. Spread throughout

clockwise from top left: Parc du Mont-Royal, Greater Montréal; Chapelle Notre-Dame-de-Bon-Secours, Vieux-Montréal; the Grande Seminare de Montréal, Centre-Ville

The Beaux-Arts building instead houses many of the temporary exhibits. With its sweeping marble staircase, maple woodwork, and Victorian light fixtures, it's the perfect environment for viewing exhibits like Tiffany Glass, Van Dongen, and the groundbreaking show Yves Saint-Laurent.

The converted Erskine and American United Church, which opened in late 2010, is the museum's Canadian pavilion, and the building itself is a national historic site. Admission is half-price after 5pm on Wednesdays and Thursdays.

MAP 2: 1380 rue Sherbrooke W., 514/285-2000, www.mbam.qc.ca; Tues. 11am-5pm, Wed.-Fri. 11am-9pm, Sat.-Sun. 10am-5pm; $20 adults, $12 children and young adults 13-30, children 12 and under free

Musée McCord

Even before David Ross McCord began trolling the country for historical artifacts in 1878, his family, who had been collecting since their arrival in Canada around 1760, had done a good deal of the work for him. By 1921, when the McCord Museum was established, his collection contained 15,000 objects.

Since then the collection has grown, and the museum now has nearly 1.5 million objects, all of which are housed in a classic Arts and Crafts building adjacent to McGill University. Designed by Percy Erskine Nobbs in the early 20th century, it has been the museum's home since 1971. The facade leads to a modern interior—in fact the original structure is almost completely unrecognizable once you pass through the foyer.

The three floors of exhibition space house two temporary exhibits and the permanent collection Simply Montréal, an exciting exhibit of artifacts that traces the history of the area from the early days of discovery.

Anyone who enjoys looking at stuff will enjoy the McCord. The ephemera from bygone eras allows the viewer to understand the cultural and social aspects of the city's life. And much of its life is represented here, from crossbows, helmets, and armor from the explorer days to the Montréal of the 1920s through the 1940s, when American Prohibition turned it into a swinging hot spot—the cocktail napkins and menus are here to prove it.

Interactive multimedia features can be found throughout the museum and offer a unique way to look at the exhibitions. To the left of the entrance is a charming café; the intimate Salle des Amis (Friends' Room) is particularly welcoming. Admission is free Wednesdays after 5pm.

MAP 2: 690 rue Sherbrooke W., 514/398-7100, www.mccord-museum.qc.ca; Mon.-Tues. and Thurs.-Fri. 10am-6pm, Wed. 10am-9pm, Sat.-Sun. 10am-5pm; $14 adults, $10 seniors, $8 students, children free

Place Ville-Marie

One of the most controversial projects the city has ever encountered, Place Ville-Marie was part of Mayor Jean Drapeau's plan to create a new, modern metropolis. Designed by I. M. Pei (who would go on to become one of the most recognized architects of the 20th century) and Henry N. Cobb, the international-style tower was completed in 1962 and was originally the head offices of the Royal Bank. Its construction marked the move of the city's financial district from Old Montréal's rue St-Jacques to downtown. Rising 47 stories, the four cross-shaped towers made up the world's largest and most complex office building—indeed, the complex itself has 52 different postal codes.

Though no longer the only skyscraper in the downtown core, it remains one of the most recognizable. Inside, over 80 stores and boutiques connect the tower to the railway station and Métro. This is the starting point of the mythical and complicated Underground City. Since it allows access to the Métro and a nightclub, the concourse is open later than the shops.

High above is Altitude 737, a panoramic restaurant and one of the city's hottest clubs, whose revolving lights sweep over the city and can be seen from 50 kilometers away.

MAP 2: 1 Place Ville-Marie, 514/866-6666, www.placevillemarie.com; shops Mon.-Wed. 9:30am-6pm, Thurs.-Fri. 9:30am-9pm, Sat. 9:30am-7pm, Sun. noon-5pm; free

Centre-Ville Est   Map 3

Chinatown

With the railroad boom of the 1800s came a wave of Chinese immigration to the city. Dating back to the 1860s, Montréal's Chinatown is far smaller than many of those found in other parts of North America but, despite its size, it remains a vital and culturally important neighborhood. The center of traditional festivals and holidays for the city's Asian communities, it also has its own Chinese hospital and community center.

An exquisite red arch on the corner of St-Laurent and René-Lévesque marks the entrance to Chinatown, which borders downtown and the Quartier International and sits just north of Vieux-Montréal. Originally a residential neighborhood, it is now a commercial district with restaurants, bakeries, stores, and

The Underground City

Montréal's Underground City has turned from legendary to legend. Though it is true that below the city's streets and skyscrapers there are 32 kilometers of underground tunnels to explore, it is not true that there are entire apartment buildings that exist exclusively within this subterranean matrix, or that the city's inhabitants never have to go outdoors.

In 1957, urbanist Vincent Ponte was the first to envision this underground metropolis when his underground pedestrian walkways were included in developer William Zeckendorf's plans for Place Ville-Marie. At the time, the plan only covered seven acres, but Harvard-educated Ponte's self-sufficient pedestrian complex would soon lead to his nickname as the "multilevel man." What started as a solution to cover old railway tracks soon became an integral part of the city's urban planning. Since Ville-Ma-

rie opened in 1962, the subterranean city has grown to include 120 exterior access points and over 12 square kilometers.

Universities, banks, museums, Métro stations, condos, and hotels are all accessible through the underground complexes, but its most important and obvious function is as a huge underground mall. Linking three major shopping tunnels, it is the bloodline of winter commerce, allowing consumers to browse and buy in a temperature-controlled environment. Exploring the many tunnels and passageways can be interesting—especially when you realize just how far you can go—but the main draw of Montréal's underworld is that it allows you to avoid the bitter, freezing cold. In fact, for many Montréalers figuring out how to get from point A to point B without going outside has become something of an art.

traditional crafts—this is the place to pick up authentic Japanese and Chinese china—many of which are concentrated on rue de la Gauchetière. In the summertime this pedestrian-only street fills up with a number of outdoor stalls.

Though Chinatown was established by the Chinese immigrants who came to Canada to work on the railway and in the mines, there was also an influx of Vietnamese-Chinese refugees, many of them French-speaking because Vietnam was under French colonial rule until 1941. As a result, there are now many Vietnamese restaurants throughout the area and it's a great place to pick up some of the best *bánh mì* sandwiches in the city.

A Holiday Inn at the edge of Chinatown designed in the style of a pagoda is a slightly kitschy but nonetheless sweet homage to the community and culture.

MAP 3: Bordered by blvd. René-Lévesque, ave. Viger, blvd. St-Laurent, and rue Jeanne-Mance

★ Musée d'Art Contemporain

Established in 1964 at the height of Québec's Quiet Revolution and abstract art boom, the Musée d'Art Contemporain (MAC) had various homes before settling into its own modern building in 1992.

Part of the Place des Arts, Canada's only cultural complex devoted to both visual and performing arts, the MAC's subtle concrete facade is the perfect foil for the columns and glass of Salle Wilfrid Pelletier next door.

Entering through the unassuming door, you're bathed in light from a domed skylight around which the museum's restaurant is placed. With over 7,000 works in the permanent collection, including works by some of the biggest names in Québec art—like Paul-Émile Borduas, Claude Tousignant, and Jean-Paul Riopelle—it also hosts some of the most exciting, interesting, and boundary-pushing exhibits by Canadian and international artists, such as Marcel Dzama and Bruce Nauman. Grab a drink, catch a live up-and-coming local act, and see the latest exhibit on the first Friday of every month at Friday Nocturnes. Or, relax in the cool of the museum while watching an artistic version of MTV at their summer-long Music Video projection series. Admission is free after 5pm on Wednesdays.

MAP 3: 185 rue Ste-Catherine W., 514/847-6226, www.macm.org; Tues.-Sun. 11am-6pm, Wed. 11am-9pm; $12 adults, $10 seniors, $8 students

Place des Arts

Taking up an entire block of the downtown core, Place des Arts is a multi-venue arts center and the home of four of the city's largest production companies—the Orchestre Symphonique de Montréal, the Opéra de Montréal, Les Grands Ballets Canadiens de Montréal, and the Jean-Duceppe theater company. The Musée d'Art Contemporain is right next door. The site recently underwent major reconstruction in order to include a sixth concert hall, L'Adresse Symphonique, dedicated to musical performances by the Montréal Symphony, and to remodel the Grand Foyer, which greets visitors to the complex.

Opening in September 1963, just four years shy of Expo 67, at the height of Montréal's construction and architectural boom, the inauguration concert featured Canadian conductor Wilfrid Pelletier and Indian conductor Zubin Mehta.

Running along rue Ste-Catherine, the Esplanade is the site of many of the city's outdoor cultural happenings. It is here that you'll find the International Jazz Festival's main stage, free movie screenings during the Montréal World Film Festival, and a host of other free summer festival events. Indeed, the block in front of the Esplanade is virtually shut down to regular traffic and even bikes from June to September. The Esplanade's stairs are a choice spot for a meeting point or to simply sit and people-watch, and the fountain at the top is often surrounded by office workers and visitors cooling off, their feet dangling in the basin.

MAP 3: 175 rue Ste-Catherine W., 514/842-2112, www.laplacedesarts.com; hours vary

Quartier Latin and the Village

Map 4

Église St-Pierre-Apôtre

With its flying buttresses, stained-glass windows, and open nave, this neo-Gothic church constructed in 1851 is one of the most traditional in the city. Inspired by Brooklyn's Holy Trinity, it was the first church to be designed by Victor Bourgeau—who would go on to become one of the most prolific church architects in Québec. It is still considered his masterpiece.

Bourgeau's materials were unusual; he used stone throughout, and even the pillars are made of limestone. Step inside, however, and you realize just how nontraditional this church really is. Decorated with rainbow banners, it's known for its gay-friendly Sunday services as well as its overall support of the gay community. Set alight in July 1996, a flame burns permanently in the Chapel of Hope, the first chapel in the world dedicated to the memory of victims of AIDS.

MAP 4: 1201 rue de la Visitation, 514/524-3791, www.stpierrapotre.org; Mon.-Fri. 10:30am-4pm, Sat. noon-5pm, Sun. 9:30am-4pm; free

La Grande Bibliothèque

One of the most interesting buildings in the city, La Grande Bibliothèque (the National Library) was completed in 2005. Set on the former site of the Palais de Commerce, a serious concrete eyesore, the library invigorated the area and gave it a much-needed boost of elegance.

Designed by the architectural team of Patkau from Vancouver and Croft-Pelletier/Gilles Guité from Québec City, the two architectural studios beat out 36 other international firms to win the contract. The 6,000 U-shaped plates of frosted glass create the glacial green color seen on the outside of the building, which is reminiscent of the glacial ice found in the far north. It was the first time this type of glass was used in North America.

Light filters into the great hall, which is supported by three concrete pillars and runs the length of the structure. From the great hall you enter into the working area of the library, featuring sleek, glass elevators and elongated stairs that are the centerpiece of the building. Yellow birch wood, one of Québec's official emblems, is used throughout to separate areas and diffuse sound. It is complemented by the classic yet modern library desks by Michel Dallaire Design.

With close to three million users, it's one of the most popular libraries in the French-speaking world and regularly hosts art exhibitions. Ninety-minute tours are available free of charge, but check before you go since the schedule changes monthly. Self-guided tours are also available for download from the library's website.

MAP 4: 475 blvd. de Maisonneuve E., 514/873-1100, www.banq.qc.ca; Tues.-Fri. 10am-10pm, Sat.-Sun. 10am-6pm; free

Rue Amherst

In the heart of the Village this delightful street is an excellent place to browse and grab a bite. The stunning finds in the antiques stores here span from the 1930s to the 1960s. Fans of mid-century modern design, beware; there's an assortment of it here and at some of the best prices you'll find on the East Coast. Sputnik and Cité Déco top the lists for best kitsch and mid-century modern respectively, but for old rotary phones, stackable cafeteria chairs, and Expo 67 memorabilia—the perfect gift for any fan of design—Seconde Chance is unrivaled.

Alongside the antiques are stores featuring up-and-coming designers; Québécois designer Dinh Bà's store can be found on this strip. Follow the street all the way south toward the port and check out the 200-year-old walls of the Molson Brewery, which look sturdy enough to defend an entire city, let alone a beer factory.

MAP 4: Between blvd. de Maisonneuve E. and rue Ontario E.

★ Rue Sainte-Catherine Est

This is the heart of one of the largest gay villages in North America, the center of the week-long pride celebration Divers/Cité, and overall life of the party. People of all sexual orientations flock to the bars and clubs along Ste-Catherine Est, making it one of the liveliest nightlife spots in the city.

Occupying what was once a poor, working-class neighborhood, the Village first started to grow during the late 1960s and early '70s, with the opening of many gay-owned and gay-friendly businesses. At the time, however, it was kept rather discreet, and in the lead-up to Expo 67 and the 1976 Olympic Games, Mayor Jean Drapeau conducted raids on bathhouses and saunas, further relegating the gay community to the margins—or at least out of the public eye.

By the early 1980s, though, things started to change, with gay bars opening up and drawing a new generation of gays to the neighborhood. It's now an active community, one whose importance is recognized by all levels of government.

Though gay and lesbian residents live in every corner of the city, the Village remains the center of activity for the LGBTQ community. Between June and September Ste-Catherine is closed to traffic, becoming one long pedestrian-only strip.

MAP 4: Between rue Berri and ave. Papineau

Le Quartier des Spectacles

Le Quartier des Spectacles is the center of attention during festival season. From Les FrancoFolies de Montréal in early June to the Montréal World Film Festival in late August this square kilometer of the city has been the hub for shows and performances for over a century. Revamped, revitalized, and newly christened, Le Quartier des Spectacles has over 80 cultural venues, from performance halls to art galleries. The area stretches between rue City Councillors, boulevard St-Laurent, rue Sherbrooke, and boulevard René-Lévesque. The **Place des Arts** complex remains the centerpiece with the addition of a brand-new concert hall **(L'Adresse Symphonique),** and the new area encompasses many existing venues, like the **Monument-National,** and the **SAT,** as well as new buildings like sleek arts hub **Le 2-22,** with galleries, radio stations, arts associations, and a bookstore.

UQÀM

Architect and urban designer Dimitri Dimakopoulous was one of the most sought after architects in the country, having designed award-winning buildings from coast to coast. In 1974, along with his ACORP associates, he undertook the project to create an urban campus for the relatively new Université du Québec à Montréal (commonly referred to as UQÀM). It subsequently won the city's Prix d'Excellence award in Architecture for that year.

Situated in the Quartier Latin, the campus Dimakopoulous created is an urban one, seamlessly integrated into the city's existing architecture. As such, the school features two former churches that have been incorporated into the design. Vastly different in styles and even materials, they add a unique twist to the modern brick structures and can be seen and explored on Ste-Catherine and St-Denis.

Established in 1969, UQÀM is the product of a merger between the fine-arts-focused École des Beaux-Arts de Montréal and the classics college Collège Sainte-Marie. It continues to be the preeminent Francophone arts university in the province, with special schools in fashion, feminist studies, and environmental studies.

MAP 4: Rue Ste-Catherine E., 514/987-3000, www.uqam.ca; free

Plateau Mont-Royal

Map 5

Avenue du Mont-Royal

By the end of the 1800s, avenue du Mont-Royal was a bustling thoroughfare linking two smaller villages, De Lorimier and Coteau-Saint-Louis. Once marked only with nine homes, including two dairies, a cart-maker, and a cobbler, it's now the main, and hippest, artery of the Plateau, lined with trendy bars, restaurants, and boutiques.

Made famous by novelist and playwright Michel Tremblay and his depiction of the area as a mostly working-class French-Canadian neighborhood, it has maintained a Francophone population but is no longer as working-class as it once was. Residents today are sometimes chided for being "bobo," a sort of French hipster, both bourgeois and bohemian. The population, however, likely has a lot to do with the impeccably preserved traditional houses and the area's numerous great restaurants.

At the far east end of the street you'll find the Stade Olympique, whose gleaming white tower is an impressive view, jutting into the air over the avenue. It can be seen from just about any point.

To help visitors explore, free bicycles are available from early June to late August. You can find them at Place Gérald-Godin, just in front of the Mont-Royal Métro station.

MAP 5: Between ave. du Parc and ave. Papineau

Carré Saint-Louis

This square links St-Laurent and St-Denis Streets and is bordered by a number of grandiose 19th-century houses. During that period, the area attracted wealthy French-Canadian families, a legacy that remains today—the majority of the Second Empire homes around the square are beautifully kept up and retain much of their charm even 200 years later.

Artists were also drawn here, including important French-Canadian poet Émile Nelligan, who was influenced by French Symbolists like Charles Baudelaire and Paul Verlaine, who made his home here.

Though not a destination on its own, the square has a nice fountain and a number of pathways lined with trees and park benches. In the summer, the kiosk on the west side of the square sells ice cream and other refreshments, making it a great place to stop and take in the scenery.

MAP 5: Bordered by rue St-Denis, ave. Laval, and rue du Square Saint-Louis

Affectionately called the Main by locals, boulevard St-Laurent was first cobbled together from streets that were established by both the French and the British regimes. When Montréal was still a fortified city, the Main was located inside the walls; it was only with the advent of the Grand Porte St-Laurent, which provided a single route out of the walled city, that it became known as St-Laurent road. In 1792, it became the official division between east and west—a division it still marks today—and the street was renamed as St-Laurent du Main.

Though it is the physical division of east and west, historically, it has also divided the city by language—French to the east, English to the west. Over 11 kilometers long, it runs nearly the entire width of the island of Montréal, which is 14 kilometers from north to south, and it is to this long street that waves of immigrants have flocked.

From the mid-1900s onward the Main became the home of the Jewish community, which migrated north from what is now Chinatown. Waves of more immigrants followed, including Italians, Portuguese, Poles, Greeks, Chinese, Latin Americans, and most recently Africans and people from the Caribbean, all of whom have left a distinct mark on the strip.

Once the center of industry, with factories and retail businesses lining the Main from one end to the other, this national historic site is best known for its restaurants, bars, clubs, and live venues.

MAP 5: Blvd. St-Laurent between blvd. René-Lévesque and blvd. St-Joseph

Parc LaFontaine

An oasis in the middle of the Plateau, Parc LaFontaine's 40 hectares have everything from tennis to *pétanque* courts, outdoor skating to baseball fields. Bordering the Village in the south and directly in the middle of the quarter, the park draws people from all over the city no matter the season.

The houses that border the park might look fancy, but most of them, and indeed most of the buildings in the city, don't have gardens, so Montréalers flock, or more precisely, bike to the green space to picnic with friends, catch a performance at the outdoor theater, jog along its shaded path, or come simply to be outdoors.

Old maps of the park have suggested that it was once used as a shooting range, but by 1909 the city had turned the land into a public park that looked not unlike the one that exists today. It was named after Louis-Hippolyte LaFontaine, a politician and the first prime minister of the United Province of Canada, whose writings contributed to the founding of the confederation.

MAP 5: Rue Rachel E. and ave. du Parc LaFontaine; daily 6am-10pm; free

clockwise from top left: Musée McCord, Centre-Ville; fruit stands at the Marché Jean-Talon, Petite Italie; Place Royale, Vieux-Montréal

A few blocks east of the Main is rue St-Denis, a largely Francophone street that traverses virtually the whole north-south length of the island. It is filled with restaurants, independent boutiques, and cafés, and the vibe here is undoubtedly French-Canadian. Hang out in this area for any length of time and you're sure to start to feel the English and French differences.

Though only a few blocks apart, the architectural contrast between boulevard St-Laurent and rue St-Denis is vast. Where St-Laurent's buildings have been informed by immigration and industry, St-Denis's remain relatively unchanged and stereotypically Montréal. Limestone buildings with steep, outdoor staircases and peaked roofs make St-Denis feel much more residential than St-Laurent.

This street is the center for performing arts in the French-language community. You'll find some of the biggest theaters here, including Theatre Rideau Vert and, farther north, the renowned National Theatre School.

MAP 5: Between rue Sherbrooke and ave. du Mont-Royal

Mile End and Petite Italie Map 6

Chiesa della Madonna della Difesa

Built in 1919 by Italian immigrants from Molise, in the southern part of Italy, the Madonna della Difesa (Our Lady of Protection) commemorates a miracle said to have occurred in Casacalenda, Italy, at the end of the 19th century. The creation of the church, built in a Romanesque style and in the shape of a Greek cross, was instrumental in centering the Italian community closer to rue Jean-Talon.

The design of the church, a designated national historic site of Canada, was based on drawings by artist Guido Nincheri. It was built by architect R. Montbirant. Inside, the church is decorated with Nincheri's frescoes, one of which features a pre-World War II Benito Mussolini signing the Lateran Accords. The church is central to the Italian community in the area; even those who have moved away return occasionally for mass.

Next door to the church is Dante Park, dedicated to the 14th-century *Divine Comedy* poet. It features a bocce court, where you'll often find groups of older Italian men playing from noon to midnight.

MAP 6: 6800 ave. Henri Julien, 514/277-6522; daily 10am-6pm; free

Church of Saint-Michael and Saint-Anthony

The most prominent landmark in Mile End, this Byzantine-style Roman Catholic church stands out thanks to its unique architecture. Inspired by Istanbul's Hagia Sophia (though now a mosque, it was originally a Greek Orthodox basilica), architect Aristide Beaugrand-Champagne integrated many different styles, including Roman and Gothic elements into the design and topping it off with a dome and a minaret-style tower typical of Islamic mosques.

Steps lead up to the front door, and inside the dome is decorated with a Guido Nincheri fresco, depicting Saint Michael watching the fall of the angels.

Built in 1915 for the large Irish Catholic population, it was originally called Saint-Michael's; by the mid-1960s, however, the Mile End's Polish population had grown so large that it merged with the existing congregation and Saint-Anthony was added to the name to mark this change. Today, the church is mainly frequented by the area's Polish, Italian, and Greek communities, and services are given in a number of languages. Standing on the corner of St-Urbain and St-Viateur Streets, it's commonly, though incorrectly, called St-Viateur Church by the locals.

MAP 6: 5580 rue St-Urbain, 514/277-3300; daily 10am-6pm; free

★ Marché Jean-Talon

Constructed in the 1930s as a make-work project during the Depression, the market is as busy and central nowadays as it was then. Open seven days a week and nearly 365 days a year, this farmers market goes way beyond expectations. With a number of permanent stores (among them a fishmonger, two bakeries, a cheese shop, a wine store, and numerous specialty shops) surrounding the market, you need not shop elsewhere.

It's an ideal place to browse in the summer; you can snack as you pass by the various stands, tasting many of the fruits and vegetables before you buy. If you're looking to sample locally grown produce, pick up some Québec sausage or ice wine, or buy some goat cheese off the back of someone's truck—and trust me it's worth it—this is the place to do it. Come winter the market moves indoors but stays just as busy. At the start of sugaring-off season in early March the crowds are out in droves drinking in the sunshine, listening to a few street performers, and happily eating maple syrup on a stick.

MAP 6: 7070 ave. Henri Julien, www.marche-jean-talon.com; Mon.-Wed. 7am-6pm, Thurs.-Fri. 7am-8pm, Sat. 7am-6pm, Sun. 7am-5pm; free

Sailing Up the St-Lawrence

One of the most inspired ways to travel between Montréal and Québec City is by boat cruise. Sure, it's not the most cost- or time-effective (a single trip lasts about eight hours), but it is one of the most romantic. And the views of the St-Lawrence and the villages that dot its banks easily beat out those of the highway.

When it comes to choosing a company or cruise there are a few different options. **The CTMA Group** (www. ctma.ca) offers a week-long trip from Montréal with stops in other regions of the province, like Gaspé and the Îles-de-la-Madeleine, before a day in Québec City. **Croisières AML** (www. croisieresaml.com), meanwhile, offers great options for simple day-long cruises with early-morning Montréal departures that get you to Québec in time for dinner.

All companies offer a variety of cruise times and types—everything from a brunch cruise and a bus ride back to Montréal to a night in Québec with a cruise back the following day—allowing flexibility in your travels. The trips, however, do not take place every day, so make sure to plan well in advance and check the websites for exact dates and schedules.

Greater Montréal
Map 7

ÎLE SAINTE-HÉLÈNE AND ÎLE NOTRE-DAME

These two islands in the stream of the St-Lawrence River are easily reached in a number of different ways. By Métro, the stop is Parc Jean Drapeau; by car, the direction is Parc Jean Drapeau; or by bike, see www.routeverte.com for directions.

★ Biosphère

Designed by visionary architect R. Buckminster Fuller, this geodesic dome is the most iconic structure left from Expo 67. Fuller was seen as an eccentric for his philosophical approach to design and his views on creating a synergy between the environment and technology, but his works were beyond their time. Because he had successfully built a few geodesic domes across the United States, when he approached the American government in 1963 with his plans for the American Pavilion for the 1967 World's Fair, they immediately responded.

With the invention of the geodesic dome, Fuller created the most efficient structure ever, using one-fiftieth of the materials normally used in conventional architecture. This perfect form would become one of the biggest attractions at the fair—a futuristic monorail that originally passed through it also added to its appeal—and is still one of the most breathtaking sights in the city. It was originally covered in thin acrylic panels, but repairs to the structure in 1976 set the whole of the skin ablaze in a matter of minutes. The panels were never replaced.

Popular with architecture buffs and kids alike, the 20-story-high building remained empty until 1995, when a new structure was built inside the Biosphère that would become an environmental museum of the same name. The only one of its kind in North America, this unique museum, which caters to children, is aimed at raising awareness for environmental issues such as air and water quality, biodiversity, and sustainable development. The structure itself uses sustainable energy resources, such as solar panels, wind turbines, and a geothermal heating system.

MAP 7: 160 chemin Tour-de-Isle, Île Ste-Hélène, 514/283-5000, www.biosphere. ec.gc.ca; Nov.-May Tues.-Sun. 10am-6pm, June-Oct. daily 10am-6pm; $12 adults, $8 students and seniors, children 17 and under free

Casino de Montréal

If you happen to catch a glimpse of the casino at night, you're in for a treat. Bathed in a golden light, it's a sparkly mirage in the St-Lawrence. Housed in the former French and Québec Expo 67 Pavilions, the casino is the largest in Canada, with over 3,000 slot machines and 120 gaming tables.

Modeled after sculpture, the French Pavilion was criticized for its numerous tall fins, accused of being merely tacked on. The Québec Pavilion meanwhile was made of glass, and by night acted as an illuminated display case. Today it is these exact traits that contribute to the casino's impressive exterior. The interior, though, is atypical for a casino and features lots of windows and low ceilings.

If you get tired of the game of chance, there are plenty of other things to keep you occupied, including four restaurants, three bars, and a cabaret. The eatery Nuances is the casino's top dining spot and a regular award winner. For a bit of Vegas in Montréal, take in a show at the cabaret, which has regular musical and dance performances.

MAP 7: 1 ave. du Casino, Île Notre-Dame, 514/392-2746, www.casinosduquebec. om; daily 24 hours; free

Musée Stewart

This former British Army garrison now serves as a museum dedicated to Canada's past. Built in 1820, the fort is the most important historical military site in Montréal—in fact, the arsenal is still in use. During the summer months, daily military parades and demonstrations are given on the fort's grounds, and in a nod to both French and English heritage, both the Franche de la Marie and Olde 78th Fraser Highlanders are represented.

The permanent collection History and Memory draws a picture of the old and new worlds by establishing links in technological and societal advances with events in early Canada. Using artifacts like navigational tools, prow figureheads, sedans, and playing cards, the museum also tells us of our ancestors' daily lives. Guides in period costume help us envision the fort's daily life, and the old barracks are still open to visitors.

Founded in 1955, the museum underwent a major reconstruction and reopened in 2011. The striking glass tower, with amazing views of the downtown skyline, and the impressive permanent collection are the most visible of this refurbishment.

MAP 7: Vieux Fort, Île Ste-Hélène, 514/861-6701, www.stewart-museum.org; May-Oct. daily 10am-5pm, Oct.-May Wed.-Mon. 10am-5pm; $13 adults, $7 students, children under 7 free

Parc Jean-Drapeau

Named after the mayor who turned Expo 67 into a reality, Parc Jean-Drapeau consists of two islands, Ile Sainte-Hélène and Ile Notre-Dame; the second was built using rock excavated to make way for the Montréal Métro.

A green paradise on the Métro line, the islands were the site of Expo 67, and though you'll find some relics remaining—like Buckminster Fuller's geodesic dome and the Québec and French Pavilions, now the site of the city's casino—most of the pavilions were destroyed in the 1970s to make room for a large basin used for water events during the 1976 Olympics. Today the basin still exists and is a great place to try your hand at rowing, canoeing, and dragon boating. Just beside the Jean-Drapeau Métro station you'll find the Jean-Drapeau Aquatic Complex with an Olympic-size pool and diving board to match. They're open for public swims from May-September.

If open water is more your thing, the park also has a beach, which includes boat rentals, beach volleyball, and the like. There are also 25 hectares of gardens, originally created for 1980s Floralies Internationales horticultural fair. The grounds were designed by some of the world's best landscape architects and boast 5,000 rose bushes. Not a bad place to stop and smell the roses.

MAP 7: Île Ste-Hélène and Île Notre-Dame, 514/872-6120, www.parcjeandrapeau. com; daily 6am-11pm; free

La Ronde

Situated on the eastern tip of Ile Sainte Hélène, La Ronde opened as part of Expo 67 and has since grown to become the second-largest amusement park in Canada. Previously owned by the City of Montréal, it was bought by Six Flags in 2001. Though little of the quaint, original park remains, the frontier town of "Fort Edmonton" is still in use and is now the entrance to le Monstre (the Monster), the highest double wooden roller coaster in the world.

Throughout June and August the park plays host to an international fireworks competition with countries from all over the world competing for top spot, judged by a public jury. Though you don't have to be at the park to see the fireworks—anywhere near the river will do—it's fun to sit on the Ferris wheel and watch the explosions in the night sky.

As at most amusement parks, much of the food is overpriced, and though it's close to downtown and easily reached by Métro, there are no food options in the area.

MAP 7: 22 chemin Macdonald, Île Ste-Hélène, 514/397-2000, www.laronde.com; mid-May-Oct. hours vary; $53 adults (taller than 54 inches), $37 children (shorter than 54 inches), $37 seniors, children 2 and under free

MONT-ROYAL

Chalet du Mont-Royal

Sitting on the top of Mont-Royal and looking out over downtown, this structure was a make-work project during the Depression. Commissioned by then-mayor Camillien Houde, the chalet was inaugurated in 1932 and is decorated with paintings tracing the history of the city. The impressive artworks, along with the chalet's spacious interior and exposed wood beams, make it look more like a vast dining hall than a mountaintop chalet. Reward your climb to the top with a cold water or popsicle from one of the vendors who hang around out front (the chalet is only equipped with vending machines).

Just in front is the Belvedere Kondiaronk, named after a Huron First Nations chief who signed the Great Peace Treaty. It is the biggest lookout on the mountain, with sweeping views of downtown and beyond. On a clear day, you can see parts of Old Montréal, the bridges that traverse the St-Lawrence, and the mountains southeast of the city, including Mont-Saint-Bruno and Mont-Saint-Grégoire.

MAP 7: 1196 voie Camillien-Houde, 514/872-3911; daily 10:30am-4pm; free

Cimetière Mont-Royal

One of the first rural cemeteries in North America, Mont-Royal Cemetery was incorporated in 1847. Though the first burial took place here in 1852, two years before the opening of its Catholic counterpart, Mont-Royal is the smaller of the two, taking up 165 acres of the mountain. In 1901 it became the site of Canada's first crematorium.

Predominantly Protestant, it is the final resting spot of many of the city's English-speaking founding fathers, including John Molson and John Redpath. Other famous Canadians, including hockey player Howie Morenz and author Mordecai Richler, are also buried here. One of the more famous graves is that of Joe Beef—now the namesake of a popular restaurant—otherwise known as

Charles McKiernan, who owned a canteen on the port and was known for giving food to the homeless and housing them in his 100-bed dorm. He died in 1889.

Though distinctly different, you can access both Notre-Dame-des-Neiges and Mont-Royal cemeteries through a small path found behind the war monument and marked with two cannons. It's a particularly popular spot for joggers as well as those delving into their family's past.

MAP 7: 1297 chemin de la Forêt, 514/279-7358, www.mountroyalcem.com; daily 8:30am-4:30pm; free

Cimetière Notre-Dame-des-Neiges

Covering a fair portion of the Mont-Royal and following the mountain's natural landscape is Notre-Dame-des-Neiges Cemetery, the biggest in Canada and the third largest in North America. It is traditionally Catholic and Francophone, while its smaller counterpart, Mont-Royal Cemetery, is Protestant and Anglophone. It was founded in 1854, and more than one million people have been interred here.

Because of its garden-like character, it is a great place to have a stroll, be it on a hot summer day or on freshly fallen snow. You can enjoy the flora (it has almost 6,000 trees), the fauna (squirrels, groundhogs, raccoons, foxes, and more), and, of course, the quietness of the dwellers. Among them, you'll come across the tombs of various prominent Montréalers, from doomed poet Émile Nelligan to hockey star Maurice Richard and some of the most important Canadian politicians.

The direction of the main chapel and office is indicated by the white dots on the ground from three access points: entrance Côte-des-Neiges, entrance Decelle (by the university), and entrance Camillien-Houde (the other side of Beaver Lake). There you can get maps and information.

MAP 7: 4601 chemin de la Côte-des-Neiges, 514/735-1361, www.cimetierenotredamedesneiges.ca; Apr.-Oct. daily 8am-7pm, Nov.-Mar. daily 8am-5pm; free

Croix du Mont-Royal

On the eastern side of the mountain in Parc du Mont-Royal is a large, illuminated cross. If you'd forgotten about the city's Catholic roots, this acts as a pretty good reminder. It's no coincidence that the cross faces east, either. It symbolizes the appropriation of the area by the French-speaking population, who historically, and even today, live in the east.

In December 1642, the city, then Ville-Marie, a small, fortified settlement on the banks of the St-Lawrence, experienced what could've been a disastrous flood. To ward off disaster, founder

Paul de Chomedey de Maisonneuve and others prayed to the Virgin Mary, pleading with her to make it stop and promising to erect a cross in her honor if she intervened. Divine or not, the flood receded and the settlement was saved. Keeping his word, de Maisonneuve carried a large wooden cross from the settlement all the way to the top of Mont-Royal, where it was erected on January 6, 1643.

In 1924, Sulpician priest Pierre Dupaigne decided to re-create the cross and designed one that included an observation platform. The arms and base of the cross are cut in stone and illuminated with lightbulbs. The cross today is illuminated by LED lights that glow in a range of colors, signifying such events as the death of the Pope, Saint-Jean-Baptiste Day (Québec's national holiday), and even AIDS awareness.

Rising 251 meters above sea level, the cross is made of 26 tons of steel and is visible from 80 kilometers away.

MAP 7: East side of Parc du Mont-Royal

Lac aux Castors

Near the top of Mont-Royal, you'll find Lac aux Castors (Beaver Lake), an artificially constructed watering hole perfect for winter skating and summer pedal-boating. Facing the lake is a pavilion built in 1961 by architects Hazen Size and Guy Desbarats. It was seen as one of the most innovative buildings in the province. Its zigzagged roof and glass facade make it a modern-day landmark, one that stands in stark contrast to the bucolic surroundings.

Newly revamped, with a fancier cafeteria and a casual fine-dining restaurant on the second floor, it is no longer just the place where you rent skates in the winter and boats in the summer. Though the public is still encouraged to bring their own snacks, the various food options are a plus, especially if you've just walked all the way up. The addition of the restaurant also makes Beaver Lake an ideal winter date spot.

MAP 7: Chemin Remembrance, 514/849-2002; free

★ Parc du Mont-Royal

Montréal's namesake and an integral part of city life, Mont-Royal rises out of the heart of the metropolis. The first European to climb Mont-Royal was French explorer Jacques Cartier, who climbed it with the help of the Hochelaga First Nations tribe in 1535. When writing about it to the king of France, he referred to it as Mount Royal and the name stuck. Though it was often used as a spot for recreation, it wasn't until 1876, after a mass culling of trees for firewood outraged citizens, that the area was designated a park.

Consisting of 200 hectares and 234 meters tall at its highest point, the park was designed by famous American landscape architect Frederick Law Olmsted, who also designed New York's Central Park.

From the late 1880s to 1920, the Mount Royal Funicular Railway carried sightseers to the top. What was once the site of the old track is now a popular lookout spot—Belvédère Camillien-Houde. Known as "Lovers Lookout," this place is a popular stop for couples, who like to canoodle here once the sun sets. Looking out east over the city, you'll see both Olympic Stadium and the oil refineries in Anjou.

Crisscrossed by a number of trails, the mountain is frequented by runners, bikers, dog-walkers, and, in winter, cross-country skiers. It's also a popular sledding place, and stacks of hay line the base along avenue du Parc come winter. The Sunday Tam-Tam is a tradition that started in the late 1970s with an African drumming workshop that is still going strong. In the summer, the public congregates weekly at the base of the Sir George-Étienne Cartier statue, near avenue du Parc and Duluth, to drum, dance, and generally indulge their inner hippie.

MAP 7: Via voie Camillien-Houde (from east) or via rue Remembrance (from west), foot access along ave. du Parc, 514/843-8240, www.lemontroyal.qc.ca; daily 6am-11pm; free

★ St-Joseph's Oratory

Set into the northern slope of Mont-Royal, this Roman Catholic basilica can be seen from various points in the city, though it stands out the most when you catch it from the window of an airplane. The largest church in Canada, it was built by the recently sainted Brother André Bessette, whose healing powers he attributed to St-Joseph.

Frail all his life, Brother André always believed in the healing and aiding power of the saint and soon recommended others to pray to him when they fell ill. Wanting to honor St-Joseph, Brother André began building a small chapel in 1905. It was soon too small for the number of visitors that came, so they started work on a second, larger chapel, which was completed in 1917, and today it is still part of the basilica and is known as the Crypt. Somehow, though, the Crypt was not enough, and in 1924, work on the basilica was officially underway. It was completed over 40 years later in 1967.

Built in the Italian Renaissance style, its dome was modeled on the Duomo in Florence. There are 233 steps from the gates to the doors of St-Joseph's Oratory; shuttles are available for those who are unable to make the journey themselves. As you enter at crypt level you'll find the Votive Chapel, lined with the wooden crutches of those that Brother André healed. The Crypt Church itself features low, arched ceilings and a statue of Joseph instead of a cross over the altar. Above, the basilica is stark compared to most, with the dome rising 195 feet and adorned with stained-glass images depicting events in Canada's religious history in which St-Joseph is thought to have intervened.

Out back you'll find Oratory Gardens, with oversized Stations-of-the-Cross and a lush green surrounding. Brother André's wooden chapel is still on the premises, on the other side of what is now a parking lot, and is open to the public. In 1910 the chapel underwent renovations and a room was added on top that would become Brother André's living quarters; they are today as he left them.

Ninety-minute guided tours are offered in several languages; call for times.

MAP 7: 3800 chemin Queen Mary, 514/733-8211, www.saint-joseph.org; daily 7am-9pm; tours June-Aug. daily 10am and 2pm, Sept.-Oct. Sat.-Sun. 10am and 2pm; free

HOCHELAGA-MAISONNEUVE

Biodôme

Part of the former Olympic complex, the Montréal Biodôme is housed in the old velodrome, where cycling and judo events took place in 1976. It was designed by French architect Roger Taillibert, who designed the entire plan for the massive Olympic park. From above the shape is reminiscent of a stingray with its flat, aerodynamic shape.

Opened in 1992, it re-creates four ecosystems found in the Americas: the tropical and Laurentian forests, the St-Lawrence marine system, and the polar regions of the Arctic and Antarctic. In these re-created environments the animals live in partial freedom, adding a dimension of reality that you don't always find in a zoo. The ecosystems also blend into one another so that you slowly migrate from one area to the next—from the hottest to the coldest—as you explore the ecosystems. The Laurentian forest, in particular, is worth visiting as it represents the diverse vegetation and wildlife that surrounds Montréal. Unlike the other ecosystems, it also changes with the seasons.

MAP 7: 4777 ave. Pierre-du-Coubertin, 514/868-3000, www.biodome.qc.ca; June-Aug. daily 9am-6pm, Sept.-May daily 9am-5pm; $18.75 adults, $17.50 seniors, $14 students, $9.50 children 5-17, children 4 and under free

Insectarium de Montréal

Founded by retired notary, George Brossard, the insectarium has a unique history. Obsessed with insects even as a child, Brossard studied law, eventually working as a notary, making a decent living and retiring in his late 30s in order to travel the world as an insect hunter. Before the museum existed, the majority of the collection was housed in Brossard's basement

Established in 1990, directly inside the city's Jardin Botanique (Botanical Garden), it is the largest insectarium in North America and among the largest in the world. Appealing to a certain kind of kid who's enthralled by, instead of creeped out by, creepy-crawlies, the collection features both live and mounted insects. Observe a live insect community in the Busy Bodies exhibit, and go inside the nests of ants, bees, and termites. Bugs from Africa; Australia; North, South, and Central America; and Asia, including spiders, walking sticks, and beetles can be observed in the Live Collection room, and a number of butterflies are displayed among the Mounted Collection. Entrance to the Jardin Botanique is free with a ticket to the Insectarium.

MAP 7: 4581 rue Sherbrooke E., 514/872-1400, www.ville.montreal.qc.ca/insectarium; Nov. 1-May 14 Tues.-Sun. 9am-5pm, May 15-Sept. 9 daily 9am-6pm, Sept. 10-Oct. 31 daily 9am-9pm; $16 adults, $14.75 seniors, $12 students, $8 children 5-17, children 4 and under free

★ Jardin Botanique

Facing Montréal's Olympic Park is the Jardin Botanique, 185 acres of outdoor gardens. Founded in 1931 by mayor Camillien Houde, it was the brainchild of Brother Marie-Victorin, a De La Salle brother and noted botanist who established the Botanical Institute at the Université de Montréal in 1920—he's also a relative of writer Jack Kerouac and was born Conrad Kirouack. After years of tirelessly campaigning, Marie-Victorin got his garden and Houde used out-of-work Montréalers to make the garden a reality. Designed by Henry Teuscher, a Berlin-born landscape architect and horticulturalist, it consists of 30 thematic gardens and 10 exhibition greenhouses. Its goal is to educate the general public as well as students of horticulture and to conserve endangered plant species.

Though all the gardens are worth a visit, the most popular are the Chinese and Japanese gardens, both of which were designed by architects from their respective countries. Pieces used in the Chinese garden were even shipped over from China. Every September and October, the Chinese gardens are the site of a wonderful exhibition of Chinese lanterns. The show is so popular that the gardens are open until 9pm to accommodate the crowds. There is free admission to the gardens November-May 14.

MAP 7: 4101 rue Sherbrooke E., 514/872-1400, www.espacepourlavie.ca/jardin-boutanique; Nov. 1-May 14 Tues.-Sun. 9am-5pm, May 15-Sept. 9 daily 9am-6pm, Sept. 10-Oct. 31 daily 9am-9pm; $16 adults, $14.75 seniors, $12 students, $8 children 5-17, children 4 and under free

Planétarium Rio Tinto Alcan

The newly constructed Planétarium Rio Tinto Alcan opened its doors to the public in 2013. It's part of Space for Life, the largest natural sciences museum complex in Canada, which includes the Biodôme, Insectarium, and Botanical Garden. The planetarium's architecture is impressive; its dome is an over-sized silo covered in luminescent steel. Inside, it's all about light wood and slate floors. Designed by local architectural firm Cardin Ramirez Julien, it's also one of the city's greenest buildings, using sustainable material and incorporating the latest green initiatives.

Visitors can explore the universe in two different ways—through poetry and science, thanks to the plantetarium's shows *Continuum* and *From the Earth to the Stars*. Both explore the cosmos and the universe, but each has its own take. Both shows are included with the price of admission.

MAP 7: 4801 ave. Pierre-du-Coubertin, 514/868-3000, www.espacepourlavie.ca; Sat. 9am-9:30pm, Sun. 9am-6:30pm; $19 adults, $18 seniors, $14 students, $10 children

★ Stade Olympique

Built as the main stadium for the 1976 Olympics, the Stade Olympique hosted both the opening and closing ceremonies as well as equestrian and athletic events. The structure, designed by French architect Roger Taillibert, is one of the most impressive sights in the city and considered one of the best examples of organic architecture in the world. As impressive as it is, however, it doesn't quite erase the fact that its construction put the city into some serious debt.

With its saucer-like shape and swooping roof, the stadium is a looming reminder of the problems that plagued its construction and the debt the city incurred in the process. Its nickname, The Big O, refers not only to the stadium's dough-nut-like shape but also to the amount of money it cost the city. In fact, the city didn't pay off its stadium debt until 2006, but even that didn't stop people from referring to it as The Big Owe.

The former home of the much-missed Montréal Expos baseball team, the stadium now stands mainly empty, hosting the occasional concert or sporting event when the city's smaller stadiums cannot accommodate the crowds. On the cheerier side, the aquatic pavilion is still in use and has regular free swims; check the website for times. Guided tours of the stadium are also available.

MAP 7: 4141 ave. Pierre-du-Coubertin, 514/252-4737, www.rio.gouv.qc.ca; Nov. 1-May 14 Tues.-Sun. 9am-5pm, May 15-Sept. 9 daily 9am-6pm, Sept. 10-Oct. 31 daily 9am-9pm; $15 adults, $12.50 seniors and students, $7.50 children 5-17, children 4 and under free

There are a number of reminders that Montréal was once hoisted onto the world stage as an example of the "City of the Future." Hosting both the World's Fair and the Olympics within 10 years of each other formed a futuristic sensibility for the city. What turned out to be one of the most popular world exhibitions in history rightfully put the spotlight on the city. Mayor Jean Drapeau was instrumental in securing the city the attention it deserved. Montréal had so impressed the world that it won the bid for the 1976 Summer Olympics.

What started as an ambitious project became too much for the city to handle, and partway through preparations, the provincial government had to take over. Bad management and planning led to a loss of three years' worth of building, and by 1973 the project was already behind. Though the Olympics themselves went off without a hitch, they left the city and its citizens reeling from a massive deficit, one that isn't altogether the fault of the Games.

Drapeau famously said that the Olympics could no more incur a deficit than a man could have a baby, and in some ways he was right. What he did wrong, however, was include the costs of basic infrastructure improvements with that of the Olympic construction. Though the final bill was $1.3 billion, much of that went into the roads and Métro system still in use today.

Tour Olympique

The Olympic tower with its moving funicular and observation deck didn't open until 1987, 11 years after the Olympic Games. At the time, the malfunctioning only added to the city's Olympic hangover, but today it's a unique way to see the city. Built at a 45-degree angle, the tower is 175 meters high and accessible only by a two-level funicular that rides the rails to the top at 2.8 meters per second and works using hydraulics. Once you get to the top, you enter the observatory, exhibition hall, and reception hall, which occupied the three upper floors of the tower. The view from the observation deck is unique, offering a near-panoramic view of the city and its surroundings; on a clear day you can see as far as 80 kilometers away, even catching sight of the Laurentians.

Though the stadium and tower are connected, they operate as separate entities, which means admission to one won't get you into the other.

MAP 7: 4141 ave. Pierre-du-Coubertin, 514/252-4737, www.rio.gouv.qc.ca; mid-June-Sept. daily 9am-7pm, Sept.-Dec. and Mar.-mid-June daily 9am-5pm; $15 adults, $11.25 seniors and students, $7.50 children 5-17, children 2-4 free

LACHINE CANAL
Marché Atwater

A public market since it opened in 1933, the art deco building designed by Ludger Lemieux is one of the most striking in the area. Located on the Lachine Canal, the two-floored market is home to butchers, general-food stores, and fresh produce stalls that migrate outside during the summer. Though it has long been the community's home for daily staples, it's also been the site of social and sporting events, including wrestling, as well as political speeches. Mayor Camillien Houde and Québec premier Maurice Duplessis both spoke here to roaring crowds. A large room on the second floor, which seats up to 1,000 people, can still be rented.

MAP 7: 138 rue Atwater, www.marche-atwater.com; Mon.-Wed. 7am-6pm, Thurs.-Fri. 7am-8pm, Sat.-Sun. 7am-5pm; free

Restaurants

Highlights

★ **Best Brunch:** It can be hard to find unpretentious brunch in Vieux Montréal but the kids behind **Le Gros Jambon** have figured it out (page 100).

★ **Most Worthwhile Splurge:** Leave the well-worn tourist path behind for the cornflower blue walls and delectable menu of **Tuck Shop** (page 113).

★ **Best Japanese:** Stepping into **Kazu,** a downtown *izakaya,* is like stepping into a tiny back-alley eatery in Shibuya, complete with soju cocktails and cramped seating (page 113).

★ **Most Quintessential Montréal Restaurant:** The rustic, hearty, over-the-top dishes at **Joe Beef** have become synonymous with the city's cuisine. One meal here is all you need to understand what makes dining out in Montréal so unique and exciting (page 115).

★ **Best Place to Challenge Your Tastebuds:** A new week means a new menu at the **SAT Foodlab.** The weekly themed menus created by chefs Michelle Marek and Seth Gabrielse will blow your mind. The stripped-down atmosphere and patio are the icing on the top (page 118).

★ **Best Place for a Date:** Grab a seat at the bar, knock back a special cocktail, and let the folks at **Le Chien Fumant** make you a good home-style meal (page 132).

★ **Best British/French Mashup:** Chef Derek Dammann goes for homey, sincere dishes that are out-of-sight at his new gastropub **Maison Publique** in the heart of the (very French) Plateau (page 132).

★ **Best Croissants:** If you're looking for an authentic taste of Europe, look no further than Mile End's independent bakery **Boulangerie Guillaume** (page 138).

★ **Best Sandwich:** The timeless and iconic **Wilensky's Light Lunch** is where you'll find the signature double-grilled salami and bologna sandwich with mustard, along with hand-mixed soda pop (page 145).

★ **Most Unique Dining Experience:** Once you place your order of Southern staples, like fried chicken and collard greens, the good people at **Dinette Triple Crown** pack the whole thing into a picnic basket and send you to a park to chow down (page 146).

PRICE KEY

$ Entrées less than CAN$15

$$ Entrées CAN$15–25

$$$ Entrées more than CAN$25

Montréal is known for its amazing restaurants and range of diverse culinary delights, with more ethnic and rough-and-tumble options than Québec City. Strong ties to French cuisine remain, so many eateries offer a table d'hôte, and a café is a place where you can drink your espresso standing up, sit down with a café au lait, or grab a hearty bite to eat.

Boundaries are blurred between café, bar, and restaurant, with a lot of places serving all three functions, depending on the time of day. Most cafés follow the French model and serve breakfast, lunch, and dinner, so don't be surprised if you find a place that makes a great cappuccino and croissant in the morning and duck confit at night. Restaurant as late-night-party-bar is a long-standing tradition in the city, so remember that when heading out you might need to only head to one place. Liquor licensing can be bizarre in the city; some restaurants serve full meals but not alcohol, while other places can only serve alcohol as long as it's accompanied by a snack, like nachos or nuts. Many restaurants also have a bring-your-own policy, which allows diners to bring their own store-bought vintage to the table.

Ethnic food is available throughout the city and is often your best late-night bet—that or fast food. Some areas are obviously ethnic, like Little Italy (Petite Italie) and Chinatown, but both a Koreatown and a second Chinatown are growing on the western edge of downtown. The best Indian and Pakistani food can be found in Parc Extension (known locally as Parc Ex), northwest of Little Italy, while Greek is a Mile End staple. Some ethnic food, though, can be hard to find; good Mexican and Japanese options are few and far between.

What Montréal does do well, however, is rustic Québécois fare in an exciting, boisterous atmosphere. There is a real emphasis on market fresh in the city, and though it can sometimes translate to higher prices, it's worth it. At times it seems Montréal suffers from a lack of good midrange restaurants, but that's not exactly true. Many neighborhood bistros—or bars for that matter—offer delicious and affordable meals that are likely to exceed your expectations.

Though menus are often written in French, they are usually accompanied by an English translation, and, if there's something that needs clarifying, servers will gladly translate anything on the menu. Keep in mind that although you might originally be greeted by the waitstaff in French, it is perfectly fine, and normal, to switch to English. If you're comfortable, adding a French word here or there, like *merci,* is always welcome.

Many restaurants are closed earlier in the week, on Mondays and/or Tuesdays. Diners start late, especially later in the week or on weekends; it's not unusual to sit down to a meal at 10 o'clock at night. In fact, some of the city's best restaurants keep their kitchen open past midnight. There's no smoking in restaurants or cafés, though it is fair game if you are sitting on an outdoor terrace.

When dining in Vieux-Montréal and the Old Port, watch out for tourist traps. Go for something a little more pricey or very low-key to avoid over-paying. There are enough top-notch restaurants in the area for every budget, so resist resorting to the first place you see.

The food choice in Montréal is expansive, and as you get to know the city you'll recognize a few of its own chain restaurants, as well as international ones, but the real culinary wizardry is found in the neighborhood bistros. Take a chance on smaller, intimate eateries; you won't be disappointed.

Vieux-Montréal

Map 1

CAFÉS

Café Titanic $
Once you step foot into this bustling café filled with dark wood, exposed brick walls, and upcycled metro chairs, you'll be hungry if you weren't already. Serving the 9-5 crowd, it's especially busy between noon and 1:30pm. Go later to avoid the hubbub and enjoy your lunch in a more laid-back atmosphere. True to its name, the sandwiches are "titanic," so bring your appetite or a friend. They're on view in a huge, open display case; you can choose from a lineup of rich but satisfying flavors. "Bacon Butty," anyone? For

something lighter, try the soup of the day, often served with a crispy oil-drenched baguette. Coffee here is some of the best in the area and always elegantly served. Treat yourself to a slice of decadent-but-worth-it carrot cake.

MAP 1: 445 rue St-Pierre, 514/849-0894, www.titanicmontreal.ca; Mon.-Fri. 8am-4:30pm

Le Cartet $

This open-concept dining hall offers a great selection of hot (grilled salmon, seafood lasagna) or cold (salade niçoise, salmon tartare, grilled chicken sandwiches) lunches. Take out or eat in at one of their long, inviting communal tables. The ambience is one of urgency and fever pitch during the week, when business deals are going down and office workers come to get their needed morning coffee. The weekend crowd is much more diverse, with locals and family and friends meeting up before an afternoon in Vieux-Montréal. Since many places in the neighborhood are closed on weekends, the popular brunch features mimosas and dishes like the hearty country breakfast, which comes in a skillet. The walls are lined with local and international fine foods, making it a perfect spot to grab a gift for your favorite foodie. If you like your coffee with a bit of kick, make sure to ask for a double shot.

MAP 1: 106 rue McGill, 514/871-8887; Mon.-Fri. 7am-7pm, Sat. 9am-4pm

Olive & Gourmando $

To enter Olive & Gourmando is to enter a lunchtime institution. From the fresh-from-the-oven bread to the array of mouthwatering goodies (the Valhorna chocolate brioche is divine) that greet you at the front counter, this place has the title of best lunch in Old Montréal on lockdown. It was started by two former chefs from Toqué!, and the atmosphere is casual but chic, with heavy wood tables, comfy seats with leather accents, and deep red walls. The dining room is always packed with tourists, office workers, and locals. In fact, on weekdays just getting takeout can be chaotic—but the food is worth the wait. Many of the dishes incorporate vegan and organic ingredients, so you know exactly what you're getting in your grain-fed chicken sandwich.

MAP 1: 351 rue St-Paul W., 514/350-1083, www.oliveetgourmando.com; Tues.-Sat. 8am-6pm

COMFORT FOOD

Brit and Chips $

With its old-school stools, blackboard menu, and white-shirted, bow-tied staff, Brit and Chips oozes the charm of a lost era. This tiny neighborhood chip shop, which has only six tables and counter space for about 20, serves five different kinds of fish, everything from cod to salmon, as well as English staples like steak and kidney pie and Scotch eggs. This is comfort food at its most authentic. Takeout is wrapped in newspaper-print wax paper, and no matter the hour of the day, you'll find construction and office workers alike chowing down on the fries and fish straight from the fryer. They also have salads.

MAP 1: 433 rue McGill, 514/840-1001, www.britandchips.com; Mon.-Sat. 8am-11pm

★ Le Gros Jambon $

A slice of Americana in the middle of Old Montréal, Le Gros Jambon (the big ham, in English) could be ripped right out of the 1950s. With its counter seating, authentic milkshake maker, Route 66 wallpaper, and various nostalgic ephemera, Gros Jambon feels like a diner. Open for breakfast, lunch, and dinner, they serve usual diner fare—French toast, Nathan's hot dogs, grilled cheese—with a twist; coconut, pecan crumble, and lobster appear on the menu. There's always a delectable array of baked goods, and if you find yourself there at dinner, don't pass up the BDLT—bacon, duck confit, lettuce, and tomatoes.

MAP 1: 286 rue Notre-Dame W., 514/508-3872, www.legrosjambon.com; Tues.-Fri. 7:30am-11pm, Sat. 10am-11pm, Sun. 10am-4pm

SoupeSoup $

A few steps up into this dining room just off McGill, you'll find an open-concept space decorated with simple wooden tables, old movie posters, and chairs reminiscent of your high school cafeteria. This Montréal-based chain now has five establishments in neighborhoods around the city. For a simple, cost-effective lunch in Old Montréal, you can't do better than a hearty soup (especially come mid-January). Eat in or take out; the menu changes daily and offers a variety of seasonal soups, salads, and sandwiches. A single order of soup is served with a generous slice of bread. Other locations are at 1228 rue St-Denis, 80 rue Duluth, 7020 rue Casgrain, and 2183 rue Crescent.

MAP 1: 649 rue Wellington, 514/759-1159, www.soupesoup.com; Mon.-Fri. 11am-4pm, Sat.-Sun. 11am-4pm

FRENCH
Boris Bistro $$

Housed in a nondescript office building—through whose foyer you walk to access the restaurant and the bathroom—the setting isn't ideal. But come the warmer months (mid-May-mid-October), the outdoor terrace is a great place for alfresco dining. Wood tables, bistro chairs, and beige umbrellas give the restaurant (partially hidden behind the ruins of an old storefront) a relaxed elegance.

On weekdays the place is packed with diners on a business lunch, but it calms down on weekends and is the perfect place to bring a large group—though those under 18 aren't allowed on the terrace after 8pm. Classic French dishes like duck *magret,* beef tartare, and shoestring fries are a good bet, and the vibe, even inside on a cold winter day, is always lively.

MAP 1: 465 rue McGill, 514/848-7595, www.borisbistro.com; Mon.-Fri. 11:30am-11pm, Sat.-Sun. noon-11pm

Chez L'Épicier No. 311 $$$

Chef and owner Laurent Godbout opened this cozy, storefront restaurant in 2000. Since then, Godbout and his restaurant have received glowing reviews from diners and critics alike, citing his "terroir" cooking as some of the best in the city. Local produce is a main ingredient in much of the dishes, but Godbout also likes to incorporate more unusual, less-local flavors like soybean broth and pepper from Madagascar. With bright blue walls, lots of windows, and his Les Saveurs de L'Épicier products on sale, the atmosphere is relaxed and more casual fine dining than uptight. If you enjoyed the meal, pick up a locally sourced product, like maple vinegar, as a keepsake.

MAP 1: 311 rue St-Paul E., 514/878.2232, www.chezlepicier.com; daily 5:30am-10pm

Le Club Chasse et Pêche $$$

Set on an unassuming side street in Old Montréal and with its rounded and tiled doorway, Le Club Chasse et Pêche looks more like a forgotten Portuguese diner than one of the best restaurants in the city. All that changes, however, when you enter its warm, cavernous, and clubby interior with quasi-famous animal-inspired lighting fixtures by Antoine Laverdière. Attracting young professionals and foodies to splurge, the restaurant has an ambience that is decidedly grown up and sophisticated with a boys' club edge. The menu changes weekly but there are a few constants, such as scallops and risotto (though the manner in which they're prepared never stays the same).

MAP 1: 423 rue St-Claude, 514/861-1112, www.leclubchasseetpeche.com; Mon.-Fri. 11:30am-2:30pm, Tues.-Sat. 6pm-10:30pm

Jardin Nelson $$

Conveniently located on Place Jacques-Cartier in a historic building that dates back to 1812, this seasonal restaurant's real gem is its courtyard. Enormous parasols save diners from the occasional rain shower and, along with the overflowing gardens and nightly live jazz, heighten the restaurant's intimate atmosphere. The menu

offers everything from crepes to pizza, osso bucco to salmon lasagna, but the ambience and surroundings are the real draw.

MAP 1: 407 Place Jacques-Cartier, 514/861-5731, www.jardinnelson.com;
May-Canadian Thanksgiving Mon.-Fri. 11:30am-10pm, Sat.-Sun. 10am-11pm

Le Marché de la Villette $$

Part store, part restaurant, Le Marché de la Villette, is a slice of
old time France in Old Montréal. Opened in 2002, this family-run
establishment offers a number of typical French products (charcuterie, cheese, baguettes), as well as hearty French meals on the
weekends. The decor, with its worn floorboards, exposed bricks
and beams, and low ceiling, goes perfectly with the food. This is
your go-to for lunch (quiches, salad with pâte), afternoon coffee, or
weekend dinner, with options like homemade foie gras and fondue.

MAP 1: 324 rue St-Paul W., 514/807-8084, www.marche-villette.com; Mon.-Thurs.
9:30am-6pm, Fri. 9:30am-10pm, Sat. 8:30am-10pm, Sun 8:30am-6pm

Les 400 Coups $$$

Both a nod to the address and to the Francois Truffaut film of the
same name, Les 400 Coups is also a French expression meaning to
push the limits. Having been voted one of Canada's best restaurants,
they're sticking with that meaning. Though the cuisine is French at
its base with beef tartar, rabbit, and duck, chef Marc-André Jetté's
flair for marrying these ingredients with surprising companions,
like anchovy, yuzu, and dates, sets the menu above and beyond the
competition. If the food doesn't transport you to Paris, the black
walls, white marble bar, and mural of Parisian neighborhood St-
Germain-des-Prés will. They also have an affordable Friday lunch
menu, so there's no excuse not to try for yourself.

MAP 1: 400 rue Notre-Dame E., 514/985-0400, www.les400coups.ca;
Tues.-Wed. 5:30pm-10:30pm, Fri. 11:30am-1:30pm, Thurs.-Sat. 5:30pm-11pm

INDIAN
Gandhi $$$

Traditional Far East fare is this restaurant's specialty. There's a re-
finement to these classic Indian dishes. Tandoori chicken, lamb
tikka, and the homemade chutney are particular standouts. Quiet
and relaxed, Gandhi is perfect for couples craving a romantic
Indian meal. Carved Hindu statues reveal themselves throughout
the restaurant, but there's nothing kitschy here, just bistro-style
seating, lots of natural light, and white, sparsely decorated walls.
Gandhi gives off an air of easy comfort.

MAP 1: 230 rue St-Paul W., 514/845-5866, www.restaurantgandhi.com; Mon.-Fri.
noon-2pm and 5:30pm-10:30pm, Sat.-Sun. 5:30pm-10:30pm

ITALIAN
BEVO 💲💲

Part pizzeria, part nightclub, BEVO perfectly encompasses the Montréal nightlife mentality. The Italian standards are all here—fried calamari, spaghetti carbonara, veal scaloppini—but it's the wood-fired pizza that stands out, if only because you can order it well into the night. The red, neon lighting and loud music add a bit of a nightlife edge to the decor and attract a crowd of young professionals in their 20s and early-30s. Though cocktails are reasonable, in the $9-12 range, beer (especially locally brews) is exceptionally over-priced, so best to indulge your inner Carrie Bradshaw.

MAP 1: 410 rue St-Vincent, 514/861-5039, www. bevopizza.com; Sun.-Wed. 4pm-11pm, Thurs.-Fri. 4pm-3am, Sat. 3pm-3am

Graziella 💲💲💲

Chef and owner Graziella Baptista creates memorable northern Italian dishes in her namesake restaurant on the west extremity of Old Montréal. Simple, honest, and prepared to perfection, the house specialties include the osso bucco, red wine risotto, and the (potato-free) gnocchi. The dining room itself is light-filled and airy with modern minimalist decor, appealing to mature diners and those looking for a quiet, refined meal. Keep an eye on your spending and skip dinner in favor of the reasonably priced lunchtime table d'hôte. But no matter when you dine, cap the meal off with what might be the best cannoli in the city.

MAP 1: 116 rue McGill, 514/876-0116, www.restaurantgraziella.ca; Mon.-Fri. noon-2:30pm and 6pm-10pm, Sat. 6pm-10pm

Mangiafoco 💲💲

This pizza joint and "mozzarella bar" is located in a stunning Beaux-Arts building on rue St-Paul. The Art Nouveau-inspired typography immediately catches the eye, as does the decor, which is totally unique thanks to its molded steel seating, light wood bar, and numerous hanging lights. Luckily, the food lives up to the decor with their wood-fired pizzas declared some of the best in the city, and an antipasto of house-cured porchetta and a fresh pea salad with mint that is sure to please even the most discerning Italian. Fun fact: It's owned by Jean-François Stinco, the guitarist in the pop punk band Simple Plan.

MAP 1: 105 rue St-Paul W., 514/419-8380, www.mangiafoco.ca; Mon.-Fri. 11:30am-2pm and 5pm-11pm, Sat.-Sun. 5pm-11pm

Porchetta 💲

Created by the team behind the seafood-only Muvbox, Porchetta offers nothing but meat. Located in a converted shipping container at the base of rue McGill in the Old Port, Porchetta is open

clockwise from top left: Europea, Centre-Ville; raw goodness at Crudessence, Plateau Mont-Royal; Maison Publique, Plateau Mont-Royal

throughout the summer and offers the Italian delicacy known
as the porchetta sandwich. Using locally farmed meat, the sandwich is served with deep fried zucchini, fresh potatoes, or a lentil salad. Other menu options include pork sausages and rapini salads. Seating is limited to a few stools and benches that pop up along with the restaurant, so consider getting your lunch to go and finding a spot overlooking the water.

MAP 1: Place du Génie, www.muvboxconcept.com; May-Oct. daily 11:30am-9pm, weather permitting

Venti Osteria 🌑🌑🌑

Named after Italy's 20 regions, and not the Starbucks size, Venti Osteria is a classic Italian eatery in a classic Québécois neighborhood. The open-plan restaurant features exposed brick walls, banquet seating, a chalkboard menu, and an open kitchen where you can watch the chefs cook up everything from squid ink spaghetti to charred brussels sprouts to breaded veal cutlets. The casual, relaxed atmosphere attracts locals and tourists alike, and staff are friendly and accommodating. Though reservations aren't necessary, they are recommended.

MAP 1: 372 rue St-Paul W., 514/284-0445, www.osteriaventi.com; Tues.-Wed. 11:30am-2pm and 5:30pm-10pm, Thurs.-Fri. 11:30am-2pm and 5:30pm-11pm, Sat. 5:30pm-11pm

POLISH
Stash Café 🌑🌑

If it's stick-to-your-ribs comfort food you're after, look no further than Stash Café. Since opening over 30 years ago, it's become a veritable Montréal institution and the only place to get your fill of borscht, pierogies, and *wódka*. For those unfamiliar with Polish cooking there's the "primer," a table d'hôte menu that'll introduce you to the basics of the hearty cuisine. The exposed stone walls, bench seating, Polish theater posters, and live pianist give the space a homey feel—the perfect setting for filling up on a cold winter night.

MAP 1: 200 rue St-Paul W., 514/845-6611, www.stashcafe.com; Mon.-Fri. 11:30am-11pm, Sat. noon-11pm

QUÉBÉCOIS
Toqué! 🌑🌑🌑

Since opening in 1993, Normand Laprise's Toqué! has almost single-handedly changed the culinary landscape of Montréal. Known around the globe for his use of Québécois ingredients, partnerships with local producers, and boundary-pushing creations, Laprise's restaurant should not be missed if you're a fool for new culinary experiences. The menu includes such notable dishes as pork shoulder with black pudding, foie gras with wild mushrooms, and beet mousse with caramel sorbet.

It's situated on the cusp of Old Montréal and the Quartier International, and the subtle and minimalist decor only adds to the overall sophistication of the atmosphere. The website may note attire as casual but ignore it; this is your opportunity to dress up. They recently added a more affordable lunch menu, but no matter when you're dinning, reservations are a must.

MAP 1: 900 Place Jean-Paul-Riopelle, 514/499-2084, www.restaurant-toque.com; Tues.-Fri. 11:30am-2pm and 5:30pm-10:30pm, Sat. 5:30pm-10:30pm

SEAFOOD

Le Bremner $$$

Run by culinary whiz-kid Chuck Hughes, the man behind Garde Manger, Le Bremner continues to keep the party and excellent food coming. Situated on the eastern edge of Vieux-Montréal in an inconspicuous location down a few steps, the restaurant has a cavernous vibe, with stone walls, dark wood tables, low ceilings, and a hidden back patio. Everything on the menu is fresh from the sea (or just about) and cooked to perfection; you can't go wrong with the fried halibut or the lobster pizza, one of the house specialties. Though not quite as raucous as Garde Manger, the staff still want you to have a great time and you'll likely leave feeling as though you've been hosted by friends.

MAP 1: 361 rue St-Paul E., 514/544-0446, www.crownsalts.com/lebremner; Mon.-Sat. 6pm-11pm

Garde Manger $$$

A former sailor's bar, this restaurant/hot spot/makeshift nightclub retains its working-class charm with shabby-chic decor and a rough-and-tumble menu that includes such culinary classics as the fried Mars bar. Since opening in 2006, it has maintained its reputation as one of the wildest restaurants in the city—so no matter when you go, expect a rowdy crowd and come expecting to join them. Reservations are a must, and so is a stab at the seafood platter, if you can convince your dining companions over the raucous crowd. Though the kitchen closes at 11:30pm, the party continues till the wee morning hours.

MAP 1: 408 rue St-Francis-Xavier, 514/678-5044, www.crownsalts.com/gardemanger; Tues.-Sun. 6pm-3am

Muvbox $

Muvbox brings new meaning to the word snack cart. This ex-shipping container transforms into a solar-powered seasonal restaurant complete with seating, counter space, and a stone oven with the flip of a switch. It's a sight to behold and would be worth checking out

Food Trucks Take to the Streets

The summer of 2013 was a glorious occasion for the city of Montréal. After 66 years, the city's food truck ban was lifted and citizens could once again grab food from roving vehicles and eat their meals while perched on stairs, spare bits of lawn, and concrete bollards around town.

This has been a serious struggle for the chefs and patrons who've been ardently petitioning the city since 2010. The leader of the debate, and the granddaddy of the food truck movement, is **Grumman 78,** a taco truck created by Marc-André Leclerc, Hilary Cerf, and Gaëlle Cerf in 2010. The team had the best tacos in town but was unable to sell them around town, thanks to the food truck ban. Unafraid of the challenge, the trio instead started catering events and taking over restaurants as a pop-up event. They now have their very own brick and mortar establishment in the St-Henri neighborhood (630 de Courcelle), but ordering from their truck is still the best way to do it.

When the city finally changed its archaic rules, 27 food trucks were selected to hit the roads. They can be found throughout the city from May to September, but they spend a lot of time in the Old Port and at the Quartier des Spectacles during festivals. Keep your eyes peeled for grilled-cheese addicts **P.A. & Gargantua,** hot dog purveyors **Chaud Dogs,** classic Québécois from **Ôsœurs Volantes,** and the gluten-free goodies from **Le Point Sans G.** There are also trucks from iconic eateries **St-Viateur Bagel** and Au Pied du Cochon's **Camion Pied de Cochon** on the prowl.

The curious can taste it all during the monthly event **First Fridays,** when the food trucks gather at the Olympic Stadium (4141 rue Pierre de Coubertin) on the first Friday of every month during the summer. You can find out all you need to know about when, where, and who at the Food Truck Association's website (www.cusinederue.org).

even if they didn't serve some of the best lobster pizza and lobster rolls you've ever tasted. Everyone flocks here, from office workers to tourists, and its location next to the water gives it an easy, breezy vibe. Local artists Seripop were commissioned to design the outside of the container, which means Muvbox is eye-catching even when it's closed up.

MAP 1: Place du Génie, www.muvboxconcept.com; May-Oct. daily 11:30am-9pm, weather permitting

SPANISH

Barroco $$$

Head-chef Benjamin Léonard's menu takes inspiration from all over Europe, but what all those flavors create has a distinctly Spanish bent. The paella is one of the most popular dishes here and with good reason: Stuffed with squid, shrimp, and scallops, it's got a freshness not always found in this dish. Situated in a historic building, the restaurant has a great ambience, with its stone walls and beamed ceiling giving the baroque touches a rustic feel. Staff are helpful, accommodating, and willing to clear up any menu questions. Slightly off the regular tourist path, it attracts a lot of locals.

MAP 1: 312 rue St-Paul W., 514/544-5800, www.barroco.ca; daily 6am-11pm

STEAKHOUSE

Gibby's $$$

Located in the Youville Stables, which once belonged to the Sisters of Charity, the setting for this classic Montréal steakhouse dates back to 1740. Stone walls, original beamed ceilings, and numerous fireplaces are dotted throughout the six separate dining rooms, which include a cocktail lounge and a secluded outdoor courtyard. If your preference is for surf, not turf, they've also got an excellent seafood selection. And though the steak is said to be the best in the city, their prices, reminiscent of expense-account heydays, tend to keep more discerning diners away. There is something about the atmosphere that makes it particularly attractive for special family get-togethers—it's a popular wedding spot—and romantic dinners. Chalk it up to the cozy fireplace and classic fine-dining service.

MAP 1: 298 Place d'Youville, 514/282-1837, www.gibbys.com; Mon.-Fri. 5:30pm-10pm, Sat.-Sun. 5pm-10:30pm

Centre-Ville   Map 2

AMERICAN

Dunn's Famous Deli $

Opened in 1927, Dunn's is a Montréal staple. The long narrow dining hall, banquette seating, and wood ceiling beams give the place the feel of an old ski chalet, which is confusing for a smoked meat joint. Open 24 hours, seven days a week, this is a late-night or early-morning staple. A favorite with downtown shoppers, pre- or post-movie diners, and those just leaving the bars, Dunn's has a no-nonsense staff; they can be a little short at times. The deli counter selections offer a great choice of classic deli fare, and you can't go wrong with any one of their five club sandwiches.

MAP 2: 1249 rue Metcalfe, 514/395-1927, www.dunnsfamous.com; daily 24 hours

M:brgr $$

Past meets present at this gourmet burger restaurant with sleek banquettes running along a backdrop of old sepia photos of Montréal. Created by Moishes, an upscale steakhouse, M:brgr is its cosmopolitan offspring. Choose from a list of truly gourmet burgers, including Kobe beef and tuna, and pile on the gourmet with toppings like smoked gouda, grilled asparagus, caramelized onions, and foie gras. Hamburgers are the focus, but they also have gourmet mac and cheese, Michigan hot dogs, and an assortment of salads. Despite the messy nature of the food, diners usually come dressed to be seen, and the music can sometimes make you feel as though you're dining in a club.

MAP 2: 2023 rue Drummond, 514/906-2747, www.mbrgr.com; Mon.-Thurs. 11:30am-11pm, Fri.-Sat. 11:30am-midnight, Sun. noon-9pm

BREAKFAST
Griffintown Café $

Serving brunch, lunch, and dinner, and with live music Tuesday through Saturday evenings, the Griffintown Café attracts families, artists, and music lovers. Situated on a newly revitalized strip of Notre-Dame West, this is a great place for the first meal of the day since they offer an eclectic brunch selection that includes mac and cheese, crab cakes, and a breakfast burger with a beef, duck, and lamb patty topped with a fried egg and aged cheddar.

MAP 2: 1378 rue Notre-Dame W., 514/931-5399, www.griffintowncafe.com; Tues.-Fri. 11:30am-10pm, Sat. 10am-10pm, Sun. 10am-3pm

CAFÉS
Café Myriade $

This is without a doubt the best coffee you'll find in downtown Montréal. Serving blends from Canada's top roaster, 49th Parallel, and using a Mirage coffee maker—the only one of its kind in Canada—they take their coffee seriously, but in taste, not pretension. The decor too is well thought out, with lots of wood and large, open windows letting in a ton of light, which is needed in the winter months. During the summer there's a small terrace out front. The vibe is friendly and the baristas are eager to please. As it's surrounded by Concordia University, expect to find yourself among students during the school year.

MAP 2: 1432 rue Mackay, 514/939-1717, www.cafemyriade.com; Mon.-Fri. 8am-8pm, Sat. 9am-8pm, Sun. 10am-6pm

Café Nespresso $

Sleek and modern, this two-floor café and store is the only place in Montréal to relax with a cup of one of Nespresso's premium blends or pick up a supply of their coffee pods. Barely half a block from the Musée des Beaux-Arts, it attracts a mature, adult crowd. This is not the kind of place where children run around, and the atmosphere can be a bit cold at times. If you're familiar with the brand, however, you'll know what you're getting here: perfectly delicious coffee in an upscale surrounding.

MAP 2: 2045 rue Crescent, 514/939-1717, www.nespresso.com; Mon.-Wed. 9am-6:30pm, Thurs.-Fri. 9am-9pm, Sat. 9am-6pm, Sun. 10am-5pm

CHINESE
Qing Hua Dumpling $

People from the Asian community and Chinese food fans in general have been raving about this hole-in-the-wall ever since its doors opened. Situated on a small street—south of rue Sherbrooke and north of boulevard de Maisonneuve—this Chinese eatery whose main decorative element is a window into the kitchen is worth seeking out, especially if you're in the mood for a mind-altering meal. With the restaurant's owner hailing from the port city of Dalian, known for its dumplings, you know you're getting the real goods when you step inside this unassuming restaurant. The dumplings are fried or boiled and stuffed with just about any combination you can imagine; the classic pork and cabbage ones are some of the best.

MAP 2: 1676 ave. Lincoln, 438/288-5366; daily 11am-11pm

COMFORT FOOD
Le bOucan $$

An American smokehouse in the heart of Little Burgundy, Le bOucan serves up Stateside classics like mac and cheese, Cajun shrimp, pork ribs, and barbecue chicken. Though the menu skews south, the beers are decidedly Canadian, with a number of local brews available. The decor is fairly casual with repurposed wood on the walls, banquettes, bar stools, and diner-style napkin dispensers on each table, which you'll need for their 5 Napkin Burger. Everything here is super causal, including the plates, which are reminiscent of the kind that used to be found in every local diner. This place is often busy, so call ahead for reservations and if you're visiting in the summer try and nab a table on their outdoor patio.

MAP 2: 1886 rue Notre-Dame W., 514/439-4555, www.leboucan.com; Tues.-Wed. and Sun. noon-10:30pm, Thurs.-Sat. noon-midnight

FRENCH
Europea $$$

If you're looking to sample the work of a "Grand Chef," that is a chef who's been recognized by the French governing body of top chefs, look no further than Europea. Executive chef Jérôme Ferrer is one of the few who hold the title in the city (Normand Laprise of Toqué! is the other), and Europea is one of the few places that offers a contemporary French menu that seems untouched by other fleeting restaurant fads (no chalkboard menu here). Situated in a grand old Brownstone downtown, the three-floor restaurant is a sprawling affair with the rooms decked out in various styles. The serving staff is of an old school persuasion, in matching suits and scarves, and wouldn't look out of place handing you a boarding pass. Accordingly, the service is impeccable, your water glass is always full, your delectable lobster bisque amuse-bouche served hot, and your seared foie gras expertly cooked on a sizzling river rock in front of you. It's all about the tasting menu here and the selection is generous, even at lunchtime.

MAP 2: 1227 rue de la Montagne, 514/398-9229, www.europea.com; Mon.-Thurs. noon-3pm and 5:30pm-10:30pm, Fri.-Sat. noon-3pm and 5:30pm-11pm, Sun. 5:30pm-10:30pm

Le Paris $$

Open since 1956, this French bistro in the middle of downtown Montréal has changed little over the years, while the surrounding area has changed a lot. With its striped white and burgundy awning and simple, cursive sign, Le Paris is a bit of Old World charm in the center of a modern city. The red banquettes and simple decor only add to the pleasure of the food, which includes classics like beef bourguignon and *poule au pot* (chicken in a pot). Many of the clientele are older French patrons, so you know this place serves great French food and has been doing it for years.

MAP 2: 1812 rue Ste-Catherine W., 514/842-7128, www.leparismontreal.com; Mon.-Thurs. noon-3pm and 5:30pm-10:30pm, Fri.-Sat. noon-3pm and 5:30pm-11pm, Sun. 5:30pm-10:30pm

ITALIAN

Liverpool House $$$

The only thing that marks the spot at this restaurant, which forgoes a sign, is a large, glowing L. This unaffected atmosphere is reflected inside with original moldings, antique hooks on which to hang your coat, and old brass lighting fixtures. The second venture by the people who brought us Joe Beef, Liverpool House, despite the name, serves a good amount of Italian fare, like veal scaloppini and traditional pasta dishes.

MAP 2: 2501 rue Notre-Dame W., 514/313-6049, www.liverpoolhouse.ca; Tues.-Sat. 6:30pm-close

Nora Gray $$$

Co-owned by Emma Cardarelli and Ryan Gray, who happen to be ex-Liverpool House chef and sommelier, respectively, Nora Gray is one of the city's hottest new restaurants. Located on an unassuming strip facing a nondescript townhouse, Nora Gray is immediately noticeable by is discreet hand-painted sign. This chic and cool vibe continues inside where the decor is sleek with dark, paneled walls, banquettes, and low lighting, all of which works in tandem with Cardarelli's modern take on Italian cuisine. Take advantage and try something from every portion of the menu, including the cocktail section, which has a number of great options for a perfect start to your meal. The pasta here is near perfect, flavorful and filling but never heavy. With capacity topping out at 50, the place is

clockwise from top left: smoked meat sandwich at Schwartz's, Plateau Mont-Royal; Joe Beef, Centre-Ville; Le Biblioquet, Mile End

MAP 2: 1391 rue St-Jacques W., 514/419-6672, www.noragray.com; Tues.-Sat. 5:30pm-11:30pm

Pizzeria Geppetto ❸❸

On the same bustling strip as Joe Beef, Burgundy Lion, and the Corona Theatre, Pizzeria Geppetto is often packed. The restaurant itself is open and spacious, with banquette seating along their signature red walls, tables in the center, and dark wood chairs along the bar. In the summertime, patrons take over a sizable chunk of the sidewalk, dining alfresco at bistro tables. Must-try dishes here include octopus in chickpea puree and their wood-fired pizzas, including the purist's margherita and the adventurous Hawaii 5-0. Call ahead for reservations and expect a packed room.

MAP 2: 2504 rue Notre-Dame W., 514/903-3737, www.geppettopizza.com; Mon.-Tues. 11:30am-10pm, Wed.-Fri. 11:30am-11pm, Sat. 5pm-11pm, Sun. 5pm-10pm

★ Tuck Shop ❸❸❸

Going off the beaten tourist path to eat at this restaurant in the up-and-coming St-Henri neighborhood is totally worth it. Not only will you get to see a different side of the city, but you'll get to indulge in some incredible food. Taking over a narrow storefront, Tuck Shop has the vibe of an old French farmhouse, with cornflower blue wood paneled walls and a giant blackboard announcing wine and cocktail options. The menu changes almost daily, depending on the season, but some staples include a fish taco starter and homemade ravioli, both of which are guaranteed to please. Check out their Twitter feed for daily menu updates (@TuckShopMTL). Clientele range from twentysomething foodies to well-heeled fiftysomethings depending on the day and time; either way, there is always great ambience.

MAP 2: 4662 rue Notre-Dame W., 514/439-7432, www.tuckshop.ca; Tues.-Sat. 6pm-11pm

JAPANESE
★ Kazu ❸❸

Montréalers are virtually starving for authentic Japanese food, so when this place popped up in 2010 it was no surprise that it became an instant hit. Anyone who has eaten in an authentic Japanese *izakaya*—or visited a reasonable facsimile—knows there's nothing quite like it. From the hurried pace of the staff to the cold beers and hamburger patties, Kazu is a little slice of Japan in the heart of Montréal, and that includes the limited seating. Because it has only three tables and a handful of stools, you may be forced to wait in line, along with a sizable portion of the city's Japanese population, before sitting down and digging in to your 48-hour pork and ramen bowl.

MAP 2: 1862 rue Ste-Catherine W., 514/937-2333; daily noon-3pm and 5:30pm-9:30pm

LEBANESE
Boustan $

There are a lot of Lebanese restaurants in Montréal, but nothing comes close to Boustan, smack-dab in the center of downtown, barely a block from Concordia University and on the main clubbing strip. You'll find everyone from students to office workers and late-night revelers stopping in to this fluorescently lit, three-table fast-food counter. The standbys, like falafel, shawarma, and shish kebabs, are all as tasty as the next; even the vegetarian pita is worth a try. But no matter what you order, make sure to say "yes please" to the secret sauce. If you want to look like a local, get it to go.

MAP 2: 2020 rue Crescent, 514/843-3576, www.boustan.ca; daily 11am-4am

Garage Beirut $

There's an authentic feel to Garage Beirut, from its simple decor—white walls and wood tables and chairs—to its delicious grilled meats and delectable *mezzes* (small dishes); everything feels and tastes homemade. In a city where the majority of our Lebanese food is dished out by local chain restaurants, the simple tastes offered at Garage Beirut make you feel spoiled. The grilled meats are a must here, as is the hummus, which will never quite taste as good elsewhere. Portions are reasonable, not huge, which just means that there's more room for their homemade baklava. Located near Concordia University, this place is popular with students and locals grabbing an affordable bite before heading to the cinema.

MAP 2: 1238 rue Mackay, 514/564-2040; Mon. noon-3pm, Tues.-Fri. noon-3pm and 5pm-10pm, Sat.-Sun. 11am-3pm and 5pm-10pm

PUB GRUB
Burgundy Lion $$

At this classic-style British pub—it even has popular Brit-Pop nights—the people are always warm, welcoming, and drinking a pint. Typical public house grub like Lancashire pot, bangers and mash, fish and chips, and the requisite Sunday roast are all on the menu. But as at modern British counterparts, expect gastropub fare: less grease, more cuisine. The weekend brunch is a treat and can be served with a choice of English muffins or crumpets and even a serving of Scotch eggs (a hard-boiled egg rolled in sausage and deep fried). The decor features dark wood, exposed brick, and a fire in winter.

QUÉBÉCOIS

★ Joe Beef ⚫⚫⚫

Named after Charles "Joe Beef" McKiernan, a popular 19th-century innkeeper, Joe Beef is one of the hottest places to dine in Montréal, and with good reason. Its name has become synonymous with fresh, hearty fare. The oysters are popular, as are dishes like lobster pasta, when it's available—regional ingredients mean the menu changes often. Co-owners Allison Cunningham, Frédéric Morin, and David McMillan have since gone on to conquer the rest of the strip with Liverpool House and McKiernan. The atmosphere is casual chic: brick walls, simple dark-wood tables, and a huge blackboard menu.

MAP 2: 2491 rue Notre-Dame W., 514/935-6504, www.joebeef.ca; Tues.-Sat. 6:30pm-close

STEAKHOUSE

Queue de Cheval ⚫⚫⚫

Top 40 hits and techno blare out of the speakers at this steakhouse, which is easily one of the most expensive in the city. But if you love steak and enjoy a good splurge once in a while, this is an ideal place. A little ostentatious at times, the vibe is lively, young, and oddly masculine, but the staff are always attentive and knowledgeable. They recently moved into new digs in a former downtown nightclub, further cementing their party mindset and atmosphere. If you're not one for a party-like dinner vibe, the lunchtime table d'hôte is a prefect time to get a taste.

MAP 2: 1234 rue de la Montagne, 514/390-0090, www.queuedecheval.com; Mon.-Wed. 11:30am-2:30pm and 5:30pm-10:30pm, Thurs.-Fri. 11:30am-2:30pm and 5:30pm-11:30pm, Sat. 5:30pm-11:30pm, Sun. 5:30pm-10:30pm

TURKISH

Avesta ⚫

The first thing you'll notice about this restaurant is a woman methodically rolling out dough in the storefront window. What she's rolling, and what features in almost all of the dishes, is lavash, a thin, doughy flatbread that'll just about melt in your mouth. Dip this bread into any of a large selection of *mezzes* (small dishes) or try it folded around some spinach and feta in *gozleme* (Turkish crêpes). West of the regular tourist path, Avesta is full of locals in the know, and the service couldn't be more accommodating. The atmosphere here is casual, comfortable, and inviting, with traditional crafts accenting the seating and walls. Relax after your meal with a strong Turkish coffee and some baklava.

MAP 2: 2077 rue Ste-Catherine W., 514/937-0156, www.restoavesta.com; daily 11am-11pm

VEGETARIAN

Bonny's $

Dedicated to organic, vegetarian meals, this eatery also caters to vegans and those with other similar dietary restrictions. Seating composed of church pews, an open kitchen, and a wall covered with logs adds to the restaurant's charm. The soup of the day is served in a giant teacup. Burgers, sandwiches, and salads make up the majority of the menu, but there are also daily specials for more dinner-like fare. Their desserts tend to be simple but no less inviting, and the crispy rice square in particular tastes like a healthier version of a homemade recipe. They also have a takeout counter for those on the run.

MAP 2: 1748 rue Notre-Dame W., 514/931-4136, www.bonnys.ca; Mon.-Fri. 11:30am-3am, Sat.-Sun. 9am-3am

Burritoville $

Serving the most basic of Mexican fare—quesadillas, tacos, and burritos—this vegetarian restaurant is a downtown haven of sorts for non-meat eaters. In an old townhouse, the dark-wood accents make it look more like a pub than a Mexican place, but it does have an inviting, relaxed vibe. Across from Concordia University, it's an ideal spot for students or those looking for a simple and healthy bite to eat. Offering organic and locally grown ingredients, it's also environmentally friendly, and if you pop in for a bite later in the night you might also catch some live music.

MAP 2: 2055 rue Bishop, 514/286-2776, www.burritoville.ca; Mon.-Sat. 11am-11pm

Centre-Ville Est **Map 3**

CAFÉS

Pikolo Espresso Bar $

Pikolo is an apt name for this sliver of an espresso bar. With a few stools and tables along the walls and a teeny mezzanine with seating at the back, Pikolo is a great place to grab a coffee to go or drink a short espresso (though you can also nab a seat on the bench out front). Located on the edge of downtown and the McGill University Ghetto (where most McGill students live), it's one of your best bets for great coffee in the area.

MAP 3: 3418B ave. du Parc, 514/508-6800, www.pikoloespresso.com; Mon.-Fri. 7am-7pm, Sat.-Sun. 9am-7pm

CHINESE

Maison Kam Fung $

Hidden in a nondescript, all-purpose complex on the edge of Chinatown, Maison Kam Fung is the go-to place for dim sum, but it also offers Cantonese and Sichuan dishes. Maison Kam Fung takes up prime real estate on the corner unit, and you can often see the packed house before you even step in the building. No matter the time, this place is always bustling, so expect a line for Sunday morning dim sum. Evenings are when you can grab an authentic Cantonese and Sichuan meal, and though there'll still be a crowd, this one will be full of community locals.

MAP 3: 1111 rue St-Urbain, 514/878-2888, www.restaurantlamaisonkamfung.com; daily 7am-3pm and 4:30pm-10pm

Niu Kee $

Niu Kee, a local favorite, is brightly lit, teeny tiny, and concealed on the second floor of an nondescript building. But the northern Chinese dishes will make your mouth water for days after. The key to many of these dishes is the out-of-this-world spice; those who like it hot, like it here. The kung pao chicken is one of the spiciest. If you've got a delicate palate, come prepared and order the dumplings, garlic eggplant, or sizzling beef. The crispy spicy garlic fish, however, can and should be enjoyed by everyone. Ordering can be a bit confusing, however, if you don't speak Mandarin; luckily, the menu has photos.

MAP 3: 1163 rue Clark, 514/868-1866; Mon.-Fri. noon-11pm, Sat.-Sun. 11:30am-11:30pm

DESSERT

Pâtisserie Harmonie $

Fifty different kinds of sweets are on offer at this Chinese bakery. It's an ideal spot to pop in and grab a mango cake, a few rounds of egg custard, or a deliciously moist slice of Japanese cheesecake. Buns are their hallmark, though, so sample both the savory (barbecue pork, curried beef) and the sweet (red bean cake, taro, and sesame). With no seats and no counter space, this is a take-out place. You'll see recent shoppers, from tourists to the local Chinese community, digging in to their sweets as they wander the streets.

MAP 3: 85 rue de la Gauchetière W., 514/875-1328, www.patisserieharmonie. com; daily 8am-9pm

FRENCH

Brasserie T! $$

Opened in the brand-new Quartier des Spectacles, Brasserie T! is the bistro brainchild of Toqué!'s Normand Laprise. Housed in a sleek, all-glass, corridor-like building, it cozies up to the Musée d'Art Contemporain and looks out onto the sleek low fountains of the new *quartier*. Serving dishes like burgers and Montréal sausage, this place has been packed since it opened with businesspeople during lunch hours, curious tourists, and young professionals. It provides an excellent alternative to Laprise's super good and super expensive usual fare. Reservations are recommended, no matter the time of day.

MAP 3: 1425 rue Jeanne-Mance, 514/282-0808, www.brasserie-t.com; daily 11:30am-midnight

KOREAN
Chez Bong $

Half a flight of stairs leads down to this eatery in the heart of Chinatown. You'll find a menu full of Korean cuisine. The modest decor consists of a few long, communal tables, wood-paneled walls, and lighting that gives the place a yellowish hue. It is usually packed with locals, and the atmosphere is decidedly relaxed. Though it's not exclusively Korean barbecue, you can still get your fill here and cook your marinated beef or chicken to your desired degree right at your table. Other dishes, however, like the seafood omelet, kimchi pork stir-fry with tofu, and a big bowl of classic *pho* all go down a treat.

MAP 3: 1021 blvd. St-Laurent, 514/396-7779; Tues.-Sun. 11am-9pm

QUÉBÉCOIS
★ SAT Foodlab $

Located on the top floor of the Société des Arts Technologiques (the SAT for locals), Foodlab is run by über-talented chefs Michelle Marek and Seth Gabrielse, whose weekly special menus will blow your mind. Based on a decided theme, like Chinese New Year or Summer in the South of Italy, the menus offer a couple of choices for appetizers, mains, and one dessert. The no-frills decor, with uncomplicated high wooden tables and chairs, ensures you get a great view of the open kitchen where the chefs work their magic. Portions are reasonable, so order more than one dish. There's also a rooftop terrace in the summer, which is almost always packed. It's one of the best places to grab a drink and, of course, a bite downtown.

MAP 3: 1201 blvd. St-Laurent, 514/844-2033 ext. 225, www.sat.qc.ca/en/foodlab; Mon.-Fri. 5pm-11pm

Quartier Latin and the Village

Map 4

AMERICAN

Kitchenette $$$

This family-run bistro—owner and chef Nick Hodge is from Texas, his wife and her parents are Québécois—mixes both backgrounds and cuisines with gratifying results. The relaxed atmosphere and minimal and welcoming decor—dark wood bar, antique white columns, and lots of windows—are the backdrop for dishes like beer-braised short ribs, smoked organic chicken pot pie, and sourdough grilled cheese. Though both lunch and dinner can draw a crowd, from those on a business lunch to foodies on a budget taking advantage of the lunch special, the menus vary. Drop in at lunch and try the fish tacos, rumored to be the best in the city.

MAP 4: 1353 blvd. René-Lévesque E., 514/527-1016, www.kitchenetterestaurant.ca; Mon. 11am-3pm, Tues.-Fri. 11am-11pm, Sat. 5pm-11pm

BAKERIES

Le Mie Matinale $

This artisanal bakery, whose name means morning bread, offers everything from muffins to croissants, which are consistently good. This cozy spot also serves homemade soups. At Christmastime, stop by the café, with its exposed brick walls, bistro chairs, and welcoming staff, for some of their stollen, a German Christmas cake. It's so popular with the local community that it can be ordered online. One quirk about this place, however, is their dedication to Dalida, a popular French singer from the early 1960s; her image completely fills one long wall, and her music is on heavy rotation.

MAP 4: 1371 rue Ste-Catherine E., 514/529-5656, www.lamiematinale.ca; Tues.-Sat. 8:30am-7pm, Sun. 9am-5pm

CAFÉS

Autour d'un Pain $

This café in the Village is a nice alternative to the standard chain coffee shops. The modern decor disguises the fact that this place is all about tradition. From their loafs to their croissiants, Autour d'un Pain (the name means "around a loaf") uses simple and traditional ingredients like salt, yeast, flour, and water to create their breads. This place smells wonderful because they bake their breads and pastries fresh each morning. Stop in for a quick continental breakfast or grab a coffee and a treat for the road.

MAP 4: 1219 rue Ste-Catherine E., 514/509-7676; Tues.-Fri. 8am-6:30pm, Sat. 8am-5pm

La Brioche Lyonnaise $

The crêpes in this stone-walled bistro are the perfect dish, no matter the time of day. With a selection of both savory *(sarrazin)* and sweet *(froment),* they range from the simple (ham and cheese) to the gourmet (smoked salmon and pesto). Filled with bistro tables and chairs and with a big, green backyard terrace, this is a popular place for studying students or hungry movie- and theater-goers; a French cinema and playhouse are across the street. The ambience is decidedly French, with patrons lingering over espressos and dipping pastries into bowls of café au lait. The café also serves a number of quiches, sandwiches on baguettes, and homemade gelato.

MAP 4: 1593 rue St-Denis, 514/842-7017, www.labriochelyonnaise.com; Sun.-Thurs. 8am-10pm, Fri.-Sat. 8am-midnight

Porquoi Pas Espresso Bar $

Need a pick-me-up after a morning of browsing rue Amherst's antique shops? Pourquoi Pas has got you covered. From the checkerboard floor to the Te Aro beans they make their coffee with, this place is no-nonsense. Locals come here to get their daily fix of espresso, and it's served to them promptly with a small glass of mineral water to clean the palate. For the latte-inclined, orders come with a fancy steamed milk design. Tony and Tyler, the baristas and owners, are both friendly and passionate about what they do, so if you want to talk beans, these are your people. Though there is Wi-Fi and a few treats on offer (small tarts and cookies), seating is sparse and it's much more an espresso bar than a coffee shop.

MAP 4: 1447 rue Amherst, 514/419-9400; Mon.-Fri. 7:30am-7pm, Sat. 9am-5pm

DESSERT

Juliette et Chocolat $

There's a bit of a joke surrounding Juliette et Chocolat, that the place is filled 90 percent of the time with 90 percent women. And it's partly true, but only if you fill the remaining 10 percent up with men on dates or digging into a hearty, homemade crêpe. The main draw is the chocolate, which can be ordered in an array of ways—shots, milkshakes, cocktails—and from an array of places—Madagascar, Ecuador, Ghana. The decor is like a warm, chocolate-y hug with dark walls, low lighting, and intimate tables. Started by the sweet-loving Juliette of the title, the St-Denis location is the original, but you can now find two more locations, one in Outremont (377 Laurier W., 514/510-5651) and a giant one on the Plateau (3600 St-Laurent, 438/380-1090).

MAP 4: 1615 rue St-Denis, 514/287-3555, www.julietteetchocolat.com; Sun.-Thurs. 11am-11:30pm, Fri.-Sat. 11am-midnight

121

FRENCH
O'Thyme $$

This BYOB restaurant in the Village offers a nice alternative to some of the more boisterous eateries in the area. Situated on an unassuming strip of de Maisonneuve not far from Amherst, O'Thyme has high ceilings, lots of banquette seating, and picture windows that let in tons of light. The menu is written on the chalkboard walls and mains include staples like filet mignon and *magret de canard*. The atmosphere is inviting and the staff knowledgeable and friendly. With seating for approximately 50 people, however, it's not the best choice for larger groups.

MAP 4: 1112 blvd. de Maisonneuve E., 514/525-3443, www.othym.com; Mon.-Fri. 11:30am-2:30pm and 6pm-10pm, Sat. 6pm-10pm, Sun. 5:30pm-9:30pm

Au Petit Extra $$

Chef Natalie Major's classic French dishes are always a crowd pleaser. Though the menu varies depending on the season, it always features staples like steak frites, *foie de veau*, and *magret de canard*. The atmosphere is casual but elegant and often full of lively clientele; the venue has the feel of a great neighborhood bistro, which is exactly what it is. If you're in the mood for a full meal, opt for the table d'hôte, available at either lunch or dinner and always a great deal.

MAP 4: 1690 rue Ontario E., 514/527-5552, www.aupetitextra.com; Tues.-Fri. 11:30am-2pm and 5pm-10pm, Sat.-Mon. 5pm-10pm

QUÉBÉCOIS
Mâche $

Serving up Québécois comfort food in the heart of the student-strewn Quartier Latin, Mâche offers a variety of provincial classics like poutine (fries, gravy, cheese), *ragoût de pattes de cochon* (pork meatballs and potatoes), and pâté chinois (ground beef, mashed potatoes, etc.), as well as North American faves like mac and cheese and grilled cheese (with fries, obviously). Wood-paneled walls, stools reminiscent of hockey benches, and a couple of flat screens give it a slight sports bar feel. It's a few steps below street level, and during the summer there's a sidewalk patio. Take advantage of the good beer prices on local brews like Boreal and the very un-local Sapporo.

MAP 4: 1655 rue St-Denis, 514/439-5535, www.restaurantmache.com; Mon.-Wed. and Sun. 11:30am-10pm, Thurs.-Sat. 11:30am-11pm

SOUTH AMERICAN

Mezcla $$$

This nuevo latino restaurant mixes Peruvian staples like ceviche with popular South American dishes like *chicharrón*, and all in a boisterous and pleasing atmosphere. Located on a quiet street in the Village, Mezcla is tastefully decorated with lots of light wood, floor-to-ceiling picture windows, and an open kitchen, which can sometimes be the focus of your evening in a negative way. Seafood lovers will enjoy the range of dishes on the menu and anyone with a sweet tooth should try their (decidedly Québécois) maple syrup soufflé. Though most of the dishes are prepared with local products, the wine list is distinctly South American.

MAP 4: 1251 rue de Champlain, 514/525-9934, www.restaurantmezcla.com; Tues.-Sun. 6pm-11pm

TEA

Camellia Sinensis $

Started by four men who, quite simply, just loved tea, the aim of Camellia Sinensis was to bring quality teas from all over the world to tea lovers in Montréal. Each year the four head off to different corners of the world to find the best tea there is, and each year, the menu changes accordingly. The salon in the Quartier Latin is a cozy spot full of red cushions on which to sit cross-legged and enjoy a pot of one of the 10 types of teas available.

MAP 4: 351 rue Emery, 514/286-4002, www.camellia-sinensis.com; daily noon-10pm

Plateau Mont-Royal **Map 5**

AMERICAN

L'Anecdote $

This all-purpose diner is a cute place full of mismatched chairs, checkerboard floors, and old-style counter seating. It's open from breakfast to dinner, seven days a week. The menu is extensive, offering everything from filling and delicious crêpes and omelets to fried fish and fancier dishes like ravioli. And though the fancier dishes can be tempting, what's really great here is the classic diner grub, like the club sandwich or a burger and fries. Frequented by locals, especially those with kids, the atmosphere is one of a typical diner, inviting and unpretentious.

MAP 5: 801 rue Rachel E., 514/527-7697; Mon.-Fri. 7:30am-10pm, Sat.-Sun. 9am-10pm

What Is Poutine?

In order to *really* understand Quebéc culture, you have to understand poutine. In recent years the province's proudest export is a greasy, heavy treat best eaten after the bars have shut down for the night.

Consisting of fries, gravy, and fresh cheese curds, poutine can be found on menus throughout the province, from chichi restaurants where it's likely served with foie gras to McDonald's and Burger King. Despite the dish's popularity, its origins remain hotly debated, with a number of greasy spoon owners declaring themselves the true inventor.

Whether the first poutine was created in the town of Drummondville or Warwick, no one will ever know for sure. But one part of the origin story remains the same: The invention of poutine hinges on customers adding fresh cheese curds to their fries.

Cheese is one of the province's biggest industries and because of this fresh cheese curds are found in greasy spoons and corner and small grocery stores all over the province. The curds have a slightly rubbery texture, a mild but salty taste, and look like a wad of chewed gum. You can tell whether the cheese is fresh or not by the sound of the squeak it makes when chewed— the squeakier, the fresher.

Since the fries and cheese together taste a little dry, a gravy is added to the mix—enough so that you taste it, but not so much that it looks like a stew. The gravy also helps to melt the cheese and turns the whole thing into a glorious mess.

Maverick chefs Martin Picard of Au Pied du Cochon and David McMillan of Joe Beef have helped turn poutine from a greasy-spoon staple into a culinary classic. Their unique takes on the dish (foie gras poutine and lobster poutine, respectively) have elevated it in the minds of foodies everywhere, and, as a consequence, you can now find Quebéc's beloved dish on menus all over the world.

Le Barbare ❶

The microbrew beers and killer weekend brunches make this a worthwhile stop, morning, noon, or night. The open, rustic interior is welcoming, as is the large front window that's open late into the night when it's warm enough. A gathering spot for a young, fun-loving Francophone crowd, it can get rowdy on weekends. The brunches feature the usual savory and sweet suspects, and the evening menu offers hearty fare.

MAP 5: 4670 rue St-Denis, 514/288-8377; Mon.-Fri. noon-midnight, Sat. 9am-3pm and 5:30pm-10:30pm, Sun. 9am-3pm

Patati Patata ❸

With only 13 seats along the windows and serving counter this could be the smallest restaurant in the city, and yet somehow they manage to serve what seems like a bazillion people a night. Seriously. This is one of the hottest restaurants on the strip, and the line, especially in the summer, is usually out the door with everyone from students to families and intrigued tourists. If you're lucky enough to grab a seat, get one at the counter and watch the cooks/waiters as they flip mini burgers, stir up tofu stir-frys, and load the toppings on one of their huge poutines. Service is brisk, and when it's busy, even the stools feel cramped. If it's nice out, skip the seat and take your order to the nearby Parc Jeanne-Mance instead. They accept cash only.

MAP 5: 4177 blvd. St-Laurent, 514/844-0216; Mon.-Fri. 9am-11pm, Sat.-Sun. 11am-11pm

Schwartz's $

This is the oldest deli in Canada; so when the term "Montréal institution" is used to describe this place, it is warranted. Opened in 1928, Schwartz's Hebrew Delicatessen remains largely unchanged, right down to its location, placemat menus, banquette seating, gruff waiters, fast service, and fluorescent lighting. Using tried and true methods, the cooks smoke the meat daily in a special blend of spices to give it that Schwartz's taste. The basic smoked-meat sandwich, coleslaw, and fries combination is the only way to go. You should, however, expect to wait, no matter the weather: Be it -30° or 30°, there is always a line down the block.

MAP 5: 3895 blvd. St-Laurent, 514/842-4813, www.schwartzsdeli.com; Sun.-Thurs. 8am-12:30am, Fri. 8am-1:30am, Sat. 8am-2:30am

CAFÉS

Café Névé $

Taking over the corner spot that used to belong to a bike repair shop, Café Névé is a great addition to this strip of rue Rachel, linking St-Laurent and St-Denis. The large, open space is sparsely decorated with shabby-chic decor and a couple of well-placed flatscreens (perfect for watching the game). Run by three young guys, the vibe is youthful and cool, but it's also a favorite for families—no one's going to be uptight about your tantrum-throwing four-year-old. Everything is reasonably priced, from the eggs Benedict to the lattes. The place is also open late, for those wanting a quiet place to grab a light dinner. The one drawback? The bicycle seat stools may look cool but they are decidedly difficult to sit on.

MAP 5: 151 rue Rachel E., 514/903-9294, www.cafeneve.com; Mon.-Thurs. 8am-10pm, Fri. 8am-9pm, Sat. 9am-9pm

Café Santropol $

Renowned for serving some of biggest sandwiches and milkshakes in the city, Café Santropol is a laid-back place that's always welcoming. Started in 1976, in an attempt to stop a derelict building from being torn down, it has become a staple in the city and caters to everyone from students to aging hippies. In the summer, the prime seating is in their quaint backyard with views of Mont-Royal. The coffee here is fair-trade organic, and it's so popular, you can now pick up a pound or two on your way out the door, or at the local grocery store.

MAP 5: 3990 rue St-Urbain, 514/842-3110, www.santropol.com; daily 10:30am-10pm

Chez José $

Small and ambitiously decorated—hey, at least you're not bored waiting for your order—this tiny café serves up sandwiches, soups, salad, smoothies, homemade pastries, and an affordable and great weekend brunch. Students, artists, and neighborhood locals pop in for a coffee and enjoy the laid-back atmosphere and service. Found on Duluth, which is rife with BYOBs but not many café's, José's is a multicolored coffee-serving haven. Grab a latte to go, or sit by one of the open windows and people-watch as you sip.

MAP 5: 173 ave. Duluth E., 514/845-0693; Mon.-Fri. 7am-6pm, Sat. 8am-6pm, Sun. 9am-6pm

La Distributrice $

On the southeast corner of Mont-Royal and St-Denis is the city's smallest coffee shop. More of a nook than a shop, La Distributrice is a take-away window tucked underneath the stairs of another establishment. Perfect for those who like to have their coffee on the go, this place offers everything from lattes to espressos to tea and homemade donuts. It's a convenient and cool alternative to chain coffee shops.

MAP 5: 408 ave. du Mont-Royal E.; Mon.-Fri. 7am-7pm, Sat. 8am-9pm, Sun. 9am-7pm

Flocon Espresso $

This tiny coffee shop, owned by the same team as Café Névé, is ideal for a quick cup of joe or an iced latte for your stroll around the Plateau. Two single, long, light-wood tables run the length of the long narrow space and are the only seats in the house. The baristas are bilingual and are great at making each drink especially individual ("flocon" means snowflake). Their lattes are particularly delicious, as are their savory scones.

MAP 5: 781 ave. du Mont-Royal E., 514/903-9994, www.floconespresso.com; Mon.-Fri. 7:30am-7pm, Sat.-Sun. 9am-7pm

DESSERTS

Cocoa Locale $

Reema Singh is the one-woman show behind this sweet boutique cake shop. Stepping in here feels like you've just stepped into your friend's kitchen, which is exactly the idea. A display counter at the front full of cakes (chili chocolate is popular), cupcakes, and brownies is the only thing that separates customers from Singh, who bakes her goodies right here in the shop. Special touches, like a mint-green rotary phone and the pink walls, give it a nostalgic feel. Since it's such a small operation, it's first-come, first-served for everything, so those wanting a cake for a special day should order ahead.

MAP 5: 4807 ave. du Parc, 514/271-7162, www.cocoalocale.com; Wed.-Sun. noon-6pm

Pâtisserie Kouign Amann $
This bakery specializes in *kouign amann*, a hard-to-pronounce treat from Brittany in northern France. Like all good things, it consists largely of butter and sugar and tastes so good you'll want to eat two. This is a teeny-tiny place that seats about six on a good day. Weekend strollers pop in to warm up or grab a treat to go. It's well known among locals, but its cuteness also attracts tourists. Cozy and welcoming, it also serves coffee, sandwiches, croissants, and quiches, and is a great place for a light lunch. The whole operation takes place directly behind the counter, so you can watch the chefs work as you bite into your little piece of French heaven.

MAP 5: 322 ave. du Mont-Royal E., 514/845-8813; Mon.-Wed. 7am-7pm, Thurs.-Fri. 7am-8pm, Sat. 7am-6pm

FRENCH

L'Academie $$
This is the place to go if you're dining in a large group. It's three stories high and located on the corner of Duluth and St-Denis, and it's not unusual for this BYOB restaurant to have a line around the corner. Decorated with subtle earthy tones like gray and beige, it feels and looks more upscale than you'd expect. It serves grilled meats and fish with an array of pastas.

MAP 5: 4051 rue St-Denis, 514/849-2249, www.academie.ca; daily noon-10pm

Au Cinquième Péché $$$
When a restaurant's name is "Fifth Sin," you know you're heading into gluttonous territory. A French bistro to a T, its walls are adorned with black-and-white photos of early-20th-century Paris, and the vibe is refined, sophisticated, and unpretentious. Chef Benoit Lenglet serves up contemporary French cooking with a twist of nouvelle cuisine. Everything they serve is worth tasting, which says a lot because they change their menu regularly. Locals love this place for its value and atmosphere. A tip for frugal travelers: The end-of-the-week lunchtime table d'hôte offers three dishes at a fraction of the regular cost.

MAP 5: 4475 rue St-Denis, 514/286-0123, www.aucinquiemepeche.com; Tues.-Wed. 5:30pm-10pm, Fri. 11:30am-2:30pm, Thurs.-Sat. 5:30pm-11pm

clockwise from top left: Tuck Shop, Centre-Ville; Wilensky's Light Lunch, Mile End; Café Olimpico, Mile End

Be Your Own Sommelier

Unique to Montréal are BYOBs, otherwise known as Bring Your Own Bottle restaurants, where diners are invited to bring their own wine instead of choosing from the restaurant's wine list. These restaurants are popular with groups and, it has to be said, young university students. But it doesn't have to be a rowdy night; many BYOBs have some of the best chefs in the city, and depending on where you go, the atmosphere can be either casual or refined. No matter where you end up dining, however, this is a great way to enjoy a meal without the sometimes-pricey wine lists.

Though you might find this elsewhere, in Montréal you won't be charged a corking fee, so your $12 bottle of wine will only cost you $12. Bring-your-owns can be found around the city, but Duluth and Prince Arthur, both charming cobblestone streets, have the highest concentration. Duluth has the most choices in the city, but some options are mediocre. One standout is **La Colombe,** a great, elegant corner bistro. If you are with a group, the three-story **L'Academie** is always accommodating.

Prince Arthur has a number of different restaurants serving various cuisines, with Greek cuisine the most popular. Though none of these will reach the apex of culinary experiences, the restaurants at least offer good value for a decent meal, and sidewalk dining in the summertime is hard to beat.

Farther north on rue Rachel, you'll find small, Parisian-esque bistro **Au 917,** seafood restaurant **Le Poisson Rouge,** and **Les Infideles,** probably one of the most refreshing and interesting restaurants in the neighborhood.

Up in the Plateau, Gilford is a picturesque street full of irresistible BYOBs: **Le Quartier Général** is one of the best on the scene and is almost always packed, while **Le Pégase** (1831 Gilford, 514/522-9487, Tues.-Sun. 5:30pm-11pm) is perfect for a romantic meal. **Chez Doval** serves simple, classic Portuguese fare and has a dedicated fan base. One of the most popular with locals and visitors alike is **Pizzeria Napoletana,** a lively, busy pizza parlor and Italian eatery in Little Italy. They don't take reservations, however, so you might be in for a wait.

La Colombe $$$

Located on the end of a busy restaurant strip, this bring-your-own-wine restaurant is both romantic and elegant. Popular with both gourmet and classical diners, it serves French fare with a North African flavor. Dishes like venison in blueberry sauce, lamb shank, and escargots are favorites. Most mains come as a table d'hôte with soup, appetizer, and dessert for approximately $50. With exposed brick walls, low lighting, and seating topping out at 45 people, it's a small restaurant with a neighborhood feel. Open since 1990, it is starting to look a little tired, but the service is still attentive, and the dining room is often packed.

MAP 5: 554 ave. Duluth E., 514/849-8844; Tues.-Sat. 5:30pm-10pm

L'Express $$

If L'Express isn't the best French bistro in the city, then it is somewhere close. From the unnamed facade—look down, the restaurant's name is spelled out in the sidewalk tiles in front—to the floor-to-ceiling front window, it looks exclusive and inviting all at once. Inside, the tables are populated with regulars, which gives the place a jovial, comfortable atmosphere. Chef Joel Chapoulie, who has presided over the kitchen for close to 20 years, is renowned for dishes like his fish soup with Gruyère croutons and veal liver with tarragon. Top off the meal with a *île flottante*, a meringue and custard delight. Many of the city's chefs come for late-night bites, if you needed more of an endorsement.

MAP 5: 3927 rue St-Denis, 514/845-5333, www.restaurantlexpress.ca; Mon.-Fri. 8am-2am, Sat. 10am-2am, Sun. 10am-1am

Les Infideles $$$

Things here are kept simple, from the white walls and low gray banquettes to the French menu inspired by local ingredients. Venison medallions with poached pear, maple pork loin, and goat cheese cheesecake feature on chef Louis Legault's menu, all to be paired with a wine of your own choosing at this bring-your-own-bottle restaurant. One of the more upscale places in the category, it's a huge hit with locals. The ambience is subtle and romantic, and the service always hits the mark. You can't go wrong with the four-course tasting menu ($50).

MAP 5: 771 rue Rachel E., 514/528-8555, www.lesinfideles.ca; Wed.-Fri. 11:30am-2pm and 6pm-10pm, Sat.-Tues. 6pm-10pm

Laloux $$

A young, ambitious staff handles the kitchen at this casual but elegant bistro. The menu is focused on Québécois and Montréal flavors, using local produce and artisanal suppliers for creations like veal sweetbreads, lobster salad, and duck *magret*. Their dessert menu is also well regarded and includes creations such as cheesecake made of goat cheese with local rubharb. The staff is young and so are many patrons—many of whom dine here before hitting up Pop!, the wine bar next door. Located slighly off the beaten path, it's a neighborhood staple, appealing mostly to those with discerning palates. Their midday table d'hôte is a great deal.

MAP 5: 250 ave. des Pins E., 514/297-9127, www.laloux.com; Mon.-Thurs. 11:30am-2:30pm and 5:30pm-10:30pm, Fri. 11:30am-2:30pm and 5:30pm-11:30pm, Sat. 5:30pm-11:30pm, Sun. 5:30pm-10:30pm

Au 917 $$$

Established in 1985, this BYOB restaurant is one of the best in the city. With its authentic French bistro fare—beef bourguignon, grilled sole, duck à l'orange, and chocolate-covered profiteroles for dessert—it's been attracting Plateau locals with refined palates since it first opened its doors. Dark wood interior, cozy banquette seating, and a single wall lined with mirrors—everything stays true to its French aesthetic, including the white-shirted, mostly Francophone waiters who serve you with an air of nonchalance. Though often packed, things stay relatively calm and low key.

MAP 5: 917 rue Rachel E., 514/524-0094, www.au917.com; daily 5pm-midnight

JAPANESE

Big In Japan $

If you're in the mood for ramen noodles, mochi ice cream, and edamame, this place is for you. This no-nonsense *izakaya* in the middle of the Plateau is a great bet for all your junk Japanese food cravings. Patrons fill the food-court seating, bar stools, and the handful of banquettes every night of the week, giving this place a truly boisterous atmosphere. Popular with twentysomethings and university students, Big In Japan offers cold and cheap beers and lots of affordable bites. It's also the sister restaurant to the sort-of-secret bar with the same name.

MAP 5: 3723 blvd. St-Laurent, 514/847-2222, www.biginjapan.ca; Mon.-Fri. 11am-3am, Sat.-Sun. 4pm-3am

Isakaya $$$

Chef Shinge Minagawa stays true to his Japanese roots with classic dishes like soba and ramen noodles and calf's liver, which you'll be hard-pressed to find elsewhere in the city. He's known for hand-picking his seafood; the fish is fresh and perfect in either a roll or as tartare. The appetizer menu is filled with distinctly authentic fare like *yakitori, gyoza,* and *chawanmuhi.* Long and narrow—a bit of a trend in Montréal—the venue has a sushi bar running the length of one wall and bistro-style seating along the other. The relaxed, minimal decor with low lighting attracts an eclectic clientele, from university students and office workers to the artistically minded.

MAP 5: 3469 ave. du Parc, 514/845-8226, www.bistroisakaya.com; Tues.-Thurs. 11:30am-2pm and 6pm-9:30pm, Fri. 11:30am-2pm and 6pm-10:30pm, Sat. 5:30pm-11pm, Sun. 5:30pm-9pm

LATE-NIGHT EATS

La Banquise $

Poutine capital of Montréal, La Banquise serves 25 different kinds of poutine, 24 hours a day, seven days a week. For the uninitiated, poutine (fries smothered in gravy with cheese curds) is the unofficial food of the province. Initially opened in 1968 as an ice cream shop, La Banquise soon started to serve typical *crasse croute* fare (junky snack food in Québec) and started dishing out poutine in

Gibeau Orange Julep

For Montréalers, there's nothing quite like the **Orange Julep** (7700 Décarie, 514/738-7486, summer daily 24 hours, winter limited hours), a huge, two-story orange ball that sits near the Décarie highway and serves classic fast food. You can't go wrong with the standard club sandwich, as well as the world-famous orange drink. It was started in 1932 by Hermas Gibeau, who constructed the orange itself in 1945. Rumor has it he wanted to move both his business and his family into it (who wouldn't want to grow up in a giant ball?). A symbol to many Montréalers, it draws the curious and long-time residents. Since it's open 24 hours in the summer, there's no better place to grab a late-night bite.

the 1980s. Brightly painted walls, wooden banquettes, and boisterous company is what you'll find, no matter the time of day. Since it's open all night, this place is busiest at four in the morning with revelers enjoying a poutine of their choice and maybe a hot dog before heading home.

MAP 5: 994 rue Rachel E., 514/525-2415, www.restolabanquise.com; daily 24 hours

MIDDLE EASTERN
Kaza Maza $

On the first floor of what was once a residential building, Kaza Maza is a comfortable, low-key eatery that also doubles as a performance space. Open and sparsely decorated, it serves up some of the best, simple and yummy Middle Eastern food in the area. Tapas-style *mezzes* (small dishes) are their forte, with a selection of both hot and cold; though the *basturma mezze* and the thick *muhammara* are the standouts. For something a bit different, try the pistachio *kefta*, which mixes the nut with minced beef, lamb, and pine nuts.

MAP 5: 4629 ave. du Parc, 514/844-6292, www.kazamaza.ca; Tues.-Thurs. 5pm-midnight, Fri. 5pm-2am, Sat. 11am-2am, Sun. 11am-midnight

PORTUGUESE
Chez Doval $$

This is traditional Portuguese cooking in a traditional Portuguese barebones atmosphere; wainscoting on the walls and burgundy tablecloths pass for decor here. Satisfying customers since 1974, this bring-your-own-wine restaurant is a neighborhood staple with diehard regulars from all walks of life. The specialty here is the grill, so no matter what you get—sardines, octopus, chicken—it will be infused with a char-grilled flavor and is going to be delicious. The simply prepared seafood, like clams and mussels, is a standout, as is the Portuguese troubadour who serenades the diners on most nights.

MAP 5: 150 rue Marie-Anne E., 514/843-3390, www.chezdoval.com; daily 11:30am-midnight

Rotisserie Romados $

The line of locals is usually out the door and for a good reason. Rotisserie Romados serves the best grilled chicken in town, and that's about all they serve. It's cooked just right—salty, spicy, and juicy—and you can smell the tastiness all the way down the block. There are only three seats, so the best deal is to get your half chicken, fries, rice, and salad—which will likely be a soggy mess buried under the perfect fries—to go and head to Parc Jeanne-Mance for some alfresco dining. The atmosphere is best summed up by one word: smoky. Hot as Hades in the summer, the interior is all white, with a Virgin Mary or a painted Portuguese folk-chicken here and there.

MAP 5: 115 rue Rachel E., 514/849-1803; daily 11am-8pm

QUÉBÉCOIS

★ Le Chien Fumant $$$

Started by three young culinary whiz kids, this is one of the best new restaurants in the city. Situated on the corner of a quiet street, the long, narrow restaurant is virtually all windows, but it stays cozy even in the deepest of winter with hearty fare like flat iron steak, fried chicken, and stewed rabbit. Using local, market-fresh ingredients, the menu changes regularly. The youthful atmosphere invites a youthful crowd, and most nights it's full of late-twenty-somethings eating at the bar, but it's also a popular family spot for brunch. Start your meal with one of the cocktails—the bar is artfully hung from the ceiling. Make reservations.

MAP 5: 4710 rue de Lanaudière, 514/524-2444, www.lechienfumant.com; Tues.-Sat. 6pm-2am, Sun. 10am-2pm and 6pm-2am

★ Maison Publique $$$

The new home of chef Derek Dammann is much more in line with his homey, sincere dishes than his previous (now defunct) endeavor DNA. Where as his previous restaurant was a swanky joint in the middle of the Old Port, Maison Publique ("Public House") is a rowdy, corner restaurant with a gastropub feel on a quiet, residential street in the heart of the Plateau. With its open kitchen and shabby-chic interior, it's hard not to love the place for its uncomplicated realness. That's not to say the menu isn't ambitious: Dammann mixes classic British (he worked at Jamie Oliver's Fifteen in London and the celeb chef backed the project) and French flavors to create some truly unique dishes like horse carpaccio and strawberries with cheddar. Eating here is an absolute must.

MAP 5: 4720 rue Marquette, 514/507-0555, www.maisonpublique.com; Wed.-Fri. 6pm-10pm, Sat.-Sun. 10:30am-2pm and 6pm-10pm

Au Pied du Cochon $$$

Since opening in 2001, this bustling Plateau bistro specializing in a uniquely meaty, hearty Québécois fare hasn't been quiet. Chef Martin Picard and his restaurant are now household names in the province thanks to outrageous dishes, like Foie Gras Poutine, Duck in a Can, and Stuffed Pied du Cochon with Foie Gras, which cater to a carnivorous crowd. The name, by the way, means "the pig's foot." The open, warmly lit restaurant, with an open kitchen down one side, wood tables, and counter seating, piques the interest of even the least carnivorous. Always lively, it's a popular place for group get-togethers and riotous dinners. It gets full, however, so plan ahead.

MAP 5: 536 ave. Duluth E., 514/281-1114, www.restaurantaupieducochon.com; Tues.-Sun. 5pm-midnight

Le Quartier Général $$$

Putting a new spin on the tried-and-true bring-your-own-wine model, Quartier Général offers a menu full of originality and quality. On a quiet, residential street in the Plateau, there's no better setting for the food than this minimal and chic restaurant. Ingredients tend toward local with Stanstead rabbit and venison steak, written up on the blackboard menu. But no matter your order, the generous mains come with a choice of soup or salad. It's popular with couples and groups wanting a nice dinner without breaking the bank, and the atmosphere is warm and welcoming. Call ahead for reservations.

MAP 5: 1251 rue Gilford, 514/658-1839; Tues.-Sat. 6pm-11pm

Réservoir $$

Conveniently located, this restaurant and bar helmed by Dany Bolduc is known for its exquisitely put together plates and fantastic microbrews. The basic principles are locally sourced ingredients and unique pairings. It's fairly small, with the entire front made up of window; you can see the vats from the street. An early proponent of Montréal chic, with a chalkboard menu and casual wooden seating, it draws a diverse crowd from Plateau-ites to young professionals. It's a popular brunch spot, and you won't find anything like it in the city, with choices like seared halibut over polenta and chorizo. In the evenings, stop in for a drink and something from the snack menu, which includes everything from olives and mixed

Montréal Takeout

On warm summer nights there's nothing better than eating alfresco. But dining outdoors doesn't mean you have wait in line at the hottest restaurant hoping to nab a table on the cramped, sidewalk terrace. In Montréal, smart diners take their meal to go. The reason? Parks.

The city is full of large, beautiful parks just begging for you to spread out a checkered tablecloth, pop open a bottle of white, and chow down. As soon as the warm winds begin to blow, picnicking becomes its very own pastime, with diners covering the city parks. City bylaws allow alcohol, as long as it is enjoyed as part of a bona fide picnic (once the food is gone, put the alcohol away to avoid getting a ticket); so other than the table service, you sacrifice nothing. Packing your own picnic, even if it's as simple as a baguette, a roast chicken, and a bottle of your favorite wine, is a great, affordable way to enjoy an evening.

nuts—perfect with a microbrewed blanc beer—to fried cod and Gruyère grilled cheese.

MAP 5: 9 ave. Duluth E., 514/849-7779, www.brasseriereservoir.ca; Mon.-Thurs. 3pm-3am, Fri. noon-3am, Sat.-Sun. 10:30am-3am

Salle à Manger ❸❸❸

Specializing in market-fresh French cuisine with a twist, with dishes like scallop ceviche and venison tartare, Salle à Manger is spacious, light-filled and, as the name suggests, has the atmosphere of an upscale cafeteria. Whether you're dining with a small or large group, prepare to share (an entire roasted suckling pig serves 12). With the menu divided into three sections—appetizers, mains, and deluxe mains—picking off of each other's plate is expected. But don't let the cafeteria analogy fool you: Set in the heart of the Plateau with floor-to-ceiling front windows, this is a place to be seen, and the young and hip flock here for late-night meals and the chic, unpretentious atmosphere.

MAP 5: 1302 ave. du Mont-Royal E., 514/522-0777, lasalleamanger.ca; Tues.-Sat. 6pm-2am

SEAFOOD

Le Poisson Rouge ❸❸

True to its name, the interior of this bring-your-own-wine restaurant is a rich, deep red, with banquette seating and mirrors along one wall to make the cozy dining room seem all that much bigger. Specializing in seafood—the name means "red fish"—they offer dishes like scallops in coconut milk, grilled tuna steak, and lobster bisque, as well as some turf selections. The intimate setting, relaxed familiar ambience, and attentive staff will make you feel like you've been coming here for years.

SOUTHERN
Icehouse $$

From talented Houston-bred chef Nick Hodge, who brought us the American-style bistro Kitchenette, comes some true down-home Texan cooking. It's a tight-squeeze into this corner restaurant that's full of wood-paneled walls, heavy-duty benches, red-and-white checkerboard print, and wall-mounted paper towel dispensers, which you'll need since this place has dispensed with plates. Your order of popcorn shrimp, fish tacos, or juicy ribs is served one of two ways: in a checkerboard paper container or in a bucket that is promptly dumped on your table for you to attack hands-on. It's best to hit this place in summer when the patio allows for more breathing space. No matter when you go, the place is bound to be jumping with bartenders serving up cold Micheladas, beer cocktails made with a light beer, Clamato, lime, and homemade Tabasco, to just about every customer.

MAP 5: 51 rue Roy E., 514/439-6691; Tues.-Sat. 5pm-1:30am

SPANISH
Club Espagnol de Québec $$

As the name suggests, this is a place to congregate for the city's Spanish population, but everyone else is invited to join in the festivities. On the second floor of what looks like a rather official storefront, an unassuming door leads you upstairs, where the decor is about as relaxed as you'd expect. Large tables usually filled with groups of family and friends take up the main dining area; but just in front of the windows, there's a small enclave perfect for smaller groups. In keeping with the community atmosphere, tapas are the menu's main feature and should be shared among dining companions.

MAP 5: 4388 blvd. St-Laurent, 514/842-6301; Tues.-Sun. 11am-1am

Pintxo $$

Pintxo is the Basque word for bite-size food, which is what this restaurant does best. The subdued setting—white tablecloths, exposed brick walls, and large works of art—makes it an ideal place for a leisurely meal, but things get lively later in the evening. Though they serve a variety of mains, consider making a meal out of the *pintxos* themselves. The *pintxo de foie con su cebolla confitada* is a perfect example: Set on tiny circles of bread, it's a mixture of foie gras, raisins, honey, and onion confit. Popular with groups who are ready to share, Pintxo attracts young professionals and mature diners.

MAP 5: 256 rue Roy E., 514/844-0222, www.pintxo.ca; Mon.-Tues. and Sat. 6pm-11pm, Wed.-Fri. noon-2pm and 6pm-11pm, Sun. 6pm-10pm

La Sala Rosa 💲💲

Frequented by hipsters and elders of the Spanish community alike, this trendy restaurant represents the diversity of the neighborhood. Tapas are the main draw, though they also make a mean paella. You can also opt for the chorizo, garlic shrimp, or grilled sardines. Their sauce is perfect for dipping the endless bread. Diners should not miss out on the fried goat cheese with honey and caramelized onions. Every Thursday diners are treated to a live flamenco performance.

MAP 5: 4848 blvd. St-Laurent, 514/844-4227, www.lasalarosa.com; Tues.-Sun. 5pm-11pm

STEAKHOUSE
Moishes 💲💲💲

Moishes was started in 1938, by Moishe Lighter, a Jewish-Romanian immigrant. Lighter was part of the immigrant community that helped shape the Main, and his tradition of smoking meat would turn Moishes into one of the best steakhouses in Montréal. Its position in the community means it's *the* place for important family celebrations. The menu is heavy on the meat—from filet mignon to sweetbreads. The elegant (but not stuffy) atmosphere and upscale prices mean you will feel most comofortable if you dress up a little. If you like the idea but hate the price, they've got a fabulous After 9 O'Clock menu that's well worth your hard-earned cash.

MAP 5: 3961 blvd. St-Laurent, 514/845-3509, www.moishes.ca; Mon.-Fri. 5:30pm-11pm, Sat.-Sun. 5pm-11pm

VEGETARIAN
ChuChai 💲💲💲

ChuChai is the grand dame of vegetarian and vegan restaurants in the city, specializing in vegetarian Thai cuisine. There's nothing you can get here that you couldn't have in a regular Thai restaurant, and with about triple the taste. Fake duck, chicken, and shrimp are all on the menu and supremely delicious, same goes for the melt-in-your-mouth fried spinach. The choice of diehard vegans wanting to indulge in a refined meal, ChuChai also appeals to all Thai-food lovers, since, meat or not, they serve some of the best Thai in the city. The vibe here is fine dining. If you want casual, head next door to their sister restaurant, **Chuch Végéthaïexpress** (4094 St-Denis).

MAP 5: 4088 rue St-Denis, 514/843-4191, www.chuchai.com; Sun.-Wed. 5pm-10pm, Thurs.-Sat. 5pm-11pm

Crudessence 💲

The first living food restaurant in Québec, Crudessence's menu fuses Latin, Asian, and Mediterranean flavors to create unique dishes that include ingredients like blue-green algae and hemp seed.

Located in a narrow storefront on a sleepy strip of Rachel, it has a summer terrace that is a great place to enjoy your quinoa salad and a cup of Kombucha, fizzy living tea. They now have a second, similarly decorated downtown location (2157 rue Mackay). Since they specialize in health food, it's not unusual to see the place full of diners in workout gear as well as locals in the mood for something healthy. A stone's throw from Parc Jeanne Mance and with prepared foods available for takeout, this is a great option for a midsummer picnic meal.

MAP 5: 105 rue Rachel W., 514/510-9299, www.crudessence.com; Sun.-Wed. 11am-9pm, Thurs.-Sat. 11am-10pm

Aux Vivres $$

Since its humble beginnings as a tiny hole-in-the-wall, Aux Vivres has been praised for its unique take on vegan dining. Now located in a bright, open space on the Main—they even have a nice backyard terrace—it serves the most wholesome and filling vegan food at brunch, lunch, and dinner that you'll find in the city. It's not just vegans and vegetarians that frequent the joint, however; regular diners are those craving a healthy, satisfying meal. Everyone will enjoy the Dragon Bowl, while reluctant vegetarians should go for the BLT. Save room for dessert and try a slice of their uncheesecake.

MAP 5: 4631 blvd. St-Laurent, 514/842-3479, www.auxvivres.com; daily 11am-11pm

Mile End and Petite Italie Map 6

BREAKFAST AND BRUNCH

Café Souvenir $

This neighborhood bistro is a stylish and comfortable place to grab a bite. An eclectic clientele of posh older women from the neighborhood, young professionals, and families of all ages fills the bar stools, the banquette seating, and the sidewalk terrace. Open for breakfast seven days a week, it has an assortment of dishes including eggs, pancakes, or a simple croissant. The menu stays casual for lunch and dinner, with hearty salads, burgers, couscous dishes, and lasagna available.

MAP 6: 1261 ave. Bernard, 514/948-5259, www.cafesouvenir.com; daily 7am-11pm

La Croissanterie Figaro $

Full of round, marble-topped tables, gilded light fixtures, and wrought-iron chairs, this corner café and bistro is a little bit of Paris in Outremont. The long, wooden counter adds to the art deco interior and Old World feel, and the menu too is decidedly Parisian, offering homemade croissants, coffees, and a reasonably priced lunch and dinner table d'hôte with selections like quiche Lorraine and roast beef. The spacious, leafy outdoor terrace is a great place to meet friends for drinks in the evening.

MAP 6: 5200 rue Hutchison, 514/278-6567, www.lacroissanteriefigaro.com; daily 7am-midnight

Vieux Vélo $

This is one of the best spots to grab your morning bite. Vieux Vélo's Formica-topped tables, old wooden school chairs, and 1970s hanging lamps have a lived-in feel to match its relaxed attitude. Located between Mile End and Little Italy, it serves breakfast and brunch all day, every day. Their best-loved creations are their killer Benedicts—like the bacon, brie, avocado—and stellar coffee. Lines are a sure thing come the weekend, since this place is popular with locals of all creeds. In fact, Montréalers like this place so much that Vieux Vélo opened Café Odessa next door (65 rue Beaubien E.), making it even more convenient to grab one of their perfect lattes.

MAP 6: 59 rue Beaubien E., 514/439-5595; Tues.-Fri. 8:30am-4pm, Sat.-Sun. 9am-4pm

CAFÉS

★ Boulangerie Guillaume $

Okay, technically, this place isn't a café—it's a bakery, with some of, if not the best, baguettes, croissants, sourdough loaves, and

Bagel Wars

Once the home of the city's Jewish community, Mile End is today known for two things: indie musicians and bagels. The legacy continues with two iconic bagel shops, **St-Viateur Bagel Shop** (263 rue St-Viateur, 514/276-8044) and **Fairmount Bagel** (74 Fairmount W., 514/272-0667, www.fairmountbagel.com), both of which operate 24 hours a day, seven days a week. With only a single city block between them, these two shops have similar histories.

Founded in 1957 by Myer Lewkowicz, who brought his recipe with him when he emigrated from Eastern Europe, St-Viateur has since expanded to include cafés in both the Plateau and Notre-Dame-de-Grâ neighborhoods, as well as a second, smaller bakery about half a block down.

The origins of Fairmount Bagel, however, go much farther back. Opened in 1919 by Isadore Shlafman, off a back alley on the Main, it was the first bagel bakery in Montréal. When it moved to its current location on Fairmount in 1949, it was renamed "The Original Fairmount Bagel Bakery." The Shlafman family continues to run the business to this day.

Unlike the big, doughy New York bagel, Montréal bagels are smaller, denser, and covered in sesame seeds. There's no everything, no cinnamon raisin—the only choice you get here is plain, poppy, or sesame, and that's on the days when there is a choice. Made around the clock, using a wood-fired oven and hand-rolled dough, they are always hot and delicious and are best when dipped in whipped cream cheese. Since the early days, there has been a silent but ongoing competition between the two shops, and both have their diehard customers. To an outsider the differences between the two are negligible, but ask any Montréaler and they'll likely have a preference.

chocolatines you can get in the city. Opened in 2010 by the cool and tattooed Guillaume of the title, the bakery has been serving clients ever since. The selection of breads is marvelous with both organic and non-organic options. And their French goodies—chaussons aux pommes, brioche, chouquetes—rival any you'll find in France. Of course, they also serve coffee to wash down those treats and they have delectable sandwiches you can grab if you're on the go, which you will be because this place has no seating except for a small bench out front.

MAP 6: 17 ave. Fairmount E., 514/508-3199, www.boulangerieguillaume.com; Wed.-Fri. 7am-7pm, Sat.-Sun. 7am-5pm

Café Italia $

If you grew up in a boisterous family—especially an Italian one—you'll feel right at home here. Waiters and baristas banter back and forth with each other and the customers at this always-busy spot. The no-frills decoration and relaxed serving ethos allows for more focus to be put on the coffee, which is always perfect. If you're lucky enough to grab a seat, get one of their sandwiches, made on a hearty bun, with meat, tomatoes, and roasted mushrooms. The place also has a couple of TVs, usually showing sports, but if Italy's playing, grab a coffee to go, because this place gets crazy.

MAP 6: 6840 blvd. St-Laurent, 514/495-0059; daily 6am-11pm

Café Olimpico $

The line at this neighborhood café can sometimes look intimidating, but it moves fast thanks to the no-nonsense staff who bark at you from their post at the espresso machine. Everybody comes here, from local hipsters to local cops, and on weekends it's taken over by young families who come to socialize. Dedicated to coffee, the place sells a few extras like cold drinks, biscotti for dipping, and slices of lemon cake, and they don't mind a bit if you bring in a hot bagel or two to enjoy with your latte. Don't expect a large cup of joe, however; this place exclusively serves espresso and its derivatives.

MAP 6: 124 rue St-Viateur W., 514/495-7046; daily 7am-midnight

Café Sardine $

If you're in the mood for homemade donuts, you're in for a treat. Squeezed between two very fine establishments—nose-to-tail restaurant Lawrence and bakery Guillaume—Sardine is a perfect link, serving up great coffee and treats in a relaxed atmosphere. The dark wood, high tables, and banquette seating give this café a different vibe than most. Saddle up to the bar and put in your order for a nice iced latte and a selection of the day's fresh donuts. The flavors change daily, but there's always at least three different options and they are always extremely delicious. The huge front window opens up in the summer, making it a great place to read and snack.

MAP 6: 9 ave. Fairmount E., 514/802-8899; Mon.-Fri. 8am-5pm, Sat.-Sun. 9am-5pm

Club Social $

Originally a private club, Club Social opened to the public back in the late-1990s, but a host of men from the Old Country still occupy most of the tables. Just a few doors down from Café Olimpico, the baristas here are often young women from the neighborhood who politely ask for your order. Both Café Olimpico and Club Social are usually packed with locals, and most have an allegiance to one place or the other, though their menus are about the same. See which ambience suits you best.

MAP 6: 180 rue St-Viateur W., 514/495-0114; daily 7am-midnight

COMFORT FOOD

Comptoir 21 $

There's something about this fish-and-chips restaurant that evokes another time. Maybe it's the hand-drawn sign on the window, the U-shaped counter made of reclaimed wood, or the blue-and-white checkerboard linoleum, either way the simple menu and friendly staff are bound to make you think of simpler times. The batter here is light and greasy, just the way a fried fish should be. Of course, they have other items on the menu, like fried calamari, burgers, salads, and the requisite poutine, but the real star is the fish and chips served with coleslaw, a slice of lemon, and a tasty tartar sauce. It's a winner every time.

MAP 6: 21 rue St-Viateur W., 514/507-3474, www.comptoir21.com; Mon.-Fri. 11:30am-11pm, Sat.-Sun. noon-11pm

DESSERT
Le Bilboquet ⊙
This is quite possibly the best ice cream shop in the city. The line here is down the street on hot summer nights. A couple of park benches are scattered outside and there are a few counter stools and wrought-iron tables inside, but for the most part, the interior is taken up with ice cream cases. A chalkboard menu gives you the list of flavors and the (mostly) teenage staff will let you try a few until you find one you like. Unique flavors like King Kong (banana and chocolate), Cacophonie (white chocolate and cashew nuts), and Brouhaha (brownie bits and two types of caramel) are enough to keep you coming back again and again. They also carry other sweets, including cookies, cakes, and cupcakes, and they make a mean banana split.

MAP 6: 1311 ave. Bernard, 514/276-0414; Mar.-Dec. daily 11am-midnight

FRENCH
Les Deux Singes de Montarvie ⊙⊙⊙
On summer evenings the floor-to-ceiling windows of this tiny bistro are rolled wide open, letting the life of the street mingle with the lively diners inside. There's something decidedly quirky about this restaurant that gives it a vibrant atmosphere. This vibrancy translates to the food as well, like the lobster sausage main, which tastes every bit as unique and complex as it sounds. Every wine that is listed by the bottle is also available by the glass—a nice touch you don't always find.

MAP 6: 176 rue St-Viateur W., 514/278-6854; Mon.-Wed. 11am-2pm and 6pm-10pm, Thurs.-Sat. 11am-2pm and 6pm-11pm, Sun. 9am-2pm

Hôtel Herman ⊙⊙⊙
Co-owned by Dominic Goyet, one of the owners of Salle à Manger, with Ariane Lacombe and chef Marc-Alexandre Mercier, Hôtel Herman is quickly racking up points as one of the top restaurants in the city. Located on St-Laurent, the decor is effortless chic with no-nonsense wood slats along one wall, exposed brick on the other, and touches of industrial design with the steel counter and gun-metal

gray dining-room chairs. It's the food that keeps the people (twenty- and thirtysomething young professionals, as well as diehard food-ies) coming back. Mercier, who was sous chef at Salle à Manger and Noma in Denmark, proves himself worthy of his own restaurant with a menu that includes local lamb with celeric, celery, and net-tles; Québec lobster with radishes; and marinated trout with fresh cream and pumpernickel bread. The dishes may sound simple, but the tastes are complex, leaving customers savoring every flavor.

MAP 6: 5171 blvd. St-Laurent, 514/278-7000; Mon.-Sat. 5pm-midnight

Kitchen Galerie $$$

Just west of Marché Jean Talon, along a boring strip of the busy av-enue, is Kitchen Galerie, anything but a boring restaurant. Simply decorated with white walls and black and red accents, it's run by two co-owners who bustle around the restaurant as chefs, maî-tre's, sommeliers, waiters, and dishwashers. And yet they find the time to create some of the freshest and most unique dishes. The evening's dishes are based on market availability, and the menu changes accordingly. But they always offer a choice of two appetiz-ers, six mains, and three desserts as part of their affordable table d'hôte. The small space fills up fast, so call ahead.

MAP 6: 60 rue Jean-Talon E., 514/315-8994, www.kitchengalerie.com; Tues.-Sat. 6pm-11pm

Lawrence $$

At Lawrence, chef Marc Cohen adds to the restaurant's casually chic atmosphere with his simple and delicious dishes and a classic brunch on weekends. The evening and lunch offerings feature ev-erything from seared mackerel to beef-and-bone marrow pie, but the menu changes often. Lawrence is ideally located in a cozy cor-ner spot, with windows on both sides of the restaurant, allowing light to come in at all times of the day. Inside, plaid banquettes and long wooden tables compliment the soft gray walls.

MAP 6: 5201 blvd. St-Laurent, 514/503-1070; Wed.-Fri. 11:30am-3pm and 5:30pm-11pm, Sat. 10am-3pm and 5:30pm-11pm, Sun. 11am-3pm

Leméac $$$

Open and spacious, this is one neighborhood bistro that can, and does, accommodate a crowd. Built on great bistro fare like steak frites, *foie de veau,* and blood pudding, Leméac goes just that little bit further with homemade desserts and Québec specialties like local cheese. Depending on when you go, the clientele varies from ladies who lunch to young professionals having a late bite before heading out on the town. The atmosphere is always a little reserved, however, in that classic French way. A little on the pricier side, it's popular for its $22 après 22 ($22 after 10pm) table d'hôte.

MAP 6: 1045 ave. Laurier W., 514/270-0999, www.restaurantlemeac.com; Mon.-Fri. noon-midnight, Sat.-Sun. 10:30am-midnight

143

GREEK

Cava ❸❸❸

In Greek, *cava* means either land or earth, so it is no surprise that just about everything on the menu here is meat. Opened by the owners of Milos, Cava is opulent, with a dark-wood bar, aging cured meats and cheeses displayed in the wall-to-wall fridge, and a wait-staff dressed in pinstriped aprons over white shirts and jeans. The opulence matches its expensive menu, and the crowd follows suit, always dressed chicly and well-put-together. The swank surroundings translate to the ambience, and everything has an expensive air. Menu standouts include the slow-cooked veal shank, the lamb chops, and the sirloin.

MAP 6: 5551 ave. du Parc, 514/273-7772, www.cavarestaurantmontreal.com; Mon.-Sat. 5:30pm-midnight

Milos ❸❸❸

Serving what is considered by some to be the best seafood in the city, Milos is ubiquitous for its pricey dishes and cool surroundings. It's on a strip of avenue du Parc that, despite the name, doesn't quite fit with the dishes' price tags. Milos's sleek black exterior stands out, and so do dishes like the wine-marinated octopus, crab cakes, and *tsipoura,* fresh from the Aegean Sea. Super-affordable lunch and after 10pm specials are also available.

MAP 6: 5357 ave. du Parc, 514/272-3552, www.milos.ca; Mon.-Fri. noon-3pm and 5:30pm-midnight, Sat. 5:30pm-midnight, Sun. 5:30pm-11pm

ITALIAN

Bottega Pizzeria ❸❸

Located on a side street in Petite Italie (Little Italy), this modern upscale setting is welcoming, with the heat of a real wood fireplace burning in the background. Using traditional Neapolitan methods—which attract lots of traditional Italians—Bottega makes some of the most authentic pizza in the city, and their wine list is exquisite. Following tradition, they offer a number of *sfizis,* typical Neapolitan appetizers; try the giant meatball, you won't be disappointed. For dessert go for a gelato, the perfect cap to a Neapolitan meal.

MAP 6: 65 rue St-Zotique E., 514/277-8104, www.bottega.ca; Tues.-Sun. 5pm-midnight

Lucca ❸❸❸

Italians love Italian food, and they're often the majority at this neighborhood staple. Classy and rustic all at once, this is the swankiest of restaurants in the area, with the prices to prove it. Lucca might not be the cheapest Italian in town, but it is one of the best. Their deceptively simple cuisine is what customers come back for, such as the seafood linguine with clams, shrimp, and fish. Because they use market-fresh ingredients, dishes often change, but staples like risotto, pasta, and meat dishes are always available, as is their heavenly tiramisu for dessert.

MAP 6: 12 rue Dante, 514/278-6502; Mon.-Fri. noon-3:30pm and 6pm-10:30pm, Sat. 6pm-10:30pm

Le Petit Italien $$

This busy neighborhood restaurant is a saving grace on nights when you simply don't feel like cooking. One wall is filled with jars of tomato sauce while the other is mirrored, to give the allusion that this tightly packed restaurant is bigger than it looks. Casual fine dining is the aim and it hits the mark every time. Their homemade pastas are a great choice on a bitterly cold winter night—the gorgonzola linguine is especially satisfying—but they also have a great selection of meat and fish and a reasonably priced table d'hôte. In summer there's an outdoor sidewalk terrace.

MAP 6: 1265 ave. Bernard, 514/278-0888, www.lepetititalien.com; Mon.-Wed. 11:30am-10pm, Thurs.-Fri. 11:30am-midnight, Sat. 9:30am-midnight, Sun. 9:30am-11pm

Pizzeria Napoletana $$

Located in the heart of Little Italy since 1948, Pizzeria Napoletana is everyone's favorite bustling, boisterous, bring-your-own-wine pizza joint. They don't take reservations and there's usually a line, but things move quickly inside. Although it's quirkily decorated—there's a fake tree with sprawling branches and a thick trunk in the middle of the room—they serve 34 different types of pizza and pasta, including their signature Napoletana with anchovies. Service is fast and efficient if not totally attentive, though they'll happily uncork two bottles of wine at once.

MAP 6: 189 rue Dante, 514/276-8226, www.napoletana.com; daily 11am-11pm

LATE-NIGHT EATS

Chez Claudette $

There's nothing quite like Chez Claudette, a 24-hour diner that caters to late-night revelers of any persuasion, and that includes vegans. This old-style diner tucked away on a quiet part of one of the city's fancier strips is so perfectly timeless that you'll forget you're feeding your face at four in the morning. Their menu is extensive and includes the regular greasy spoon breakfast, but you can never go wrong with their poutine and a club sandwich, either the regular or vegan kind.

MAP 6: 351 ave. Laurier E., 514/279-5173; Sun.-Wed. 10am-midnight, Thurs.-Sat. 24 hours

145

LUNCH COUNTERS
Dépanneur Le Pick-Up $

If you're up for a food adventure, find your way to Dépanneur Le Pick-Up. In Québec a *dépanneur* is a corner store, and that's exactly what this place is: a corner store with a food counter and outdoor seating in the summer. A little off the beaten path, tucked away on a residential street, Dépanneur Le Pick-Up is known for its amazing pulled pork sandwiches—both vegetarian and regular style—and its weekend brunches. Hipsters rub elbows with old-time regulars who frequented the place when it just did coffee and eggs over easy. Now, it's the site of some of the best culinary events in the city.

MAP 6: 7032 rue Waverly, 514/271-8011, www.depanneurlepickup.com; Mon.-Wed. 7am-7pm, Thurs.-Fri. 7am-9pm, Sat. 9am-7pm, Sun. 10am-6pm

★ Wilensky's Light Lunch $

Not much has changed since Moe Wilensky opened this lunch counter in 1932, housed in the current location since 1952. You'd be forgiven for thinking its origins were earlier. Nine counter stools make up the only seating in the place, and the decor can only be described as nonexistent. If timelessness were an ambience, they'd have it in spades. Act like a regular and get the house special, a double grilled salami and bologna sandwich with mustard—mustard is compulsory, as a sign inside makes clear—on a kaiser bun, which tastes as delicious as it sounds. Immortalized by Mordecai Richler in *The Apprenticeship of Duddy Kravitz*, the sodas here are all old-fashioned and mixed by hand.

MAP 6: 34 ave. Fairmount W., 514/271-0242; Mon.-Fri. 9am-4pm

MEXICAN
Maïs $$

Tacos are extremely difficult to find in the city and Maïs has them in spades, along with spicy Micheladas and just about any tequila-based cocktail you can think of. The (brief) menu is broken down into three sections: starters, tacos, and salsas. Though the selection isn't exhaustive, it offers choices for both omnivores and vegetarians, and when the food arrives, it is delicious. The decor is industrial-chic with low, steel benches along long communal tables, with more private two-person tables along the wall or at the bar. The staff are friendly for the most part, but sometimes they seem more preoccupied with themselves than the diners. This place fills up quickly and doesn't take reservations, so get here early if you don't fancy a wait.

MAP 6: 5435 blvd. St-Laurent, 514/507-7740, www.restaurantmais.com; Tues.-Wed. 5pm-11pm, Thurs.-Sat. 5am-midnight

MIDDLE EASTERN

Le Petit Alep $$

Simply delicious—there's no better way to describe the food on the menu here, from their coffee to their meats, which are always tender and juicy, to the *fattouch* salad that comes with a nice kick. The relaxed atmosphere is reflected in the magazines that hang on the wall and the newspapers nearby that you are welcome to bring to your table while you dig into a filet brochette. If you're feeling fancy, pop next door to big Alep (199 rue Jean-Talon E., 514/270-6396) and enjoy your Syrian meal in slightly more romantic and upscale surroundings.

MAP 6: 191 rue Jean-Talon E., 514/270-9361; Tues.-Sat. 11am-11pm

SOUTHERN

★ Dinette Triple Crown $$

Montréal's great at creating unique dining experiences, and the experience you'll get at Dinette Triple Crown is unlike any other. The brainchild of an ex-chef of Dépanneur Le Pick-Up, another excellent, quirky restaurant, Dinette is all about Southern comforts and alfresco dinning. Situated on the edge of Little Italy, it eschews the local trend and instead offers traditional Southern dishes like pulled pork, fried chicken, collard greens, pan-fried cornbread, and even a biscuit sandwich made with fried chicken, gravy, and cheese. If that doesn't make your mouth water, maybe this will: The staff pack your order up in a picnic basket, complete with checkered tablecloth, and send you on your way. Luckily, there's a park kitty-corner to the restaurant where you can enjoy your meal under the stars, complete with a bottle of your own choosing (alcohol is permitted in Montréal parks, as long as it's accompanied by a meal). All of this makes for a memorable dinner—just remember to please return the basket after your meal.

Map 6: 6704 rue Clark, 514/272-2613; daily 11am-9pm

VEGETARIAN

Le Cagibi $

Situated on the corner of St-Laurent and St-Viateur, Le Cagibi is in the heart of hipsterville. But don't let that put you off; it is also one of the coziest cafés in the area, serving affordable vegetarian meals and good coffee all day long. At night, the back room transforms into a performance space with everything from live shows to stand-up comedians and public talks. If you drink, however, you must eat, so make sure to bring an appetite. Though Montréal is

queer-friendly, Le Cagibi is especially so for a younger LGBT crowd.
They accept cash only.

MAP 6: 5490 blvd. St-Laurent, 514/509-1199, www.lecagibi.ca; Mon.
6pm-midnight, Tues.-Fri. 9am-1am, Sat. 10:30am-1am, Sun. 10:30am-midnight

La Lumière du Mile End $

This tiny restaurant with bench seating, lots of light, and a café
ambience caters to vegans with a number of delicious options on
the menu, including black bean and quinoa burgers and the Whoa
Black Betty wrap with olive tapenade and roasted red peppers.
Though the fare here is modest, everything is fresh and usually
served with nacho chips and a side salad. There's a small garden
out back, open in the summer months, and the place also serves a
great vegan brunch on the weekend.

MAP 6: 214 rue Bernard W., 514/585-7453; daily 11am-8pm

Le Panthère Verte $

Falafels, falafels, falafels. Sure, this place does other stuff like tofu
steak, tempeh, and a veggie burger, but their falafels reign supreme—or your money back. Owner Chaim, an Israeli native, gives
the falafels a traditional twist that adds up to a fresh and healthy
sandwich. Maybe it's the whole-wheat pita or the fact that you can
get a shot of wheat grass with your meal, but no matter what it is,
the food here is both delicious and good for you. The decor is low
key, with a few tables cut out into funny, not-so-practical shapes,
and a clientele that ranges from new-age hippies to parents grabbing a quick dinner for the family. It's such a runaway success that
they've opened a second location downtown (2153 rue Mackay).

MAP 6: 66 rue St-Viateur W., 514/903-7770, www.lapanthereverte.com; Mon.-Fri.
11am-8pm, Sat. 11am-5pm

Nightlife

Montréal is known for its nightlife. Whether you're catching the latest emerging bands, dancing till the early morning, or sharing drinks with friends on a *terrasse* (patio), there's no shortage of places or things to keep you busy. Many cafés, restaurants, and live venues double as nightlife hot spots when the sun goes down. If you're looking for something unpretentious and fun, these are the kinds of joints that you should seek out.

Those looking for a flashy night out at the club should head directly to St-Laurent; the lower part of this strip on the boundary of downtown and the Plateau has long been one of the top places to see and be seen. Restaurants that double as nightlife hot spots are especially popular in this area; servers are even known to get in on the party at these types of venues.

Chockablock with bars and nightclubs, rue Crescent may be enticing but should be avoided—unless you're an 18-year-old out-of-towner enjoying your first taste of freedom, in which case, party on. As in any popular strip, there are definitely some more sophisticated and worthwhile spots, like Newtown, but migrating farther east to St-Laurent will give you a more authentic Montréal experience.

Legal drinking age in Québec is 18. Kids who are from the province are usually well behaved, but because the drinking age is much lower than that in the States or even neighboring provinces, many teenagers come to Montréal for the clubs, especially during New Year's and spring break. They tend to stick to the same area,

Look for ★ to find
recommended nightlife.

Highlights

★ **Best Dance Club:** Amazing views of the city skyline and some impressive architecture make **New City Gas** the best place to go dancing (page 153).

★ **Best Gastropub: Dominion Square Tavern** is one of the oldest taverns in the city. It has now been renovated into a sleek gastropub that serves a great mix of food and drink (page 156).

★ **Best 5 à 7:** Hidden on a quiet downtown side-street, the laid-back atmosphere and high-school cafeteria feel make **Furco** the place to hit after the office (page 158).

★ **Most Surprising:** A nondescript red door leads you into the wonderful world of the **Big In Japan Bar** (page 169).

★ **Most Versatile Venue:** Drink, dance, and catch the latest bands at **Casa del Popolo,** where there is always something happening and it's always fun (page 171).

★ **Best Wine Bar: Pullman** boasts a stunning interior and extensive wine list featuring 300 wines (with 50 wines by the glass), making this the best spot in the city for a classy but laid-back night out (page 174).

★ **Best Beer Garden:** Only open during the summer, **Alexandraplatz Bar** is a fleeting pleasure that shouldn't be missed (page 174).

★ **Best Microbrews:** Taste real Québécois beer at **Dieu du Ciel,** an unpretentious neighborhood staple (page 175).

★ **Unique Decor:** At dive bar **Notre Dames des Quilles,** you can drink and bowl (page 176).

★ **Best Gay Bar:** It's good times all around at the **Royal Phoenix Bar,** an LGBT favorite in the Mile End (page 177).

however, like the aforementioned rue Crescent, so if you head off the beaten path, you'll soon lose them.

Live music is a big part of going out, especially in a city known for its indie rock scene. Whether you're into minimal electro, hip-hop, metal, or even bluegrass, there's a club or a DJ night for you. The Plateau is the best area to catch emerging or lesser-known bands, both Canadian and international. If you're wandering the area at night, you'll likely come across a show or three. Most venues have a small cover charge, under $20, so if you like what you hear, it is usually worth it.

Since it is such a nightlife spot, Montréalers tend to go out late. It's not unusual to head out for an evening at midnight, or even later. That being said, Montréalers also love a good after-work drink. Happy hour is referred to as a 5 à 7, meaning cheaper drinks between five and seven in the evening.

No matter what you're up for—a quiet night sipping scotch, or hitting the clubs until the wee hours of the morning—Montréal's got you covered.

Vieux-Montréal

Map 1

BARS

Le Confessional

This inviting neighborhood bar has more swank than you'd expect from its unassuming front door. With a richly decorated interior, enhanced by soft lighting, this bar has the cozy feel of an old-time pub. Hosting a number of diverse events, everything from stand-up comedy to live performances, rock nights to R&B, Le Confessional has something to offer everyone and the crowd reflects that. Depending on the night's event, the place might be packed with old-school hip-hop fans or young professionals winding down after work.

MAP 1: 431 rue McGill, 514/656-1350, www.confessional.ca; Tues.-Wed. 9pm-3am, Thurs.-Sat. 5pm-3am; no cover

Le Philémon Bar

One of the hottest bars in Vieux Montré, Philémon attracts a huge range of clientele, everyone from thirtysomething hipsters to fortysomething suits out for a post-work drink. Cocktails are a popular choice, but they also have reasonably priced beers, wine, and bubbly. If you're hungry, they offer a number of delicious and affordable snacks (gravlax, oysters, pate) created by Éric Belanger, head chef at another of the city's hot spots, Buvette Buvette Chez Simone. The layout is unique with the bar in the middle of the room surrounded by bar seating, banquettes along the walls, and even prime window seats, but this makes it difficult to dance when this place gets packed around 10-10:30pm at night. DJs here typically play everything from indie bands like The XX to remixes featuring Metallica's "Enter Sandman."

MAP 1: 111 rue St-Paul W., 514/289-3777, www.philemonbar.com; Thurs.-Sun. 5pm-3am; no cover

Les Soeurs Grises

Named after a sect of nuns who helped establish the city and who still maintain a nunnery one street over, Les Soeurs Grises is all about the in-house artisanal beer and anything smoked (pork, fish, cheese—you name it, it's smoked). The decor is super modern, with white Eames DSW-style stools lining the bar and low, wooden school seating accompanying wooden tables. The vibe here is generally low key and laid-back. Though it's in Old Montréal, it's located in one of the newer buildings.

MAP 1: 32 rue McGill, 514/788-7635, www.bblsg.com; Mon.-Fri. 11:30am-2:30am, Sat. 3pm-2:30am, Sun. 3pm-midnight; no cover

Taverne Gaspar

Located in the heart of Vieux-Montréal, Taverne Gaspar is the go-to spot at the Auberge du Vieux-Port. Young and fresh, it brings a needed bit of relaxed fun to the district. Taverne Gaspar offers top-quality wines and has locally brewed beer on tap. This is a popular after-work destination for 20- and 30-somethings, so expect it to be especially crowded on Thursday and Friday nights. In summer, Taverne's *terrasse*, also known as Terrasse Sur L'Auberge, is a great place to grab a drink and take in the sights of the river and Old Port from five stories up.

MAP 1: Auberge du Vieux-Port, 89 rue de la Commune E., 514/392-1649, www. tavernegaspar.com; Sun.-Wed. 5pm-10pm, Thurs.-Sat. 5pm-midnight; no cover

Terrasse Place d'Armes

This swank cocktail bar on the roof of Place d'Armes Hôtel (formerly called Terrasse Suite 701) couldn't give you better views of the city's skyline. A DJ pumps tunes throughout the day, everything from Top 40 to bossa nova, for the mostly local clientele who slip on their best dancing shoes for an evening of open-air dancing. The service is attentive and efficient, and your drink requests are answered by a mixologist. The crowd is mostly mid-20s and up, which lends the whole affair an air of sophistication. If the weather turns, you can take refuge in the adjoining indoor lounge.

MAP 1: Place d'Armes Hôtel and Suites, 701 Côte de la Place d'Armes, 514/904-1201, www.terrasseplacedarmes.com; May-Oct. Mon.-Wed. and Sun. 11am-midnight, Thurs.-Sat. 11am-3am; no cover

Verses Sky

During the summer months, this rooftop terrace in Hôtel Nelligan is one of the top places to see and be seen. Populated with fashionable twentysomething women, young professionals still in their business suits, and, later in the evening, older Mafioso-types, this place appeals to high rollers. It's located on the roof of a boutique hotel, so drinks are on the pricier side ($10 for a cocktail), but you can't beat the 200-degree view of the city that includes the Aldred Building, Habitat 67, and Notre-Dame Basilica.

MAP 1: Hôtel Nelligan, 100 rue St-Paul W., 514/788-4000, www.versesrestaurant. com; May-Oct. daily 11am-11pm; no cover

DANCE CLUBS
★ New City Gas

This new club in the heart of Griffintown, an old working-class area that's quickly transforming into one of the city's coolest neighborhoods, takes full advantage of the building's history. Built in 1859, the original facade remains intact, as does the name. Once the headquarters of a gas company, the venue now host up to 3,000 people a week who come to party to the electrifying sounds of DJs, like Sunnery James, Victor Calderone, and Bob Sinclair, and sip on cocktails like "Birds of Paradise" (vodka, blood orange juice) created by mixologist Lawrence Picard. During the summer months, New City Gas is the place to be on Thursdays, when they open their terraces up for one of the best after-work drink experiences in the city.

MAP 1: 950 rue Ottawa, 514/879-1166, www.newcitygas.com; Thurs.-Sat. 10pm-3am; free

Wunderbar

Rumor has it that when this bar first opened they bribed local hipsters with free drinks to populate the place. Whether the rumor is true or not, it remains one of the top bars in the city and a great place to cut a rug. With a roster that includes some of the city's top DJs playing everything from top-40 mash-ups to old school slow-jams, the dance floor is always packed. The clientele is decidedly diverse—everyone from college kids to high rollers—and in keeping with the Montréal ethos, everyone is impeccably dressed, with women in up-to-the-minute fashions with a downtown edge and men looking chic but casual.

MAP 1: 901 rue du Square-Victoria, 514/395-3100, www.wunderbarmontreal. com; Tues.-Sat. 10pm-3am; no cover

LIVE MUSIC

Les Deux Pierrots

If you're looking for a truly Québécois experience, head to Les Deux Pierrots on a Friday or Saturday night. Since opening its doors in 1974, it has become one of the most well-known *boîtes à chansons* in Montréal. First springing up in the mid-1950s, *boîtes à chansons* combine well-known and home-grown songs with live entertainment in a bar setting, a phenomenon that is specific to Québec. Featuring some of the best singers (*chansonniers*) and entertainers in the province, the atmosphere is rowdy in the best way, with audience members often joining in with the antics on stage. Les Deux Pierrots has since expanded to include Le Pierrot just next door, and also has an outdoor terrace in the summer and a year-round sports bar. Don't expect a classy show bar however; like the performers themselves, this place is down to earth.

MAP 1: 104 rue St-Paul E., 514/861-1270, www.lespierrots.com; Fri.-Sat. 8:30pm-3am, Sun. 11:30am-midnight; $5

Pub St-Paul

Ideally located in a building that was established in 1875 and overlooking the Old Port, this rock bar is one of the few live venues in Old Montréal. The decor may be decidedly no-frills, but the pub grub is some of the most authentic in the area. Go for the chicken wings; they can be hard to find in Montréal. Spread out over two floors, Pub St-Paul offers live music—everything from hard rock to Top 40—every Thursday through Saturday from some of Montréal and Québec's best bands.

MAP 1: 124 rue St-Paul E., 514/874-0485, www.pubstpaul.com; daily 11am-3am; $5

LOUNGES

Terrasses Bonsecours

Just past the Cirque de Soleil tent, surrounded by water, are the four floors of Terrasses Bonsecours. A great place to rent ice skates and warm up with a hot chocolate in the winter, it transforms into a jumping, open-air hot spot come summer. Avoid the cover (and crowds) and get here early to enjoy a cocktail and watch the sunset behind the city from one of the best vantage points. By midnight, the place is packed with the bridge and tunnel crowd (local slang for suburbanites); stay and dance to the techno and R&B along with them, or head for a late-night stroll along the waterfront.

MAP 1: Quays of the Old Port, 514/288-9407, www.terrassesbonsecours.com; May-Sept. daily 3pm-3am; $5-25

Le Velvet Speakeasy

Step down into this cavernous, candle-lit bar and you'll find yourself surrounded by stone walls and low ceilings, the foundations of a 17th-century basement. Despite the mysterious setting, Velvet is all about contemporary beats, and a mix of electro, pop, and disco tunes keep the crowd moving. Velvet specializes in vodka; the drinks are affordable and the atmosphere is a far cry from the black light glitz of other Old Montréal clubs.

MAP 1: 420 rue St-Gabriel, 514/878-9782; Tues.-Sun. 10pm-3am; free-$15

WINE BARS
Dolcetto

This wine bar's nautical theme will have you thinking that you've washed ashore in picturesque Portofino, not on the shores of the St-Lawrence. Terracotta floor tiles, blue and white striped banquettes, exposed beams, and gleaming white walls evoke a seaside retreat, and though you might be far from the sea, you at least get to follow a trail of cobblestones to get here. Serving Italian tapas along with its cocktails, Dolcetto is all prosciutto, calzones, lobster cannelloni, and a good time. Crowds and couples in their early thirties can be found taking part in the establishment's delights during the week, while a slightly more sophisticated crowd shows up on the weekends. No matter the crowd, however, the upbeat decor and, of course, the prosecco, are uplifting.

MAP 1: 151 rue St-Paul W., 514/419-8522, www.dolcettomontreal.com; Mon.-Wed. and Sun. 5pm-11pm, Thurs.-Sat. 5pm-midnight; no cover

Centre-Ville
Map 2

BARS
Le Bar Soleil

Tucked away on the roof of the Hilton hotel, surrounded by concrete, this is an urban oasis thanks to a flourishing garden that offers a welcome break from the hubbub of city life. With the speakers pumping a mix of lounge and African-Cuban rhythms, reasonably priced cocktails and local beers (they also have 5 à 7 specials) will have you relaxed in no time. The small pool is an added bonus and attracts a welcome mix of sophisticated tourists and locals. The service is also low key, making you feel even further away from the city.

MAP 2: Hilton Montréal Bonaventure, 900 rue de la Gauchetière W., 514/878-2332, www.hilton.com; May-Oct. daily 11:30am-11pm; no cover

Montréal is in winter's clutches for what feels like eight months of the year, so when the thermometer finally shows a positive number, everyone is out drinking in the sunshine.

- **Le Bar Soleil:** Take an all-inclusive break at this rooftop pool, bar, and garden with great views of the city beyond.

- **Taverne Gaspar:** This rooftop terrace offers a great view of the Old Port as you sip an old-fashioned.

- **La Terrasse Place d'Armes:** Looking out onto Notre-Dame Basilica and Place d'Armes, you can enjoy your port while contemplating the great architecture.

- **Les Trois Brasseurs:** This popular local microbrewery chain has the best patio of any bar in the Latin Quarter.

- **Verses Sky:** Rivaling the view from Narcisse is Verses. It's open 11am-11pm, so you can sip your cocktail at just about any time of day.

Brutopia

This brewpub is one of the most well known and well liked in the city. Though brand-name beers are available, the microbrew selection consists of classic beers all year, including an IPA and a Raspberry Blonde, while seasonal brews include the Chocolate Stout, the Maple Rousse, and the Scotch Ale. It takes up three floors (with three outdoor terraces) of an old stone building on Crescent, and the vibe can definitely steer toward student at times. Happy hours are extended here from opening till 8pm daily, and they regularly host open mic nights and smaller, local bands.

MAP 2: 1215 rue Crescent, 514/393-9277, www.brutopia.net; Mon.-Thurs. and Sat.-Sun. 3pm-3am, Fri. noon-3am; no cover

★ Dominion Square Tavern

Built in 1926, Dominion is one of Montréal's oldest taverns. Recently renovated by new owners Alex Baldwin (of Baldwin Barmacie) and Alexander Wolosianski (of Whisky Café), it is now an old-timey, chic gastropub. Serving fare like pigs' knuckles, ploughman's lunches, and pan-seared salmon, it's the bar part of the equation that's really getting noticed, attracting everyone from Canadiens fans to moviegoers and more than a few hipsters. Tastefully decorated with a good amount of historic grit, it's a great place to grab a cocktail.

MAP 2: 1243 rue Metcalfe, 514/564-5056, wwww.tavernedominion.com; Mon.-Fri. 11:30am-midnight, Sat. 5pm-midnight; no cover

Hurley's Irish Pub

There's no shortage of Irish pubs in Montréal, but there is something to be said of an Irish pub that actually feels Irish, and few come as close to the real thing. A few steps down into Hurley's and you're surrounded by stone walls and low ceilings, with the bar taking center stage. Classic low stools and tables take up the main room, but try to nab a place on one of the comfy club chairs near the fireplace. Traditional Irish music—and that includes U2—plays just about every night of the week.

MAP 2: 1225 rue Crescent, 514/861-4111, www.hurleysirishpub.com; daily 11am-3am; no cover

DANCE CLUBS

Le Cinq

Originally built in 1859 as a personal residence (and now supposedly haunted), the enormous and, it has to be said, flashy building consists of a huge domed entrance with circular staircases carved out of white marble. The dome theme continues in the main room, as do the marble touches. Since the space is so huge, it hosts a number of different venues and includes everything from a bistro, a lounge, a club, and even an outdoor patio. The downtown location means that you'll find everyone from university students to businesspeople grabbing a drink after work. The dress code here isn't too strict; women can get away with flats, and men, dressier jeans, but make sure to freshen up before you go.

MAP 2: 1234 rue de la Montagne, 514/395-1111, www.lecinq.ca; Mon.-Wed. 11am-11pm, Thurs.-Sat. 11am-3am; $10 and up

Newtown

Opened by race-car driver Jacques Villeneuve (Newtown is the English translation of his surname), this club and restaurant occupies three floors of an impressive corner lot in the heart of the downtown club district. A mix of old and new on the outside, the venue has a huge interior, with a minimal gray and white decor and purplish lighting. Catering to the 25-and-up crowd, this is a classy joint with good food, stylish patrons, and a range of music from electro house to hip-hop and Top 40.

MAP 2: 1476 rue Crescent, 514/284-6555, www.lenewtown.com; Mon.-Thurs. and Sun. 11:30am-1am, Fri.-Sat. 11:30am-3am; free

LOUNGES

Altitude 737

Shining out over the city like a roving Bat-Signal, Altitude 737's spotlight is one of the most recognizable sights in the night sky. Situated on the top of Place Ville-Marie, the first skyscraper in downtown Montréal, Altitude 737 attracts a diverse clientele to its three-floor nightclub and lounge, with a rooftop terrace in the summer that looks out over the entire city. Each floor features different styles of music from house to Top 40.

Centre-Ville Est

Map 3

BARS

Benelux

A brewpub on the cusp of the Latin Quarter and the Plateau and situated within walking distance of three universities, Benelux couldn't be in a better position. Of course, this great location means it's usually packed to the rafters with university students getting in rounds of affordable pints. If you're up for an adventure, make sure to get the $2 samples and try everything on that day's beer menu. Chips and hot dogs act as great chasers. The decor isn't anything special, but the building itself is pretty cool: white and curved, it stands out in the best way.

MAP 3: 245 rue Sherbrooke W., 514/543-9750, www.brasseriebenelux.com; daily Mon. 2pm-3am; no cover

La Distillerie

This small neighborhood bar has quickly grown into a small chain of neighborhood bars. The downtown location, however, is the original and has a welcoming laid-back vibe. The interior is fairly bare-bones with saloon-style chairs and tables (the goal was to make you feel like you stepped into a Vegas saloon circa 1950). The drinks, however, are definitely out of the ordinary. Served in mason jars, they run the gamut from "Smokey Blues" (tequila, scotch, agave nectar) to create your own. The cocktails also come with snacks for the table (Goldfish and mixed nuts).

MAP 3: 300 rue Ontario E., 514/288-7915, www.pubdistillerie.com; daily 4pm-3am; no cover

★ Furco

Tucked on a quiet side-street in the downtown core, Furco is the new go-to spot for after-work drinks. The weekday crowd can start early and it's not unusual to find the bar packed by 5pm. Once you make it through the doors, you'll understand why. The bar, which serves food (cheese plates, tartar, grilled lamb) until midnight, has an industrial-chic vibe (exposed pipes, wood and steel stools) with just a pinch of high-school cafeteria (the round, communal bath-room sink). The vibe, and crowd, is a bit older and more mature than some other downtown places and it's also distinctly French—though the bar staff are all bilingual. A roster of DJs rotate through-out the week, playing everything from 1990s hip-hop to the latest

clockwise from top left: Pullman, Plateau Mont-Royal; view of the city from Vieux-Montréal's Verses Sky; Saint-Denis Street, Quartier latin

remixes of Top 40 hits. Despite its popularity with the après-work crowd, it also draws in clientele on the weekend, so come early and expect to stay late.

MAP 3: 425 rue Mayor, 514/764-3588, www.barfurco.com; daily 4pm-3am; no cover

Mme Lee

White subway tiles add a unique dimension to this downtown bar, which is otherwise decorated with that particularly popular look of industrial-chic: wood tabletops, steel accents, and angular, neon lighting. Taking over the location that was formerly occupied by jazz bar Jello Lounge, Mme Lee has completely remodeled the space, expanding it so that it's sprawling, spacious, and, luckily for them, often packed. This is the kind of place that can accommodate you and your seven colleagues for an after-work drink. The client base is mostly young professionals in their twenties and thirties and the vibe is casual but elegant. They have a tapas menu with a varied selection of bites (though it's heavy on the tartar) for you to munch on while you sip your cocktail.

MAP 3: 151 rue Ontario E., 438/383-7673; Mon.-Sat. 5pm-3am; free

Nyks

Just south of Ste-Catherine, surrounded by a number of big, flashy venues, you'll find Nyks, an unpretentious, rustic haven in which to kick back and have a drink. This is a serious gem with great food, after-work drink specials, and a great atmosphere with brick walls and heavy wood tables and chairs. It's a nice alternative to the crowded bars in the rest of the downtown core. Grab a bite from the varied menu; the kitchen is open until 11pm Wednesday through Saturday and never disappoints.

MAP 3: 1250 rue de Bleury, 514/866-1786, www.nyks.ca; Mon.-Fri. 11:30am-3am; no cover

Le Ste-Élisabeth

A building that was built in the 1930s, Le Ste-Élisabeth's nonde-script exterior hides a magnificent beer garden. Lush and green in the summer and surrounded by tall, ivy-covered walls, it's always hard to find a seat here. Inside, there's an old tavern atmosphere with club chairs, sofas, and striped wood floors. Even in the winter this place gets packed, and you'll sometimes find yourself yelling over the music, which ranges from Top 40 hits to Québécois rock. If you can't find a seat in the garden, there's a second-floor glassed-in terrace overlooking the outdoor one.

MAP 3: 1412 rue Ste-Élisabeth, 514/286-4302, www.ste-elisabeth.com; Mon.-Fri. 4pm-3am, Sat.-Sun. 6pm-3am; no cover

LIVE MUSIC

Les Foufounes Electriques

Lovingly called Foufs by locals, Les Foufounes Electriques means Electric Ass. It opened in 1983 with the aim of showcasing different types of art—a large metal spider still hangs over the entrance. What started as an artists' hangout has turned into a club and bar and Montréal's answer to CBGB in the 1990s, with bands like Nirvana, L7, and The Misfits taking the stage. It's still one of the best places to catch bands play and drink a cold beer, but it's also become a popular dance spot, attracting young and old rockers and punks (and some wannabes) to the dance floor.

MAP 3: 87 rue Ste-Catherine E., 514/844-5539, www.foufounes.qc.ca; daily 4pm-3am; no cover, $5-20 shows

Katacombs

This punk club has been going for years, though it only recently moved into its black, cubist digs on St-Laurent and Ontario. Catering to mainly punk, hard-core, and metal crowds, Katacombs features bands from all three genres as well as industrial DJs. The club sometimes branches out into one-off events like dress-up disco night. The venue has also hosted comedians and other non-GG Allin-type performers.

MAP 3: 1222 blvd. St-Laurent, 514/861-6151; Mon.-Thurs. 7pm-3am, Fri.-Sat. 8pm-3am, Sun. 8pm-1am; $5-15

LOUNGES

Le Bleury Bar à Vinyle

Taking up the ground floor of a former townhouse, Le Bleury (formerly Vinyl Lounge) is low lit and welcoming. Full of old antique couches, Victorian-style tables, and fringed light fixtures, it has a casual, relaxed atmosphere. The crowd here tends toward later twenties and early thirties, so it can be a nice break from clubs that attract a younger crowd. With an extensive martini list and a full bar, the place is usually filled to capacity, both inside and out.

MAP 3: 2109 rue de Bleury, 514/312-5809, www.vinyllounge.ca; Tues.-Sun. 8pm-3am; no cover

The Original Sin City

Only a few hours from the American border, Montréal has always had a tortured history with its neighbors to the south. For generations, out of work Québeckers would head across the border, looking for work in any number of small New England towns close to the frontier. After World War I, however, roles reversed and it was the Americans who came north, though they were seeking something different.

Between 1920 and 1933, Prohibition turned Montréal into a paradise for many Americans who came north in search of alcohol and found the jazz clubs, burlesque shows, gambling rooms, and brothels that went along with it. With this kind of "entertainment" unrivaled by any other North American metropolis, it quickly picked up the nickname "Sin City." The city continued its reign well into the 1940s and 1950s, even attracting popular burlesque performers like Lili St-Cyr to the town.

Despite the fact that the city is no longer a mecca for jazz clubs, or gambling, it still retains that "Sin City" vibe, though one that's on the right side of the law, thanks mainly to the city's joie de vivre. Semi-secret loft parties, live venues that double as someone's living room, and the city's numerous strip clubs show that there's still some sin left in the old city yet.

Quartier Latin and the Village

Map 4

BARS

L'Absynthe

A small, outdoor terrace invites patrons inside, where the crowd is invited to lounge in easy chairs and stare at the banister that leads to nowhere. This is, of course, after you've had a drink of the green fairy, the absinthe of the bar's name. The bartenders are adept at pouring the infamous stuff, which comes in a variety of choices. Music here tends toward hippie-er sounds like world, electronic, and late-1960s music.

MAP 4: 1738 rue St-Denis, 514/285-1738; daily 3pm-3am; no cover

Ambassade Boris

If you're in the mood for a proper Guinness or a classic Corona, Ambassade Boris won't be able to quench those particular thirsts. They do, however, have kegs of Boris lager on tap. Opened and operated by the company behind Boris beer, this restaurant and bar is ideally situated in Quartier Latin, right next to UQAM university and backing on to the Grand Bibliothèque. The decor is a strict combination of black, white, and red; the crowd, however, is harder to define. Everyone from first year university students to mid-thirties businesspeople frequent the bar. Outdoor seating runs the length of the building come summer—not a bad place to enjoy a drink.

MAP 4: 1641 rue St-Denis, 514/508-5979, www.ambassadeboris.com; daily 4pm-3am; no cover

L'Amère à Boire

Three stories tall, this artisanal microbrewery is one of the best places to grab a drink in the Latin Quarter, and not only because they give you 18 different brews to choose from. With a huge cross-section of patrons that includes university students and office workers, L'Amère has a convivial atmosphere that can sometimes be hard to find. Almost labyrinthian in design, the bar has multiple levels throughout, and the stairs are seemingly endless. There's usually one corner or another available for you to tuck yourself into. They also have a selection of tapas, though some of it can be pricey.

MAP 4: 2049 rue St-Denis, 514/282-7448, www.amereaboire.com; Sun.-Wed. 2pm-3am, Thurs.-Sat. noon-3am; no cover

Le Cheval Blanc

One of the city's last great working-class taverns, Le Cheval Blanc (The White Horse) is unlike any other bar in Montréal. It's a long-time family-run business located in a turn-of-the-20th-century building; the green Formica on the walls, bar, and tabletops is the main aspect of the decor, with the establishment simply decorated with counter stools and black bistro chairs. In 1986 it became the first brewpub in the city, and its white beer Cheval Blanc is famous throughout the province. Everyone comes here, from young artists to old regulars, and the staff is friendly. It's mainly a Francophone hangout, and you'd be hard-pressed to find a less pretentious bar in Montréal.

MAP 4: 809 rue Ontario E., 514/522-0211, www.lechevalblanc.ca; Mon.-Sat. 3pm-3am, Sun. 3pm-2am; no cover

Gotha

This cozy bar in the Village has a bit of a mid-1960s vibe with its round-backed chairs, banquette seating, and geometric pillows. Just because it is in the Village, however, doesn't mean the clientele comes exclusively from the LGBT community; patrons of all orientations can be found here.

Music on the stereo tends toward lounge, with bartenders and regulars setting the play list. Later in the week, on Thursday and Friday evenings, the bar's piano serves as the center of jazz night.

MAP 4: 1641 rue Amherst, 514/525-1270; Sun.-Thurs. 4pm-1am, Fri.-Sat. 4pm-3am; no cover

Le Saint-Sulpice

Once the home of a Victorian banker, the immense Saint-Sulpice first opened its doors as a bar in 1980. Occupying four floors of the 19th-century house, it has 10 bars in the summer and 7 in the winter, all of which have to be seen to be believed. Each floor has its own style: There's the library, the cabaret, and the cave and annex; the basement and top floors both double as dance floors. Outside, a massive outdoor terrace attracts patrons throughout the summer, and even features a babbling fountain and its own back alley entrance. Unlike most Montréal bars, this place asks for I.D., so don't forget to bring yours, regardless of age.

MAP 4: 1680 rue St-Denis, 514/844-9458, www.lesaintsulpice.ca; winter daily noon-3am, summer daily 11am-3am; no cover

Les Trois Brasseurs

Located in the heart of the Quartier Latin, this local microbrewery has branches throughout the city (in Vieux-Montréal at 105 St-Paul E., 514/788-6100, and downtown at 732 Ste-Catherine W., 514/788-6333), but this is the only location with a rooftop terrace. It's open year-round (heated in winter), and is popular with university students and office workers off the clock. The vibe is always lively and relaxed, and the service is like that too, with servers happy to bring you another pitcher and freshly chilled beer mugs. The interior isn't much—wooden tables, beer vats—but the view of St-Denis at night is perfect.

MAP 4: 1658 rue St-Denis, 514/845-1660, www.les3brasseurs.ca; Mon.-Wed. and Sun. 11:30am-midnight, Thurs.-Sat. 11:30am-2am; no cover

DANCE CLUBS

Circus

Three different rooms catering to three different sounds make up the biggest after-hours club in Montréal. Living up to its name, the club features circus performers wandering around the crowd as they dance well into the morning. DJs on the decks spin mainly house, dark house, hip-hop, tribal, and R&B, though celebrity DJs often bring their own sounds to the decks. Dress code here is less formal than most clubs in the city, but since the majority of the clientele have already been out all night, dress as though you have too. This place is popular, so lines sometimes go around the block.

MAP 4: 917 rue Ste-Catherine E., 514/844-3626, www.circusafterhours.com; Thurs. and Sun. 2am-8am, Fri. 2am-10am, Sat. 2am-11am; cover varies

La Mouche

Like all dance clubs, La Mouche (The Fly) loves its black lights and dark dance floor. Located in the Latin Quarter, it has a younger feel than some of the more sophisticated clubs for the late-twenties to mid-thirties set. The DJs here focus on real crowd pleasers: dance-hall, hip-hop, R&B, reggaeton, and Top 40 hits. It also hosts a ton of guest DJs, everyone from Jazzy Jeff to Art Department; tickets can be expensive, so make sure to check before going. There's no dress code, but you'll want to look sharp.

MAP 4: 1284 rue St-Denis, 514/686-1283, www.lamouche.ca; Fri.-Sun. 10pm-3am; guest list before midnight, $5 after midnight

Stereo

This world-renowned after-hours club may have hit a couple of road bumps in the past few years—a fire and subsequent closure in 2008 and another in 2009—but it is now back up and running at top speed. Still one of the best places in the world to party late into the night and early morning, it is known for playing house music and attracting some of the world's top DJs. Though Stereo Bar opens at 11pm, the after-hours club doesn't open its doors till after 1am, often later. With the renovations came a new DJ booth, swankier furnishings, and a couple of big screens for visuals.

MAP 4: 858 rue Ste-Catherine E., 514/286-0325, www.stereo-nightclub.com; Fri.-Sat. 11pm-late; $40

GAY AND LESBIAN

Cabaret Chez Mado

The grande dame of Montréal drag, Mado Lamothe is the proprietor and star attraction of this cabaret showcase. Performances always include silliness, dancing, music, and a little improv. Showcasing some of the best drag acts from across the city and internationally, Mado's always attracts a diverse crowd. The setup isn't particularly flashy, with a small(ish) stage, regular bar seating, and lots of black lights. Each performance is followed by a night of dancing, so come ready to bust a move. Mado herself takes to the stage every Tuesday.

MAP 4: 1115 rue Ste-Catherine E., 514/525-7566, www.mado.qc.ca; daily 3pm-3am; $10

Club Date Piano Bar

If the name didn't already attract you, the nightly karaoke battles should. Situated in the heart of the Village, this place is known for the intense level of commitment shown by die-hard karaoke fans of every walk of life.

Seat yourself at the bar or at one of the more intimate tables near the front window, which opens onto the sidewalk in the summer. Musical selections are vast and range from Led Zeppelin to Celine Dion. This place is all about the audience though, so if you're shy about your singing, sit back and enjoy the show. They accept cash only.

Club Unity

Featuring three floors, a VIP lounge, and a rooftop terrace, Club Unity is one of the bigger clubs in the Village. The casual atmosphere, epitomized by the lounge with its long benches and friendly environment, extends to the dress code as well. Music played here tends toward house, Top 40, and hip-hop, with local and international DJs taking over the decks nightly. It also plays host to special events, including drag shows, karaoke nights, and even the occasional dance troupe.

MAP 4: 1171 rue Ste-Catherine E., 514/523-2777, www.clubunitymontreal.com; Wed.-Sat. 10am-3am; $7, free before 11pm

Le Drugstore

One of the largest gay bars in the world, this six-floor complex has rooftop terraces, karaoke, pool tables, and dance floors. The decor is decidedly casual with lots of neon signs, brightly colored walls (in honor of the gay flag), and an American diner feel with jukeboxes, a popcorn machine, and old movie cameras hung about the place.

Once predominantly a lesbian bar, it now welcomes all clients, though there are "girls nights" throughout the week. The relaxed atmosphere and packed bars on the weekend attract those looking for a place to gab under the stars and cut a rug to the rock, pop, and disco tunes.

MAP 4: 1366 rue Ste-Catherine E., 514/524-1960, www.le-drugstore.com; daily 10am-3am; no cover

Sky Pub Club

This absolutely massive complex—a bit of a trend in the Village—has a ground floor pub (open for dinner 4pm-9pm), a male strip club, a dinner and drag cabaret, a hip-hop room, a huge disco, and even an outdoor terrace with a pool.

Though it caters to a mostly gay male clientele, with this kind of choice, it is hard to keep everyone away. In fact, it has girls-only nights for lesbians, and it is a popular place for straight women looking for a place to party without the bad pickup lines.

MAP 4: 1474 rue Ste-Catherine E., 514/529-6969, www.complexesky.com; daily noon-3am; free 1st floor, $4 2nd-4th floors

LIVE MUSIC

Café Chaos

Since opening its doors in 1995, Café Chaos has become a Quartier Latin staple and the best punk bar in the city. Fostering young talent from around the province and abroad, it hosts some of the wildest hard-core and punk bands currently touring. When the club is not blasting customers with live music, DJs take over the decks for nights during the week, including Metal Wednesdays. Run as a co-op, it also has a small kitchen where you can get a bite to go with you locally brewed beer, both at affordable prices.

MAP 4: 2031 rue St-Denis, 514/844-1301, www.cafechaos.qc.ca; Mon.-Fri. 3pm-3am, Sat.-Sun. 5pm-3am; $5-15

Plateau Mont-Royal

Map 5

BARS
Bar Barouf
This large, open bar will likely remind you of the windowed bistros of Paris. With marble-topped tables, bistro chairs, and reddish lighting, it has a distinct Rive Gauche vibe, compacted by the fact that finding a seat here can sometimes be a task. The gold-plated bar and beer taps give the place an added sheen, and though you can get your usual Québécois beers, like Boreal, Barouf also offers more continental choices—order a Pastis and be transported to France.

MAP 5: 4171 rue St-Denis, 514/844-0119; daily 3pm-3am; no cover

Barfly
A tiny hole-in-the-wall on the Main, this dive bar is known for its bluegrass nights and its dingy interior. Cheap beer, a pool table, and live shows throughout the week sum up the bar's appeal. During hockey season, Canadiens games can be watched on their LCD screen, an anomaly compared to the rest of the bar. High stools, a small bar, and a large round table constitute the seating arrangements. What it lacks in size, however, it makes up for in authenticity.

MAP 5: 4062 blvd. St-Laurent, 514/284-6665; daily 4pm-3am; no cover, $5-15 shows

Bar Plan B
Set in the heart of the Plateau, this modern bar, frequented by young professionals and local residents, has the feel of being at a friend's place. Leather banquette seating, club chairs, and a sizable outdoor terrace all lend themselves to a comfortable, casual atmosphere. With a number of snacks on the menu, including mixed nuts, smoked trout, and goat's cheese, it's a perfect place for a pre-dinner aperitif.

MAP 5: 327 ave. du Mont-Royal E., 514/845-6060, www.barplanb.ca; daily 3pm-3am; no cover

clockwise from top left: Les Deux Pierrots, Vieux-Montréal; neighborhood bar and live music venue Divan Orange, Plateau Mont-Royal; Le Drugstore, one of the biggest bars in the Village

Walk past here on a cold winter's night and you might miss the warm southern winds calling you in. Barraca is the city's only "rhumerie" and it has 56 different types of rum on offer—stepping in here is sure to warm you up. The bar itself has a distinct island-y vibe with low, wooden stools and tables. Long and narrow, Barraca has a cavernous feel, which, along with a couple of mojitos, helps transport you out of the city. Once the summer hits, patios open in both the back and on the street out front.

MAP 5: 1134 ave. du Mont-Royal E., 514/525-7741, www.barraca.ca; daily 3pm-3am; no cover

Biftek

A perennial favorite, this dive bar is usually full to capacity with university students and people in their twenties and thirties. Beer is the drink of choice and usually comes in a pitcher, but shooters with appetizing names like "Windex" are also a hit with patrons. Barebones "decor" includes a pool table and a jukebox. Popcorn, usually stale though somehow still delicious, is unceremoniously placed on the table along with your beer. Music preference tends toward loud, and the bar is cash only.

MAP 5: 3702 blvd. St-Laurent, 514/844-5211; daily 3pm-3am; no cover

★ Big in Japan Bar

Step through the unassuming red door, down the long corridor, and prepare to be awed when a gentleman in a tux sweeps aside the heavy velvet curtain to reveal a dimly-lit paradise. From the bottles suspended above your head to the geometric shape of the bar itself, Big in Japan Bar is utterly unique. Offering reasonably priced cocktails served by bow-tied waitstaff, the bar has a great ambience that brings to mind all the best spy movies of the 1970s. With its spacious, cushioned stools and mood lighting, Big in Japan Bar is one place you won't want to soon leave.

MAP 5: 4175 blvd. St-Laurent, 514/380-5658; daily 5pm-3am; no cover

Bily Kun

Meaning "white horse" in Czech, Bily Kun is named after a bar of the same name found by friends Fabien Lacaille and Bruce Hackenbeck during a trip to the Czech Republic. Charmed by the bar's quiet but cool ambience, and the rumor that Goethe used to come there to grab a beer at the end of a hard day, the friends returned to Montréal determined to create something similar.

Mounted ostrich heads and tiles reminiscent of an old public pool make this one of the most distinctive bars in the city. Intimate tables and a chic but unpretentious crowd make this place a must.

Brasserie Chez Baptiste

This no-nonsense Mont-Royal bar is a great place to stop in with friends and catch up over a pitcher of beer. In summertime it moves outside, like a few bars along this strip, taking over a section of the street with a makeshift terrace. Popular among young Québécois, and even some known musicians, it can often get rowdy, especially around the foosball table. The vibe is super relaxed and friendly, so this is a good place to break out some French, like *"merci"* or *"deux bieres"* (two beers). Happy hour here, known as a 5 à 7 in Québec, lasts 2pm-9pm.

MAP 5: 1045 ave. du Mont-Royal E., 514/522-1384, www.chezbaptiste.com; daily 2pm-3am; no cover

DANCE CLUBS

Blue Dog Motel

The Blue Dog is co-owned by DJ duo Team Canada, known for mix tapes that mash hip-hop, rock, and electro. The internationally known duo took over the decks, bar, and venue of a once-flagging hip-hop club and have brought it back with a vengeance. The single room is usually filled to capacity with skateboarders, hip-hoppers, and kids dying to dance all week long. Sunday is a sad excuse to stay home. If you're unsure where you're headed, just look for the sky-blue facade, which stands out against other stores and bars on the Main.

MAP 5: 3958 blvd. St-Laurent, 514/845-4258; daily 9:30pm-3am; no cover

Commission des Liqueurs

This huge dance club on the Main is one popular place. No matter how bitter the cold, there is always a line of young men and women inappropriately dressed for the climate waiting to get in. Situated in a beautiful old building (limestone, doric columns), this is where the party is. Drinks are affordable, there's a guest list to get in (you just have to send an email), and the music is everything you want to hear, from Top 40 hits to remixed 1980s classics. The clientele are rather young and often Francophone.

MAP 5: 4521 blvd. St-Laurent, 514/286-9986; Wed.-Sat. 9pm-3am; cover varies

Korova

On the second floor of a building on the Main, Korova's wall-to-wall windows look out over the traffic and night crawlers on the street below. Catering to a rock crowd, but including many a dancier pop tune, it has a definite relaxed vibe amped up with the addition of a pool table and vintage Pac-Man console. Dancing is not

MAP 5: 3908 blvd. St-Laurent, 514/904-6444; daily 10pm-3am; no cover

Le Salon Daomé

Dedicated to electronic music, this dance club and lounge has a more opulent feel than most clubs, with plush seating and sparse surroundings. Set in a loft, the electronic music featured here is more varied and off-the-beaten-track than what you'll find elsewhere in the city. Patrons are usually die-hard electronic fans seeking out the latest music in the scene.

MAP 5: 141 ave. du Mont-Royal E., 514/982-7070, www.lesalondaome.com; Tues.-Sun. 10pm-3am; $5

Tokyo Bar

This popular bar, full of young patrons, has different rooms decorated in wildly different ways, from futuristic all white to gold and glitzy; there's even an outdoor terrace on which you can dance the night away, come rain or shine. On Thursday, Friday, and Saturday nights you might find a line outside, but the bar is usually accommodating and it shouldn't take long to get in. No matter the day of the week, the music here—Top 40, '80s, hip-hop—is usually better than what you'll find at other dance clubs on the Main; at the very least, it offers you choices.

MAP 5: 3709 blvd. St-Laurent, 514/842-6838, www.tokyobar.com; Wed.-Sun. 10pm-3am; $5

LIVE MUSIC

Café Campus & Petit Campus

Once a bar frequented by students of the Université de Montréal in the 1970s, Café Campus has become one of the most frequented venues in the city. The clientele still draws from the student sector, but it is no longer as closely associated with the university; instead university kids from all over the city come here for their dance and DJ nights or to check out an indie rock show. Divided into two venues, both Petit Campus and Café Campus are busy most days of the week, though entrance to one won't get you into the other.

MAP 5: 57 rue Prince Arthur E., 514/844-1010, www.cafecampus.com; Tues.-Sat. 8:30pm-3am, Sun. 8pm-3am; $5-15, dance nights are often free before 10pm or 11pm

★ Casa del Popolo

Started by a member of über-cool ensemble Godspeed You! Black Emperor, this venue hosts both obscure and more well-known bands. It's a vegetarian café during the day, and later in the evening it transforms into a bar. True to its roots on the Main, it has authentic tin ceilings, mixed-matched furniture, and a lot of old, dark wood. Casa del Popolo recently expanded its second room, used exclusively for shows and DJ nights. No matter when you go, there is always something happening, from doo-wop nights to rock, live bands to dance parties. During the summer, head out back to the bustling terrace.

MAP 5: 4873 blvd. St-Laurent, 514/284-3804, www.casadelpopolo.com; daily noon-3am; no cover, $5-20 shows

Divan Orange

There's something about this bar that gives a particularly homey feel. It could be the regular kitchen range behind the bar and the fact that snacks include a homemade pizza, but it goes beyond that. Effortlessly bilingual, it attracts patrons from both sides of the language debate and has become, despite its small stage, one of a few places to hear bands as diverse as the folksy Fleet Foxes and local punk band Grand Trine.

MAP 5: 4234 blvd. St-Laurent, 514/840-9090, www.divanorange.org; Tues.-Sun. 4pm-3am; no cover, $5-20 shows

L'Escogriffe

This intimate, stone-walled basement bar is one of the best places to see emerging bands, which is what makes it so popular with the *branchée* (hip) Francophone crowd. Though it has a decidedly rock edge, playing mostly garage rock, '50s, '60s, and punk from the '70s and '80s, they also showcase jazz, indie rock, and electro bands. But they all come from underground scenes. Even the occasional dance night focuses on lesser-known tunes. If you're passing by during the day, grab a drink and sit on one of their two terraces.

MAP 5: 4467 rue St-Denis, 514/842-7244, www.lescobar.com; daily 8pm-3am; no cover,s $5-20 shows

O Patro Vys

Just upstairs from the ostrich heads at Bily Kun is O Patro Vys, their live-venue counterpart, which showcases more jazz and minimal-electro than punk bands. The cool elegance of the downstairs bar continues upstairs, making it a more adult venue than some. An interested and interesting crowd can usually be found, and the atmosphere is always super relaxed.

MAP 5: 356 ave. du Mont-Royal E., 514/845-3855, www.bilykun.com; Tues.-Sun. 8pm-3am; $5-25

LOUNGES

Blizzarts

One of the first places in the city to exclusively play electro-techno, Blizzarts now plays various kinds of music all week long. Large, rounded banquettes give the space a retro-futurist feel. Art exhibitions are often held here, and the vernissages can go late into the night. A casual place for dancing, Blizzarts has a small dance floor at the front that usually gets crowded. The attitude and crowd here are generally laid-back, and you're welcome to come dancing in your sneakers, or your winter boots for that matter, whatever suits.

MAP 5: 3956 blvd. St-Laurent, 514/843-4860; Mon.-Sat. 9:30pm-3am; no cover

Buonanotte

Market-fresh Italian cuisine is on the menu at this restaurant turned nightclub, known to draw a celebrity crowd—a wall is dedicated to plates signed by hot Hollywood actors. The dress code is particularly stylish; don't expect to get in here unless you're wearing heels (if you're a woman) or a suit jacket (if you're a man). The super-modern interior consists of fuchsia sofas and sleek, wooden seating. Dinner is served late into the night, so expect to finish off your Italian meal next to a crowd dancing on tables.

MAP 5: 3518 blvd. St-Laurent, 514/848-0644, www.buonanotte.com; Mon.-Wed. noon-midnight, Thurs.-Fri. noon-1am, Sat. 4pm-3am, Sun. 4pm-midnight; cover varies; bottle reservation required

Globe

Owned by the people behind Buonanotte, this restaurant and nightclub is less about the food than the waitresses that serve and then party with the patrons all night long. Though the food is decent, the real reason people come is for the late-night parties that rival those across the street at Buonanotte. If you're looking for a one-stop evening, then look no farther than Globe. With its loud techno and expense account clients, this place can get a little cheesy.

MAP 5: 3455 blvd. St-Laurent, 514/284-3823, www.restaurantglobe.com; Mon.-Wed. 6pm-11pm; cover varies; bottle reservation required

Go-Go Lounge

This psychedelic 1960s-themed bar does a nice job of staying on the good side of cheesy, with pop art themed walls, hand-shaped chairs, and lots of red lights. Known for their cocktails, this is a great place to knock back a martini based on your astrological sign. The dance floor is small and tends to get packed, so come early to avoid the crowds.

MAP 5: 3682 blvd. St-Laurent, 514/286-0882; daily 5pm-3am; $20

Wood 35

The newest of the restaurants/nightclubs on the St-Laurent strip is designed to cater to the younger generation of diners/nightclubbers. The restaurant serves up Italian dishes with a twist, while the DJs serve up a mix of funk, soul, disco, '80s, hip-hop, R&B, and classic house. The crowd is younger than what you might find at similar establishments along this strip and, much like the decor, is best described as modern and sleek.

MAP 5: 3500 blvd. St-Laurent, 514/844-0027, www.wood35.ca; Tues.-Sat. 6pm-3am; free

WINE BARS

Buvette Chez Simone

On the border of Mile End and the Plateau is Chez Simone, a very popular wine bar that offers a great selection of local charcuterie. Traditionally, *buvette* means a place to grab a drink and a light snack while you wait for your train, and though Chez Simone is nowhere near the station, the bare tabletops, low lighting, and terrace give it a similar ambience. Relaxed elegance nicely describes the feel of the place, which attracts younger, sophisticated patrons (think upwardly mobile 20-30-year-olds) with its affordable wines and charcuterie plates adorned with peach halves. No matter the day of the week, the parties here go late.

MAP 5: 4869 ave. du Parc, 514/750-6577, www.buvettechezsimone.com; Tues.-Sun. 4pm-3am; no cover

★ Pullman

The huge, crystal chandelier is likely the first thing you'll notice about this wine bar, visible through the massive front window. Situated on a bizarre strip of avenue du Parc, it faces a grocery store and is next to a Quality Inn. But Pullman is a gem in the rough. The high ceilings of this former carpet store make for a dramatic interior, full of chic, minimal furniture and stark walls. Three hundred wines are featured on the extensive wine list, 50 of which are available by the glass. Patrons here are an especially chic breed, but in a laid-back unpretentious way.

MAP 5: 3424 ave. du Parc, 514/288-7779, www.pullman-mtl.com; daily 4:30pm-1am; no cover

Mile End and Petite Italie   Map 6

BARS

★ Alexandraplatz Bar

The city's premiere beer garden is tucked away in a labyrinthian industrial neighborhood full of old warehouses and railroad tracks. Make sure to check out the map on their site before heading over. One of the most enjoyable bars in the city, Alexandraplatz is only open in summer months when the large garage door is raised to reveal a sparse, high-ceilinged space filled with long communal benches, a diagonal bar in the corner, and revelers galore. Serving everything from fancy cocktails (try the Bicycletta) to beer and wine by the bottle, the bar also has snacks like vegan hot dogs and vegetarian tacos. This place is a high priority for Montréal's coolest kids, so don't expect a mixed crowd.

MAP 6: 6731 ave. de l'Esplanade, www.alexandraplatzbar.com; May-Oct. Wed.-Sun. 4pm-3am; no cover

Bar Waverly

This sizeable bar in the Mile End has a small patio come summer and doors that open up right on to the street—you couldn't be more in on the action. A great (and popular) place to go with slightly larger groups, the bar has tons of seating, from comfy banquettes to requisite bar seating and heavy wooden chairs. The music and vibe varies depending on the day of the week. Weekdays are fairly calm, made up of locals coming in for a quiet drink, while weekends draw a bit of the bridge and tunnel crowd and can be much rowdier. If you're here on a weekend, bring I.D.

MAP 6: 5550 blvd. St-Laurent, 514/903-1121, www.barwaverly.com; Mon.-Sun. 4pm-3am; no cover

5296 Parc

Everyone loves a mystery. At least that's what the owners of this new Mile End bar must be betting on. Known around town as the "No Name Bar," this establishment has no name, no website, and no phone number. The mystery is charming (it helps that it's super easy to find) and makes this palm-treed, cane-chaired 1970s-style cocktail bar more desirable than most. The bow-tied bartenders make a mean Manhattan; sip it at the bar or lounge in the back room, decorated with low sofas and black *tadelakt* walls to look like something out of a Kasbah in Marrakesh.

MAP 6: 5295 ave. du Parc; daily 3pm-3am; no cover

★ Dieu du Ciel

This microbrewery and brasserie is one of the best places in the city to experience real Québécois beer. Full of dark wood, tiny round tables, heavy velvet curtains, and a view of the beer vats themselves, Dieu du Ciel evokes a relaxed, friendly atmosphere, especially in winter when the windows are fogged by the heat from indoors. Beer menus change often but usually include at least 15 choices, some of which are seasonal. Try the Péché Mortal (Mortal Sin), an imperial coffee stout, in the winter.

MAP 6: 29 ave. Laurier W., 514/490-9555, www.dieuduciel.com; daily 3pm-3am; no cover

Though sleeker than other brewpubs in the city, with its wooden chairs and tables and bright orange upholstery, Helm maintains a focus on the beer, with a classic and new rock edge. It's a popular place most nights of the week, and, in the summer, patrons of all ages often sit on the bar's street-level window ledge swigging a beer. Beer prices change depending on size and time of day, so if you want a real bargain, get here early and grab a bite off the bar menu. Seven micro-beers feature on the menu, alongside wines and spirits and even a few regular domestic brews.

MAP 6: 273 rue Bernard W., 514/276-0473, www.helm-mtl.ca; Mon.-Tues. and Sun. 4pm-1am, Wed.-Sat. 3pm-3am; no cover

★ Notre Dames des Quilles

A nice little dive bar just off of St-Laurent between Mile End and Petite Italie, Notre Dames des Quilles has something not all dive bars have: its very own bowling lane. In fact, directly translated, the name means "Notre Dame of Bowling." Drink prices are more than reasonable, the atmosphere completely relaxed (feel like dancing? Go right ahead), and the bowling, pretty fun. The decor is barebones (Formica tables, bingo-hall chairs, the walls an unsubtle shade of mint), but the vibe is pure Montréal and the grilled cheese sandwiches are great.

MAP 6: 32 rue Beaubien E., 514/507-1313; daily 3pm-3am; no cover

Sparrow

The bird motif wallpaper, church pews, and fireplace/DJ booth make Sparrow one of the Mile End's coziest bars. This bar has an Old World pub atmosphere that is popular with neighborhood locals and those looking for a hangout where the music isn't too loud. If you find yourself here around dinnertime, grab a burger, beef cheeks in red wine sauce, or the po' boy sandwich. After the dinner rush, Sparrow transforms into one of the busiest bars in the neighborhood, with standing room only on weekends.

MAP 6: 5322 blvd. St-Laurent, 514/690-3964; Mon.-Fri. 5pm-3am, Sat.-Sun. 6pm-3am; no cover

Vices et Versa

This neighborhood brewpub, situated on the cusp of Mile End and Petite Italie, has a definite laid-back atmosphere, though things often get rowdy later in the night. The high tin ceilings give the impression that the bar is bigger than it actually is, with its built-in wooden banquettes and long, narrow terrace. Thirty-three beers are always on tap from microbreweries from around the province, including Vices et Versa's own IPA and Cream Ale. Selections change regularly, however, so if you loved the Framboise (raspberry) last time, they might not have it this time.

MAP 6: 6631 blvd. St-Laurent, 514/272-2498, www.vicesetversa.com; Sun.-Mon. 1pm-1am, Tues.-Sat. 1pm-3am; no cover

GAY AND LESBIAN

★ Royal Phoenix Bar

This Mile End bar has quickly become one of the most happening bars in the city. Though it caters to the LGBT community, the environment is welcoming to everyone, and straight couples frequent the bar for good times and good tunes just as much as couples from the LGBT community. Come summer, clients crowd the mini sidewalk patios, the windows open, and speakers blast everything from Le Tigre to Lady Gaga. They also serve a mean weekend brunch, but come early, as it gets packed.

MAP 6: 5788 blvd. St-Laurent, 514/658-1622, www.royalphoenixbar.com; Tues.-Fri. 5pm-3am, Sat.-Sun. 11am-4pm and 5pm-3am; free

LIVE MUSIC

Il Motore

With Casa del Popolo and La Sala Rossa, Il Motore completes the holy trinity of cool Montréal venues. A collaboration between the owners of Casa and Sala and local promoters/record label Blue Skies Turn Black, it brings some of the most interesting, emerging international bands to the city and a frequently sold-out crowd. As such, it is usually full of young and not-so-young hipsters, checking out Europe's hottest new export. The atmosphere is understated cool; dark red walls and a fully stocked bar are about the extent of decoration. Seats are at a premium, though you might find a handful at the bar, so come prepared to stand. Depending on how booked they are, the weekly schedule varies, so check before coming.

MAP 6: 179 rue Jean-Talon W., 514/284-0122, www.ilmotore.ca; daily 9pm-3am; no cover, $5-20 shows

LOUNGES

Baldwin Barmacie

Cutting-edge electro and indie rock are usually on the sound system at this retro-futuristic bar. Opened by two brothers whose father used to run a pharmacy on the same spot, the name is a clever nod to the family legacy, but it also serves as the theme throughout the cocktail menu, which includes the "Pharmacien" drink. It's a popular spot for locals earlier in the week—stop by for an early evening cocktail to catch the vibe—but by the weekend, it is taken over by young professionals and trust-fund kids with a taste for dancing.

MAP 6: 115 ave. Laurier W., 514/276-4282, www.baldwinbarmacie.com; Mon.-Sat. 5pm-3am, Sun. 7pm-3am; no cover

WINE BARS

Bu

The first wine bar to open in the city, in 2003, Bu has become a neighborhood staple. Looking out on the Main, the huge storefront windows display guests as they sit in old cafeteria-style chairs, sipping their wine and munching on the tasting menu. Dim lighting and ambient sounds give it a laid-back atmosphere that attracts young professionals. Weekly, 25 wines are offered by the glass, alongside simple antipasti like olives, ceviche, and bruschetta. If eating in the minimal, contemporary dining room isn't to your liking, you can take your wine and dinner to go.

MAP 6: 5245 blvd. St-Laurent, 514/276-0249, www.bu-mtl.com; daily 5pm-1am; no cover

Whisky Café

With over 150 scotch whiskeys on their menu, the Whisky Café is a favorite of cigar and whiskey aficionados. The opulent surroundings, full of leather club chairs and rich wood, give off a cozy, masculine atmosphere, and are complemented by the adjoining cigar lounge, one of the last places in the city where you're allowed to smoke indoors. Though food is served, it is more a tasting menu than a full meal. This place is all about whiskey, and they even have designated drivers to make sure you arrive home safely.

MAP 6: 5800 blvd. St-Laurent, 514/278-2644, www.whiskycafe.com; Mon.-Fri. 5pm-3am, Sat. 6pm-3am, Sun. 7pm-3am; no cover

Arts and Culture

Look for ★ to find
recommended arts and culture.

Highlights

★ **Best Place to See the Circus:** Young and innovative, the performers and minds behind **Cirque Éloize** are an impressive and captivating bunch (page 182).

★ **Best Gallery:** Dedicated to the contemporary arts, **DHC/ART** is one of the most sophisticated galleries in the city, featuring work by contemporary arts stars like Jenny Holzer, Sophie Calle, and Cory Arcangel (page 183).

★ **Most Likely to Offer an Art/ Fashion/Music Mash-Up:** Calling itself a "gathering place for art," the **Phi Centre** more than lives up to its motto with events and exhibits that explore a ranges of disciplines (page 183).

★ **Best Dance Performance:** With both classical and contemporary pieces, **Les Grands Ballets Canadiens de Montréal** brings classical dance into the 21st century (page 187).

★ **Best Art Complex:** Get all your art viewing out of the way at the **Belgo Building.** Once a warehouse, it has since turned into a hive of artistic activity and now has five floors of independent galleries (page 189).

★ **Best Place to Thrill a Film Buff:** Home to celluloid classics and the bravest and boldest in documentary film, the **Cinémathèque Québécoise** is an absolute must if you adore the word "auteur" (page 190).

★ **Best Place to See Fancy Footwork:** The country's preeminent school and performance venue for contemporary choreography, **Agora de la Danse** is where to catch the work of ground-breaking dancers and choreographers (page 194).

★ **Best Theater: Segal Centre for the Performing Arts** offers some of the best new plays in the city. Architecture buffs will also get a kick out of the Mies van der Rohe-designed complex (page 199).

E ver since the city's musical explosion of the early 2000s, Montréal has become synoymous with up-and-coming artists, be it internationally known indie rock musicians (Arcade Fire, Grimes) or visual masters (David Altmejd, TAVA). The city attracts some of the best and brightest in a number of disciplines.

This richness translates to a thriving arts scene. No matter which neighbourhood you're exploring, you're likely to find both galleries and theaters. The city is full of smaller commercial galleries representing established and emerging artists. From Old Montréal to Little Italy, independent galleries show work from both local and international artists and offer an abundance of different styles and genres. Many hold vernissages (art openings) with complimentary drinks on Thursday evenings, making it a great time for a gallery crawl.

Fans of French theater can enjoy some of the best this side of Paris. Though not as big, Montréal's English theater scene offers diverse plays and performances by both established and independent production companies. The city even has its own Fringe Festival, one of the largest in North America.

If the province of Québec is known for one thing, it's the circus, a theatrical event you can enjoy no matter your mother tongue. There are a number of unconventional circuses in the city, from Cirque du Soleil to TOHU.

Museums tend to be concentrated in the downtown core, with some dotted throughout Vieux-Montréal and the Plateau. Large or small, many of these offer free or half-price entry at least once during the week; check with the specific museum for days and times.

Vieux-Montréal

Map 1

CIRCUS

Cirque du Soleil

The now infamous blue-and-yellow-striped Grand Chapiteau (Big Top) stands out among the rest of the more somber-colored buildings of the Vieux-Port. Started in the town of Baie-Saint-Paul by stilt-walker Guy Laliberté, Cirque's first big gig was in 1984 in celebration of Jacques Cartier's discovery of Québec, and now they have reached near world domination with shows on almost every continent and a permanent showhouse in Las Vegas. This is the only Cirque du Soleil venue in Montréal and the premiere spot to see their latest productions.

MAP 1: Quai Jacques-Cartier, 800/450-1480, www.cirquedusoleil.com; $50-260

★ Cirque Éloize

Following in the footsteps of fellow Québec-founded circus Cirque du Soleil, Cirque Éloize also boasts a big top in the Vieux-Port and a world-wide audience (nearly 4,000 performances in 30 countries). Founded in 1993 by Jeannot Painchaud, Daniel Cyr, and Julie Hamelin, the performance group combines circus arts with music, dance, and theater. Éloize, which is an Acadian word referring to the heat and lightning before a storm, breaks away from the traditional circus mold and pushes the boundaries of the art with a youthful flair.

MAP 1: Quai de l'Horloge, 514/596-3838, www.cirque-eloize.com; $30-50

CONCERT VENUES

Jacques-Cartier Pier

It's standing room only at this outdoor auditorium. Situated at the end of the pier (just behind the Cirque du Soleil tent), it looks out over the St-Lawrence and offers an open perspective on the performers. The partially walled-in structure is also equipped with a balcony for better viewing and, despite its size, has the feel of a cozier, neighborhood venue. It hosts outdoor events and concerts throughout the year, and it is here that Igloofest takes place each January.

MAP 1: Quai Jacques-Cartier, 514/496-7678, www.quaysoftheoldport.com; $15-40

GALLERIES

Darling Foundry

Known for its ambitious installations and unusual surroundings—much of the foundry remains unchanged—the Darling Foundry is both an exhibition space and artists' residence, situated in what was once the industrial heartland of the city. Part of the gallery's aim was to help rejuvenate the area, something it has accomplished with addition of the Cluny Art Bar. Exhibiting the work of both Canadian and international contemporary artists, the Foundry approaches the work on a big scale and often holds outdoor and sight-specific exhibits. Admission is free on Thursdays.

MAP 1: 745 rue Ottawa, 514/392-1554, www.fonderiedarling.org; Wed. and Fri.-Sun. noon-7pm, Thurs. noon-9pm; $5

★ DHC/ART

Since opening in fall 2007, the DHC/ART Foundation for Contemporary Art has exhibited the work of some of the world's biggest contemporary artists, including Jenny Holzer, Sophie Calle, Marc Quinn, and Cory Arcangel. Setting up shop in a converted, historic building, the gallery has an ultramodern interior, which brings the surroundings into the 21st century. In keeping with their dedication to dynamic programming, public art education classes and workshops are available. And their opening parties are, hands-down, some of the best in the city.

MAP 1: 451 rue St-Jean, 514/286-6626, www.dhc-art.org; Wed.-Fri. noon-7pm, Sat.-Sun. 11am-6pm; free

★ Phi Centre

Calling itself a "gathering place for art" just about begins to explain all the many facets of the Phi Centre. Part contemporary art gallery, cinema, recording studio, and concert hall, the newly opened center caters to every possible aspect of contemporary arts. Hard-to-find movies are often screened here, and intimate concerts with your favorite artists and weeklong fashion extravaganzas are also part of what they do here. One thing's guaranteed, the Phi Centre is unlike anything else in the city and should make it onto your to-do list, if only for you to get a glimpse of its architecturally diverse rooftop patios.

MAP 1: 407 rue St-Pierre, 514/225-0525, www.phi-centre.com; hours vary according to events; cost varies

MUSEUMS

Centre des Sciences de Montréal and IMAX Telus Theatre

Taking up an entire quay-side warehouse in the Old Port, the Centre des Sciences de Montréal (Montréal Science Center) aims to woo 9- to 14-year-olds with interactive exhibitions focusing on the

ARTS AND CULTURE
VIEUX-MONTRÉAL

environment and technology. Permanent exhibits include Science 26, which invites you to learn about scientific concepts through trial and error, and Mission Gaia, which presents you with some of the worst environmental disasters of the 20th century and asks you for solutions. The IMAX and temporary exhibits draw the biggest crowds; if you're looking to catch either, get your tickets in advance.

MAP 1: King Edward Pier, 514/496-4724, www.montrealsciencecentre.com; daily 10am-5pm; $14 adults, $13 seniors and teens, $8.50 children

Centre d'Histoire de Montréal

This converted firehouse, which served as the central fire station in 1904-1908, now holds the Centre d'Histoire de Montréal (Montréal Historical Center) and its three stories of civic history. Dating as far back as the first contact with the indigenous people in 1535 and extending to the cultural boom of the 1960s and '70s, the permanent collection looks at five important eras in the city's history through archival footage, interactive exhibits, and reconstructions. The museum also offers guided walking tours throughout the year focusing on different aspects or areas of the city.

MAP 1: 335 Place d'Youville, 514/872-3207, www.ville.montreal.qc.ca/chm; Tues.-Sun. 10am-5pm; $6 adults, $5 seniors, $4 students and children

Sir George-Étienne Cartier National Historic Site of Canada

One of the founders of the confederation, George-Étienne Cartier originally practiced law before being elected co-prime minister of the province of Canada alongside John A. MacDonald in 1858 (nine years before the confederation). Home to the Cartier family in 1848-1872, this historic site is the only Victorian house open to the public in Montréal. Tour guides in period dress show you through the house, which has been restored to match the customs of the bourgeoisie of 1860.

MAP 1: 458 rue Notre-Dame E., 514/283-2282, www.pc.gc.ca/cartier; Apr. 27-June 20 and Sept. 6-Dec. 24 Wed.-Sun. 10am-noon and 1pm-5pm, June 21-Sept. 5 daily 10am-5:30pm; $3.90 adults, $3.40 seniors, $1.90 children

THEATER AND DANCE

Centaur Theatre

Founded in 1969, the Centaur Theatre is Montréal's preeminent English-language theater company. Located in the Old Stock Exchange, which was built in 1903 by American architect George B. Post, the theater went through two major reconstructions in 1974 and 1996. As one of only a handful of English-language theater companies, Centaur's mandate is to present the plays of Montréal and Canadian playwrights. The company also consistently produces English-language productions of French-language plays by such noted Québécois playwrights as Michel Tremblay.

Theater en Français

Montréal has some of the best French theater this side of Paris. Here is a list of some of the city's top theaters.

- **Espace Go** is committed to showing plays by women playwrights. It opened as Théâtre Expérimental des Femmes in the 1980s and remains true to its roots (4890 blvd. St-Laurent, 514/845-4890, www.espacego.com).

- **Espace Libre,** dedicated to experimental theater, is considered one of the best theater companies in the city (3081 rue Ontario E., 514/521-4191, www.espacelibre.qc.ca).

- **Théâtre d'Aujourd'hui,** founded in 1968, is focused on showing new work from Québécois playwrights

(3900 rue St-Denis, 514/282-3900, www.theatredaujourdhui.qc.ca).

- **Théâtre de Quat'Sous** is a great venue to catch up-and-coming talent. The new building is as modern and daring as the company itself (100 ave. des Pins E., 514/845-7277, www.quatsous.com).

- **Théâtre du Nouveau Monde** stages traditional and modern classics and is better known as TMN (84 rue Ste-Catherine W., 514/866-8668, www.tnm.qc.ca).

- **Théâtre du Rideau Vert** is the oldest professional theater company in Québec, and it has a faithful fan base (4664 rue St-Denis, 514/844-1793, www.rideauvert.qc.ca).

MAP 1: 453 rue St-Francis-Xavier, box office 514/288-3161, www.centaurtheatre.com; $43.50 adults, $37.50 seniors, $32.50 adults under 30, $25 students

Centre-Ville

Map 2

CINEMA
Cinema Banque Scotia

A three-floor movie complex in the heart of downtown, this is your typical North American movie theater that plays the latest Hollywood releases and little else. Lines can be brutal, especially for highly anticipated films, so buy your tickets early. Tuesdays are the cheapest night to catch a flick with tickets a bargain under $10.
MAP 2: 977 rue Ste-Catherine W., 514/842-5828, www.paramountmontreal.com; $12.50 adults, $10 children and seniors

Cineplex Odeon

Montréal's Cineplex Odeon theater (AMC in the United States) may be part of a chain, but this particular cinema is different for one reason and one reason only: the Canadiens. The theater took up residence in the Forum, the hockey team's former beloved rink. The Canadiens' logo can still be seen at center ice and a few authentic stands still remain. While the architecture may be a little underwhelming, its overall grandeur is not.

MAP 2: 2313 rue Ste-Catherine W., 514/904-1250, www.cineplex.com; $13.50 adults, $11 seniors, $8 children under 12

CONCERT VENUES

Corona Theatre

Built in 1912, when silent movies and light comedy shows were the kings of entertainment, the Corona Theatre with its elaborate moldings and gold touches retains much of its 100-year-old charm. Located on a bustling strip of the city, across the street from the renowned Joe Beef, it has balcony seating and a former orchestra pit, making it perfect for getting up close with musicians like Steve Earle, Devendra Banhart, and Feist.

MAP 2: 2490 rue Notre-Dame W., 514/931-2088, www. theatrecoronavirginmobile.com; $15-30

GALLERIES

Canadian Guild of Crafts

Founded in 1906, with the aim to preserve and promote Inuit and First Nations art, the Canadian Guild of Crafts has one of the most important permanent collections of aboriginal art in Canada. Prints, tapestries, and sculpture make up the majority of the collection, along with fine ceramics, glass work, and handmade jewelry. Temporary exhibits by Canadian artists are displayed throughout the year in the gallery.

MAP 2: 1460-B rue Sherbrooke W., 514/849-6091, www.canadianguildofcrafts. com; Tues.-Fri. 10am-6pm, Sat. 10am-5pm; free

Parisian Laundry

Spacious, with floor-to-ceiling windows, exposed wood beams, and a cavernous exhibition space referred to as the "Bunker," Parisian Laundry is a massive space dedicated to contemporary art. Though focused on Canadian artists—they represent some of the best up-and-comers in the country, like Kim Dorland and Rick Leong—they are also monumental in bringing top international artists to Montréal, like Kalup Linzy and Alex Da Corte. The sheer size of the gallery allows for a unique use of space, reserving the "Bunker" for sight-specific installations.

MAP 2: 3550 rue St-Antoine W., 514/989-1056, www.parisianlaundry.com; Tues.-Sat. noon-5pm; free

MUSEUMS

Redpath Museum of Natural History

Full of dinosaur bones, mummies, African masks, stuffed animals, and even a Victorian medical teaching auditorium, the Redpath Museum is for anyone who loves old stuff. Completed in 1882, it is the oldest museum in Canada and is located on the campus of McGill University. It's known for its ethnological displays and dedication to natural history—it has extinct animals like the passenger pigeon and the dodo bird—and the Victorian display cases and dark wood are reminiscent of the British Museum in London. Indoor shoes are recommended for winter, and no flash photography is allowed in the museum.

MAP 2: McGill University, 859 rue Sherbrooke W., 514/393-4086 ext. 00549, www.mcgill.ca/redpath; Mon.-Fri. 9am-5pm, Sun. noon-5pm; $5 adults, $2 students and children

Centre-Ville Est

Map 3

BALLET, OPERA, AND THE SYMPHONY

★ Les Grands Ballets Canadiens de Montréal

Founded in 1957 by young choreographer and dancer Ludmilla Chiriaeff, Les Grands Ballets continues to be the only ballet company in the city and one of the most boundary-pushing in North America. Presenting both classical and more contemporary works, which have included *Tommy,* Les Grands remains vibrant and is currently headed by artistic director Grandimir Pankov.

MAP 3: 175 rue Ste-Catherine W., 514/849-0269, www.grandsballets.com; $50-150

Opéra de Montréal

In the years since its founding in 1980, the Opéra de Montréal has presented 91 operas, including *La Boheme, Salome,* and two world premieres. In a city full of bilingual arts, the opera is one of the few places the two languages come together. The opera house presents a handful of operas a year. There are often specials for 18- to 30-year-olds.

MAP 3: 175 rue Ste-Catherine W., 514/985-2222, www.operademontreal.com; $30-110

L'Orchestra Symphonique de Montréal

Currently led by world-renowned conductor Kent Nagano, the Montréal Symphony Orchestra was founded by Wilfrid Pelletier in 1935 and continues to be the leading company of classical music in the province and is one of the biggest and most respected in Canada. Their new specialized hall, which was inaugurated at the Place des Arts in spring 2011, ensures the sound is impeccable and is quite the feast for the eyes. Those ages 34 and under should check out their website for deals on tickets.

MAP 3: 175 rue Ste-Catherine W., 514/842-3402, www.osm.ca; $30-165

CONCERT VENUES

L'Astral

Found in the heart of the Quartier des Spectacles, L'Astral is situated in the building that now houses the International Jazz Festival. It's fitting then that L'Astral is mainly a jazz venue, with performances from international musicians throughout the week. The venue has a club atmosphere, with tables and chairs set up on the floor around the room for a more intimate setting. It also hosts a number of music-related art exhibits featuring the Jazz Festival's collection, so give yourself time to pop in and take a look.

MAP 3: 306 rue Ste-Catherine W., 514/288-8882, www.sallelastral.com; $15-50

Club Soda

Around since the 1980s, this two-floor venue has a 900-person capacity and plays host to well-known international bands whose music you'd likely recognize on the radio. Frank Ocean, Amy Winehouse, and Oasis are just some of the musicians who have graced the stage. A second-floor balcony, which is quite flashy with accents of neon blue and LCD screens, accommodates more patrons, and bars on both levels ensure the beer keeps flowing.

MAP 3: 1225 blvd. St-Laurent, 514/286-1010, www.clubsoda.ca; $15-30

Métropolis

This is the biggest venue in the city other than the Centre Bell, and tickets to shows here usually sell out fast. If a band is playing here, they've most likely made it to the top of their game. The large venue still manages to ooze a little charm with balconies and richly hued walls. Bars line the walls and TVs are in place around the venue for those whose view of the stage is obscured by a tall person.

MAP 3: 59 rue Ste-Catherine E., 514/844-3500, www.metropolismontreal.ca; $25-75

SAT

Founded in 1996, SAT is dedicated to the research, creation, production, education, and conservation of digital culture. La Société des Arts Technologiques, or the Society for Arts and Technology, is one of the most interesting and diverse venues in Montréal, hosting everything from fashion shows to electronic music nights and holiday craft fairs. The sparsely decorated, simple, modular seating is forever shifting places. The open-concept space in the newly named Quartier des Spectacles has floor-to-ceiling windows that let passersby in on the action. If it's innovative, new, and cutting edge, it's happening here.

MAP 3: 1195 blvd. St-Laurent, 514/844-2033, www.sat.qc.ca; $15-40

GALLERIES

★ Belgo Building

Once an old industrial building, the Belgo has been given a new life, thanks to the various art galleries, dance studios, and cultural organizations that have opened here. What started as a haven for struggling artists in the 1980s and '90s is today an artistic hub with five floors housing over 30 art galleries—the real draw of the place. Some of the city's most respected galleries make their home here, like **Galerie Donald Browne** (Ste. 528, www.galeriedonaldbrowne. com) and **Galerie Joyce Yahouda** (Ste. 516, www.joyceyahoudagallery.com).

MAP 3: 372 rue Ste-Catherine W.; hours vary; free

Le 2-22

Located on the hottest corner of the former red-light district, Le 2-22 is both an Côte-de-la-fabriquehitectural joy—all right angles and glass—and a hub for contemporary arts. The flagship building of the Quartier des Spectacles, it houses **La Vitrine** (Ste. 101, 866/924-5538, www.lavitrine.com), the one-stop shop for all your cultural informational needs—tickets, events, calendars, and more. In addition to offering last-minute deals and cultural expertise, the building is home to a number of different contemporary art galleries, including **Vox Centre d'image contemporaine** (Ste. 401, 514/390-0382, www.voxphoto.com), art archives, and a radio station that broadcasts from its street-level studios. Don't forget to check out the fifth-floor bar, with an outdoor terrace offering great views of the city.

MAP 3: 2 rue Ste-Catherine E.; www.artactuel2-22.com; free

THEATER

Gesù Centre de Créativité

Though it is adjacent to the Église du Gesù (Jesus in Italian), one of the oldest baroque churches in Montréal, don't expect many religion-based performances. Being in the middle of the Quartier des Spectacles means the venue plays host to a number of events and performances, everything from stand-up comedy to contemporary dance, visual arts, and events featuring traditional African and Native American music. Depending on the event, you'll either find yourself in the roomy theater below the church or in the impressive sanctuary.

MAP 3: 1202 rue de Bleury, 514/861-4378, www.legesu.com; $10-50

Théâtre Ste-Catherine

This cozy, independently run theater is a great place to catch various, usually more experimental, acts. Emerging Montréal-based playwrights often stage new work here, but you could also find yourself chuckling along with a stand-up comedian—though you may not recognize the name on the marquee. Improv nights happen here regularly, with a stellar lineup of local talent that invites audience members to get in on the action every Sunday.

MAP 3: 264 rue Ste-Catherine E., 514/284-3939, www.theatrestecatherine.com; $7-20

Quartier Latin and the Village

Map 4

CINEMA

★ Cinémathèque Québécoise

Dedicated to preserving cinema, the Cinémathèque Québécoise is the place to catch celluloid classics, hard-to-find international titles, or Kenneth Anger's experimental gems. The schedule often includes a month dedicated to a single director or type of cinema. The modern architecture of the space adds to the overall ambience of the theater and evokes Paris's very own Cinémathèque. This is a must for cinema buffs.

MAP 4: 335 blvd. de Maisonneuve E., 514/842-9763, www.cinematheque.qc.ca; $8 adults, $7 seniors, $5 children

CONCERT VENUES

Le National

On the cusp of the Village and the Quartier Latin, Le National is a great old venue on an unassuming strip. With an austere blink-and-you-miss-it marquee, the names here range from popular French and English indie rock bands to acid jazz. Audience members who are lucky enough to get up to the balcony are welcome to a seat; the rest of the venue is standing room only.

MAP 4: 1220 rue Ste-Catherine E., 514/845-2014, www.lenational.ca; $20-35

L'Olympia

Built in 1925, the Olympia theater remains one of the most majestic in the city. Once the place to go for "cinematic theater," it is now a great place to catch a band or dance the night away at a foam party—seriously. The main theater still has seats on both the main floor and the balcony, a rarity in the city.

MAP 4: 1004 rue Ste-Catherine E., 514/845-3524, www.olympiademontreal.com; $25-50

Telus Theatre

One of the city's newer venues, the Telus Theatre is located in the east end of downtown, near the Quartier Latin. Performers tend toward the R&B, hip-hop, and electronic dance music end of the spectrum. Telus hosts a number of regular DJ nights. Recent shows have included rap luminaries like RZA and Method Man. Since the building is only a few years old, it has some flashy additions, like LEDs illuminating the entrance and an impressive sound system, which many venues in the city lack.

MAP 4: 1280 rue St-Denis, 514/764-2680 or 888/608-1280, www.theatretelus. com; $15-40

MUSEUMS

Éco Musée du Fier Monde

Housed in a former public bath, the Éco Musée du Fier Monde is dedicated to the city's industrial and working-class history. Though the exhibit is fairly straightforward, it is worth the price of admission alone to see the refurbished public bath, a historic building in itself and part of the area's history. The now empty pool is one of the first things you notice about the space, which was built in 1924 for the area's working-class residents, who didn't have access to showers or bathtubs. It was later used for recreation and remained popular and in full use into the 1970s.

MAP 4: 2050 rue Amherst, 514/528-8444, www.ecomusee.qc.ca; Wed. 11am-8pm, Thurs.-Fri. 9:30am-5pm, Sat.-Sun. 10:30am-5pm; $8 adults, $6 seniors, students, and children

Plateau Mont-Royal   Map 5

CINEMA

Cinema du Parc

Found in the basement of an out-of-place shopping complex, Cinema du Parc is the best repertory theater in Montréal. Playing everything from well-known American directors like Jim Jarmusch and Woody Allen to lesser known international directors like Jacques Audiard, the best in international contemporary cinema is always on view here. Films are subtitled in both English and French; if it is an international title, double-check the language before heading off to the showing.

MAP 5: 3575 ave. du Parc, 514/281-1900, www.cinemaduparc.com; $11.50 adults, $8.5 seniors and students

Cinema Excentris

The premier French cinema in the city, it was established in 1978 and has been showing the best films in the world ever since. Conveniently located on the lower Main in the Plateau, it's also been known to host more than a few premieres. The decor is modern

clockwise from top left: line-ups outside Club Soda, Centre-Ville Est; from Cirque Éloize's production "Cirkopolis," Vieux-Montréal; Cinemathèque Québécoise, Quartier Latin

and the seating super comfy. Head here if you want to see the lat-
est hit from Québec, France, or Sofia Coppola. English films are shown with subtitles.

MAP 5: 3536 blvd. St-Laurent, 514/847-2206, www.cinemaexcentris.com; $11.75 adults, $9.25 seniors and students, $6 children

Cinema L'Amour

Montréal's foremost adults-only cinema started off as a theater hall/movie house in 1914, called Le Globe. Located at the time in the heart of Montréal's Jewish community, it was here in the 1920s and '30s that locals would flock to catch the latest Yiddish films. After a stint as a regular movie house (1930-1960s), it turned exclusively to adult films in the late-1960s and hasn't looked back since. The interior, however, remains virtually unchanged and is as opulent and, oddly, as beautiful as in its heyday.

MAP 5: 4015 blvd. St-Laurent, 514/849-2727, www.cinemalamour.com; $10.50 adults, $9.50 seniors

CONCERT VENUES

La Sala Rossa

Sitting atop super-cool Spanish restaurant La Sala Rosa is super-cool venue La Sala Rossa (see the difference? two S's). Locals often grab a bite downstairs before heading upstairs to catch an indie rock band. The open space is nothing fancy, with chairs stacked in the corner. Though mainly a live music venue, it also hosts dance nights, film screenings, and weddings.

MAP 5: 4848 blvd. St-Laurent, 514/284-0122, www.casadelpopolo.com; $15-50

La Tulipe

La Tulipe has one of the most interesting histories of any theater in the city. Built in 1913, it was a traditional music hall and movie theater (its domed ceiling makes for great acoustics) until the early 1960s, when it became a popular place to see burlesque and stand-up comedy. Today, it has returned to its roots as a music hall, with popular bands playing here from all over the world. If you've had a long day, snag a seat in the balcony, sit back, and enjoy the show.

MAP 5: 4530 ave. Papineau, 514/529-5000, www.lenational.ca; $10-35

GALLERIES

La Centrale Galerie Powerhouse

Located on a bustling strip of St-Laurent, the floor-to-ceiling windows and kooky, eye-catching window displays effortlessly draw the attention of passersby to La Centrale Galerie Powerhouse. Opened in 1973, La Centrale is an artist-run center that focuses on the work of contemporary female artists and aims to expand on the history of feminist art practices. The works displayed here are often witty and humorous as well as thought-provoking.

MAP 5: 4296 blvd. St-Laurent, 514/871-0268, www.lacentrale.org; Wed. noon-6pm, Thurs.-Fri. noon-9pm, Sat.-Sun. noon-5pm; free

MUSEUMS

Musée des Hospitalières de l'Hôtel Dieu

Tucked inside the stone walls of l'Hôtel-Dieu de Montréal, the Musée des Hospitalières de l'Hôtel Dieu looks at the history of the hospital and its medical practices.

Visitors are greeted by a 17th-century staircase before learning about early treatments and practices administered by the nurses, as well as the history of national healthcare and the hospital.

If you are visiting during the summer months, take a detour into the garden. The museum is closed from mid-December to mid-January, and reservations are required in January and February.

MAP 5: 201 ave. des Pins W., 514/849-2919, www.museedeshospitalieres.qc.ca; mid-June-mid-Oct. Tues.-Fri. 10am-5pm, Sat.-Sun. 1pm-5pm; mid-Oct.-mid-Dec. and Mar.-mid-June Wed.-Sun. 1pm-5pm; Jan.-Feb. reservations required; $6 adults, $5 seniors and students, children free

THEATER

★ Agora de la Danse

With over a hundred performances a year, Agora de la Danse is the place to see contemporary dance in Montréal. Started in the 1980s, it continues to present interesting works from both local and international choreographers and is the only venue in all of Canada dedicated to the presentation and creation of contemporary dance. The building itself is impressive, with its Beaux-Arts facade and grand staircase at the entrance.

MAP 5: 840 rue Cherrier E., 514/525-7575, www.agoradanse.com; $15-30

MAI

Promoting multidisciplinary and multicultural contemporary artists, the MAI (Montréal, Arts Interculturels) is the only venue in the city to focus on work by artists who have diverse origins and inspirations—meaning you could catch a traditional Thai dance performance one night and a psychedelic Middle Eastern post-rock band the next. The modern surroundings make it a nice place to have a drink or a coffee while you wander from the gallery into the theater to catch a play by a young, emerging playwright.

MAP 5: 3680 rue Jeanne-Mance, 514/982-1812, www.m-a-i.qc.ca; box office Tues.-Sat. 3pm-6pm; $10-35

MainLine Theater

The MainLine was originally established to produce the Montréal Fringe Festival, an event it continues to support. Nowadays, however, it is a theater company known for presenting more cutting-edge English theater, like a *Desperate Housewives*-tinged *Hedda Gabler*, a half-naked musical about Dionysus, or a play about stripping in the 1990s. Located directly above a grocery store on the Main, the surroundings might not be inspired but the plays always are.

MAP 5: 3997 blvd. St-Laurent, 514/849-3378, www.mainlinetheatre.ca; $15-30

Mile End and Petite Italie   Map 6

CONCERT VENUES
Rialto Theatre

Designed after the Palais Garnier in Paris, the Rialto Theatre is one of the most gorgeous venues in the city. Opened as a movie theater in 1924, its dark red and gold interior and near vertical balcony seating set it apart from any other theater in Montréal. Once relegated to yearly showings of *The Rocky Horror Picture Show*, it has recently been given a new lease on life and hosts everything from fashion shows to comedy shows and live gigs.

MAP 6: 5723 ave. du Parc, 514/272-3899, www.theatrerialto.ca; $15-50

Theatre Outremont

This art deco theater opened in 1929, and its music hall was subsequently filled with the voices that defined the eras that followed. Renovated to include a cinema in the 1970s, it soon became a popular repertory cinema. Today it continues to be a venue for live music and also shows the occasional movie. Performances here are more of an adult, sit-down affair.

MAP 6: 1245 ave. Bernard W., 514/495-9944, www.theatreoutremont.ca; $25-70

GALLERIES
Articule

This artist-run center, which was established in 1979, often showcases the work of local Montréal artists, though it also offers residencies for international artists. Situated in the heart of the Mile End, it takes up the street level storefront of a grand old townhouse, but the bright-green facade sets it apart from the otherwise quiet street. Exhibits here range from video and performance art to installations—one artist filled the entire floor with sand. They close for a month during the summer but they always have a window installation for passersby.

MAP 6: 262 ave. Fairmount W., 514/842-9686, www.articule.org; Wed.-Thurs. noon-6pm, Fri. noon-9pm, Sat.-Sun. noon-5pm; free

Battat Contemporary

Though "contemporary" is in its name, Battat is one of a few places outside a museum where you can occasionally see older works from the owner's private collection. Occupying the second floor of an old warehouse in an up-and-coming part of the city (Mile Ex), the collection includes the work of masters like Gustave Courbet and Francisco de Goya. The single-room format allows for an intimate viewing of the work, which also includes exhibitions by established and emerging Canadian and international artists.

MAP 6: 7245 rue Alexandra, 514/750-9566, www.battatcontemporary.com; Tues.-Fri. noon-6pm, Sat. noon-5pm; free

Galerie Simon Blais

Initially founded to exhibit abstract works and those done on paper, Simon Blais is now recognized as one of the most diverse galleries in the city, representing both established international artists like Betty Godwin as well as known Québécois artists like Claude Tousignant and Guido Molinari. Given the wide range of work exhibited, shows can be hit or miss. The Guest Artist series, which invites emerging artists to exhibit in the two-story space, is usually more rewarding.

MAP 6: 5420 blvd. St-Laurent, 514/849-1165, www.galeriesimonblais.com; Wed. and Fri. 10am-6pm, Thurs. 10am-8pm, Sat. 10am-5pm; free

Galerie Yves Laroche

This avant-garde gallery exhibits work that is influenced by subcultures, like graffiti, tattooing, comics, and cartoons, and art movements like pop-art and surrealism (think of Dali's melting clocks but with melting Mickey Mouses). Cutting edge and provocative, the work is often both dark and darkly funny. Opened in 1991, the gallery recently moved from its old historic digs in Old Montréal to a modern space in Little Italy, the perfect backdrop for the dynamic pieces on show.

MAP 6: 6355 blvd. St-Laurent, 514/393-1999, www.yveslaroche.com; Tues.-Wed. 10am-6pm, Thurs.-Fri. 10am-8pm, Sat. 10am-5pm; free

clockwise from top left: Place des Arts; Rialto Theatre, Mile End; Centre d'Histoire de Montréal

CIRCUS

TOHU

Montréal is a city full of circuses, but the TOHU is a little bit different. Founded in 2004 by En Piste, the National Circus School, and Cirque du Soleil, TOHU is one of the largest training grounds for performers of the circus arts in the world. Shows here might lack the pomp and circumstance (and the awesome costumes) of Cirque du Soleil, but you'll be hard-pressed to find performers who are more dedicated and astounding in their art.

MAP 7: 2345 rue Jarry E., 514/376-8648, www.tohu.ca; $25-50

MUSEUMS

Maison Saint-Gabriel

Situated in Pointe-Saint-Charles, a working-class neighborhood west of Old Montréal, the grounds that are now Maison Saint-Gabriel were given to Marguerite Bourgeoys in 1668. Bourgeoys used the land to start a farm and built the house to accommodate the *filles du roi,* young French women who came to Canada in the early days of the settlement to help populate the new colony.

Interpreters recreate the everyday tasks of the 17th and 18th centuries, and, in the summer, artisans recreate traditional trades on the museum's grounds. This is one of the more worthwhile interpretive museums and well worth the trip, especially if you have your own transportation. Tours are offered.

MAP 7: 2146 Place Dublin, 514/935-8136, www.maisonsaint-gabriel.qc.ca; Jan. 19-June 19 and Sept. 7-Dec. 19 Tues.-Sun. 1pm-5pm, June 20-Sept. 5 Tues.-Sun. 11am-6pm; $10 adults, $8 seniors, $5 students, $3 children

Montréal Holocaust Memorial Museum

With over 7,000 documents, photographs, and objects in its collection, the Holocaust Museum reconstructs the life of Jewish communities before, during, and after World War II, exploring the rise of Nazism, life in the ghettos, and the diaspora communities after the war. The museum was founded in 1979 by Holocaust survivors, and the history of Montréal's Jewish community is explored here as well in the testimonials and life stories of those who eventually chose Montréal as their home.

Found off of the beaten path in the residential area of Côte-des-Neiges, it was the first major museum dedicated to the Holocaust in the country, and it will take visitors a couple of hours or more to browse the museum and take in the multimedia displays. The personal artifacts (which include everything from suitcases and

postcards to stars of David and identity cards) and moving testimonials of nearly 500 survivors make for a profound experience.

MAP 7: 5151 chemin de la Côte-Ste-Catherine, 514/345-2605, www.mhmc.ca;
Mon.-Tues. and Thurs. 10am-5pm, Wed. 10am-9pm, Fri. and Sun. 10am-4pm; $8
adults, $5 seniors, students, and children

Le Musée Château Dufresne

Not far from the modern organic architecture of the Olympic
Stadium is the Musée Château Dufresne, the complete antithesis
to its surroundings with its classic Beaux-Arts style. Designed by
Parisian architect Jules Renard in 1915, the museum was originally
two houses owned by brothers Marius and Oscar Dufresne, who
were wealthy entrepreneurs.

The interior of the house remains virtually untouched right
down to murals and ceiling paintings by Guido Nincheri, best
known for his ecclesiastical works. Tours of the grand mansion
are given twice daily and are free with admission.

MAP 7: 4040 rue Sherbrooke E., 514/259-9201, www.chateaudufresne.com;
Wed.-Sun. 10am-5pm, tours 1:30pm and 3:30pm; $9 adults, $8 seniors and
students, $5 children

THEATER

★ Segal Centre for the Performing Arts

With a focus on creating a nurturing environment for developing
performers and playwrights, the Mies van der Rohe-designed Segal
Centre has a number of different stages and programs that make
it one of the most exciting places to see English theater in the city.
Independent companies use the Segal Stage as a place to refine and
perform, while bigger productions are found on the larger stage.
They also host a yearly Yiddish Theater Festival with performers
from all over the world.

MAP 7: 5170 chemin de la Côte-Ste-Catherine, 514/739-2301, www.segalcentre.
org; $25-50

Sports and Activities

When it comes to sports, Montréal can be summed up in one word: hockey. There's little the city loves more than a good hockey game, whether it's a quick game of shinny (ice hockey) on an outdoor rink or cheering on the Canadiens at the Bell Centre. From December until March, skating rinks pop up in public parks (and private backyards) across the metropolis and are ideal if you have skates on hand. If ice skating is new for you, test your skills at one of the larger outdoor rinks across the city, where you can rent skates at a nearby pavilion.

Since winter feels like it lasts forever, winter sports are a huge part of a Montrealer's daily routine. As soon as there's snow on the ground, cross-country skis are brought out of hibernation and put to good use navigating the unplowed city streets.

The city's many green spaces allow urban dwellers to indulge their inner jock. Of course, these parks provide the perfect opportunity to run, roller-blade or do yoga once the winter has disappeared.

Though all outdoor sports are popular in this city, cycling is the most prevalent. Biking is a huge part of city life, and you'll see cyclists battling the elements even in the middle of winter. The city's bike share scheme, Bixi, has helped to make cycling even more popular, not just for recreation but as an alternative to public transportation. As such, Montréal has 600 kilometers of designated bike lanes that crisscross through the city. Look for the painted bikes on the asphalt or follow fellow cyclists to find your way.

Look for ★ to find
recommended activities.

Highlights

★ **Best Way to See the City:** Get yourself a bike from **Ça Roule Montréal** and explore the city on two wheels (page 203).

★ **Best Sporting Event:** The **Montréal Canadiens** have won the most Stanley Cups of any team in the National Hockey League. Montréalers are so devoted to the team, so the fan spirit at any of their games is palpable (page 206).

★ **Best Two-Wheeled Tour:** Offering everything from family tours to hidden neighborhood gems, **Fitz and Follwell** is your best biking tour bet (page 206).

★ **Best Taste of Canadiana:** The Canadian Football League was founded in 1958, but its roots go back to 1878. Catch **Les Alouettes de Montréal** in action to see one of the country's oldest sports (page 208).

★ **Most Likely to Get You Revved Up:** Since the 1960s, the **Canadian Grand Prix** has brought the world's top drivers to the city for a week of cars and champagne, with a distinctly European flare (page 213).

★ **Best Place to Get Wet:** Located on a lush island a metro stop from downtown, **Jean-Drapeau Aquatic Complex** is the ideal place to take a dip (page 214).

Vieux-Montréal Map 1

BIKING
Bike Rentals and Tours
★ **Ça Roule Montréal**

Just in front of the Vieux-Port, Ça Roule Montréal provides a great option for hourly or daily bike rentals. If you want to explore the city's waterfront, biking is the most accessible and fastest way to do it. Different types of bikes are available, so you can pick a ride that you're comfortable with. They provide tandems, as well as bikes for children. They also offer tours of different lengths to various destinations and attractions around the city. Using the Vieux-Port as a starting point, there's no better way to see the city.

MAP 1: 27 rue de la Commune E., 514/866-0633, www.caroulemontreal.com; daily 9am-8pm; rentals $28/day, tours $22-65

Bike Paths
Lachine Canal Bike Path

Running along the base of the Vieux-Port and continuing west, the Lachine Canal bike path is one of the longest in the city. Following the river for 15 kilometers, the path enables riders to get a view of the city skyline and take in the old warehouses of what was once a bustling port. Open for cycling from April to when the snow flies, it becomes a great path for cross-country skiing in winter. One of the most popular paths in the city, it can get crowded, especially on summer weekends. Those who feel inspired to ride farther can connect with a number of adjoining paths and check their route on maps along the way. It's also a popular path for in-line skaters and walkers.

MAP 1: From Vieux-Port to chemin du Musée in Lachine

BOAT TOURS
Le Bateau-Mouche

Departing from the Old Port, Le Bateau-Mouche takes you on a boat tour of the Old Port and the surrounding islands, including sites such as the Biosphère, La Ronde Amusement Park, and Habitat 67. Hour-long tours depart three times daily, with a 90-minute cruise departing once a day around noon. Evening dinner cruises are also available, as are specialty cruises during popular events like the jazz festival.

MAP 1: Quai Jacques-Cartier, 514/849-9952, www.bateaumouche.ca; mid-May-mid-Oct. daily 11am, 2:30pm, and 4pm; $25 adult, $23 senior and student, $12 child, children under 5 free

This is the wettest and wildest of boat tours on offer in Montréal. This hour-long tour takes you from the heart of the Old Port out onto the St-Lawrence River and the Lachine Rapids for an unparalleled experience on the water. An integral part of the city's history, the rapids are part of the reason explorers stopped in Montréal. The tours offer a unique view of the city and are guaranteed to get you wet.

MAP 1: Quai d'Horloge, 514/284-9607, www.sautemoutons.com; May-Oct. daily 10am-6pm; jet boating $67 adult, $57 adolescent (13-18), $47 child (6-12); speed boating $26 adult, $21 adolescent (13-18), $19 child (6-12)

HORSE-DRAWN CARRIAGE RIDES
Calèches

These horse-drawn carriage rides are a popular way to see the city, and are commonly seen around Vieux-Montréal's two busiest squares, Place d'Armes and Place Jacques-Cartier. A tour will take you along the area's historic streets and point out buildings, areas of interest, and give you a bit of the city history. Though the summer is the obvious season for a carriage ride, the horses and their drivers work all year long, and winter rides come equipped with a heavy (sometimes fur) blanket. Take a thermos of hot chocolate for the ride during the winter.

MAP 1: Place d'Armes and Place Jacques-Cartier; daily 8am-11pm; $45 for 30 min., $75 for 60 min.

ICE-SKATING
Bonsecours Basin

Depending on the winter weather, skaters are either lucky enough to skate free on the larger open-water basin—it's approximately 1.5 times the size of a regular rink—or are restricted to a smaller pond. Either way, it's a great family or date activity on lovely cold and crisp days.

MAP 1: Bonsecours Basin, 800/971-7678; Mon.-Wed. 10am-9pm, Thurs.-Sun. 10am-9pm; $7 adult, senior, and student, $5 child; $8 skate rental, $6 helmet rental

Centre-Ville   Map 2

GYMS
Mansfield Athletic Club

Housed in a former theater in downtown, the Mansfield Athletic Club is unlike any other gym in Montréal. Open at the crack of dawn (and hours before in the winter months), it is perfect for early

Hang 10 on the River

Montréal may be surrounded by water, but anyone who's visited the city would be hard-pressed to think of it as surf heaven. There are no beachfront properties, no surf shacks, no sun-bleached beach babes. But in recent years the sport has exploded, and it's now one of the fastest growing recreation activities in the city.

It works like this: Montréal is on the St-Lawrence River, and part of that river includes the Lachine Rapids, which create large standing waves. It is on these waves that surfing has become popular. In contrast to regular surfing, the standing wave doesn't really move, the surfer does.

Between May and October two surf schools can teach you how to carve like a pro. **Kayak Sans Frontiéres** (7770 blvd. Lasalle, Lachine, 514/595-7873, www.ksf.ca) offers two-day courses as well as board and equipment rental. If you're simply curious and want to check out the scene before you sign up to ride the rapids, **Surf Montréal** (www.surfmtl.com) is a great resource on the sport and offers regular updates and suggestions for those looking for a taste of the coast 1,300 kilometers to the west.

risers, and offers top-of-the-line equipment; it even has its very own health clinic. Though day passes are available, there is a limit to how many you can buy; those in the city for a while should talk with membership about other possible options.

MAP 2: 1230 rue Mansfield, 514/390-1230, www.clubmansfield.ca; Mon.-Fri. 6am-10:45pm, Sat.-Sun. 7:15am-7:45pm; day pass $25

YMCA

Opened in 1851, the Montréal Downtown Y was the first YMCA to open in North America. Situated in downtown, the recently renovated building has a modern new interior that rivals that of any private gym. They offer a range of classes, everything from yoga to hip-hop dance, spinning to tai chi, and they have numerous facilities, including a weight room, squash courts, an indoor pool, and an indoor track. There is just about everything you need for a varied and satisfying workout.

MAP 2: 1440 rue Stanley, 514/849-8393, www.yquebec.org; Mon.-Fri. 5:30am-11pm, Sat. 8am-6pm, Sun. 8am-5pm; day pass $17

ICE-SKATING

Le Atrium 1000

Open year-round, this indoor skating rink located in the atrium of a large office tower is a great place to bring the family or enjoy a little winter sport in the middle of a heat wave. Special times are reserved for younger skaters and their parents, so if you are traveling with the kids make sure to check the site for days and times. They even offer skating lessons for adults and kids.

MAP 2: 1000 rue de la Gauchetière, 514/395-0555, www.le1000.com; June-Sept. Mon.-Fri. 11:30am-6pm, Sat. noon-9pm, Sun. noon-6pm; Oct.-May Mon. 11:30am-6pm, Tues.-Fri. 11am-9pm, Sat.-Sun. noon-9pm; $7.50 adult, $6.50 senior and student, $5.50 child

SPECTATOR SPORTS
Hockey
★ Montréal Canadiens

One of the original six teams to play in the National Hockey League, the Canadiens have won the Stanley Cup 24 times. To say that the city supports the "Habs" is an understatement; Montréalers of all stripes and creeds are devoted to the team. Despite the fact that they haven't won the cup since 1993, games routinely sell out, though scalpers can be found "buying" tickets around the entrance on game days. **MAP 2:** Centre Bell, 1909 ave. des Canadiens-de-Montréal, 877/668-8269, http://canadiens/nhl.com; $40-240

Plateau Mont-Royal
Map 5

BIKING
Bike Rentals and Tours
★ Fitz and Follwell

This bike shop and tour company in the Plateau offers a number of tours year round, including a winter snowshoe tour, but their bike tours are by far the most popular. Whether renting or signing up for a tour, this shop will have you cruising the streets on one of their infinitely cool Linus cruisers, so you'll fit in perfectly with the hipster enclaves you'll be exploring. With a number of different bike tours on offer, it's up to you where you want these bikes to take you. **MAP 5:** 115 Mont-Royal W., 514/840-0739, www.fitzandfollwell.co; Tues.-Wed. 10am-6pm, Thurs.-Fri. 10am-7pm, Sat. 10am-5pm, Sun. 11am-5pm; rentals $30/day, tours $75-100

GYMS
Club LaCité

Work out among buff university students at this gym situated in the McGill ghetto. The affordable day pass, which drops to an even more respectable $5 after 7pm, gets you into their weight room and cardiovascular center and gives you access to their tennis and squash courts (reservations required). The club even has a year-round outdoor pool, great for laps in the winter and for being seen sipping a cocktail at the swim-up bar in the summer. **MAP 5:** 3575 ave. du Parc, 514/288-8221, www.clublacite.net; Mon.-Fri. 6:30am-10:30pm, Sat.-Sun. 8am-10pm; day pass $10-20

A fast way to make friends in this town is to strike up a conversation about the city's beloved hockey team, the Montréal Canadiens. One of the oldest and most storied franchises, in not only hockey but in all North American sports, the Canadiens are one of the original six teams to make up the National Hockey League and have been around since 1909. Also known as the Habs (short for *habitant,* a term used to describe early French settlers), the Canadiens hold the record for the most Stanley Cups: The team has won the title 24 times, though the Cup has been elusive since last being hoisted here in 1993.

During the season (September to April), you can't go wrong to take in the atmosphere in most of the bars in town, which will be showing the game. Water cooler talk, newspapers, and entire radio stations are dedicated solely to discussing last night's game and dissecting coaching strategies. Passionate is an understatement when describing Hab fans, who are known to voice their opinions about anything Hab related. Sit down next to one for a game and you'll see for yourself.

The team plays out of the centrally located Centre Bell, and tickets are a hot commodity. Having sold out the last six seasons, tickets can most easily be bought from scalpers around the arena or on sites such as Craigslist. Seeing a game live, you'll find out why this city lives and dies with this team; the atmosphere is infectious and insane, and even the most lax of supporters will be olé-ing with the best of them by the end of the third period.

ICE-SKATING

Parc Jeanne-Mance

Reserved for those with their own equipment, this seasonal rink is put up by the city each winter and is one of the more sought after in Montréal, especially by those wanting to play a game of shinny (ice hockey). Directly across the street from Parc du Mont-Royal, it is easily accessible by bus and doesn't get as busy as the more popular Beaver Lake.

MAP 5: Corner of ave. du Parc and ave. Duluth W.; Dec.-Mar. daily 10am-10pm; free

Parc LaFontaine

The most idyllic place to go for a skate in the city, Parc LaFontaine's large pond offers a huge rink on which to meander and practice your camel spins and backwards technique. Hockey enthusiasts can usually be found shooting the puck off in their own corner, and beginners are able to find their own spot of ice on which to get their balance. Skate and equipment rental is available on-site at a minimal cost. Those with their own skates can skate for free.

MAP 5: 3933 ave. du Parc-LaFontaine, 514/872-2644; Dec.-Mar. Mon.-Fri. 11am-10pm, Sat.-Sun. 10am-10pm; free

SPECTATOR SPORTS
Football
★ Les Alouettes de Montréal

The team was originally founded in 1872, playing a hybrid of English rugby and football, but a game against Harvard University in 1874 changed the rules and created Canadian football. The team was rechristened the Montréal Alouettes in 1946 and has had a sometimes-troublesome history that includes name changes and a brief move to Baltimore. Back in Montréal since 1996, the team has since gone on to win two Grey Cups (the Canadian Football League's equivalent of the Super Bowl). There is a serious lack of professional sports teams in Montréal, at least compared to the enthusiasm harbored by fans, so the Alouettes are popular and the screams of the crowd can be heard far across the Plateau.

MAP 5: Molson Stadium, 475 ave. des Pins W., 514/871-2266, www.montrealalouettes.com; $15-120

SWIMMING
Sir Wilfred-Laurier Pool

This local pool situated in one of the prettiest parks on the Plateau recently underwent a well-deserved renovation and now boasts an enlarged lounging area and a brand-new wading pool for the kiddies. A popular spot for locals of all ages, it gets crowded here on weekends; weekday and evening swims are the best.

MAP 5: 5200 rue de Brébeuf, 514/872-4050; mid-June-late-Aug. daily 10:30am-8pm; free Mon.-Fri.; $4 adult, $2 senior, $1 child (18 and under) Sat.-Sun.

YOGA
Moksha Yoga

This hot yoga studio on the Main is a great place to stop in and get a serious workout. For a small fee, the public is welcome to drop in to Moksha's community classes, which are taught by new teachers and cater to all yoga levels. These are best for beginners or those just looking to drop in. Participants are asked to bring a bath towel, a bottle of water, and a yoga mat; everything except for the bottled water is available for rent on-site. Check the schedule for dates and times.

MAP 5: 3863 blvd. St-Laurent, 514/288-3863, www.mokshayogamontreal.com; Mon.-Fri. 7am-9:30pm, Sat.-Sun. 8am-8:30pm; $17 single class

A Yoga Passport

A unique concept in every way, the **Passport to Prana** (www.passport-toprana.com, $30) gives you access to 30 yoga studios all over the city and allows you 10 months to use it up. The only catch is that you can only use the card at each yoga studio once.

The idea behind the card is to allow people the opportunity to try out different studios and find the one that best suits them. For those traveling or in the city for an extended amount of time, this is a great way to get in your yoga practice.

Mile End and Petite Italie   Map 6

CROSS-COUNTRY SKIING AND SNOWSHOEING

Le Yeti

Located in the Mile End, close to the Plateau and not far from Mont-Royal, Le Yeti rents cross-country ski equipment at reasonable daily and weekly rates. During a heavy snowfall, it's not uncommon for Montréalers to cross-country ski around the city; for those visiting in winter, it is a great way to see the city. Snowshoes are also available.

MAP 6: 5190 blvd. St-Laurent, 514/271-0773, www.leyeti.ca; Mon.-Wed. 10am-6pm, Thurs.-Fri. 10am-9pm, Sat. 9:30am-5pm, Sun. noon-5pm; $12/day, $11/week

YOGA

Naada Yoga

This yoga studio based in the Mile End offers a wide variety of yoga practices, everything from restorative classes to classes where you hang upside down from their yoga wall. With lots of open space, high ceilings, and light wood, Naada exudes a feeling of calm. Their instructors are knowledgeable and often funny, so don't be surprised if they crack a joke as you're doing your twentieth sun salutation. This places uses an awful lot of props though, so be prepared to lug them to and from your mat.

MAP 6: 5540 ave. Casgrain, 514/510-3274, www.naada.ca; Mon. 10am-9:30pm, Tues.-Thurs. 7am-9:30pm, Fri. 7am-7:30pm, Sat. 10am-6pm, Sun. 10am-4:30pm; $18 single class

Greater Montréal

Map 7

BIKING
Bike Rentals and Tours
My Bicyclette

Located on the Lachine Canal, near the Atwater Market, My Bicyclette offers hourly and daily rates for adult and children's bikes. One of the best locations in the city for bike riding, the canal is 15 kilometers long and runs from the Old Port to Lake St-Louise in the west. All bike rentals come with a helmet and a map of the city. Bike tours are offered between June and October, and My Bicyclette also helps organize specialty rides and customized tours exclusively for groups; call or email ahead of time to secure a spot for both.

MAP 7: 2985 rue St-Patrick, 514/998-6252, www.mybicyclette.com; Mon.-Fri. 10am-7pm, Sat.-Sun. 9am-8pm; rentals $25-30/day

CROSS-COUNTRY SKIING
Jardin Botanique and Parc Maisonneuve

When the flowers are no longer in bloom, the Montréal botanical gardens become an urban winter wonderland. Situated out by the Olympic Stadium, the Jardin Botanique and the adjacent Parc Maisonneuve are some of the most picturesque places to cross-country ski. The mostly flat terrain includes 20 kilometers of trails that weave through both the park and the gardens and offer great views of the Biodôme and stadium. But you are required to bring your own gear.

MAP 7: 4101 and 4601 rue Sherbrooke E.; Jardin Botanique Tues.-Sun. 9am-5pm, Parc Maisonneuve daily 6am-11pm; free

Parc du Mont-Royal

Ideally located in the center of the city, Mont Royal Park transforms into one of the best places in the city to cross-country ski when the snow falls. Twenty-two kilometers worth of trails are easily accessible by public transport and offer both flat and inclined terrain, making it a perfect choice for beginners and old pros alike. Skis are available for rent from the **Beaver Lake Pavilion** (Sun.-Thurs. 9am-8:30pm, Fri.-Sat. 9am-9:30pm), but those with their own equipment are invited to simply enjoy the trails.

MAP 7: Beaver Lake Pavilion, Parc du Mont-Royal, 514/872-6559; daily 6am-11pm; free

Bixi-ing the City

In the early summer of 2009, the city of Montréal launched the **Bixi,** a public bicycle sharing system with 3,000 bikes and 300 stations located around the city. Although Bixis are already established in cities like Paris and Barcelona, Montréal was one of the first to adopt the program in North America—and with great success. By the end of the summer of 2009, the Bixi network had grown to include 5,000 bikes and 400 stations. Montréal is a bike-friendly city to begin with, and the Bixi has extended the city's love of bikes to those in Montréal for a short stay. Available from April to November it is both an ideal way to see the city and one of the fastest ways to get around.

Getting in on the Bixi action is simple; subscriptions can be purchased at any Bixi station (or online at www.bixi. com), located on street corners in just about every neighborhood of the city. Swipe your credit card to get a number code, then type that number code into the bike of your choice to unlock it, and voilà! you're ready to ride. When you get to your destination, push the Bixi into an empty slot and check for the red light to make sure it is locked in.

The idea behind the Bixi is really to get you from point A to point B, not to keep riding the same bike for the whole day. If you take the Bixi for a long morning ride along the Lachine Canal (ahem), don't be surprised when the bill comes in for $50. Bixis are ideal for short rides and the payment scheme promotes that. A single-day subscription will cost you $7, but that's just to unlock the bike; trips that last longer than 30 minutes incur a charge of $1.50 to $6 for each subsequent 30-minute period. If you see yourself using them a lot, opt for the $28 per month plan available through the website, which is worth it even if you're just visiting for a week.

If this is your first time using a Bixi, take it for a spin before you head out on the road; they're nearly indestructible, so the movement is stiffer than a regular bike. And if you think you're going to do a lot of biking, it's a good idea to bring a helmet. Montréal has specialized bike lanes, but when you're unfamiliar with a city, and the sometimes oblivious drivers, it is better to be safe than sorry.

GOLF

Club de Golf Sainte-Rose

North out of the city in the suburb of Laval is the Sainte-Rose Golf Club. Located on the Rivière des Mille-Iles and inaugurated in 1996, it was designed by course architect John Watson, one of the most renowned architects in the province. This 18-hole par-70 course has a rustic feel to it, with weather-worn pines lining the fairway and natural ponds along the course. Deceptively challenging, it's 6,400 yards in length and includes three par-5 holes.

MAP 7: 1400 blvd. Mattawa, Laval, 450/628-6072, www.golfsterose. groupebeaudet.com; May-Nov. daily dawn-10pm; $56 for 18 holes

Dorval Municipal Golf Club

This semi-private course about a 20-minute drive outside of the city is a convenient course, if not the most spectacular. Opened in 1960, it was the Elmridge Golf Club, which was moved to make room for a housing development. Seven of the original holes remain. Bordered by subdivisions and the airport tarmac, it's a popular place for a nine-hole game, or for those just getting the hang of golf. Nonmembers can tee off at specific times; call or check the site for details.

MAP 7: 1455 Cardinal, Dorval, 514/631-4711, www.golfmunidorval.com; May-Nov. daily dawn-10pm; $28 for 18 holes

Meadowbrook Golf Club

Located in the west-end borough of Côte-Saint-Luc, this 18-hole course got its start as part of the Canadian Pacific Recreation Club of Montréal in the early 20th century. Opened as a course in 1949, it's now tucked behind houses and railway tracks, though the tree-lined fairways and occasional babbling brook do a nice job of transporting players off the island. Although not the most challenging of courses, it's convenient to get to and offers a bit of an oasis without leaving the city.

MAP 7: 8370 rue Côte Saint-Luc, 514/488-6612, www.clubdegolfmeadowbrook. com; May-Nov. daily dawn-10pm; $35 for 18 holes

ICE-SKATING

Beaver Lake

The donut-shaped rink isn't the biggest or the most diverse in Montréal, but Mont-Royal provides a beautiful backdrop and makes it one of the most popular outdoor rinks in the city. This place can get packed on weekends—head here at night for a calmer atmosphere. Rental equipment is available from the pavilion, which also offers storage lockers as well as a café and a cafeteria. Hours and dates vary depending on weather conditions, so check before heading out.

MAP 7: Beaver Lake Pavilion, Parc du Mont-Royal, 514/843-8949; Dec.-Mar. Sun.-Thurs. 9am-9pm, Fri.-Sat. 10am-9pm; free

KAYAKING

H2O Adventures

Located along the bank of the Lachine Canal, H2O Adventures rents sea kayaks, pedal boats (*pedalos* in Montréal parlance), and electric boats. They also offer two-hour lessons in sea kayaking and have over 32 kinds of kayaks to choose from, including single and tandem (two-person) kayaks. Rentals are available on a first-come, first-served basis and are limited to two-hour time slots. It is a popular place in the summer, so reservations are recommended.

MAP 7: 2985B rue St-Patrick, 514/842-1306, www.h2oadventures.com; June-Sept. daily 9am-9pm, Sept.-close Mon.-Fri. noon-8pm, Sat.-Sun. 9am-8pm; kayak rental $20/hour; kayak lessons $50 Mon.-Fri., $55 Sat.-Sun.

Rolling On

The **Montréal Roller Derby League** (various locations, www.mtlrollerderby.com, May-Oct., tickets $10) was founded in 2006. Over the last few years, roller derby has made a comeback in cities all across North America, and Montréal is no exception. Consisting of three home teams—The Contrabanditas, Les Filles du Roi, and La Racaille—and two traveling teams, the league always sees a lot of action. The season runs May-October. During that time, unused ice rinks around the city fill with fans cheering on their favorite players. The matches attract so many people that the lines to get in are often down the block.

SPECTATOR SPORTS
Car Racing
★ Canadian Grand Prix

A yearly event since 1961, the Canadian Grand Prix is part of the Formula One World Championship and takes place on the Gilles Villeneuve circuit off island on Ile Notre-Dame near Parc Jean-Drapeau. Drivers cover the 2.7-mile-long circuit 70 times before crossing the finish line. A popular event—it is one of the most-watched sporting events in the world—the race attracts visitors from all over, and the three-day event has a number of street parties and events in its honor.

MAP 7: Circuit Gilles Villeneuve, Parc Jean-Drapeau, 514/350-0000, www.grandprixmontreal.com; $50-200

Soccer
Montréal Impact

We may not have a player as internationally recognizable as David Beckham or Mia Hamm, but the Montréal Impact still bring in the crowds. In a city full of citizens with strong ties to their family heritage (Italian, Greek, Portuguese), it is no surprise that soccer pulls at their heartstrings, and a subculture around the club has even started to emerge. Founded in 1992, the Impact joined Major League Soccer (MLS) in 2012.

MAP 7: Saputo Stadium, 3200 rue Viau, 514/328-3668, www.montrealimpact.com; $30-80

Tennis
Rogers Cup

Otherwise known as the Canadian Masters, and formerly called the Canadian Open, the Rogers Cup is the country's preeminent tennis tournament and annually hosts the world's top players. Established in 1881, the weeklong competition is the third longest-running tennis tournament in the world after Wimbledon and the U.S. Open.

214

Montréal splits the duty with Toronto, and the cities annually take turns hosting the men's and women's championships.

MAP 7: Uniprix Stadium, Parc Jarry, 514/273-1234, www.rogerscup.com; $25-200

SWIMMING

★ Jean-Drapeau Aquatic Complex

Three pools, including a lane pool, diving pool, and recreational pool, let you cool off from the heat of the summer surrounded by the greenery of the park. Open throughout the summer, the off-island location gives it an edge over the competition, and it's less frequented throughout the week than those in the heart of the city.

MAP 7: Parc Jean-Drapeau, Île Sainte-Hélène, 514/872-7368; mid-June-late Aug. daily 10am-8pm; $6 adult, $3 child

Olympic Pool

With seven different types of pools—a competition pool, a training pool, water polo pool, diving pool, underwater diving pool, warm-up pool, and wading pool for kids—the Olympic swimming center is without a doubt the largest and most varied of its kind in the city. Open for daily open swims, it is a must for those looking for the thrill of swimming Olympic waters; doing a few laps of the backstroke is the best way to admire the architecture. It's sometimes closed for competitions, rentals, or for holidays, so call ahead.

MAP 7: 4141 ave. Pierre-De Coubertin, 514/252-4622, www.rio.gouv.qc.ca; Mon.-Fri. 6:30am-8:55pm, Sat.-Sun. 9am-4:25pm; $7.25 adult, $6.25 senior and student, $5.50 child

Shops

Look for ★ to find recommended shops.

Highlights

★ **Best Hat Store: Henri Henri** has barely changed since it opened in 1932. It remains a dapper hat store with selections for men and women for all types of weather (page 230).

★ **Best Kitsch: Kitsch 'n' Swell** is a great place to find a unique gift or that perfect item you've been wanting for your home. And it's just really fun to browse (page 237).

★ **Best Music Store:** It's all about the vinyl, both new and used at **Aux 33 Tours** in the Plateau. Warning: You could be here for a while (page 238).

★ **Most Inspired Children's Store:** The wooden toys at **La Grande Ourse** will capture the imagination of kids of all ages (page 239).

★ **Best Kitchen Supplies:** If you're crazy about cooking (and collecting fancy stuff for your kitchen), **Arthur Quentin** is the place to pick up oyster knives and Le Cruset cookware, among other things (page 242).

★ **Best Place to Indulge Your Stationery Fetish:** If you miss the feeling of new school pens, you'll spend hours browsing the notebooks, agendas, and colorful pens at **Nota Bene** (page 243).

★ **Best Bookstore:** Small but mighty, the physical store of independent comic publishers **Drawn & Quarterly** stocks both new and classic literature and a fine selection of comics and graphic novels. It even has a reading corner and kid-friendly shelves for the tykes (page 250).

★ **Best Québécois Fashion:** The women behind **Boutique Unicorn** have a keen eye for style and trend and work by local designers. The store acts as a snapshot of current Québécois fashion (page 253).

★ **Best Men's Boutique:** Though not exclusively a men's store, **Les Étoffes** has an impeccable men's section full of the latest from some of the coolest labels around (page 253).

Montréal style is unlike anything else in Canada, and the boutiques around the city reflect that. Back in the early 20th century it was the chicest place on the continent, thanks to its position as the hub of travel. Passengers traveling to and from Europe would disembark here, bringing the latest fashions from the continent with them before traveling on to places like New York and Toronto.

Montréal remains at a crossroads style-wise, with both European and North American tendencies, all of which have been shaped by the cold winters. Anyone who has visited when the snow is piled high knows that winter fashion here is particularly idiosyncratic, one that can be summed up by puffy parkas and fur-trimmed boots.

In smaller, independently owned boutiques, there's a trend toward emerging local and international talent with an emphasis on exclusivity, so if you see it at one store, you might not be able to find it elsewhere. There's also a push to appeal to both men and women, so many boutiques are unisex and more often than not they'll also carry a range of footwear and accessories, or even fragrances, to ensure you leave with a total look. Montréal's love of classic pieces means you'll come across vintage in the unlikeliest of stores.

Even before the words sustainability and eco-friendly became part of everyday parlance, there was a tradition of artisan products and a dedication to made-in-Québec goods. Though many of the garment factories have closed, the city's flourishing design scene remains dedicated to producing products within the province. All over the city there are home decor and clothing boutiques dedicated to selling exactly that. Just as Montréal is a hotbed for artists, it's also a hotbed for up-and-coming designers, and stores throughout the city carry their work, or you might come across the designer's own eponymous boutique. Montréalers are fond of simple leather goods and handmade pieces from local jewelers.

Montréal has a torrid love affair with antiques and kitsch, one that's led to an overabundance of these types of stores. There are so many, from bizarre back-room family-run affairs to huge, engrossing warehouses full of a lot of junk and a few treasures.

For the amount of beauty products that are made and conceived close to Montréal, you'd expect more independent boutiques to pop up. For the moment, however, we have to be content with a slim (but excellent) selection. The numerous spas here help make up for the lack of beauty boutiques. If you've yet to experience the hammam, a traditional Turkish bath, this is where to take the plunge, giving you a bit of the Orient in the middle of North America.

There are a ton of great record stores in Montréal, most of them carrying a spectrum of musical styles from acid jazz to prog-rock and classic albums by Québécoise singers like Celine Dion, Isabelle Boulay, and everything in between. Fans of vinyl will find new and old albums to pad out their collection, and most of places also carry a range of CDs, both new and used.

The majority of bookstores in the city are French. There are a couple of independent English-language bookstores, though the majority of them are large chains. If you're looking for a hard-to-find title, used bookstores are your best bet.

As yet, the province's mini baby boom hasn't translated into more kid-specific stores; at the moment there are only a few great ones. Since Montréal is a bilingual city, not all children's toys are in English, so double-check the label before buying that present for your niece or nephew.

The city's main shopping district is concentrated in the downtown core, along, and underneath, rue Ste-Catherine. It's here that you'll find Montréal's shopping malls, department stores, popular chain stores, electronics shops, and the legendary Underground City that lets you explore the entire shopping mecca without stepping outside. If you want a bit of chic, head for upscale rue Sherbrooke with its high-end fashion boutiques and department stores. Still downtown, the grand buildings and wide boulevard will make you feel as though you're somewhere else entirely. But no matter where you are in Montréal, chances are you'll find a cute little neighborhood store to pop into.

clockwise from top left: secondhand finds at The Annex, Mile End; masculine minimalism at menswear store Micheal Brisson, Vieux-Montréal; boutique Espace Pepin, Vieux-Montréal

ACCESSORIES AND JEWELRY

Roland Dubuc Joaillier

Located on Place Royale in the heart of Vieux-Montréal, jeweler Roland Dubuc's store doubles as his studio, so don't be surprised if you catch him at work on a piece while you're browsing. Apart from his studio-shop set-up, what sets Dubuc apart is how he creates his jewelry. Instead of building his pieces from various materials, his work is created using a single sheet of metal. Geometric in form and elegant in design, his work has a contemporary edge that gives off a definite Montréal vibe.

MAP 1: 163 rue St-Paul W., 514/844-1221, www.rolanddubuc.com; Tues.-Fri. 11am-6pm, Sat.-Sun. 11am-5pm

BATH, BEAUTY, AND SPAS

Bota Bota

Bota Bota dropped anchor in the city's port in 2010 and hasn't look backed. Once a ferry, the Bota Bota boat has since been converted into one of Montréal's most unique spaces, and offers a number of different services including cold showers and baths, Finnish saunas, 40 types of massage, a Hammam, two basins fed by the St-Lawrence River, and your regular mani-pedi. Though all spas are created with the idea of escape in mind, stepping onto a boat just makes it that much easier. They also offer yoga and pilates. Treatment prices start at around $50.

MAP 1: 358 rue de la Commune W., 514/284-0333, www.botabota.ca; daily 10am-10pm

Scandinave Les Bains Vieux-Montréal

Taking over a large 19th-century building directly across from the Vieux-Port, the Scandinave Les Bains focuses its attention on hydrotherapy, relaxation, and massages. Modeled after traditional Scandinavian spas, the surroundings are as natural as possible, with stone walls, wood floors, and an earthy color scheme. Even the baths are a calming slate-gray. Massages, which start at $128 for 60 minutes and include access to the baths, are from the Nordic mold and include deep tissue ($138), Swedish exfoliation ($208), and hot stone massages ($198).

MAP 1: 71 rue de la Commune W., 514/288-2009, www.scandinave.com; Mon.-Fri. 7am-9pm, Sat.-Sun. 10am-9pm

Cahier d'Exercices

This upscale boutique offers only the most coveted of labels, an eclectic and avant-garde mix of internationally recognized as well as up-and-coming designers. The racks at Cahier d'Exercices ("school notebook" in English) are stocked with pieces by the likes of Dries Van Noten, Celine, and Ann Demeulemeester. It's a few steps up to the grand old space in Vieux-Montréal, whose interior has been transformed into a contemporary heaven full of sleek white shelves, a high, open ceiling, and simple, suspended steel racks. If you're browsing in the area, stop in for a peek, even if your wallet stays shut.

MAP 1: 369 rue St-Paul W., 514/439-5169, www.cahierdexercices.com; Mon.-Fri. 11am-7pm, Sat. 10am-5pm

Clusier Habilleur

More than just a store, this menswear boutique in Old Montréal (they also have a store downtown at 2041 Stanley, 514/844-3988) offers made-to-measure pieces that range from suits and tuxes to jeans, dress shirts, and even cashmere coats. Since they offer bespoke services, the staff here knows their stuff and can guess your neck size just by looking. Sip a coffee in their espresso lounge as you wait for them to get your size in a pair of multicolored Lacoste topsiders. Alongside well-known brands, the store has its own in-house Clusier line. Though it's found in Old Montréal, the boutique is distinctly modern with occasional brickwork accenting the white walls.

MAP 1: 432 rue McGill, 514/842-1717, www.clusier.com; Mon.-Wed. 10am-7pm, Thurs.-Fri. 10am-8pm, Sat. 10am-5:30pm

Espace Pepin

Owner and artist Lysanne Pepin has created a unique space where her artwork serves as a backdrop to a carefully selected array of clothing, jewelry, accessories, and lingerie. Created by local and international designers, the pieces are affordable and have a classic, relaxed appeal. White walls and shabby-chic decor invite you into the open-concept boutique that's as welcoming as a friend's apartment.

MAP 1: 350 rue St-Paul W., 514/287-5005, www.espacepepin.com; Mon.-Wed. 10am-6pm, Thurs. 10am-8pm, Sat. 10am-6pm, Sun. noon-6pm

Michel Brisson

Wanting to recreate the feel of an old haberdasher where men could shop in a relaxed atmosphere, Michel Brisson created his eponymous menswear boutique with the help of architects Saucier + Perrotte. The classic storefront in Vieux-Montréal perfectly hints at the masculine minimalism of the interior. For added drama, one room retains its original wood paneling. Sharp touches of steel and the heavy use of black nicely mimic the aesthetic of the contemporary brands the store carries, like Dries Van Noten, Rick Owens, and Acne. There's a second boutique in Outremont (1012 ave. Laurier W., 514/270-1012, www.michelbrisson.com).

MAP 1: 384 rue St-Paul W., 514/285-1012, www.michelbrisson.com; Mon.-Sat. 11am-6pm, Sun. noon-6pm

Reborn

Carrying some of the most cutting-edge designers, Reborn seems almost to echo the physical shape the fashion world so adores, with a long, skinny space that never seems to get overpopulated. Owner and buyer Brigitte Chartrand's keen eye and discerning taste mean the choices from designers like Gareth Pugh, Preen, and Rad Hourani are ever changing and ever challenging. Often dressed in all black, the staff can seem intimidating, but get them talking and you'll soon realize how well they know their stuff, including how to make you look your best. Though the shop has some pricey pieces, it also carries mid-priced goods and has great sales.

MAP 1: 231 rue St-Paul W., 514/499-8549, www.reborn.ws; Mon.-Wed. and Sat. 11am-6pm, Thurs. 11am-8pm, Sun. noon-6pm

SSENSE

This is the flagship store of online luxury retailer SSENSE (pronounced "essence"). Entering this store with the intention to buy is sure to do damage to your pocketbook. Pieces from Alexander McQueen, Balmain, and Lanvin stand out against the high-gloss black walls and well-worn gray floorboards. Taking up ideal real estate on a corner block of St-Paul, the boutique is filled with light from the store's high windows. Menswear can be found down a set of burnished steel stairs that lead to a dimly lit basement bunker, complete with stone walls and the latest from Comme des Garçons and Maison Martin Margiela. No matter your budget, this is a fashion snob's paradise.

MAP 1: 90 rue St-Paul W., 514/289-1906, www.ssense.com; Mon.-Wed. and Sat. 10am-6pm, Thurs.-Fri. 10am-9pm, Sun. noon-6pm

U&I

When owner and buyer Eric Toledando opened U&I at the tail end of the 1990s, he wanted to focus on the conceptual side of modern style. Now considered one of the best unisex boutiques in the city, it has made a name for itself carrying upscale, typically hard-to-find or emerging designers. The modern, open-concept design of the store is welcoming and the racks are perfectly balanced—not too much, not too little—making it an inviting place to browse.

Selections from labels like See by Chloé, Vivienne Westwood,
Opening Ceremony, 3.1 Philip Lim, and Comme des Garçons are
all found here, as are denim brands Acne and Paper Denim, shoes
by Chie Mihara, and bags by Denis Gagnon.

MAP 1: 215 rue St-Paul W., 514/508-7704, www.boutiqueuandi.com; Mon.-Wed.
11am-7pm, Thurs.-Fri. 11am-9pm, Sat. 10am-7pm, Sun. noon-6pm

GIFT AND HOME
Zone Orange
Art gallery, store, and café, Zone Orange is a tiny jack of all trades
just off of the busy rue St-Paul. As soon as you step into this small
boutique, you're surrounded by 100 percent Québec-made goods.
It's dedicated to local producers and to supporting the local arts,
and every product they carry (with the exception of the coffee)
comes from the province. They're displayed in white cubbies and
on long white shelves, and an espresso machine takes center stage
next to the till. The laid-back and inviting staff knows the products
and producers well and can answer most questions about who made
the product you're holding and how. Handmade paper puppets, silver jewelry, and recycled-leather bags are just some the goods you
can browse as you sip a latte and check out the latest exhibition in
the back room.

MAP 1: 410 rue St-Pierre, 514/510-5809, www.galeriezoneorange.com; Mon.-Fri.
10am-6pm, Sat. noon-6pm

Centre-Ville
Map 2

ACCESSORIES AND JEWELRY
Bleu Comme Le Ciel
This is the place to pick up costume jewelry in the city, though from
the window display, you'd never know these rocks are fake. And
that's just how owner Marie-Hélène Chartray likes it, mixing real
stones with Swarovski crystals and silver or other metals for one-
of-a-kind pieces. Women of all ages and bank accounts, and men
looking for the perfect gift, come here to find that needed piece of
affordable bling.

Taking the Côte d'Azur vibe even further, the boutique itself
mimics the coastal region, with soft, sandy-colored floors and blue
walls; even the display cases act as shells, showing off their treasured finds.

MAP 2: 2000 rue Peel, 514/847-1128, www.bleucommeleciel.com; Mon.-Wed.
10am-6pm, Thurs.-Fri. 10am-9pm, Sat. 10am-5pm, Sun. noon-5pm

Tiffany & Co.

This iconic jewelers needs no introduction. It's here that you'll find the company's most coveted collections and pieces by their most prized designers. Known for its craftsmanship and beauty, Tiffany is synonymous with family heirlooms and life's greatest events. Opened in 2012, this location can be found on the opulent stretch of Sherbrooke and is housed in the same building as the Ritz, appropriate company for the world's most beloved jewelers.

MAP 2: 1290 rue Sherbrooke W., 514/842-6953, www.tiffany.ca; Mon.-Wed. 10am-6pm, Thurs.-Fri. 10am-9pm, Sat. 9:30am-5:30pm, Sun. noon-5pm

ANTIQUES AND KITSCH

L'Ecuyer Antiques

Old traveling trunks and luggage are elegantly stacked along the walls of this beautifully decorated store, with black-and-white photos hanging on the walls. You feel as though you've just entered the corridor of a family about to go on vacation. Set designers are in love with this place, as are those with a thing for classic nostalgia pieces. The fashion-conscious will immediately have their eye on the antique Louis Vuitton or the full snakeskin set with hardly a nick on it. Owner André also has a lovely collection of walking sticks, as well as the occasional picnic set for those who want to eat alfresco in style.

MAP 2: 1896 rue Notre-Dame W., 514/932-8461; Tues.-Sat. 11am-5pm

Grand Central

The ceiling here is dripping in chandeliers. Owners Wayne and Gordon Downs have an eye for those from the 18th and 19th centuries, and at dusk, the view from outside is stunning, giving it a romantic and old-timey feel. Though lighting is their specialty—beyond chandeliers they have a range of floor lamps, desk lamps, and table lamps, they also have the furniture to match your early-20th-century hurricane lamp.

MAP 2: 2448 rue Notre-Dame W., 514/935-1467, www.grandcentralinc.ca; Mon.-Fri. 9:30am-5:30pm, Sat. 11am-5pm

Retro-Ville

Montréal's original nostalgia store—it was formerly called Nostalgia-Ville—and arguably "the only place to visit in Montréal," at least according to the unflagging owner, this store appeals to the collector in all of us. Around for over 30 years, it's stocked with everything from vintage toys to antique cookie tins, Charles and Di commemorative tea cups, old street signs, and seltzer bottles. It's less antique-y than a lot of the stores on the strip—there is something here that will trigger childhood memories for everyone.

Those with an appetite for kitsch and schmaltz would do well to stop in.

MAP 2: 2652 rue Notre-Dame W., 514/939-2007; Tues.-Sat. 11am-5pm

BATH, BEAUTY, AND SPAS
Murale

The Canadian answer to Sephora (the flagship is on Ste-Catherine), Murale is a one-stop beauty store with internationally recognized brands and emerging beauty labels. The first Murale to open in Canada, this one can be found on the ground level of Place Ville-Marie. Über-sleek and futuristic looking, the entirely white store has a high-gloss shine to it and the vibe is super modern. Taking a more holistic approach, alongside beauty and fragrance experts is a pharmacist and a dermatological skin-care center, which offers facials and other services. Those interested in checking out lesser-known brands like Gosh and Dr. Hauschka should stop in here.

MAP 2: 1 Place Ville-Marie, 514/875-1593, www.murale.ca; Mon.-Wed. 9am-7pm, Thurs.-Fri. 9am-9pm, Sat. 9am-5pm

Studio Beauté du Monde

If there's one beauty treatment in Montréal that you'll be hard-pressed to find outside of the city, it is the hammam spa. This spa is bright and open with Middle Eastern touches like rich, striped pillows and low wood furniture. The traditional Turkish bath for both men and women offers two steam rooms and a hot room. Traditional treatment, which starts at $89, involves black soap exfoliation, *rassoul* body wrap, and oil application to rehydrate your skin. Though the hammam is shared by both men and women, men are only allowed on Saturdays. Other treatments include Oriental honey waxing and facials.

MAP 2: 1455 rue Drummond, Ste. 2B, 514/841-1210, www.studiobeautedumonde. com; Tues.-Sat. 10am-7pm, Sun.-Mon. 10am-6pm

BOOKS AND MUSIC
Cheap Thrills

Established in 1971, Cheap Thrills harmoniously brings books and music together in this second-floor mecca. Specializing in jazz, avant-garde, experimental, and blues albums, they also stock the latest rock and indie rock albums on vinyl and CD. No matter what you're looking for they likely have it, since their stock of used and new vinyl and CDs is over 10,000.

Being a stone's throw from McGill University, this is an ideal place to pick up a lightly used *Norton Anthology* or annotated version of *To the Lighthouse*. The selection of used books here is so vast it almost reaches the ceiling, so don't be afraid to use the ladder provided.

MAP 2: 2044 rue Metcalfe, 514/844-8988, www.cheapthrills.ca; Mon.-Wed. and Sat. 11am-6pm, Thurs.-Fri. 11am-9pm, Sun. noon-5pm

Mediaphile

This independently owned newsstand sells a number of international daily and weekend papers and offers a wide selection of magazines in just about every language you can think of. This is a cute little place that has a homey feel; they even have wrapping paper, greeting cards, and trinkets for a last-minute gift that you can send right away because there is also a post office in the back. If you need an emergency loan while you're in town, they're even a part of Western Union. Wait, there's more—cigars. This store has a huge selection of pipes, cigars, fancy cigarettes, and all the paraphernalia that goes with them, including beautiful, and pricey, humidors. Locals come to get the dailies and browse the tabloids, and tourists pop in for a Cuban.

MAP 2: 1901 rue Ste-Catherine W., 514/939-3676; Mon.-Sat. 8am-11pm, Sun. 10:30am-11pm

Paragraphe

A long-time independent bookstore, Paragraphe was bought out by Quécécois company Archambault in the mid-aughts. Somehow, though, it's managed to retain its charm and the feel of a neighborhood bookstore. Kitty-corner to McGill University and on the northern tip of downtown, it always has a good selection of fiction and nonfiction to browse. A long-time favorite with authors—Yann Martel in particular drops in when he's in town—it hosts a number of readings and book launches throughout the year.

MAP 2: 2220 ave. McGill College, 514/845-5811, www.paragraphbooks.com; Mon.-Fri. 8am-9pm, Sat.-Sun. 9am-9pm

CLOTHING AND SHOES

Browns

It may have grown into a national chain with over 40 stores, but the history of Browns starts right here in Montréal. The first Canadian retailer to import European brands like Salvatore Ferragamo, Charles Jourdan, and Bruno Magli, it continues to carry some of the world's top shoe designers as well as their very own Browns and trendier B2 labels. In the heart of downtown, the atmosphere of the store is akin to a crowded disco, with the staff dressed to impress and the music pumping. They offer a range of men's and women's styles and have a second-floor mezzanine reserved for designer labels.

MAP 2: 1191 rue Ste-Catherine W., 514/987-1206, www.brownsshoes.com; Mon.-Fri. 10am-9pm, Sat. 10am-5pm, Sun. noon-5pm

Les Créateurs

For a bit of Japanese or Belgian minimalism head to Maria Balla's Les Créateurs, a mainstay since its debut in 1983. Balla's (well-heeled) clients know what they want, and those wants include runway pieces from designers like Yohji Yamamoto, Junya Watanabe, and Ann Demeulemeester. Pieces here are always edgy with a hint of futurism. Located in a historic Beaux-Arts townhouse on classy rue Sherbrooke, the store has ambience that is as dramatic as the pieces it carries. Among the younger, lesser-known designers that fit into Balla's no-nonsense aesthetic are Haider Ackermann and Rick Owens, both of whose outerwear adds automatic drama.

MAP 2: 1444 rue Sherbrooke W., 514/284-2102, www.lescreateurs.ca; Mon.-Wed. 10:30am-6pm, Thurs.-Fri. 10:30am-9pm, Sat. 10:30am-5pm, Sun. noon-5pm

Harricana

Designer Mariouche Gagné first started working with fur as a struggling fashion student. Having entered a competition with the Fur Council of Canada, she used her mother's old coat to create a piece and her business was born. Working with recycled fur, she transforms pieces into hats, mittens, a chic *gilet,* or a new coat entirely. The store space is modern and clean, and, though it's slightly below street level, huge windows let in lots of light. If you have a fur coat you'd like re-styled, take it with you: Gagné will transform it into something else entirely and ship it back to you.

MAP 2: 3000 rue Ste-Antoine W., 514/287-6517, www.harricana.qc.ca; Mon.-Fri. 10am-6pm, Sat.-Sun. 10am-5pm

Marie Saint Pierre

Marie Saint Pierre is a leading figure in Canadian fashion, and her creations are available in high-end boutiques from New York to Paris. But this boutique on the ritzy de la Montagne is her only flagship store in her native city. Working with a mostly neutral palette, Saint Pierre focuses instead on texture, volume, and shape, and the results are stunningly modern. The boutique itself has a strong feel with its concrete floors and smoke-like murals, though the low lighting helps give it a softer touch. Those wanting a more personal shopping experience can request an evening of private shopping.

MAP 2: 2081 rue de la Montagne, 514/281-5547, www.mariesaintpierre.com; Mon.-Wed. and Sat. 10am-6pm, Thurs.-Fri. 10am-8pm, Sun. noon-6pm

Mona Moore

Women who love shoes peer wide-eyed into this deliciously elegant shoe store, minimally decorated with only a few, well-chosen touches: sorbet-hued baroque furniture, soft-pink walls, and a simple mirror, leaning gracefully against the wall. The shoes here, mostly off the runway, take center stage and are effortlessly placed along the wall. This is not the most affordable of stores—prices are usually in the $1,000 range. But even if you're not looking to buy, just entering into the store allows you to indulge in a little fashion-world fantasy. And, of course, it helps that the staff are just as sweet and welcoming as can be.

MAP 2: 1446 rue Sherbrooke W., 514/842-0662, www.monamoore.com; Mon.-Fri. 10am-6pm, Sat. 10am-5pm

DEPARTMENT STORES

Holt Renfrew

This luxury department store, which is not for every size bank account, is housed in an illustrious art deco building. It has all the top-name designer brands from around the world. Established as a furrier in 1849 in Québec City, Holt Renfrew opened the Montréal store in 1910 and continues to be one of the few places you can find the labels Marni, Dries Van Noten, and Balenciaga. This is also the only store in Montréal to exclusively carry the designs for Denis Gagnon, one of Montréal's best designers. The Holt Renfrew Café on the ground level is a chic place to grab a light lunch or catch up with a friend over coffee.

MAP 2: 1300 rue Sherbrooke W., 514/842-5111, www.holtrenfrew.com; Mon.-Wed. 10am-6pm, Thurs.-Fri. 10am-9pm, Sat. 9:30am-5pm, Sun. noon-5pm

La Maison Ogilvy

Established in 1866 by Montréal linen merchant James A. Ogilvy, La Maison Ogilvy is a timeless Montréal institution, and its tartan bags and boxes are ubiquitous throughout the city. The only high-end department store of its kind, it carries exclusive labels like Louis Vuitton and Burberry, and those who shop here have the pocketbooks to afford it. Completed in 1912, the building itself is impressive, with a large circular staircase at the main entrance. On the fifth floor is Tudor Hall, the city's first music hall.

MAP 2: 1307 rue Ste-Catherine W., 514/842-7711, www.ogilvycanada.com; Mon.-Wed. 10am-6pm, Thurs.-Fri. 10am-9pm, Sat. 9am-5pm, Sun. noon-5pm

La Maison Simons

Started as a dry goods store in Québec City in 1840, Simons has become the quintessential Québécois department store, particularly popular among Francophones. Though the Montréal location only opened in 1999, its European-flavored products and design give it a different feel than other North American department stores and make it a shopper's staple. More compact than most, it carries everything from affordable and fashionable knitwear and accessories to lingerie and housewares. For men, there is a large suit section, and the store also carries a number of designers, like Vivienne Westwood and Dolce and Gabbana.

MAP 2: 977 rue Ste-Catherine W., 514/282-1840, www.simons.ca; Mon.-Wed. 10am-6pm, Thurs.-Fri. 10am-9pm, Sat. 9:30am-5pm, Sun. noon-5pm

229

GIFT AND HOME

Beige

One of a few stores along Notre-Dame West that sell new pieces, Beige has just about everything you need to set up house: lighting, mirrors, bedding, kitchen tables, four-poster beds, and a lounge chair to put next to the pool. The store appeals to a wide range of customers, from 20-year-olds just starting out to empty-nesters, and prices here are just as varied, from $25 for a large candle to hundreds of dollars for a custom re-upholstery. It's great for picking up a gift or something new for your home. The employees here are also interior designers and can help you with tough decisions.

MAP 2: 2475 rue Notre-Dame W., 514/989-8585, www.beigestyle.com; Mon.-Wed. 10am-6pm, Thurs.-Fri. 10am-7pm, Sat. 10am-4pm

SHOPPING DISTRICTS AND CENTERS

Les Cours Mont Royal

The crème-de-la-crème of brands can be found in this upscale shopping center. The province's sole Club Monaco is situated here, as are DKNY and Harry Rosen, Canada's top men's store. It's a former hotel, and the original ceiling mosaic and dazzling chandelier can still be seen, adding a certain amount of elegance to the main hall. Independent boutiques carrying local and well-known international brands can be found here, as well as one of the city's top spas and salons. It connects to the Métro system and other shopping centers through the Underground City. Opening times vary depending on the boutique.

MAP 2: 1445 rue Peel, www.lcmr.ca; Mon.-Wed. 10am-6pm, Thurs.-Fri. 10am-9pm, Sat.-Sun. 10am-5pm

Centre Eaton

Four floors of shops, kiosks, restaurants, and exhibition spaces make up the Centre Eaton. It is here that you'll find North American staples like Arizia, the Gap, Levi's, Old Navy, and Aldo. The largest shopping mall in downtown Montréal, it boasts 175 boutiques, services, and restaurants.

MAP 2: 705 rue Ste-Catherine W., 514/288-3710, www.centreeatondemontreal.com; Mon.-Fri. 10am-9pm, Sat. 10am-5pm, Sun. 11am-5pm

Rue Notre-Dame West

In the southwest part of the city, east of Marché Atwater, you'll find rue Notre-Dame West. Once an important route for the fur trade, it experienced an economic boom at the end of the 19th century, and homes, offices, banks, and even a library went up along the street.

By the 1950s, however, it was virtually deserted. It wasn't until the mid-1970s that independent antiques dealers started opening shops on the strip between Guy Street and Atwater Avenue, making it the street with the highest concentration of antiques stores in the city, known as the "Quartiers des Antiquaires." You can find everything here, from vintage finds to quirky trinkets to relics from the sea and 18th-century chandeliers. Stores along this strip keep their own hours, so your best bet is to head here on a Saturday afternoon.

MAP 2: rue Notre-Dame W. between ave. Atwater and rue Guy

Rue Sainte-Catherine

This is the main commercial shopping district for the city. Starting at rue Bishop in the west, stores run the length of the street till about Bleury, where it becomes the new Quartier des Spectacles. All the big-name-brand stores are concentrated here, including Apple, Nine West, Urban Outfitters, H&M, Banana Republic, and Zara. It is also along this strip that you'll find a number of shopping centers and department stores. Below ground, the majority of the Underground City is found; the various malls and department stores are all connected through walkways and shopping malls and you can walk about a third of the Ste-Catherine strip below street level.

MAP 2: rue Ste-Catherine W. between rue Bishop and rue de Bleury

Centre-Ville Est

Map 3

ACCESSORIES AND JEWELRY

★ Henri Henri

To those who say "I don't suit hats," Henri Henri's answer is that a person who doesn't suit hats simply doesn't have a head. And after nearly 80 years in business, this shop knows its stuff. Founded by Honorius Henri and Jean-Maurice Lefebvre in 1932, the store remains devoted to hats, and they've got all kinds of 'em, from a classic Panama to a fedora, from a Stetson to a Basque beret.

Part of this store's charm is its appearance, from the virtually unchanged window displays and 1930s-style awning to the all-wood interior, with hats tucked away in cubbies. Attracting old-time hat lovers and young men and women looking to be different, the service is genuine and thorough. Just try leaving without something new on your head.

MAP 3: 189 rue Ste-Catherine E., 514/288-0109, www.henrihenri.ca; Mon.-Thurs. 10am-6pm, Fri. 10am-9pm, Sat.-Sun. 10am-5pm

Maison Birks

It may not have a movie with its name in the title, or an iconic heart-shaped pendant, but Maison Birks is Canada's answer to Tiffany's—even their boxes are a particular shade of blue. Founded in 1879, this store opened on rue Ste-Catherine in 1894. It's here that you'll find men picking out an engagement ring, women trying on a pair of sapphire earrings to wear to the opera, or family members picking out a keepsake for the newborn. The interior remains virtually unchanged, except for an update or two, so it's worth popping in for a look at the turn-of-the-20th-century accents.

MAP 3: 1240 Place Philips, 514/397-2511, www.maisonbirks.com; Mon.-Wed. 10am-6pm, Thurs.-Fri. 10am-9pm, Sat. 9:30am-5pm, Sun. noon-5pm

BOOKS AND MUSIC
The Word

In the heart of the McGill ghetto, this tiny lopsided house was once a Chinese laundry. In 1973, Adrian King-Edwards and his wife started an underground bookstore out of their apartment living room, and when the laundry went up for rent, they moved the shop next door. It specializes in secondhand academic books, so literature lovers will swoon at the shop's selection, which includes titles by local authors, and the Old World feel of the interior. This is the kind of place where you could, and should, spend hours browsing the shelves.

MAP 3: 469 rue Milton, 514/845-5640; Mon.-Wed. 10am-6pm, Thurs.-Fri. 10am-9pm, Sat. 11am-6pm

DEPARTMENT STORES
La Baie

A Canadian institution, La Baie was first founded in 1670 as the Hudson's Bay Company and controlled much of the fur trade throughout North America. By the early 20th century, it had morphed into one of the biggest chain department stores in Canada. Housed in a grand red-brick building that was constructed in 1891, the Bay's seven floors offer everything from kids' shoes to perfumes, housewares to electronics, and is the Canadian home of brands like Topshop, Sandro, Sonia Rykiel, and Theory. Fans of Canadiana will do well by picking up an iconic Hudson's Bay blanket, a simple off-white blanket striped with the company's colors: green, red, yellow, and blue.

MAP 3: 585 rue Ste-Catherine W., 514/281-4422, www.thebay.com; Mon.-Wed. 10am-7pm, Thurs.-Fri. 10am-9pm, Sat. 9am-6pm, Sun. 10am-6pm

THRIFT AND VINTAGE

Eva B

Quirky and chaotic, this huge secondhand store feels like it goes on for miles, with entire sections dedicated to menswear, leather jackets, cowboy boots, dresses, hats, and even a costume trunk full of gloves. A favorite with students and those who love the thrill of searching for a good deal, the shop has a laid-back yet intense atmosphere, thanks to the sheer volume of stuff to dig through. The store itself has definitely seen better days, but the creaky floorboards and exposed brick still have their own charm. The staff leave you to your own devices, though they'll happily serve you a coffee from the on-site café.

MAP 3: 2013 blvd. St-Laurent, 514/849-8246, www.eva-b.ca; Mon.-Sat. 10am-10pm, Sun. noon-8pm

Quartier Latin and the Village

Map 4

ANTIQUES AND KITSCH

Cité Déco

Cité Déco features an exquisitely curated collection of furniture with a focus on pieces from the 1930s to the 1960s. Squeezed between other charming antique stores on rue Amherst, Cité Déco may not be the biggest store on the block but it does have some of the best finds, like Danish-designed teak dining room sets, re-upholstered Rococo chairs, art deco mirrors, and earthenware vases.

MAP 4: 1761 rue Amherst, 514/528-0659, www.citedecomeubles.com; Tues.-Fri. 11am-6pm, Sat. 11am-5pm, Sun. noon-5pm

Seconde Chance

Dwindling vintage stock has caused prices to rise in the last few years, but Second Chance keeps things budget-friendly with their kitschy but well-selected finds. Design students are frequent shoppers here, looking for inspiration or to sift through the awesome selection of Expo '67 memorabilia that includes everything from drinking glasses to travel bags.

MAP 4: 1691 rue Amherst, 514/523-3019; Tues.-Sat. 11am-5pm

Spoutnik Boutique

With lime-green walls and a packed floor-space, Spoutnik stands out among its Amherst brethren. The store offers everything from lamps adorned with mosaics, bizarre geometric wall hangings, and clustered bubble light-fixtures that would make even Lady Gaga

Secondhand Style

Montréal is full of *friperies* (second-hand shops), and each has its own interpretation of what secondhand means. Many boutiques deal exclusively with authentic pieces, while others sell goods on consignment or resell donations.

Head up to the Mile End to scope out a trinity of *friperies*, all within a few blocks of each other. **Local 23, Annex Vintage,** and **Citizen Vintage** offer some of the best vintage shopping in the neighborhood. Local 23 and Annex deal exclusively in secondhand: boots, fur hats, blouses, belts, and big 1980s earrings, as well as a large selection of menswear. Citizen Vintage offers a curated collection of secondhand duds.

West of Local 23, you'll find **Arterie,** a *friperie* and boutique dedicated to local, emerging designers. This big space was one of the first places to provide a platform for emerging Montréal designers, and though many of them have gone on to bigger and better things, most have remained loyal to their early supporter. You'll find various authentic vintage pieces for both men and women at the back of the store. They also carry kitschy pieces for the home and a range of shoes for vegetarians.

Head north on St-Laurent and you'll come across **La (Found)erie,** a vintage boutique that specializes in rare designer finds. This place also carries a number of things for the home, including artwork by local artists.

Connoisseurs of vintage will get a kick out of **Friperie St-Laurent.** With elegant window displays full of hatboxes and trench coats, Friperie St-Laurent deals in vintage finds from the 1940s-1970s. It's a great place to look for a fur stole or a leather jacket; the men's selection here usually outweighs the women's, though they do have a great collection of accessories. Pieces here are timeless, so you're likely to find a gem.

Folles Alliées has a selection of evening and casual wear for both men and women. Vintage tuxes hang casually on the frame of the changing room. Looks here are distinctly *Mad Men,* with full-skirted, calf-length dresses for women and casual short-sleeve button-downs for men. Some of the best finds in the store are in the display case at the cash register. Costume jewelry, vintage frames, and evening bags beg a closer look.

It's all about the hunt at **Eva B.** This sprawling boutique on the lower Main has been among the top go-to places for vintage for the past decade. Racks of leather and jean jackets are flanked by rows of vintage cowboy boots. Selection and prices run the gamut. If you're willing to dig, there's a trunk or two full of goodies to sort through. They've also got a small café at the front.

If you like the look of vintage but don't like the idea of scrounging through seemingly unending racks of the stuff to find it, then head down to **Era Vintage.** This bright boutique is a refreshing change, with the clothes organized by color, giving the place the look of a candy store. Owner Élaine Léveillée has an excellent eye for both pieces and merchandising; nothing in this store looks (or smells) vintage. Every garment is dry cleaned and pressed before being hung on the rack. Details are everything here—there's even an on-site seamstress who can alter a piece for you.

lustful. There's a definite 1960s and '70s feel to the goods, with lots of stainless-steel lamps and Formica kitchen tables, but you'll also find more classic goods, like elegant teak desks and simple chandeliers. Prices vary greatly but you should be able to find something that fits your budget.

MAP 4: 2120 rue Amherst, 514/525-8478, www.boutiquespoutnik.com; Tues.-Wed. and Sat. noon-5pm, Thurs.-Fri. noon-6pm

ARTS AND CRAFTS
DeSerre

Started by Omer DeSerre in 1908, this was a hardware store and a department store before it was influenced by the École des Arts des Apliques (now a part of UQÀM) in the 1950s and started to carry a range of art materials. Still near the original location at Ste-Catherine and St-Denis, it's still popular with art students and hobbyists and is now a national chain. This is one of the largest in the city (other locations are at 1500 McGill College and 1515 rue Ste-Catherine W.). It has two floors of art and craft supplies and is the perfect place to pick up everything from needlepoint kits to acrylic paints and frames.

MAP 4: 334 rue Ste-Catherine E., 514/842-3021; Mon.-Wed. 9:30am-6pm, Thurs.-Fri. 9:30am-9pm, Sat.-Sun. 10am-5pm

BOOKS AND MUSIC
Atom Heart

With a large selection of rock and electronic albums, a dedication to vinyl, and the latest underground releases, Atom Heart could easily be branded a music-snob's paradise—and that's the way they like it. Long and narrow and completely white, the minimal interior puts the attention on the music. A regular stop for UQÀM students and Francophone cool kids, this is a great place to check out albums by local groups or get introduced to some ultra-cool Francophone artists. The staff might be a bit cold at first, but drop a few band names and they'll soon warm up.

MAP 4: 34-B rue Sherbrooke E., 514/843-8484, www.atomheart.ca; Mon.-Wed. 11am-7pm, Thurs.-Fri. 11am-9pm, Sat. 11am-5pm, Sun. noon-5pm

SHOPPING DISTRICTS AND CENTERS
Rue Saint-Denis

The vibe of the stores on rue St-Denis, the major Francophone shopping district, is distinctly different from that on St-Laurent, even though they consist of similar elements—independent boutiques and a mishmash of restaurants and furniture stores. Because this is the French side of the city, it is no surprise that cafés and restaurants, most of them with their own sidewalk terraces, are more plentiful here—the perfect cure for mid-browsing fatigue.

Get Crafty

There is little that brings Montréalers together more than a craft fair. Held throughout the year, with an abundance around the holidays, these fairs take all shapes and sizes, with vendors traveling from all over to attend.

The biggest show of all, attracting international vendors, is **Le Salon des Mètiers d'Art** (www.metiers-d-art.qc.ca/smaq, Dec., free), which takes at Place Bonaventure come winter. It houses over 400 professional exhibitors and the 200,000 people who come to take it all in. Running throughout December, the fair encompasses traditional and artisan crafts, such as blown-glass jewelry, felted winter accessories, and handmade bed linens.

After Mètiers, **Souk at SAT** (www.souk.sat.qc.ca) is the second most popular pre-Christmas craft fair. Attracting a diverse clientele of hipsters and suburban parents, this show always strikes a perfect balance of vendors, with an emphasis on local producers. Greeting cards and ceramics are on sale here, as is the work of a number of emerging designers. The only trick with this fair is walking away with gifts for anyone but yourself. This place gets packed, so if you want to browse without heating up, check your winter coat before you shop.

Held during the weeklong September music festival Pop Montréal, **Puces POP** (www.popmontreal.com) attracts a hipster crowd of shoppers and sellers with young crafters coming from all over Canada and the United States to participate. It's usually held in a church basement, and there's a definite nostalgic feel to the whole event, but the work on sale is top-notch and includes everything from cupcakes to screen prints, from natural beauty products to toys. A pre-Christmas edition is usually held mid-December, with a third event in the spring.

Organized by a group of local designers, the **Smart Design Mart** (www.smartdesignmart.com) runs a few times a year and aims to put local designers of housewares, clothing, and jewelry, as well as artists, in the spotlight. The vendors are less about traditional crafts and more about a platform for new talent.

Major Québécois designer Philippe Dubuc's eponymous boutique is situated here, as are a number of high-end designer home stores. Québécois chains like Bedo, Le Château, Jacob, and Zone are here, as are outposts for the Gap, Mexx, Lululemon and Urban Outfitters, making it the perfect antidote to downtown.

MAP 4: Between blvd. de Maisonneuve and ave. Mont-Royal

Plateau Mont-Royal

Map 5

ACCESSORIES AND JEWELRY

M0851

The minimalist leather creations from this Montréal-based brand may have leaked into international territory—they have stores in New York, Paris, and Antwerp—but they remain a strong part of the city's design scene and their creations continue to be made in Montréal. Known for its bags (once you've seen one, you'll notice their style anywhere), this boutique also sells other leather goods, including outerwear. The open-concept store on the Main, with wooden shelves and unfinished floors, is always welcoming.

MAP 5: 3526 blvd. St-Laurent, 514/849-9759, www.m0851.com; Mon.-Wed. 10am-6pm, Thurs.-Fri. 10am-7pm, Sat. 10am-5pm, Sun. noon-5pm

Oz Bijoux

Working mostly in sterling silver, jeweler Monic Dahan creates unique handmade pieces that are both capricious and stunning. At this St-Denis boutique, all four plain white walls are filled with glass display cases and there is a huge semicircle display case in the middle. The display cases show off the intricacy of the work, which features natural stones like onyx, turquoise, and quartz crystals. The staff is knowledgeable, and two large cats are often found sprawled on the counter, warming themselves under the fluorescent spotlights.

MAP 5: 3933 rue St-Denis, 514/845-9568, www.ozbijoux.com; Mon.-Wed. 11am-6pm, Thurs.-Fri. 11am-9pm, Sat.-Sun. 10am-5pm

ANTIQUES AND KITSCH

Couleurs

This store's modern aesthetic might trick you into thinking you've walked into the wrong place. Tucked away on busy St-Denis, a simple sign in their trademark sea-foam green (okay, so that may tip you off) leads you down a few stairs into this little piece of mid-20th-century heaven. Calling itself both a store and a gallery, Couleurs brings the already "modern" furniture into the 21st-century with new upholstery and contemporary styling, letting you see the timeless style in a set of cornflower blue stoneware mugs, without associating it with the teachers' lounge.

MAP 5: 3901 rue St-Denis, 514/282-4141, www.couleurs.qc.ca; Mon.-Wed. noon-6pm, Thurs.-Fri. noon-9pm, Sat. 11am-5pm, Sun. noon-5pm

★ **Kitsch 'n' Swell**

Step inside this fantasyland of kitsch and you're surrounded by leopard-print walls, fringed light fixtures, and hook-rugs of flamenco dancers. This place is so stuffed that you could easily lose yourself for a good hour or two. Dedicated to kitsch from the 1940s up to the '70s this store is unlike anything you've seen before. Once you've pulled yourself away from the hypnotizing leopard-print, however, there's a ton of great, unique items that could easily work in your home, like a teak side table or a set of themed highball glasses.

MAP 5: 3968 blvd. St-Laurent, 514/845-6789, www.kitschnswell.ca; Mon.-Wed. noon-6pm, Thurs.-Fri. noon-9pm, Sat. 11am-5pm, Sun. noon-5pm

ARTS AND CRAFTS
A La Tricoteuse

This charming corner store is minimally decorated with pops of color from the wool exploding out of the white, square cubbies that line the walls. Catering to the more mature knitter, the shop sells wool on the more expensive end, but the quality is always top-notch—though don't expect to find anything too psychedelic. They also offer a range of patterns, needles, and other tools for the trade and will help you work out a problem, or get started if you're new to the pastime.

MAP 5: 779 rue Rachel E., 514/527-2451; Wed.-Fri. 10:30am-6pm, Sat. 10:30am-5pm

BATH, BEAUTY, AND SPAS
Espace Nomad

Offering massage and organic body treatments, Espace Nomad is one of only a few green spas in the city. It's situated on the Main in the heart of the Plateau. The atmosphere is relaxed, but the surroundings are distinctly more modern and design-oriented than some places, with vibrantly colored walls contrasting with earth-tone furniture. Organic treatments include body wraps and scrubs, and they also offer private yoga classes. Prices start at $75 for an hour-long massage and organic treatments.

MAP 5: 4650 blvd. St-Laurent, 514/842-7279, www.espacenomad.ca; Mon. 10am-6pm, Tues.-Sat. 10am-10pm, Sun. 11am-9pm

BOOKS AND MUSIC
Beatnick Music

Die-hard record collectors and vinyl fanatics come from far and wide to check out the selection at Beatnick. Heck, they've even got their own online store, but nothing beats heading into this cavern of sound and listening to a rare Northern Soul album on their turntables. Everything here revolves around the album, from the walls full of vinyl to the fastidiously organized shelves. The staff's knowledge is encyclopedic and their tastes individual. Of course, they also carry a number of CDs and the latest albums, usually on vinyl, by well-known contemporary bands.

MAP 5: 3770 rue St-Denis, 514/842-0664, www.beatnickmusic.com; Mon.-Wed. 11am-7pm, Thurs.-Fri. 11am-9pm, Sat.-Sun. 11am-6pm

Multimags

This citywide chain has seven stores around Montréal where locals come to get their morning papers and peruse the selection of international magazines. Other central stores are located at the bus terminal at 1717 rue Berri and 370 avenue Laurier West (514/272-9954). They also carry stationery, including Moleskin notebooks, greeting cards, art books from publishers like Taschen and Phiadon, as well as other novelty items. Though the choice is generally the same at each store, it sometimes varies; ask the knowledgeable staff if you're looking for something specific.

MAP 5: 825 ave. du Mont-Royal E., 514/523-3158; Mon.-Wed. 8am-10pm, Thurs.-Sat. 8am-11pm, Sun. 9am-10pm

Paul's Boutique

Started with just 100 vinyls and 20 CDs in 2001, Paul's Boutique has since grown to 20,000 vinyls and has taken over the two floors of a sagging, shabby house on Mont-Royal, filled to the rafters with every kind of music available. The shop is named for the store's owner, not the iconic Beastie Boys album—though the band has visited. The interior is chaotic, with fake sharks and disco balls hanging from the ceiling and the walls are painted bubble-gum pink. From the albums of a prepubescent Celine Dion to Hawkwind's entire back catalogue, vinyl fiends are sure to find something here. The staff can be grumpy, so don't expect the warmest welcome, but don't take it personally either.

MAP 5: 112 ave. du Mont-Royal E., 514/284-7773; Mon.-Wed. and Sat. 11am-6pm, Thurs.-Fri. 11am-9pm, Sun. noon-5pm

★ Aux 33 Tours

An alternative name for this shop could be Dedicated to Vinyl. They specialize in Japanese pressings and the love for the old 33 is strong in this store and is reflected in their vast selection of both new and used vinyl. They carry just about every type of music you can think of and have an impressive collection of hardcore and metal albums. With its location in the heart of the Plateau, it's not unusual to see early morning lines of people waiting to get gig tickets or spend their hard-earned cash on the annual Record Store Day. They've got a pretty swell collection of CDs, too.

MAP 5: 1373 ave. du Mont-Royal E., 514/524-7397, www.aux33tours.com; Mon.-Wed. 10am-7pm, Thurs.-Fri. 10am-9pm, Sat.-Sun. 10am-6pm

239

CHILDREN'S STORES

Bummis

Expecting and new parents in Montréal love Bummis. Started as a cloth-diaper business in the 1980s, it has since expanded into a specialized boutique for parents and their newborns. The walls are still stacked with cloth diapers, but they now carry a multitude of items like breastfeeding bras, pumps, changing table pads, booties, books on parenting, natural skin-care products, and mini-sleepers—many things are made in-house. The space has a warm feeling with exposed brick and two big comfy couches.

MAP 5: 4302 blvd. St-Laurent, 514/289-9415, www.boutiquebummis.com; Mon.-Wed. 10am-6pm, Thurs.-Fri. 10am-8pm, Sat. 10am-5pm, Sun. noon-5pm

Au Diabolo Jeux et Jouets

This fully stocked toy store is one of the best places in the city to pick up everything from card games to princess costumes. With bright colors and cartoony windows and a register surrounded by silly things like bouncy balls, whoopee cushions, and yo-yos, it's immediately obvious that this place caters to kids. The staff is friendly, bilingual, and usually closer to your kid's age than you are. However, most of the books on sale are in French only, which is great if you want to teach your kid a new language.

MAP 5: 1390 ave. du Mont-Royal E., 514/528-8889; Mon.-Wed. 10am-6pm, Thurs.-Fri. 10am-8pm, Sat. 10am-5pm, Sun. noon-5pm

★ La Grande Ourse

Unlike at any other children's store in the city, practically all the toys sold in La Grande Ourse are made of wood and crafted by local artisans. The store's aim is to inspire children to use their imagination during play, so most of the toys have simple gestures and expressions. Plainly decorated with white walls, the small store's shelves are filled with toys. There are pull-along toys and rocking horses for toddlers, and kitchen sets, sailboats, and dollhouses for older children. Despite the nondescript decor, the store is full of wonder and excitement, and the staff is willing to answer parents' questions or play with the little ones. But parents aren't the sole customers—those looking for unique gifts are regulars.

MAP 5: 263 ave. Duluth E., 514/847-1207; Tues.-Wed. noon-6pm, Thurs.-Fri. noon-9pm, Sat.-Sun. noon-5pm

CLOTHING AND SHOES

Deuxième Peau

The decoration in this small, bottom-floor boutique, which specializes in swimwear and lingerie, is minimal, letting the prettiness of the garments stand out. Supporting women of all shapes and sizes, bras come in sizes AA to G from European brands like Princess Tam-Tam, Simon Pérèle, Aubade, and Chantal Thomas. Swimwear comes in a range of different sizes and includes pieces from Seafolly and Sunfair. Though they will happily measure you to determine proper bra size, owner Zoé Mitsakis's keen eye (along with a little bit of prodding) is better than any tape measure.

MAP 5: 4457 rue St-Denis, 514/842-0811, www.deuxiemepeau.com; Mon.-Wed. 10:30am-6pm, Thurs.-Fri. 10:30am-9pm, Sat. 10:30am-5pm, Sun. noon-5pm

Dubuc

Philippe Dubuc, known for his menswear designs, was the first Canadian designer to be asked to present at Paris Fashion Week. Dubuc's eponymous St-Denis boutique is, like most of his collections, almost entirely black and slate gray, with rough stone taking up the bottom half of the walls. The boutique takes up an entire row house, with a floor for menswear, a floor for accessories, and one for his atelier (but that's off-limits to the public). His pieces are precise and impeccably cut and tailored.

MAP 5: 4451 rue St-Denis, 514/282-1424, www.dubucstyle.com; Mon.-Wed. and Sat. 11am-6pm, Thurs. 11am-7pm, Fri. 11am-9pm, Sun. noon-5pm

Duo

One of the top men's boutiques in the city, Duo first opened its doors in 2003 and became so successful it has since expanded to take over the shop next door. The sleek modern interior is the perfect backdrop for the exclusive lines the store carries. Labels available here are more upscale than what you'll find at most boutiques and include Dior Homme, Raf Simons, Y3, and Moncler. Alongside suits and clothes for the every day is a range of watches, fragrances, and footwear.

MAP 5: 30 rue Prince-Arthur W., 514/848-0880, www.boutiqueduo.com; Mon.-Wed. and Sat. 10am-7pm, Thurs.-Fri. 10am-9pm, Sun. noon-7pm

École Militaire

Opened in 2012, this store is more sophisticated than its age suggests. Catering to the man who likes to mix high culture with low, École Militaire (aka Military School) offers a number of classic guy brands—Brooklyn Tailors, St-James—alongside streetwear brands like Kitsuné and Still Good. Located one block east of the Main, this thoroughly modern store is full of light, thanks to the floor-to-ceiling windows and immaculate white walls. The setup is also sparse, with goods arranged on simple wooden tables. Framed art and steel racks line the walls, with their selection of trousers hung casually from hooks instead of stuffy old hangers.

MAP 5: 3764 rue St-Dominique, 514/439-1664, www.ecolemilitaire.net; Mon.-Wed. noon-7pm, Thurs.-Fri. noon-9pm, Sat.-Sun. noon-6pm

Ibiki

Minimal is the best way to describe both the decor and the clothing for sale at Ibiki. The store's aim is to sell menswear and womenswear that'll become a prized possession. The spacious two-story store on the Main features brands such as A.P.C. and Minimarket. Prices are affordable but not cheap, though their sales are great and they carry a number of well-priced accessories and magazines.

MAP 5: 4357 blvd. St-Laurent, 514/509-1675, www.ibiki.co; Mon.-Wed. noon-7pm, Thurs.-Fri. noon-9pm, Sat.-Sun. noon-5pm

John Fluevog

The chance to buy a warehouse full of early-20th-century shoes gave designer Fluevog his start, and his style has become unmistakable. Women's shoes often sport a rounded toe and an exaggerated spoon heel (wider at the top and bottom but narrower in the middle), while his colorful men's brogues and desert boots are some of his best, remaining classic but with a modern touch. The design and ambience of this store, however, are fairly unremarkable, with beige throughout and shoes displayed on walls and on a low circular table at the front; the footwear is the main focus. Clients and staff are always a little bit kooky, bold enough to wear something out of the box.

MAP 5: 3857 rue St-Denis, 514/509-1627, www.fluevog.com; Mon.-Wed. 10am-6pm, Thurs.-Fri. 10am-9pm, Sat. 10am-5pm, Sun. noon-5pm

Kanuk

Designed and made in Québec, Kanuk was established in 1974 by a few outdoor enthusiasts who realized the only way to get a winter coat warm enough for the province's climate was to make it themselves. Specializing in outerwear, this Plateau store is brightly lit and spacious with floor and wall space dedicated to coats, accessories, and other outerwear. There are 35 parka models to choose from in a range of colors. A parka from this place may be pricey—they start around $500—but it will last you a lifetime. The staff is more than happy to help you figure out the type and fit that will work for you and they know the products inside and out.

MAP 5: 485 rue Rachel E., 514/527-4494, www.kanuk.com; Mon.-Wed. 9am-6pm, Thurs.-Fri. 9am-9pm, Sat. 10am-5pm, Sun. noon-5pm

Lustre

Owner and designer Yasmine Wasfy creates both the Lustre line and her own eponymous label, which can be found in this independent boutique full of one-of-a-kind pieces. Designs are fresh and young—think of a great, well-tailored shift with a cutout back or an on-trend black-lace blouse. Popular with women in their twenties and early thirties with a DIY aesthetic, the store's various decorations, art, and accessories have a definite vintage feel. Whimsical scarves and bags can be found next to locally made jewelry and hats. The service is sweet and friendly, and Wasfy herself can sometimes be found doling out tailoring advice or picking out the perfect accessory.

MAP 5: 4068 blvd. St-Laurent, 514/288-7661, www.lustreboutique.blogspot.com; Mon.-Wed. noon-7pm, Thurs.-Fri. noon-9pm, Sat. noon-6pm, Sun. noon-5pm

Scandale

One look at the whimsical storefront and window displays of this boutique on the Main and you know Scandale is no ordinary store. A St-Laurent staple since the early 1980s, the store is dedicated to the unique vision of designer Georges Lévesque, whose idiosyncratic creations oscillate between the supremely elegant and the supremely...Lévesque. He's a fan of mixing patterns (tartan is a favorite) and styles, and much of this is reflected in the store's surroundings. Cluttered with dresses and displays, the store gives off a dark and brooding yet somehow joyful vibe. The staff is helpful and they often have clear ideas of what will suit you best, before you've even had a chance to contemplate.

MAP 5: 3639 blvd. St-Laurent, 514/842-4707, www.boutiquescandale.ca; Mon.-Wed. and Sat. 11am-6pm, Thurs. 11am-7pm, Fri. 11am-9pm, Sun. noon-5pm

GIFT AND HOME
★ Arthur Quentin

Couples in the know come here to pick out their wedding registry. The selection here is classic yet unconventional, with many of the products imported from France. The store is divided into three distinct mini-stores: a British-style haberdashery, cookware, and tableware. These mini-boutiques help you keep your focus as you browse everything from leather bags to red-checkered canister sets and fine bone china. All three rooms are modest in size and pretty much filled to capacity, so each space demands a bit of concentration. Can't find the tea towels? They're hung up inconspicuously next to the doorframe.

MAP 5: 3960 rue St-Denis, 514/843-7513, www.arthurquentin.com; Mon.-Wed. 10am-6pm, Thurs.-Fri. 10am-9pm, Sat. 9am-5pm, Sun. noon-5pm

Chez Farfelu

This place is a little crazy. Best described as a five-and-dime on steroids, it has a definite nostalgic feel with its rows of lollipops and candy machines, and notebooks and coffee mugs emblazoned with 1960s comic-strip heroes. They also stock a bunch of jewelry and novelty items, like blow-up chairs shaped like frogs. Over half the merchandise seems to be neon. A good portion of the store is dedicated to gift-wrapping your finds. Across the street at number 838, you'll find slightly tamer gifts for the kitchen and bathroom, including peel-and-stick decals for tiles and motif beach towels.

MAP 5: 843 and 838 ave. du Mont-Royal E., 514/528-6251; Mon.-Wed. 10am-6pm, Thurs.-Fri. 10am-9pm, Sat. 10am-5pm, Sun. 11am-5pm

Interversion

It doesn't get any more local than the Québec-designed and -made furniture at Interversion. The pieces are made from local materials and are often in a limited series or are one-of-a-kind pieces that blur the lines between furniture design and functional art. This huge showroom is set up to mimic real rooms, giving it a welcoming, homey atmosphere that makes you want to sink into an oversized wooden rocker. The helpful and friendly floor staff are also designers and will gladly answer any and all of your questions.

MAP 5: 4273 blvd. St-Laurent, 514/284-2103, www.interversion.com; Mon.-Wed. 10am-6pm, Thurs. 10am-9pm, Fri. 10am-7pm, Sat. 10:30am-5pm, Sun. noon-5pm

★ Nota Bene

The classic storefront windows of this chic stationery shop are always filled with covetable items like a classic, oversize Stendig calendar or notebooks in a rainbow of colors from Mark's Tokyo Edge. A stationery-lover's dream, this place carries notepads, agendas, pens, paper, and everything in between, from the top-quality international companies all over the world, including Lamy pencils, Atoma notebooks, Faber Castell, and graph-paper notebooks from Sweden's elusive Whitelines. A mezzanine level at the back of the store serves as an art gallery, with work by local artists featured regularly.

MAP 5: 3416 ave. du Parc, 514/485-6587, www.nota-bene.ca; Mon.-Fri. 11am-7pm, Sat. 11am-5pm

3 Femmes et 1 Coussin

Specializing in tableware, 3 Femmes et 1 Coussin offers a number of dinnerware lines, many of which are imported directly from Europe. The dishes on sale here are almost exclusively white and their shapes are always slightly out of the ordinary. To show off the white china, the walls are beautifully covered in bright damask prints, and the simple layout ensures the china stays unbroken. In

clockwise from top left: M0851 on St-Laurent Boulevard; Mile End florist; chic stationary shop Nota Bene, Plateau Mont-Royal

contrast to the stark dishes, the glassware here is bright and colorful with a number of tumblers, champagne flutes, and wine glasses available in sparkling primary colors. It's the go-to place for locals and small restaurants. It also offers unique gift ideas.

MAP 5: 783 rue Gilford, 514/987-6807, www.3f1c.ca; Mon.-Wed. 10am-6pm, Thurs.-Fri. 10am-7pm, Sat. 10am-5pm

Zone

Montréalers with a taste for affordable design are lucky; when they want to add a little pizzazz to their homes, they don't have to schlep all the way out to Ikea to do it. Instead they can hit up this small local chain—there are only four stores province-wide—for everything from fridge magnets to Bodum coffee makers, shower curtains to loveseats, and everything in between. Urban and young, this two-floor store is airy, all white, the largest in the city, and offers the best selection of the store's modern design pieces.

MAP 5: 4246 rue St-Denis, 514/845-3530, www.zonemaison.com; Mon.-Wed. 10am-6pm, Thurs.-Fri. 10am-7pm, Sat. 10am-5:30pm, Sun. 10am-5pm

GOURMET TREATS

Le Canard Libéré

If you like the idea of local food, check out Le Canard Libéré (The Liberated Duck), exclusively dedicated to duck products produced in nearby Lac Brome. Sausages, pâtés, duck fat, smoked duck, dried duck, duck pasta, even duck wings seasoned with garlic and honey are available in this sparse, open boutique with a huge counter and refrigerated display cases showing off the assorted products. If all the duck is making you hungry, have a seat at one of the few tables and dig into the duck of the day.

MAP 5: 4396 blvd. St-Laurent, 514/286-1286, www.canardsdulacbrome.com; Mon.-Wed. 10am-6pm, Thurs.-Fri. 10am-8pm, Sat. 10am-5pm, Sun. 11am-5pm

Les Chocolats de Chloé

Chloé Germain-Fredette is the artisanal chocolatier behind this quaint and slightly quirky chocolate shop in the Plateau. This all-wood interior is modern, with chocolate-filled shelves lining one wall and freshly made chocolate in a case on the other. The products are made in-house using Valrhona chocolate as a base and infusing it with unlikely flavors, including fig and balsamic vinegar, raspberry, hibiscus, cardamom, saffron, pastis, lemon, and even basil. With over 30 different flavors, whose availability changes depending on the season, the best-seller is still Fleur de Sel. Those with a sweet-tooth and 98 percent of kids can't get enough of this stuff. In winter, stop in for a rich and thick cup of homemade drinking chocolate, with or without marshmallows.

Sabor Latino

When the owners realized that just as many people, whether locals or tourists with an eye for food, were popping in to get a quick bite to eat as were coming to get their groceries, they renovated this place to make the hot food the centerpiece. Now there's a cute dining area with simple chairs and a table that lets you eat your *churro* in-house. Specializing in South American foods, they carry at least 2,500 Latin American products, everything from hot sauces, beans, and corn meal to Arepa. Stop in to pick out your favorite South American salsa and get Peruvian, Colombian, or Salvadoran tamales while you're at it.

MAP 5: 4387 blvd. St-Laurent, 514/848-1078, www.saborlatino.ca; Mon.-Wed. 8am-6pm, Thurs.-Fri. 8am-9pm, Sat.-Sun. 8am-5pm

La Vieille Europe

The intoxicating smell of cheese and coffee hits you as soon as you walk into this veritable institution on the Main. With over 300 cheeses and 30 different types of coffee, it's no wonder that this is the go-to place for Montréal chefs and foodies looking for that particular ingredient. It specializes in products from France, Germany, Eastern Europe, Scandinavia, and England, so you can pick up pickled herring, sauerkraut, camembert, and black currant jam all at the same place, and it attracts a number of expats or passing tourists led by their nose. They also have a selection of sandwiches available from the deli counter; you can't go wrong with the Polish sausage—perfect for a quick lunch.

MAP 5: 3855 blvd. St-Laurent, 514/842-5773; Mon.-Wed. and Sat. 7:30am-6pm, Thurs.-Fri. 7:30am-9pm, Sun. 9am-5pm

SHOPPING DISTRICTS AND CENTERS

Boulevard Saint-Laurent

A number of independent, mainly fashion boutiques are concentrated here starting at the corner of boulevard St-Laurent and rue Sherbrooke, and moving steadily north. Historically an immigrant neighborhood and the dividing line between the western (English) and eastern (French) sides of the city, St-Laurent has stores with a real mix of influences, so you can pick up everything from a $400 pair of shoes to a vegetable steamer to an authentic lava lamp. When day turns to night, St-Laurent is a major hot spot, with late-night falafel and pizza joints often found next to high-end boutiques. As you head farther north on the strip, the boutiques change from clothing to housewares and furniture. Between rue Rachel and

MAP 5: blvd. St-Laurent between rue Sherbrooke and rue St-Viateur

THRIFT AND VINTAGE
Folles Alliées

Men and women can leave this cave of vintage well turned out in everything from medieval costumes to 1930s evening wear. The racks, display cases, shelves, and even the floor are stuffed with secondhand finds, making for a chaotic, vintage mess. Giving off the vibe of a hoarder's closet (moth balls included), this small, narrow store is always full of eccentrics, both behind and in front of the till, who are not afraid to indulge their inner Don Draper, Daisy Buchanan, or Holly Golightly.

MAP 5: 365 ave. du Mont-Royal, 514/834-4904; Mon.-Wed. 11am-6pm, Thurs.-Fri. 11am-9pm, Sat. 11am-6pm, Sun. noon-5pm

Friperie St-Laurent

Arbiters of vintage style should make a stop at this friperie on the Main. Elegant yet quirky window displays are sure to entice you into the well-laid out store full of cubbies and glass shelves, on which accessories like clutch bags and shoes are artfully displayed. A vintage soundtrack with jazz and 1960s pop fills the nostalgic atmosphere. The staff practice what they preach and are usually decked out in rare vintage finds and will help you find some gems as well. Carrying some of the best secondhand men's selections in the city, it's a great place to pick up a leather jacket or a silk tie from the 1940s.

MAP 5: 3976 blvd. St-Laurent, 514/842-3893; Mon.-Wed. 11am-6pm, Thurs.-Fri. 11am-9pm, Sat. 11am-5pm, Sun. noon-5pm

Mile End and Petite Italie   Map 6

ACCESSORIES AND JEWELRY
Maison Montures

The destination for four-eyed cool kids, Maison Montures (it means "house of frames" in English) specializes in eyeglasses and sunglasses, and carries a number of deadstock glasses from the 1970s and 1980s. High ceilings, white walls, wood floors, wood shelves, and winter-scene wallpaper are your backdrop to browsing and posing in any number of frames and shades. If vintage Cazal's aren't your vibe, they also carry a number of modern brands, including Retro Super Future, Dior, YSL, and Persol.

MAP 6: 174 rue Bernard W., 514/507-8282, www.lesmontures.com; Sat.-Mon. noon-5pm, Tues.-Wed. noon-6pm, Thurs.-Fri. noon-8pm

ANTIQUES AND KITSCH
Monastiraki

It's hard to classify just what Monastiraki is. Part gallery, part antique shop, comics shop, and all kitsch, it's unlike any store you've been in. Owned by local artist, cartoonist, and all around nice guy Billy Maveras, who knows the merchandise inside and out, it has undergone a complete revamp in the last couple of years, one that has cleared the floor space enough for you to enter without knocking into something. The antiques and collectibles, like back issues of *The New Yorker* and *Gourmet*, are still all here, only now they're just a little bit organized.

MAP 6: 5478 blvd. St-Laurent, 514/278-4879, www.monastiraki.blogspot.com; Mon.-Wed. noon-6pm, Thurs.-Fri. noon-8pm, Sat.-Sun. noon-5pm

Style Labo

Style junkies beware: This new addition to the scene strikes a distinct balance between the old and the modern, the high end and the low end. When it's warm enough, a number of goodies are out on the sidewalk to tempt you, so passing by can leave you with a mid-20th-century school desk and an $80 hole in your wallet. Industrial pieces like galvanized steel desks and wall-mounted clocks from decommissioned factories are displayed next to a row of Pantone mugs in 25 different shades. They also sell old jewelry overstock and brightly patterned pillows to play off ultra-modern Design House lamps. Office supply fetishists can rejoice—tables are cluttered with vintage in-and-out trays, pencil sharpeners, and even manual desk calendars.

MAP 6: 5765 blvd. St-Laurent, 514/658-9910, www.stylelabo-deco.com; Mon.-Wed. 10:30am-6pm, Thurs.-Fri. 10:30am-7pm, Sat. 10:30am-5pm, Sun. 11:30am-5pm

ARTS AND CRAFTS
Effiloché

This knitting and sewing lounge—the name means unraveled in English—has been around for the better part of five years and has the lived-in feeling of your grandparents' kitchen. The bare, wooden floors, cubbies full of wools in an appetizing range of colors and textures, and big, comfy antique couches in the middle for kitting and chatting give the whole space a welcoming atmosphere. There's even a sewing room set up with machines in the back, as well as drawers full of punchy, quirky fabrics and trimming.

MAP 6: 6252 rue St-Hubert, 514/276-2547, www.effiloche.com; Tues.-Wed. 11am-7pm, Thurs.-Fri. 11am-9pm, Sat. 10am-5pm, Sun. noon-5pm

This family-owned and -operated business goes back to 1927, when it was started by founder Leo Laurent Lozeau as a wedding photography and film processing business. Since then it has become a retail outlet of anything and everything related to photography; whether you've got a problem with your old SLR or are looking for a reliable digital point-and-click, they've got you covered. The big, modern interior with good lighting and subtly red walls is a good backdrop for all the digital wares. The bilingual workers really know their stuff, and if you're looking to rent out equipment for a specific project, they can help with that too.

MAP 6: 6229 rue St-Hubert, 514/274-6577, www.lozeau.com; Mon.-Wed. 8am-6pm, Thurs.-Fri. 8am-9pm, Sat.-Sun. 9am-5pm

Au Papier Japonais

A seriously beautiful store, with soft lighting and reels of *washi* hanging off the wall, Au Papier Japonais—or the Japanese paper store, as locals call it—carries over 500 different kinds of Japanese paper. It is not, however, the only type they stock; they also have paper from Nepal, India, Mexico, and Montréal, as well as journals, photo albums, and even kimonos for you to wear. One of the store's biggest draws, however, are its courses, which cover everything from simple bookbinding and box-making to Japanese gift-wrapping and paper-quilting.

MAP 6: 24 ave. Fairmount W., 514/276-6863, www.aupapierjaponais.com; Mon.-Sat. 10am-6pm, Sun. noon-4pm

BATH, BEAUTY, AND SPAS

Lise Watier Institut

One of the biggest names in Canadian beauty, Lise Watier's Institut offers everything from massages and facials to pedicures and blow-outs. Starting in 1972, Watier first made waves as a makeup artist, and her eponymous line of cosmetics is available at this modern, silvery, almost space-age Outremont store. Her fragrance Neiges has been a bestseller in the province since it debuted in 1993. Women pop in for a quick pedicure or stop by for a touch-up before heading out. If you're looking for a day of pampering, they have a number of packages available at various price points. They also offer special treatments for men and can teach you how to do your own makeup in a simple one- or two-hour lesson ($45-100).

MAP 6: 392 ave. Laurier W., 514/270-9296, www.institutlisewatier.com; Mon. 8:30am-5pm, Tues.-Wed. 8am-6pm, Thurs.-Fri. 8am-9pm, Sat. 7:30am-5pm, Sun. 10am-5pm

Savon Populaire

A wide array of organic, sustainable soaps line the walls at this small, charming store in Little Italy. Made of all natural ingredients, these vegetable-based soaps first got their start as Christmas gifts in owner Alysia Melnychuk's kitchen. Melnychuk's business has since expanded beyond just soaps to include exfoliating scrubs, body butter, lip balms, and even shampoo. Fragranced with essential oils like lemon ginger, mint, anise, lavender, and chamomile, the smell in the store is inviting, not overpowering. Melnychuk also offers soap-making workshops and courses on skin care and essential oils.

MAP 6: 273 St-Zotique E., 514/270-0539, www.savonpopulaire.ca; Mon.-Wed. 10am-6pm, Thurs.-Fri. 10am-8pm, Sat. 10am-5pm, Sun. 11am-5pm

BOOKS AND MUSIC

★ Drawn & Quarterly

Possibly one of the best bookstores on the continent—seriously—Drawn & Quarterly is the physical extension of the art and graphic novel publishing house of the same name. Located in a turn-of-the-20th-century building, it has an old-store feel with tables full of books, low and accessible wooden shelves, and exposed bricks, making the whole place cozy. It's filled with locals just passing by, and the staff couldn't be sweeter. Carrying graphic novels and comics, gorgeous art books, literature, and kids' books (they have their own kid-size corner), this place offers everything a bibliophile could ask for. It's also a popular spot for book launches for local and bigger-name authors like Adrian Tomine, William Gibson, Tavi Gevinson, and too many more to mention.

MAP 6: 211 rue Bernard W., 514/279-2224, www.drawnandquarterly.com; Mon.-Tues. 11:30am-6pm, Wed.-Sat. 11am-9pm, Sun. 11am-7pm

Phonopolis

If the storefront of this record store on one of the Mile End's coolest strips looks vaguely familiar, that's because its monthly window displays mimic the covers of new releases. Don't be surprised if you brush past a member of Plants and Animals on your way in. Carrying new and used vinyl and CDs, the shop has a great collection of indie rock, obscure bands and labels, and vintage finds—unsurprisingly it's popular with local hipsters. The interior isn't much to speak of, just albums lined up on the walls. The atmosphere is detached and cool with some Springsteen or new sensation playing on the stereo.

MAP 6: 207 rue Bernard W., 514/270-4442, www.phonopolis.ca; Tues.-Sun. noon-7pm

In business since 1984, secondhand bookstore S.W. Welch was a longtime staple on the Main before relocating to the Mile End in 2007. Locals spend hours browsing the shelves or pop in to take a look at the New Titles table. The topics range from transportation to science fiction, sexuality to Canadiana, though they also have a large selection of poetry, fiction, and children's books. The walls are lined with bookshelves, and they often have a display outside. Many titles come from people in the neighborhood, and it's not unlikely to find a brand-new title on the shelves.

MAP 6: 225 rue St-Viateur W., 514/848-9558, www.welchbooks.com; daily 11am-7pm

CHILDREN'S STORES

Boutique Citrouille

Started by a couple of Parisian parents, Boutique Citrouille is chockablock with wooden toys. In fact, this midsize store is so full of toys that it's a miracle that any parent can pull their child out of here—and vice versa. Anyone eco-conscious or even just with a weakness for old-fashioned toys will immediately fall for this place. But just because the toys here are wooden doesn't mean they're any less modern; you can still get helicopters, tea sets, kites (not wooden), cranes, and of course plush stuffed animals.

MAP 6: 206 ave. Laurier W., 514/948-0555, www.boutiquecitrouille.com; Mon.-Wed. 10am-6pm, Thurs.-Fri. 10am-8pm, Sat. 10am-5pm, Sun. noon-5pm

CLOTHING AND SHOES

Atelier B.

Owned and operated by designers and best buds, Catherine Métivier and Anne-Marie Laflamme, Atelier B. is a workshop/boutique featuring the label's seasonal collections for men and women. The store has an industrial feel with a long heavy counter at the cash register, and gunmetal gray cabinets and drawers placed throughout. The space is open and has lots of room for browsing. Atelier B.'s simple and clean design aesthetic matches perfectly with the boutique's decor. If you're looking for wardrobe staples like winter coats or well-tailored shirts, this place is ideal. All merchandise is made on the premises at the back of the store. They also carry a few novelty items like *Dazed & Confused* and *Monogram* magazines, and posters by local poster artists.

MAP 6: 5758 blvd. St-Laurent, 514/769-6094, www.atelier-b.ca; Tues.-Wed. noon-6pm, Thurs.-Fri. noon-8pm, Sat.-Sun. noon-5pm

Belle et Rebelle

Those wanting a picture of the current state of Québécois design, or those looking for ethical and organic clothing, will get a good picture of it here. Committed to Québécois design, this boutique carries the work of over 60 young designers, all of whom work and live in the province. Though the ambience is nonexistent, the helpful staff and range of products give the store some depth. Clothing, bags, jewelry, and even shoes are available, the majority of which are made in Montréal. Ranging from casual, ethical T-shirts by Oom to the simple, classic dresses of Birds of North America and the repurposed leather purses of Cokluch, every type and style is represented.

MAP 6: 6321 rue St-Hubert, 514/315-4903, www.belleetrebelle.ca; Mon.-Wed. 10am-6pm, Thurs.-Fri. 10am-9pm, Sat. 10am-5pm, Sun. 11am-5pm

Billie

No matter the time of day, the floor-to-ceiling glass storefront of this boutique gives you a full view of the lovely girly finds inside. Elegant but youthful, the decor consists of a number of small, cabin-style cubbies, a long dresser topped with perfectly selected accessories, and a luxurious satin-walled changing room that makes you feel as though you've just stepped into a Chanel purse. Pieces here are from a number of designers, everything from Paige to J Brand to Orla Kiely, but the look is distinctly soft and feminine, with occasional edgier pieces.

MAP 6: 1012 ave. Laurier W., 514/270-5415, www.billieboutique.com; Mon.-Wed. noon-6pm, Thurs.-Fri. noon-8pm, Sat.-Sun. 11am-5pm

Bodybag by Jude

Working out of her atelier in the back room of her eponymous boutique, which is light and airy in all white with large floor-to-ceiling windows, designer Judith Desjardins creates both her Bodybag and j.u.d.e. labels. A regular at Montréal Fashion Week, Desjardins first came to international prominence in 2002 when Nicole Kidman wore one of her dresses on David Letterman. At the time punky and streetwise, Bodybag has since evolved into a line of well-tailored classics with a bit of an edge that appeal to young, streetwise women. Though the selection is concise, the easy-to-wear pieces tie in with any wardrobe.

MAP 6: 17 rue Bernard W., 514/274-5242, www.bodybagbyjude.com; Mon.-Wed. 11am-6pm, Thurs.-Fri. 11am-8pm, Sat. 11am-5pm, Sun. noon-5pm

Boutique Oxford

Boutique Oxford, in the heart of the Mile End, is the city's first conceptual shoe store. Marrying their love of shoes with their love of mags, the team behind the store offers a curated selection of affordable men and women's shows with a side of your favorite newsstand staples. Nike, Swear London, Generic Surplus, and Treton are just some of the brands that line the store's long, sleek, shelf-covered walls. A buffed and glossed concrete floor, exposed brick wall, and pine shelves give it a modern, cool feel. With over 100 magazine titles on offer as well as novelty socks, these guys aim to please.

MAP 6: 174 rue St-Viateur W., 438/382-3555, www.boutiqueoxford.com; Sat.-Mon. noon-5pm, Tues.-Wed. noon-6pm, Thurs.-Fri. noon-8pm

★ Boutique Unicorn

It can be hard to find a name that works in both French and English, so when boutique owners Mélanie Robillard and Amélie Thellen finally stumbled on Unicorn the name stuck. Since opening in 2008, it has become a hit with fashionable women from both cultures. Full of modern classics, the store recently expanded to include a room dedicated to shoes and accessories. The boutique, which is effortlessly decorated with a damask-covered couch and other repurposed and black-lacquered finds, is devoted to local and Canadian designers.

MAP 6: 5135 blvd. St-Laurent, 514/544-2828, www.boutiqueunicorn.com; Mon.-Wed. noon-6pm, Thurs.-Fri. noon-8pm, Sat.-Sun. 11am-5pm

La Canadienne

When the weather is nice, Montréalers do their best to ignore the fact that winter is coming, but when the first frost arrives, stylish women get themselves to La Canadienne. Producing boots that are on-trend, comfortable, waterproof, and, most importantly, warm, for nearly 50 years, this flagship store on Laurier is big and glossy with lots of windows and a sleek gray interior. It may be the go-to brand for stylish and functional winter boots, but it also carries a range of sandals, heels, coats, and bags, all made with the same attention to detail and practicality.

MAP 6: 273 ave. Laurier W., 514/270-8008, www.lacadienneshoes.com; Mon.-Wed. 10am-6pm, Thurs.-Fri. 10am-9pm, Sat. 10am-5pm, Sun. 11am-5pm

★ Les Étoffes

Started by a chic young couple, this new boutique on the Main carries a range of menswear and womenswear from contemporary, hard-to-find labels like Australia's Lover and Montréal's own Naked and Famous Jeans. There's a modern aesthetic to the store, but it also has a welcoming warmth, thanks to the rich, dark-blue wall and wooden fixtures. There's a real sense of timelessness in the pieces on sale here.

MAP 6: 5253 blvd. St-Laurent, 514/544-5500, www.lesetoffes.com; Tues.-Wed. and Sat.-Sun. noon-6pm, Thurs.-Fri. noon-8pm

General 54

What opened as a secondhand store is now dedicated to local designers. At last count, they were up to 30 unique designers. Finds include everything from jewelry to coats and dresses, though you can still find vintage pieces like shoes and accessories. Artfully curated antique furniture doubles as display cases for handmade leather goods, while jewelry pieces are often pinned on the wall and you'll find silk-screened pillowcases coming out of old hatboxes. The atmosphere is low key, with local indie rock or classic oldies playing in the background, and the staff is always ready to offer a hand or an opinion.

MAP 6: 5145 blvd. St-Laurent., 514/271-2129, www.general54.blogspot.com; Mon.-Wed. and Sat.-Sun. noon-6pm, Thurs.-Fri. noon-7pm

Lyla

This two-floor boutique on quietly chic Laurier is the go-to place for top-quality lingerie and swimwear. It was started by sisters Sophie and Esther Paquette in 1983, and the staff here is knowledgeable and especially dedicated to helping you find the suit or bra that best fits your form. The store's atmosphere is reserved but elegant, and European lingerie from Princess Tam Tam, Eres, and Andres Sarda hangs tantalizingly along the wall. The bathing suits have a bit more spunk, with fun pieces by Jean-Paul Gaultier and punchier, Pucci-inspired looks from New York-based Milly. They also carry a number of evening wear pieces and beach accessories.

MAP 6: 400 ave. Laurier W., 514/271-0763, www.lyla.ca; Mon.-Wed. 10am-6pm, Thurs.-Fri. 10am-9pm, Sat. 10am-5pm

GIFT AND HOME

CO

With an eye to the ecological, this boutique on the Main specializes in art and design pieces that are sustainable. Owner Sarah Richardson has a great eye, and the pieces are sharply modern while remaining green. Pieces include cardboard bookcases and shelving, as well as organic cotton pillows printed with a picture of a penguin or a gorilla that could just as easily be dragged around by a toddler as they could sit coyly on your couch. The range of products displayed on simple white shelves throughout the Zen-like store is impressive, from pencil cases and political potato mashers to coffee tables and hanging light fixtures; prices range accordingly from $20 to hundreds of dollars.

MAP 6: 5235 blvd. St-Laurent, 514/277-3131, www.galerie-co.com; Tues.-Thurs. and Sat. 10am-6pm, Fri. 10am-7pm, Sun. noon-5pm

Jamais Assez

Practical and modern are two traits you'll find belong to most of the goods in this bright, open, and modern St-Laurent store. But there is also a fair amount of whimsy in what they stock—a yellow bookcase custom-made for your collection of *National Geographic* magazines, a rocking horse in the shape of a dodo bird, a wine rack with a spot for glasses, a spiral umbrella rack, or a designer kitty litter box. Much of the stock is made in Montréal or Québec, and the staff is very knowledgeable about where their products are from.

MAP 6: 5155 blvd. St-Laurent, 514/509-3709, www.jamaisassez.com; Tues.-Thurs. 11am-6pm, Fri. 11am-8pm, Sat. 11am-5pm

Quincaillerie Dante

The word *quincaillerie* means "hardware," but don't run into this corner shop expecting to find the shelves full of nuts and bolts and the walls adorned with 50 different kinds of hammers. Established in 1956, Quincaillerie Dante was the first Italian-owned and -operated hardware store in the city, and it's still run by the same friendly family. They are on a first-name basis with most of their clients. Though they carry a few crucial tools, they also have an assortment of kitchenware, like pots, pans, delicate china, stovetop espresso makers—and then there are the rifles. Alongside the cutesy latte bowls and oyster knives, there's a locked gun case offering a selection of hunting rifles and camouflage supplies. It's a bit jarring to be browsing the *Tintin* mugs next to a display case of hunting knives, but that's the kind of juxtaposition that's made this place such an important neighborhood store—it has everything.

MAP 6: 6851 rue St-Dominique, 514/271-2057; Mon.-Wed. 9am-6pm, Thurs.-Fri. 9am-9pm, Sat. 9am-5pm, Sun. 11am-5pm

Les Touilleurs

Styled to look like a cross between an art gallery and a dream kitchen, Les Touilleurs displays its wares along white walls, stacked on butcher-block tables, and neatly put away in perfect cubbies. From cookware to tableware, small kitchen appliances like old-fashioned scales to scoops for your coffee canister, this store has the chicest stuff for your kitchen. Owners François Longré and Sylvain Côté also offer cooking workshops, and most of the staff are self-proclaimed foodies, so not only will they tell you which pot to cook pot roast in, they'll also give you insider tips on their favorite restaurants.

MAP 6: 152 ave. Laurier W., 514/278-0008, www.lestouilleurs.com; Mon.-Wed. 10am-6pm, Thurs.-Fri. 10am-7pm, Sat. 10am-5pm, Sun. 11am-5pm

GOURMET TREATS

Fromagerie Hamel

If you love cheese, you'll love Fromagerie Hamel. Established in 1961, it continues to be one of the most well stocked cheese stores in the city. Locals come here to stock up on weekly specials and have a taste at the sample counter, while tourists pop in for a light meal at the on-site café. A huge, U-shaped display case featuring wheels of cheese from all over the world takes up the majority of the store, with workers behind the counter busily cutting cheese and serving the clients. They also sell things to pair with your cheese, like meat, crackers, spreads, and freshly baked bread.

MAP 6: 220 rue Jean-Talon E., 514/272-1167, www.fromageriehamel. com; Mon.-Wed. and Sat. 8am-6pm, Thurs. 8am-8pm, Fri. 8am-9pm, Sun. 8:30am-5:30pm

Genevieve Gadbois

Chocolatier Genevieve Gadbois's tiny boutique with its steel, walk-up counter is reminiscent of an ice cream shop. Stepping up to the window, you make your selection from a precise menu that includes chocolates from places like Madagascar, Cuba, and Tanzania, and from flavors like chai, extra-virgin olive oil, and maple syrup. Your order comes to you perfectly packaged in a neat little box and ready to eat. Locals pop in for a warming hot chocolate or rich ice cream in summer.

MAP 6: 162 rue St-Viateur W., 514/394-1000, www.chocolatsgg.com; Mon.-Wed. 10am-6pm, Thurs.-Fri. 10am-9pm, Sat.-Sun. 10am-5pm

Gourmet Laurier

Calling itself the "Queen mother of fine foods in Montréal," Gourmet Laurier offers an exclusive range of products from both inside and outside of the province. The decor and layout of this specialty grocery store look like most, but their shelves, in-house coffee, delicatessen and cheese counters filled with local products like foie gras and Québec Brie tell a different story. Some well-to-do patrons do all their shopping here, but most locals pop by to get specialty products like French comfort food, including Pépito cookies, Gallettes St-Michel, Banania drink mix, and Mousline mashed potatoes.

MAP 6: 1042 ave. Laurier, 514/274-5601, www.gourmetlaurier.ca; Mon.-Wed. 9am-7pm, Thurs.-Fri. 9am-9pm, Sat. 9am-6pm, Sun. noon-5:30pm

La Guilde Culinaire

One of the most exciting places to open up in recent years, La Guilde Culinaire is both a kitchen store and a cooking school. It's a few steps up into this store, which proudly displays its Nespresso machine in the window—chances are you'll be offered a compli-mentary coffee before the door behind you even shuts. Modern and uncluttered, the all-white store has top-of-the-line cookware and the sleekest kitchen utensils you've ever seen. Fine groceries, such as olive oil from La Belle Excuse or a box of Christophe Morel's mac-aroons, are also available and momentarily distract you from the beautiful kitchen setup in the back room, where they teach classes.

MAP 6: 6381 blvd. St-Laurent, 514/750-6050, www.laguildeculinaire.com; Tues. and Sun. noon-5pm, Wed. and Sat. 10am-5pm, Thurs.-Fri. 10am-8pm

Milano

Around for over 50 years, Milano is an Italian supermarket in the middle of Little Italy, making it *the* place to get things like olive oil, balsamic vinegar, and Christmastime panettone. It's always bustling with locals yelling at each other in Italian and patrons shouting back and forth with workers. The setup here is different than pretty much any grocery store you've been in before. Instead of aisles, it's set up with little islands around the store overflowing with packages of imported Italian coffee, 10 different kinds of arborio rice, and jars of roasted vegetables. They also have a mean selection of cheeses at great prices and a range of stove-top espresso makers.

MAP 6: 6862 blvd. St-Laurent, 514/273-8558; Mon.-Wed. 8am-6pm, Thurs.-Fri. 8am-9pm, Sat.-Sun. 8am-5pm

Aux Plaisirs du Bacchus

Devoted to Roman god Bacchus's drink of choice, this charming store in Outremont has anything you could ever want to do with wine. Corkscrews of any size, shape, and dimension, as well as wine buckets, cabinets, decanters, and glasses—even those designed specifically for tasting—are all displayed here. The staff are real wine aficionados and they take every aspect of the drink seriously; they will even help you design and build your very own wine cellar to meet both your needs and your budget.

MAP 6: 1225 ave. Bernard W., 514/273-3104, www.auxplaisirsdebacchus.com; Mon.-Wed. 10am-6pm, Thurs.-Fri. 10am-8pm, Sat. 10am-5pm, Sun. noon-5pm

THRIFT AND VINTAGE

The Annex

From boots to jackets, wide belts from the 1980s, and more than a few plaid shirts for men, The Annex is the newest vintage store to open in the Mile End. Run by the same women who take care of neighboring General 54, it draws a number of hipsters and thrift lovers of any age. Filled with finds like old chests of drawers, wooden rocking chairs, and old luggage, the store has a homey, nostalgic feel. Sales associates here are pretty hands-off, but if you're looking for an honest opinion, they'll be happy to dish it out. Music here is usually indie rock, though CBC talk radio often sets the mood.

MAP 6: 56 rue St-Viateur W., 514/271-2129; Mon.-Wed. and Sat.-Sun. noon-6pm, Thurs.-Fri. noon-7pm

Arterie

Located in an old Victorian building, Arterie has classic deep storefront windows that feature some of the best displays in the neighborhood—think dressmaker forms in vintage garb next to a tray of cocktails. They sell a bit of everything, including vintage martini shakers, handmade cards, and vegan shoes, but the focus is on vintage pieces and work from emerging designers for both men and women. Large and open, with wood floors and high ceilings with beautiful moldings, the store is welcoming and laid-back, and the salespeople are always friendly.

MAP 6: 176 rue Bernard W., 514/273-3933, www.arterieboutique.blogspot.com; Tues.-Fri. noon-6pm, Sat.-Sun. 11am-5pm

Citizen Vintage

One of the newer vintage stores on the block, Citizen Vintage has a distinctly curated feel. Shopping here is less about searching for a great find and more about searching the great finds hanging on the racks. The all-white space, with great high-ceilings, also gives it an airy feel, rare for secondhand stores in this town. Popular with men and women, the shop has a dedicated menswear section as well as a couch for tired shoppers to stop and rest a while. They also host a number of art shows and events.

MAP 6: 5330 blvd. St-Laurent 514/439-2774, www.citizenvintage.com; Mon.-Wed. 11am-6pm, Thurs.-Fri. 11am-7pm, Sat.-Sun. 11am-5pm

La (Found)erie

Located on the border of Petite Italie, this vintage store carries a number of designer finds—Ferragamo boots, Gucci purses, Diane von Furstenberg scarves—as well as home accessories and artwork by local artists. The floor-to-ceiling windows allow for lots of light and awesome windows displays—look out of the cat-head mannequins—while a brocade couch, vintage mirrors, and hardware-style fittings give the store a nostalgic yet practical edge. They host a number of events, including gift-basket workshops during the holidays. Appealing to young men and women with a thing for vintage but an eye on trends, the collection is regularly updated to reflect what's happening both on the catwalks and on the street. The (small) staff is friendly, helpful, and always up for a chat.

MAP 6: 6596 blvd. St-Laurent, 514/507-7755; Tues.-Fri. 11am-9pm, Sat.-Sun. 11am-6pm

Local 23

The latest boots and shoes line the windowsill of this second-hand floor, and the huge, seasonal selection lines the walls. It's divided by item (menswear, skirts, dresses, blouses), and you'll find a number of scores here, including vintage fur hats or berets come winter. An old record player has been transformed into a jewelry display case, and luggage adds a bit of old-time flavor. It's staffed by a number of vintage-savvy young women who will help you dig through the latest finds, while their well-thought-out get-ups add to the ultra-cool vibe.

MAP 6: 23 rue Bernard W., 514/270-9333; Mon.-Wed. and Sat.-Sun. noon-6pm, Thurs.-Fri. noon-7pm

Greater Montréal Map 7

BATH, BEAUTY, AND SPAS
Strom Spa Nordique
For a mini-getaway without actually going too far outside of the city, you can't get any better than this. Trickier to get to than some places, it's worth the hassle. Situated on Nuns Island, this Scandinavian spa is all clean, slate-gray lines in bucolic surroundings. The thermal baths are restorative and look out over a large pond and forest. Seven kinds of massages are offered ($79 for 60 minutes), including Thai, Swedish, and hot stone therapy, and an additional $34 will get you a thermal experience. A brand-new spa, it's distinctly modern with a professional and helpful staff.

MAP 7: 1001 blvd. de la Forêt, Île-des-Soeurs, 514/761-2772, www.stromspa.com; daily 10am-10pm

CHILDREN'S STORES
Oink Oink
There's something about the selection of toys and games at this store that makes you think it wasn't made for kids at all but for the adults that accompany them. Painted bright green with a rainbow-striped awning, the exterior is an anomaly in this somber neighborhood. The bright color continues inside, matching the store's atmosphere of exuberance and fun. Just as silly and kid-like as the clients, the staff likes to have a good time and knows their products inside out.

MAP 7: 1343 ave. Greene, Westmount, 514/939-2634, www.oinkoink.com; Mon.-Sat. 9:30am-6pm, Sun. noon-5pm

CLOTHING AND SHOES
Abe & Mary's
On the outer edge of the city, just two Métro stops from the end of the line, you'll find Abe & Mary's. Often described as "a bit of L.A. in Montréal," the massive 7,000-square-foot store is full of high-end goods and surrounded by car dealerships. They stock enough jeans to fill an entire wall, and enough chic designer

goods to occupy a second floor. Designer pieces might not fit everyone's budget, but luckily they also carry novelty items and beauty products. If it all gets a bit overwhelming, have a seat at the in-house café and regroup with a cupcake and a coffee.

MAP 7: 4175 rue Jean-Talon W., 514/448-6223, www.abeandmarys.com; Mon.-Fri. 10am-6pm, Sat. 10am-5pm, Sun. noon-5pm

Envers

Adored for his bespoke tailoring and three-quarter-length coats for men, local designer Yves Jean Lacasse's work always involves an ethnic, romantic, or historical twist. Lacasse is not afraid of color, and his clientele vary from flamboyant artists to conservative businessmen with an eye for tailoring. The ambience of the boutique is definitely creative but masculine as Lacasse mixes subtle hues like gray and black with rich pops of color. The boutique also carries accessories and swimwear. Though best known for menswear, the boutique also has a range of pieces from Lacasse's womenswear line.

MAP 7: 4935 rue Sherbrooke W., Westmount, 514/935-7117, www.yvesjeanlacasse.com; Mon.-Wed. 10am-6pm, Thurs.-Fri. 10am-9pm, Sat. 10am-5pm

La Gaillarde

Opened in 2000, La Gaillarde (which means "strapping young woman" in English) was one of the first boutiques in the city dedicated to ecological fashion. Over a decade later it is still unparalleled in its commitment, with a selection of recycled and repurposed accessories and clothes for both men and women. One step into this modern, newly renovated store with sleek black floors, immaculate white walls, and antique lights and you'll be hooked. The clothes are inventive and contemporary; nothing about them screams "eco." To ensure you leave with a bit of their ethics, organic and free trade coffee, tea, and chocolate sit enticingly at the cash register for one last impulse buy.

MAP 7: 4019 rue Notre-Dame W., 514/989-5134, www.lagaillarde.blogspot.com; Tues.-Wed. 11am-6pm, Thurs.-Fri. 11am-9pm, Sat.-Sun. 11am-5pm

THRIFT AND VINTAGE

Era Vintage

This is one of the best vintage stores in the city. Owner Élaine Léveillée lovingly color coordinates her merchandise—including many designer pieces from labels like Lanvin, Gucci, and YSL—making it all the more beautiful when seen through the floor-to-ceiling windows. The natural light gives it a bright, open feel that is enhanced by the white walls and simple displays. Chic, modern, and elegant is the feel it gives off, and the customers often fall into that category. Nothing here looks old or secondhand, just cared for. Staff will approach you in a similar manner—helpful when you need them to be but otherwise as enthralled by their surroundings as you are.

MAP 2: 1001 rue Lenoir, 514/543-8750; Mon.-Tues. noon-4pm, Wed.-Fri. 11am-6pm, Sat. 10:30am-4:30pm

FAIRMONT LE REINE ELIZABETH

Hotels

Montréal has accommodations for any size budget. But depending on the time of year, you might find you're paying for more than what you're getting. There's no disputing that Old Montréal is the ideal location, as there's nothing quite like walking out of your hotel and onto the cobblestone streets. However, it's one of the more expensive areas in the city, so a night or two in this quarter might not fit every budget. Research Old Montréal's numerous boutique hotels, stylish modern accommodations, and intimate inns and you'll find a price that works.

The majority of international chain hotels, like Holiday Inn and Marriott, are concentrated on rue Sherbrooke between University and avenue du Parc, but there are lots of other options, including smaller inns, hostels, and independent hotels, usually found in the eastern or western end of the downtown core, that provide visitors with a distinct experience.

Being a student hub, the Quartier Latin is full of budget options and the rowdier, party-on-your-doorstep crowd that usually comes with them. Still, larger hotels and smaller intimate boutique-style inns can be found here, and all are within walking distance to downtown and the Plateau, making it a great choice for those who want to see the city by foot, bike, or Métro.

When choosing accommodations, don't forget location. Old Montréal might be pretty, but if you're coming to enjoy the city's nightlife in the middle of January, come expecting to cab it back to your hotel nightly. If you want to be able to roll out of bed and into the party, a hotel closer to the spots you want to hit might be wiser.

Highlights

★ **Best-Kept Secret:** The huge rooms, aerodynamic furniture, and minimalist design of **Hôtel Gault,** tucked away in a quiet corner of Old Montréal, make it perfect if you're looking for your own private paradise in the city (page 266).

★ **Best Design:** One of the first boutique hotels in the city, **Hôtel St-Paul** has bold interiors that remain cutting edge—and the location is unbeatable (page 267).

★ **Best Boutique Hotel:** Modern design and a youthful attitude meet classic, Old Montréal architecture at **Le Petit Hôtel** (page 268).

★ **Most Romantic Hotel:** The opulent Louis XIV-inspired decor and charming Old Montréal setting of **Pierre du Calvet** make it perfect for a couple's weekend away (page 268).

★ **Most Historical Room:** Yoko Ono and John Lennon holed up in room 1742 of the **Fairmont Queen Elizabeth** during their famous 1969 peace protest. Request the same suite and make your own history (page 269).

★ **Most Likely to Make You Extend Your Stay:** Designed with the comfort of guests in mind, **Hôtel Le Germain** makes you feel like you're entering your own private loft. The hotel also boasts a 24-hour gym, a four-star restaurant, and panoramic views of the city (page 270).

★ **Best Classic Hotel:** In the heart of Montréal's swanky rue Sherbrooke, the **Ritz-Carlton** is as opulent as ever. Its top-hatted doorman, sharply dressed staff, and afternoon tea are guaranteed to transport you to a different era (page 272).

★ **Best Contemporary Hotel:** Ideally located on the edge of the Plateau Mont-Royal and downtown, the **Hotel 10 Montréal** has a sleek, modern design and stunning Gaudi-like art nouveau architecture that will make you feel like you're stepping into a luxury European hotel (page 273).

★ **Best Budget Boutique Hotel:** Wonderfully located and with a sharp, contemporary decor, **Hotel Zero 1** raises the bar on affordable luxury (page 275).

★ **Best LGBT-Friendly Inn: Sir Montcalm** is a charming B&B located in the heart of the Village. With a number of exquisitely designed rooms, this hotel offers an oasis in the city (page 278).

Some of the best rates can be found in the suburbs or close to Montréal's Trudeau Airport. But even though public transit is (generally) fast and efficient, there's little reason to stay so far outside of the city center. If you're booking online double-check the address before hitting the confirmation button.

The farther north of rue Sherbrooke you go, the harder it is to find accommodations. Though a few hotels are available in the Plateau, residential areas like the Mile End and Little Italy offer very few options, most of which are independently run bed-and-breakfasts or rental apartments—accommodations that don't suit everyone's taste but can be ideal if you're planning on visiting for an extended amount of time.

Hostels can be found throughout the city and are a great option for those traveling on a budget. Though dorms are popular with student travelers, a number of the hostels offer private rooms and cater to more mature travelers.

CHOOSING A HOTEL

Because it's a large North American city, Montréal has hotels with all the usual amenities travelers are used to, like air-conditioning in the summer and standard double beds. Some, however, follow a more European model and offer a single queen-size bed for double occupancy. Breakfast is usually, but not always, included. And those expecting a daily buffet may be disappointed with some hotels that offer a simple continental breakfast with fresh pastries, coffee, and juice instead. If breakfast at the hotel is going to set you back more than $10 per person, you can most likely find a more palatable and affordable breakfast option not far from your accommodation.

Though most hotel websites can be trusted to give authentic photos, it is always a good idea to check visitor review sites like www.virtualtourist.com for feedback before booking. Tired-looking decor might have been recently updated, or a five-star hotel might no longer be up to standard.

Parking in the city can be a hassle, and expensive, so double-check to make sure your hotel offers parking or at the very least a reasonably close alternative. Street parking is usually safe, but watch out for unusual parking rules—like having to move the car for an hour each day. Finding a spot close to the hotel isn't always easy.

HOTELS

Vieux-Montréal

Map 1

Auberge du Vieux-Port $$$

Overlooking the waterfront, this boutique *auberge* (inn) offers a number of rooms, as well as self-sufficient lofts and apartments (often walk-ups) that are a short distance away from the main building. It's decorated with rustic touches—exposed ceiling beams, wrought-iron balconies—so the feel is more homey than modern, like visiting a friend's summer home. The in-house restaurant, Taverne Gaspar, boasts both a rooftop terrace (with a panoramic view of the river) and a downstairs bistro, complete with remnants of the city's original fortifications.

MAP 1: 97 rue de la Commune, 514/876-0081, www.aubergeduvieuxport.com

L'Hôtel Champs-de-Mars $

On the eastern border of Vieux-Montréal, this establishment has a long history as a hotel. Built in 1889, it first opened its doors as Hôtel le Relais, and its street-level tavern soon became a popular meeting place for sailors and port workers alike. Though it's anything but fancy, it has a family-run feel and is an affordable option for those who want the experience of staying in the historic quarter. It also offers a filling American-style breakfast, which is not always the easiest amenity to find.

MAP 1: 756 rue Berri, 514/844-0767, www.hotelchampsdemars.com

★ Hôtel Gault $$$

A 19th-century textile store in Old Montréal was converted into Hôtel Gault, one of the most scenic and serene boutique hotels in the city. The 30 spacious rooms (300-1,000 square feet each) come complete with movable ergonomic workstations and heated slate bathroom floors, essential for Montréal winters. The hotel is also pet-friendly, and guests are welcome to bring along their treasured feline or canine companion. Though luxury is everywhere you step in the Gault, it's understated: From the reproduction midcentury modern furniture to the bar that greets you at reception, nothing about the place is ostentatious.

MAP 1: 449 rue Ste-Hélène, 514/904-1616, www.hotelgault.com

Hôtel Le St-James $$$

Madonna, Victoria Beckham—this is where the celebrities stay when they come to Montréal. Decorated with lovingly preserved antiques, four-poster beds, and marble-accented bathrooms, the St-James has gone to great lengths to create a luxurious, European atmosphere. Located on the cusp of Vieux-Montréal and the modern

Quartier International, this former merchants bank still has many of its defining features, including John Hammond's 1930 murals, which are an ode to hydroelectric energy, and the idiosyncratic window treatments that grace each of the building's eight floors. If you are looking for a unique spa experience, theirs is located in the bank's former vault.

MAP 1: 355 rue St-Jacques, 514/841-3111, www.hotellestjames.com

LHotel Montréal [$$]

Situated on what was once "Canadian Wall Street," this Second Empire-style building, erected in 1870, was originally the Montréal City and District Savings Bank. It also housed the law office of Jean Drapeau, who would later become the city's mayor. The hotel has a focus on art; works by Warhol, Litchenstein, and Christo are on view throughout the premises, and each room is uniquely decorated, mixing modern decor with the existing architectural elements, such as the ceiling friezes. The hotel offers indoor parking—a perk, especially if you're visiting in winter.

MAP 1: 262 rue St-Jacques, 514/985-0019, www.lhotelmontreal.com

Hôtel Nelligan [$$$]

Occupying two buildings that date back to the 1830s, the hotel features an indoor Mediterranean-style atrium and has a more traditional approach than some of the other boutique hotels in the area. The dark-wood furniture and earthy palette give every one of their 120 rooms a sophisticated gravitas. Judging from the modest facade, you'll be surprised to find their rooftop terrace offers some of the best views (and cocktails) the city has to offer.

MAP 1: 106 rue St-Paul W., 514/788-2040, www.hotelnelligan.com

★ Hôtel St-Paul [$$]

As you enter the sleek lobby of this Beaux-Arts building, you'll notice the large marble fireplace, which seems to appear almost out of nowhere. Opening in 2001, the St-Paul was one of the first converted buildings in the area and led the way for further reconstruction and rejuvenation. The warm, monochromatic and minimalist decor, accented with leather, suede, and fur (a nod to Québec's past and the frigid winters) makes it one of the first "design" hotels in the city. It also offers services like valet parking and babysitting that you'd expect from a luxury hotel. Even if you're not staying, pop into Hambar, the hotel's restaurant, for a drink and a peek at the gorgeous interior. It also has an outdoor patio, located next to the hotel.

MAP 1: 355 rue McGill, 514/380-2222, www.hotelstpaul.com

Airbnb

Montréal's residential neighborhoods are quickly becoming tourist attractions, especially among younger visitors, thanks to the popularity of musicians and artists like Grammy-award-winners Arcade Fire and singer/songwriter Grimes, who live and work in these areas. For those looking to immerse themselves in the city's cultural epicenter—otherwise known as the Mile End—your best bet is to rent a room or an apartment via **Airbnb** (www.airbnb.com).

The website, founded in 2008, allows people to rent out their living spaces for short-term stays to guests. Guests can either rent a room or an entire apartment or house, depending on their needs.

Since the majority of hotels in the city are located downtown, and can often times be prohibitively expensive, renting your very own apartment for a short-term stay could be the best alternative.

★ Le Petit Hôtel $$

The simply-named Le Petit Hôtel takes a relaxed approach to the boutique hotel concept. Recently opened on rue St-Paul West, it has a hipper, younger atmosphere with a café on the first floor that turns into a bar in the evening (or the afternoon, if you need it), as well as a mini-spa offering massages. Rooms come in small, medium, large, or extra large, and inside, they are sleek and modern—white duvets, splashes of color, iPod-docking systems—with traditional touches like exposed brick walls and cathedral ceilings.

MAP 1: 168 rue St-Paul W., 514/940-0360, www.petithotelmontreal.com

★ Pierre du Calvet $$$

Just in front of Chapelle Notre-Dame-de-Bon-Secours, this ancestral mansion was built in 1725 and maintains its Old-World charm thanks to the sumptuous decor—there is something Louis XIV about the bedrooms—and the use of family heirlooms and antique furniture. Named for Pierre du Calvet, who immigrated to Canada in 1758, it's one of the oldest buildings in Montréal to offer accommodations. An outdoor terrace and fireside library with exposed beams are nice additions, as is the inclusion of the coat of arms of the Trottiers (who rejuvenated the premises and still run the hotel), featuring the motto My House Is Your House.

MAP 1: 405 rue Bonsecours, 514/282-1725, www.pierreducalvet.ca

Place d'Armes Hôtel and Suites $$

Mixing elements from the 1880 structure with contemporary design, the hotel, which was the first of its kind to open in Vieux-Montréal, offers a fine balance of classic and modern—brick walls and industrial lighting fixtures meet colonial furniture—giving it a cozy, yet luxurious atmosphere. Looking out onto Place d'Armes and the Notre-Dame Basilica, Aix Cuisine du Terroir restaurant's rooftop terrace offers stunning views. The hotel also has an in-house hammam spa. Take advantage of the complimentary cheese and wine during afternoon cocktail hour on Terrasse Place d'Armes.

MAP 1: 55 rue St-Jacques W., 514/842-1887, www.hotelplacedarmes.com

W Hotel ❸❸❸

Already established in the United States, this high-fashion world-class hotel muscled its way into Vieux-Montréal in 2004 with its ultramodern and sleek design. The 1960s-modernist architecture of the converted Banque du Canada building gives the hotel a sort of timeless edge and allows it to blend in seamlessly with the existing structures in the Quartier International. Though some aspects of the place might make your eyes roll—the Wow Suites, the Whatever/Whenever button, the glass-walled shower—there is no denying this is one of the city's most enviably hip addresses.

MAP 1: 901 rue du Square-Victoria, 514/395-3100, www.whotels.com

Centre-Ville Map 2

Château Versailles ❸❸

An intimate hotel in a grand old house on the western end of downtown, Château Versailles is a great option if you're looking for a cozy but lavish atmosphere. Each room and suite is uniquely decorated, giving the hotel the feel of an old manor house. The decor itself falls somewhere between contemporary and classic, with big, heavy furniture, modern art, and opulent touches like gilded mirrors. They also serve afternoon tea and offer a babysitting service.

MAP 2: 1659 rue Sherbrooke W., 514/933-3611, www.chateauversaillesmontreal. com

★ Fairmont Queen Elizabeth ❸❸❸

One of the most famous hotels in the city, the Fairmont Queen Elizabeth has been the temporary home of Queen Elizabeth II, Nelson Mandela, and Mikhail Gorbachev. And it was here in 1969 that Yoko Ono and John Lennon staged their infamous "Bed-In" in suite 1742 and wrote and recorded "Give Peace a Chance." Opened in 1958, this world-class luxury hotel is an imposing structure and has over 1,000 rooms, 100 of which are suites. A classic Montréal hotel, it is directly connected to the train station and is accessible through the Underground City.

MAP 2: 900 blvd. René-Lévesque W., 514/861-3511, www.fairmont.com

L'Hôtel du Fort ❸❸

In the western part of downtown, close to the Center for Canadian Architecture and the old Forum, this independent hotel offers standard rooms at reasonable rates. Situated on a busy side street, with access to the highway, it's a good option for those who want easy access in and out of the city. The staff is friendly, bilingual, and often helpful. The rooms themselves are standard hotel fare, clean and neat, and some afford views over the city. It also has an underground parking lot.

MAP 2: 1390 rue du Fort, 514/938-8333, www.hoteldufort.com

L'Hôtel Espresso ❸

This former Days Inn in the heart of downtown, within walking distance to Vieux-Montréal and close to the Métro, has been renovated and given a boutique hotel touch. Warm earth tones are found throughout the hotel, from the lobby to the rooms, which have a comfortable but sleek and modern feel with parquet floors and crisp white duvets. Not all the rooms have been renovated, however, so some are terribly outdated and have seen better days. Amenities include a 24-hour gym, sauna, reasonably priced on-site massage facilities, and an outdoor pool in summer.

MAP 2: 1005 rue Guy, 514/938-4611, www.hotelespresso.ca

L'Hôtel le Crystal ❸❸

Newly opened in the heart of downtown, and looking out over the Centre Bell, this gleaming glass tower boasts 131 spacious suites with free Wi-Fi and flat-screen TVs. Contemporary in design, the furnishings are modern and monochromatic. There is also a pool and spa on the premises. Since it's situated kitty-corner to the Centre Bell, members of the Canadiens are sometimes residents here, so don't be surprised if you bump into one of them in the elevator or hot tub.

MAP 2: 1100 rue de la Montagne, 877/861-5550, www.hotellecrystal.com

★ Hôtel Le Germain ❸❸

Once an office building, this austere concrete structure—certainly a product of the 1970s—was renovated in 1999 to become Hôtel Le Germain. Totally redesigned to give their clients the feel of entering their own private loft, the boutique hotel's decoration is all dark wood, earth tones, and glass. With a full gym, spa, and restaurant, all of which are staffed by experienced practitioners in their fields, their facilities are considered some of the best in the city. Panoramic views of Montréal only add to the hotel's charm.

MAP 2: 2050 rue Mansfield, 514/849-2050, www.germainmontreal.com

clockwise from top left: Hôtel Gault, Vieux-Montréal; classic meets contemporary at Le Petit Hôtel, Vieux-Montréal; a historical home is the site of the regal Pierre du Clavet Hotel

Marriott Château Champlain $$

With 38 floors, the Château Champlain is the tallest hotel in the city and one of the most interesting architecturally. Designed by Roger D'Astous and Jean-Paul Pothier, it was completed in time for Expo 67. It was set apart by its arched windows, which won it the unfortunate nickname "the cheese grater." Now owned by Marriott, the lobby features a golden ceiling made up of numerous domes. Similar opulent touches can be found throughout the hotel. Located on the outer edge of downtown, it looms over the Cathedrale Marie-Reine-du-Monde.

MAP 2: 1050 rue de la Gauchetière, 514/878-9000, www.montrealchateauchamplain.com

Le Méridien Versailles $$

Among the grandiose buildings of the city's Golden Square Mile, Le Méridien Versailles is a boutique hotel set in a striking, modern building. With its classic but relaxed decor (think overstuffed couches and lots of light), it offers a modern take on comfort. Located downtown but away from the hustle and bustle of the area's noisier streets, Le Méridien has a number of amenities, including a 24-hour gym, a spa, and valet services.

MAP 2: 1808 rue Sherbrooke W., 514/933-8111, www.lemeridienversailleshotel.com

Le Petit Prince $$

This small, four-bedroom bed-and-breakfast located on a quiet, secluded street just south of the downtown core is a nice break for those wanting to be close to the action. It's located in a Victorian townhouse that was built in 1876, and the wood floors, stone work, and impeccably designed rooms give it a unique and welcoming charm. It's steps away from the Métro and within walking distance to Old Montréal. Breakfast is made to order, and in summer you can enjoy it on their quiet outdoor terrace.

MAP 2: 1384 ave. Overdale, 514/938-2277, www.montrealbandb.com

★ Ritz-Carlton $$$

Opened in 1912 on posh rue Sherbrooke, the Ritz-Carlton is still "La Grande Dame" of Montréal hotels, as it's the only Canadian hotel of its era still in existence. Started by five investors who wanted to capitalize on the city's carriage trade, this luxury hotel still has a wrought-iron awning and top-hatted doormen that greet guests on the rich, blue carpet. The imposing Beaux-Arts building is as elegant as when it first opened. Still the top choice for those who can afford it, it underwent a huge renovation in 2010 to ensure the interior is as stunning as the exterior. In homage to a past era, condos are still for rent on the top floors.

Sofitel Montréal $$

Set on the Golden Square Mile, close to McGill University and the Musée des Beaux-Arts, it may be part of a chain but French-owned Sofitel is one of the sleekest and most stylish hotels in the downtown core. Tall and lean with huge windows, its ultra-modern design continues inside with a minimalist decor, stained-glass windows in the lobby, and contemporary art throughout. This is a European chain, so room sizes are slightly smaller than their North American counterparts, and the per-room Internet charge is a bit of a letdown. The hotel of choice with European travelers, it's also pet friendly.

MAP 2: 1155 rue Sherbrooke W., 514/285-9000, www.sofitel.com

Centre-Ville Est   Map 3

Holiday Inn Select $

There's a lot of European flavor in Montréal hotels, but this place is a little different. Located in Chinatown on the edge of Vieux-Montréal, it has an Asian theme. As the rooftop pagodas indicate, the Far East aesthetic runs throughout, with a water garden and more pagodas and paper lanterns in the foyer. The rooms are standard, with queen-size beds, TVs, and windows onto Vieux-Montréal or Chinatown. Kitty-corner to the Métro, but right next to a highway, it's within walking distance to downtown and the Vieux-Port, and visitors can take advantage of their indoor pool, gym, and spa services.

MAP 3: 99 ave. Viger W., 514/878-9888, www.yul-downtown.hiselect.com

★ Hotel 10 Montréal $$

A great mix of old and new, Hotel 10—formerly Opus Montréal—has some of the most stunning architecture in the city. Located on the corner of St-Laurent and Sherbrooke, it is the perfect distance between downtown and the Plateau. Originally built in 1914 by Joseph-Arthur Godin, the art nouveau-style building was the first poured-concrete structure in North America. Incorporating the existing structure into the new design, Hotel 10 balances sleek design and decor with Old-World charm. The friendly and bilingual staff is always helpful and the in-house bar has a great outdoor terrace and is a popular hangout.

MAP 3: 10 rue Sherbrooke W., 514/843-6000, www.hotel10montreal.com

Hostels

If you're looking for alternatives to the swanky boutique hotels of Old Montréal and the hotel chains of downtown, there are a number of great hostels and bed-and-breakfasts in the city.

Those looking to stay in Old Montréal without the hefty price tag should look no farther than **Auberge Alternative de Vieux-Montréal** (358 rue St-Pierre, 514/282-8069, www.auberge-alternative.qc.ca, $25 dorm room, $75 private room). This converted warehouse still retains the arched windows and high ceilings of its 1875 construction. Decorated with an eclectic collection of found or made objects, the hostel's dorms and private rooms are brightly colored, enlivening the old stone walls. Conveniently located in the western part of Vieux-Montréal, close to rue McGill, it's easily accessible by Métro and within walking distance to downtown. It is three floors up to the reception area, so be prepared to lug your bags.

Visitors looking to be close to the downtown action should check out **L'Auberge Apéro** (1425 rue Mackay, 514/316-1052, www.aubergeapero. com, $21-24 dorm room), an affordable, popular alternative to less-than-favorable cheaper hotels. Clean and minimally decorated, it is relatively small, with only 18 beds available in an old building built in the 1880s. It boasts an outdoor terrace as well as knowledgeable and bilingual staff.

The center of activity for Francophone students, the Latin Quarter has a number of hostels, though if you're well out of university, choose carefully; the area and the hostels themselves can get rowdy. Location-wise it is perfect, a stone's throw from the Plateau and close to downtown. All the choices here have a truly French vibe.

Your best choice for the Latin Quarter, and possibly the city, is the **M Montreal** (1245 rue St-Andre, 514/845-9803, www.m-montreal. com, $20 dorm room, $80-125 private room). With exposed brick walls, modern decor, TVs in just about every room, a bumping bar, and complimentary breakfast, this hostel is one of the best in the city for young travelers.

Offering private rooms and small apartments, **Auberge de Jeunesse Alexandrie** (1750 rue Amherst, 514/522-9420, www.alexandrie-montreal.com, $22 dorm room, $70-90 private room) in the Latin Quarter is in the center of the action and a good choice for those traveling in small groups. The same goes for **Hostel Montréal Central** (1586 rue St-Hubert, 514/843-5739, www.hostelmontrealcentral. com, $27 dorm room, $40-90 private room), though it has more of a student vibe with an outdoor terrace and in-house restaurant and bars.

For a more residential location, the Plateau is perfect. Once you get used to the laid-back pace and tree-lined streets, you might not want to venture downtown. Close to Parc La-Fontaine in the eastern Plateau and open June 1-August 31, **La Gîte du Parc Lafontaine** (1250 rue Sherbrooke E., 514/522-3910, www.hostelmontreal.com, $28 dorm room, $65-80 private room) offers private rooms or dormitory beds in a classic-style townhouse. If you're visiting at a different time of year, check out **La Gîte du Plateau** (185 Sherbrooke E., 514/284-1276, www.hostelmontreal.com, $28 dorm room, $75-90 private room), which is run by the same people, offers the same amenities, and is located closer to the downtown core.

Hotel Quartier des Spectacles 💲

Located in the heart of the newly christened Quartier des Spectacles, this boutique budget hotel is located on a small block populated by sex shops and tattoo parlors. But never judge a book by its cover: Once inside, the exposed brick walls, tidy reception area, and comfortable, clean rooms dispel any unease. It is superbly located within walking distance of both Old Montréal and the Plateau; the one drawback would be just how close you want to be to the action. During the summer months (June-late-Aug.), this area is the heart of the festival season and things can get rowdy.

MAP 3: 17 rue Ste-Catherine W., 514/849-2922, www.hotelquartierdesspectacles. com

★ Hotel Zero 1 💲

This brand new hotel in the downtown core, right near the Quartier des Spectacles with views overlooking Chinatown and Vieux-Montréal, is just what the city needed. A former university residence, the building has been converted into a stylish boutique hotel. Best of all, it's affordable. The design is clean and sleek with lots of concrete, dark wood, and punches of yellow and white to lighten the mood. The majority of the rooms, all of which come with a mini-kitchenette, offer unobstructed views of the city's skyline. Get some fresh air on their third-floor patio or enjoy your morning coffee in the ground-floor atrium. Though the hotel doesn't have a restaurant, it's close to many eateries and offers complimentary morning coffee and muffins as a concession.

MAP 3: 1 blvd. René-Lévesque E., 514/871-9696, www.zero1-mtl.com

Quartier Latin and the Village

Map 4

Auberge Hotel Le Jardin d'Antoine 💲

You'd be hard-pressed to find a location that's closer to the action. Located around the corner from the Métro and the bus station (where even those flying into town will be deposited) and within walking distance to the main shopping district and the Plateau, this hotel makes navigating the city super simple. The rooms have a cozy, country vibe (paisley quilts and wrought-iron bed frames) as well as free Wi-Fi and air-conditioning, a savior come summer. The room rate includes a generous buffet breakfast.

MAP 4: 2024 rue St-Denis, 514/843-4506, www.aubergelejardindantoine.com

Auberge Hotel Le Pomerol $

This may not be the biggest hotel on the block, but what it lacks in size it makes up for in convenience and affordability. The modestly sized rooms are minimally decorated, with a smattering of contemporary touches. The staff is friendly, helpful, and fully bilingual. Well situated, it's within walking distance to the Village, Vieux-Montréal, the Quartier des Spectacles, and the Plateau. The continental breakfast is delivered to your room in a picnic basket.

MAP 4: 819 blvd. de Maisonneuve E., 514/526-5511, www.aubergelepomerol.com

Celebrities Lovely Hotel $

The name might sound a little silly, but Celebrities Lovely Hotel is just that, a lovely, movie-themed hotel in the Latin Quarter. Situated in an old Victorian mansion built in 1897, the house has been renovated to turn it into a small boutique hotel. Taking inspiration from *Breakfast at Tiffany's,* shots of Audrey Hepburn adorn almost all the rooms and give it its glamorous atmosphere. Portraits of Holly Golightly and a pink and white color scheme make it more the spot for a girls' weekend than a romantic getaway.

MAP 4: 1095 rue St-Denis, 514/849-9688, www.celebritieshotelmontreal.com

L'Hôtel Gouverneur Place Dupuis $

This moderately priced hotel isn't anything spectacular, but because it's situated in the Latin Quarter, close to the Village, Old Montréal, Berri-UQÀM Métro station, and within walking distance to the Plateau and downtown, it's a great option for those looking for affordable accommodations. Though the rooms are showing a bit of wear and tear, they are large, comfortable, and a great choice for families. The 18-floor high-rise also affords great views of the city and the St-Lawrence River, and an indoor pool and gym sweeten the pot.

MAP 4: 1415 rue St-Hubert, 514/842-4881, www.gouverneur.com

L'Hôtel Lord Berri $

Located in the Latin Quarter, just steps away from the Berri-UQÀM Métro station and Old Montréal, L'Hôtel Lord Berri is a non-smoking hotel with 154 rooms and features amenities like free Wi-Fi and parking nearby (though space is tight). The hotel was recently renovated with a few modern touches here and there, but the decor remains fairly standard. Regardless, you can expect a clean hotel with a friendly and helpful staff and a great location.

MAP 4: 1199 rue Berri, 514/845-9236, www.lordberri.com

L'Hôtel St-Denis $

Built in the 1920s, L'Hôtel St-Denis is in the center of the action, not far from downtown and only a block away from the Berri-UQÀM

Plateau and Mile End, it's perfect for the self-sufficient traveler looking for a no-frills bed. Bathrooms and the kitchen are shared, but the cozy rooms and the location above one of the city's hottest bars is worth it. Guests also get free passes to see bands playing during their stay, and the location alone, near tons of affordable restaurants and within walking distance of the city's coolest addresses, sweetens the deal.

MAP 5: 4871 blvd. St-Laurent, 514/284-0122, www.casadelpopolo.com

clockwise from top left: treat yourself to a night at the newly revamped Ritz Carlton, Vieux-Montréal; Place d'Armes Hôtel and Suites; Fairmont Queen Elizabeth, Centre-Ville

Métro station. The rooms themselves, which are your standard hotel fare, have been freshened up with a recent renovation. Some guests might find the rooms to be noisy in the summer due to the air-conditioners. Parking is available just around the corner and Wi-Fi is free for guests. Breakfast isn't included at the hotel, but since it's next to a number of cafès and restaurants, finding a good meal is hardly a problem.

MAP 4: 1254 rue St-Denis, 514/849-4526, www.hotel-st-denis.com

La Loggia $

Located on Amherst in the center of the Village, this charming bed-and-breakfast serves up both art and breakfast. Situated in a three-story early-20th-century townhouse, the five rooms are all uniquely decorated with antique chairs, modern art, and personal touches, like vibrant cushions or Persian rugs, all of which give it a homey vibe. Close to the Plateau and Berri Métro station, the hotel offers packages that include private yoga classes, personal trainer sessions, or a course in sculpture. Breakfast is made with local, fair-trade, and organic ingredients and is served on the terrace in the summer.

MAP 4: 1637 rue Amherst, 514/524-2493, www.laloggia.ca

★ Sir Montcalm $$

This ultra-chic bed-and-breakfast in the Village—think matte black walls, sleek white linens, and ambient lighting—may cater to the LGBT community, but anyone with an eye for design will be instantly smitten. It's a perfect blend of comfortable yet polished. Perks include a day pass to the local gym, access to the gorgeous patio in summer, and a filling four-course breakfast. Close to Vieux-Montréal and the Métro, it's an urban oasis that's sure to please.

MAP 4: 1453 rue Montcalm, 514/522-7747, www.sirmontcalm.com

Plateau Mont-Royal

Map 5

Anne Ma Soeur Anne $

Situated in the middle of the Plateau close to Parc LaFontaine and the restaurant-filled avenue Duluth, this hotel is a good option for those traveling on a budget or those looking to stay in the heart of the action. The no-frills, studio apartment-sized rooms are comfortable enough, and most come equipped with Murphy beds that you can fold into the wall when not in use. Since it's directly above a jazz club, the noise, especially on weekends, will keep some guests up at night. The small rooms also come equipped with a micro kitchen for some simple self-catering.

MAP 5: 4119 rue St-Denis, 514/281-3187, www.annemasoeuranne.com

Auberge de la Fontaine $

This turn-of-the-20th-century townhouse looks out onto Parc LaFontaine, one of the most pleasant spots in the city. Three floors of rooms offer an intimate place to stay in a residential, mainly Francophone area. Though parking can be a bit of a hassle—the hotel only has three spots, the rest are on the street—it is situated on a bike path and is perfect for anyone wanting to bike the city. A buffet breakfast and free Wi-Fi are available, and guests also have access to the kitchen after hours, where they can help themselves to tea, coffee, and various snacks.

MAP 5: 1301 rue Rachel E., 514/597-0166, www.aubergedelafontaine.com

Gingerbread Manor $

Just off of Carré St-Louis between St-Denis and St-Laurent and located in a Victorian three-story townhouse built in 1885, this charming bed-and-breakfast is a different way to see the city. With large bay windows, original molding (it's named after the period's "gingerbread" ornamental details), and an attached carriage house, it harkens back to a bygone golden age. All five rooms are fitted with either a king or queen bed, have hardwood floors, and are uniquely furnished. Only one, however, has a private bath. A hot breakfast includes croissants and fruit salad, and they also have bikes available to rent.

MAP 5: 3445 ave. Laval, 514/597-2804, www.gingerbreadmanor.com

L'Hôtel de l'Institut $

As this is the training ground for future hotel staff, you're unlikely to find better service in the city. A recent renovation has modernized this 35-year-old hotel to rival the sleek design of just about any hotel in Montréal. With only 42 rooms, it is relatively small, but each room has its own balcony, affording views of the city. Ideally located in the Plateau, it is within walking distance to downtown and is directly above a Sherbrooke Métro station. The sole drawback is the slightly overpriced parking, which isn't always available.

MAP 5: 3535 rue St-Denis, 514/282-5120, www.ithq.qc.ca

Pensione Popolo $

The owners of cafè and music venue Casa del Popolo have opened a small, European-inspired pensione above the cafè (look for the red door). Ideally located on the border of the

Excursions from Montréal

Look for ★ to find
recommended sights and activities.

Highlights

★ **Most Multicultural Cottage Country:** Jewish, Francophone, and English populations pioneered the summer existence of **Sainte-Agathe-des-Monts,** and to this day all three cultures can be seen in the town, making it the most culturally diverse in the region (page 293).

★ **Best Rock Climbing:** Experienced and inexperienced climbers alike come to **Parc Régional Val-David and Val-Morin,** the site of the best rock climbing in Québec, as well as some delicately preserved ecology (page 294).

★ **Best Place to See the Leaves in Fall:** There's no better way to see the seasons change than riding or walking along the **Parc Linéaire Le P'tit Train du Nord,** which is 230 kilometers long and cuts through the Laurentians (page 294).

★ **Best Kid-Friendly Sight:** Over 1,000 animals call the **Granby Zoo** home. With unique attractions like Hippo River, it's a great day out for the kids (page 300).

★ **Best Children's Museum:** Interactive exhibits at the **Museum of Science and Nature** in Sherbrooke beautifully mix history and art (page 300).

★ **Best Summer Stage:** Located in the picturesque town of Knowlton, **Theatre Lac Brome** is one of the most respected English summer stages in the province, with performances of classic and contemporary plays (page 302).

★ **Best Place to Tune Up Your Gregorian Chant:** Located on the banks of Lake Memphremagog, **Abbaye St-Benoît-du-Lac** is home to 50 monks who produce some of the tastiest cheese and gourmet goods in the region. A bonus: They'll also let you pray with them and join in a little Gregorian chant three times a day (page 303).

★ **Most Likely to Give You Vertigo:** One of the longest pedestrian suspension bridges in the world can be found at the **Parc de la Gorge-de-Coaticook.** The bridge sits 50 meters above the gorge (page 304).

★ **Most Unexpected Way to Explore the Region:** Few people associate Québec with wine, so following **La Route des Vins** to the many wineries in the region will give you a totally different perspective on the region and its geography (page 304).

★ **Best Place to Hit the Slopes:** It's the scenery that stays with you after you've slalomed your way down the 60 picturesque alpine trails at **Ski Mont Sutton** (page 307).

One of the greatest things about Montréal is its proximity to nature. Montréalers are always heading out of the city for some antiquing, apple-picking, and cycling in the Cantons de l'Est (Eastern Townships in English) or leaving the office en route to some of the best skiing on the East Coast and a cozy chalet weekend in the Laurentides (the Laurentians).

Depending on which way you leave the island—to the mountains in the north, or the valleys in the south—you're headed for some diverse geography. To the southeast, you'll find the lowlands, lakes, and rolling hills, populated with a number of wineries and towns, each with their own—often British-influenced—style. Located 80 kilometers from Montréal and bordering on New Hampshire and Vermont, certain parts of the Eastern Townships can seem almost indistinguishable from some of their American counterparts. The covered bridges, Victorian gingerbread houses, and antiques stores give it a certain Anglophone touch you don't always see elsewhere in the province.

This was a predominantly English area until the 1970s, and English and French are spoken so fluently here it can be hard to figure out the native from non-native speakers. On your way out of the city, drivers will pass three unique Monteregian hills. Mont St-Hilaire, Rougemont, and Yamaska explode out of the otherwise flatlands; these mini-mountains, created by what many think may have been intrusions of long extinct volcanoes, are now accessible ski stations in the winter.

Leave Montréal to the north and you'll soon be in the thick, dense boreal forests and driving through the foothills of the Laurentian mountains, first colonized in the mid-1800s. It was a priest, Antoine Labelle, who saw the area's potential and pushed to exploit it. Saddened by the number of French Canadians moving south of the border for work, he convinced mills and logging companies and their workers to move north into the mountains. The opening of the northern railway Petit Train du Nord in the late 1800s also pushed development.

Today, this region remains particularly close to the hearts of many Montréalers, and it has become a popular place to retire. Amid the woods and the lakes and mountains are a number of cottage towns and, of course, some of the most accessible ski slopes in the province.

PLANNING YOUR TIME

All of these excursions from Montréal, to the south and to the north, can be made in a day by car. Though, those who have the time should think about staying a night or two in the region for more exploring. The Laurentians, approximately an hour's drive north of the city, in particular offer a number of different types of escapes, and you could spend weeks hiking the various trails, canoeing some of the area's bigger lakes, and camping out in a different area each night.

The Cantons de l'Est, meanwhile, are great for a day out of town or a romantic getaway; it all depends on what you're looking for. Camping is popular here as well. The quaint inns and many towns to explore allow for a more relaxed visit, and because it's barely a 90-minute drive from the city, it's ideal for those on a short stay. This region is great to hit if you have a bit of time when traveling between Montréal and Québec. If you want to make a stop on your way out of the city, the town of Chambly, with its 18th century fort, is a great place for a pit stop.

Weekends are always busiest no matter the time of year or whether you're heading north or to the southeast. If you're flexible in your travel times, avoid the crowds and opt for a midweek excursion, then head back to the city for the weekend. Between December and March 15 snow tires are the law for any vehicle registered in the province, so if you're driving a rental you'll be covered. But if you've got your own set of wheels, sticking to major (read, plowed) roads and avoiding dirt tracks is the safest bet. Many of the roads, especially those that lead to out-of-the-way, privately owned chalets and cottages, rely on local residents to shovel and plow them.

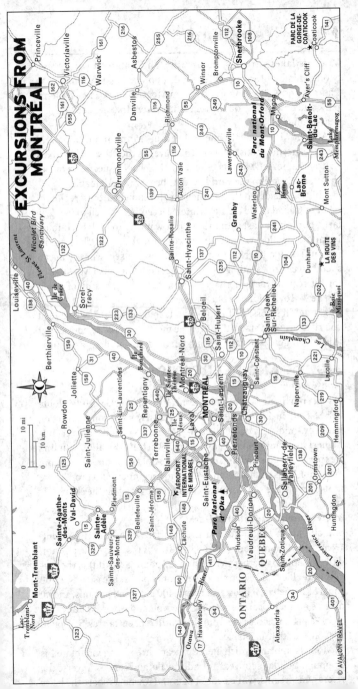

EXCURSIONS FROM MONTRÉAL

© AVALON TRAVEL

Mont-Tremblant

With its lakes, streams, mountains, and untamed wilderness, Mont-Tremblant is one of the most popular destinations in the Laurentians. A 90-minute drive from Montréal, it boasts a national park and an internationally renowned resort that attracts tourists year-round.

Autumn is an ideal time to head up to the mountains and catch the tremendous colors of the leaves as they turn. The mixed Laurentian forest, with its boreal and big woods species, is one of the most diverse in the world, and its beauty is undeniable.

This is considered the premier ski and snowboarding region in Eastern Canada, and during winter (December-March in particular), sport enthusiasts, and those just wanting to kick back in an Icelandic sweater with a drink next to a roaring fire, flock to the region. Though the biggest draw is the resort itself, where you can spend an entire vacation and never get bored, it's also worth visiting the region's many heritage buildings and churches, all of which can be discovered in the old towns.

Though it's possible to do Mont-Tremblant in a day, provided you rise early and stay late, to get the most out of the region, stay at least one night, especially if you plan on doing outdoor activities.

SIGHTS AND RECREATION

Mont-Blanc

Just over an hour's drive from Montréal is **Mont-Blanc** (1006 Route 117, St-Faustin-Lac-Carré, 800/567-6715, www.skimontblanc.com, late Nov.-mid-Apr. daily 8:30am-3:30pm, $45 adult), the second-highest mountain in the Laurentians. Boasting 41 trails, including 5 expert trails, it also has a major ski school and is one of the more affordable hills in the region, perfect for beginners and pros. There is also an on-site spa, the perfect answer to a day on the slopes.

Mont-Tremblant National Park

Smack dab in the middle of the Laurentian mountains, **Mont-Tremblant National Park** (819/688-2281, www.sepaq.com/pq/mot, daily 24 hours, weather permitting, $7 adult, $3 child) is the biggest and oldest of the province's national parks. Measuring 1,500 square kilometers, it boasts six rivers, 400 lakes and streams, and 40 diverse animal species, including the wolf and moose. The park is so vast that it is accessible from three different entrances: St-Donat, St-Côme, and de la Diable.

Mont-Tremblant, which literally means "trembling mountain," is a popular holiday spot year-round; kayaks and canoes traverse the rivers and streams, while pedal-boats and rowboats share the lakes with fishers and swimmers. Over 150 kilometers of hiking trails are available as well as 59 kilometers of mountain biking tracks. These turn into cross-country skiing and snowshoeing trails in the winter. Unique to the park is the Via Ferrata du Diable, a mix of hiking and climbing that takes you through part of the park that is not accessible otherwise.

If there's one northern pastime you have to indulge in, it's dog-sledding. Not far from the park's Diable entrance is **Nordic Adventure Dog Sledding** (Place St-Bernard, 819/681-4848, www.tremblantac-tivities.com, $132). Offering the ultimate in Jack London fantasies, the guides here will teach you how a powerful team of eight har-nessed huskies is steered and stopped before you hop on the sled to experience the ride firsthand. The two-hour ride winds up moun-tains, across frozen lakes, and through thick forest with a quick stop for hot chocolate to warm you up.

Mont-Tremblant Resort

Just next door to the national park is **Mont-Tremblant Resort** (1000 Chemin des Voyageurs, Mont-Tremblant, 888/738-1777, www.trem-blant.ca, late Nov.-mid-Apr. daily 8:30am-3:30pm, $80 adult), the premier ski resort in Eastern Canada and one of the best-known spots in the region. The first lodge and ski lift opened here in 1939, and no one has looked back since. The view from the mountain remains just as stunning now as then, and you can see the whole countryside from atop the 95 runs and numerous lifts. Acres of ramps, rails, and jumps are also available. Come for the day or stay over night in one of the resort's brightly colored Disney-fied versions of a mountain town. In summer, activities like biking and hiking take over the hills.

Ville de Mont-Tremblant

The actual village from which everything else got its name, the town of **Mont-Tremblant** (877/425-2434, www.villedemont-trem-blant.qc.ca) is a nice change of pace from the hustle and bustle of the resort. Established in the late 1800s, Mont-Tremblant was one of many new villages founded by Father Antoine Labelle, who encour-aged city folk to colonize the country. Since the late 1930s it has be-come a popular village, and the stores and restaurants reflect that. Take a stroll down the main strip, or pop into the **Maison des Arts et de la Culture Saint-Faustin** (1171 rue de la Pisciculture, 819/688-2676, www.maisondesarts.ca, Wed.-Sun. 11am-5pm) to see the latest in the region's arts. Those visiting in the summer can get a taste of local life at **Le Marché d'Été de Mont-Tremblant village** (1875 chemin du Village, July-Sept. Sat. 9:30am-1pm), the seasonal local market.

RESTAURANTS

There are tons of restaurants in and around Mont-Tremblant Resort, but there are also plenty of independently run places worth checking out—many of them located in old converted houses—only a 10- to 15-minute drive away. If you head into downtown Mont-Tremblant, stop at **Couleur Café** (415 rue Léonard, 819/681-0723, www.couleurcafe.ca, Mon.-Fri. 8am-6pm, Sat. 8am-5pm, Sun. 9am-5pm, $6-8) for a coffee, where the java is fair-trade and roasted on-site.

Not far away, **Seb l'Artisan Culinaire** (444 rue St-Georges, 819/429-6991, www.resto-seb.com, daily 6pm-close, table d'hôte $50) is modern yet romantic. This converted old house is the setting for dishes made with fresh local ingredients, like smoked organic duck breast and bison steak. The food is hearty but delicate, and the wine list is full of soon-to-be favorites.

Those lusting after some Québec seafood should head to **Le Cheval de Jade** (688 rue de St-Jovite, 819/425-5233, www.chevalde-jade.com, Tues.-Sat. 5pm-10pm, $25-40), with delicacies like oysters and scallops and black cod on the menu. Situated in a house that was built in 1925, the restaurant has an elegant, relaxed vibe. Though known for seafood, Le Cheval de Jade also offers a unique specialty, duckling *à la Rouennaise,* a French dish in which the duck carcass is squeezed in a "duck press" that extracts the juices. A hard-to-find delicacy, even in France, it's a must for any hardcore foodie. Call ahead to make a reservation for the dish, which serves two for $100.

There's no better place to dig into traditional, hearty Québécois grub than in the backcountry, surrounded by woods and mountains. Southeast of the ski hills is **La Tableé des Pionniers** (1357 rue St-Faustin, Saint-Faustin-Lac-Carré, 855/688-2101, www.lat-ableedespionniers.com, Sat.-Sun. 8:30am-2pm). This traditional Québec sugar shack has been revamped to include a lighter breakfast menu and an updated atmosphere. Though the log cabin remains, gone are the servers' checkered shirts. Luckily they still offer the traditional sugar shack menu, which includes dishes such as "scrunchies," eggs and sausages in maple syrup, baked beans, and maple taffy; it's sure to put you in the best kind of food coma.

HOTELS

When it comes to hotels in Mont-Tremblant, the obvious choice is the **Fairmont Mont-Tremblant** (3045 chemin de la Chapelle, 866/540-4415, www.fairmont.com, $250-525), with its luxurious rooms, great views, and the convenience of skiing down the mountain and right up to your hotel. The spa and restaurant with a roaring winter fire are the icing on the cake.

Built in 1942 by Joe and Mary Ryan, the founders of the

clockwise from top left: Parc de la Gorge-de-Coaticook; local wine at Vignoble d'Orpailleur, Cantons de l'Est; Abbaye St-Benoît-du-Lac is known for its cheeses, Cantons de l'Est

Mont-Tremblant Resort, **Château Beauvallon** (6385 Montée Ryan, 888/681-6611, www.chateaubeauvallon.com, $150 and up) is equally as luxurious as the Fairmont but off the well-beaten path. Offering 70 different suites, Beauvallon has a secluded feel with views of Lake Tremblant.

Many of the best places to stay are small inns a few minutes away from the mountain. Looking out over Lac Mercier, the **Auberge la Porte Rouge** (1874 chemin du Village, 819/425-3505, www.aubergelaporterouge.com, $184-234) looks and feels more like a friend's cottage than a midsize inn. In a nice surprise, the rates include a gourmet dinner and hearty breakfast.

If bed-and-breakfasts are more your thing, the **Crystal Inn** (100 Joseph Thibault, 819/681-7775, www.crystal-inn.com, $120 and up) offers an intimate and unique experience. Each of the four suites is decorated according to the healing powers of different crystals—agate, amethyst, sun stone—and each room has its own fireplace and is decorated with hand-painted murals. Breakfast and a session at the in-house nature spa are also included.

If you prefer to be self-sufficient, check out the stylish and modern cabins and suites available for rent from **Côte Nord Tremblant** (141 Chemin du Tour du Lac, Lac-Supérieur, 819/688-5201, www.cotenordtremblant.com, $150 and up), located just outside of Mont-Tremblant. The lake views, tennis courts, and modern vibe will give you a totally different perspective on the region. And these accommodations will be easier on your pocketbook if you're traveling with a group.

INFORMATION AND SERVICES

Covering all aspects of the area, including the resort and the old Mont-Tremblant village, **Tourisme Mont-Tremblant** (877/605-4746, www.tourismemonttremblant.com) has all the information you need to get your bearings in the area. Local maps and even package deals are accessible on-site, and it also has links to the chamber of commerce and detailed information on getting to and from the area. Once there, the **Tourist Information Bureau** (5080 Montée Ryan, daily 9am-5pm) will be able to help you with anything else.

GETTING THERE
By Air

Boutique airline **Porter** (888/619-8622, www.flyporter.com) offers direct flights to Mont-Tremblant International Airport from major U.S. and Canadian hubs, including Boston, Chicago-Midway, New York-Newark, Toronto Island Airport, and Ottawa. There's even a flight from Montréal that will take all of 25 minutes in the air. Many of these flights are only offered December-March. Shuttles are available from the airport to the resort and town.

All international and national flights to Montréal arrive at **Pierre Trudeau International Airport** (www.admtl.com) in Dorval. A shuttle bus service offered by **Skyport** (800/471-1155, www.skyportinter-national.com, $70 one-way) departs Trudeau for Mont-Tremblant during skiing season, mid-December to mid-April. Check the website for exact rates and times.

By Bus

A coach is available daily from Montréal's main bus terminal, **Gare d'Autocars** (1717 rue Berri 514 842-2281, www.stationcentrale.com). The trip with **Galland** (514/333-9555, $65 round-trip) takes about 2.5 hours and will deposit you at a gas station/convenience store an easy walk to the resort. Tickets are available from the bus station website www.stationcentrale.com.

By Car

Driving from Montréal to Mont-Tremblant couldn't be simpler. Take Highway 40 West to Highway 15 North and drive straight for about 90 minutes. After Sainte-Agathe, Highway 15 becomes Route 117 North; continue untill you get to Mont-Tremblant.

GETTING AROUND

The easiest way to get around Mont-Tremblant is by car. If you don't have your own, there is a **Performance Laurentides Budget** (1345 Route 117, 888/357-3157, www.budget.ca) rental agency in the center of town. Public buses are available for a cost of $2 per ride; the schedule and routes can be found on the chamber of commerce's website (www.ccdemonttremblant.com).

Lower Laurentians

Even closer to the city than Mont-Tremblant, about an hour or so drive from downtown, there are different areas to be explored that are perfect for an entire day, or even just an afternoon. Still part of the Laurentians, the geography overall is slightly flatter, and though a few ski hills can still be found, you won't find bigger mountains than those in the north. Instead, the Lower Laurentians are populated with towns and villages and summer homes laid out along the shores of freshwater lakes. Forests and low mountains still define the area, but it's the lakes and villages that set it apart.

Many of the places could be visited individually in a day, or if you get an early start or stay out late, a few places that are closer together, like Sainte-Agathe-des-Monts and Val-David, are doable in a single day. If you want to take advantage of the area but only have a day to spare, pick a single town and spend the day exploring by foot. Returning to the city along smaller roads is also a great way to feel like you're getting the most out of your day.

SIGHTS AND RECREATION

Oka

Northwest of the city, just off the island, is **Oka National Park** (2020 chemin Oka, 450/479-8365, www.sepaq.com/pq/oka, $10 adult). Easily accessible (it's about a 45-minute drive east of the city), it offers outdoor recreation year-round. In June-September locals flock to the beaches on the shores of Lac des Deux-Montagnes for a swim or to try their hand at windsurfing, one of the lake's popular sports. Another one of the park's biggest draws is the wetlands, where marshes mingle with the boreal forest. Explore them by walking the Grande Baie trail, or canoeing through the Rivière des Serpents. In 1742, the Sulpicians defined their presence in this area when they built the Way of the Cross. Revisit the stone structures and chapels by walking the 4.5-kilometer Calvaire d'Oka path. In winter, the park offers 47 kilometers of cross-country skiing trails and 16 kilometers of snowshoeing. Throughout summer the park is accessible by Route 644 in the east and Highway 640 in the west, with the latter closed during winter.

The **Marina d'Oka** (257 rue des Anges, 450/479-8323, www.marinadoka.com, mid-May-mid-Oct.) is one of the more picturesque marinas in the area. Located on Lac des Deux-Montagnes, accessed by downtown Oka, the marina has a small shop that sells boating accessories and decorative items, as well as seafaring wear. A small, lakeside bistro is a great place to grab a bite and look out over the water.

Saint-Sauveur

Head north out of the city and in less than an hour you'll hit Saint-Sauveur. Incorporated in 1855, the village and the surrounding ski hills have since become a weekend destination. There's still a feel of an old downtown main street with many of the stores situated in converted houses. Though they've since been turned into restaurants and stores, many of them are dedicated to sports gear and winter wear with a few dedicated to antiques.

Those looking to nab a bargain are likely to find it at the city's many outlet stores. Nike, Diesel, Guess, La Senza, and Reebok can all be found at **Les Factoreries** (100 Guindon, 800/363-0332, www.factoreriestanger.com, Mon.-Wed. 10am-6pm, Thurs.-Fri. 10am-9pm, Sat.-Sun. 10am-5pm).

The town also plays host to a yearly celebration of music and dance. Around since the early 1990s, the **Festival des Arts de Saint-Sauveur** (www.fass.ca, late July-early Aug.) has everything from contemporary to hip-hop dance and traditional music from around the world. Many of the events are free.

Also in summer, **Parc Aquatique du Mont St-Sauveur** (350 ave. St-Denis, 450/227-4671, www.parcaquatique.com, $35 adult, $28 youth, $18 child) is one of the area's biggest attractions. One of Canada's largest water parks, it features rafting, a wave pool, a tidal-wave river, and slides. They also have lots of non-water fun like alpine-slides and zip-lining.

Thanks to a few hard-working snow machines, **Mont-Saint-Sauveur** (350 rue St-Denis, 450/277-4671, www.montsaintsauveur. com, Dec.-late Apr., $55) has one of the longest winter seasons in the country, with hills and snowboard runs open well into April and sometimes even May. The hills also have nighttime lighting for after-work runs, and the latest attraction is a year-round alpine roller coaster.

★ Sainte-Agathe-des-Monts

Continue farther north on Route 117 and you'll reach the quaint town of **Sainte-Agathe-des-Monts** (www.ville.sainte-agathe-des-monts.qc.ca), established in 1849. Situated on **Lac des Sables,** it's one of the most popular cottage towns in the region. By the 1860s it was a thriving, mostly Francophone community that eventually grew to include many Anglophone residents. Today, it's one of the most diverse towns in the region, with a large population of English-speaking and Jewish summer residents who were originally drawn here in the early part of the 20th century, not only for the town's proximity to Montréal but also for the good, clean mountain air (part of Mordecai Richler's *The Apprenticeship of Duddy Kravitz* was set here). For a fair number of years one of the town's main draws was its benefits for the ill and convalescing and those suffering from tuberculosis. The Laurentian and Mount Sinai Sanatoriums were both located here, and you can see their influences reflected in the architecture of old homes equipped with large covered balconies and solariums.

At the end of the main street (rue Principale)—lined with the original Catholic church and restaurants and boutiques that have been refurbished to capture their original glory—you'll find the Lac des Sables and the **Croisières Alouette** (866/326-3656, www.croisiere-alouette.com, late May-late Oct., $16). A staple in the area since the 1940s, these 50-minute cruises give you a bit of context by pointing out historical sights, celebrity homes, and features of the landscape. They're especially nice in fall when the leaves are multicolored.

Val-David

Few towns in this region have the same hippie commune vibe as **Val-David** (www.valdavid.com), which is slowly but surely changing into a younger and slightly more accessible boho one. Nestled in the Laurentians, this former mill town has become known for the amateur artists that work and live here. The town offers self-guided tours that point out public art works and take you to a number of artist studios. Since the town is highly concentrated, it's fairly easy to get around, with many of the sites next door to each other. The **Centre d'Exposition de Val-David** (2495 rue de l'Église, 819/322-7474, www.culture.val-david.qc.ca, summer daily 11am-5pm, winter Wed.-Sun. 10am-5pm) holds regular exhibits by local and regional artists with exhibitions changing regularly.

Those interested in the history of the town's architecture can guide themselves around the various historic buildings, including **Magasin Général Alexis-Guindon** (2475 rue de l'Église), a general store built in 1919 that remains virtually unchanged, and **Moulin Georgine-du-Perré** (1267 rue de la Sapinière), a private residence that was built to resemble an old French mill, with stone work and circular roof.

★ Parc Régional Val-David and Val-Morin

For the best climbing on the country's east coast head to the **Dufresne Sector** of the **Parc Régional Val-David and Val-Morin** (1165 chemin du Condor, 888/322-7030, www.parcregional.com). The site of the first ever rock climbing competition in Québec, the park now has over 500 routes, including walls for those just beginning to learn and walls that'll challenge those who've been doing it for a lifetime. Dedicated to preserving the local ecosystem—it was created largely by locals—it is also a great place to bird-watch, check out the native plants, hike through in the summer, and cross-country ski in the winter.

★ Parc Linéaire Le P'tit Train du Nord

After drawing people to the region in the mid-1800s, Antoine Labelle's second feat was the construction of a railway (built between 1891 and 1901) that carried visitors and holiday makers from the outer reaches of the city all the way into the northern Laurentians. It was this advancement that allowed the area to grow. Made obsolete 100 years later by highways and cars, the old railway is now the **Parc Linéaire Le P'tit Train du Nord** (800/561-6673, www.laurentians.com/parclineaire), a 230-kilometer-long recreational trail running from Saint-Jérôme to Mont-Laurier.

Providing a north-south crossing, it's most used by cyclists in the summer, many of whom spend days exploring the region. If cycling's not your bag, inline skating and hiking are also permitted on the trail and will still let you see the beauty of the area and the stunning vistas the trail offers. In winter, snowmobiling is allowed between Labelle and Mont-Laurier, and cross-country

Pick Your Own: Apple Orchards

Vergers (apple orchards) flourish in Québec, and from September to late October the Eastern Townships are full of different varieties of apples ready to be picked. The perfect afternoon outing, especially if you're with the kids, apple-picking offers a great escape from the city as well as a closer look at the leaves in all their autumn glory. Orchards can be found throughout the Townships, but here are a few that are just a short drive from Montréal. Though most orchards are open throughout the week in high season, call ahead if you're unsure of times, since opening hours are often dependent on weather conditions.

- **Cidrerie et Verger Léo Boutin:** A-710 Rang de la Montagne, Mont St-Grégoire, 450/346-3326, www.vergerboutin.com, daily 8am-4pm

- **Verger du Flâneur:** 1161 La Petite Caroline, Rougemont, 450/469-0505, Sept.-Oct. daily 9am-5pm

- **Verger du Flanc Nord:** 835 chemin Rouillard, Mont St-Hilaire, 450/464-7432, www.vergerduflanc-nord.com, mid-Aug.-mid-Oct. daily 8am-7pm

- **Verger du Pavillon de la Pomme:** 1130 Sir Wilfrid Laurier, Mont St-Hilaire, 450/464-2654, www.pavillondelapomme.com, daily 9am-6pm

- **Vergers et Cidrerie Denis Charbonneau:** 575 Rang de la Montagne, Mont St-Grégoire, 450/347-9184, www.vergersdc.qc.ca, Sept.-Oct. daily 9am-4pm, Oct.-Sept. Sat.-Sun. 9am-4pm

skiing is possible between Saint-Jérôme and Val-David. All along the trail, the old railway stations have been converted into cafés, repair shops, and information centers. There are campsites along the way, and the park will help you arrange baggage transport.

Village du Père Nöel

The spirit of Christmas, and Santa himself can be found throughout the year at **Village du Père Nöel** (987 Morin, 819/322-2146, www.noel.qc.ca, June-Sept. daily 9am-5pm, Dec.-Jan. daily 11am-5pm, $20 adult and child). This outdoor children's play park offers a ton of activities for kids ages two and up. A tree house, electrical train, goat run, zip line, and slides are open no matter the weather, and kids will get a kick out of winter skating and Santa's house, where they can meet the man himself.

RESTAURANTS

Before heading out for a morning of apple-picking in Oka, dig into breakfast at the orchard's restaurant. **O'Verger Gourmand** (4354 chemin Oka, Oka, 450/472-2463, www.vergerduparc640.populus.org, Fri.-Sun. 7:30am-1:30pm, $20) serves weekend brunch using fresh, seasonal ingredients. Brightly decorated with lots of light, it's a perfect place for families with kids.

Orange & Pamplemousse (120 rue Principale, Saint-Sauveur,

450/227-4330, www.orangepamplemousse.com, Wed.-Thurs. and Sun. 8am-3pm and 5pm-9pm, Fri.-Sat. 8am-3pm and 5pm-10pm, $20) in Saint-Sauveur is a modern bistro with an outdoor patio in summer. They serve breakfast staples like eggs Benedict and crêpes and dynamic dinner fare like veal with maple syrup and cranberries and lamb with walnuts and honey, all at reasonable prices.

For more classic bistro fare, there's **La Bohème** (251 rue Principale, Saint-Sauveur, 450/227-6644, www.restoboheme.com, daily 5pm-10pm, $20), a dark, cozy neighborhood staple with a bar that's often busy. The dishes here include mussels and fries and New York steak.

In Val-David you can smell the deliciousness of the freshly baked bread at **La Vagabonde** (1262 chemin de la Rivière, Val-David, 819/322-3953, www.boulangerielavagabonde.com, daily 8am-6pm, $10) from around the block. Organic homemade breads (chocolate and cranberry loaf, sourdough rye) and pastries (croissants, *chocolatines*) are the specialties here, but they also offer great sandwiches and soups, and they whip up a mean latte.

The minimal design of **Les Zèbres** (2301 rue de l'Église, Val-David, 819/322-3196, www.restaurantleszebres.com, Thurs.-Sun. 5pm-close, $30) means it is essentially a glass-walled cabin that looks both totally out of place and totally at home in this natural setting. The menu of market-fresh food changes regularly, so heading to the restaurant for a specific dish is not the point; instead, it's all about the modern design and vibrant ambience. It is often packed, so call ahead for a reservation.

HOTELS

When it comes to spending the night in **Oka National Park** (2020 chemin Oka, 450/479-8365, www.sepaq.com/pq/oka) the only accommodation choice you have is your tent or theirs. That being said, the park does offer rental Huttopia tents ($109 per night), which are large enough for a family of four and have a kitchen, two bunk areas, and even wood floors—perfect if you're not in the mood for roughing it. You can reserve tents through the park's website.

In the middle of Saint-Sauveur Valley and overlooking the ski hill is **Hotel St-Sauveur** (500 chemin des Frênes, 450/227-1800, www.hotelstsauveur.ca, $99-300), a modern hotel that mixes cozy, antique-style furnishings and minimal design. It's a great option, especially if you're traveling in a group. Each unit has a fireplace, balcony, and a kitchen where you can whip up your own breakfasts.

Reminiscent of an old ski chalet—peaked roofs, stone walls in the foyer—the **Manoir Saint-Sauveur** (246 chemin du Lac Millette, Saint-Sauveur, 800/361-0505, www.manoir-saint-sauveur.com, $169-350) is located in the middle of the village, with views overlooking the slopes. Those staying in summer can hang out at the outdoor pools or play a round of tennis before heading off for an afternoon hike.

Luxuriously decorated rooms are all fitted with an espresso machine, Wi-Fi, and views of the surrounding hills.

Staying true to the area's roots, **Auberge du Lac des Sables** (230 rue St-Venant, Sainte-Agathe-des-Monts, 800/567-8329, www.aubergedulac.com, $169-300), with its back to the forest and with a view of the lake, exudes good, clean mountain air. Though the interior is nothing spectacular, it has a cozy, cottage feel that is perfectly at home in the surroundings.

The Laurentians have been a vacation destination since vacations became a thing, so why not stay at the most storied of hotels? **Hôtel la Sapinière** (1244 chemin La Sapinière, Val-David, 800/567-6635, www.sapiniere.com, $166-250) in Val-David was built in 1936 by Mayor Léonidas Dufresne to advance tourism in the region. It remains the quintessential Laurentian hotel. The charming country-style hotel has a cottage feel with antique-style furniture, stone walls, exposed ceiling beams, and fireplaces in many of the rooms. As in the early days, the emphasis here is on the cuisine, which you can enjoy while looking out over the lake.

INFORMATION AND SERVICES

Each town has its own tourist center with all the information you need for the town and surrounding area. **Oka National Park's Discovery and Information Center** (450/479-8365, www.sepaq.com/pq/oka, mid-May-mid-Oct. daily 8am-5pm) is located just inside the Route 644 entrance. There's also the easily accessible **Oka National Park's Le Littoral Visitors Centre** (450/479-8365, www.sepaq.com/pq/oka, year-round daily 8am-5pm), which has a ski shop, waxing room, first-aid services, and a restaurant.

Saint-Sauveur's Tourist Office (605 chemin des Frènes, 450/227-3417, daily 9am-5pm) covers all aspects of the region, including the slopes. **Sainte-Agathe-des-Monts's Tourist Office** (24 rue St-Paul, 888/326-0457, www.sainte-agathe.org, summer daily 9am-6pm, winter daily 9am-5pm) is open year-round.

In Val-David, road maps, brochures, and souvenirs are all available at **Val-David Tourist Office** (2525 de l'Église, 888/322-7030, ext. 235, mid-May-mid-Oct. and mid-Dec.-mid-Mar. 9am-5pm).

GETTING THERE AND AROUND
By Bus
All of the Laurentians can be reached from the city with **Galland** (514/333-9555) coach lines. Trips (and tickets) are available daily from Montréal's main bus terminal, **Gare d'Autocars** (1717 rue Berri 514/842-2281, www.stationcentrale.com). To Oka the trip takes about 45 minutes and costs $22 round-trip. The same coach that takes you to Mont-Tremblant will also take you to Saint-Sauveur in about 90 minutes ($38 round-trip), Sainte-Agathe-des-Monts in

clockwise from top left: Lac des Sables in Ste-Agathe-des-Monts, Lower Laurentians; the Eastern Townships offer great recreation including boating and skiing; the Parc Linéaire Le P'tit Train du Nord, Lower Laurentians

By Car

Driving is by far the easiest and fastest way to get here and get around, especially if you want to see more than one village or are taking equipment like ski gear. From Montréal, take Highway 40 West to Highway 15 North and watch out for the signposts. All of the towns are easily accessible off of Highway 15 (which eventually becomes Route 117 North). To get to Oka, take Highway 15 to Highway 13, then head west on Highway 640; road signs will help you along the way.

Cantons de l'Est

Southeast of the city, you'll find the low, rolling hills, flatlands, and picturesque towns of the Cantons de l'Est (the Eastern Townships). Traditionally the home of the Abenaki Amerindians, the Eastern Townships were later colonized by the United Empire Loyalists, who sided with the British during the American Revolution. Though many of the town's roots started with the Loyalists, it wasn't until the turn of the 19th century that immigration from the United States exploded, especially by wealthy folk looking for a place to build their dream summer home. This distinct patrimony is what sets the Eastern Townships apart from the rest of the province, and it can still be seen today in the architecture, culture, and language.

Interesting towns and villages can be found throughout the region. Since many of them are also close to one another, you can easily visit one or two in a day. Depending on what sights you're attracted to, an afternoon or day in the region is enough time to get the overall feel of the place. If you want to do a bit more serious exploring, it's better to spend at least one night in one of the many towns, and a weekend is ideal for those interested in cycling around the region or exploring the area's many wineries.

SIGHTS
Granby

One of the bigger towns on the Eastern Townships map, Granby (www.ville.granby.qc.ca) has a lovely old main street (called rue Principale) that you can stroll along, browsing the shops and cafés and seeing some of the area's older architecture. Built on the textile, lumber, and dairy businesses, it is one of the more commercial towns, but the main attraction is the Granby Zoo.

Ride the Orford Express

Russia may have the Trans-Siberian Railway, but the Eastern Townships have the **Orford Express** (720 rue Minto, Marché de la Gare, 866/575-8081, www.orfordexpress.com, May-late Oct. Wed.-Sun., $76-100). Mixing a little sightseeing with a gourmet meal, the train takes you through the countryside of the Eastern Townships from Sherbrooke, through Magog, to Eastman, and back.

The train ride offers views of the region that you might not get otherwise. The train consists of three restaurant-coach cars; each one is decorated to recall the good old days of rail travel, with white tablecloths, soft lighting, and sumptuous curtains on the windows of the main car. The latest edition to the trains is the lounge car, with panoramic windows that give you an unobstructed view of the landscape.

Three different journeys are available: a weekend brunch, a late-afternoon lunch (Le P'tit Plaisir Gourmand), and a dinner meal (Le Souper à Brunante), all served as three-course meals. They include dishes like chef's quiche, duck confit, veal carpaccio, guinea fowl, and puff pastry with snails and mushrooms.

For those interested in the view but not so interested in the meal, they offer specially priced l'Escapade tickets at the station depending on availability.

★ Granby Zoo

The **Granby Zoo** (1050 blvd. David-Bouchard, 877/472-6299, www.zoogranby.ca, late May-Aug. daily 10am-7pm, Sept.-Oct. Sat.-Sun. 10am-5pm, $35 adult, $23 child) is home to over 1,000 animals. Watch the hippopotamus swimming underwater in the Hippo River, feed the sharks, see the gorillas in their very own valley, and get to know the kangaroos as they hop around.

Sherbrooke

The largest city in the Eastern Townships and the region's commercial center, Sherbrooke (www.ville.sherbrooke.qc.ca) has a downtown core filled with shops and restaurants. First settled by Loyalists in 1793, it was originally an English-speaking town, but today the majority of the city's 200,000 residents are Francophones. It also has a large student population and is the home of two universities, the Francophone Université de Sherbrooke and the Anglophone Bishops University, which became part of the city in 2002 when Lennoxville merged with Sherbrooke.

★ Museum of Science and Nature

Some of the best sights in the city are the many museums. Kids (and parents) get a chance to learn about southern Québec's natural surroundings at the **Museum of Science and Nature** (225 rue Frontenac, 819/564-3200, www.naturesciences.qc.ca, early Sept.-mid-June Wed.-Sun. 10am-5pm, mid-June-early Sept. daily 10am-5pm, $13 adult, $9 child), where interactive exhibits teach kids about everything from river ecology to renewable energy.

Musée des Beaux-Arts de Sherbrooke
Situated in the old Eastern Township Bank, the **Musée des Beaux-Arts de Sherbrooke** (241 rue Dufferin, 819/821-2115, www.mbas.qc.ca, summer Tues.-Sun. 10am-5pm, winter Tues.-Sun. noon-5pm, $10 adult) has a diverse collection of works dating from the 19th up to the 21st century from both Canadian and Québécois artists.

La Société d'Histoire de Sherbrooke
Discover the history of the town and the people who created it through the permanent exhibits at **La Société d'Histoire de Sherbrooke** (275 rue Dufferin, 819/821-5406, www.histoiresherbrooke.org, early Sept.-mid-June Tues.-Fri. 9am-5pm, Sat.-Sun. 1pm-5pm, mid-June-early Sept. Tues.-Fri. 9am-5pm, Sat.-Sun. 10am-5pm, $7). The center also offers a number of tours, including a self-guided one of the downtown streets ($7 with iPod and map) and a tour of the Frontenac Power Station ($7).

Réseau Riverain
Explore the area's riverside with a stroll (or ride) along the **Réseau Riverain.** This bike and walking path runs alongside the Magog River for 18 kilometers. Starting at Blanchford Park, it takes you through the Magog River Gorge and has panels all along the pathway pointing out interesting points and historical facts.

Lion d'Or
Beer fans should pop into the **Lion d'Or** (2 rue de College, Lennoxville, 819/562-4589, www.lionlennoxville.com, Sun.-Mon. 4pm-midnight, Tues.-Sat. noon-3am) for a well-pulled pint of Lion's Pride, the pub's flagship dark brown brew. It opened in 1973, and they started brewing their own in 1986, making the Lion d'Or the oldest microbrewery in Québec. Call ahead for a guided tour and an "après-tour" tasting (Mon.-Fri. noon-4pm, $7.50/person).

Lac Brome
Surrounding the lake of the same name, the town of Lac Brome is made up of seven smaller villages. One of the more popular tourist destinations is the village of **Knowlton,** whose downtown core is full of restaurants, boutiques, antiques dealers, and cafés, which are set in restored Victorian buildings.

The town is also known for the Lac Brome duck. Reared in the area, the duck is found on menus throughout the region and is celebrated with the yearly **Duck Festival** (www.canardenfete.ca), which takes place in the month of September. Visitors are given the chance to taste the world-renowned duck, enjoy concerts and the farmers market, and watch a winner waddle its way to victory at the duck race.

Brome County Historical Museum

Stop into the **Brome County Historical Museum** (130 chemin Lakeside, 450/243-6782, www.bromemuseum.com, mid-May-mid-Sept. Mon.-Sat. 10am-4:30pm, Sun. 11am-4:30pm, $5 adult, $3 senior and student) in the center of town to check various artifacts connected to the area's past, including a rare World War I Fokker plane.

★ Theatre Lac Brome

During the summer months, **Theatre Lac Brome** (9 Mont-Echo, Knowlton, 450/242-2270, www.theatrelacbrome.ca) becomes one of the best summer stages in the province, presenting a number of works in English, from classics like *Pygmalion* and *Our Town* to pieces by Canadian playwrights and a number of its own commissioned works. They also have other events, including musical performances happening throughout the year.

North Hatley

Sitting on the northern shore of Lake Massawippi, North Hatley is one of the most beautiful towns in the region. A popular summer resort, it first attracted aristocrats, savvy businessmen, and other rich, mostly American tourists in the mid-1800s. The town's popularity grew even more with the opening of the railway in the 1880s and it became a haven for many American playboys during Prohibition. Today, much of that history remains in the architecture, with many of the grand old homes converted into hotels and bed-and-breakfasts.

Though the year-round population here is under 1,000, it is home to a few antiques shops, artist studios, folk art shops, and a few galleries, including **Galerie Jeannine Blais** (102 rue Main, 819/842-2784, www.galeriejeannineblais.com, Nov.-mid-June Thurs.-Mon. 10am-5pm, mid-June-Oct. daily 10am-5pm), devoted entirely to art naïf.

English plays take over the summer stage at **Théâtre Piggery** (215 chemin Simard, 819/842-2431, www.piggery.com), and musical acts can be seen all year. In summer, cool off on the shores of the lake with a dip or a day out boating. North Hatley is a quiet town, and there isn't much in the way of sights, but that hasn't stopped it from being one of the most sought-after places in the region; those thinking of visiting and staying should book well in advance.

Sutton

Nowhere is the historic influence of the United Empire Loyalists more prominent than in Sutton. Located about 20 minutes from the

Border Crossing: Stanstead, Québec

Stanstead is one of those rare places that is actually located on a border—the division line between the United States and Canada literally cuts right through the town.

Settled in the 1790s by the Taplin family, who came north from New England looking for affordable land, Stanstead and its counterpart, Derby Line, Vermont, have always had a long and intertwined history. On Canusa Street, the border cuts right down the middle, so the homes on the south side are in America and those on the north side are in Canada, with the American and Canadian Customs situated at the west end of the street. The stone building now facing Customs was once a post office; cut in two by the border, it was the only international post office in the world, with two different counters: one serving Vermont and the other serving Québec.

One of the town's greatest attractions is the **Haskell Free Library and Opera House** or **La Bibliotheque Gratuite de Haskell** (93 Caswell Ave., Derby Line, VT, and 1 rue Church, Stanstead, QC, 819/876-2471, www.haskellopera.com, Tues.-Wed. and Fri.-Sat. 10am-5pm, Thurs. 10am-9pm). A gift of Martha Stewart Haskell in memory of her late husband, who was a prominent merchant, the cultural center was deliberately built across the border in order to give residents of both sides equal access to culture and the arts.

The library is located on the first floor and the music hall on the second, with the original notion that one would pay for the other. Opened in 1904, it is unlike anywhere else; where else you can watch a performance where one-half of the audience and the performers on stage are in another country entirely.

Though the border might be one of the more interesting things about the town, it's not the only thing. It's called the Capital of Granite, and many of Montréal's most famous buildings, including Sun Life (1155 rue Metcalfe), were made with granite from the nearby quarry. And like many towns in this region, it is unbelievably picturesque with a number of historical homes and scenic surroundings. The only difference here is, when you go for a stroll in the town, you need your passport.

U.S. border (its neighbor is Richford, Vermont), this small town is a unique spot in the Eastern Townships with a quaint town center that's full of remnants of British architecture. It is situated at the base of Mount Sutton, a popular skiing spot. Visitors to the area can explore the town's heritage by taking a tour of the **Township Trail** (www.chemindescantons.qc.ca), which invites you to follow in the footsteps of the town's early settlers who first arrived here in 1802. A four-kilometer-long walking tour will show you many important sites and point out certain architectural influences. Pick up a map at the **Sutton Tourist Office** (24 A, rue Principale Sud, Sutton, 800/565-8455, daily 9am-5pm).

★ Abbaye St-Benoît-du-Lac

Founded in 1912, overlooking Lake Memphremagog, **Abbaye St-Benoît-du-Lac** (819/843-4080, www.st-benoit-du-lac.com, church daily 5am-8:30pm, shop Mon.-Sat. 9am-10:45am and 11:50am-4pm) is home to more than 50 monks who continue to work and live here. Designed by Dom Bellot, the abbey is known throughout the province for the monks' cheeses—they make 10 different types, including Blue Ermite and Fontina—jams, cider, and other goods that are made on the premises. Those looking for a quiet place for contemplation can stay at their men's hostel; there's also a women's hostel in a nearby nunnery. The public is invited to join the monks in daily prayer and Gregorian chant (daily 7:30am, 11am, and 5pm).

Coaticook

In the southernmost part of the Eastern Townships, bordering on the United States, is the town of Coaticook. Though the town is full of quaint buildings, there are few sights here; instead, people come for the scenic surroundings.

★ Parc de la Gorge-de-Coaticook

Parc de la Gorge-de-Coaticook (135 rue Michaud, 888/524-6743, www.gorgedecoaticook.qc.ca, summer daily 9am-5pm, winter Mon.-Fri. 11am-5pm, Sat.-Sun. 9am-5pm) is best known for its magnificent suspension bridge, one of the longest pedestrian suspension bridges in the world. It sits 50 meters above the gorge. There is more to this park than the breathtaking views (though admittedly they are the main attraction). Hiking and mountain biking trails are available throughout the summer, as is horseback riding, with horses and gear available for rent by the hour. In winter, the main attractions are snowshoeing and sledding. Stay at one on the park's campsites, or rent one of their on-site cabins.

★ La Route des Vins

Not far from the American border, in the Brome-Missisquoi lowlands, you'll find over 120 kilometers of wineries. Inaugurated in 2003, **La Route des Vins** (888/811-4928, www.laroutedesvins.ca) takes you through the valleys and bends of a picturesque region with a winery at almost every corner. Seventeen wineries can be found on this route, and maps can be picked up at the region's tourist centers. All of the wineries are open June-October, with some of them open throughout the year.

Québec's specialty is ice wine, a dessert wine that is semi-sweet and produced from grapes that have been frozen on the vine. **Vignoble Chapelle Ste-Agnès** (2565 chemin Scenic, Sutton, 450/583-0303, www.vindeglace.com, June-Oct. Wed. and Sun. 1:30pm, reservations required otherwise, $25 tasting tour) has a monastic feel with its Romanesque stone chapel and vaulted stone cellars.

Domaine Pinnacle (150 chemin Richford, Frelighsburg, 450/298-1226, www.domainepinnacle.com, May-Dec. daily 10am-5pm,

Jan.-Apr. Sat.-Sun. 10am-5pm, tastings $2 and up) produces one of the best-known ice wines in the region in the shadow of Mount Pinnacle. The winery's 1859 farmhouse is an inviting place for a tasting.

A unique selection of wines is available to taste at **Val Caudalies** (4921 rue Principale, Durham, 450/295-2333, www.valcaudalies. com, mid-May-Nov. Wed.-Sun. 10am-6pm, Dec. Sat.-Sun. 10am-6pm, Jan.-May reservation only, tastings $2 and up), where they make everything from rosé to ice cider, cider liqueur, and Vidal semi-dry white wine. Visitors are invited to pick apples and grapes in their vineyards and orchards.

Your eye will likely be caught by the number of large glass bottles that line the roof at **Vignoble d'Orpailleur** (1086 rue Bruce, Dunham, 450/295-2763, www.orpailleur.ca, May-Oct. daily 9am-5pm, Nov.-Apr. daily 10am-4:30pm, tour with tasting $9-20). The bottles contain one of their specialties, La Part des Anges, a sweet wine reminiscent of porto that ages on the roof's edge for 24 months. In addition to ice wine and a tasty Vin Gris, they also produce a Brut, one of the few places in the area to do so.

The only producer of chardonnay in Québec is **Vignoble Les Pervenches** (150 chemin Boulais, 450/293-8311, www.lespervenches. com, June-Oct. Wed.-Sun. 10am-4pm, free, self-guided tours). It's also one of the few organic wineries in the region. Along with chardonnay, they produce two varieties of red using traditional methods.

Producing dry whites, rosés, and reds, **Domaine Vitis** (1095 chemin Nord, Bromont, 450/263-4988, www.domainevitis.com, May-Dec. Wed.-Sun. 10am-5pm, tours 10am, noon, 2pm, and 4pm, $10-20) is one of the largest wineries in the region, offering tours throughout the day. Don't pass up a tasting of their Glace Noire, a dark, fruity ice wine that is unlike the others from the area.

RESTAURANTS

If one microbrewery in Sherbrooke isn't enough for you, check out hip **Siboire** (80 du Dépôt, Sherbrooke, 819/565-3636, www.siboire. ca, daily noon-close, $20), located in the downtown core. The high ceilings and open floor plan make it a welcoming place to grab a pint. Four permanent beers and two seasonal types are made on the premises. You can also enjoy them on the sidewalk *terrasse*. For a sweet treat, head over to **Savoroso** (720 rue Minto, Sherbrooke, 819/346-2206, www.savoroso.com, winter daily 10am-6pm, summer daily 10am-10pm, $10) in the train station market. A popular place for gelato in the summer, it also serves up coffees, pastries, sandwiches, and salads, making it perfect for a light lunch.

In Knowlton, pick up some fresh, homemade bread at **Panissimo** (291-A rue Knowlton, Knowlton, 450/242-2412, daily 8am-5pm,

$10), where they specialize in traditional French baguettes and aromatic focaccia. Gourmands and cheese fiends will love **Brie et Cie** (291-C rue Knowlton, Knowlton, 450/242-2996, daily 10am-5pm, $10 lunch, $25 dinner), a small café and bistro that has a wide selection of international and local cheeses, as well as specialty foods. Go for breakfast or try their Québec cheese plate. They also serve a select number of dishes on Saturday night; call ahead to reserve.

As the saying goes, when in Brome...you have to try Lac Brome duck, and there's no better place to taste it than at Knowlton's **Le Relais** (286 chemin Knowlton, Knowlton, 450/242-6886, www.aubergeknowlton.ca/relais, daily 11am-10pm, $25). Located in Auberge Knowlton, it has an entire menu dedicated to the local delicacy, as well as a number of standard dishes.

North Hatley's **Pilsen** (55 rue Main, North Hatley, 819/842-2971, www.pilsen.ca, Mon.-Sat. noon-11pm) is one of the livelier restaurants in the area. Located on the water, this pub and restaurant serves classic pub grub like bangers and mash as well as finer selections like grilled salmon and ribs. Get a taste of local ingredients and cooking at the upscale **Plaisir Gourmand** (2225 Rte. 143, North Hatley, 819/838.1061, www.plaisirgourmand.com, Oct.-June Thurs.-Sun. 6:30pm, June-Oct. Wed.-Sun. 6:30pm); go for gold with the seven-course tasting menu or opt for à la carte selections like braised lamb and roast boar.

After a day on the hills, or hiking the trails, there's nothing better than a satisfying meal. The chef at Sutton's **Auberge des Appalaches** (234, chemin Maple, Sutton, 450/538-5799, www.auberge-appalaches.com, Tues.-Sun. 6pm-9pm) uses local ingredients to create delectable French bistro dishes, such as stuffed rabbit and grilled calves liver. The restaurant has a homey, rustic feel and a wine list that includes local favorites.

Coaticook is well known for its cheeses, and **Fromagerie La Station** (440 chemin de Hatley, Compton, 819/835-5301, www.fromagerielastation.com, June-Nov. daily 10am-5pm, Dec.-May Thurs.-Sun. 10am-5pm) specializes in raw organic milk cheese and gives tours of their workshop and farm. Try the freshest goat cheese you'll ever taste at **Domaine de Courval** (825 chemin de Courval, Waterville, 819/837-0062, Wed.-Mon. 11am-5:30pm). This artisanal *fromagerie* has five different flavors of rich but delicate cheese, as well as two aged varieties and a triple cream. A map of all the local *fromageries* is available at the tourist office.

Anyone who grew up in Québec likely has a soft spot for **Coaticook Ice Cream** (1000 rue Child, Coaticook, 800/846-7224, www.laiteriedecoaticook.com, Oct.-Mar. Mon.-Sat. 8am-6pm, Apr.-May Mon.-Wed. 8am-6pm, Thurs.-Sat. 8am-9pm, Sun. 11am-6pm, June-Sept. Mon.-Sat. 8am-10pm, Sun. 11am-10pm). Established in 1940, the small business has grown to become one of the biggest in the region, but they still make it the way they used to, with real cream. Their *bar laitier*, or ice cream bar, is open all year round and has all the latest flavors on hand for you to choose from, as well as other products for you to check out, like their Capricook goat cheese and Québec cheddar.

RECREATION
Bicycling

Spanning 5,000 kilometers and linking all parts of the province, **La Route Verte** (800/567-8356, www.routeverte.com) is the ultimate cyclist's dream. Initiated in the late 1990s, most of the major cycling trails in Québec, like those that travel alongside the St-Lawrence River or head deep into the Laurentians, are part of this linking route. The proximity of the towns in the Eastern Townships and the area's lower-lying lands, however, make it an ideal spot to use the Route Verte, even for the most occasional of bikers. Bring your own ride with you or rent one for the day from rental outlets in Lac Brome, Sherbrooke, Orford, Sutton, and Granby.

Skiing

Ski hills can be found not too far from the city; they are great for hitting the runs after work or for a day-long outing.

Not too far from the town of Magog is **Mont-Orford** (4380 chemin du Parc, 866/673-31, www.orford.com, Dec.-Apr. Mon.-Fri. 8am-4:30pm, Sat.-Sun. 9:30am-4:30pm, $57 day pass), one of the best skiing spots in the province. With the fourth highest summit in Québec, it consists of three mountains (Orford, Giroux, and Alfred Desrochers) and 61 trails.

Rising over the western shores of Lake Memphremagog, **Owl's Head** (40 chemin du Mont Owl's Head, 800/363-3342, www.owlshead.com, Dec.-Apr. daily 8:30am-4pm, $45 day pass) offers 45 trails of varying difficulty, with the majority in the intermediate range, and is about 80 minutes outside of Montréal.

Even closer to the city, about a 45-minute drive away, is **Ski Bromont** (150 Champlain, 866/276-6668, www.skibromont.com, Dec.-Apr. Sun.-Thurs. 8:30am-10pm, Fri.-Sat. 8:30am-10:30pm, $55 day pass). Taking over Mont Brome, Mont Spruce, and Pic du Chevreuil, it is the largest illuminated alpine ski resort in North America, making it ideal for night runs. In the summer (June-Sept.), the same hills are home to an extensive water park.

★ Ski Mont Sutton

Opened in 1960, **Ski Mont Sutton** (671 Maple C.P. 1850, 866/538-2545, www.montsutton.com, Dec.-Apr. Mon.-Fri. 9am-4pm, Sat.-Sun. 8:30am-4pm, $60 day pass) was started by a family who wanted to pursue their favorite pastime. Nowadays it's one of the most popular ski resorts in the area and with good reason. Located a little over an hour's drive from the city, it has 60 trails that cut through the woods, giving it a tranquil atmosphere. They also offer ski packages for weekday visits.

HOTELS

A century-old house makes sleeping in Sherbrooke a welcoming experience at **Le Marquis de Montcalm** (797 rue Générale-Montcalm, Sherbrooke, 819/823-7773, www.marquisdemontcalm.com, $104-135). The five rooms at this bed-and-breakfast are charmingly decorated with antiques and personal touches like the hand-painted mural in the Place de Voges room.

Built in 1849, **Auberge Knowlton** (286 chemin Knowlton, Knowlton, 450/242-6886, www.aubergeknowlton.ca, $125-167) has been fully renovated but still holds much of that Old-World charm, with hardwood floors and country pine furniture. Looking out on Lac Brome, it's also got one of the best views in the village. Breakfast isn't always included.

Auberge du Joli Vent (667 chemin Bondville, Lac Brome, 866/525-4272, www.aubergedujolivent, $125-145) is a great little bed-and-breakfast with charming, brightly colored rooms and a fine-dining restaurant on-site. Surrounded by nature, the B&B even has an outdoor pool, which is great when traveling with kids.

North Hatley's reputation as a place for vacationing aristocrats is safe with **Auberge La Raveaudière** (11 chemin Hatley, North Hatley, 819/842-2554, www.laraveaudiere.com, $130-175), an elegant guesthouse in an old Victorian home. Along with seven guest rooms it has two acres of gardens, a comfortable living room, a large, open patio, and it backs onto the local golf course.

Located just outside of North Hatley on Lake Massawippi is **Manoir Hovey** (575 chemin Hovey, North Hatley, 800/661-2421, www.manoirhovey.com, $250-820), one of the most charming inns in the region. Modeled after George Washington's Mount Vernon home, it was built at the turn of the 20th century and has 40 comfortably luxurious rooms, a pool, two beaches, touring bikes, an exercise room, and complimentary haute-cuisine dinners and breakfasts.

Located on a hill, up a winding, ice-prone driveway sits **Domaine Tomali-Maniatyn** (377 chemin Maple, Sutton, 450/538-6605, www.maniatyn.com, $150-180), a striking bed-and-breakfast that's designed to charm. Though it's not far from the ski hills of Mont Sutton, the quiet here is undeniable. The large chalet has a number of suites available with views overlooking the countryside. An indoor salt-water pool and hearty, homemade breakfast seal the deal.

North of Coaticook is **Le Bocage** (200 Moe's River Rd., Compton, 819/835-5653, www.lebocage.qc.ca, $90-490), a charming Victorian home that's been converted into a welcoming four-room bed-and-breakfast. Handmade quilts lie atop pine bed frames, giving the place a country farm feel. Breakfast is served in a cozy, stone-walled dining room or outside on the terrace.

INFORMATION AND SERVICES

Coming from Montréal, stop off at the **Regional Tourist Office** (Autoroute 10, exit 68, 800/355-5755, www.easterntownships.org, June-Sept. Mon.-Fri. 8am-10pm, Sat.-Sun. 9am-5pm, Sept.-June Mon.-Fri. 8:30am-4:30pm), the first center in the Eastern Townships region. Though some towns have their own tourist centers, larger centers can be found in **Granby** (111 rue Denison E., Place de la Gare, Granby, 800/567-7273, daily 9am-5pm).

Sutton Tourist Office (24-A rue Principale S., Sutton, 800/565-8455, daily 9am-5pm), **Sherbrooke** (785 rue King W., 800/561-8331, www.destinationsherbrooke.com, mid-Aug.-mid-June. Mon.-Sat. 9am-5pm, Sun. 9am-3pm, mid-June-mid-Aug. daily 9am-7pm), and **Coaticook** (13 rue Michaud, 866/665-6669, www.tourismecoaticook.qc.ca, mid-Aug.-mid-June Mon.-Fri. 8am-10pm, Sat.-Sun. 9am-5pm, mid-June-mid-Aug. Mon.-Fri. 8:30am-4:30pm).

GETTING THERE AND AROUND
By Bus
A coach is available daily from Montréal's main bus terminal, **Gare d'Autocars** (1717 rue Berri, 514 842-2281, www.station-centrale.com). **Galland** (514/333-9555) takes travelers to most major spots in the Eastern Townships, including to Sherbrooke's main bus station (two hours and 5 minutes, $65 round-trip), Knowlton's Depanneur Rouge (483 rue Knowlton, two hours and 10 minutes, $43 round-trip), and Magog (90 minutes, $56 round-trip).

Smaller towns, including Sutton, Cowansville, Farnham, and Knowlton, can be reached by **Veolia Transport** (877/348-5599, www.destinationknowlton.com), which departs from Montréal's main bus terminal twice on weekdays and three times a day on weekends (including Friday). The trip to Knowlton takes 2.5 hours and costs $36 round-trip.

By Car
The simplest way to travel to the Eastern Townships and around is by car. Head out of Montréal by the Champlain Bridge, then head for Autoroute 10 East. The roads are clearly marked with signs for the Cantons de l'Est, but they can sometimes come up quickly, so keep your eyes peeled. Once on Autoroute 10 all

the towns are easily accessible; it's just a matter of watching for the right exits.

Once you've arrived, getting from one town to the next is just as simple. Many of the small, country roads are signposted, ensuring you get from Lac Brome to North Hatley by the quickest way possible. Depending where you are, you might have to get back on Autoroute 10 to reach your next destination.

QUÉBEC CITY

Sights

The only fortified city left in North America, Québec City is like no other place on the continent. Constructed on the top of Cap Diamant, a cliff that looks out over the St-Lawrence River, the city is defined by its natural hills and cliffs, though from afar it's not always easy to notice. Québec City is the cradle of Canadian society, where in 1608 the first settlers arrived. Led by Samuel de Champlain, they built the first habitation on the site that's now called Place Royale. It was under French rule until 1759, when it fell to the British at the Battle of the Plains of Abraham, but this political feat did not alter the existing French-Canadian culture and way of life. Despite 100 years of British rule and the eventual founding of the Canadian Dominion, the city's ties to the early settlers remain remarkably intact. It's this lineage and incredible architectural heritage that give it its own unique (albeit European) feel.

Quebéc City is divided into two main areas, Haute-Ville (Upper Town) and Basse-Ville (Lower Town). They are easy to differentiate thanks to their geography. Upper Town constitutes the area on the top of the cliff, while Lower Town constitutes everything below it. It's in Upper Town that you'll find Les Fortifications, the walled defenses that encircle Old Québec's Upper Town and many of the biggest sights, including Château Frontenac and La Citadelle.

Directly below, between the cliff and the river, is Vieux-Québec's Basse-Ville (Old Québec's Lower Town). This is where the first European settlement was established, near Place Royale, and where historic areas like the Vieux-Port (Old Port) and the Quartier du

Highlights

★ **Most Iconic Sight:** The most photographed hotel in the world, **Château Frontenac** has become an indelible image of Québec City (page 317).

★ **Best Views:** Stroll along the top of **Les Fortifications** for the most stunning views of the city from both within and outside of the historic walls (page 319).

★ **Best Museum:** Dedicated to the history of Québec, **Musée de la Civilisation** offers an in depth look at Québécois culture (page 327).

★ **Most Historic Sight:** The site of the first settlement in Québec, **Place Royale** is the birthplace of both the French-Canadian nation and Canada itself (page 328).

★ **Most Picturesque Neighborhood:** Once home to Irish immigrants and dock workers, **Quartier du Petit-Champlain** has been revived and rejuvenated by a co-op of artists (page 330).

★ **Most Unusual City Street: Rue Sous-le-Cap** is a charming three-meter-wide street that runs along the cliff-face, lined with tiny old cottages (page 330).

★ **Best Collection of Québécois Art:** With a 19th-century prison incorporated into its design, the **Musée National des Beaux-Arts du Québec** beautifully mixes history and art (page 334).

★ **Most Patriotic Site:** The **Parc des Plaines d'Abraham** is the site of the historic 1759 battle between the French and British, an event that changed the course of North American history (page 336).

★ **Most Historical City Street:** Learn about the city's history in the older buildings that line **rue Saint-Jean** as you wander down what is now one of the busiest commercial streets in the city (page 341).

Petit-Champlain are situated. Getting from the lower to the upper part of the city isn't complicated, provided the winding, hilly streets aren't sheets of ice. Taking the Escalier Frontenac (Frontenac Stairs) is the easiest way, but the funicular and the brand-new Ecobuses offer some good alternatives.

Though separated by a cliff, Vieux-Québec is quite small and dense, so it's easy to cover by foot. In fact the best way to get around the city, in winter or summer, is by walking. Expect to get quite a workout, though, thanks to the hilly geography. No matter where you are in the city, if you want to get down or up, there are likely stairs involved, or at the very least, a city bus. Due to the density of the city, even peripheral areas like the Plains (just outside of the walls in Upper Town) and Saint-Roch (the city's coolest post code, located in Lower Town) are only a 15-minute walk from Vieux-Québec.

Of course, Québec is a vastly different city with a completely different landscape in winter than in summer. Many sites close during the winter or have truncated hours. What constitutes the different seasons, however, is a complicated matter. A good general rule of thumb is the following: Summer hours usually run from June 24, Saint-Jean-Baptiste day and the province's national holiday, to Labor Day, the first Monday in September. Winter hours, meanwhile, could start as early as Labor Day or Canadian Thanksgiving (the second Monday of October) and run until May or June. Many of these dates fluctuate according to the weather, so make sure to double-check hours if there's a particular sight you want to visit.

With so many interesting historical sites just about everywhere you turn in Québec City—even a stroll down Faubourg Saint-Jean Baptiste is a lesson in the city's evolution—there's no time for a dull moment.

Vieux-Québec's Upper Town

Map 8

Basilique-Cathédrale Notre-Dame-de-Québec

It was on this site, high above the St-Lawrence River, that explorer Samuel de Champlain built Québec's first church in 1647. Later, in 1664, the Basilique-Cathédrale Notre-Dame-de-Québec became the first parish church in North America. It was given the title of cathedral 10 years later, when the diocese of Québec was established with the arrival of Monsignor de Laval, the first bishop of New France.

Destroyed by fire during the English conquest in 1759, it was

Confession: Québec City's Love Affair with Churches

If you weren't convinced about the Catholic Church's involvement in the development of New France, you will be after a trip to Québec City. There are so many churches in the city that a single trip alone couldn't cover them all. Most are free and open to the public for both prayer and sightseeing.

- **Chalmers-Wesley United Church:** A neo-Gothic Protestant church, this one was completed in 1853 and was designed by architect John Wells. Its steeple is the tallest inside the walls of Old Québec at 164 feet above the sidewalk (78 rue Ste-Ursule).

- **Chapelle Historique Bon Pasteur:** Designed by Charles Baillairgé in 1868, the slanting roof hides an ornate baroque-style interior (1080 rue de la Chevrotière).

- **Église Saint-Dominique:** Run by Dominican monks, this church and former monastery boasts a stunning wood-beamed ceiling reminiscent of medieval architecture (175 Grande-Allée).

- **Holy Trinity Anglican Cathedral:** Inspired by St-Martin's in the Fields in London, this was the first Anglican cathedral to be built outside of the British Isles (31 rue des Jardins).

- **Sanctuaire Notre-Dame-du-Sacré-Coeur:** Tucked back from the road, this slender, neo-Gothic church was built in 1901 by François-Xavier Berlinguet and is renowned for its stained-glass windows and marble plaques that line the walls (71 rue Ste-Ursule).

- **St. Andrew's Presbyterian Church:** This congregation had its start among the Scottish Fraser Highlanders that were part of Wolfe's Army in 1759 (106 rue Ste-Anne).

entirely reconstructed a few years later, only to be remodeled again in 1843, by Thomas Baillairgé. Inspired by Sainte-Geneviève in Paris, Baillairgé, whose father François designed the church's interior, gave it a neoclassical facade. That, too, had to be reconstructed when the church was once again ravaged by fire—arsonists used the fire to steal priceless paintings—in 1922. During this rebuilding period, however, the builders tried to stay as true as possible to the original building, working off of François Baillairgé's original 18th-century drawings for the interior. Despite the fact that it has been rebuilt a number of times, the bell tower and portions of the walls are from the original structure.

Long and narrow, the interior is a soft buttery yellow with a high arched ceiling, lined with windows and intricate moldings. A stunning gold-plated baldaquin stands at the altar, and other items include paintings of the Virgin Mary that date back to the French regime, the bishop's original throne, and a chancel lamp that was a gift of Louis XIV.

Between 1654 and 1898 over 900 people were buried in the crypt below the church, including 20 bishops and four governors. It's also rumored that Samuel de Champlain himself is buried nearby; archaeologists have been searching for the grave for over 50 years.

Hour-long guided tours of the crypt and basilica are available but must be reserved in advance, so call ahead.

MAP 8: 16 rue de Buade, 418/692-2533, www.notredamedequebec.org; Nov.-Apr. Mon.-Fri. 7:30am-4pm, Sat. 7:30am-6pm, Sun. 8:30am-6pm; May-Oct. Mon.-Fri. 7:30am-5pm, Sat. 7:30am-6pm, Sun. 8:30am-6pm; free

★ Château Frontenac

Proudly holding the title of "most photographed hotel in the world," Château Frontenac is one of the most stunning buildings in Québec. The fortress-like architecture and its location on the top of the Cap Diamant, a bluff overlooking the St-Lawrence, give it an especially majestic feel.

Built in 1893, it is part of a chain of "château style" hotels that were constructed across the country by the Canadian Pacific Railway. Since Québec was one of the North American ports before the long trip across the Atlantic, the hotel was designed to rival any European counterpart and grab the attention of travelers. The building's architect, Bruce Price, drew from both the Middle Ages and Renaissance and used elements like the turrets found on Scottish castles and the bastion towers of French châteaus.

Named after Louis de Buade de Frontenac, who was governor of New France twice between 1672 and 1698, the hotel sits on the site of what was once Château St-Louis, the official residence of the governor of New France and later home of the British governors. The ruins of the many incarnations of the residence lie just in front of the hotel.

It has been the temporary residence of everyone from Queen Elizabeth II to Charles Lindburgh, as well as the site of Alfred Hitchcock's *I Confess*, but the hotel's proudest moment took place in 1943. It was the site of the Québec Conference of World War II, where U.S. president Franklin D. Roosevelt, British prime minister Winston Churchill, and Canadian prime minister William Lyon Mackenzie King discussed the eventual invasion of France.

MAP 8: 1 rue des Carrières, 866/840-8402, www.fairmont.com/frontenac; daily 24 hours; free

La Citadelle

The largest British fortress in North America, La Citadelle is also the largest defense on the continent to have never seen battle. Covering 2.3 square kilometers and perched on the edge of the cape at the highest point in the city, overlooking the St-Lawrence, this strategically placed defense is an imposing figure, standing out along the rolling plains and the copper roofs of Vieux-Québec.

Built under the direction of British officer Lieutenant-Colonel Elias Walker Durnford, the design is entirely French. Modeled in the style of military engineer Vauban, it is shaped like a

A Tour of One's Own: Québec City's Best Walking Tours

There's more than one way to see the city, but the best way to see it is on foot. Here are a few fun, kookier ways to get to know the town.

If you like to be spooked, **Ghost Tours of Québec** (418/692-9770, www.ghosttoursofquebec.com) is for you. Reservations are recommended for these nighttime tours that whisk participants down darkened streets while talking about the city's 400-year-old history and all the ghosts and hauntings that go with it. Guides will even take visitors into one of the most haunted buildings in the city, though taking a pass and staying outside is totally okay. Learn about the previous job experience needed to qualify for the job of executioner in the 1600s, or how the murder of an American in Québec could be the source of an unexplained haunting.

Equally exciting but slightly less grim, **La Compagnie des Six Associés** (418/692-3033, www.sixassocies.com) offers a handful of walking tours, all with a different theme. They often involve a stop at a bar. Lust and Drunkenness is one such tour; it will take you past and into some of the forgotten brothels and taverns of the 19th century and give you an idea of how both the rich and the poor spent their free time and money. Things get a little darker with their Crime and Punishments tour, which lets visitors follow the wife of a French torturer through the streets by lantern-light as they learn about various crimes, the criminals, and inevitably their punishment.

If you love the history but hate the gore (well, some of it anyway), **Les Tours Voir Québec** (866/694-2001, www.toursvoirquebec.com) hits up all the important sights on their Grand Tour. The architecture, the events, the history—it's all here, along with a few lesser-known sights. If you're not quite full yet, take a second helping and try their Food Tour, which looks at the influence of British, French, and Amerindian cooking in the kitchen. Of course, a taste of local wine, beer, chocolate, cheeses, pastries, and crêpes will only give you a better idea of exactly how this whole mix has come together.

Fed up with walking? **Tours Ludovica** (418/655-5836, www.toursludovica.com) does the work while you sit back and relax. Guides ride around on bikes while visitors sit and enjoy the scenery, in a sort of mash-up between a rickshaw and a horse-drawn carriage. Going off map, Tours Ludovica offers tours of lesser-known areas like Saint-Roch, Saint-Sauveur, and Limoilou. A ride out to Saint-Sauveur lets visitors take in the historical architecture of a neighborhood that—had Samuel de Champlain's plans gone through—would have become a large city called Ludovica. It's here that you'll find many old seminaries and other church buildings as well as the Hôpital Général de Québec, the city's original hospital and the oldest building in the city. Up-and-coming Limoilou can also be explored by pedicab; let the guide lead you through the history of this emerging neighborhood before hopping out to grab a coffee at one of the sidewalk cafés.

four-pointed star and as such has no blind spots. Construction on the Citadelle started in 1820, took 30 years to complete, and incorporated two existing buildings from the French regime, the oldest of which is a battery dating back to 1750. The winding gate that is used as entrance into the Citadelle is also the only real gate remaining from the French regime, and is reminiscent of what all gates into the city were once like.

Though it never saw any action, the Citadelle continues to be the official residence of the Royal 22e Régiment, the only Francophone infantry regiment in the Canadian Forces Regular Force. The low stone barracks are a mix of English and French influences with symmetric casement windows and doors and pitched tin roofs. A brand new museum, completed in 2014, commemorates the regiment's 100th anniversary. Housed in a historic building on the site, the museum is dedicated to the regiment's distinguished military history. Starting with the early days and Québec's most important battles, the exhibits continue up to the modern day with the regiment's tour in Bosnia and other United Nations missions. One exhibit is dedicated to the war heroes of the 22e Régiment who fought in World Wars I and II, summarizing their duties, showing personal artifacts, and in one case showing a spy's various identity cards.

As early as the 1860s there was talk of tearing down the Citadelle, but then Governor General Lord Dufferin refused, instead pointing to the fortifications' historical importance. Since that time, his residence became the official residence of the governor general of Canada. It is here too that Georges Vanier, the first French-Canadian governor general and a war hero, was laid to rest in a battery turned chapel.

Since it is still an active military residence, the only way to get inside the Citadelle is to take a tour. Both the regiment and city get equal tour time, and though there's a lot to see, the most interesting aspects, such as the barracks and doors that lead inside the walls, are off-limits.

MAP 8: 1 Côte de la Citadelle, 418/694-2815, www.lacitadelle.qc.ca; bilingual tours Apr. daily 10am-4pm, May-Sept. daily 9am-5pm, Oct. daily 10am-3pm, Nov.-Mar. daily at 1:30pm; $10 adults, $9 seniors and students, $5.50 children, children 7 and under free

★ Les Fortifications

Québec is the only fortified city in North America, and its walls encircle the entirety of Upper Town, covering 4.6 kilometers, which you can walk for free. The Fortifications offer some of the most stunning views of the city and environs and are a great place to hang out in the summer and have a picnic or take a break from sightseeing. One of the best places to start is at the St-Louis Gate on rue St-Louis. As it's here that you're mostly likely to recognize the ramparts. As you walk along the walls, every angle of the city can be explored, from the defenses of the Citadelle to the lookouts over the river. Lined with cannons and grass-covered in spots, the stone walls of the Fortifications frame the city in a way that transports visitors back to the days when they were a practical defense against attacks. It's along this part, surrounding the Citadelle, where you'll find the best views.

Built in a classic urban style, the Fortifications are characterized by the geometry of flanking and the adaptation of the walls to the city's topography, which sees the walls grow in height and depth at different parts. Though Québec was a bustling city by 1700, its defense system was inadequate, and the city was a maze of temporary and permanent structures. It wasn't until the fall of Louisbourg, a fort in Cape Breton off the coast of Nova Scotia, in 1745, that serious consideration was given to the state of the Fortifications. It was Governor Beauharnois who, following Chaussegros de Léry's designs, authorized a new enceinte that permanently closed the city to the open countryside.

In the late 19th century, citizens complained about the impracticality of the gates, complaining that they stopped circulation and were a nuisance—the gates would close at curfew, and, up until the British troops left, the ramparts were for military and pedestrian use only. Though Lord Dufferin, then governor general of Canada, understood their complaints, he also saw the historical importance of the fortifications—during the summer-long siege of Québec, it was these walls that kept the citizens from British invasion—and instead suggested the gates be dismantled and then rebuilt to make them wider.

The Interpretation Centre of the Fortifications of Québec is located by the St-Louis Gate, beneath the city's ramparts. It offers information about the history of the city's defenses as well as exhibits and guided tours, which depart from Terrasse Dufferin.

MAP 8: 2 rue d'Auteuil, 418/648-7016; Interpretation Centre May-Sept. daily 10am-6pm; tours June 1-24 daily 2pm, June 25-Sept. 6 daily 10am and 2pm, Sept. 7-Oct. 11 2pm; Interpretation Centre $4 adults, $3.50 seniors, $2 children; tours $9.80 adults, $7.30 seniors, $4.90 children

Musée de l'Amérique Francophone

Entering the modernized foyer of the museum you're almost not prepared for the historic chapel that you enter shortly after. Full of green marble pillars, beautiful stained-glasses windows, golden busts of important members of Québec's history, and a 1753 organ, the most alluring part of this exhibit is the baroque music that is played throughout the day.

After a bit of maze-like wandering—through the chapel, into an elevator, and across an outdoor walkway—you arrive at the building that houses the Musée de l'Amérique Francophone, an old building that once belonged to the Séminaire de Québec. The first exhibit on the ground floor looks at the history of the seminary itself, with artifacts like old keys, chalices, and furniture that once belonged to the seminary.

Moving on to the museum's permanent collection, visitors get a well-rounded view of the history and trajectory of the Francophone population, not just in Canada but within the whole of the continent. It retraces the roots of Francophone explorers and guides who helped explore the United States and found American cities like Detroit, Pittsburgh, Buffalo, and St. Louis.

The design of the exhibit is modern and easy to navigate, even in high season when there are more crowds. For the most part, however, it's rarely overcrowded and visitors can wander the exhibits at their leisure.

MAP 8: 2 Côte de la Fabrique, 418/692-2843, www.mcq.org; early Sept.-mid-June Tues.-Sun. 10am-5pm, mid-June-early Sept. daily 9:30am-5pm; $8 adults, $7 seniors, $5.50 students, $2 children, children under 12 free

Musée des Ursulines

Founded in 1639 by Marie de l'Incarnation, an Ursuline nun, and Madame Marie-Madeline de Chauvigny de la Peltrie, a rich widow, the Couvent des Ursulines is the oldest school in North America dedicated to the teaching of women. Girls still study at this institution, which now boasts a museum and a chapel alongside the schoolrooms and courtyard playgrounds.

The first Ursuline nuns landed in Québec on August 1, 1639, and soon started teaching, though at the time the French-Canadian population was so small, the majority of their students were First Nations girls. Just outside of the convent's walls is the Musée des Ursulines de Québec, which tells the story of these pioneer women who were both teachers and students. Newly reopened and renovated, the new permanent collection, The Young Ladies' Academy, allows visitors into the heart of the boarding school and the daily lives of the nuns and pupils that passed through the convent's halls. Artifacts from the time of the French regime are also on view, including teaching materials, personal objects, and sacred artwork.

When French governor Montcalm died after the Battle of the Plains of Abraham, he was buried in the convent chapel by night so as not to arouse suspicion. For a long time his skull was part of the museum's permanent collection, to the delight of visiting schoolchildren.

Despite the simple, austere pews found in the small Ursuline chapel, it has some of the most beautiful sculpted wood in Québec. The carvings were created by master craftsman Pierre-Noël Levasseur between 1723 and 1739, and it was the Ursulines themselves who gilded the carvings, which now adorn the nave of the chapel. The tomb of founder Marie de l'Incarnation can also be found here. The chapel is open to the public from May to October, and entry is free.

MAP 8: 12 rue Donnacona, 418/694-0694, www.museedesursulines.com; May-Sept. Tues.-Sat. 10am-noon and 1pm-5pm, Sun. 1pm-5pm, Oct.-Nov. and Feb.-Apr. Tues.-Sun. 1pm-5pm; $8 adults, $6 seniors and students, $4 children

Parc de l'Artillerie

The position of the Parc de l'Artillerie, looking out over the west of the city and across the St-Charles River, has made it a strategic military site since the late 17th century. Four vastly different buildings trace the city's history from the French regime right up to the 1940s. Of the four buildings that make up the site, the Dauphine Redoubt is the most striking, with massive white supports that plunge down the side of a hill. Built in 1712 and completed in 1748, it was army barracks both before and after the British conquest and eventually became the home of the superintendent. During the summer, characters in period costume bring the barracks to life with demonstrations and tours through the rooms, which have been decorated to reflect various periods in the building's evolution.

Kitty-corner to the Redoubt is the interpretation center, a former foundry used to make an arsenal for the Canadian military, from the Boer War up to World War I and II, and even the Korean War. The site now holds a 200-year-old scale model of Québec. Constructed in 1806-1808, by draftsman Jean-Baptiste Duberger and John By, a military engineer, it was sent to England in 1810 to convince the British government that the city needed new fortifications. Alongside uncovered ruins, there are artifacts that were found on and around the site, including toothbrushes, children's toys, and belt buckles.

MAP 8: 2 rue d'Auteuil, 418/648-7016, www.pc.gc.ca; early May-early Sept. daily 10am-6pm, early Sept.-Oct. daily 10am-5pm; $4 adults, $3.50 seniors, $2 children

Parc du Cavalier-du-Moulin

This tiny little park tucked away at the end of a quiet residential street is one of the city's best-kept secrets. Passing through the park's wrought-iron gates, visitors enter onto Mont-Carmel, the spot of an old windmill (*moulin* in French). Originally a military outpost, the small 1,500-square-meter park was one of the few defenses constructed by the French military in the 17th century. This small defensive outpost was then named "cavalier," a nod to its solitary position. In 1663, the windmill was erected here and included in the military fortification. By 1700, with the building of the first surrounding walls, *le cavalier du moulin* was no longer needed.

Nowadays the park acts as a window onto history, allowing visitors to imagine a city that once had nothing but fields beyond this hillock. It's adorned with a cannon to remind people of its past life as a military defense; the cannon juts out over the hill, directed at the houses and winding streets beyond.

clockwise from top left: the Fontaine de Tourny, Parliament Hill; the Funiculaire du Vieux-Québec, Vieux-Québec's Lower Town; the Séminaire de Québec, Vieux-Québec's Upper Town

Place d'Armes

The history of Place d'Armes is the history of Québec. Once situated behind Château St-Louis, which was at the time also a fort,
it was in this public square, safely behind the defenses, that the
military would perform their various parades and military inspec-
tions. When construction of the Citadelle was undertaken in 1820,
however, the military moved and the regular parades went with it,
moving instead to the Parc de l'Esplanade in front of the fortress
and running alongside the city walls.

Though it lost its military importance, the square continued to
be a popular meeting place, and in 1915 a monument was erected
to the notion of faith. Dedicated to the Récollets, the first religious
community to live in New France, the monument today stands in
the shadow of the Château Frontenac at the center of a bustling
square surrounding by busy restaurants and cafés.

MAP 8: between rue du Trésor and rue du Fort

Séminaire de Québec

Established in 1663 by Monsignor François de Laval, the first
bishop of New France, to train young men for the priesthood,
this seminary was expanded five years later to include the Petit
Séminaire, which, in a push to Gallicize the indigenous population,
accepted both Indian and French students to study at the Collège
des Jésuites. It continued to be the training ground of future priests
right up until the conquest, when its connection to the priesthood
was somewhat lost. The studies instead began to focus on the liberal
arts, and the school began accepting students who didn't want to
become priests. By 1852 the college part of the Séminaire de Québec
became the University of Laval.

Laid out according to 17th-century principles, the *séminare*
has various wings, all of which center around interior courtyards
(you can enter one through the Musée l'Amérique Francophone).
Though the time periods vary there is continuity in the architecture, with stone masonry covered with stucco, casement windows,
steep roofs with dormers, and raised firewalls evident in all of the
buildings. The bursar's wing in particular is interesting. Designed
from 1678 to 1681 and restored in 1866 after a fire, its vaulted
kitchen is still intact, along with the chapel of Monsignor Briand,
who was bishop of Québec in 1766-1784.

Today, it remains both a school and seminary, with Laval's school
of architecture located on the site and priests who continue to live
here and dedicate their lives to the church.

MAP 8: 1 rue des Remparts, 418/692-3981, www.seminairedequebec.org

Along the front of Château Frontenac, looking out over the St-Lawrence River and across to Lévis, is the wide boardwalk of Terrasse Dufferin. Created in 1879 by the governor general of Canada, Lord Dufferin, the 671-meter-long promenade was designed by Charles Baillairgé, the same designer behind the kiosks and street lamps that line the boardwalk.

It was during his summer stay at the Citadelle, now at the opposite end of the promenade, that Lord Dufferin conceived of the idea to build the boardwalk, a place for residents and visitors to take their daily stroll. The use of wooden planks gives the whole thing an air of summer, even in the middle of winter. Though he left his post in 1879, Dufferin himself inaugurated the project and put down the first stone.

Beneath the *terrasse* lie the ruins of the former St-Louis Fort and Château, which was destroyed by fire in 1834. Visitors are able to visit the excavation site thanks to a new interpretation center, cleverly hidden by the boardwalk. Only a few steps down and you're face-to-face with the foundations of the original building and some of the artifacts they uncovered here.

During the winter, a huge slide is built at the Citadelle end of the *terrasse* and children of all ages line up to take a super-fast ride down *les glissades* overlooking the frozen river.

MAP 8: Intersection of rue des Carrières and Place d'Armes

Vieux-Québec's Lower Town

Map 9

Église Notre-Dame-des-Victoires

The oldest stone church in Québec, Église Notre-Dame-des-Victoires was built on Place Royale in 1688, on the site of l'Abitation, Québec's first building. In the basement of the church you can still see one of the building's walls, and archaeological digs have uncovered one of the building's original turrets in the church's facade. The king's storehouse also stood on this site, and it was this particular location that attracted François de Laval, the bishop of New France. For years Laval requested a chapel be built on the site of the king's storehouse, an extension of Upper Town's Notre-Dame-de-Québec church, but it was his successor, Monsignor de Saint Vallier, who would see the work completed in 1723.

Designed by Claude Baillif, the church was originally named l'Enfant Jesus, but it's name was changed twice. In 1690 the British admiral Phipps was defeated by Governor Frontenac, and the

Sky High: Édifice Price

Completed in 1931, Édifice Price is the only skyscraper in Vieux-Québec. Built as the headquarters for Price Brothers Limited, one of the biggest printing companies in Québec at the time, it was designed by Montréal firm Ross and Macdonald. Despite heavy criticism from the public, the government ignored accusations that it wasn't protecting Québec's historic area—two historic houses were demolished to make way for the new building—and gave the company a building permit anyhow.

Completed within a year, the art deco building is reminiscent of the Empire State Building in New York, though much smaller. The design uses setbacks to gradually taper the building's width. Unlike the Empire State Building, however, the roof is classical in design, with a château-style steepled copper roof that blends well with its surroundings. The interior includes bas-reliefs that depict the origins of the Price company, which was forced into bankruptcy during the Depression.

Since 2001, the 16th and 17th floors have become the official residence of the premier of Québec, and the two-floor apartment includes a 14-guest dining room, two bedrooms, and offices. Decorated to reflect the province's history, it boasts maple hardwood floors, traditional Québec style furnishings, and paintings by local artists.

church was renamed Notre-Dame-de-la-Victoire. In 1711, the city was again saved when the fleet of Admiral Walker, on its way to attack Québec, was shipwrecked in the St. Lawrence. This time the name change was easy; they made it plural. Despite two failed attempts, the British would eventually destroy the church in 1759 during the siege of Québec. The subsequent reconstructions were meticulous and took place in 1762-1766 under the eye of Jean Baillairgé.

The interior itself is rather austere, with a few pews and a tiny, circular staircase leading up to the organ. Designed by students of Thomas Baillairgé, it was constructed in 1854-1857 and features several paintings from the 17th, 18th, and 19th centuries. The oldest part of the church is the tabernacle; originally found in the Sainte-Geneviève Chapel, it dates from 1724. Unique to Québec, the frescos on either side of the main altar retrace the history of the church and city, and were done by local painter and decorator Jean-M. Tardivel. The most striking church accent, however, is the single ex-voto, a model of a vessel that arrived in 1664, transporting the Carignan Regiment and the Marquis de Tracy, which hangs suspended over the pews.

MAP 9: Place Royale, 32 rue Sous-le-Fort, 418/692-1650, www.notredamedequebec.org; daily 9am-5pm; tours May-Oct., reservations required mid-Oct.-Apr.; free

La Fresque des Québécois

Reaching nearly three stories tall and at 420 meters high, La Fresque des Québécois is the largest and most historical trompe l'oeil in the city. Unveiled in 1999, it took 12 artists to complete the immense mural that cleverly shows the city's history and its important figures. Sixteen important Québécois are featured in the painting, including historical figures like Jacques Cartier, Samuel de Champlain, and Lord Dufferin, as well as cultural icons like singer/songwriter Félix Leclerc and politician Louis-Joseph Papineau. Also shown in the mural are typical Québécois buildings through whose windows the important figures peek. One of the gates figures prominently, as do the famous L'Escalier du Casse-Cou and the province's four seasons.

A popular tourist sight (it's fun to try and slip yourself in among the historical figures), it kicked off a trompe l'oeil craze around the city, and many buildings are now covered in historically clever murals.

MAP 9: Place Royale

Funiculaire du Vieux-Québec

The only funicular of its kind in North America, the Funiculaire du Vieux-Québec was built in 1879 and designed by William Griffith. Wood-covered and steam-powered, it operated six months a year as an alternative to horse and buggy, transporting passengers and merchandise from Lower Town to Upper Town. The arrival of electrical power in 1907 meant it could work year-round, which it did until 1945, when the wooden structure caught fire and was subsequently rebuilt with metal shelters. It lets passengers off and on at Terrasse Dufferin.

Transportation is still its main function, though today it transports more tourists than merchandise since it allows incomparable views of Lower Town, the port, and Lévis, across the water.

The entrance of the funicular is situated in a historical house, built in 1683 by Québec architect Baillif, that once belonged to one of the country's first European explorers, Louis Jolliet. Jolliet, along with Father Jacques Marquette, was the first European to explore and map the Mississippi River. Jolliet lived here until his death in 1700.

MAP 9: 16 rue du Petit-Champlain, 418/692-1132, www.funiculaire-quebec. com; early Sept.-June 19 daily 7:30am-11pm, June 20-early Sept. daily 7:30am-midnight; $2.25

★ Musée de la Civilisation

In the heart of the port district, not far from the shores of the St-Lawrence and surrounded by historical buildings, the modern facade of the Museum of Civilization strikes out against its surroundings. Designed by Moshe Safdie, the architect behind Montréal's Habitat 67, the front of the museum is built into an incline, tucking the museum away and adding a touch of nature, with a glass roof and greenery sprouting from along the sides. Inaugurated in 1988, the museum is dedicated to the history, present, and future of Québec civilization, as well as that of cultures from around the world.

Inside, the harmony with the surroundings continues with a large open lobby, full of glass and light. The three-story building accommodates 10 exhibits simultaneously, 3 of which are permanent exhibits rooted in the region's history. Le Temps des Québécois is an overview of the history of this nation within a nation, from the first explorers to Expo 67. It's a fun exhibition with bits of pop culture—like videos of iconic TV presenters and shows from the 1980s and 1990s—placed within context next to religious iconography, old tramway signs, sabers, and World War II ration boxes. Presented in conjunction with the National Film Board of Canada (the NFB), historic films, political speeches, and important cultural events are shown on film here.

With a focus on the province as a whole, Territoires looks at the various regions of the province and the problems the areas, and their inhabitants, face. Not an overly optimistic exhibit, it examines issues like suburban sprawl and the Amerindians' lost connection to the land, and tries to provide solutions. The breathtaking photos and videos of the regions give visitors a good overview of the expansive province.

Those wanting to learn more about Québec's First Nations will enjoy Encounter with the First Nations, which looks at the 11 different tribes that inhabit the province and includes videos, artifacts—a birch canoe, a tepee, Inuit sculpture—as well as a look at the history and migration patterns of the particular tribes. Admission is free on Tuesdays November-May.

MAP 9: 85 rue Dalhousie, 418/643-2158, www.mcq.org; mid-June-early Sept. daily 9:30am-6:30pm, early Sept.-mid-June Tues.-Sun. 10am-5pm; $15 adults, $14 seniors, $10 students, $5 children, children 11 and under free

★ Place Royale

For all intents and purposes this is the birthplace of Canada—or more specifically the birthplace of the French-Canadian civilization. It was here that Samuel de Champlain, founder of Québec, built l'Abitation, the first establishment in Québec, and though the structure itself is long gone, slate stones mark where the building once stood. As early as 1623, the square started to take on a life of its own alongside the settlement's second habitation. A military parade ground, marketplace, and the surrounding houses burned to the ground during a fire that destroyed Lower Town in 1682.

One of the best views of the city is from across the river in the city of Lévis. Get there by hopping on the **Québec-Lévis Ferry** located right on the port (10 rue des Traversiers, 877/787-7483, www.traversiers.gouv. qc.ca, $3.25 adult, $2.25 child, $7.75 car). The views of the city are stunning, especially at night, and the 10-minute trip on the commuter ferry will give you a new appreciation for the city's geography. The ferry runs all year long, several times an hour 6am-6pm and hourly 6pm-2:30am. In July-August, a bus tour to Lévis is also available and includes such sights as Fort No. 1, which was built by the British as a defense between 1865 and 1872.

Place Royale got its name in 1686 when Intendant Jean Bochart de Champigny erected a bust of King Louis XIV in its center. As in all towns in France, it was the custom to have a square dedicated to royalty, but unlike in France, there was nothing ceremonious about the square or its surroundings; in fact, the merchants complained that the bust took up valuable space, and so it was removed and placed at the intendant's house.

Damaged during the Seven Years' War, the square was gradually rebuilt, and by the 19th century the square was part of an urban complex that included warehouses, two markets, and a number of businesses. Up until the early 20th century many of the buildings went through major transformations; floors were added, roofs were flattened, storefront windows were built on the ground floor. It wasn't until an economic downturn in the 1960s forced the city to reconsider its purpose that the area was restored.

After restoring a few buildings (the Chevalier hotel, the Maison Fornel, and the Notre-Dame-des-Victoires church), the government decided it wanted to recreate the ambience of the early 17th century and went about completely renovating the buildings to closely resemble how they would have looked during the French regime. Following the detailed plans of the original structures, the buildings were rebuilt using Norman construction with firewalls, stone, spirits to hold up the walls, and ladders on the roofs.

Set on the same square is the Place Royale Interpretation Center. Opened in 1999, it's in the former home of merchant François Hazeur as well as part of the Smith home next door. Exhibits here include a scale model of the original settlement, which would've been situated just outside the modern glass doors. Built against Côte-de-la-Montagne—the steep road established by Samuel de Champlain in 1623—it also houses a public staircase that links the Lower Town with the street above. Admission is free on Tuesdays November-May.

MAP 9: 27 rue Notre-Dame, 418/646-3167, www.mcq.org; mid-June-early Sept. daily 9:30am-5pm, early Sept.-mid-June Tues.-Sun. 10am-5pm; $7 adults, $6 seniors, $5 students, $2 children, children 12 and under free

★ Quartier du Petit-Champlain

The charming restaurants, quaint boutiques, and tourist-packed cobblestone streets of this picturesque neighborhood often belie its rich and interesting history. The oldest street in the city, rue du Petit-Champlain in the 17th century was little more than a dirt path down which residents would walk to get their water. Over the next 200 years, the street would grow to become a bustling area full of houses and businesses of many working-class families and men who worked in the port.

In the mid-1800s, the area saw an influx of immigrants. The Irish Potato Famine saw the Irish fleeing the country in boatloads and consequently arriving in Québec, one of the first ports of call. Many of these immigrants stayed, settling on la rue du Cul-de-Sac and la Petit rue Champlain, calling it instead Little Champlain Street. In time, the Francophones adopted the name as well, turning it into rue Petit-Champlain. This was a poor, working-class neighborhood, and the reconstruction of the nearby Place Royale in the 1970s forced a change in Petit-Champlain as well. The low rent meant that many artists had moved into the area, and it was the artists who rejuvenated it, financing renovations themselves and doing much of their own work. Since none of the buildings were entirely destroyed, a walk through this quarter gives visitors a view of the city's architecture through the ages, with buildings from different eras lovingly preserved.

At one end of rue Petit-Champlain you'll find L'Escalier du Casse-Cou, or the Breakneck Stairs, a narrow and steep set of steps that are one way to get from Upper Town to Lower Town. First built in 1660, the steps are squished between two buildings and can get icy in winter. The unusual name is rumored to come from American soldiers during their attempted invasion. At the other end of the street, you'll find La Fresque de Petit Champlain, which represents the life and history of the area, including the 1759 siege and the fires that came with it.

MAP 9: Between rue du Petit-Champlain and Place Royale

★ Rue Sous-le-Cap

La rue Sous-le-Cap, which means "street beneath the cape," is unlike any other street in the city and totally enchanting. Wedged between the cliff face and the backs of the houses that face rue St-Paul, it was the only road that pedestrians could use at the beginning of the 19th century to get from their homes in this section of Lower Town to the Côte du Palais, a winding street that would take

Bunge du Canada

Bunge Silo

A number of imposing silos occupy the far end of Québec City's port. Known as the **Bunge of Canada** (300 rue Dalhousie), these grain silos have been in operation for more than 40 years, enabling Canadian and American shippers to store a massive amount of grain before sending it overseas. They are some of the only silos in the eastern region of the country and a reminder of the city's history as a bustling and crucial port. The Bunge du Canada remains an important part of the city's landscape and its economic strength.

them to Upper Town. What today are the backs of houses fronting on rue St-Paul used to be front entrances of homes along the waterfront, and during high tide, the roadway would be submerged under water.

The narrow street, which measures three meters across, was also at one time the city's red-light district, with a number of brothels operating on the street. Characterized by the stairs and walkways that cover almost all of the street, it's here that you'll find tiny, slightly crooked houses and some of the prettiest private patios in the city.

MAP 9: Behind rue du Sault-au-Matelot; between rue de la Barricade and rue St-Paul

Vieux-Port de Québec

At the base of Cap Diamant, where the waters of the St-Lawrence and St-Charles Rivers converge, the Vieux-Port de Québec (Old Port) is steeped in history. Lined with buildings that are both old and new, it maintains a connection to the past while looking to the future. The basins that once accommodated large cargo and passenger ships are now marinas docked with pleasure cruisers and sailboats, though the old locks of Louise Basin are still in use.

During its heyday in the 19th century, it was one of the world's five biggest ports, a hub of activity with commerce and transatlantic voyages. It was and still is a major contributor to the economic development of the region. Ships from here deal in commercial trade with over 60 countries, and the city is a popular cruise destination. On the very outskirts of Petit-Champlain, one of the areas that border the Vieux-Port, are some of the city's oldest defenses. Low walls, cannons, and a moat are the only remnants of what was once part of the Lower Town's fortifications. To celebrate the city's 400th anniversary in 2008, the waterfront was rejuvenated with a number of bike paths that follow the water's edge and takes cyclists right in to the Old Port. It's here along the quays and among the docked boats that people stop for an ice cream or a cold drink in the summer and look back at the city that stands, perfectly lit, on the hill. The newly built Vieux-Port Interpretation Centre presents exhibitions related to the timber trade and shipbuilding, and characters in period costumes evoke a sense of history as they tell old-time tales. Guided walking tours of the port are also available. **MAP 9:** 100 Quai St-André, 418/648-3300; May-Aug. daily 10am-5pm, Sept.-Oct. daily noon-4pm; free

Parliament Hill and the Plains Map 10

Fontaine de Tourny

Fontaine de Tourny was a gift from La Maison Simons (one of the oldest department stores in the province) to Québec City for its 400th anniversary in 2008. It came to its place in front of the Parliament by a circuitous route. Created in France in 1854, it won an award at the Universal Exposition in Paris the following year before being installed, in 1857, in the heart of Bordeaux in the Allées de Tourny. By 1960, however, the city no longer wanted the fountain, which was in a state of near disrepair. It was dismantled and stored in the Château Larivière near Bordeaux before being sold to a Parisian antiques dealer at the beginning of the 21st century.

During a trip to Paris in 2003, Peter Simons, president of the department store, discovered it in a flea market and had it shipped to Québec for restoration. Measuring seven meters high and four meters wide, it's adorned with 43 jets and decorated with statues, by sculptor Mathurin Moreau, of one man and three women symbolizing water, which matches well with the history of the port city. Five other statues were made from the same mold and can be found in cities across Europe, including Geneva in Switzerland and Porto in Portugal.

La Grande-Allée

Dubbed the "Champs d'Elysées of Québec," La Grande-Allée is one of the larger boulevards in the city and is the city's nightlife hot spot. It's lined with grand Victorian mansions, and the homes have been converted into cafés, restaurants, and nightclubs. Once lined with terraced houses, it was the chichi neighborhood of Québec, but many of those homes were torn down to make way for the Hôtel du Parlement, found on the south end of the *allée,* just in front of the St-Louis Gate.

It is the Grande-Allée that separates the rest of the city from the Plains of Abraham, which run along its back. The architecture of the strip's buildings is still stunning, with much of the stonework dating from the late 19th century.

MAP 10: Between Fontaine de Tourny and rue de l'Amérique Française

Hôtel du Parlement

The Parliament Building, house of the National Assembly of Québec, is one of the most impressive buildings in the province's capital city. Located on one of the highest spots of Upper Town, just outside the city walls, the quadrilateral building was constructed between 1877 and 1886 by the French architect Eugène-Étienne Taché. Inspired by the Louvre in Paris, the style of building, Second Empire neo-French Renaissance, is unique in North America. The front of the building also features a pantheon representing the province's rich history.

Incensed by the Durham Report, in which the British Lord said that the French-Canadians could not be civilized because they had no history, Taché included 15 statues depicting important figures in the province's history, to show that they did indeed have a strong past. Figures include Samuel de Champlain, Louis de Buade de Frontenac, James Wolfe, the Marquis de Montcalm, and, at the very top, an indigenous family. As the province's political life continues to grow, so does the number of statues; there are now 22 in front of the Parliament Building.

Since it is still a functioning government office, the only way to see the interior of the building is to take a free guided tour. At 30 minutes long, the tour provides a great opportunity to appreciate the unique architecture of the building, as well as gain insight into Québec's history and political scene. Make sure to have a photo I.D. with you, however, otherwise you won't pass the security check. In the summer, outdoor tours are also given to discover the surrounding gardens, which highlight the many trees and flowers of Québec and also give an overview of the many sculptures. All tours leave from the visitors center.

MAP 10: 1045 rue des Parliamentaires, 866/337-8837, www.assnat.qc.ca; first Tues. of Sept.-June 23 Mon.-Fri. 9am-4:30pm; June 24-first Mon. of Sept. Mon.-Fri. 9am-4:30pm, Sat.-Sun. 10am-4:30pm; free

Manège Militaire

This iconic piece of Canadiana was destroyed by fire in 2008, and though 90 percent of the museum's artifacts were saved, only the shell of the historic drill hall remains. Built in 1887, between the Plains of Abraham and the Grande-Allée, the Manège Militaire is home to the Voltigeurs de Québec, a primary reserve regiment founded in 1862. It was designed by Eugène-Étienne Taché, who also designed the Parliament Building, and the architectural style is inspired by the French chateaus of the 14th and 15th centuries, with circular turrets, pointy roofs, and high dormer windows. This particular style, extremely unique in North America, is recreated in countless other important structures in the country. It is one of the most recognized Canadian military buildings in the world.

MAP 10: 805 ave. Wilfrid-Laurier

★ Musée National des Beaux-Arts du Québec

Located in the middle of the Plains of Abraham, Musée National des Beaux-Arts du Québec holds the largest existing collection of Québec art, with works dating from the 17th century onward. The major focus here is on fine art, and the exhibits rarely revolve around the work of contemporary artists, though plans for a new addition will hopefully change that.

The musuem consists of three distinct structures: the Gérard-Morisset Building, the Charles-Baillairgé building, and the Grand Hall. Each has its own atmosphere and the work exhibited therein reflects that. Inaugurated in 1933, Gérard-Morisset is classical in style. It was designed by architect Wilfrid Lacroix and built in a neo-Italian Renaissance style. The first of the buildings to hold the museum's collection, it's full of white marble, wide Victorian steps, sculpted ceilings, and columns, and it's here that you'll find permanent collections dedicated to Québécois artists like Emile Bourdos and others.

Much less conventional is the Charles-Baillairgé building, a former prison. It was incorporated into the museum in 1991 but retains a number of cells, which visitors are invited to explore. Opened in 1867, the prison was modeled after the Auburn Penitentiary in New York state and was all about rehabilitation through isolation. Overpopulated from the beginning, it sheltered not only criminals but the poor and needy. Despite its old-fashioned design, it housed inmates until 1970.

The Grand Hall joins these two structures with its pyramid like glass facade, which adds light and airiness to the entire structure.

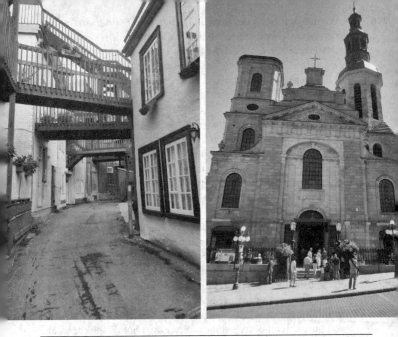

clockwise from top left: the hidden rue Sous-le-Cap, Lower Town; Basilique-Cathédrale Notre-Dame-de-Québec, Lower Town; the Musée National des Beaux Arts, Parliament Hill and the Plains

A monument directly out front of the museum commemorates the place where General James Wolfe was shot and killed.

MAP 10: Parc des Champs-de-Bataille, 418/644-6460, www.mnba.qc.ca; June-Aug. Thurs.-Tues. 10am-6pm, Wed. 10am-9pm, Sept.-May. Tues. and Thurs.-Sun. 10am-5pm, Wed. 10am-9pm; $18 adults, $16 seniors, $10 youth (13-30), children 12 and under free

Observatoire de la Capitale

It might not look like much on the outside, but on the 31st floor of the building is one of the best views of the city. Perfect for a general overview of Québec, at 221 meters high the *observatoire* is the highest spot in Québec and offers 360-degree views of the city and its environs.

As you look out over the city at various vantage points, you will see important buildings and monuments, pointed out and explained on the easy-to-read plaques that adorn the windows. Sights like the far-off Québec bridge are easily seen, along with the Laurentian mountains and the St-Lawrence River. Alongside points of interest, the Observatoire de la Capitale also gives you information on the province and its history, such as the destruction of Chinatown, which took place to make way for highways to the suburbs. Temporary exhibits, including photographs of local sights, are also on view.

MAP 10: 1037 rue de la Chevrotière, 418/644-9841, www.observatoirecapitale. org; Feb.-Canadian Thanksgiving daily 10am-5pm; $10 adults, $8 seniors and students, children 12 and under free

★ Parc des Plaines d'Abraham

It was here on the Plains of Abraham on September 13, 1759, that the French fell to the British, forever changing the course of North American history. After Champlain's arrival in 1608, there were skirmishes on and off with the British, who at the time were fighting for control of the North American colonies against the French, but it wasn't until 1759 that the real battle took place.

Led by General James Wolfe, the British army advanced up the St-Lawrence in the spring of 1759, setting up camp north of Québec. During that summer, they laid a near constant siege on the city, destroying houses and monuments but not breaking French general Montcalm's reserve. For all intents and purposes, life continued within the walls of the city amid the bombardments and fires. The siege lasted three long months. With winter approaching, Wolfe discovered the Canadians were awaiting a shipment of supplies from France to arrive on September 13. The supplies never arrived, but Wolfe continued with his plan regardless, maneuvering his men through the hard-to-navigate narrows in rowboats and mounting the cliff by way of a dried-up creek. By the time the Canadians

The longest cantilever bridge in the world, the Pont de Québec is also the easternmost bridge to cross the St-Lawrence River. Measuring 987 meters long, 29 meters wide, and 104 meters high, it has three highway lanes, one rail line, and one pedestrian walkway, and connects Québec City in the north with Lévis in the south.

Before the bridge was completed, after two disasters, the only way to get from one side of the St-Lawrence to the other was by ferry. Politicians and government officials were looking into building a bridge as early as 1852, but it wasn't until the turn of the century that construction got underway, headed by the Phoenix Bridge Company out of Pennsylvania.

In the summer or 1907, with three years of work nearing completion, the bridge collapsed, killing 75 workers, the majority of which were Mohawk steelworkers from the Kahnawake reserve near Montréal. Though engineer Norman McClure had noticed abnormalities in the foundation structure, his eventual call to halt production never made it to Québec. That same afternoon the southern arm and central section collapsed into the river in 15 seconds.

After a Royal Commission of Inquiry, construction started on a second bridge. This time construction was headed by three engineers: Canadian H. E. Vautelet, Maurice Fitzmaurice from Britain (who worked on the construction of the Forth Bridge in Scotland), and Chicago's Ralph Modjeski. With the bridge nearing completion, the central span was raised into position on September 11, 1916, only to crash into the river, killing 13 workers. Because it was in the midst of World War I, rumors quickly spread that it was German sabotage. It soon became clear, however, that it was another unfortunate accident.

Reconstruction started almost immediately after the collapse and the project was granted special permission to use steel, which was in high demand because of the war effort. After nearly 20 years of construction, the bridge opened for rail traffic on December 3, 1919. Today it is still one of the most impressive engineering feats in North America. Though it's not visible from downtown Québec City, those traveling to and from Québec City by Autoroute Duplessis or heading for a stroll beside the river in Parc de la Plage Jacques-Cartier will get a stunning view of the bridge in all its glory.

arrived on the battlefield, the British army was already in formation. It was all over in 15 minutes. Wolfe was shot and killed on the spot, but Montcalm was only wounded; he was rushed back inside the city walls, where he was taken to a friend's house and died the following day. Five days later, Québec capitulated.

The peculiar name Plains of Abraham can be traced as far back as 1635, when Abraham Martin, a pilot of the St-Lawrence and a friend of Samuel de Champlain, was given 12 acres of land in the area and an additional 20 acres 10 years after. Today there is little trace of the battle on the rolling green hills of the plains that border the cliff above the river. The grandiose stone building set back from the Plains houses the interpretation center, which offers a multimedia exhibit of its history, from the battle to its popularity with prostitutes in the 19th century and as a choice spot for duels, hangings, and the Stanley Cup playoffs. The park itself was part of the 300th anniversary celebrations and was designed by Frederick Todd. Many of the cannons that line the park were gifts from other nations to remind people that this was once a battlefield.

If you're interested in doing more than just strolling and picnicking in the park, you can head to the **Discovery Pavillon** on the Plains where you can visit the Odyssey exhibit about the battle ($10 adults, $8 seniors and students, 12 and under free).

MAP 10: 835 ave. Wilfrid-Laurier, 418/649-6157, www.theplainsofabraham.ca; daily 10am-5pm; free

Tours Martellos

In 1807 the United States Congress closed U.S. ports to all exports and restricted imports from Britain because of British and French interference with U.S. merchant ships during the Napoleonic Wars. Dubbed the American-Anglo crisis, it prompted Sir James Craig, then governor in chief of Canada, to increase the city's fortifications. Built between 1808 and 1812, four Martello towers were constructed around Québec as defenses and were positioned at various points outside of the city walls, mostly along the Plains of Abraham.

Round in shape, with limited openings, the west sides of the towers were built stronger than the east sides, based on the idea that if an attack were to happen, it would likely come from the west. In the event that the Martellos were under siege from the east, the eastern wall could easily be battered down and the men would be able to escape and continue fighting.

The smooth sandstone was cut in such a way that the constructions are perfectly rounded. Each Martello has a single door, placed at 4.5 meters above ground, 2.5 times the height of men at that time. It was originally reached by a ladder.

They became obsolete in the 1860s but continue to stand as monuments of and windows onto the city's past. Tour Martello 1, located on the Plains of Abraham, hosts an exhibition in summer (mid-June-early Sept.) inviting visitors to discover the military history and examine the lives of the soldiers who occupied the towers. Tour Martello 2, located not far from the Plains on the corner of Taché and Wilfrid-Laurier, invites you to drink beer in 19th-century style while you discuss the appropriate punishment for a British solider with the locals. These are hosted daily July-August and on weekends from late August to early September. An adult must accompany those under 18.

MAP 10: Parc des Champs-de-Bataille, 418/648-5371, www.ccbn-nbc.gc.ca; mid-June-early Sept. daily 10am-5pm; $14 adults, $10 seniors and students, $4 children (included with entrance into Plains of Abraham's Odyssey tour)

Saint-Jean-Baptiste and Saint-Roch

Église Saint-Jean-Baptiste

Built in 1882, this parish church is one of the most stunning in Québec City. Situated outside of the walls in Saint-Jean-Baptiste, a neighborhood that at the time was home to blue-collar workers of both French-Canadian and Irish origin, it's now surrounded by shops, restaurants, and residential homes.

A fire destroyed the previous church and much of the neighborhood in 1881, and the job of rebuilding the church was passed on to Joseph-Ferdinand Peachy. Of mixed Québécois (his mother) and Irish (his father) descent, Peachy was an ideal choice for an architect in this region. First learning the craft under Thomas Baillairgé, he started his own architecture firm in 1866. Inspired by both a church built in the 12th century and Église-de-la-Sainte-Trinité in Paris (which was built a mere 10 years earlier), Église Saint-Jean-Baptiste is a combination of very distinct styles: neo-Renaissance, neo-Roman, and Second Empire.

Though the facade is unmistakably Second Empire, and almost a direct copy of the Sainte-Trinité, the interior styles are subtler. The gallery features semicircles under the windows as well as triptychs in the arcade, both neo-Roman elements. Neo-Renaissance, meanwhile, can be seen in the use of blue pastel for the roof and in the placement of the window.

The church opened to the public in 1884, but it wasn't until 1896 that the church would be completely finished. Staying close to its parish roots, much of the financing for the church came from the public, and many of the church's embellishments, from the pews to the baldaquin, were made in Québec City, by members of the parish. Only three elements came from outside of the province: the Italian ceramic floor tiles, the paintings of the stations of the cross, and the three types of white marble that are used throughout, on the pillars and for the statues. Even the organ was built by local Napoléon Déry in 1885, though it was reconstructed by the Casavant brothers in 1921.

MAP 11: 400 rue St-Jean, 418/525-7188, www.jeandominique.org; Mon.-Sat. noon-4pm, Sun. 11am-4pm; tours daily; free

Jardin Saint-Roch

Once an empty dirt lot, the Jardin Saint-Roch has become a symbol for the ongoing revitalization of the Saint-Roch (pronounced ROCK) area in the city's Lower Town. Inaugurated in 1992, it was

New Québec: Up-and-Coming Limoilou

Like its neighbor Saint-Roch, Limoilou is fast becoming one of the coolest neighborhoods in the city. Full of cozy bars and cafés, artist boutiques, kid-friendly restaurants, and some of the best food shops in Québec City, it's an ideal place to spend the day wandering and scouring for antiques.

Situated across the St-Charles River, it is one of the oldest boroughs in the city. The first thoroughfare, now called 1e avenue (1st Avenue) was built in 1665. The area was entirely rural up until the end of the 19th century. Its proximity to downtown and placement alongside the river allows for an exceptional view of the city. It's a predominantly residential neighborhood, and the majority of shops and cafés are found in Vieux-Limoilou, easily reached by crossing the rue du Pont in Saint-Roch. Inspired by the grid system used in New York, the streets and avenues are numbered. The majority of cafés and shops are concentrated on 3e avenue, a continuation of rue du Pont on the other side of the St-Charles River. Cafés and neighborhood shops are on 1e avenue, while 2e avenue is perfect for taking in the old Victorian architecture and apartment blocks with spiral staircases, reminiscent of those in Montréal's Plateau.

Open and bright with a modern, minimalist decor, **Le Fun en Bouche** (1073 3e ave., 418/524-7272, www.lefunenbouche.com, Tues. 9am-2pm, Wed.-Sun. 8am-2pm, $10) is a neighborhood bistro in the heart of Vieux-Limoilou. Head here for the daily brunch and try the eggs Benedicts or French toast. The lunch selections include bagel with smoked trout and blueberry port spread, and smoked chicken, leek, and parmesan quiche. If you're in the mood for something to warm you up, **Soupe et Cie** (522 3e ave., 418/948-8996, www.soupecie.com, daily 11am-9pm, $15) has hearty soups and open-faced sandwiches on the menu. Closer to the community, this long restaurant with brick walls, old chandeliers, and tons of bright cushions is a cozy place to grab a bite. Despite its chic decor, it's kid-friendly—in fact, kids rule here and their exuberance and chitchat make up most of the ambience.

Just down the block is **Hosaka-Ya** (491 3e ave., 418/529-9993, Tues.-Fri. 11:30am-2pm and 4:30pm-9pm, Sat.-Sun. 4:30pm-9pm, $10), a relaxed Japanese restaurant inspired by the traditional *izakaya*. The menu is more well-rounded than most, offering classic dishes like *gyoza* and udon noodles as well as seasonal sushi dishes. They've also opened a **Ramen** (75 St-Joseph E.) in St-Roch. If you're looking for a drink, stop into **Le Bal du Lézard** (1049 3e ave., 418/529-3829, www.lebaldulezard.

one of the first places to get a much-needed facelift. With the opening of the park, the centerpiece of which is a waterfall featuring local stone, other businesses came to the area, taking up residence in old warehouses and factories and transforming them into workable, creative environments.

Displayed in the park are busts of René Richard, Alfred Pellan, and Horatio Walker, three important Québécois painters. Though their styles differed wildly, they represent the diversity and the richness of art and culture in Québec. The park is now surrounded by gaming companies, art studios, galleries, and theaters.

com, daily 2pm-3am), a friendly little neighborhood bar that's been a staple here since 1985. It has a laid-back feel and features a foosball table and nice sidewalk *terrasse* come summer. For a cozy, rustic bar, you can't do much better than **La Souche** (801 Chemin de la Canardière, 418/742-1144, www. lasouche.ca, Mon.-Wed. 11am-1am, Thurs.-Fri. 11am-3am, Sat. 3pm-3am, Sun. 3pm-1am, $7), or "The Stump" in English. This local bar offers a number of local brews in a relaxed, stump-strewn setup. They also have a patio come summer.

Decked out in red and green table-cloths and multicolored streamers adorning the walls, **Restaurant la Salsa** (1063 3e ave., 418/522-0032, Tues.-Sat. 11:30am-10pm, $15) is one of the most authentic Mexican restaurants in the city. The interior might border on kitsch, but their *pupusas*, enchiladas, and tamales are nothing but classic. Cheese lovers should make a stop at **Yannick Fromagerie** (901 3e ave., 418/614-2002, www.yannick-fromagerie.ca), which specializes in specialty cheese from Québec, while a fresh baguette from **La Fournée Bio** (1296 ave. 3e, 418/522-4441, Mon.-Wed. 7am-6:30pm, Thurs.-Fri. 7am-7pm, Sat.-Sun. 7am-5:30pm, $10) acts as the perfect accompaniment. Open for over 14 years, La Fournée Bio is an artisanal organic bakery that makes everything from croissants to sourdough and even serves a good cup of coffee.

New on the scene is **La Planque** (1027 ave. 3e, 418/914-8780, www. laplanquerestaurant.com, Tues.-Fri. 11:30am-2pm and 5:30pm-close, Sat. 5:30pm-close, $25), a casual fine-dining restaurant with a young, superstar chef whose creations, like scallop "ratatouille" and roasted pig's foot, garnered the establishment a nomination for best new Canadian restaurant in 2013, as well as clients from across the St-Charles River.

For a bit of antiquing, head into **Le Retour du Passé** (500 1e ave., 418/524-8885, www.leretourdupasse. net, Mon.-Sat. 9am-5pm, Sun. 9am-4pm), an antiques store that deals in old electronics like radios, clocks, and record players, as well as the usual mishmash of stuff. **Aarticle 721** (721 3e ave., 418/742-4333, Tues.-Sun. 11am-6pm) specializes in locally made products for the home and for the child, man, or woman in your life. They've got everything from pine-apple printed pillows to googly-eyed baby onesies. **La Boutique du Skate** (412 3e ave., 418/781-2030, Tues.-Fri. and Sun. noon-5pm, Sat. 10am-4pm) has a selection of skateboarding shoes as well as a huge selection of boards—perfect if you're traveling with your teen.

MAP 11: Between Côte d'Abraham and blvd. Charest at rue du Parvis and rue de la Couronne; daily 24 hours; free

★ Rue Saint-Jean

This section of rue St-Jean, part of the area known as Faubourg Saint-Jean-Baptiste, is a continuation of the St-Jean found within the city's historic walls. And though these two sides of the street—within and without the walls—are linked by a shared past, their appearance and history are markedly different. The word *faubourg* refers to "outskirts" in English, and during the early days of the city, when its gates were opened in the morning and closed in the evening, that's exactly what Faubourg Saint-Jean Baptiste was, an outskirt with no services or protection available from the city center once the gates were locked.

In the beginning of the 18th century, craftsmen built their workshops and homes along the inside walls of the fortifications. In 1745, however, the defenses were expanded, forcing many to move. This construction pushed them outside of the walls and they quickly established themselves and took their trades to the *faubourg*, bringing commerce to the area for the first time. In 1845, however, the first of two fires would decimate the area. Two churches, three schools, and 1,300 homes were burned to the ground during the 1845 fire, which subsequently led to the widening of the street. This and other fire prevention measures, such as restrictions on the layout of foyers in homes, were soon put into practice. In 1881 the area was hit with a second fire, and in just seven hours the church went up in flames and 5,000 were left without homes. This time the architectural restrictions were more drastic and wood was banned in construction.

These two disasters and the resulting architectural restrictions, coupled with a meshing of cultures that came later (the working-class Protestants and Catholics), have created the vibrant street today. The *faubourg* remains a vital part of day-to-day life as one of the busiest commercial streets in a busy residential neighborhood. As you wander along the street, the city's history is mapped out before you in the various architectural styles and businesses telling the story of each important epoch.

MAP 11: Between Autoroute Dufferin and ave. Salaberry

Rue Saint-Joseph

From the end of the 19th-century until the 1960s, this was one of the most important commercial streets in the city. Akin to Fifth Avenue in New York, it was the chichi shopping district, the home of upscale shops and historic department stores. The construction of large shopping centers on the outskirts of town in the 1950s and '60s, however, drew consumers out of the downtown core. Soon the stores left too, moving to new digs in the suburban malls, leaving the stores boarded up and the street run-down.

With hopes of luring business and shoppers back to the street, the city decided to turn it into the closest thing they could to a mall. In 1974, they covered the majority of the street with a Plexiglas arcade. Instead of drawing business, however, the new scheme attracted the marginalized and disenfranchised—the arcade was ideal shelter against the elements. Except for department store Laliberté and the Brunet pharmacy next door, who resisted the original exodus, most businesses consisted of cheap cafés and diners and five-and-dime stores.

It was Mayor Jean-Paul L'Allier, who governed for four terms, who would eventually bring business back to the area and the street. His first gamble was convincing Université Laval to move its art school from its campus on the fringes of the city to an old, unoccupied corset factory. The gamble paid off, and slowly but surely other businesses, drawn by incentives, returned to the strip. Sections of the Plexiglas eyesore, however, remained. It was fully removed for the city's 400th anniversary in 2008, but there are still sections along this diverse and interesting street where you can see where the arcade roof once sat.

MAP 11: Between rue St-Dominique and rue Caron

St-Matthew Church and Cemetery

Distinctly English with its slender steeple and neo-Gothic stonework, reminiscent of medieval English parish churches, St-Matthew Church and Cemetery stands out in an otherwise French-influenced Faubourg St-Jean Baptiste. The first cemetery in the city to exclusively bury Protestants, it encircled the church and was in use from 1772 to 1860. It is the burial place of many of the earliest English settlers in Canada and is the oldest cemetery in Québec City.

The church was originally the city gravedigger's house. It was only in 1822 with the arrival of French-speaking Protestant immigrants from the Channel Isles that services started to be held in French. By 1827, the services had become so popular, with a French service in the morning and an English one in the evening that the house was modified into a chapel. Destroyed by the great fire of 1845, it was rebuilt into today's incarnation by John Cliff. The interior, which now houses a public library, maintains its late-19th-century architecture with its exposed beams, rounded moldings at the top of the arcades, and delicate embellishments in the stonework.

Today it is a public library, and visitors can stroll among the bookshelves and admire the preserved interior, which has remained virtually untouched.

MAP 11: 755 rue St-Jean, 418/641-6798, www.bibliothequesdequebec.qc.ca; Mon.-Tues. and Thurs. noon-5:30pm, Wed. noon-8pm, Fri. 10am-5:30pm, Sat.-Sun. 1pm-5pm; free

Greater Québec City   Map 12

Aquarium du Québec

Staying true to its roots, this aquarium specializes in boreal and arctic wildlife, though over 10,000 animals call this place their home. It's divided into eight areas, both indoor and outdoor, and the main attraction is the Awesome Ocean, a glass tunnel through a massive seawater tank that allows visitors to get up close and personal with the marine life. Species from Québec wetlands and the St-Lawrence River are also here, along with polar bears, harp seals, and walruses from both coasts in the Arctic display. The newest addition is a tropical exhibition space showcasing jellyfish, stingrays, seahorses, and other southern species.

First opened in 1956 as a marine biology laboratory and research center, it soon attracted visitors eager to see the species that occupied the two aquariums. Continuing its slow growth over the next 40 years, the sight was given a major renovation in 2002 that saw it expand with outdoor gardens and seal and polar bear viewing pools. Located just outside of the city in Sainte-Foy, this is a great attraction for families and has drawn over eight million visitors.

In summertime kids can cool off in the adjoining water park or clamber their way through the Abre-en-Abre pathway adventure.

MAP 12: 1675 ave. des Hôtels, Sainte-Foy, 866/659-5264, www.sepaq.com/aquarium; June-early Sept. daily 10am-5pm, early Sept.-May daily 10am-4pm; $17 adults, $15.50 seniors, $8.50 children 3-17

Restaurants

Look for ★ to find
recommended restaurants.

Highlights

★ **Best Views:** Le Café de la Terrasse in Château Frontenac is in a picturesque setting looking out over the St-Lawrence (page 351).

★ **Best Place to Get a Taste of the North:** The menu at **Chez Boulay Bistro Boréal** is full of game and fish, with a focus on meats that are sustainable and come from the northern part of the province (page 353).

★ **Best Late-Night Eats:** Credited with popularizing poutine, **Chez Ashton** is Québec's preeminent fast-food joint and the ideal spot to refuel after a night on the town (page 356).

★ **Best Tasting Menu:** One of the best haute cuisine restaurants in the city, **Restaurant L'Initiale** features tasting menus with local food in a down-to-earth, modern interior (page 360).

★ **Most Authentic Québécois Grub:** Established in 1975, **Buffet de l'Antiquaire** serves heaping portions of traditional cuisine and some great breakfasts in a tiny 1950s-style diner (page 361).

★ **Best Upscale Bistro:** Situated on a tiny street in the Vieux-Port, **L'Échaudé** has both an elegant and relaxed atmosphere with classic bistro dishes (page 361).

★ **Best Café:** Brûlerie Saint-Roch is packed for a reason: The lattes here are the best and the ambience is effortlessly cool (page 370).

★ **Most Authentic Crêpes:** Run by an expat from Brittany, **Crêperie Le Billig** serves up the best crêpes in the city, which are even more delicious when you down them with cider (page 372).

★ **Most Bang for Your Buck:** Eat among savvy locals at **Le Clocher Penché,** where the bistro fare is made with fresh, regional ingredients and the bill is always a pleasant surprise (page 373).

★ **Most Likely to Surprise:** Both the wine and food menu change regularly at **Le Moine Échanson,** an unassuming restaurant that's all about getting you to discover new flavors from various corners of the globe (page 373).

PRICE KEY

$ Entrées less than CAN$15
$$ Entrées CAN$15–25
$$$ Entrées more than CAN$25

With the most restaurants per capita in the country, Québec City has no shortage of choice when it comes to dining. The challenge here isn't finding a decent place to eat, it's deciding which ones you have time for. The number of noteworthy, award-winning chefs and restaurants in Québec, well respected for its gastronomy, can be both tiring and exhilarating. Whether serving up a simple breakfast or an intricate haute-cuisine meal, chefs tend toward *terroir,* cooking that uses local produce and ingredients. In this region of the province those ingredients include wild game, such as elk, red deer, and bison, and seafood like scallops and cod.

Whereas the big trend at Montréal restaurants is market-fresh cuisine cooked by up-and-coming chefs in a boisterous atmosphere, the trend in Québec is more traditional, with a focus on details and inventive preparation, though a few young, breakout stars can be found, mostly in the Saint-Roch section of town. Even the decor of some of the city's best restaurants can feel a little staid and reserved—few, if any, of the city's restaurants turn into nightclubs once the tables have been cleared. The ones that do, however, can be found on the Grande-Allée, just outside the old walls.

Since so many of the restaurants offer top-quality ingredients and service, the price tag can also be high, though it's often worth it. One way to circumvent the cost without sacrificing the experience is to order the table d'hôte, which gives you the option of a three-course meal, usually appetizer, main, and dessert, for a set price. Another option is to go to one of the more expensive restaurants for lunch. Following the French tradition, restaurants here serve lunch well into the afternoon (service ends around 2pm), often with a specific lunchtime menu. Also in the French tradition is the city's love affair with cafés and bakeries; like in Montréal, they are abundant and delicious.

Barely a street goes by that doesn't feature a cute, independent café or two, most of which serve delectable pastries, light lunches, and choice coffee. Though you can always get your coffee to go, it's rare to see resident Québeckers striding along with their lattes; in fact, there are only two Starbucks in the city, and other chain coffee shops are just as rare. Bakeries, too, can be found in every neighborhood, each offering its own take on freshly-baked bread and pastries.

There are a couple things, however, that the Québec culinary scene is lacking: vegetarian and ethnic restaurants. Though some restaurants offer a vegetarian option, many do not, and doing research ahead of time is sure to save some frustration. Vegetarians who eat fish have abundant choices, but vegans will be sorely disappointed. When it comes to ethnic eats in Québec, Asian cuisines are the most popular; there are good Chinese and Vietnamese restaurants available. Japanese is a little harder to find, but the restaurants that do exist have excellent sushi, thanks to the abundance of fresh fish.

The city is no stranger to tourists, and menus in Québec are often written in English. Even when they're not, there's no reason to be shy; servers are happy to translate for you. A lot of fuss can be made about the dangers of falling into a "tourist trap" when you're visiting a city like Québec, but the reality is, most restaurants, regardless of the number of tourists at their tables, are adept at making some seriously good meals. Whether you're enjoying a tasting menu by one of the top chefs or eating meat pie by candlelight in a laid-back bistro, you'll always find a lively and welcoming atmosphere—the city's most charming and infectious trait.

Vieux-Québec's Upper Town

Map 8

ASIAN

Apsara [$$]

If you're fed up with bistro fare and all this "Europe in North America" business, head over to Apsara for some traditional Asian cooking. The decor here doesn't stray far from typical dining rooms, with its white tablecloths and wicker chairs, but a sense of the Far East is evoked in the golden statues, Thai artwork, and traditional masks featured throughout the restaurant. The ambience is quiet and calm with traditional music playing in the background and impeccable service. Apsara specializes in Cambodian, Thai, and Vietnamese cuisine, and with five or six mains available from each region, deciding on a single dish can be tough. Those facing a bout of indecision should go for the Apsara Plate, featuring dishes from each country, including Khemara beef from Cambodia and Vietnamese shrimp d'Anam.

MAP 8: 71 rue d'Auteuil, 418/694-0232, www.restaurantapsara.com; Mon.-Fri. 11:30am-2pm and 5:30pm-10:30pm, Sat.-Sun. 5:30pm-10:30pm

Chez Soi La Chine $

The sign at the entrance reads Authentic Chinese Food, a simple but bold statement in a city that isn't overflowing with ethnic food choices. It's located on the down slope of a hilly street, and the sidewalk cuts in front of the door at nearly a 45-degree angle. Inside, the yellow paper lanterns and traditional Chinese music are just about the only Asian touches in this otherwise sparse restaurant. Despite its austerity, it's one of the best Asian restaurants in the city, serving up traditional Chinese fare that is both filling and tasty. It's popular with young locals and the city's Asian community, and specialties like duck with Chinese mushrooms, crispy chicken, and perfectly steamed pork dumplings keep customers coming back. There is, however, one ingredient this place is missing: alcohol. It's a BYOB venue, so don't forget to bring a bottle of wine or beer with you to dinner.

MAP 8: 27 rue Ste-Angèle, 418/523-8858; Tues.-Fri. noon-2pm and 5:30pm-10pm, Sat.-Sun. 5:30pm-10pm

CAFÉS AND CHEAP EATS

Café-Boulangerie Paillard $

Modern and open, the long communal tables of this pastry shop, bakery, and *sandwicherie* are cafeteria-like in style, but the tall ceilings and lots of light make it feel effortlessly spacious. In traditional New York style, you must line up to order, be it a fresh Paillard salad with walnuts, blue cheese, and pears or a frothy cappuccino and almond croissant. They're known for their macaroons, those sweet, one-bite-and-you're-done cookies; they come in a rainbow of colors and flavors and rival any that you'd find in the tiny back lanes of Paris.

MAP 8: 1097 rue St-Jean, 418/692-1221, www.paillard.ca; daily 7am-9pm

Chez Temporel $

Established in 1974, this two-story café on rue Couillard, a quaint and winding side street, has become an institution. A favorite with students and artists, it is frequented by locals who come here to grab a quiet coffee or light lunch, offering a nice alternative in the otherwise touristy and busy part of Old Québec. It's simply decorated, with wood tables, brick walls, and work by local artists on the wall, and the food follows suit with homemade croissants, muffins, soups, salads, and quiches.

MAP 8: 25 rue Couillard, 418/694-1813; daily 7am-1am

Le Petit Coin Latin $

Just inside the city walls on a steep side street you'll find Le Petit Coin Latin, one of the oldest cafés in Québec. Stone walls, a fireplace, and burgundy banquettes give it an intimate, homey atmosphere. Like its surroundings, the food here is unpretentious and includes Québécois classics like *tourtière au caribou* (caribou pie) and *tarte au sucre* (sugar pie). It's a popular place for breakfast and brunch, especially in the summer when the garden terrace is open out back; their plentiful omelets and *pain doré* will leave you stuffed. In winter, order the hearty and warming raclette.

MAP 8: 8½ rue Ste-Ursule, 418/692-2022; Mon.-Fri. 8am-11pm, Sat.-Sun. 7:30am-11pm

Les Trois Garçons $$

Started by three friends (hence the name, which means "Three Guys" in English) who wanted to create an eatery that towed the line between Parisian bistro and New York diner, Les Trois Garçons serves gourmet burgers and the like. Located on a bustling strip of rue St-Jean, the restaurant has a pleasant sidewalk patio in the summer that's almost always packed; its casual dining style is a nice change compared to some of the city's stuffier (and pricier) dining rooms. Outfitted in red, white, and black, it has a slight 1950s diner feel thanks to the art deco metal railing on the second floor that lets you oversee the diners below. The crowd here are in the know when it comes to food trends, and you'll often see diners chowing down on a Trio of Mini Burgers—the best way to taste them all.

MAP 8: 1084 rue St-Jean, 418/692-3900, www.bistro3garcons.com; Mon.-Wed. 7am-10pm, Thurs.-Fri. 7am-11pm, Sat. 8am-11pm, Sun. 8am-10pm

CRÊPERIES

Casse-Crêpe Breton $

No matter the time of day, the line at this bustling crêperie on St-Jean is usually out the door. Luckily, it moves pretty fast and customers are soon seated in the banquettes that line the restaurant's walls or at the bar with a full view of the action. Open since 1983, it can sometimes feel like an upper-class fast-food joint, in the swiftness of service and the way they churn out the crêpes. Choose from a list of suggestions—egg, bacon, mozzarella—or build your own with fillings like berries, chocolate, asparagus, and swiss cheese. While it's not the best crêperie in the city, it's a good choice for a quick and inexpensive meal.

MAP 8: 1136 rue St-Jean, 418/692-0438, www.cassecrepebreton.com; daily 7am-10pm

FRENCH
Le Café Buade $

Established in 1919, Café Buade is the oldest restaurant in the city. Not far from Château Frontenac and facing the Notre-Dame-de-Québec Cathedral, it's a popular place with both tourists and long-time regulars. Serving basic family restaurant fare like pasta, pizza, and prime rib, it may not be the best meal you'll eat in the city but it won't break the bank either. If you do find yourself intrigued by the homey and warm atmosphere, opt for a classic club sandwich or one of their generous breakfasts, available daily until noon.

MAP 8: 31 rue de Buade, 418/692-3909, www.cafebuade.ca; May-Sept. daily 7am-11pm, Oct.-Apr. daily 7am-9pm

★ Le Café de la Terrasse $$$

Situated in Château Frontenac with stunning views of the St-Lawrence, Le Café de la Terrasse is luxury without the price tag. Overseen by Baptiste Peupion, the newly appointed executive chef at Le Champlain, the café's haute-cuisine sibling, the menu varies according to season and tends toward regional gastronomy. The wine list too stays close to home and features many Canadian selections. The restaurant runs along the facade of the hotel, with picture windows onto the river. The soft green decor, reminiscent of a summerhouse, is welcoming and sumptuous. Mains include classics like beef Wellington and lamb with marinated herbs, and buffets are often theme-based, like the lavish brunch buffet. Backpackers and mature travelers alike come here to grab a pre-dinner or post-skiing cocktail, especially in winter when the city of Lévis is lit up across the water.

MAP 8: 1 rue des Carrières, 418/691-3763, www.fairmont.com/frontenac; daily 7am-2pm and 5:30pm-10pm

Le Champlain $$$

Chef Baptiste Peupion, originally from Paris, was appointed executive chef in early 2013 and has revamped the menu by adding touches of local *terroir* cooking to the traditional French cuisine. The storied restaurant (and hotel) went through a major overhaul in 2013-2014, and Peupion's dishes follow suit with a mix of contemporary and classic flavors. Located in the historic Château Frontenac, it has gorgeous views of the river and boasts a glass-roofed sun lounge. With patterned carpets, luxurious chandeliers, and rich

clockwise from top left: Brûlerie Saint-Roch; sidewalk terrasse at Lapin Sauté, Vieux-Québec's Lower Town; late-night eats at Chez Ashton

wood paneling, the decor is traditionally elegant. Though new flavors have been added to the menu, it retains much of its original charm, including the century-old tradition of afternoon tea, which is served June-October Thursday-Saturday. Reservations and smart casual attire are a must.

MAP 8: 1 rue des Carrières, 418/266-3905, www.fairmont.com/frontenac; daily 6pm-10pm

★ Chez Boulay Bistro Boréal $$$

This new addition to rue St-Jean is unlike any other dinning experience in the city. Jean-Luc Boulay, chef and owner of Saint-Amour, has teamed up with up-and-comer Arnaud Marchand to create a restaurant that's centered on cooking and delicacies from the northern, or boreal, region of the province. The menu is chock-full of game and fish, with a focus on meats that are sustainable. Standout dishes include confit bison cheeks, confit goose legs, and seared black cod with shellfish mousse. The decor is sleek and black with lots of banquette seating and chic white walls in the open concept dining room. Weather permitting, there's also an outdoor patio. Stop in for a three-course lunch if you fancy experiencing the boreal flavors with a smaller price tag.

MAP 8: 1110 rue St-Jean, 418/380-8166, www.chezboulay.com; Mon.-Fri. 11:30am-10:30pm, Sat.-Sun. 10am-10:30pm

Chez L'Autre $$

Opened in 2012, this low-key brasserie is the perfect antidote to fussy tasting menus. Located in Le Capitole, a theater/hotel that's also home to Italian restaurant Il Teatro, L'Autre has a prime location just outside the old walls on the Place d'Youville. In the summertime, the flower baskets overflow with color and the *terrasse* is bustling. It's the interior, however, that defines the restaurant. The black and white decor—white walls, white bar, black bistro chairs—is simply elegant and sets the tone for the menu, which features classic French bistro fare. Foie gras torchon, salmon tartar, and beef tenderloin with béarnaise sauce all make an appearance on the menu.

MAP 8: 964 rue St-Jean, 418/694-1199, www.lecapitole.com; daily 11am-10:30pm

La Crémaillère $$$

Just in front of City Hall, you'll find award-winning restaurant La Crémaillère. Situated in a historic Victorian townhouse, the rooms of the restaurant have been diligently restored to show the intricate moldings and woodwork of a bygone era. The rich, patterned upholstery contrasts nicely with the white walls, giving the setting a bit of a modern kick. Taking inspiration from both French and Italian traditions, dishes are classic in presentation and flavor.

House specialties include roasted rack of lamb, milk-fed veal, and lobster in champagne sauce. The atmosphere is elegant and romantic, making it perfect for a date night.

MAP 8: 73 rue Ste-Anne, 418/692-2216, www.cremaillere.qc.ca; Mon.-Fri. 11:30am-2:30pm and 5pm-10pm, Sat.-Sun. 5pm-10pm

Les Frères de la Côte ⓢⓢ

A cheerful and festive ambience oozes from this restaurant full of bon vivants. Located on one of the busiest corners in Old Québec, the casual dining room, decorated with checkered tablecloths and banquette seating, can be a bit cramped at times, with neighboring diners squished in beside each other. This is all part of the lively atmosphere, which in summer extends to a tiny sidewalk *terrasse*.

Cuisine here runs the gamut from *bavette de cheval* (horse flank) and osso bucco to thin-crust pizzas and mussels with fries.

MAP 8: 1190 rue St-Jean, 418/592-5445; Mon.-Fri. 11:30am-10pm, Sat.-Sun. 10am-10pm

Le Pain Béni ⓢⓢⓢ

Le Pain Béni is all about mixing influences. Located in the 200-year-old Auberge Place d'Armes, the dining room's stone walls are juxtaposed against the ultramodern design of bright orange chairs and simple table settings, creating a fresh and modern take on fine dining. On the menu you'll find dishes inspired by both French and Italian traditions, including lamb ravioli, beef tartare, goose leg confit, and parsnip gnocchi. With popular music on the sound system creating a laid-back ambience, there are few places that mix fine cuisine and contemporary atmosphere so well.

MAP 8: 24 rue Ste-Anne, 418/694-9485, www.aubergeplacedarmes.com; May.-Sept. daily 11:30am-10:30pm; Oct.-Apr. Mon. 11:30am-2pm, Tues.-Fri. 11:30am-2pm and 5:30pm-10pm, Sat. 5:30pm-10pm

Le Patriarche ⓢⓢⓢ

Situated in a converted heritage home that was built in 1827, Le Patriarche retains the feeling of an old house, giving it an especially warm and romantic atmosphere and making it a choice spot for couples. It specializes in *gastronomie du terroir,* and the service here is unique: Each course is served as a trio of dishes, sort of like a choose-your-own tasting menu. An order of Québec lamb, for example, comes as mini-servings of roasted lamb rack, pan-fried lamb loin, and braised lamb tongue. Since Patriarche emphasizes *terroir* cooking, wild game features on the menu, but they also have one of the better vegetarian selections, offering three mini-dishes that change daily.

MAP 8: 17 rue St-Stanislas, 418/629-5488, www.lepatriarche.com; July-Aug. daily 5:30pm-10pm, Sept.-June Wed. and Sat.-Sun. 5:30pm-10pm, Thurs.-Fri. 11:30am-2pm and 5:30pm-10pm

355

Le Saint-Amour ❸❸❸

Le Saint-Amour is one of the most renowned restaurants in Québec. Chef Jean-Luc Boulay has won all the honors, the most recent of which was a visit by Sir Paul McCartney. After his historic concert for the city's 400th anniversary in 2008, the former Beatle and noted vegetarian came here with his band. The French-inspired dishes are creative, though, sadly, not vegetarian-friendly. Try the homemade terrine cooked "sous-vide," stuffed and roasted Scallops from the Iles of Madelaeine, or the red deer seared and served with wild mustard seeds. Art nouveau touches can be found throughout the restaurant, framing the mirrors and illuminating the bar with a beautiful stained-glass mosaic. Watch the kitchen magic happen through the open kitchen design and sip a glass of red from their exquisite wine list, reputed to be one of the best in the country.

MAP 8: 48 rue Ste-Ursule, 418/694-0667, www.saint-amour.com; Mon.-Fri. 11:30am-2pm and 6pm-10pm, Sat. 5pm-10pm, Sun. 6pm-10pm

ITALIAN

Conti Caffe ❸❸❸

The resolutely modern decor of this Italian-style restaurant is a breath of fresh air compared to many restaurants in Old Québec that stick to a staid, traditional look. The little brother of Le Continental, from which it took its name, Conti Caffe has an atmosphere that is younger, more relaxed, and more fun than that of its older counterpart. It serves Italian dishes like veal parmigiana and spaghetti carbonara, and specialties include lamb chops, filet mignon, and pan-fried sea scallops. Of course, the classic brick and stone walls still add an air of charm and romance, but the rich blue walls and contemporary furnishing are a vibrant touch.

MAP 8: 32 rue St-Louis, 418/692-4191, www.conticaffe.com; daily 11:30am-11pm

Le Continental ❸❸❸

Waiters in white dinner jackets prepare mains tableside, making Le Continental the pinnacle of fine dining. Set in an elegant Victorian house, Le Continental is a traditional, rather formal restaurant known for impeccable service and unmatched cuisine. Blending Italian and French traditions, the restaurant is known for its flambé dishes, which include shrimp with whiskey, orange duckling, and flambé sirloin. Other classic dishes include braised veal sweetbreads and steamed snow crabs. Though there is no formal dress code, this is the time to break out your dinner jacket and dress shoes.

RESTAURANTS
VIEUX-QUÉBEC'S UPPER TOWN

MAP 8: 26 rue St-Louis, 418/694-9995, www.restaurantlecontinental.com; Mon.-Fri. noon-3pm and 6pm-11pm, Sat.-Sun. 6pm-9pm

Il Teatro $$

With one of the most eye-catching terraces in the city—with overflowing flower pots and a view of St-Jean Gate—Il Teatro is a no-brainer when it comes to dining alfresco and is popular with theater-goers and tourists alike. It's located in the magnificent Capitole de Québec theater (hence the name), and the interior is modern and welcoming with brick walls, simple decoration, and huge windows that look on to Place d'Youville. Chef Serge Gagné, despite his not-too-Italian name, has been cooking some of the best Italian food in the city for the past 18 years. The risotto al mascarpone and scaloppini del capo are some of the best dishes, and the tuna steak with pepper is perfect for fish lovers. Cap the night off with a cappuccino, a slice of *panforte,* and a stroll around the city's walls.

MAP 8: 972 rue St-Jean, 418/694-9996, www.lecapitole.com/en/restaurant.php; daily 7am-2am

LATE-NIGHT EATS

★ Chez Ashton $

Founded in 1969 by Ashton Leblond, Chez Ashton is fast food *à la québécoise.* Sure you can get your burgers and fries here, but what Ashton prides itself on is its poutine. It's the single culinary achievement of the region (origins remain obscure and hotly debated), and Mr. Leblond helped popularize the combination of French fries, cheese curds, and brown gravy that has since gone on to conquer the rest of the province. Add shredded turkey and green peas onto the rest and you have a *galvaude,* a popular selection here. The decor is typical of fast-food chains—neon lights, vinyl banquettes, and a crowd of starving late-night revelers. You can find many Chez Ashton locations in the city, including one in Saint-Roch (830 blvd. Charest, 418/648-0891) and one near the Parliament (640 Grande-Allée, 418/522-3449).

MAP 8: 54 Côte du Palais, 418/692-3055, www.chez-ashton.com; Sun.-Wed. 11am-2am, Thurs. 11am-4am, Fri.-Sat. 11am-4:30am

QUÉBÉCOIS

Aux Anciens Canadiens $$

Located in the oldest house in the city (built in 1675), Les Anciens Canadiens is firmly planted in Québécois tradition. It's not hard to fall for its charm, with its white-washed walls, red roof, and miniature stature. It's a huge tourist destination. Servers are dressed in slightly unconvincing old-timey costumes, and the food on the menu is traditional Québécois—that is to say, plentiful and heavy.

Despite the kitschy costumes and themed dining rooms, the food is excellent. If you want to discover everything about traditional regional cooking, try the Trapper's Treat (meat pie with a pheasant and bison casserole) or the Québec Tasting Platter (meat pie with meatball and pig's knuckle ragout and baked beans). As for dessert—well, you'd better like maple syrup.

MAP 8: 34 rue St-Louis, 418/692-1627, www.auxancienscanadiens.qc.ca; daily noon-9:30pm

Vieux-Québec's Lower Town

Map 9

CAFÉS AND CHEAP EATS

Les Cafés du Soleil $

Over 40 kinds of coffee, some from as far as India and Japan, line the walls of this Vieux-Port café. Dedicated to the art of coffee and coffee making, this popular neighborhood café, full of locals and browsing tourists, was originally a store selling espresso makers and other coffee accessories and making some *allongée* (long espresso) on the side. It only became a full-fledged café when they decided to make sandwiches and snacks for the customers who were spending more and more time hanging out and sampling their coffee. A small but lively place, it's usually packed with regulars. Besides coffee, they also offer sandwiches, salads, soups, and pastries, as well as a selection of teas.

MAP 9: 143 rue St-Paul, 418/692-1147; winter Mon.-Fri. 7am-5:30pm, Sat. 8:30am-5:30pm, Sun. 10am-5:30pm; summer Mon.-Wed. 7am-7pm, Thurs.-Fri. 7am-10pm, Sat.-Sun. 8:30am-10pm

CRÊPERIES

Café Bistro du Cap $$

On a narrow cobblestone street backing onto the sheer cliff face, Café Bistro du Cap is in a gem of a spot. With a small *terrasse* out front and a modest, no-frills interior, the entire atmosphere is unpretentious and intimate. This is a small operation run by a couple; he runs the kitchen while she runs the front of the house, so selection here isn't huge and is often determined by the availability. Praised by both locals and tourists, their menu includes items like pan-fried salmon, lamb shank, and chowder. They are especially known for their crêpes. Savory or sweet, the crêpes are some of the best in the city, and perfect for a mid-afternoon snack.

MAP 9: 67 rue du Sault-au-Matelot, 418/692-1326; Tues.-Sun. 11:30am-2:30pm and 5:30pm-9:30pm

A Quick Guide to Québécois Food

Over the past 400 years or so Québec has developed its own cuisine; some foods are variations on old French recipes and some are creations that are uniquely their own. In the early days of the colony much of Québec society relied on hunting and fishing for sustenance, and wild game is still a big part of cooking in the region. Here's a quick guide to some of the more common but obscure foods you may come across.

- **Caribou:** This is one of the more popular meats, and you'll find it on menus across the city. It's an especially popular ingredient in meat pies.

- **Caribou (the drink):** During the city's world-famous annual Winter Carnival this stuff is available in all the SAQs (liquor stores). This mixture of port, vodka, black-currant liqueur, and maple syrup might be tough to get down but it will keep you warm and give you enough courage to tackle *les glissades*—the enormous toboggan run on Terrasse Dufferin.

- **Cheese Curds:** This is the special cheese they put on top of poutine, but it is also eaten on its own as a snack and can be found at most corner stores. Made from fresh cheddar, it has a rubbery texture and squeaks when it's chewed.

- *Cheval:* Though it's not as common a meat here as in Belgium, horse can still be found on menus across the city, mostly likely listed as *bavette de cheval,* horse steak. Similar to beef in consistency, it is both sweeter and more tender.

- *Cretons:* If you order a traditional Québécois breakfast, there's a good chance you'll find a serving of this on your plate. A salty pork product, it's made by boiling the pork in milk with onions and spices until its consistency is halfway between a spread and a pâté. It's best eaten on toast.

- **Foie Gras:** Made from duck and goose liver (the name literally means "fatty liver"), this typical French dish has turned into an industry in Québec. Locally produced foie gras is now a staple in most

FRENCH

Café du Monde $$

Café du Monde is in the Vieux-Port on a quay that juts out into the river. Aiming to bring a little Rive-Gauche (Left Bank) to Québec, the interior is precisely decorated with black and white checkered tiles, walls of wine, and even black-apron-clad servers (who have tempered their accents in some cases) to really give diners that Parisian feel. Though the atmosphere isn't entirely convincing—since when is the Rive-Gauche surrounded by grain silos and shipping relics?—the food is, with mains like mussels, salmon tartare, and rabbit hindquarter transporting you across the Atlantic in no time.

MAP 9: 84 rue Dalhousie, 418/692-4448, www.lecafedumonde.com; Mon.-Fri. 11:30am-11pm, Sat. 9am-11pm

bistros and restaurants serving haute cuisine.

- ***Galvaude:*** A variation on poutine, this dish adds chicken and peas to the fries, gravy, and cheese for a more "rounded" meal.
- ***Grand-père dans le Sirop:*** A popular dessert during the Great Depression, this is essentially a sweet dumpling made by boiling batter in sugar water, then serving it doused with maple syrup. Translated it means "Grandpa in the syrup."
- ***Guedille:*** Found mostly in *casse-croûtes* (snack shacks), *guedilles* are hot dog buns stuffed with lettuce, mayonnaise, and just about anything else, including egg, chicken, and fries. Commonly found outside of the cities, it's one version of Québec's take on fast food.
- ***Oreilles de Crisse:*** Translated this means "Christ's ears." Made from fried salted pork, they've been a snack since the time of Nouvelle France. Variations on this can be found in upscale restaurants across the province, especially those that specialize in *terroir* cooking.
- **Poutine:** Fries, gravy, cheese curds—this is the unofficial national dish of Québec. Though poutine has recently been embraced by food lovers everywhere, it was invented in this region and remains close to locals' hearts.
- ***Ragoût de Pattes de Cochon:*** This stew made with pig's feet is part of the *réveillon,* or Christmas meal. A variation on this includes *ragoût de boulettes,* which means meatballs, though likely made with pork and not beef.
- ***Tourtière:*** Otherwise known as meat pie, this is likely the most common of all the dishes as well as the oldest. Records show that it was first being made in Québec as early as 1611. It's usually made with beef or pork, but different regions in the province have different versions. In Montréal, it's a shallow pie filled with ground pork, while in the Lac-Saint-Jean region, north of Québec City, the pie is deeper and made with wild game like moose, caribou, elk, and hare. It's called *cipaille* in most restaurants.

Le Cochon Dingue [$][$]

Started in 1979, French bistro Le Cochon Dingue (The Crazy Pig) has become one of the most popular restaurants in the city. Famous for mussels, steak frites, and pork filet mignon, they also serve breakfast and lunch, with daily specials. Though they've since opened other outlets, including one near rue Cartier (46 blvd. René-Lévesque, 418/523-2013), the original establishment is still the most charming, with brick walls, sharp white tablecloths, and bistro chairs. It's both elegant and relaxed. In summer, their sidewalk *terrasse* takes up almost the entire street, with Le Petit Cochon Dingue at number 24, serving coffees and sweets.

MAP 9: 46 blvd. Champlain, 418/694-0303, www.cochondingue.com; Mon.-Fri. 7am-11pm, Sat.-Sun. 8am-11pm

Lapin Sauté ❸❸❸

Run by the same people who own Le Cochon Dingue, Lapin Sauté (Jumping Rabbit) is more laid-back and romantic than its bustling neighbor. Located in a turn-of-the-20th-century home, the small dining room—it seats 32—has a rustic feel with a low, wood ceiling and a stone fireplace. The food here is rustic as well, specializing in country-style cuisine. Their specialty is rabbit, served in a pie, a cassoulet, or roasted with maple and raspberry sauce. They also have a refined kids' menu that includes grilled salmon and Caesar salad.

MAP 9: 52 rue du Petit-Champlain, 418/692-5325, www.lapinsaute.com; Mon.-Fri. 11am-10pm, Sat.-Sun. 9am-10pm

Le Quai 19 ❸❸

Located in an old stone warehouse in the heart of the Vieux-Port, Le Quai 19 (formerly Le 48 St-Paul) couldn't be in a better location. In summer, the large *terrasse* with chic black umbrellas and overflowing flowerpots is one of the most enviable places in the city. Forgoing typical French cuisine to focus on local produce and flavors, the new menu puts an emphasis on freshness, with the majority of the dishes featuring such treats as fish from New Brunswick, veal from Charlevoix, and chanterelle mushrooms from Québec. The interior is cozy but chic with the old gray stone walls providing an austere backdrop to the simple white banquette seating and black tables.

MAP 9: 48 rue St-Paul, 418/694-4448, www.lequai19.com; daily 7am-11am, 11:30am-2pm, and 5:30pm-11pm

★ Restaurant L'Initiale ❸❸❸

One of the most renowned restaurants in the city, this is a must for those who enjoy haute cuisine and is frequented by foodies from the world over. There is no set menu but various tasting menus that change with the seasons and the local products available. Known for his innovative dishes, head chef Yvan Lebrun marries unlikely flavors, such as suckling pig with squash, and crispy sweetbreads with mustard kidneys. Housed in a century-old building, the interior of l'Initiale is distinctly modern with a sleek comfortable design. The entire restaurant follows a beige and cream color scheme and this subtly works in achieving a rich atmosphere.

MAP 9: 54 rue St-Pierre, 418/694-1818, www.restaurantinitiale.com; Tues.-Fri. 11:30am-2pm and 6pm-9pm, Sat. 6pm-9pm

ITALIAN
La Pizz ❸❸

The delicious thin and crispy crust may be the trademark of this pizza joint, but the secret of their success is their ingredients. Fresh vegetables from the Marché du Vieux-Port and imported French cheese are mixed to produce unique flavor combinations, like tomato, bacon, egg, and Emmenthal or tomato, crème fraîche, leeks, scallops, and Emmenthal. The restaurant on St-Paul, which has a homey feel with bistro chairs and warm red walls, has been so successful that they recently opened another place right on Place Royale (3A Place Royale, 418/692-3003), making it a default tourist destination. So you can now eat your Frenchified 'za on the oldest spot in Canada.

MAP 9: 299 rue St-Paul, 418/692-5005, www.la-pizz.com; mid-Oct.-late May Mon.-Wed. 11:30am-2pm, Thurs.-Fri. 11:30am-10:30pm, late May-mid-Oct. daily noon-10:30pm

QUÉBÉCOIS

Brynd Smoked Meat $$

Located on the former spot of the famous Thomas Dunn Pub, Brynd specializes in smoked meat sandwiches, a well-known Montréal specialty. This Québec variation, a smoked meat sandwich on rye served with "class" (the "class" seems to apply solely to the fact that you can choose between fries or salad and you don't have to wait in line for an hour to order), is one of the best in the city. The decor is minimally chic with mirrors lining the walls and the wooden banquettes filled with local office workers and hungry tourists. The waiters in all black duds are especially cool and congenial.

MAP 9: 369 rue St-Paul, 418/692-4693, www.brynd.com; Sun.-Tues. 11am-9pm, Wed.-Thurs. 11am-10pm, Fri.-Sat. 11am-11pm

★ Buffet de l'Antiquaire $

Set among the chichi bistros and idyllic antiques stores of rue St-Paul, the Buffet de l'Antiquaire is a no-frills diner. Established in 1975, it serves up breakfasts and traditional Québécois grub like *ragoût de boulettes* (meatballs, potatoes, and gravy), *pâté à la viande* (meat pie), and *cipaille* (game meat pie). Usually the busiest place on the block, it's adored by locals and tourists alike for its old-time charm—diner stools, vinyl banquettes, and line cooks in full-view. The all-day-long breakfast is served in heaping amounts and with their unforgettable homemade jam. In summer, tables and chairs are set up on the sidewalk outside for a makeshift patio.

MAP 9: 95 rue St-Paul, 418/692-2661; daily 6am-11pm

★ L'Échaudé $$

With a stainless-steel bar and tables covered with butcher paper, the vibe at this Vieux-Qubébec bistro strikes the perfect balance of relaxed elegance. A new team behind this established name means almost everything (save for the decor) has undergone a makeover. A revamped menu—lobster tempura with risotto, mackerel with

clockwise from top left: French bistro Les Bossus, Saint-Roch; Le Clocher Penché, Saint-Roch; Le Café Buade, Vieux-Québec's Upper Town

mustard sauce—puts the focus on organic and locally sourced food, while the wine list is selected from a sustainable vineyard. Touches of classic bistro fare remain, however. As does the restaurant's dedication to excellent value. They recently introduced a specially priced after-9pm menu, perfect for tasting their wares at a fraction of the price.

MAP 9: 73 rue du Sault-au-Matelot, 418/692-1299, www.echaude.com; Mon.-Sat. 11:30am-2pm and 5pm-10pm, Sun. 10:30am-2:30pm and 5pm-10pm

Laurie Raphaël [$][$][$]

At Laurie Raphaël it's all about infusing the flavors and aromas of the region into the cuisine. Dishes include scallops, beef with truffle dressing, veal with zucchini flower, and orange soufflé. But, of course, the menu changes depending on the season, so check before booking. Those on a budget should try the "Chef! Chef!," a three-course meal ($30 at lunch, $60 at dinner) improvised by head chef Daniel Vézina. The interior is luxurious and inviting thanks to the subtle color palette, with tones of grays and sand; floor-to-ceiling windows open onto the dining room, but gauzy, sheer curtains afford the perfect balance of privacy and light. Reservations are a must.

MAP 9: 117 rue Dalhousie, 418/692-4555, www.laurieraphael.com; Tues.-Fri. 11:30am-2pm and 6:30pm-10pm, Sat. 6:30pm-10pm

Panache [$][$][$]

Situated in the Auberge St-Antoine, this former 19th-century warehouse has been transformed into one of the most inviting dining rooms in the city, with exposed wood beams, stone walls, and original wood flooring. A wrought-iron staircase leads to a second dining level, with tables tucked away under the eaves for an intimate and romantic setting. Using local ingredients and taking much of his inspiration from the fresh produce available, chef Julien Dumas creates dishes that cater to the season and the palate. Foie gras, veal sweetbreads, and local Québec cheese, however, can always be found on the menu. Reservations are recommended.

MAP 9: 10 rue St-Antoine, 418/692-1022, www.restaurantpanache.com; Mon.-Tues. 6:30am-10:30am and 6pm-10pm, Wed.-Fri. 6:30am-10:30am, noon-2pm, and 6pm-10pm, Sat.-Sun. 7am-11am and 6pm-10pm

SSS [$][$]

The latest endeavor from the people who brought you Toast!, SSS (Simple, Snack, Sympathique) is more relaxed and hipper (not counting the name) than its progenitor. Drawing a young, fashionable crowd, it has two different rooms: a small bar lounge with high tables, red accents, and lips on the wallpaper, and an adult dining room with stone walls, black-lacquered floors, and crisp white tablecloths. The main menu is French-influenced and heavy on the meat, with dishes like ribs, New York cut steak, and pasta with duck confit. The relaxed atmosphere, along with a late-night kitchen cooking up snacks like grilled chicken curry, gourmet hot dogs, and burgers, makes it a great choice for an evening cocktail or late dinner.

MAP 9: 71 rue St-Paul, 418/692-1991, www.restaurantsss.com; daily 11:30am-2pm and 5pm-midnight

Toast! 🟠🟠🟠

Located in the heart of the Vieux-Port in the Priori hotel, Toast! offers modern cuisine in a picturesque setting. The atmosphere here is hip, with warm, orange-hued lighting illuminating the 200-year-old stone walls. Using French and Italian influences, dishes include vegetarian risotto with stuffed zucchini, salmon with smoked sour cream, and red deer bacon. For dessert, they offer a selection of cheeses, including a Québec cheese plate, *croque monsieur*, and a sheep's milk plate with figs and rye bread. In the summer, a large terrace is open out back, drawing everyone from young families to passing tourists and young professionals.

MAP 9: 17 rue du Sault-au-Matelot, 418/692-1334, www.restauranttoast.com; Mon.-Fri. 11:30am-2pm and 6pm-10:30pm, Sat. 6pm-10:30pm, Sun. 10:30am-10pm

SEAFOOD

La Cabane Lobster Shack 🟠🟠

It's all about low-key seafood at this casual and hip restaurant overlooking the Vieux-Port. As the name suggests, lobster, or *homard* in French, is the main attraction here, but it's not presented in the fussy way we once imagined. Instead it's served in typical Québécois dishes such as poutine or on a hotdog bun as a lobster roll. If you're not a fan of the lobster, there are a number of mussel dishes to try as well as bistro staples like steak and fries. No matter what you order, it's bound to taste pretty good if you can nab a seat on their sunny patio and wash the whole meal down with a local beer.

MAP 9: 115 Quai St-André, 418/692-1010; Sat.-Wed. 5pm-9pm, Thurs. 5pm-10pm, Fri. 11am-11pm

Café Riviera 🟠🟠

Located next to the Silo de la Bunge, this is the hangout for wannabe sailors and those who actually own boats docked in the marina. Even if you left your Breton shirt and Top Siders at home, a trip to Café Riviera is worth it for the outstanding view of the city alone. It's owned by Captain Bernier, and has the seafaring qualities—blue-checkered tablecloths, lanterns hanging from the ceiling, boat miniatures—you'd expect a restaurant owned by a captain would have. Dishes here range from classic (fries and pasta) to haute snacks (shrimp poutine, lobster sandwiches) and sophisticated meals (filet mignon). It's open throughout the summer.

MAP 9: 155 rue Abraham-Martin, 418/694-4449, www.riviera-quebec.com; May-Sept. Mon.-Fri. 9am-10pm, Sat.-Sun. 8am-10pm

Marie-Clarisse $$$

There are only 12 tables, each set with a blue tablecloth and yellow flowers, in this cozy, romantic restaurant that occupies the ground floor of a 340-year-old house. Situated at the bottom of L'Escalier du Casse-Cou, the stone walls, wooden floors, and blazing fire in wintertime only add to the warm atmosphere. One of the top restaurants in the city for fish and seafood, it also offers fine meat dishes like chestnut and maple duck breast and calf's sweetbread. The menu changes daily according to the fresh fish available, but the specialty remains the *marmite de poisson sauce rouille* (fish soup with bouillabaisse).

MAP 9: 12 rue du Petit-Champlain, 418/692-0857, www.marieclarisse.qc.ca; winter daily 6pm-10pm, summer daily 11:30am-2:30pm and 6pm-10pm

Parliament Hill and the Plains

Map 10

CAFÉS

Bügel Fabrique des Bagels $$

Bügel Fabrique des Bagels makes the best Montréal-style bagels in Québec City—wood fired and smothered in sesame seeds. The small neighborhood staple is decorated with old church pews, and lively patrons give it a homey, comfy atmosphere. In the summer the tiny outdoor patio is the perfect place to chow down on one of their breakfast bagels, like *le poussin,* a bagel with an egg (served daily until 2pm), or dig in to one of their sandwich creations with smoked chicken and curried mayonnaise. Vegetarian meals are served, as well as soups, salads, and desserts.

MAP 10: 164 rue Crémazie W., 418/523-7666; Mon.-Wed. and Sat. 7am-7pm, Thurs.-Fri. 7am-9pm, Sun. 7am-6pm

Le Fastoche $

This great *sandwicherie,* located in the Halles du Petit-Quartier on the upscale rue Cartier, has been turning sandwich making into an art since 2008. This take-away counter caters to workers on lunch or locals needing a quick bite. Creative sandwiches with a unique blend of ingredients include the baguette with duck, port, and blueberries and the prosciutto with two pestos. If you're looking for something more substantial try the *boite-à-lunch,* which comes with salad, dessert, and a drink. Close to the Plains of Abraham, it's a great place to pick up a last-minute picnic.

MAP 10: 1191 ave. Cartier (Halles du Petit-Quartier), 418/948-3773, www.sandwicheriefastoche.com; Mon.-Fri. 9am-7pm, Sat. 9am-6pm

DESSERTS

Glacier Aberdeen $

This ice cream shop, tucked into a nook behind avenue Cartier, is one of the best in the city, and locals flock here from all over the city just for a scoop. It has just a slim, long hallway and a walk-up window, so customers savor their treats on the sunny terrace. Across the street, a statue by a local artist also attracts some ice cream eaters. Sundaes, sorbets, frozen yogurts, and milkshakes are all made here, but the place is especially known for its soft-serve ice cream coated with Belgian chocolate and a trickle of maple syrup.

MAP 10: 90 rue Aberdeen, 418/648-6366; mid-Apr.-mid-Sept. daily 10am-midnight

FRENCH AND QUÉBÉCOIS

Bistro B $$$

Bistro B's large picture windows overlook avenue Cartier and the sleek yet overstuffed sofas of the restaurant's outdoor lounge area come summer. Opened in 2012, it's a great place to grab a fancy cocktail—they regularly post their latest creations on a chalkboard in the window to entice passersby—or a casual yet sophisticated meal. The interior is large and spacious, with the high wooden chairs and tables populating the open-concept restaurant. Even the kitchen is open for all to see, with the stools along the chef's counter being the most sought after in the place. Just as the atmosphere is casual, so is the menu. Hand-written daily above the kitchen, it features everything from veal in truffle oil to arugula risotto and Cæsar salad with blood sausage and a poached egg.

MAP 10: 1144 ave. Cartier, 418/614-5444, www.bistrob.ca; Mon.-Fri. 11:30am-2pm and 6pm-11pm, Sat.-Sun. 10am-2pm and 6pm-11pm

Café Krieghoff $$

No matter the time of day, this place is always packed with both locals and tourists. Named after a famous early-Canadian painter who lived in the area, Café Krieghoff serves everything from your basic breakfast (eggs, toast, potatoes) to bistro-style dinners (quiche lorraine, grilled salmon). Neither the food nor the coffee is out of this world, and, beyond the hustle and bustle, the ambience is lacking, but the prime real estate (on the popular avenue Cartier close to the Plains of Abraham and Fine Arts Museum) and the large front and back terraces keep customers coming back. They also have a small seven-room B&B, which occupies the top two stories, a great choice if you're looking for something cozy and intimate.

MAP 10: 1091 ave. Cartier, 418/522-3711, www.cafekrieghoff.qc.ca; Mon.-Fri. 7am-10pm, Sat. 8am-11pm, Sun. 8am-9pm

Graffiti 💲💲💲

This chic and modern restaurant—exposed brick, soft lighting, modern furnishings—serves dishes influenced by both Italian and French traditions. Chef Robert Saulnier is known for his personal touch, which includes creations like veal sweetbread in pastry with candied apples, and roast rack of lamb with sun-dried tomato risotto. Located in the food emporium Les Halles des Cartier, it's popular with neighborhood locals and especially young couples and groups of friends in their late twenties, early thirties. On Sunday, they serve a decadent brunch; pop in for the poached eggs and blintzes.

MAP 10: 1191 ave. Cartier, 418/529-4949; Mon.-Thurs. 11:30am-2:30pm and 5pm-10pm, Fri. 11:30am-2:30pm and 5pm-11pm, Sat. 5pm-11pm, Sun. 9:30am-3pm and 5pm-11pm

Restaurant du Musée des Beaux-Arts 💲💲

One of the first things you notice when you enter the Musée des Beaux-Arts is the restaurant, located just off the entrance hall. The clink of glasses and plates and wafting aromas immediately grab your attention (especially if you're hungry). Featuring regional cuisine and local, organic produce, mains include pork breast, halibut, and stuffed portobello mushrooms. The atmosphere inside is fairly subdued with sparsely designed chairs and simple white tablecloths. During the summer, however, the *terrasse* out back has a stunning view of both the St-Lawrence and the Plains. It's a perfect spot for lunch, and dinner is served once a week, on Wednesday nights when the museum is open late.

MAP 10: Parc des Champs-de-Bataille, 418/644-6780, www.mnba.qc.ca; Thurs.-Tues. 10am-5pm, Wed. 10am-8:45pm

INTERNATIONAL

Le Cosmos 💲💲💲

Right next to the Voo Doo Grill, Le Cosmos shares the same fusion spirit and exotic decor. Dishes here are international, from General Tao chicken to burgers and pastas. It's a trendy and hip restaurant. The decor has organic influences with a sort of *Space Odyssey: 2001* vibe and is a bold mix of neon tree-like columns, illuminated pictures of forests, and an aquarium that runs the length of the floor. The contemporary furniture is 1960s-inspired. Bordering on kitsch, somehow it all seems to work. They have a great selection of cocktails and a big *terrasse* on Grande-Allée on which to knock one back.

MAP 10: 575 La Grande-Allée E., 418/640-0606, www.lecosmos.com; Mon.-Thurs. 7am-midnight, Fri. 7am-1am, Sat. 8am-1am, Sun. 8am-midnight

Voo Doo Grill ❸❸❸

Part of a big complex that houses famous Le Maurice nightclub, the Voo Doo Grill serves international food that, despite the name, tends toward Asian and fusion. As if that weren't confusing enough, the decor, once Africa-inspired with roaming drum circles, has recently been replaced by an art deco look, full of cast iron, fur, and gilded mirrors. Specialties of the house, however, haven't changed, so you can still get the same filet mignon, tandoori shrimp, and snow-crab cakes, all of which are better than what you'd expect. They also have a great selection of wine, over 200 choices. Customers, from traveling businesspeople to twentysomething students, come for dinner and stay to burn off the calories on the dance floors of Le Maurice and Le Charlotte Ultra Lounge, where the door fee is waived with proof that you ate at Voo Doo.

MAP 10: 575 La Grande-Allée E., 418/647-2000, www.voodoogrill.com; Mon.-Fri. 11am-midnight, Sat.-Sun. 5pm-midnight

ITALIAN

Casa Calzone ❸❸

If you're looking for Québec City's Little Italy, look no further than Casa Calzone. The red-checkered tablecloths, postcards of Italy on the wall, Italian music, and bottles of chianti subtly let you know you've arrived. Pastas and homemade pizzas are always good, but the real standouts here are their famous calzones. The proud owner often makes the rounds of the tables just to make sure what you've ordered has sent you to food heaven. Don't forget to please him as much as he pleased you and leave your comments on the wall provided.

MAP 10: 637 La Grande-Allée E., 418/522-3000, www.casacalzone.com; winter Mon.-Sat. 11:30am-2pm and 5:30pm-10pm, summer daily 11:30am-11pm

Milano Pizza ❸❸

This pizza joint's reputation as one of the best in Québec City has been cemented over the last 40 years, thanks to the neighborhood regulars who drop in at least once a week. Though it's not gourmet (black olives are the fanciest topping), it's always fresh and delicious, and the unpretentious attitude keeps bringing people back. It's just off avenue Cartier, and for late-night cravings, it's the perfect place, especially during the summer when they often close after 1am.

MAP 10: 194 rue Crémazie W., 418/529-2919; Mon.-Thurs. 11am-1am, Sat.-Sun. 11am-midnight

Morena $

Part specialty store, part casual restaurant, Morena is your go-to place for authentic and delicious Italian staples. Whether it's a creamy latte to go, fresh homemade linguine ready to be thrown in the pot, or a can of San Marzano tomatoes, this place has you covered. There are only about six tables in the store and they're nearly always filled with neighborhood locals who pop in for a quick bite of their lasagna Bolognese or eggplant Parmesan. A great place to grab lunch or dinner, it's also a popular spot for brunch on the weekends, serving everything from two eggs the way you like them to baked eggs in tomato sauce.

MAP 10: 1040 ave. Cartier, 418/529-3668, www.morena-food.com; Mon.-Wed. 8am-7pm, Thurs.-Fri. 8am-8pm, Sat.-Sun. 8am-6pm

JAPANESE

Métropolitan Eddie Sushi Bar $$$

This restaurant's name might be lost in translation, but they got everything else right at this authentic Japanese restaurant on Cartier. The large, open dining room is painted white with dark wood accents in the door and window frames. The rest of the decor is kept simple with the tables and chairs almost precisely matched to the existing wood, evoking a particularly Zen ambience. Though you can still order your California and kamikazi rolls here, the emphasis is on traditional Japanese sashimi and sushi with *unagi, tobiko,* and scallops featured on the menu.

MAP 10: 1188 ave. Cartier, 418/649-1096, www.eddiesushi.com; Mon.-Fri. 4:30pm-10:30pm, Sat. 5pm-11:30pm, Sun. 5pm-10:30pm

TEA

Sebz Thés and Lounge $

The interior of this teahouse makes up for the exterior on the busy and less than picturesque boulevard René-Lévesque. The vibe here is more relaxed than British afternoon tea, and the friendly atmosphere makes it popular with local residents and students alike. More than 150 teas from China, Japan, India, and Africa are available. Detox Tuesdays are popular with regulars, as are the infusion blends, which they roast and blend on the spot.

MAP 10: 67 blvd. René-Lévesque E., 418/523-0808, www.sebz.ca; Mon.-Sat. 10am-9pm, Sun. 10am-6pm

Saint-Jean-Baptiste and Saint-Roch

Map 11

BAKERIES

La Boîte à Pain §

This artisanal bakery has freshly baked bread all day long and the smell lures in just about anyone who passes by. The pastries are also awesome, from the croissants to the *pains aux chocolates* to the brioche. They also serve sandwiches—try the tomato, mozzarella, and basil—delicious soups spiced with curry, and great salads. Though the interior is nothing fancy, it does have a few nondescript chairs and tables where locals and weary tourists recharge with a coffee and a treat.

MAP 11: 289 rue St-Joseph E., 418/647-3666, www.boiteapain.com; Mon.-Fri. 6:30am-8pm, Sat.-Sun. 6:30am-5:30pm

Le Pain Grüel §

This self-proclaimed *"boulangerie creative"* makes its breads and pastries by hand and with some of the healthiest ingredients. All breads are made using sourdough, but a variety of flours and ingredients are added according to the season. The results: multigrain bread, cheese bread, bread with nuts. They even have a bread with chocolate and dried pears. The ambience is all business, with a simple counter and not much else. This is a take-away place, so you can feel French and eat your baguette as you stroll the street.

MAP 11: 375 rue St-Jean, 418/522-7246; Tues.-Fri. 6am-6:30pm, Sat. 6am-5pm

CAFÉS

★ Brûlerie Saint-Roch §

This is one of the best cafés in the city, and the line starts early in the mornings when regulars pop in to get their usual before heading off to work. Ideally located on a corner lot, it has two walls of picture windows with bars and seats along both that are usually occupied. If it's not too packed, try to grab a seat on the tiny second-floor mezzanine that looks out over the action. Front and center when you enter is the gleaming Nuova Simonelli (the espresso machine), backed by a wall of coffee beans ready to be ground. The lattes here are outstanding—it's all in the foam—and the sandwiches and pastries are mouthwatering. There is a second location on rue St-Jean (881 rue St-Jean, 418/614-3359).

MAP 11: 375 rue St-Joseph E., 418/529-1559, www.brulerie-st-roch.com; Sun.-Wed. 6:30am-11pm, Thurs.-Sat. 6:30am-midnight

Café Babylone $

With different events happening here almost every night of the week, Café Babylone is a great place to take in a different kind of show. Local musicians hit the tiny stage to try out new material, and on Tuesday nights you can stop by to hear everything from slam poetry to storytelling. Most of these events are pay-what-you-can. During daylight hours, it's a cozy café serving Turkish specialties as well as sandwiches, salads, and even breakfasts. The atmosphere is laid-back and so is the decor; most of the furniture has been salvaged from secondhand shops.

MAP 11: 181 rue St-Vallier E., 418/523-0700, www.cafebabylone.com; Mon.-Fri. 10am-10pm, Sat. 9am-10pm, Sun. 9am-3pm

Librairie St-Jean-Baptiste $

A bookshop and café in one, Librairie St-Jean-Baptiste is one of the latest additions to the street. Situated in a building that dates from the early 1900s, the bookstore, dealing in mostly used books, has quickly become a meeting point for local artists and students. There's also a small café, where you're invited to while away the afternoon in this inviting and relaxed atmosphere. Snacks, including sandwiches, soup, and grilled cheese, are also available.

MAP 11: 565 rue St-Jean, 581/999-0951, www.librairiesjb.com; daily 11am-9pm

Nektar $

At Nektar, coffee is an art. Baristas here are experts and will explain the ins-and-outs of a good cup of joe to you, all in a thinly veiled attempt to lure you into tasting their *grands crus,* the latest vintage of coffee. If they succeed in getting you to taste the Nektar, you'll have a hard time going back to your Starbucks Breakfast Blend. Despite their devotion to java, they also have pastries, crêpes, and pizzas on hand in the off chance you might want something solid. The interior is a bit of a letdown; chocolate brown walls give the place a cozy feel in winter, but in warmer months it all seems a bit too dark.

MAP 11: 235 rue St-Joseph E., 418/977-9236, www.lenektar.com; Mon.-Wed. 7am-11pm, Thurs.-Fri. 7am-midnight, Sat. 8:30am-midnight, Sun. 9:30am-9pm

Pain et Passion $

Located in what used to be a cookie factory, this Mediterranean grocery store offers pretty much everything. Alongside various kinds of homemade bread, you'll find deli, pastry, and cheese counters. They've also got hot meals, salads, pastas, and good coffee. Locals come here for special ingredients or for a quick and easy take-away dinner. Grab a seat at one of the few tables and eat among the old artifacts, imported European products, and old factory decor, and lounge in the laid-back, almost soothing atmosphere. They also offer nice breakfasts on weekends 10am-2pm.

CRÊPERIES

★ Crêperie le Billig $

This is the most authentic crêperie in Québec City—some even say it's better than the ones found in France. It was founded by a true Breton, and authentic *galettes* made of organic buckwheat flour and sweet crêpes made of sarrazin are both available. First-timers should try the classic crêpe suzette, flambéed with Grand Marnier. Don't forget to wash your sweet or savory crêpe down with a cider. The lively and boisterous ambience is palpable since the place is always full of locals packed into the seven tables or taking up the one or two outside tables in the summer. Reservations are a must.

MAP 11: 526 rue St-Jean, 418/524-8341; Tues.-Sat. 11am-9pm, Sun. 11am-3pm

DESSERTS

Tutto Gelato $

This 100 percent authentic Italian *gelateria* comes from the heart of a 100 percent authentic Italian. When owner Giacomo Donati moved to Canada he brought with him gelato recipes and lots of them. All the gelato here is homemade, and with over 100 recipes, there's always a different flavor to try, including matcha, saffron cream, ginger, sea-salt caramel, and all the classics. Modern and sleek, this slim take-away counter also has cakes, biscuits, coffees, and even homemade soy milk ice cream.

MAP 11: 716 rue St-Jean, 418/522-0896, www.tuttogelato.ca; late Apr.-early Oct. daily 10:30am-8pm or midnight depending on the weather

FRENCH

Au Bonnet d'Âne $$

Situated in what was once the local general store, this café and restaurant is a local favorite. It's not hard to imagine a shopkeeper behind the dark, heavy bar, or think of the long bay windows, now comfortable banquettes, as filled with stuff for sale. The relaxed, sometimes boisterous atmosphere is laid-back and inviting. Old artifacts line the shelves, the menu is written on the mirror behind the bar, and old photos hang on the walls. The burgers are some of the best. Their weekend brunch is always hearty, but refined. A small *terrasse* on the side is a great spot in the summer.

MAP 11: 298 rue St-Jean, 418/647-3031, www.aubonnetdane.com; Mon.-Fri. 11am-10pm, Sat.-Sun. 8am-10pm

Les Bossus $$

This is a classic French bistro, from its checkered-tile floor to the waiters in long black aprons to the menu that lists everything from breakfast to dessert. Simply decorated, the narrow restaurant has a long bar on the right, an entire wall with banquette seats on the left, and black-lacquered chairs and tables in the middle. All this might look very elegant, but everything here stays simple and relaxed. Not convinced? Bossus in English means "The Hunchbacks." The diners here are diverse—businesspeople, locals, and tourists. They come to eat bistro classics like tartare, *boudin noir*, duck confit, and filet mignon. Les Bossus also serves an excellent breakfast.

MAP 11: 620 rue St-Joseph E., 418/522-5501, www.lesbossus.com; Mon.-Fri. 11am-10pm, Sat.-Sun. 9am-10pm

Le Cercle ❸❸

Defying all conventions, Le Cercle is a restaurant, a bar, a café, and a performance venue, and is the go-to place for the young and hip. With its concrete floors, light wood interior, and floor-to-ceiling windows, it is one of the city's coolest restaurants. Serving both tapas-style munchies (try the grilled sardines and rabbit shoulders—seriously) and mains (smoked salmon tartare and veal smoked ribs), it's also one of the more popular brunch places in town. It may not be surprising to learn that they serve up some of the most sought-after cocktails (at brunch you can order an entire carafe of mimosas), but one surprising twist about Le Cercle is the wine cellar. It blends in so well, you barely even notice the $1,600 bottles of Château Pètrus stacked up against the wall.

MAP 11: 228 rue St-Joseph E., 418/948-8648, www.le-cercle.ca; Tues.-Fri. 11:30am-3am, Sat. 10am-3am

★ Le Clocher Penché ❸❸

If you ask Québec City residents what their favorite restaurant is, or at least which one gives you the best bang for your buck, they'll tell you Le Clocher Penché. It's set in an old bank, and the washrooms are where the big safe used to be. The ever-changing menu includes dishes like roasted snails, scallops with spaghetti squash, and black pudding with apple chutney. They use all local, fresh products. It's called Clocher Penché (Leaning Belfry) because the church next door has a slanted bell tower. Large windows open onto the street in summertime and give the dining room lots of light no matter the time of year. The light wood chairs and tables give the whole atmosphere a delightful airiness. Reservations are recommended.

MAP 11: 203 rue St-Joseph E., 418/640-0597, www.clocherpenche.ca; Tues.-Fri. 11:30am-2pm and 5pm-10pm, Sat. 9am-2pm and 5pm-10pm, Sun. 9am-2pm

★ Le Moine Échanson ❸❸

First the translation—*échanson* means "cup-bearer," an officer whose duty was to serve the drinks at a royal table. *Moine* means "monk." The concept at this *bistro à vin* is to discover a new wine region of France every time you visit. The menu, using Québécois and French products, varies according to season and climate. For example, you'll be in Savoy and Alsace in winter, the Mediterranean in summer (including Greece, Portugal, Spain), and Québec in fall.

It's small and cozy with wood tables, a chalkboard menu, and lots of natural light; the ambience here transports you to France without crossing the Atlantic. In summer, prime tables are available outside to let you appreciate the vibe of Faubourg Saint-Jean-Baptiste. A favorite with couples or friends on dates, it can get packed, so reservations are a good idea.

MAP 11: 585 rue St-Jean, 418/524-7832, www.lemoineechanson.com; Sun.-Mon. 5pm-10pm, Tues.-Wed. 11:30am-2pm and 5pm-10pm, Thurs. 11:30am-2pm and 5pm-11pm, Fri. 11:30am-2pm

Versa $$$

One of the first restaurants to open in the revitalized Saint-Roch neighborhood, this oyster bar headed by young chef Christian Veilleux is the only one of its kind in the city. It looks just as much like a club as a fine dining establishment. The centerpiece of the dining room is a long communal table illuminated by a modern disco ball. The atmosphere is hip and young. Aside from the oysters, mains include seared sweetbreads and baby-back ribs. In summertime the floor-to-ceiling window slides open and revelers mingle on the tiny, cobblestone street.

MAP 11: 432 rue du Parvis, 418/523-9995, www.versarestaurant.com; Mon. 11:30am-2pm, Tues.-Fri. 11:30am-close, Sat. 5pm-close

JAPANESE

Yuzu Sushi Bar $$$

This sushi bar is named after a small Japanese citrus fruit whose delicate grapefruit-meets-mandarin flavor is often found in fusion cooking. There could be no better symbol for what Yuzu does: blend traditional Japanese with North American flavors. The interior of this modern sushi bar is just peachy, with the color on the walls, the plush upholstery of the chairs, and even the pink hues of the wooden tabletops. It's frequented by young, chic professionals. Dishes like tempura, beef sashimi, and dragon rolls are all available here, but where Yuzu differs is with its specialties and tasting menus, which mix flavors like blue fin tuna with pesto and salmon tartare with quinoa salad.

MAP 11: 438 rue du Parvis, 418/521-7253, www.yuzu.ca; Mon.-Wed. 11:30am-2:30pm and 5pm-10pm, Thurs.-Fri. 11:30am-2:30pm and 5pm-11pm, Sat. 5pm-11pm

MIDDLE EASTERN
Le Carthage $$

Named after the ancient African city, Le Carthage serves fine Tunisian cuisine. The atmosphere is laid-back and the surroundings majestic; the slightly curved ceiling and intricate moldings give the whole room an exotic feel. Seating here is North African as well, and low chairs and tables adorned with colorful plush cushions invite you to take your shoes off and relax. Bring your own wine to accompany dishes like tahini, royal couscous, or *merguez* and quail brochettes. On weekends, enjoy traditional music and belly-dancing as you sit back and finish your meal with some sticky baklava.

MAP 11: 399 rue St-Jean, 418/529-0576; Tues.-Fri. 11am-2pm and 5pm-11pm, Sat.-Mon. 5pm-10pm

Le Sultan $

Decorated with hookahs and gilded tea pots, Le Sultan looks like something out of *Arabian Nights*. It's super casual; you can get takeout or eat in one of their brightly decorated rooms. It's the perfect place for a Moroccan mint tea. Their simple food is fresh, healthy, and delicious, and their *shish taouk "gigot d'agneau"* is not to be missed. A salon at the back is welcoming; leave your shoes at the door and let yourself sink into the cushions. They accept cash only.

MAP 11: 467 rue St-Jean, 418/525-9449; Mon.-Thurs. 11:30am-11pm, Fri. noon-midnight, Sat.-Sun. noon-11pm

QUÉBÉCOIS
Chez Victor $

The ambition of this self-proclaimed burger gourmet is to make a hamburger a "piece of art." And so far, everybody in Québec—artist or not—would agree that they make the best burgers in town. The salmon burger, duck burger, and wild boar burger are interesting takes on the old standard. Vegetarians get choices as well, a rarity in Québec, with tofu, nut and spinach, and cereal burgers available. The success led them to open new restaurants, including one in the Vieux-Port (300 rue St-Paul, 418/781-2511), but the one on St-Jean remains the best and definitely worth the walk, with its stone walls, low ceiling, and casual atmosphere.

MAP 11: 145 rue St-Jean, 418/529-7702, www.chezvictorburger.com/st-jean; Sun.-Wed. 11am-9pm, Thurs.-Sat. 11am-10pm

Le Comptoir $

One of the main things about Québécois food—be it at one of the best restaurants in the country or a typical neighborhood diner—is that it always comes back to comfort. And that's what Le Comptoir (the Counter) serves up: satisfying comfort food in a comfortable setting. Located on St-Jean, this cute restaurant—it's all red and white banquettes and bar stools line the windows—offers two stories of cozy charm for you to settle in with your friends and family. Most of the clientele can be placed in three categories: locals, journalists (the offices of the Francophone version of Canada's national broadcasting network is just across the street), and families (what kid will say no to a burger?). The menu, too, aims to please. They have two specialties here, the very British fish and chips and smoked meat, a popular Montreal staple. The fish is as fresh as anything you'd find on the coast of Maine, while the smoked meat comes directly from Montréal's own Lester's. Of course, their burgers and club sandwiches hit the spot too.

MAP 11: 849 rue St-Jean, 418/614-5522; daily 11am-10pm

Snack Bar St-Jean $

Snack Bar St-Jean is a rare find: a place that can satisfy your craving for burgers and fries just as easily at 4am in the morning as at noon. Open till 5am seven days a week, this snack bar is all about being here for you when that craving for grilled cheese hits. This modern diner is nicely, if not overly, decorated with low sturdy wooden tables and chairs that can stand up to a lot of abuse. There's even a backyard patio come summertime, the perfect place to kick back with your enormous and ingenious poutine club (a club sandwich dumped on a pile of fries and covered in gravy, essentially). Everything here is over the top and that's part of the charm. If you're watching your calories, this place is best to be avoided (though they do have a rather demure toasted tomato sandwich on the menu). This is a place to revel in your love of the fatty and fried. Come for the "Gangbang Burger," featuring both a beef and chicken patty, but stay for the other crazy creations that come out of the kitchen.

MAP 11: 780 rue St-Jean, 418/522-4727, www.snackbarsaintjean.com; daily 10am-5am

Taverne Steakhouse Le Tonneau $

Opened in 1939, Taverne Steakhouse Le Tonneau, one of the oldest restaurants in the city, has witnessed a lot of history. Rumor has it that the first separatist powwows were held here, when St-Joseph was still slightly unsavory. Most recently, it's witnessed the cleanup of the area, and though it's been cleaned up itself, it has managed to retain its unique personality and clientele. The Formica tables and refrigerators in imitation wood, paired with the long bar, give it the air of an urban saloon. The regulars are still here, but they're surrounded by a younger, hipper generation. Smoked meat, liver, poutine, and blood pudding are popular, as are new additions like beef and salmon tartare. If you manage to eat the hulking 72-ounce sirloin steak in less than an hour, the boss picks up the tab. You have been warned.

MAP 11: 732 rue St-Joseph E., 418/525-9337; daily 11am-3am

TEA

Camellia Sinensis $

Québec City deserves its own branch of this great Montréal-based teahouse and it's no surprise to find it here on St-Joseph. Tea tasters travel the world to find the best and rarest of teas. More than 180 fresh teas are kept in store, and they come from as far way as Japan, India, China, and Taiwan. This small store is set up like an old sweet shop with a counter, and the soft green walls are filled with silver tea tins. The shelves in heavy dark wood give it a feel of gravitas. Tea being a serious business for them, the owners organize a number of tea-centered activities, including tastings, workshops, and even classes on traditional tea ceremonies.

MAP 11: 624 rue St-Joseph E., 418/525-0247, www.camellia-sinensis.com; Mon.-Wed. and Sat. 10am-6pm, Thurs.-Fri. 10am-8pm, Sun. 10am-5pm

VIETNAMESE

La Petite Boîte Vietnamienne $

The brainchild of young chef Thi Cam Nhung Lê, La Petite Boîte Vietnamienne brings together Western and Eastern influences. Vietnamese classics, like *phô,* the national soup, alternate with Québécois dishes that Nhung Lê then revisits, like duck breast with Hanoi spices and mussels in Vietnamese spices. It's a must among local adventurous eaters and those wanting a change from bistro fare. The tiny dining room is simply decorated with rich red walls and paper lanterns; seats are also available at the bar, where you can watch the chef at work and sip a mojito, her own drink of choice.

MAP 11: 281 rue de la Couronne, 418/204-6323; Tues.-Fri. 11am-10pm, Sat. 4pm-10pm

Nightlife

Québec City might have more historic sights but Montréal has it trumped when it comes to nightlife. Though the rejuvenation of the Saint-Roch neighborhood has led to new hipster venues and interesting bars, La Grande-Allée remains the epicenter of the city's nightlife, with dance clubs and bars chockablock along the strip. The late-night scene, however, still lacks a certain amount of diversity. Sure, you can always catch a band or find a place to dance the night away, but the selection can feel limited compared to most major North American cities. Nightlife here tends to stick to the neighborhood bar, and it is in these small establishments that you'll find the city's true ambience.

One facet of Québec's nightlife that you won't find much of in Montréal, however, is *chansonniers* (singer/songwriters). These folk singers perform in *boîtes à chansons* ("music boxes"). These venues, deeply entrenched in Québécois identity, give singers and songwriters a platform to sing about their heritage and experience and were first popular shortly after World War II. Famous *chansonniers* have included Félix Leclerc and Raymond Lévesque, who helped popularize this new form of folk music in the 1950s. It's still popular today, and there are venues in the city dedicated solely to supporting emerging songwriters, who sing both old classics and new material. Those looking for a uniquely Québécois experience should make time to check out one of these performances, even if the lyrics remain something of a mystery.

Montréalers love to antagonize Québeckers by calling it a "town," rather than a city, and though it can feel small at times, that isn't

Look for ★ to find recommended nightlife.

Highlights

★ **Best Place to Find Your Sea Legs:** With 50 different cocktails and an interior that makes you feel like you're drinking in the captain's cabin, **Bar Ste-Angèle** will soon have you swaying with the ship (page 381).

★ **Best Terrace:** With cocktails in mason jars, imported beer on tap, and a large patio that looks onto the old walls, **Le Sapristi** is your go-to for alfresco drinks (page 382).

★ **Most Incomprehensible Good Time:** You might not understand the lyrics to the songs sung at **Le Pape-Georges,** but the energy at this *boîte à chansons* is infectious (page 386).

★ **Best Dance Club:** The sheer size of the dance floor and variety of music at **Le Maurice** will keep you dancing all night long (page 387).

★ **Best (and Only) Place to Smoke Indoors:** With its walk-in humidor and selection of over 200 cigars, **Société Cigare** lets smokers enjoy their stogies in dignified surroundings (page 388).

★ **Best Microbrew: La Barberie** is socially and environmentally conscious, so you can down your tasting selection of eight beers guilt free (page 389).

★ **Best Place to Skip the Meal:** Pitchers of beer are served in watering cans at **La Cuisine,** which cooks up full-on dance parties that rage on well into the night (page 390).

★ **Most Authentic Québécois Tavern: Taverne Jos Dion** is one of the oldest bars in the city. Head here for the live accordion music and stay for the cheap beer (page 392).

★ **Best Drag Show:** Gay bar and night-club **Le Drague** is nothing but unadulterated fun, and the dance floor is always packed with people letting loose (page 394).

★ **Best Game Selection:** Head downstairs to the Game Bar at **Le Boudoir** for some old-school Pac-Man and new-school sounds (page 395).

always a bad thing. When the city comes alive at night, it's in the numerous bars and taverns in neighborhoods all over the city. Even in the deepest of winter the bars are packed with men and women downing pints from local breweries. Many of the bars also feature regular live music that ranges from jazz trios to local rock acts, and if you feel like dancing, chances are you aren't alone. Québeckers are always up for a good time, so it doesn't take much to get the city's population out of their seats, even if there's no actual dance floor.

Those in the mood for neon lights, thumping bass, and big crowds should head to La Grande-Allée, the city's biggest boulevard, which is full of historical buildings that have been converted into bars and dance clubs. The legal drinking age is 18 throughout the province, and this is the place where teens can be found reveling in their newfound freedom. If you're looking to dance but want something more *branchée* (trendy), head over to Le Drague, the city's gay club, for some guaranteed fun. Though smaller than the clubs found in Montréal, Québec nightlife still offers a variety of events and a good time without discrimination.

When looking for a place to pop in for a nightcap or hear some local music, don't be afraid to wander along quiet side streets or go beyond the old city walls—it's in these places that you'll find the most authentic ambience and the most affordable beer.

Vieux-Québec's Upper Town

Map 8

BARS
★ Bar Ste-Angèle
Cocktails here come in a rainbow of colors and a multitude of flavors, including Red Devil, Blue Angel, and Kamikaze. With 50 cocktails to choose from, which you can get by the pitcher, they all start to become tempting after a while. They also have an extensive selection of imported beers and scotch. The bar is designed to resemble the cabin of a ship; there's a lot of heavy woodwork, tiny windows, and mini tables. Small and often packed, it's the perfect retreat when it's super cold or rainy out. Live jazz plays Thursday, Friday, and Saturday nights.

MAP 8: 26 rue Ste-Angèle, 418/692-2171; daily 8pm-3am; no cover

L'Ostradamus
It's not every day that a popular student bar is found in a historic building. Designed by Eugène-Étienne Taché and built in 1890,

L'Ostradamus takes up two floors of this impressive Victorian structure, which is hidden on the twisty-turny rue Couillard. The all-wood interior gives it a warm though distinctly bar-like feel. The young and hip have been flocking here for the cheap drinks and fun atmosphere since it opened in 1973. The top floor is a show lounge dedicated to showcasing new music, stand-up comedy, and other events, while the vibe on the first floor is more relaxed, perfect for beer with friends.

MAP 8: 29 rue Couillard, 418/694-9560; daily 4:30pm-3am; no cover

★ Le Sapristi

Owned by the team behind burger joint Les Trois Garçons, brand new bar Le Sapristi is a much needed breath of fresh air. Taking over the coveted corner spot on St-Jean just inside the old walls, Le Sapristi serves up delectable mixed drinks made all the more desirable because they're casually served in old mason jars. On tap you'll find a number of local brews alongside European staples like Newcastle Brown Ale and 1664 Blanc. The crowd is mostly full of twentysomethings and thirtysomethings, many of whom stop off for an after-work drink and bite. Stone walls, rustic but nicely finished wood tables and chairs, and a newly refurbished copper ceiling pull the whole casual vibe together. If you get hungry, they also serve some mean pizzas and charcuterie plates. In the summer there's not one but two *terrasses* to choose from, one out front offering a great view of the St-Jean gate and a larger one around the side that's perfect for whiling away the hours with friends.

MAP 8: 1001 rue St-Jean, 418/692-2030, www.sapristi.ca; daily 11am-3am; no cover

LIVE MUSIC
Boîtes à Chansons
Les Yeux Bleus

If you want to experience the peculiarly Québécois institution of *boîtes à chansons*, this is the place to do it. It was in these small filled-to-capacity rooms that emerging Québécois singers first got their start in the 1950s, and the tradition continues to this day, especially at Les Yeux Bleus (The Blue Eyes), the most popular venue for *chansonniers* in the city. Situated at the end of a courtyard off of St-Jean, the room here gets packed early with audiences of all ages. Even if you don't understand a word of what the musician three feet from your table is singing, you'll witness the magical effect it has on the audience.

MAP 8: 1117½ rue St-Jean, 418/694-9118; daily 8pm-3am; no cover

Jazz Bars
Le Charles Baillairgé Jazz Bar
Situated in the Hotel Clarendon, the Charles Baillairgé Jazz Bar continues the 30-year tradition originally started here by L'Emprise. Found on the street level of the hotel, the large, open-concept bar with low lights, bucket chairs, and a small stage makes for an intimate atmosphere. With jazz groups playing almost every night, the stage has hosted such legendary names as Diana Krall and John Zorn and continues to be a showcase for Québec's emerging and established jazz musicians.

MAP 8: 57 rue Ste-Anne, 418/692-2480, www.hotelclarendon.com; daily 7pm-10:30pm; no cover

LOUNGES
St-Laurent Bar and Lounge
Like its sibling establishments Le Champlain and Café de la Terrasse, Château Frontenac's St-Laurent Bar affords the same great views of the St-Lawrence River. Unlike its siblings, however, this is the only establishment that is exclusively a bar (though light meals are available from the restaurants). The circular, rich wood bar is the centerpiece of the St-Laurent, with massive picture frame windows that look out onto the *terrasse* and river beyond. The seating is placed around the bar, and old wingback-style chairs are the standard. Evening or afternoon, the cocktail reigns supreme, with a number of classics on the menu like whiskey sours, gin fizz, and Tom Collins, as well as a list of martinis like the Winston Churchill or F. D. Roosevelt, all named after illustrious guests. Dress code is smart casual. Men in sleeveless shirts will be turned away.

MAP 8: 1 rue des Carrières, 418/266-3919, www.fairmont.com/frontenac; daily 11:30am-1:30am; no cover

PUBS
Pub St-Alexandre
If you like beer, then you'll love Pub St-Alexandre. It's the English pub of Québec City, with mahogany paneling, big mirrors, and an "olde British pub" facade to prove it. Pub St-Alexandre has been here for more than 20 years and offers the largest selection of beer in the province. More than 250 beers are available, mostly from Ireland, Britain, Germany, and Belgium. They also carry a selection of 40 single malts. It's a hangout that attracts both locals and tourists. If you find yourself confounded by choice, the servers are all beer experts.

MAP 8: 1087 rue St-Jean, 418/594-0015, www.pubstalexandre.com; daily 11am-3am; no cover

clockwise from top left: Pub St-Patrick, Upper Town; Le Pape-Georges, Upper Town; LGBT hot spot Le Drague, Saint-Jean-Baptiste and Saint-Roch

Pub St-Patrick

Pub St-Patrick is hard to miss, with its ideal location and large, usually packed *terrasse* full of students, tourists, and professionals still in their suits after work. Inside this bustling pub is some of the most fascinating architecture. The building dates back to 1749, and several of the rooms are made completely of stone, and feature vaulted ceilings. Once used as barracks during the French regime, they are now some of the coziest places to sip a pint of Guinness. Imported beer is a specialty here and you'll find Harp, Kilkenny, and Smithwick's on tap, as well as an outstanding scotch selection.

MAP 8: 1200 rue St-Jean, 418/694-0618; daily 11:30am-3am; no cover

Vieux-Québec's Lower Town

Map 9

BARS

L'Oncle Antoine

Right next to Place Royale, L'Oncle Antoine is one of the coolest looking bars in the city. Located in the cellar of one of the oldest buildings in the city, it dates back to 1754, and the vaulted brick ceilings and walls make you feel like you're hanging out in an old bunker. In wintertime, a raging fireplace gives a unique ambience and keeps things cozy. Fifty different beers are on tap, including local specialties like Fin-du-Monde, and bar snacks like hot dogs and nachos are also available.

MAP 9: 29 rue St-Pierre, 418/694-9176; winter daily 11am-3am, summer daily 10am-3am; no cover

Taverne Belley

Located in a hotel of the same name, Taverne Belley looks out over the marina and the farmers market. In the summer, the outdoor *terrasse* attracts everyone from office workers to cyclists looking for a refreshing drink and a rest. Opened in 1933, it also has a popular *pétanque* court just in front of the *terrasse*, to which players flock daily in the summertime. True to its name, the Belley is really all about the beer, and there are a number of imported and local microbrews available. There's also a large selection of wines and port to sip next to the fireplace as you take in the warm wintertime ambience.

MAP 9: 249 rue St-Paul, 418/692-4595; daily 8am-midnight; no cover

LIVE MUSIC
Boîtes à Chansons
★ Le Pape-Georges

It's easy to miss Le Pape-Georges, one of the best and only *boîte à chansons* bars in Vieux-Québec's Lower Town; it's hidden down a little back lane, off the popular rue Petit-Champlain. Though it calls itself a wine bar, the crowds don't come here for the selection of wines, ports, and microbrewery beers alone. They come instead for the ambience of this welcoming bar, located in a historical house built in 1790. The patrons gather around small tables and huddle up against the stone walls to hear the songs of *chansonniers* (folk singers) and jazz bands. While you listen, snack on some Québec cheese and charcuterie, or a pot-au-feu in the winter.

MAP 9: 8 rue du Cul-de-Sac, 418/692-1320; summer daily noon-3am, winter Mon.-Wed. 4pm-3am, Thurs.-Sun. noon-3am; no cover

Parliament Hill and the Plains
Map 10

BARS
L'Inox

Founded in 1987, L'Inox is the beer institution of Québec. Formerly located in the Vieux-Port, it recently moved up to the nightlife mecca of the Grande-Allée. Its new interior is modern with high ceilings and basic bar seating. In respect to the forefathers of New France, L'Inox tries to hold up the long tradition of brewing and drinking beer, which has existed in Québec since the early days of the colony. The big vats are visible at the back of the bar and patrons are more than welcome to go downstairs for a more personal visit. Come and savor a Viking or a Trouble-Fête (with coriander and citrus flavors), brewed on the spot, and enjoy it with one of their famous European hot dogs.

MAP 10: 655 La Grande-Allée E., 418/692-2877, www.inox.qc.ca; Apr.-Oct. daily noon-3am, Nov.-Mar. daily 3pm-3am; no cover

Le Jules et Jim

Just like the famous François Truffaut film from which it took its name, this little *bar de quartier* has become a classic. Since it's a popular neighborhood bar, the patrons are mostly locals, and there's no better place to soak up the city's authentic atmosphere. Clearly stuck on the notion of French classics, music here tends toward Edith Piaf, Jacques Brel, Georges Brassens, and the like. The low wooden tables and deep red velvet banquettes give it an added Old-World charm.

MAP 10: 1060 ave. Cartier, 418/524-9570; daily 3pm-3am; no cover

DANCE CLUBS

Le Charlotte Ultra Lounge

This club is in what used to be the attic of this grand old house, which is now a nightlife complex. It's named after former premier Maurice Duplessis's secretary, Charlotte, with whom he is suspected of having an affair—in this very attic! Québec political scandal aside, the ambience here tends toward chill, compared to the dance floor action in the main bar. Retro and pop nights are popular here. Appealing to a mid-twenties to late-thirties crowd, the interior is refined and rich with padded walls, velvet couches, and fur throws.

MAP 10: 575 La Grande-Allée, 418/647-2000, www.mauricenightclub.com; Sun.-Tues. 9pm-3am, Wed.-Sat. 8pm-3am; $5 cover

Le Dagobert

Set in a huge castle-like house on the Grande-Allée, the "Dag" as it's known has been an institution for more than 30 years. Inside there are two distinct sounds: The first floor has a rock vibe with regular live shows by cover bands, while the second floor is a full-blown club with a huge dance floor, neon lights, and a mezzanine running along its edges. It's here that you'll catch sets by some of the world's best DJs. The crowd is younger than what you'll find at Maurice, with many of them barely over the drinking age. During the summer, a line forms quickly for entrance onto the *terrasse*, so get here early to avoid it.

MAP 10: 600 La Grande-Allée E., 418/522-0393, www.dagobert.ca; daily 9pm-3am; no cover

★ Le Maurice

Le Maurice is housed in the former headquarters of the Union Nationale, a conservative political party headed by Maurice Duplessis (hence the name), which governed the province throughout the 1940s and '50s. The epicenter of a good 70 percent of the city's entire nightlife, this complex includes Le Charlotte Ultra Lounge, Voo Doo Grill, and Société Cigare. The complex's main attraction remains Le Maurice, with its immense dance floor and eclectic music, everything from electro to salsa and rock to R&B. It is a good place to lose yourself in the beat. Come winter don't miss the famous Iceothèque, the ice disco that takes up the entire front *terrasse*.

MAP 10: 575 La Grande-Allée E., 418/647-2000, www.mauricenightclub.com; Sun.-Wed. 8pm-3am, Thurs. 11pm-3am, Fri. 8:30pm-3am, Sat. 10pm-3am; $5 cover Wed.-Sat.

LIVE MUSIC
Boîtes à Chansons
Rideau Rouge

This former lounge has since transformed itself into a *boîtes à chansons,* complete with makeshift stage and stage lights bright enough to make even the most amateur of open mic performers feel like a burgeoning star. It's a few steps down into this club; luckily, there's usually a hostess waiting to usher you down from the street. Once in the club, it's all neon lights and slate walls. Chandeliers hung over the bar illuminate the suspended glasses like so many crystals. There's also ample floor space for spectators to stand and watch the show, or you can take a seat at one of the many tables that line the walls. If live music makes you hungry, you're in luck. They also have a menu populated with a variety of burgers.

MAP 10: 1147 ave. Cartier, 418/977-6843, www.rideaurouge.ca; daily 11am-10pm; free-$20 cover

Les Voûtes Napoléon

With its stone arches and low ceiling this *boîte à chansons* has a cozy albeit cave-like feel. Located in the basement of what used to be Restaurant Bonaparte (and is now the Savini), it's a great place to listen to some traditional Québécois music. The stage is so tiny, there's little room for a backup band for the singers who pass through here, so instead they're backed by a modest-sized sound system. It's busy from the moment it opens to the moment it closes, so don't be surprised if the crowd ends up singing louder than the musician. Shows usually start around 10pm.

MAP 10: 680 La Grande-Allée E., 418/640-9388, www.voutesdenapoleon.com; daily 8pm-3am; no cover

LOUNGES
★ Société Cigare

If you're nostalgic for the days when you used to be able to light up as you sipped your vintage cognac, then Société Cigare is sure to put a smile on your face. The only place in Québec City where you're allowed to smoke indoors, Société Cigare is part of the huge nightlife complex on Grande-Allée that includes Le Maurice and Voo Doo Grill. Customers can choose from a selection of over 200 brands of cigars, including Cuban Cohibas and Dominican Ashtons, from the Société's walk-in humidor. The soft lighting, all-wood bar, and leather club chairs give the bar a distinctly masculine feel. Smokers can choose from a range of scotch, port, and cognac to go with their cigars, and those with their own stogies are free to cut and light them here, as long as they get a drink to go with them.

MAP 10: 575 La Grande-Allée E., 418/647-2000; daily 1pm-3am; no cover

PUBS

Blaxton Pub and Grill

A former sports bar, Blaxton has reinterpreted itself as a classy neighborhood joint with the logo to prove it. If you want to see the game, however, this is still your best bet. Big-screen TVs are scattered throughout the wood and brick bar, which is populated with high stools and tables. Always a lively place, things get especially busy during weekday happy hours; this is an ideal spot to catch the game. The crowd tends to be younger, with most clients in their twenties or thirties. Shunning pub fare for more standard American food, they serve pizza, burgers, chicken, New York-style steaks, and ever-so-elusive chicken wings.

MAP 10: 1179 ave. Cartier, 418/522-9955, www.blaxton.com; Mon.-Fri. 11:30am-3am, Sat.-Sun. 3pm-3am; no cover

Pub Galway

This charming Irish pub in what was traditionally the English-speaking part of town is a little slice of Ireland, full of wood paneling, stained-glass windows, and smaller tables and chairs. It's not hard to imagine yourself in a country pub some 3,000 miles away. With a selection of 15 different whiskeys and over 20 different kinds of (mostly imported) beer, they also serve up pub classics like Irish poutine (it involves whiskey), fish and chips, and Irish stew with Guinness. The staff knows the regulars by name but still gives newcomers the same warm welcome.

MAP 10: 1112 ave. Cartier, 418/522-5282, www.pubgalway.com; daily 10am-3am; no cover

Saint-Jean-Baptiste and Saint-Roch

Map 11

BARS

★ La Barberie

This artisanal microbrewery started out as a small co-op in 1996 and now exports its beer to bars throughout the province. Situated in the heart of Saint-Roch, the brewery and bar—technically their tasting salon—are right next door to each other, so you know exactly where your pint is coming from. The owners, who are passionate about their beer but also dedicated and involved in the local community, made just about every inch of the bar and the rustic interior—wood tables, lots of light—to feel welcoming. First time visitors should try the tasting carousel featuring eight different

Local Brews

When you order a beer in Québec, there's a decent chance the beer you're ordering hasn't traveled more than 300 kilometers—the distance between Québec City and Montréal. Even brands that after a while start to feel as commonplace as Labatt and Budweiser come from some local, Québec-owned and -run brewery. There's a proud history of beer in the province, and the more time you spend in bars, the more you notice it.

Beer has been a part of Québécois culture for as long as Québécois culture has existed. When the first colonists arrived in Québec City from France at the beginning of the 17th century, they brought with them the tradition of brewing and were soon replicating century-old production techniques in the new world. In Québec though, they replaced hops with spruce, which made the particularly tangy spruce beer. An integral part of their diet, beer was full of important vitamins and nutrients that helped the colonists fend off scurvy. By the late 1640s, the Jesuit priests, headed by brother Ambroise, were brewing their own for themselves and the community.

People carried on brewing their own throughout the colony, and it wasn't until 1671 that Intendant Jean Talon opened the Brasserie du Roi, the first brewery in Québec City. Made entirely of Québec products, it was shipped as far away as the Caribbean and Europe. After that, home brewing started to die out in the French regime for one reason or another and only started to resurface again in the late 1700s with the arrival of British rule. With the Brits came true life-long brewers who were making beer here as early as 1791.

It's this mix of British and French (as well as some Belgian) brewing techniques that makes Québec beer so unique. Each micro- and independent brewery has its own distinct flavors and blends that can be traced back to brewing practices from one tradition or another. Some well-known local breweries include: La Barberie, Microbrasserie de l'Ile d'Orléans, and L'Inox.

draft beers. And if the weather is nice, drink them out on the sidewalk *terrasse*.

MAP 11: 310 rue St-Roch, 418/522-4373, www.labarberie.com; daily noon-1am; no cover

★ La Cuisine

Started in 2006, this brightly decorated spot with a retro feel is a daytime restaurant and nighttime hot spot. The restaurant formula goes like this: five meals per night (changing every week), all at the same price and all home-cooked. Québécois classics like *pâté chinois* and lasagna are staples on the menu, which is all made to reproduce home-cooked comfort food. Truth be told, however, most people who go to La Cuisine (The Kitchen) have likely never eaten here. It's a place to drink and dance the night away, especially among *branchée* twenty- and thirtysomethings. Music here tends toward popular indie hits and classic '80s (we're talking Blondie, Elvis Costello, the Jesus and Mary Chain) with a few Top 40 tunes thrown in for good measure.

MAP 11: 205 rue St-Vallier E., 418/523-3387, www.barlacuisine.com; Mon.-Thurs. 11am-1am, Fri. 11am-3am, Sat. 2pm-3am, Sun. 2pm-1am; no cover

391

Fou-Bar

Open since 1984, Fou-Bar is a veritable institution in the Faubourg Saint-Jean-Baptiste area, hosting everything from art exhibitions and vernissages to comedy nights, musical improv events, and concerts. People of all ages meet up here. Many musicians have regular nights here and the beer on tap is almost all from local breweries. Like all bars worth their weight, it also has a foosball table at the back.

MAP 11: 525 rue St-Jean, 418/522-1987, www.foubar.ca; daily 3pm-3am; no cover

Mo

In Japan, sushi bars have built-in taps that spout hot water; at Mo's in the hip Saint-Roch region, the built-in taps spout beer. This new breed of urban tavern mixes a minimalist design aesthetic—cream leather couches, geometric light fixtures—with classic cheap beers, and attracts hip young professionals and beer lovers. Local Québec brew Belle Gueule is available from the taps, and Mo stays true to its tavern roots and offers big 325-milliliter bottles of Tremblay and Labatt 50, a particularly Québec phenomenon. A large sidewalk *terrasse* is an inviting place in the summer, though sadly, no table taps here.

MAP 11: 810 blvd. Charest E., 418/266-0221, www.moresto.ca; Sun.-Tues. 11:30am-midnight, Wed.-Sat. 11:30am-1am; no cover

La Ninkasi

This two-floor bar in the middle of the action on St-Jean has a nice terrace out back with a view of the St-Matthew cemetery next door. A popular student hangout, with a boisterous vibrant atmosphere, it's dedicated to promoting Québec music and local beer, making it one of the best spots to catch emerging bands in the city. DJs take over the sound system on Thursdays and Fridays, so stop by if you're in the mood for a dance or two. With big-screen TVs, foosball, and pool tables, it's also a great place to watch hockey or any other big-time sports game.

MAP 11: 811 rue St-Jean, 418/529-8538, www.laninkasi.ca; Mon.-Fri. 2pm-3am, Sat.-Sun. noon-3am; no cover

Le Sacrilège

This popular bar on St-Jean draws a range of clients, from *fonctionnaires* (civil servants) and drunkards in the afternoon to university students at night. Everybody mixes here for the famous 5 à 7—Québec's version of happy hour. They have a good choice of microbrewery beers on tap. Thanks to stone walls, long, almost pew-like seats, and small round tables, the entire atmosphere is welcoming and unpretentious. Out back you'll find one of the biggest and best terraces in the city. Music here tends toward rock and indie music with particular DJs taking over the decks and switching things up.

MAP 11: 447 rue St-Jean, 418/649-1985, www.lesacrilege.com; daily noon-3am; no cover

Les Salons d'Edgar

Part billiard room, part bistro, part tango club, Les Salons d'Edgar wears a number of different hats. Once a theater, it has since been converted into one of the most diverse bars in the city, though it's still the hangout of choice for established Québécois actors and up-and-coming stars. Located in the front of the house, the bistro is fairly typical with heavy velvet curtains adorning the windows and candles on each table. In the second room, however, it's a whole different story. The electric blue walls of the billiard room are in striking contrast to the restaurant, but somehow it works. The five pool tables are never free for long, so make sure to grab a drink while you wait your turn. On Sundays, from 6pm onward, it turns into a tango club for amateurs and old pros alike.

MAP 11: 263 rue St-Vallier E., 418/523-7811, www.lessalonsdedgar.com; Sept.-June Wed.-Sun. 4:30pm-2am; no cover

Scanner

This punk-edged alternative bar is quiet in the afternoon but gets wilder at night when the garage-rockers, punks, indie-kids, and rockabillies come to hang out. It's a no-nonsense bar with screens projecting videos and artwork, loud music on the stereo, arcade games, pool tables, and two different kinds of foosball—European and North American. They have some of the best-priced microbrewery beer in the city and typical Québécois snack foods like nachos and hot dogs to go with it. Bands play here most weekends— think metal, punk, country—so check the site. They also have free Wi-Fi, if you're looking for an afternoon beer but still need to get some work done.

MAP 11: 291 rue St-Vallier E., 418/523-1916, www.scannerbistro.com; Mon.-Sat. 11am-3am, Sun. 3pm-3am; no cover

★ Taverne Jos Dion

Set in the heart of the working-class district of Saint-Sauveur, Taverne Jos Dion stands as a testament to taverns of a bygone era. Opened in 1933, it is the oldest tavern in Québec and, according to some, in North America. In fact women have only been allowed since 1986, when the government forced their hand, telling them to either accept women or close. Wanting to be democratic, they put it to a vote and *les habitués* (the regulars) voted to keep the

bar open, and subsequently let the women in. It remains, however, decidedly masculine and is a good place to watch sports games as well as drink your weight in beer, which is ridiculously cheap. Live accordion music is featured on Thursdays and Fridays to give it an even more authentic touch.

MAP 11: 65 rue St-Joseph W., 418/525-0710; Mon.-Sat. 8am-3am, Fri. 11am-3am, Sat. 2pm-3am, Sun. 2pm-1am; no cover

Le Temps Partiel

Run as a co-op, this is Québec City's alternative bar, as the website says: *une place différente pour des gens différents* (a different place for different people). In a past life, it was known as the Fourmi Atomique, a mythic place located in Old Québec whose walls collapsed in 2001. The bar relocated to the current location while waiting for a reconstruction that never came, hence the name Temps Partiel—it was supposed to be temporary. In many ways, the big square room with artwork occasionally on the wall still looks temporary, but the music (punk, indie, and electro), cheap beer, and alternative events like video projections, concerts, DJs, and exhibitions keep customers coming back. They also have free pool on weekends.

MAP 11: 698 rue d'Aiguillon, 418/522-1001, www.letempspartiel.com; daily noon-3am; no cover

GAY AND LESBIAN

Bar Le St-Matthew

Two former gay bars, Taverne 321 and the 889, have come together to create the Bar Le St-Matthew, a small, welcoming bar in Upper Town. Located on a small side street, the gay-friendly bar is popular with both gay and straight locals who pop in for affordable drinks. The atmosphere is laid-back with simple decor, pool tables, and a friendly staff. During the summer, the *terrasse* is open for cocktails alfresco.

MAP 11: 889 Côte Ste-Geneviève, 418/524-5000; daily 11am-3pm; no cover

★ Le Drague

Le Drague takes up most of the real estate on this small cobblestone street that constitutes the city's Village Gai (gay district). It's divided into four different sections, and each area of the club has its own vibe, from the quiet bar Verrière to the dance floor intensity of the main room, from the men-only vibe of Zone3 to the Cabaret with almost nightly performances. The events calendar is packed and includes weekly drag acts, karaoke, quiz games, and country dancing. Most people, though—gays, straights, lesbians, and transsexuals—come to dance like fools to the house and Top 40 hits that blare out over the crowded dance floor.

LIVE MUSIC
Jazz Bars
Le Largo
This Mediterranean restaurant turns into a jazz club later in the night. Long and narrow, with floor-to-ceiling picture windows that open out onto the street in the summer, the interior is exuberantly decorated with plush, bright-red banquettes, blond-wood floors, and lots of light from exquisite chandeliers. Live jazz is played here almost every night of the week, with bigger-named musicians taking the Thursday through Saturday evening time slot. Many of the musicians are local, but well-known bands are also known to pass through. You don't have to eat here to enjoy the music; those solely interested in the performance should head here around 10pm.

MAP 11: 734 rue St-Joseph, 418/529-3111, www.largorestoclub.com; daily noon-1am; free-$20 cover

LOUNGES
★ Le Boudoir
This two-floor lounge in the heart of Saint-Roch has multiple personalities, each attracting a diverse clientele. Upstairs, it's a restaurant by day and a lounge by night; most people skip the meals, however, and come solely for the ambience. Windows roll open in the summer onto the tiny rue du Parvis, giving the dark bar a bit of ambient lighting when the sun sets. Mixing the feel of a gentleman's club with 1960s futurism, the decor is distinctly modern and perfectly suited to the clientele of young professionals. Downstairs it's a different story. Called the Game Bar, it features 1980s arcade games like Pac-Man and Donkey Kong as well as foosball and darts. Wii and Playstation 3 can also be found, hooked up to a screen on the dance floor. This venue draws a younger, hipper crowd; nights here include iPod battles and DJ sets by international DJs as well as popular musicians.

MAP 11: 441 rue du Parvis, 418/524-2777, www.boudoirlounge.com; Mon.-Fri. noon-3am, Sat.-Sun. 4pm-3am; free-$20 cover

PUBS
Pub Nelligan's
A little known fact about Québec: It has quite a bit of Irish heritage. In fact, an estimated 40 percent of French-speaking Québecers have Irish ancestry, and Nelligan's is here to help celebrate that ancestry. Located on an unassuming side street, it's easy to miss the 200-year-old building that houses this cozy local. Like all Irish pubs, the atmosphere here is inviting, with the bar stools taken up by pub

NIGHTLIFE SAINT-JEAN-BAPTISTE AND SAINT-ROCH

regulars. The decoration is fairly barebones, but there's no lack of wood or handwritten Jameson signs. Take a seat near the window and down pints of Irish beer to your heart's content. They've got a number of Irish brews on tap, including Guinness, Kilkenny, Smithwick's, and Harp.

MAP 11: 789 Côte Sainte-Geneviève, 418/704-7817, www.pubnelligans.ca; daily 4pm-3am; no cover

Greater Québec City   Map 12

BARS

Le Pub de l'Université Laval

If you're a student looking for a place to party, hop the bus out to Université Laval to find your kindred spirits. Barely 15 minutes by bus, Le Pub de l'Université Laval is the campus hot spot. Located in the Pavillon Alphonse-Desjardins, it has the usual student bar vibe, nondescript tables and chairs, and TVs mounted on the walls. What it lacks in ambience, however, it makes up for in cheap beer. Drink specials are available throughout the week, including weekends, when the entire bar turns into one gigantic dance floor.

MAP 12: 1312 Pavillon Alphonse-Desjardins, Cité Universitaire, Sainte-Foy, 418/656-7075, www.cadeul.ulaval.ca/pub; Mon.-Fri. 11am-2am, Sat. 5pm-2am; no cover

DANCE CLUBS

L'Ozone Laurier

Outside of the city center, close to the malls of Sainte-Foy and the campus of Université Laval, is L'Ozone. Situated in a hotel of the same name, this lounge and dance club has become a popular place thanks to a number of cool after parties—this is where the Black Eyed Peas came after their performance at Festival d'Été, and French rap group TTC has also made an appearance. Appealing to university students and twentysomething Sainte-Foy residents, the vibe is youthful and energetic. The decor is minimalist chic, with stone walls, low leather couches, and neon lights. With hip-hop, house, Top 40, and hits from the '80s and '90s on rotation, the two dance floors are always bumping when the party gets underway around 10 at night. A second Ozone can be found on the Grande-Allée (270 La Grande-Allée E., 481/529-7932, www.ozonehotelbar.com), but it is more of a bar than a club.

MAP 12: 2810 blvd. Laurier, Sainte-Foy, 418/652-2020, www.ozonehotelbar.com; daily 7pm-3am; $5-20 cover

Arts and Culture

Highlights

★ **Best Place to Get Bookish:** The library at the **Morrin Centre** is well stocked and cozy (page 401).

★ **Most Intimate Venue:** Catching a show at **Le Théâtre du Petit Champlain,** with its 140-seat capacity, means you're practically in on the act (page 403).

★ **Best Art Complex:** Home of the opera, the orchestra, the ballet, and theater company Théâtre du Trident, **Grand Théâtre de Québec** is the center of all things high culture in Québec City (page 406).

★ **Best Mix of Art and Culture:** **Méduse** is a hub for all things cultural, from photography galleries to multi-disciplinary acts (page 408).

★ **Best Contemporary Gallery:** **Morgan Bridge** focuses on emerging artists whose work is often illustrative, street-inspired, and humorous (page 409).

Nowhere is the spirit of Québec culture more evident than in its arts. Though the province counts for just over 24 percent of the entire Canadian population, the cultural community is diverse and thriving. Québec City is the center for Francophone arts in the country, and the latest in theater and performing arts can be found here, as well as a strong visual arts community. There is an emphasis on homegrown talent, and though you'll often find European influences and artists, the Québec artist is championed. And why not? The culture here is so rich and unique, it doesn't need to depend on outside sources.

Since Québec is a predominantly Francophone city, English productions are rarely mounted, and it's in music, visual art, and dance that the language barriers come tumbling down. And with many of the most cutting-edge producers creating and exhibiting in cultural hot spot Méduse, you barely have to leave the building to catch it all. Once almost exclusively defined by traditional and artisinal work, the contemporary art scene has grown over the past decade. There are now a number of cool, boundary-pushing galleries that feature the more experimental works by local and international visual artists.

Tradtional arts and crafts still play a major role in the city's visual arts scene. Take the opportunity to explore the many galleries that showcase traditional Québécois and First Nations artwork, as it's some of the finest in the province.

Vieux-Québec's Upper Town

Map 8

CONCERT VENUES

Le Capitole

Opened in 1903, this playhouse retains many of the architectural charms that made it so illustrious back then: a sweeping marble staircase, gold trimmings, and balustrades. Originally the place to see the biggest music hall and vaudeville acts, Le Capitole is mainly a venue for movie screenings and concerts. Tributes to bands like Emerson, Lake, and Palmer and Supertramp are popular, as are classic French singers like Charles Aznavour. It's here that you'll also catch long-running performances like the *Elvis Story* and *Ring of Fire* (the Johnny Cash musical), often shown with English subtitles.

MAP 8: 972 rue St-Jean, 800/261-9903, www.lecapitole.com; $30-120

Palais Montcalm

Built in 1932, this art deco building just outside of the walls was originally a public pool before being converted into a concert hall. After undergoing major reconstruction in 2007, Palais Montcalm has emerged as one of the main centers for artistic life in the city. Seating close to 1,000, this is the home stage of chamber orchestra Les Violons du Roy (the King's Violins) as well as the site of many jazz, classical, and world music concerts.

Along with the large auditorium, it also has a multipurpose café/theater and café/bar.

MAP 8: 995 Place d'Youville, 877/641-6040, www.palaismontcalm.ca; $20-60

GALLERIES

Galerie d'Art Brousseau and Brousseau

Founder Raymond Brousseau first started collecting Inuit art in 1956 after receiving a sculpture as a present. In 1974 he opened his first gallery, and it has since become one of the most respected commercial galleries dealing in Inuit art. The large, open space with carpeted floors is a blend between store and gallery, but the aim here is to display the works in the best light possible. Works from four specific regions (Kitikmeot, Kivalliq, Nunavik, and Baffin) are available, each with their own style and materials. The staff here are all expertly qualified in specific fields.

MAP 8: 35 rue St-Louis, 418/694-1828, www.sculpture.artinuit.ca; daily 9:30am-5:30pm; free

★ **Morrin Centre**

Military barracks, city jail, and an English college make up the past lives of this cultural center dedicated to preserving and sharing the history of Anglophone culture in Québec. Built during the French regime in 1712, the original structure was used to house French troops and eventually prisoners of war. The current neoclassical structure was built in 1808 and was the first jail in Canada based on the ideas of prison reformer John Howard. Converted in 1868, it became the first English college in the city. Today, visitors can see remnants of these histories as they tour the Victorian library and head down to the old jail cells.

MAP 8: 44 Chaussée des Écossais, 418/694-9147, www.morrin.org; Tues. noon-9pm, Wed.-Fri. and Sun. noon-4pm, Sat. 10am-4pm; tours June-Sept. Mon.-Sat. 11am and 3pm, Sun. 1:30pm; tours $9 adult, $7 student, children under 8 free

Musée Bon Pasteur

This congregation of nuns, the Good Shepherd Sisters of Québec, was established by a mother of three, Marie Fitzbach, in 1856. Started as a women's shelter, it soon became a place of refuge for marginalized women and abandoned children in the 19th and 20th centuries. Housed in a structure that was built in 1878, the museum takes up three floors. Exhibits look at the past and future of the congregation, with many personal artifacts of the founders and their predecessors as well as a trip through the trials and tribulations facing Québec women throughout the congregation's history.

MAP 8: 14 rue Couillard, 418/694-0243, www.museebonpasteur.com; Tues.-Sun. 1pm-5pm; $3 adult, $2 senior, $2 student, children 12 and under free

Musée du Fort

Situated in the shadow of the Château Frontenac, the Musée du Fort, located in a historic house, features a 30-minute multimedia show that recreates the six sieges of Québec City and the Battle of the Plains of Abraham. Other highlights include a model of the city as it was in 1759 at the time of British conquest, as well as a small exhibit of weapons, uniforms, and military badges.

MAP 8: 10 rue Ste-Anne, 418/692-2175, www.museedufort.com; Feb.-Mar. and Nov. daily 11am-4pm, Apr.-Oct. daily 10am-5pm, Dec.-Jan. closed; $8 adult, $6 senior, $6 student

Québec Experience

As the name suggests this exhibit invites you to experience the history of Québec City—but in 3D. Admittedly, the technology is in need of an update, and what was once state-of-the-art now feels like a throwback to the late-1980s. Still, if you're into a bit of kitsch

Open-Air Gallery Rue du Trésor

Back in the 1960s, a group of art students looking for a place to show their work got together and started hanging their pieces on the walls of a narrow alleyway not far from Château Frontenac.

Called **Rue du Trésor** (Treasure Street, www.ruedutresor.qc.ca), it is one of the oldest streets in the city and has been around for three centuries. At the time of the French regime it was along this street that the colonists would pass in order to reach the Royal Treasury, where they paid their taxes. After the British conquest, the street was no longer so important and instead served its purpose as a service alley.

In fact, when the students started using it as an open-air art gallery, it was little more than a shortcut. Today, 36 different artists exhibit their work, and some of those original students are still here, selling their picturesque watercolors of Québec City scenes or abstract etchings of something completely indefinable. What started out as a ballsy venture has turned into a popular spot for emerging and established artists to show off and sell their work. Locals and tourists alike come here looking for a little piece of the city to take home with them.

(which is a must in Québec), this show presents all the major events, from the falling bridge to rifle crossfire, and real falling water.

MAP 8: 8 rue du Trésor, 418/694-4000, www.quebecexperience.com; mid-May-mid-Oct. daily 10am-10pm, mid-Oct.-mid-May daily 10am-5pm; $9.50 adult, $7 senior and student, children under 6 free

Vieux-Québec's Lower Town

Map 9

CONCERT VENUES

L'Agora du Vieux-Port

Looking out on to the St-Lawrence River, this outdoor theater couldn't be better located. Built down into the ground, the sunken stage and raised seating give it the air of a natural amphitheater. With seating for just over 4,000 (22 reserved for wheelchairs), it is one of the largest venues in the city, and its location near the Champlain bike path means an audience of passersby. It's open throughout the summer season from June to September, and shows here include everything from rock concerts to comedy shows and have included performers like Green Day and Bill Cosby. Events are cancelled when it rains.

MAP 9: 84 rue Dalhousie, 418/691-7211, www.agoraportdequebec.ca; free-$120

Situated in the pretty Quartier du Petit-Champlain, this small venue was built in the mid-19th century and was originally used as a theater, but since 1994 it's become a mecca for emerging and established artists. It consists of two smaller stages: La Salle Ulric Breton, which seats 140, and the Mezzanine, which seats 90. The shows are always intimate. The exposed brick walls and balcony seating give both rooms a cozy, cavern-like atmosphere. Many popular, and cool, French-language performers play here as well as the occasional English-language band. They also host shows by the Québec Gospel Choir come the holidays (it's a lot rockier than it sounds) as well as comedy acts.

MAP 9: 68 rue du Petit-Champlain, 418/692-2631, www.theatrepetitchamplain. com; free-$25

GALLERIES

Atelier Guy Lévesque

Self-taught artist Guy Lévesque takes inspiration from traditional theater like Commedia dell'Arte, Japanese nô theater, and the Venice Carnival to create his leather masks. Using a mold technique that dates back to the Middle Ages, the masks consistently take on a personality of their own. Entering his gallery and workshop, visitors are able to see the work in process, and it gives them a better understanding of how his vision comes together. Though masks are his specialty, he also creates sculpture and chairs, mostly out of metal and leather.

MAP 9: 79 rue du Sault-au-Matelot, 418/694-1298, www.guylevesque.com; Mon.-Sat. 10am-5pm; free

Galerie Madeleine Lacerte

Housed in an old car garage on a corner lot in the Vieux-Port, Galerie Madeleine Lacerte is one of the most prominent contemporary art galleries in Québec City. It was founded by Madeleine Lacerte in 1986, and her son Louis Lacerte is now the gallery director. It's dedicated to supporting Québec and Canadian artists on both national and international levels. The artists they represent are all based in Canada. Exhibits range from painting and photography to installation and conceptual pieces and feature both established and emerging artists. They continue to be on the forefront of contemporary art.

MAP 9: 1 Côte Dinan, 418/692-1566, www.galerielacerte.com; Mon.-Wed. 9am-5pm, Thurs.-Fri. 9am-6pm, Sat.-Sun. noon-6pm; free

Galeries d'Art Beauchamp and Beauchamp

Six commercial galleries make up this large collection of exhibition spaces located in the Vieux-Port. Each gallery has its own mandate,

top: Le Capitole, Vieux-Québec's Upper Town; bottom: Rue de Tresor

allowing for a huge variation in the types and the prices of work, as well as its own layout; some galleries have so many pieces on the walls you can barely see the wall. The galleries represent over 140 artists, particularly local ones. Both classical and contemporary works are on view here, as well as photography. Though typical closing time is 6pm, they often stay open much later in summer.

MAP 9: 10 rue du Sault-au-Matelot, 877/694-2244, www.galeriebeauchamp.com; daily 9:30am-6pm; free

MUSEUMS
Maison Chevalier

Built by trader and ship owner Jean-Baptiste Chevalier in 1752, the Maison Chevalier incorporates other buildings that date back to 1675 and 1695. A great example of early New France architecture, the house features firewalls, high chimneys, and vaulted cellars. Ravaged by fire, the house was rebuilt in 1762 and was run as an inn throughout the 19th century. Inside, you'll find exposed wood beams, wide wooden floorboards, and stone fireplaces. The permanent exhibit A Sense of the Past focuses on life in the 18th and 19th centuries, and English guidebooks are available at the front desk. One weird fact: The facade, which looks out on the St-Lawrence River, was originally the back of the house.

MAP 9: 50 blvd. Champlain, 418/646-3167, www.mcq.org; Tues.-Sat. 10am-5pm; free

Musée Naval de Québec

This small museum in the Vieux-Port is dedicated to the city's naval history. The new permanent exhibit Meanders looks at the major historic events that have taken place on the river, from the first Amerindian settlements to the numerous invasion attempts by the British to the German U-boat attacks that happened in her waters.

Personal stories add a human face to the history, and objects include bows and arrows, 18th-century muskets, and a model of the hull of a World War II warship. It also hosts various traveling exhibitions.

MAP 9: 170 rue Dalhousie, 418/694-5387, www.museenavaldequebec.com; July-Aug. Tues.-Fri. and Sun. 10am-noon and 1pm-4pm, Sept.-June Tues.-Fri. 1pm-4pm; free (donations accepted)

THEATER
La Caserne Dalhousie

This center for the multidisciplinary arts was established by Robert Lepage and his creative collaborators—actors, writers, set designers, technicians, opera singers, and puppeteers—in 1997. The ultramodern venue looks almost mechanical, with visible pipes, scaffolding, and stairs. It's used primarily as a workspace for the company, called Ex Machina, to try out and create new performances. They occasionally hold public events to show off new works.

MAP 9: 103 rue Dalhousie, 418/692-5323, www.exmachina.qc.ca; cost varies

Parliament Hill and the Plains

Map 10

CINEMA

Cinéma

This repertory cinema, located above a pharmacy, might bring you back to your adolescence if you grew up watching unlikely films in unlikely places. It's devoted to screening original films that have never before been screened in Québec City, and the emphasis here is on classics, modern-day masterpieces, and of course, independent features. With 117 seats, it's intimate without being uncomfortable. English films are screened with French subtitles, but no matter the language, this place is for film buffs.

MAP 10: 1019 ave. Cartier, 418/522-1011, www.cinemacartier.com; $11 adult

MUSEUMS

Maison Henry-Stuart

Take afternoon tea and cake in this charmingly authentic 19th-century cottage. Built in 1849 for Mrs. William Henry, the wife of a rich wood merchant, the house today is found on one of the biggest boulevards in the city, but inside it has retained its elegant and rich decor. Tours of the garden and house give visitors an idea of what life was like for well-to-do English families in Québec at the turn of the 20th century, and tea time is part of the hour-long tour.

MAP 10: 82 La Grande-Allée W., 418/647-4347, www.actionpatrimoine.ca; tours mid-June-early Sept. daily on the hour 11am-4pm; $8 adult, $3 child 6-12

THEATER

★ Grand Théatre de Québec

The largest arts complex in Québec City, the Grand Théatre was built to commemorate the country's centennial in 1967. Designed by Montréal-based architect Victor Prus, the large concrete structure opened in 1971. Home to the Québec Symphony Orchestra, l'Opéra de Québec, and the Théâtre du Trident, it's here that most large-scale performances happen, whether it's a dance piece by the Ballet du Québec, a rock extravaganza like Jason Bonham's Led Zeppelin Experience, or a concert by Québec indie rock kings Karkwa.

MAP 10: 269 blvd. René-Lévesque E., 877/643-8131, www.grandtheatre.qc.ca; $20-120

Saint-Jean-Baptiste and Saint-Roch

Map 11

CONCERT VENUES

Le Cercle

Le Cercle is the Québec City version of Montréal's Sala Rosa. Not only does it serve up a mean meal and cool bar atmosphere, but it's also the place where you'll find the coolest music shows. This St-Roch staple is all concrete floors, high ceilings, great acoustics, and even better acts. If you want to dance the night away to the sounds of Berlin's latest electro sensation, this is your destination. Since it's one of the few places to catch new music in the city, it's become quite popular. Get your tickets ahead of time and if you want a decent view, arrive early. In addition to live music, they also host a number of film and art events.

MAP 11: 228 rue St-Joseph E., 418/948-8648, www.le-cercle.ca; $10-30

Impérial de Québec

This theater and concert hall in Saint-Roch has a long history. Originally the site of the neighborhood's cemetery, this was a factory before becoming a theater with a second-floor art gallery in 1912. Rebuilt under new ownership in 1917, in the style that was popular at the time—a flat, square marquee, and the Imperial's sign illuminated and protruding from the center of the building—it's this facade that still exists and is one of the few theaters in Québec that recall the golden age of silent films. Inside, the old-time charm remains, with balustrades adorned with winged cherubs and moldings framing the stage. It's a midsize venue; bands like Gwar and Broken Social Scene have hit the stage along with cabaret acts and the occasional movie screening.

MAP 11: 252 rue St-Joseph E., 418/523-2227, www.imperialdequebec.com; $15-50

GALLERIES

Centre Materia

This artist-run center is dedicated to the field of fine crafts. With an aim to broaden the public's familiarity with and recognition of this art form, they host a number of openings and exhibits by diverse artists, everything from glasswork to textiles. Both emerging and established artists exhibit here, but unlike conventional galleries, Materia doesn't represent the individual artists. Located in a bright, open space on the busy boulevard Charest, the gallery has an industrial feel with white walls and exposed pipes and ceiling beams.

MAP 11: 395 blvd. Charest E., 418/524-0354, www.centremateria.com; Wed. and Fri.-Sun. noon-5pm, Thurs. noon-8pm; free

Galerie d'art Factory

Representing both established and emerging local talent, Factory has a distinctly contemporary edge, in both the artwork hanging on its walls and in the surroundings themselves. Large picture windows showcase the many large-scale works suspended in front of rough brick walls above a polished concrete floor. A pristine white couch located in the middle of the room invites visitors to linger and contemplate the metal sculptures and day-glo paintings. It's also perfect for lounging and sipping during one of the gallery's vernissages.

MAP 11: 837 rue St-Joseph E., 418/561-2558, www.galeriefactory.com; Wed. and Sat.-Sun. noon-5pm, Thurs.-Fri. noon-8pm; free

Le Lieu

Situated in Saint-Roch, this artist-run center was established in 1982 and focuses on multidisciplinary arts. The floor-to-ceiling windows of the sparse space look out onto the street—perfect for catching the attention of passersby. Le Lieu works with artists both at home and abroad, and the contemporary work shown here focuses on practices like installation, performance, and audio and visual art. It's often quite conceptual. It's rare that you'll see a painting hanging on these walls. They also host Rencontre Internationale d'Art Performance (RAIP), a yearly international festival dedicated to performance art.

MAP 11: 345 rue du Pont, 418/529-9680, www.inter-lelieu.org; daily 1pm-5pm; free

★ Méduse

Established in 1995, Méduse is an arts complex filled with galleries, studios, and offices dedicated to arts and culture. Made up of linked buildings, some of them modern, others refurbished historical structures, it's the home of 10 different businesses, from a radio station to art galleries. L'œil de Poisson, which exhibits contemporary works, and VU, the only gallery in the city dedicated to contemporary photography, are always worth checking out. Dance company La Rotonde often performs in the center's *salle multi*. This hub has become integral to all forms of the city's contemporary arts scene, and if you want to check out a specific space, check the times before you leave since they often vary.

MAP 11: 541 rue St-Vallier E., 418/640-9218, www.meduse.org; Wed.-Sun. noon-5pm; free

Morgan Bridge takes the idea of what we perceive an art gallery to be and turns it on its head. With a strong connection to graffiti and skateboard culture—spray paint is sold in the gallery, along with zines, and many of the artworks are created on skate decks—the work is subversive, exciting, and out of the ordinary. It's not all street art though; throughout the space you'll find art naïf and work that tows the line between graphic and street art. In short, this is where you'll find the work of emerging underground artists in Québec.

MAP 11: 367 rue du Pont, 418/529-1682, www.morganbridge.ca; Wed. and Fri. noon-6pm, Thurs. noon-7pm, Sat.-Sun. noon-5pm; free

THEATER

Théatre La Bordée

Established in 1976 by a group of young actors directly out of theater school, this independent theater company situated in Saint-Roch mounts four productions a year. Walking the line between classical and experimental, their aim is to produce excellent theater that is also accessible to a large public. They focus on plays from Québec, but there is also a variety in their programs, and past seasons have included productions of Shakespeare's *Richard III*, Dumas' *Le Reine Margot*, and *The Pillowman* by Irish playwright Martin McDonagh. Consisting of two presentation halls, an Italian-style theater that seats 350 and one that seats 60, the settings are decidedly intimate. All productions are in French.

MAP 11: 315 rue St-Joseph E., 418/694-9721, www.bordee.qc.ca; $35 adult, $30 senior, $25 under 30

Greater Québec City   Map 12

CINEMA

Le Clap

If you can get past the unfortunate name, Le Clap is a great repertory cinema that plays films that don't always get wide distribution in the province. It plays English movies with French subtitles. Fans of international and art-house cinema will enjoy their selection of festival hits from festivals like Cannes, TIFF, and Festival Nouveau Cinéma. With none of the bells and whistles you find at bigger name cinemas, the smaller auditoriums and intimate setting aren't for everyone.

MAP 12: 2360 chemin Ste-Foy, 418/653-2470, www.clap.qc.ca; $12 adult, $9 senior and student, $8 child

Sports and Activities

Québec City was blessed with huge green spaces, a waterfront, and a cliff face perfect for scaling. In fact, the city is so hilly that sometimes even a trip to the local store can feel like a hike. Blame the instense inclines, the promise of mountains looming to the north, and the beauty of one of the world's largest rivers. This is city that embraces its proximity to nature. Quebeckers are no strangers to the sporting goods store and they bring their partiuclar love of sports, like canoeing and skiing, to an urban environment.

Québec has a strong connection to the outdoors, even when the ground is buried under four feet of snow. Cross-country skiing and snowshoeing are part of getting around in the city. What better way to see the historical sights than skiing from one place to the next? There's no shortage of outdoor skating rinks, many of which are frozen rivers and ponds. Ice-skating is an idyllic and truly Canadian pastime. Not far from the city center are a number of mountains, pefect for exploring with snowboards and downhill skis.

The city is on one of the largest waterways in North America, so boating is a popular sport, and in summer the St-Lawrence is dotted with white sails and even the occasional sea kayak.

Though it's one of the hilliest cities in Canada, Québec City is also home to two of the longest bike paths in the country, running alongside the river; a trip down the Promenade Champlain is like a mini-break from the city. And, of course, come winter the bike path becomes one of the best ski trails.

Highlights

★ **Best Winter Sledding:** At 250 meters high, the **Glissades de la Terrasse Dufferin** is the biggest (and only) winter slide in Québec City; speeding from the top down to the *terrasse* at speeds of up to 70 kilometers per hour has been a tradition since 1884 (page 414).

★ **Best Bike Path:** Running alongside the St-Lawrence River and through Cap Blanc and various parks, **Corridor du Littoral** is a great path for exercise and to see some of the lesser-known parts of the city (page 414).

★ **Best Place for Snow Sports:** With everything from cross-country skiing to ice-skating and snowshoeing available, **Parc des Plaines d'Abraham** is your outdoor sports paradise (page 416).

★ **Best Place to Have a Picnic:** Once the grounds of the governor-general's residence, **Parc du Bois-de-Coulonge** boasts groomed gardens and amazing views of the St-Lawrence that are still worthy of royalty (page 420).

★ **Best Summer Activity:** Nothing says summer like a game of baseball. **Les Capitales de Québec** are among the best in the Can-Am league (page 421).

Vieux-Québec's Upper Town

Map 8

BOAT TOURS

Croisière Dufour

This company offers two different cruises in and around Québec. La Touristique is a 90-minute historical tour that will take visitors from the Vieux-Port along the coast of the Île d'Orléans and Montmorency Falls and allows for waterfront views of Château Frontenac and Cap Diamant. The Image Mill cruise allows you to take in Le Moulin à Images multimedia event from the water; with panoramic windows and three terraces, it gives you a different take on the spectacle. They also offer longer cruises into the Charlevoix region to see the whales and the fjords.

MAP 8: 57 rue Ste-Anne, 800/463-5250, www.dufour.ca; May-Oct. daily 1:30pm, mid-July-mid-Aug. daily 1:30pm and 3:30pm; $64 adult, $59 senior and student, $29 child, children under 6 free for 90-minute cruise

ICE-SKATING

Patinoire de la Place d'Youville

Located directly in front of the Palais de Montcalm, this outdoor skating rink is a veritable winter wonderland once the snow has settled. A great place to bring the kids, it is frequented by tourists and locals alike who want to go for a skate in the shadow of the old city walls. Skate rental and sharpening are available during opening hours, as is a warm changing room fitted out with lockers, but visitors have to bring their own padlock.

MAP 8: 995 Place d'Youville, 418/641-6256; late Oct.-mid-Mar. Mon.-Thurs. noon-10pm, Fri.-Sat. 10am-10pm; free

MINIATURE GOLF

Golf Touristique de Québec

Sign in at the clubhouse to receive your specialized club and ball before hitting the Upper Town links. A way of combining history with golf, this nine-hole course (rumor has it, it's a par 4) has you teeing off at various points around the city's fortifications (which are for the most part covered in grass), through its historic back streets, and even up along the walls of the Citadelle. A round takes approximately two hours and the course is open come rain or shine.

MAP 8: Parc-de-l'Artillerie, 2 rue d'Auteuil, 418/977-2453, www.golftouristique. com; June-Sept. daily 10am-5pm; $15 adult, $13 senior, $13.50 youth, children under 8 free

SLEDDING
★ Glissades de la Terrasse Dufferin

This entertainment of sliding down a steep 250-meter run at speeds of up to 70 kilometers per hour has been around since 1884. The Glissades de la Terrasse Dufferin *(les glissades)* are a Québec tradition. In front of the Château Frontenac, with great views of the St-Lawrence, families line up in full winter regalia to ride a toboggan down to the base of the wooden structure. Up to four people can ride down on a single toboggan, though you're also allowed to try it solo and in pairs. A mini-sugar shack full of refreshments is available on the spot. Lines can be long, especially on weekends, so be prepared to wait.

MAP 8: Terrasse Dufferin, at rue des Carrières and Place d'Armes, 418/829-9898; mid-Dec.-mid-Mar. daily 11am-11pm; $2 pp per ride

SWIMMING
Parc de l'Esplanade

This children's wading pool is in the heart of Vieux-Québec's Upper Town. Situated in the shadow of the Fortifications, the wading pool is simple, with hardly any bells and whistles; still, it's the perfect place to let the kids cool off and let off some steam in the middle of the day. A children's playground can be found just a little further along.

MAP 8: Parc des Plaines d'Abraham, 418/523-5695; mid-June-mid-Aug. daily 11am-4pm; free

Vieux-Québec's Lower Town
Map 9

BIKING
Bike Paths
★ Corridor du Littoral

This 48-kilometer bike path stretches all the way from Saint-Augustin-de-Desmaures west of Québec City way to Chute Montmorency to the east. Running alongside the St-Lawrence, the path includes the Promenade Samuel Champlain; redone for the city's 400th anniversary in 2008, this section of the path is located below the Plains of Abraham and includes various parks and rest stops. It takes you along Cap Blanc, a charming working-class area built directly against the cliff.

Though it's mainly a bike path, runners, walkers, in-line skaters, and those in wheelchairs are free to use the path for both recreation and mobility. Open throughout the year, it becomes an ideal place to snowshoe and cross-country ski in winter.

MAP 9: St-Augustin-de-Desmaures to Chute Montmorency, 418/641-6290, www.routeverte.com; free

Bike Rentals and Tours
Cyclo Services

Offering both rentals and tours, Cyclo Services has different types of bikes on offer, including hybrids, road bikes, tandem, and children's bikes. All rentals come with a helmet, lock, and a map. Located across the street from the Corridor du Littoral, it couldn't be easier to jump on your bike and go. Five bike tours are available throughout the summer season; some, like the one through Lower Town and the Vieux-Port, stay closer to home, while others, like Huron-Wendake, take you farther afield. Prices vary and times change often, so call or email ahead. For those with their own wheels, an on-site mechanic is available seven days a week.

MAP 9: 289 rue St-Paul, 418/692-4052, www.cycloservices.net; daily 9am-9pm; tours May-Oct. 9am-9pm; $35 per day

Écolocyclo

Located at the Marché du Vieux-Port, Écolocyclo is perfectly situated on the Corridor du Littoral, the longest bike path in the city. The majority of their rental fleet bikes are mountain and city bike hybrids, with at least 21 speeds, perfect for those steep Québec streets. They also offer electric bikes to help give your pedaling a bit of a push, as well as tandems, trail-a-bikes for children, and recumbent bikes for those who want to give laid-back riding a try. Though they don't offer tours, they will give you suggested routes to try, and all of their bikes are available for rentals of up to three days, at reasonable prices—perfect for getting around.

MAP 9: Marché du Vieux-Port, 160 Quai St-André, 418/692-2517, www.ecolocyclo.net; May-Oct. daily 9am-6pm; $17-45/hour

BOAT TOURS
Croisière AML

Cruises are available on the *Louis Jolliet*, a restaurant boat that can take you as far north as the Charlevoix region. Divided into day and night cruises, options include the brunch cruise with activities for kids, a tour of Île d'Orléans, a fireworks cruise, and a five-course dinner cruise. The captain's lounge, three dining rooms, and terraces are on board as well as a gift shop and a bistro. Entertainment is part of every cruise and guide Louis Jolliet—an early Canadian explorer—will reveal all the area's secrets. An orchestra plays in the evenings; passengers can dance the night away.

MAP 9: Quai Chouinard, 10 rue Dalhousie, 866/856-6668, www.croisieresaml.com

Departing from the Vieux-Port, Croisières Coudrier offers some unique and interesting tours. Many of the cruises are also educational. Learn about Québec's own Ellis Island, Grosse-Île, a quarantine station between 1832 and 1937 and the home of Irish immigrants; passengers will have a chance to visit the island. Or experience the charms of Isle-aux-Grues by bike and taste their well-known cheese. Apple-picking and five-course dinner cruises are also available, as is a sightseeing tour, which lets you see the city from the river.

MAP 9: Bassin Louise, Pier 19, 180 rue Dalhousie, 888/600-5554, www. croisierescoudrier.qc.ca; May-mid-Oct. Sat.-Sun. 1:30pm, July-Aug. daily 3:30pm; $32 adult, $30 senior and student, $15 child, children under 5 free for 90-minute cruise

GYMS

Planète Fitness Gym

This 24-hour gym is open seven days a week and offers à la carte memberships that allow up to 10 visits. Longer memberships are available for three months up to a year. Along with a weight and cardio room, they also offer a number of classes, including crossfit, spinning, and toning, many of which start as early as seven in the morning.

MAP 9: 400 blvd. Jean-Lesage, 418/523-0284, www.planetefitnessgym.qc.ca; daily 24 hours

Parliament Hill and the Plains

Map 10

CROSS-COUNTRY SKIING AND SNOWSHOEING

★ Parc des Plaines d'Abraham

Come winter, this historical sight becomes an outdoor sport paradise. For beginners and pros, the 12.6 kilometers of cross-county trails and the 3.8-kilometer (round-trip) trails for snowshoers are the best place to experience winter in the city's own backyard. Four classic trails, made up of one easy trail and three intermediate ones, are open. Those without their own equipment—boots, poles, skis, and snowshoes—can rent them from the Discovery Pavilion. A waxing room and two heated rest areas are available around the plains, and they also offer cross-country ski lessons.

MAP 10: Discovery Pavilion, 835 rue Wilfrid-Laurier (equipment rental), 418/648-2586, www.ccbn-nbc.qc.ca; late Dec.-mid-Mar. daily 8:30am-4pm; free

ICE-SKATING

Parc du Musée

This outdoor skating rink, directly in front of the Musée des Beaux-Arts and right on the Plains of Abraham, is a great place to bring the kids. Easily accessible and popular with locals, it was completely renovated in 2011. Skaters should bring their own skates and equipment, since there are no rental facilities on the premises.

MAP 10: Parc des Champs-de-Bataille; late Oct.-mid-Mar. daily 11am-6pm; free

SWIMMING

Piscine Parc du Musée

Located on the Plains of Abraham, this public pool and wading pool were renovated in 2011, giving them a brand new look. Conveniently located right on the Grande-Allée, it's easily accessible from all points in the city. A haven for locals, this is a great place to bring the kids, especially to let them go a little wild after an afternoon at the museum.

MAP 10: Parc des Champs-de-Bataille; mid-June-mid-Aug. daily noon-7pm; free

YOGA

Ashtanga Yoga Québec

A number of different types and levels of classes are available at this Ashtanga yoga studio located in a local community center. Guided classes are available for beginners to intermediate and for regular practitioners. Courses run throughout the day, seven days a week, typically starting at 6:30am and ending at 7:30pm. Those already comfortable with their yoga and just looking for a place to practice are welcome to drop in; there are free practice times available throughout the week.

MAP 10: Centre Culture et Environnement Frédéric Back, 870 ave. de Salaberry, 418/682-0654, www.ashtangaquebec.com; Mon.-Sat. hours vary by season; $16 per class for nonmembers

Greater Québec City   Map 12

AMUSEMENT PARKS

Mega Parc des Galeries de la Capitale

A child's paradise, this amusement park in the middle of a mall is designed for toddlers through tweens. Twenty different rides are waiting for kids to take them for a whirl, from physical fun like the Magic Castle's ball pit, slides, and rope games and the Baby Jungle's plush obstacle course to more traditional fairway staples like mini-bumper cars, a miniature train, a merry-go-round, Ferris wheel, and a rollercoaster. For kids wanting a bit more sport, there's also a climbing wall, an ice rink, and mini-putt. Each ride requires a varying number of tokens, anywhere from two to six, with each token costing 50 cents.

MAP 12: 5401 blvd. des Galeries, 418/627-5800, www.mega-parc.com; Sept.-mid-June Mon.-Wed. noon-5pm, Thurs.-Fri. noon-9pm, Sat. 9:30am-5pm, Sun. 11am-5pm; mid-June-Aug. Mon.-Wed. 10am-5pm, Thurs.-Fri. 10am-9pm, Sat. 9:30am-5pm, Sun. 11am-5pm

BIKING
Bike Paths
Corridor des Cheminots

Intersecting with the Corridor du Littoral just outside Saint-Roch, the Corridor des Cheminots is 22 kilometers long and takes riders from the city to Haute Saint-Charles in the north. Since it passes through various areas, including the St-Charles River and Wendake Village, riders can view a diverse landscape. Open to cyclists, walkers, runners, and inline skaters, it becomes a popular place for cross-country skiing and snowshoeing in the winter.

MAP 12: North of Estuaire de la Riviere St-Charles to Haute Saint-Charles, 418/641-6412, www.routeverte.com; free

CLIMBING
Le Champlain and Le Pylône

For experienced climbers only, this natural climbing wall can be accessed from rue Champlain. Located just outside of the city, near the Pont de Québec, are two cliffs perfect for climbing. This outdoor climbing area is a popular place with local climbers and caters to both learners and intermediate climbers. Le Pylône is the beginner area with 5.8 routes, while Le Champlain, 30 feet high by 200 feet long with lots of overhanging routes, is great for experts. Known as the "School of Rock," it's a great place to practice, especially since the rock face is made up of difficult gritstone.

MAP 12: Near Pont de Québec

Roc Gyms

Opened in 1993, Roc Gyms is a climbing school that offers indoor climbing lessons. Over 75 climbing lines are available in the main room, while two bouldering rooms are also available on-site, as are a number of indoor aerial courses. Those that are already experienced climbers can sign up for courses in outdoor and ice-climbing. Located in Limoilou, it's easily accessible from downtown and Vieux-Port.

MAP 12: 2350 ave. du Colisée, 418/647-4422, www.aventurex.net; Mon.-Sat. 10am-10pm, Sun. 10am-6pm; $18 day rental with equipment

GOLF

La Tempête

Situated across the water in the city of Lévis, La Tempête is one of the top courses in the metropolitan area (of course, the green fees reflect this). It hosted the World Skins tournament in 2009 and has been called the first 18-hole golf course of international caliber in the area. Designed by golf architect Darrell J. Huxham, the 7,203-yard course is topped with a luxurious clubhouse and high-class restaurant.

MAP 12: 51 rue des Trois Manoirs, Lévis, 418/832-8111, www.golflatempete.com; May-Nov. daily dawn-10pm; $95-155 for 18 holes

ICE-SKATING

Pointe-aux-Lièvres

When the St-Charles River, which separates Saint-Roch from Limoilou, freezes over, it becomes a natural skating rink, measuring 1.5 kilometers long. It's here that you'll find people playing pickup hockey and families teaching the youngest members how to skate. If you want a real Canadian experience, there's nothing like plopping your bum on a cold park bench to lace up your skates. Of course, a warm changing room and heated pavilion with hot chocolate and skate rental are also available.

MAP 12: 5 rue de la Pointe-aux-Lièvres, 418/641-6345; late Oct.-mid-Mar. daily 24 hours; free

PARKS

Domaine Maizerets

Situated just across the St-Charles River, Domaine Maizerets is both a public park and a historic site. Bought by the church in 1705, the land served as a farm and some of the church's old buildings are still standing. Tours of the beautifully landscaped gardens and arboretum are available, and concerts are often held on the park grounds. Two bike trails, Corridor des Cheminots and Corridor du Littoral, cut through the park, and in the winter it's a popular place for skating, cross-country skiing, snowshoeing, and tobogganing.

MAP 12: 1248 ave. de la Verendrye, 418/660-7357, www.domainemaizerets.com; free

Parc Cartier-Brébeuf

South of Saint-Roch, this national historic site commemorates both the winter of 1535, when Jacques Cartier and his shipmates spent the season near the Iroquoian village of Stadacona, and the site of the Jesuit missionaries' first home in Québec. Commemorative monuments are set up around the park, which is divided into east and west by a small river. With 6.8 hectares, it's a popular place for outdoor sport and a bike path cuts through most of it.

An interpretation center is open on-site from early May to early September, offering guided tours and various family activities.

MAP 12: 175 rue l'Espinay, 888/773-8888, www.pc.gc.ca; free

Parc de la Plage Jacques-Cartier

Located outside of the city, just on the other side of the Québec Bridge, this waterfront park gives visitors direct access to the St-Lawrence River. The winding paths and roads that take you to the shore, coupled with the boulders and pebbles that line the beach, make you feel as though you're somewhere else entirely. Since swimming is prohibited, boating is the summer's most popular sport, along with the 2.5 kilometers of hiking trails.

MAP 12: 3636 chemin de la Plage Jacques-Cartier, Ste-Foy, 418/641-6300; May-Oct.; free

★ Parc du Bois-de-Coulonge

The former home of the governor-general of United Canada, Spencer Wood was bought by the Québec government in 1870 and was home to the province's lieutenant-governors until 1966. Though a fire destroyed the main residence, the splendid gardens remain, including a park that runs along the St-Lawrence, offering great views of the city. The park is a favorite for picnicking, self-guided tours, and its three kilometers of hiking trails. There's also a children's playground and sledding in winter.

MAP 12: 1215 Grande-Allée W., 800/442-0773; free

Parc Linéaire de la Rivière St-Charles

Starting at the Vieux-Port and running on for a total of 32 kilometers, this park runs along the banks of the St-Charles River, covering both urban and natural environments. Open year long, it has 4 kilometers of bike and rollerblade paths, ice-skating, snowshoeing, and 10 kilometers of cross-country skiing in winter. An interpretation center is located in the middle of the park.

MAP 12: 332 rue Domagaya, 418/691-4710, www.societerivierestcharles.qc.ca; free

Parc Victoria

Situated at the southern tip of Saint-Roch on the banks of the St-Charles River, Parc Victoria has been one of the few green spaces in the area since 1897. Almost completely surrounded by water, the small park was named after Britain's Queen Victoria. It provides excellent views of the river and it's here that you'll catch a baseball game by Les Capitales de Québec.

MAP 12: Rue Robert-Rumilly, 418/641 6654; free

Baseball
★ Les Capitales de Québec

Members of the Can-Am Baseball League, Les Capitales are one of the most successful teams in the league. Making the playoffs almost every year since they entered the league in 1999, they garnered league titles in 2006, 2009, and 2010.

They play at the Stade Municipal, which seats approximately 5,000 and is located in Parc Victoria. The stadium opened in 1938 and has a long history within local baseball legend. This rich history and the affordable tickets ($10, $15 box seats) give you the feeling that you're still in touch with what sports used to be and should be.

MAP 12: Stade Municipal, Parc Victoria, 418/521-2255, www.capitalesdequebec. com

Football
Le Rouge et Or

This university football team has amassed a strong following in a city craving more spectator sports. Le Rouge et Or (the Red and the Gold, which are the school colors) won the Vanier Cup, the highest distinction for a Canadian university football team, four times in six years (2003, 2004, 2006, and 2008). They also hold the record for the longest winning streak in Canadian Interuniversity Sport football with 19 consecutive wins. If you happen to be visiting in the fall, a trip to Sainte-Foy to see a game is worth it; the bleachers are always packed and the energy is palpable.

Université Laval's outdoor stadium can hold up to 10,000 spectators it but fit double that in 2005 with standing room only. Their loyal fan base has also mastered the art of tailgating, getting to the stadium parking lot early on game day mornings.

MAP 12: PEPS de l'Université Laval, 2300 rue de la Terrasse, 418/656-7377, www.rougeetor.ulaval.ca

Hockey
Remparts de Québec

Ever since they won the Memorial Cup (the Canadian Junior Championships) in 2006, the Remparts, Québec's Major Junior Hockey team, have become the hottest show in town. And things will probably stay that way so long as this crazy-about-hockey city doesn't have an NHL team. Their home rink is the Colisée Pepsi, the former home of les Nordiques (RIP), which moved to Colorado in 1995.

They're coached by former goalie Patrick Roy, considered one of the best goalies in the history of the game. Roy, who ranks with Celine Dion as far as Québec hero hierarchy goes, brings a colorful edge to the team. Famous Remparts alumni include legendary player Guy Lafleur, ex-Nordiques Michel Goulet, left-winger Simon Gagné, center Mike Ribeiro, and right-winger Alexander Radulov.

MAP 12: Colisée Pepsi, 250 blvd. Wilfrid-Hamel, 418/525-1212, www.remparts. qc.ca

WATER SPORTS

Baie de Beauport

A world of boating fun is only a five-minute drive from downtown Québec City. Though swimming in the river is forbidden, a ton of boating and beach activities make you feel like you're on the coast. Canoe, kayak, sailboard, dinghy, and catamaran rentals are offered at various rates and lengths, and those looking to learn how to sail can sign up for classes. Beach soccer and volleyball courts are free for all to use and the large children's park keeps the kids busy.

MAP 12: Eastern end of blvd. Henri-Bourassa, 418/266-0722, www. baiedebeauport.com; mid-June-mid-Aug. daily 10am-9pm

Shops

Highlights

★ **Best Hat Store: Bibi et Compagnie** has approximately 3,000 men's and women's hats for all kinds of weather and in all kinds of styles (page 430).

★ **Unique Gifts:** Connoisseur of kitsch, Mr. Blouin carries everything from old milk jugs to vintage magazines at the cabin-esque **Magasin Général P.L. Blouin** (page 433).

★ **Best Store for Romantic Gifts: Pont Briand Joallier** has a number of beautiful, handcrafted pieces perfect for that special someone (page 435).

★ **Best Artisanal Crafts:** Carrying the work of over 125 local artisans, **Boutique des Métiers d'Art** is a perfect one-stop shop for everything from jewelry to salad bowls (page 436).

★ **Best Place to Rock:** If you're a fan of rock, specifically garage, punk, hardcore, and indie, and specifically on vinyl, then **Le Knock-Out** has got you covered (page 446).

★ **Best Toy Store:** Parents can let kids run wild and kids can let parents do the same at toy emporium **Benjo** (page 447).

★ **Most Accommodating:** Located in a former bank, women's boutique **Esther P** not only carries a number of stylish lines, but has a couch on hand for weary shoppers (page 447).

★ **Best Selection of Local Designers:** Dedicated to local designers, **Jupon Pressé** exclusively carries lines from some of the province's most exciting emerging designers and does it with some fun in a bright, eclectic boutique (page 448).

★ **Best Design:** Known for its cutting-edge, sartorial choices, menswear boutique **Philippe Dubuc,** with its mirrored walls, high ceiling, and austere displays, is the last word in cool (page 449).

★ **Best Outdoor Gear:** If you're headed for an outdoor adventure, **Mountain Equipment Co-op** has everything from bike gear to arctic sleeping bags to get you ready (page 453).

Québec has a long history with commerce. As the site of the first settlement in New France, its entire founding was based on trade with the Amerindians, and as the colony grew, trade became vital to its survival. Its genetic makeup as a commercial city is still apparent, and over the centuries it has created some of Canada's most recognized stores and brands.

Many of those same stores exist today. Holt Renfrew, La Maison Simons, and J. A. Moisan (the oldest grocery store in North America) are businesses that first bloomed in Québec and whose rich past can still be seen when you enter their establishments.

With all that history, however, it's important to have something new, and the revival of rue St-Joseph in Saint-Roch has been one of the most important developments of the past few years. The area was abandoned by businesses that opted for the malls of the late 1950s, but new customers and retailers are now emerging in the area. Filled with young, modern stores and independent boutiques, it has given the city a much-needed boost of cool. Rue St-Jean, outside of the walls, is experiencing a similar rejuvenation, with youthful stores popping up, many with an eye on local products and design.

Unlike most major Canadian cities, when it comes to the downtown core, Québec sticks to its roots. Here, stores like H&M, Gap, and Zara are relegated to the malls, about a 15-minute drive away. Though some chains can be found (mostly in Upper Town), they are few and far between. Instead, the historic houses and beautiful

Beaux-Arts buildings are small independent boutiques or established businesses.

There are independent jewelry stores throughout Québec City. Rue Petit-Champlain has a good mix of high-end and more artsy offerings. In fact, these are the two main kinds of jewelry stores found all over the city: super kitsch costume jewelry and high-end designer pieces. One thing that remains the same in upscale or costume jewelry is that it's all handcrafted.

If you're on the hunt for antiques, look no further than the narrow cobblestone rue St-Paul, where just about every other store is dedicated to antiques. If you're looking for something specific, it's best to pop into them all. Just about every single store is stocked full of everything from antique bedposts to silverware.

Though Québec doesn't have crafts in the traditional sense, there is a certain aesthetic found in the various artisanal works. A mix of materials is one element, as is an unexpected juxtaposition of colors and shapes. Inuit art, though not exclusive to the province, can also be found in a number of arts and craft shops, since northern Québec is home to many native and Inuit tribes.

If you're looking for a relaxing massage or facial, look no further than your hotel: Most have exquisite facilities. For those that don't, there are a few spas within the city that offer everything from quick therapeutic massages to daylong adventures in pampering.

Unlike in Montréal, English books are hard to come by in Québec City. Although most hotels carry a few national and international English-language papers, finding anything more than a bestseller can be tough. Magazines, however, are much easier to find, and both European and North American versions are readily available.

If you want to pick up some vintage Félix Leclerc after an inspiring night at a *boîte à chansons,* head along rue St-Jean, where you'll find both new and used vinyl and CDs. The implosion of the record industry has been tough on Québec's independent music stores, but a few gems remain.

Many of the stores that line the streets of Vieux-Québec's Upper and Lower Town cater to tourists. Though many of them strive to have their own personality, a lot blend into one another. The stores included in this chapter, however, all offer something a bit different and less well known.

It's not surprising that in a city so defined by its food, its best markets revolve around farmers and fresh produce. And though winters can be harsh, the farmers markets keep going all year long.

Québec City spends at least six months out of the year under snow, so that may explain why there are two stores dedicated entirely to Christmas decorations. Situated kitty-corner to each other, snowy landscape or not, these places are packed even in the summer.

In high tourist season during the summer, boutiques in Upper and Lower Town stay open late, some even as late as midnight, if the crowds are still out. In winter, stores often close early, or for months at a time, depending on the nature of their business. If there's a store you particularly want to visit, it's always best to call ahead, especially in the off-season.

Vieux-Québec's Upper Town

Map 8

ACCESSORIES AND JEWELRY

Zimmermann

Having studied jewelry design and gemology in Paris, Michel Zimmermann returned to Québec in the late 1970s to open his very own jewelery shop. Zimmermann's has since become one of the most respected jewelers in the business, known for unique hand-crafted gems. The pieces are all meticulously handcrafted without the use of any cast, working exclusively with 925/1000 silver and 18-carat gold or platinum. Styles vary from simple, leaf-shaped earrings to detailed wedding bands and teardrop birthstone pendants.

MAP 8: 46 Côte de la Fabrique, 418/692-2672, www.zimmermann-quebec.com; Mon.-Wed. and Sat. 9:30am-5:30pm, Thurs.-Fri. 9:30am-9pm

ARTS AND CRAFTS

Boutique Canadeau

Situated in the heart of Vieux-Québec's Upper Town, this small boutique located in a historic building offers high-end pieces from artists in the region. Stone and ivory carvings, both Inuit and local, are some of the more sought-after pieces, as are intricately carved chess pieces. It's a popular tourist shop, and handmade hunting knives are among the less conventional items, as are woven and knitted goods like the handmade sweaters reminiscent of the kind Bill Cosby made famous in the 1980s.

MAP 8: 1124 rue St-Jean, 418/692-4850, www.canadeau.com; summer daily 10am-7pm, winter daily 10am-6pm

Galerie d'Art les Trois Colombes

Situated in a beautiful historic house complete with a red-peaked roof and white-washed facade, Galerie d'Art les Trois Colombes is one of the most picturesque of arts and craft stores. Filled with selections from both Québécois and Canadian arts and crafts, it also carries works by Inuits and Amerindians, including thick-wool parkas trimmed with fur and moccasins and mukluks in both child and adult sizes. Authentic snowshoes, soapstone sculptures, and weavings occupy the downstairs, while, upstairs, visitors will find handmade hats, rag dolls, and sweaters.

MAP 8: 46 rue St-Louis, 418/694-1114; Mon.-Wed. 9:30am-7pm, Thurs.-Sun. 9:30am-9pm

Lambert & Co.

This teeny-tiny store, approximately two meters wide, in the interior courtyard of Château Frontenac is a splendid gem. The emphasis here is on quality not quantity, and their finely made, striped wool socks, black-and-red checkered blankets, and fur-trimmed hats have become a recognized brand in this region. Alongside the cozy woolen goods (and pillows that make great souvenirs), they also sell a few natural beauty products, like moisturizer, body wash, and shampoo, for both people and their pets.

MAP 8: 1 rue des Carrières, 418/694-2151, www.lambertco.ca; Mon.-Fri. 10am-7pm, Sat.-Sun. 9:30am-6:30pm

BATH, BEAUTY, AND SPAS

Boutiuqe & Spa Signé Prevonia

Located inside the Hôtel Manoir Victoria, this full-service spa offers manicures ($52), pedicures ($73), and signature treatments like Cocoon facials ($100), Jin Shin Do massage ($100), and maple body scrubs ($85). A 30-minute Swedish massage will set you back $65. It's frequented by hotel guests, but nonguests may also make a reservation here. Many of the treatments use products made with local, organic maple sugar, and a day-package to the spa also gives visitors access to the hotel's gym, sauna, and indoor pool, all of which have an early-20th-century, Turkish-bath feel with mosaic tiles and arched columns around the pool.

MAP 8: 44 Côte du Palais, 800/463-6283, www.manoir-victoria.com; daily 9am-9pm

Payot Institute

Opened in 2010, the Payot Institute is located in the Château Frontenac, but you don't have to be a hotel guest to benefit from the treatments offered by this renowned institution. Started by Dr. Nadia Payot, the first woman to graduate from the Lausanne School of Medicine in France in 1913, the spa offers treatments that go beyond the regular massages and facials to include an entire beauty philosophy. Facial acupuncture, a face and body scrub with caviar, myrrh and amyris, and Dr. Payot's signature facial, which includes 42 specialized movements designed to halt aging, hair elixir, and precious oils are all available. They also offer a number of treatments designed specifically for men, including foot, hand, and nail care. The decor is soft gray with hints of purple, which complements the institute's calm atmosphere. The prices are at the high-end of the scale.

MAP 8: 1 rue des Carrières, 418/977-7790, www.fairmont.com; Mon.-Thurs. 8:30am-8pm, Fri.-Sat. 8:30am-9pm, Sun. 9am-5pm

BOOKS AND MUSIC

Archambault

One of the biggest music stores in the province, Archambault has 15 stores throughout Québec and sells everything from CDs and DVDs to books, magazines, newspapers, video games, and musical instruments. Deep red walls are the backdrop for this location's selection of small instruments and musical accessories. It was founded in 1896 by Edmond Archambault, who wanted to open a sheet music store; he teamed up with piano man and musical instrument specialist J.A. Hurteau to create the first Archambault retail outlet. Locals pop in here to pick up a new release or get strings for their guitar.

MAP 8: 1095 rue St-Jean, 418/694-2088, www.archambault.ca; Jan.-May Sun.-Wed. 9:30am-6pm, Thurs.-Sat. 9:30am-9:30pm; June-Dec. daily 9:30am-9:30pm

Librairie Pantoute

Founded in 1972 by a bunch of counterculture kids, Librairie Pantoute (its name means "not at all" in Québécois lingo) is one of the most important independent bookstores in the province. Situated in the heart of Upper Town, this location has high ceilings and walls full of bookshelves. They carry popular English titles, mostly best-sellers like John Grisham and Ken Follett, although they usually have a title or two by still popular but slightly lesser-known authors. No matter what you're looking for, the well-informed, usually bilingual staff will be able to help.

MAP 8: 1100 rue St-Jean, 418/694-9748, www.librairiepantoute.com; Mon.-Sat. 10am-10pm, Sun. noon-10pm

Maison de la Presse Internationale

If it is published on a daily, weekly, or monthly basis, they likely have it here. From periodicals to newspapers to magazines and specialized reviews in a number of languages—English, Spanish, Russian, German, Arabic—this is your best bet for finding your favorite daily. *Le Monde, le Figaro,* the *New York Times,* the *Wall Street Journal,* and the *International Herald Tribune* can all be found here. If you want something with a bit more meat, they also have books, including paperbacks, usually bestsellers, in English. Also set up partially as a gift shop, it sells postcards and trinkets and offers money exchange.

MAP 8: 1050 rue St-Jean, 418/694-1511; Mon.-Sat. 7am-11pm, Sun. 8am-11pm

Die-hard comic fans will want to make Première Issue a definite stop on their map. Sitting at a 45-degree angle in Vieux-Québec's Upper Town directly across from Les Fortifications, this comic book paradise is filled with back issues of DC and Marvel comics, as well as cult classics like *The Watchman*. Local fans can be found browsing and reading or having an intense discussion about *Tintin* with staff. The atmosphere is laid-back with a bit of whimsy. Though they also carry comics from Québec and France, known as *bande dessinée*, the focus here is on classic English-language comics.

MAP 8: 27A rue d'Auteuil, 418/692-3985, www.librairiepremiereissue.com; Mon.-Fri. 10am-7pm, Sat. 10am-5pm, Sun. 11am-5pm

CHILDREN'S STORES

Boutique l'Échelle

Established in 1966, this chaotic boutique just inside of the old walls carries old-time toys. Marionettes, matryoshka dolls, model cars, trains, and stuffed animals line the walls, alongside traditional Québécois wood toys like spoons for playing traditional songs and the *gigueux*, a wooden doll that is made to dance the jig on a platform. Board games for all ages and in both English and French are available, as are party favors and balloons.

MAP 8: 1039 rue St-Jean, 418/694-9133, www.boutiqueechelle.com; summer daily 10am-11pm, winter Mon.-Wed. 10:30am-5pm, Thurs.-Fri. 10:30am-9pm, Sat. 10am-5pm, Sun. noon-5pm

CLOTHING AND SHOES

★ Bibi et Compagnie

If you ask the owner of this headwear wonderland tucked down a quiet side street how she would describe her store, she will tell you, "I sell hats. That's it. Point final." And she's right. Men's hats, women's hats, they are all available here from panamas to fedoras, caps to cloches, and in an array of colors and sizes, stacked up along the shelves or modeled by body-less mannequins. The service is hands-off, unless customers show real interest, and the atmosphere quite sober, depending on the mood of the staff, who are mostly mature women who look lovely in hats.

MAP 8: 42 rue Garneau, 418/649-0045, www.bibietcie.com; Feb.-Oct. Mon.-Sat. 9am-7pm, Sun. 10am-6pm; Nov.-Jan. Thurs.-Sun. noon-7pm

La Maison Darlington

One of the oldest boutiques in Québec, it's named after an English tailor who took over a business that sold military garments and turned it into a wool and cashmere boutique. The antique till and specialized wooden sweater shelves are reminders of times past

clockwise from top left: menswear boutique Philippe Dubuc, Saint-Roch; Laliberté, Saint-Jean-Baptiste and Saint-Roch; toy wonderland Benjo, Saint-Jean-Baptiste and Saint-Roch

and though the styles may have changed since he opened in 1872, the ethos remains the same and you'll find a range of accessories, toques, berets, mittens, and scarves of only the highest-quality from brands such as Ballantyne, Johnston of Elgin, and Tilley Endurables. Dapper gentlemen who still wear caps are fans, as are well-heeled older women who come for their cozy knits.

MAP 8: 7 rue de Buade, 418/692-2268; Mon.-Wed. 9:30am-6pm, Thurs.-Fri. 9:30am-7pm, Sat. 9:30am-5pm, Sun. 10am-5pm

DEPARTMENT STORES

La Maison Simons

One of the city's most important businesses, La Maison Simons was started in 1840 by 17-year-old John Simons, who opened a dry goods store near Porte St-Jean. Thirty years later, in 1870, the store moved to a new location close to the basilica, and here it has remained. Though opened in the late 19th century, it has a definite art deco feel, with a beautiful, concave ceiling made of pearl glass. A large section of the building has recently been remodeled and features high-ceilings, sleek, white modern stairs, and a live DJ on weekends. They carry a number of labels, both mid-range (Canada Goose) and luxury (Kenzo, Chloe) as well as their private label collection. Locations can be found at Place Ste-Foy (2450 blvd. Laurier, 418/692-3630) and Galeries de la Capitale (5401 blvd. des Galeries, 418/692-3630).

MAP 8: 20 Côte de la Fabrique, 418/692-3630, www.simons.ca; winter Mon.-Wed. 9:30am-5:30pm, Thurs.-Fri. 9:30am-9pm, Sat. 9:30am-5pm, Sun. noon-5pm; summer Mon.-Sat. 9:30am-9pm, Sun. noon-5pm

GIFTS AND HOME

Boutique Artisans Canada

Open since World War II, this large, open boutique in Vieux-Québec's Upper Town has subsequently been run by three generations of the Théberge family. It stocks jewelry, leather goods, fur hats, plush toys, sweaters, T-shirts, and outerwear. The majority of the lines are made and designed in Québec. It's recommended by the *New York Times* as a store to visit, and staff will remind you of this designation. The back of the store is dedicated to toy soldiers, and they have a huge collection of figurines, including the French battling the English at Waterloo and on the Plains of Abraham.

MAP 8: 30 Côte de la Fabrique, 418/692-2109, www.artisanscanada.com; summer daily 9am-10pm, winter daily 10am-6pm

Boutique Claude Berry

Open since 1981, Boutique Claude Berry specializes in European earthenware. Situated just in front of the basilica, this is the only store in the city dedicated to this particular kind of ceramics.

Walking in here can be a bit of a visual overload; patterned platters, teapots, cups and saucers, and tableware are set out before you, each item perfectly displayed so as to give visitors the optimal view of the pattern. At this family-run business, service is hands-off unless you get too close to the products. This is the only store in North America to carry Faience d'Art de Gien earthenware.

MAP 8: 6 Côte de la Fabrique, 418/692-2628, www.claudeberry.com; mid-Sept.-mid-May Mon.-Wed. 9:30am-6pm, Thurs.-Fri. 9:30am-9pm, Sat.-Sun. 10am-7pm; mid-May-mid-Sept. daily 9am-9pm

La Boutique de Noël

No matter the time of year, it's always Christmas at La Boutique de Noël. In a three-story building whose facade is permanently decorated with fairy lights, the interior is painted a deep hunter green with red trim and high-flying angels. Fully decorated Christmas trees line the aisles, while the walls are hung with an almost inconceivable number of ornaments, from Disney characters to sophisticated icicles and everything in between. They also carry Nativity scenes, stockings, tinsel, and anything else you want to hang on your tree. If you're unsure of the number of days left until the big event, this place has a running countdown.

MAP 8: 47 rue de Buade, 418/692-2457, www.boutiquedenoel.ca; Jan.-Apr. daily 10am-5pm, May-June and Oct. daily 9am-10pm, July-Aug. daily 8am-midnight, Sept. daily 9am-11pm, Nov.-Dec. daily 9am-9pm

Boutique Le Sachem

A silent statue of a native chief greets you at the entrance of this boutique, setting the tone for what's inside. This entire store is filled with Amerindian-inspired pieces, from moccasins to hunting knives, traditional woven blankets, and fur hats, even some à la Davy Crockett. One of the most serious gifts on display, however, has to be the stuffed wolf retailing for a cool $4,000. If you can get past the overwhelming kitsch of the place, there are some nice traditional crafts to be found.

MAP 8: 17 rue des Jardins, 418/692-3056; summer daily 9am-9pm, winter daily 10am-6pm

★ Magasin Général P.L. Blouin

Without a doubt one of the best stores in the city, Magasin Général P.L. Blouin is filled with novelty items and pieces of historic kitsch. Old Québec license plates line the walls, along with models of old cars. They stock everything here, from brand-new checkered hunters' caps to vintage magazines, old Coca-Cola paraphernalia, and magnetic Elvises. Owner Mr. Blouin is a connoisseur of kitsch, and people wanting to get rid of 40 years' worth of junk in the attic come to him first.

MAP 8: 1196 rue St-Jean, 418/694-9345, www.magasingeneralplblouin.
com; Nov.-Apr. Sun.-Wed. 9am-6pm, Thurs.-Sat. 9am-9:30pm; May-Oct. daily
9am-10pm

GOURMET TREATS

Confiserie C'est si Bon

This picturesque shop has the feel of an old-time *confiserie*, or
candy shop. The shelves are lined with containers full of candy,
old-fashioned treats, novelty cups and saucers, magnets, and bowls,
making it a great place to pick up a gift. Homemade chocolate,
fudge, and hot chocolate are made on the premises and there's also
an emphasis on local products like spices, teas, candies, and maple
goodies. It's been open for over 20 years, and just about everything
here is for sale, from the antique display case to the squares of maple
sugar candy sitting temptingly at the cash register.

MAP 8: 1111 rue St-Jean, 418/692-5022; summer daily 9am-9pm; winter
Mon.-Wed. 9am-5pm, Thurs.-Fri. 9am-9pm, Sat.-Sun. 9am-5:30pm

Les Délices de l'Érable

Everything here is drizzled with maple, from the blueberry gelato
to the fleur du sel. Part store, part café, one side of this large, open
store is dedicated to pastries, coffees, desserts, and gelatos, while
the other is filled with rows of gourmet maple syrup, maple cookies,
maple pork rub, coffees, teas—you get the idea. A small seating area
at the back is a pleasant place to try a taste of their hot maple-flavor
milk, but the real draws here are the gourmet products.

MAP 8: 1044 rue St-Jean, 418/692-3245, www.mapledelights.com; fall and spring
Mon.-Thurs. 7am-9pm, Fri. 7am-10pm, Sat. 9am-10pm, Sun. 10am-10pm; winter
Mon.-Thurs. 7am-8pm, Fri. 7am-9pm, Sat. 9am-9pm, Sun. 10am-9pm; summer
Mon.-Fri. 7am-midnight, Sat. 9am-midnight, Sun. 10am-midnight

MARKETS

Artisans de la Cathédrale

This outdoor market runs throughout the summer on the grounds
of the Holy Trinity Anglican Cathedral, in the shadow of Château
Frontenac. The cozy, makeshift stalls erected here put you in direct
contact with the artist or crafter who made the goods, making the
shopping and browsing experience all the more memorable. The
products are completely unique and different than what you'll find
in other artisan and gift shops. Vendors sell everything from jewelry to sweaters to glass and woodwork.

MAP 8: 31 rue des Jardins, www.artisansdelacathedrale.com; mid-June-early
Sept. daily 10:30am-10pm

If you're tired of museums but still want a trip back in time, head to **J. A. Moisan** (699 rue St-Jean, 418/522-0685, www.jamoisan.com, daily 9am-10pm), the oldest grocery store in North America, established in 1871. The Victorian-era look of the store has been meticulously recreated. Every little detail has been accounted for, from the crisp white shirts of the serving staff to the large wooden framed display cases, to the tin roof, wooden shelves lined with goods, and the French music from the 1930s and '40s piping in over the speakers.

When it first opened, Moisan's aim was to offer the area's well-to-do clients gourmet foods, and that tradition continues today with items like char-cuterie, imported foie gras, biscuits, chocolates, and even soaps, filling the walls of the two-room grocery store. What has changed, however, is the addition of a small café near the entrance, where locals come to grab a quick lunch or indulge in a fresh pastry and coffee. Built in the early 1800s, it is one of the oldest buildings in St-Jean and was one of the few structures that wasn't destroyed by the great fire of 1881, which decimated the area. Though it retains a Victorian aesthetic, it is still a functioning grocery store, with locals popping in to get their morning bread and fresh produce. It may look and feel like the oldest grocery store in North America but it is also very modern.

Vieux-Québec's Lower Town

Map 9

ACCESSORIES AND JEWELRY
★ Pont Briand Joallier

Open for over 40 years, this high-end jeweler located in a historic stone house in Petit-Champlain is one of the city's best. The super-sleek interior with white display cases built into the walls gives it an added bit of glamour. The pieces here, many of which are made by Québec artisans, are exquisitely crafted with a wide range of styles and materials available, from rough-hued gold rings set with brilliant turquoise from the exclusive Louis Perrier collection to refined platinum engagement rings with a simple butterfly setting.

MAP 9: 48 rue du Petit-Champlain, 418/977-5800, www.pontbriand.net; winter daily 10am-5:30pm, summer Mon.-Sat. 10am-9pm, Sun. 10am-6pm

ANTIQUES
Antiquités Bolduc

Owned and staffed by a young helpful and friendly couple, Stéphanie and Frédéric Bolduc, this small antique store situated in an old stone house is bright, uncluttered and artfully laid out with furniture, chandeliers, and just about anything else. Clocks and sconces line the walls, while tables, cabinets, and dressers are topped with children's toys, rotary telephones, firefighters' helmets, china tableware, steak knives, and vanity sets.

MAP 9: 89 rue St-Paul, 418/694-9558, www.lesantiquitesbolduc.com; Mon.-Fri. 9:30am-5pm, Sat. 10:30am-5pm, Sun. 11am-5pm

Boutique aux Mémoires Antiquités

A staple on the strip since the 1970s, Boutique aux Mémoires Antiquités is filled with treasures like Victorian furniture, oil lamps, old office desks, glittery chandeliers, and other curiosities. The low tin ceilings add even more charm to the crowded space in this historic building. The owner has a keen eye for finery, so fans of Tiffany lamps, fine silverware, and dinner china should keep their eyes peeled here. Though most of the stuff will look like it could come from anywhere, just about all of the finds here are directly from Québec's past.

MAP 9: 105 rue St-Paul, 418/692-218; Mon.-Sat. 9:30am-5pm

Maison Dambourgès

Named after a French shopkeeper who was also the head colonel of the militia in 1790, Maison Dambourgès is one of the larger stores on the street. Specializing in 19th-century pine country furniture from Québec and folk art, the store is perfectly curated. The large store is spacious compared to others on the strip and has a country feel. Just about everything here looks like it was fished out of an abandoned farmhouse in the country, and the owners have an impeccable eye for everything from stoneware jugs and weather vanes to old pine hutches with peeling paint and armoires built for the sole purpose of cooling pies.

MAP 9: 155 rue St-Paul, 418/692-1115; Mon. and Thurs.-Fri. 11am-5pm, Sat.-Sun. 11am-4pm

ARTS AND CRAFTS

★ Boutique des Métiers d'Art

Devoted to the work of Québécois artisans, the Boutique des Métiers d'Art showcases the work of over 125 craftspeople, all members of the Québec Craft Council. Situated on the famous Place Royale, it couldn't be better located, with huge, floor-to-ceiling windows and shelves and display cases lining the stone walls. Everything is well plotted out. Goods here are divided by materials and include wood, ceramic, metals, and glass, though other materials can be found in the work throughout the shop. Whether it is simple wood kitchen utensils you're looking for, a tin candelabra, or a unique silver pendant, you'll find it here.

MAP 9: 29 Place Royale, 418/694-0267, www.metiers-d-art.qc.ca; June 24-late-Aug. daily 9:30am-9:30pm; Sept.-Dec. Sat.-Wed. 9am-6pm, Thurs.-Fri. 9:30am-9pm; Jan.-late-Apr. daily 9:30am-6pm; May-June 24 Sat.-Wed. 9:30am-6pm, Thurs.-Fri. 9:30am-9pm

437

Pauline Pelletier

Pauline Pelletier's ceramic and porcelain artwork is both unconventional yet modern. Using unusual shapes as a base, a square teapot for example, the ceramic is then smoke-fired to create the final effect, giving it a marbled finish. The unusual pieces of art, popular with tourists and locals alike, include vases, tea sets, and serving platters. The colors are unconventional—navy blue, red, and jade, many with a touch of rich gold adorning the edges. The boutique, open since 1983, also carries the work of other Québec artisans and jewelers, giving it a more dynamic atmosphere and added quirkiness.

MAP 9: 38 rue du Petit-Champlain, 418/692-4871, www.paulinepelletier. com; Oct.-May Mon.-Wed. 9:30am-5:30pm, Thurs.-Fri. 9:30am-9pm, Sat.-Sun. 9am-5pm; June-Sept. daily 9am-9pm

Soierie Huo

This unique shop is run by artist Dominique Huot, who has been creating her one-of-a-kind silk products since the late 1970s. A descendant of Québécois artist Charles Huot, Dominique uses natural silk and wool fibers to create her scarves and men's ties. The designs on many of the scarves are spontaneous, though she continually recreates certain themes, including abstracts, florals, and maple leaves. The shop itself is quite small with the scarves predominantly displayed throughout.

MAP 9: 91 rue du Petit-Champlain, 418/692-5920, www.soieriehuo.com; summer daily 9:30am-8pm, winter daily 9:30am-5pm

CLOTHING AND SHOES

Atelier La Pomme

This store, located in the quaint Petit-Champlain district, carries lines by Québécois designers, from young, lesser-known labels like Véronique Miljkovitch (whose bias-cut dresses and asymmetrical shapes have won her the adoration of fashion insiders) to the mixed-textile playfulness of Myco Anna. Situated in a historic building, the interior is plain, featuring white walls with red trim. Carrying both men's and women's wear, it's a popular tourist shop for watches, jewelry, leather bags, and seasonal products like fur coats and hats, all made in Québec.

MAP 9: 47 rue Sous-le-Fort, 418/692-2875; Sept.-June Sat.-Wed. 10am-5pm, Thurs.-Fri. 10am-9pm; July-Aug. daily 9am-9pm

Le Capitaine d'Abord

If you need a pea coat or a striped Breton sweater this is a good place to start, whether you're a man or a woman. The goods here all have a nautical flair and evoke Cape Cod even when it's mid-January outside. The bright blue walls, low ceilings, and high-gloss wood floors give the vague impression you're on a ship, but the thick, knitted sweaters and heavy down jackets will remind you of the weather outside. They are exclusive carriers of yachting brands like Paul & Shark, Armor-Lux, and Meyer, and if you're sailing the St-Lawrence, this is the only store you need.

MAP 9: 59 and 63 rue du Petit-Champlain, 418/694-0694, www.capitainedabord. com; Sun.-Tues. 9am-6pm, Wed.-Sat. 9am-9pm

Fourrures Richard Robitaille

Established in 1894, Richard Robitaille is a family business passed down through four different generations. While visitors are invited to browse the luxurious fur coats and hats (worn just as much by men and women in this province), the real draw here is to see how the coats get made. Serge Richard repairs and makes fur coats from scratch and invites you to see the process, from the skins to the final product, at the store's Eco Musée. Richard will tell you about different hunting methods and species, and the evolution of fur in fashion, all while creating a brand-new look.

MAP 9: 329 rue St-Paul, 418/692-9699, www.economusees.com; Mon.-Sat. 9:30am-4pm

Oclan

This two-floor store on the tiny rue de-Petit-Champlain carries contemporary designer brands, including Martinique for men and Michael Kors for women. Entering the menswear section, you'll find a fairly small floor space tastefully packed with the latest from GStar, J Lindeberg, and Energie, among others. Down a camouflaged staircase you'll reach the women's floor (which you can also enter or exit from the larger rue Champlain), similar in size but much more stocked, with pieces from Velvet, In Wear, and Nougat, among others.

MAP 9: 67½ rue du Petit-Champlain, 418/692-1214, www.oclan.net; Sat.-Wed. 10am-6pm, Thurs.-Fri. 10am-9pm

GIFTS AND HOME
Machin Chouette

This place takes things you love but seemingly have no real use for, like that first pressing of the Grateful Dead's "Anthem to the Sun," and turns them into something useful like a CD rack. The brainchild of Lise Maheu, this large, open boutique in the Vieux-Port has some great pieces, from the aforementioned vinyls-turned-CD racks. They also turn old butter boxes into ottomans and teapots into lights and carry various kinds of furniture, from old country pine tables to contemporary pieces that would look just as good in a loft as in a 19th-century townhouse.

MAP 9: 225 rue St-Paul, 418/525-9898, www.machinchouette.com; Mon.-Wed. and Sat. 10am-5pm, Thurs.-Fri. and Sun. 10am-6pm

Pot en Ciel

This split-level store in Petit-Champlain carries ceramics and kitchenware. On the lower floor they carry an array of charming things for the home, including mugs with mustaches, checkered canisters, and artisanal pieces like carved owls and polar bears, as well as a few gourmet products like dried pasta imported from Italy and loose-leaf teas from France. On the upper level, it's all serious kitchen stuff like baking sheets, cookie cutters, and French brands like Emile Henry, as well as a range of Bodum presses.

MAP 9: 27 rue du Petit-Champlain, 418/692-1743; July-Aug. daily 9am-10pm, Sept.-June Sun.-Wed. 9am-6:30pm, Thurs.-Sat. 9am-9:30pm

GOURMET TREATS

La Fudgerie

As the name suggests, this place is a fudge fanatic's fantasy. Well established outside of the city, this cozy, old-timey store is the company's first in downtown Québec. The low ceilings, old wood floors, and exposed ceiling beams make you feel as though you're stepping into the past, a feeling added to by the workers in pristine white coats who circle the store with a platter offering tastes of their divine homemade fudge. Nougat, gourmet hot chocolate, and candied pecans are also made here.

MAP 9: 16 rue du Cul-de-Sac, 418/692-3834, www.lafudgerie.com; Mon.-Wed. 9:30am-5:30pm, Thurs.-Fri. 9:30am-9pm, Sat.-Sun. 9:30am-5pm

Madame Gigi Confiserie

This sweets shop in Petit-Champlain boasts one of the most dangerous sounding treats—chocolate pizza. With floor-to-ceiling windows and display cases prettily decorated with the day's chocolate special, this place will easily break your resolve and lure you in to try their various goodies, including fudge, chocolate-dipped fruit kebabs, and Belgian chocolate. In summer, they also have homemade ice cream, and their homemade jam is available year-round.

MAP 9: 84 rue du Petit-Champlain, 418/694-2269; winter Mon.-Wed. 9am-5:30pm, Thurs.-Fri. 9am-9pm, Sat.-Sun. 9am-6pm; summer daily 9am-11pm

O Petites Douceurs du Quartier

Less exciting than some of the other gourmet stores, this bright, feminine shop—it's all creams and soft pinks—in Petit-Champlain

clockwise from top left: Jupon Pressé, Saint-Jean-Baptiste and Saint-Roch; Le Capitaine d'Abord, Vieux-Québec's Lower Town; the most famous commercial street, Rue du Petit-Champlain at Lower Town

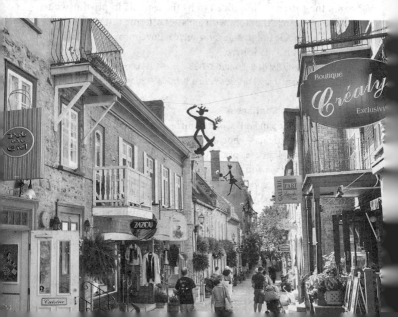

carries old-fashioned sweets and local products. Creamy nougats, flavored oils, spices, fair-trade chocolate, sweets, teas, and spreads (such as Verger du Sureau's organic jams and jellies) are some of the goods available. They also carry non-foodie gifts like beauty products from Blue Lavender and small ceramics for the home.

MAP 9: 51 rue du Petit-Champlain, 418/692-4870; Apr.-Aug. Mon.-Sat. 9:30am-9pm, Sun. 9:30am-5pm; Sept.-Oct. Mon.-Wed. 9:30am-5:30pm, Thurs.-Fri. 9:30am-9pm, Sat.-Sun. 9:30am-5pm; Nov.-Mar. Sat.-Wed. 10am-5pm, Thurs.-Fri. 10am-9pm

La Petite Cabane à Sucre de Québec

This little shop at the end of the rue du Petit-Champlain is all kitted out in wood paneling, both inside and out. Exclusively selling maple goods, it is the downtown extension of a sugar shack outside of the city. "The little sugar shack" sells maple syrup, maple candy, ice cream, maple lollipops, nougat, butter and spreads, and a ton of other maple products.

MAP 9: 94 rue du Petit-Champlain, 418/692-5875, www.petitecabaneasucre. com; winter Sat.-Wed. 10am-5pm, Thurs.-Fri. 10am-9pm, summer daily 9am-9pm

MARKETS

Le Marché du Vieux Port

Located right on the marina, this is the city's largest farmers market. A tradition that's been going on since 1841, the Marché du Vieux Port continues the practice of country farmers bringing their goods to city dwellers. Everything available here is locally grown and produced, and many of the products are organic. You'll find everything from fruits and vegetables to cheese, meats, and seafood to wine and beer. If seeing all that food makes you hungry there are a number of places to grab a sandwich or a light lunch. There's also a section dedicated to gifts and artisanal goods, including handmade jewelry, knitted scarves and socks, artwork, and leather goods.

MAP 9: 160 Quai St-André, 418/692-2517, www.marchevieuxport.com; Jan.-mid-Mar. Thurs.-Sun. 9:30am-5pm; mid-Mar.-Sept. Mon.-Fri. 9am-6pm, Sat.-Sun. 9am-5pm; Oct.-late Nov. daily 9am-5pm; late Nov.-Dec. Sat.-Wed. 9am-5pm, Thurs.-Fri. 9am-9pm

SHOPPING DISTRICTS AND CENTERS

Quartier du Petit-Champlain

Full of artisanal shops, many of which double as artists' workshops, Quartier du Petit-Champlain is the perfect place to support the local arts and pick up some unique gifts. It's run as a co-op, and there is a real neighborhood spirit and camaraderie here due in part to the fact that many of these stores have been here since its inception in the late-1980s. Expect to find silk scarves, leather goods, gourmet fudge, maple syrup, expensive handmade jewelry, and more.

MAP 9: Between Place Royale and rue Petit-Champlain

Rue Saint-Paul

This narrow cobblestone street in the Vieux-Port is Québec City's antiques row. With the exception of a few cafés, bars, and restaurants, almost all of the stores here are filled with antiques. There is a real emphasis on classic antiques—that is to say, don't expect to walk in and find a midcentury modern gem (though it could happen). The pieces aren't often dated later than the 1940s, and even objects from that period can be hard to find. Instead, the focus in many stores is on traditional Québécois antiques.

MAP 9: Between rue St-Pierre and rue Rioux

Parliament Hill and the Plains

Map 10

ARTS AND CRAFTS

Ketto

Located in a skinny corner house decorated with deep blue trim, lots of flower pots, and their unmistakable yellow sign, Ketto has an aesthetic all its own. In the late 1990s, Onge was working at a ceramic store when the pieces with her cutesy, big-headed, stick-limbed characters painted on them started flying off the shelves. Today, Ketto carries hand-painted ceramics, jewelry, clothing, glassware, and stationery all with Onge's signature style. The interior can be a bit chaotic, but everything is perfectly laid out, with a simple wood cabinet full of cups and saucers taking up almost an entire wall.

MAP 10: 951 ave. Cartier, 418/522-3337, www.kettodesign.com; Mon.-Wed. and Sat.-Sun. 10am-5pm, Thurs.-Fri. 10am-9pm

BATH, BEAUTY, AND SPAS

Izba Spa

This spa mixes traditional Russian Banya treatments (steam baths) with therapeutic massage. Banya treatments here involve a humid environment in which the person starts to perspire; soaked oak leaves are then warmed and used to stroke, brush, and tap the body before a honey rub is used to draw out toxins and soften the skin. Trained and certified staff will give you a 60-minute Izba massage that starts at $90, or a deluxe Izba with facial and seawater wrap

for $175. The stone walls, low lighting, and vaulted ceilings give it
an especially luxurious feel.

MAP 10: 36 blvd. René-Lévesque E., 418/522-4922, www.izbaspa.qc.ca; Mon.-Tues. 9am-7pm, Wed.-Fri. 9am-10pm, Sat.-Sun. 9am-5pm

BOOKS AND MUSIC

Sillons Le Disquaire

This is one of the best independent music stores in the province, open since 1984; what they lack in floor space they make up for in the huge choice. It's close to the Plains of Abraham. The staff here are highly knowledgeable and can advise you on everything from Ye-Ye pop to the latest Québec rock sensation. The selection is contemporary with 15,000 to 20,000 CDs available in-store. Listening booths are set up around the store.

MAP 10: 1149 ave. Cartier, 800/287-7455, www.sillons.com; Mon.-Fri. 10am-9pm, Sat. 10am-5pm, Sun. 11am-5pm

CLOTHING AND SHOES

Urbain Prêt-à-Porter

This corner boutique in a well-heeled part of town carries fashion-forward brands aimed at women of various ages. The decor changes throughout, from the deep gray walls and designs that cater to more mature women, to an adjoining white space that features younger brands like Miss Sixty and Nolita. The store also has its own shoe section, with seasonal footwear from the likes of Diesel and Ilse Jacobsen, among others, as well as a wall dedicated to denim.

MAP 10: 996 ave. Cartier, 418/521-1571; Mon.-Wed. 10am-6pm, Thurs.-Fri. 10am-9pm, Sat. 10am-5pm, Sun. 11am-5pm

GIFTS AND HOME

Zone

This modern living and design store carries an array of products, all chic, sleek, and sophisticated for your home. The all-white store is artfully decorated with stock arranged as you might arrange it in your own home. Recently expanded, the store now takes up not only the corner lot but the one next to it, with mirrors, chandeliers, table lamps, drinking glasses, tableware, shower curtains, jewelry boxes, cool wall clocks, and furniture from kitchen tables to small couches and chairs.

MAP 10: 999 ave. Cartier, 418/522-7373, www.zonemaison.com; Mon.-Wed. 9:30am-6pm, Thurs.-Fri. 9:30am-9pm, Sat. 9:30am-5:30pm, Sun. 10am-5pm

MARKETS

Les Halles du Petit Quartier

Less like a market than a mini-gourmet shopping center, Les Halles du petit Quartier is a brick and mortar building filled with great shops. It's popular with locals. An organic fruit and produce stand, a fishmonger, butcher, cheese shop, fresh pasta shop, a pastry, and a bakery shop all offer top-quality products. It also boasts not one, but two coffee shops where you can take a break with a cappuccino; get one to go as you carry on with your browsing.

MAP 10: 1191 ave. Cartier, 418/688-1635, www.hallesdupetitquartier.com; Mon.-Wed. and Sat. 7am-7pm, Thurs.-Fri. 7am-9pm, Sun. 7:30am-7pm

Saint-Jean-Baptiste and Saint-Roch   Map 11

ACCESSORIES AND JEWELRY

Mademoiselle B

This narrow storefront would be easy to miss if it weren't for the floor-to-ceiling windows and old-fashioned sign that pops out over the door. Situated in a newer building in the Saint-Roch neighborhood, Mademoiselle B has an Old-World charm with dark chocolate parquet floors, soft pink walls, and plush velvet display shelves. In keeping with the romantic interior, the costume jewelry here is very girly, with collections coming from France, the south of Italy, and, of course, Québec.

MAP 11: 541 rue St-Joseph E., 418/522-0455; Mon.-Wed. 10am-5:30pm, Thurs.-Fri. 10am-9pm, Sat. 10am-5pm, Sun. 11am-5pm

Rose Bouton

A lot of time could be spent in this kitschy store filled with overwhelming amounts of jewelry and accessories and vibrantly decorated with bubble-gum pink walls, bright florals, pink fun fur, and circle motif wallpaper. Expect to find fabric-covered earrings, hand-drawn pins, long-fringe pendants and earrings, and bracelets and necklaces made with buttons, the store's namesake *bouton*. A fun and vibrant store, it also carries seasonal accessories like bags, scarves, and hats.

MAP 11: 387 rue St-Jean, 418/614-9507, www.boutiquerose.blogspot.com; Tues.-Wed. 11am-5pm, Thurs.-Fri. 11am-9pm, Sat.-Sun. 11am-5pm

ANTIQUES

Déjà Vu

Specializing in furniture and objects from the 1930s to the 1970s, the selection at Déjà Vu is much more mid-century modern than what you'll find in most antique stores in the city. Full of Formica tables, colored glass cocktail sets, and electric blue sectionals from the late 1950s, it's a fun place to stop in if only because the act is akin to a 20th-century flashback. Unlike flea market finds, the treasures here have been lovingly and expertly restored by owners Marie-Claude and François Gagnon. Prices can be higher than anticipated, but knickknacks and anything to do with cocktail hour—ice buckets, martini shakers—are well-priced and the perfect unique souvenir.

MAP 11: 834 rue St-Joseph E., 418/914-2483, www.dejavumeubles.com; Tues.-Wed. 10am-5pm, Thurs.-Fri. 10am-8pm, Sat. 10am-5pm, Sun. noon-5pm

ARTS AND CRAFTS
Point d'Exclamation
Founded by Diane Bergeron of Euphory Design in 2004, Point d'Exclamation was at the forefront of the movement to champion Québec-based designers. Nowadays, the entire neighborhood is full of shops dedicated to locally produced and designed goods (Jupon Pressé, Code Vert, Rose Bouton), but it was Bergeron and her eye for local artisanal work that got the ball rolling. The boutique carries the work of 30-40 local designers at any one time, and the goods range from jewelry to accessories and clothes. The all-white interior is a bit too bright at times but puts the focus on the work, while their constantly-changing storefront window is always a feast for the eyes.

MAP 11: 762 rue St-Jean, 418/525-8053; Sat.-Wed. 10am-6pm, Thurs.-Fri. 10am-9pm

BATH, BEAUTY, AND SPAS
Cosmétiques Bloomi
This sleek and modern cosmetics store is reminiscent of the international chain Sephora. Products are beautifully arranged on white high-gloss lacquered shelves and the whole interior is given an added bit of warmth thanks to the exposed brick walls. It carries high-end makeup lines, a large range of perfumes, and just about any color of polish you could want. Pop in to get a manicure or pedicure, your makeup done for a special occasion, or just to get some tips from the beauticians, who are always ready to give you some pointers and a bit of a touchup.

MAP 11: 507 rue St-Joseph E., 418/529-7470, www.bloomi.ca; Mon.-Wed. 9:30am-5:30pm, Thurs.-Fri. 9:30am-9pm, Sat. 9:30am-5pm, Sun. 11am-5pm

La Quintessens
This urban spa in Saint-Roch is great for a massage or a quick bit of pampering. The decor is relatively simple, with the rooms filled with massage tables and not much else. Though they offer treatments, the focus is on massage, and five different kinds are available: Swedish, Californian, Amma (also known as Japanese massage), Thai-yoga massage, and massage with hot stones.

Hour-long massages cost $65 and body wraps, including chocolate, algae, and sea salt, are $75. They also offer half-hour lunchtime massages (11:30am-1:30pm, $25) and 15-minute chair massages ($15).

MAP 11: 656 rue St-Joseph E., 418/525-7270, www.quintessens.ca; Mon. noon-5pm, Tues.-Fri. 10am-7pm, Sat. 10am-5pm

BOOKS AND MUSIC
CD Mélomane

Established in 1996, this is the best record store in the city. Totally unpretentious, the staff here simply know their stuff, with certain clerks knowing the store's entire stock almost by heart. New and used CDs are available, as are racks upon racks of vinyl, which take up the majority of the space. Brick arches divide the store. They'll happily transfer your cherished 33s, 45s, and 78s onto CD.

MAP 11: 248 rue St-Jean, 418/525-1020, www.cdmelomaneinc.supersites.ca; Mon.-Wed. and Sat. 10am-5pm, Thurs.-Fri. 10am-9pm, Sun. noon-5pm

★ Le Knock-Out

Vinyl is king at this Saint-Roch record store. Tired of having to buy vinyl on the Internet, owners Jean-Philippe Tremblay and Roxann Arcand decided to open a store dedicated to genres and media they most wanted to hear played. Specializing in rock (indie, math, pop), garage, punk, and local, the shop has an impressive collection of both new and used records. The space is open concept and airy: There's even a foosball table near the large floor-to-ceiling window and a makeshift stage where shows are played at the back. The walls are lined not only with music but also books, zines, DVDs, and magazines about the bands and genres they love. The walls are fairly sparse, but the work of Mathieu Plasse, illustrating the history of rock through outfits, is pretty much all you need.

MAP 11: 832 St-Joseph E., 581/742-7625; Tues.-Wed. 11am-6pm, Thurs.-Fri. 11am-9pm, Sat. 11am-5pm, Sun. noon-5pm

Librairie Phylactère

Comics and graphic novels are a huge part of Francophone culture. Just think of Tin Tin. Librairie Phylactère (the name means "speech bubble" in English) is here to cater to that love and is the go-to stop in the city for all of your graphic novel needs. Whether you're looking for the latest Manga or Adrian Tomine, chances are you'll find it in this Saint-Roch boutique. Comic book artwork adorns the walls and there are a few comfy seats for reading but otherwise they let the books be the focus.

MAP 11: 685 rue St-Joseph E., 418/614-2443; Tues.-Wed. 10:30am-6pm, Thurs.-Fri. 10:30am-9pm, Sat.-Sun. 10:30am-5pm

★ Benjo

You could spend all day at this 25,000-square-foot store, and that's exactly the point. It's filled with educational toys, accessories for infants, model trains, planes, automobiles, party favors, candy, books, and a whole lot of costumes; if it's meant for children you'll likely find it here. Take the kids to lunch at the Benjo restaurant, or sign them up for a ceramic painting, jewelry, or paper-making workshop. The staff is always helpful and delightfully off-kilter, as is mascot Benjo, a frog, whom the kids can meet on weekends (Sat.-Sun. 11:15am-3:15pm).

MAP 11: 550 blvd. Charest E., 418/640-0001, www.benjo.ca; Mon.-Wed. 10am-5:30pm, Thurs.-Fri. 10am-9pm, Sat.-Sun. 9:30am-5pm

CLOTHING AND SHOES

Boutique Lucia F.

Tucked down a quiet side street in Saint-Roch, Boutique Lucia F. is a vintage store carrying everything from old 45s to women's pumps. Owned by a young graduate of design, there is an easy feel to how the whole place has been put together; bags line the windowsills, hats are pegged on the exposed brick wall, and old mismatched sitting room chairs are placed throughout the store. Styles for men and women are carried, and the majority of prices are $10-20. And if you like that magazine rack currently holding scarves, well, you can likely buy that too.

MAP 11: 422 rue Caron, 418/648-9785; Wed.-Fri. 11am-6pm, Sat. 11am-5pm

★ Esther P

Located in a former bank, women's boutique Esther P is one of the most stunningly designed stores on St-Jean. The store carries labels that are typically hard to find in Québec City—James Perse, French Connection, Ella Moss, Graham & Spencer. Owner Esther Pichette's aim is to dress women of all ages. The boutique has an open-concept feel with high ceilings that show off the original moldings, blonde-wood floors, punches of red, and lots of windows and glass to keep things modern.

MAP 11: 873 rue St-Jean, 418/704-7774, www.estherp.com; Mon.-Wed. and Sat. 10am-6pm, Thurs.-Fri. 10am-9pm, Sun. 11am-5pm

Fanamanga

Fans of manga and cosplay congregate at this store turned hangout that brings a touch of Tokyo to Québec. It's filled with Gothic Lolita outfits, cosplay accessories, manga, magazines, Japanese treats like Okonomiyaki chips, curry-flavored sweets, and any number of trinkets, dolls, and ephemera associated with the culture. The stools at the bar are usually filled with fans in cosplay, sipping their bubble-tea and bobbing their heads to the Visual Kei videos playing on the TVs above. They also have a karaoke box you can rent by the hour that has songs in Japanese, English, Korean, Chinese, and Vietnamese.

MAP 11: 383 rue du Pont, 418/614-5052, www.fanamanga.com; Tues.-Wed. 10:30am-5:30pm, Thurs. 10:30am-10pm, Fri. 10:30am-11:30pm, Sat. 11am-11:30pm

Flirt

As the name suggests, this brightly colored boutique is all about clothes that bring out your inner flirt, specializing in lingerie for both men and women. The walls are lined with intimate apparel hanging tantalizingly in rows. The store prides itself not only on the many hard-to-find European brands they import, like Eva Racheline and Parah, but also on the fact that they carry hard-to-find sizes, including the line Empreinte, for the fuller-busted woman. Those looking for swimwear can pick from lines here like Cristina and Canadian company Shan. They also offer made-to-measure, but you must make an appointment first.

MAP 11: 525 rue St-Joseph E., 418/529-5221, www.lingerieflirt.com; Mon.-Wed. 9:30am-5:30pm, Thurs.-Fri. 9:30am-9pm, Sat.-Sun. 10am-5pm

★ Jupon Pressé

This inviting women's boutique on St-Jean is dedicated to emerging designers from Québec City, Montréal, and beyond. Brightly decorated with purple walls, flashes of yellow, bright floral wallpaper, and an inflatable moose head, the shop has an especially clean layout with pieces from designers like Eve Gravel, Supayana, and Valérie Dumaine. Nicely hung and spaced, nothing looks too crowded. T-shirts are perfectly piled on Formica tables, while accessories are laid out deliciously on cake plates; jewelry is displayed like art, framed and hung on the wall, though always easily accessible. Along with things for you to wear, they also carry cute, kitschy finds for the home.

MAP 11: 790 rue St-Jean, 418/704-7114; Mon.-Wed. 10am-6pm, Thurs.-Fri. 10am-9pm, Sat.-Sun. 10am-6pm

Kitsch

Hit this boutique up if you're a young woman who is always on trend, faithfully follows Queen Bey, and wishes Nasty Gal was your own personal closet. Carrying everything from Cheap Monday jeans to silky, floral bomber jackets and Ain't Laurent (without Yves) T-shirts, this store caters to the coolest looks and latest pieces. Owned by two super stylish and savvy mavens, this is their second location (the first Kitsch is located in Sherbrooke) and can be found on the über-hip St-Joseph, just a few doors down from that dictator of cool, Urban Outfitters. Curved, white furniture, like the kind you'd find in an 8-year-old's bedroom is used as display cases, while the rest of the space is open and airy. The shop's staff is eternally youthful, but also extremely helpful and competent, so don't be shy.

MAP 11: 425 rue St-Joseph, 418/528-2222, www.boutiquekitsch.com; Mon.-Wed. 10am-5:30pm, Thurs.-Fri. 10am-9pm, Sat. 10am-5pm, Sun. 11am-5pm

Lobo Lavida

Fans of vintage will get a kick out of this high-ceilinged store, filled to the gills with vintage and consignment pieces. From a pair of barely worn knee-high boots to hats from the 1930s and authentic RayBan aviators, this store has it all. Situated in what was once an old house, the entire first floor has been taken over with display cases full of costume jewelry and purses, with clothes lining the walls and on carousels in the center of the room. The prices are reasonable, and those usually put off by secondhand goods should know that everything here has been cleaned, ironed, and hung according to color.

MAP 11: 511 rue St-Jean, 418/521-3397; summer Mon.-Wed. and Sat. 11am-7pm, Thurs.-Fri. 11am-9pm, Sun. noon-6pm; winter Mon.-Wed. noon-5:30pm, Thurs.-Fri. 11am-8pm, Sat. 11am-5:30pm

★ Philippe Dubuc

This Québec City boutique of Montréal-based designer Philippe Dubuc couldn't be sleeker. The long, narrow store is like a mirrored corridor with all-white floors, ceilings, and walls giving it an extra modern kick. Distinctly masculine clothes are represented in the store, made all the more cool by its location in the Saint-Roch neighborhood. Though Dubuc is primarily a menswear designer, fashion-forward women shouldn't think twice about trying on a piece or two in this fabulous hall of mirrors.

MAP 11: 537 rue St-Joseph E., 418/614-5761, www.dubucstyle.com; Tues.-Wed. 10:30am-5:30pm, Thurs.-Fri. 10:30am-9pm, Sat. 10:30am-5pm, Sun. noon-5pm

Schüz

Casual shoes for men and women can be found at this relaxed boutique on St-Jean. Steve Madden, Tsubo, and Chinese Laundry are available for women, while men's brands include Asics, Onitsuka Tiger, and Camper for both sexes. Though there is definitely more of a choice for women, men looking for something unfussy, masculine, and modern, or just a new pair of everyday sneakers, are sure to find it here. The decor is minimal with the shoes displayed on the wall and the center of the room taken up with seating and seasonal displays. Winter boots are one of their specialties, so they always have a range of styles for both sexes come autumn.

MAP 11: 748 rue St-Jean, 418/523-4560, www.schuz.ca; mid-June-mid-Oct. Mon.-Sat. 10am-9pm, Sun. 11am-7pm; mid-Oct.-mid-June Mon.-Wed. and Sat. 10am-6pm, Thurs.-Fri. 10am-9pm, Sun. 11am-5:30pm

top: Librarie St-Jean-Baptiste; **bottom:** Déjà Vu, Saint-Jean-Baptiste and Saint-Roch

Signatures Québécoises

This relatively new shop in Saint-Roch is dedicated to local designers. If you're interested in a snapshot of Québécois fashion as it's made here, then this shop is a must. Taking over the semi-basement of a church, the space has been completely refurbished and modernized, so much so that you'd never realize you were in a church basement. Open and sprawling, the space features the work of a number of different designers and different styles and price ranges. Expect everything from street-wear brands like Lady Dutch and Kärv to specialty brands Yoga Jeans and Blank and higher-end designers like Stacey Zhang, Harricana, and Tavan & Mitto. The clothes and accessories suit just about any age and style, though there's much less choice for men.

MAP 11: 560 rue St-Joseph E., 418/648-9976, www.signaturesquebecoises.com; Mon.-Wed. 10am-5:30pm, Thurs.-Fri. 10am-9pm, Sat.-Sun. 10am-5pm

Swell & Ginger

Proof that Saint-Roch is indeed the fastest (and coolest) growing neighborhood in the city, style savvy womenswear boutique Swell & Ginger put down roots here in mid-2013. Modern, open, and sparsely decorated with heavy wood tables and steel fixtures, the boutique would fit right in in New York's East Village or London's Portobello Road. Labels include Rich and Skinny Jeans, Tiger of Sweden, and House of Harlow. Don't let the label love mislead you, however. Prices are surprisingly reasonable.

MAP 11: 765A rue St-Joseph E., 581/742-7080, www.swellandginger.com; Mon.-Wed. 10am-6pm, Thurs.-Fri. 10am-9pm, Sat. 10am-5pm, Sun. 11am-5pm

Tohu Bohu

Though this store specializes in upscale footwear and carries lines like Emilio Pucci, Kate Spade, and Marc by Marc Jacobs, it's not just a shoe store—they also do pedicures. With a name that means "confusion" and "hubbub," Tohu Bohu may surprise you. The store's dynamic streamlined design—plush gray banquettes mixed with high-gloss, red-and-black shelving and illuminated cubbies—puts the emphasis on the shoes and bags. Come to browse or come just for a pedicure or manicure, which you can enjoy while you eat; their pedi-sushi deal allows you to chow down on dinner from Yuzu while you get your toes prepped for those new peep-toes.

MAP 11: 775 rue St-Joseph E., 418/522-1118, www.tohubohu.ca; Mon.-Wed. 10am-5:30pm, Thurs.-Fri. 10am-9pm, Sat.-Sun. 10am-5pm

DEPARTMENT STORES

Laliberté

In May 1867, 24-year-old Jean-Baptiste Laliberté founded a modest fur shop that by the beginning of the 20th century was one of the best fur stores in North America. From its humble beginnings, the store eventually grew to become an arresting five-floor department store with huge arched windows and a corner clock tower looking over St-Joseph. When many stores upped and moved to the new malls outside of town, Laliberté was one of the few that stayed. Though the store has since been scaled back (the unused floors are now lofts), Laliberté continues to be a leader in furs. Bring your old furs to be remodeled here or browse their seasonal collections.

MAP 11: 595 rue St-Joseph E., 418/525-4851, www.lalibertemode.com; Mon.-Wed. 9:30am-5:30pm, Thurs.-Fri. 9:30am-9pm, Sat. 9:30am-5pm, Sun. noon-5pm

GIFTS AND HOME
Balthazar

This two-floor home and design store in Saint-Roch brings together modern furniture, trendy kitchen utensils, and various objets d'art to place around your home. Super sleek in design, the over-100-year-old building has been meticulously redesigned so that the black slate staircase to the second floor blends in seamlessly with the ground floor walls lined with products like vases, espresso cups, and kitschy alarm clocks. Filled with brands that come from all over the world that are typically hard to find in the city, the store also carries collections from Québécois design firms.

MAP 11: 461 rue St-Joseph E., 418/524-1991, www.baltazar.ca; Mon.-Wed. 10am-5:30pm, Thurs.-Fri. 10am-9pm, Sat. 10am-5pm, Sun. 11am-5pm

GOURMET TREATS
Champagne Le Maître Confiseur

This chocolate and sweets shop has a few unique specialties. With only a few marble-topped tables to sit at, this fairly small store serves up some of the best marzipan treats in the city and also offers a range of fine sugar-free chocolate made in the European tradition in flavors that range from saffron to goat cheese with honey. Port glasses made of chocolate are the ultimate companion to the aged wine, as are their buttery French biscuits. The most unusual treat, though, is the cherry blossom—cherries soaked with champagne and cherry kirsch, covered in dark chocolate, and topped with a chocolate-dipped marshmallow. Totally decadent.

MAP 11: 783 rue St-Joseph E., 418/652-0708; Mon.-Fri. 8am-9pm, Sat.-Sun. 10am-6pm

Choco-Musée Erico

Established in 1987, this artisanal chocolatier is one of the most decadent stops in the city. Chocolate lines the walls in this quaint kitchen and boutique, with an array of seasonal treats (like nachos dipped in chocolate) on one side, and displays of freshly made chocolates (with flavors like chestnut cream, rum, and allspice) on the other. Line up to get your gourmet hot chocolate, ice cream, or one of their many desserts—the brownies and chocolate cake here are said to be among the best in the province. The adjoining room is the Chocolate Museum, which gives you a history of the treat, lets you taste some wares, and allows you to watch the magic being made in the kitchen.

MAP 11: 634 rue St-Jean, 418/524-2122, www.chocomusee.com; Mon.-Wed. and Sat. 10am-5:30pm, Thurs.-Fri. 10am-9pm, Sun. 11am-5:30pm

Epicerie Européenne

This shop was founded in 1959 by two Italians, nostalgic for their homeland. The massive wooden shelves are stocked with imported products. Italian coffees, olive oils, pestos, and balsamic vinegars take center stage, while at the back you'll find a cheese and meat counter, where you can order a great panini—but hurry up, they go fast. Along with the groceries, they also sell imported kitchen accessories, coffee makers, crockery, and the famous French Laguiole knives. Stop in and try one of their specialties, an authentic *espresso ristretto*—the shortest coffee around.

MAP 11: 560 rue St-Jean, 418/529-4847, www.epicerie europeenne.com; Mon.-Wed. 9am-6pm, Thurs.-Fri. 9am-9pm, Sat. 9am-5pm

OUTDOOR GEAR

★ Mountain Equipment Co-op

Better known as MEC, this co-op was started by a couple of Canadian climbers in the 1970s and now has almost three million people as registered members. You must sign up to become a member in order to make a purchase, but the five bucks good-for-life membership pays for itself by the time you get to the checkout. The open-concept store design give you lots of room to roam the goods, which include everything from cycling gear to hiking boots, tents to sleeping bags. Even rental equipment is available; there really isn't a better store dedicated to the outdoors (unless you want to hunt). Eco-friendly and pro-sustainability, the store hires clerks that are friendly, patient, and know their stuff.

MAP 11: 405 rue St-Joseph E., 418/522-8884, www.mec.ca; Mon.-Wed. 10am-7pm, Thurs.-Fri. 10am-9pm, Sat. 9am-5pm, Sun. 10am-5pm

SHOPPING DISTRICTS AND CENTERS

Rue Saint-Jean

Whether inside or outside the walls, rue Saint-Jean is Québec City's main shopping street. In Vieux-Québec's Upper Town you'll find a string of well-known stores, including Québec chains, women's stores Jacob, San Francisco, Le Château, and internationally recognized brands like Crocs, American Apparel, and Foot Locker. It's also along this strip that you'll find magazines and bookstores selling English-language material. If you want to shop like the locals, check out the independent clothing boutiques and record stores in Faubourg Saint-Jean-Baptiste, a continuation of the same street; you'll find interesting shops just beyond the fortifications.

MAP 11: Between rue Couillard and ave. Salaberry

Rue Saint-Joseph

The main shopping strip in the Saint-Roch neighborhood, this street has an illustrious past that has recently been revived. Once the Fifth Avenue of Québec City, it is now the city's coolest shopping district. You won't find many well-known chains here except for the recently opened Urban Outfitters, the only store of its kind in the city. Independent lingerie boutiques can be found as well as some great shoe stores, home stores, and other fashion-forward boutiques. The best children's store in the province, Benjo, is also located here, with a VIP entrance especially for the little ones.

MAP 11: Between rue St-Dominique and rue Caron

Greater Québec City   Map 12

BOOKS AND MUSIC

La Maison Anglaise

The only bookstore dedicated to English books in Québec City is in Place de la Cité, one of the mega malls on the outskirts of town. The staff knows their English-language stuff and is always ready to help. The selection is, unsurprisingly, unbeatable, from *New York Times* best-sellers to literary fiction, humor, philosophy, travel, and kids books. It might not be as big as your local Barnes & Noble but it does have the most comprehensive collection of English books in the city and the atmosphere is quiet and calm—like it should be.

MAP 12: Place de la Cité, 164-2600 blvd. Laurier, 418/654-9523, www.lamaisonanglaise.com; Mon.-Wed. 9:30am-5:30pm, Thurs.-Fri. 9:30am-9pm, Sat. 9:30am-5pm, Sun. 11:30am-5pm

CHILDREN'S STORES

Univers Toutou

A special treat for kids of all ages, this store is located in one of the malls outside of the city. Over 20 different kinds of plush toys are available, from teddy bears to rabbits, moose, and pigs. Once the selection has been made, the plush is then stuffed and given a passport with its date and place of birth printed inside. The staff is kid-friendly and excited about helping kids pick a companion. Choices hang at kid-level all around the brightly decorated store.

Clothing like bathrobes and boxers and accessories like sunglasses
and jewelry can added to give the new plush toy a bit of its own
personal style.

MAP 12: Galeries de la Capitale, 5401 blvd. des Galeries, 418/623-5557, www.
plushfactory.com; Mon.-Wed. 9:30am-5:30pm, Thurs.-Fri. 9:30am-9pm, Sat.
9am-5pm, Sun. 10am-5pm

DEPARTMENT STORES
Holt Renfrew

Originating on rue Buade in Vieux-Québec's Upper Town, this
high-end department store is now the only branch of Holt Renfrew
in Québec City. Opened at this location in 1965, it retains its elegance, with high ceilings, simple design, and the designer brands
customers have come to expect. This location also offers fur services, which include everything from proper storing and cleaning
to alterations and remodeling. Made-to-measure tailoring is available here as well.

MAP 12: Place Ste-Foy, 2452 blvd. Laurier, 418/656-6783, www.holtrenfrew.com;
Mon.-Wed. 9:30am-5:30pm, Thurs.-Fri. 9:30am-9pm, Sat. 9:30am-5pm, Sun.
11am-5pm

OUTDOOR GEAR
Latulippe

With over 70 years of history, Latulippe is one of the highly regarded stores in the region when it comes to gear for hunting and
fishing. What used to be just a tiny, family-run store was recently
renovated and is now a large, modern, two-floor store with everything you need for an outdoor adventure—boots, bags, tents,
waterproof outerwear, and accessories. They even have gear for
snowmobiling and ammunition, guns, and knives for hunting. And
the staff is always full of advice and helpful tips, so just ask.

MAP 12: 637 rue St-Vallier W., 418/529-0024, www.latulippe.com; Mon.-Tues.
8:30am-5:30pm, Wed.-Fri. 8:30am-9pm, Sat. 9am-5pm, Sun. 11am-5pm

SHOPPING DISTRICTS AND CENTERS
Galeries de la Capitale

About a 20-minute drive from downtown Québec City, Galeries
de La Capitale is one of the most fascinating malls in the province
(especially for kids). Opened in 1981, it was the brainchild of businessman Marcel Adams and was filled with Canadian department
store heavyweights Eaton's, The Bay, Simons, and Woolco. Today, it
has 280 stores, 35 restaurants, the biggest IMAX theater in Canada,
and an indoor amusement park. Called Le Mega-Parc, it has 20
rides, including a Ferris wheel, roller coasters, a skating rink, and
smaller rides and games that will make kids go wild.

MAP 12: 5401 blvd. des Galeries, 418/627-5800, www.galeriesdelacapitale.com; Mon.-Wed. 9:30am-5:30pm, Thurs.-Fri. 9:30am-9pm, Sat. 9:30am-5pm, Sun. 10am-5pm

Laurier Québec

The biggest of the three malls, Laurier Québec, formerly called Place Laurier, is three levels high and boasts 350 stores. Opened in 1961, it is the largest mall in eastern Canada and one of the city's top tourist attractions. Well-known stores like Old Navy, H&M, The Bay, Nike, Aldo, and American Apparel are all situated here, as are specialized boutiques including Laine, which carries wool and other knitting materials, and Vision Rock, where you can get a tattoo while you pick up a KISS wall-clock and T-shirt from your favorite hard-rock band. Laurier Québec offers free shuttle service between Vieux-Québec and the mall as well as to the nearby Aquarium du Québec.

MAP 12: 2700 blvd. Laurier, 418/651-5000, www.laurierquebec.com; Mon.-Wed. 10am-5:30pm, Thurs.-Fri. 10am-9pm, Sat. 9am-5pm, Sun. 10am-5pm

Place de la Cité

Part of the large shopping complex on boulevard Laurier in Sainte-Foy, Place de la Cité stands out thanks to the 17-story office building that's attached to the mall's concourse. It's the home of 150 stores and restaurants, and you'll find independent boutiques including Simone Paris, which caters to sizes 6-18; Québécois label Myco Anna; and Corset Corsaire, carrying exclusive prêt-à-porter labels from Europe. La Maison Anglaise, the only bookstore dedicated to English books in the region, is located here, as are sports stores including O'Neill, Sport Select, and Québec brand Chlorophylle.

MAP 12: 2600 blvd. Laurier, Sainte-Foy, 418/657-6920, www.placedelacite. com; Mon.-Wed. 9:30am-5:30pm, Thurs.-Fri. 9:30am-9pm, Sat. 9am-5pm, Sun. noon-5pm

Place Ste-Foy

One of the three shopping malls that make up the impressively large complex in the region close to Université Laval just outside of the city, Place Ste-Foy is also one of the oldest. Built in 1958, it is considered the best shopping center in Québec City for upscale boutiques and labels. Canada's preeminent luxury department store, Holt Renfrew, has been located here since 1965, and among the mall's 135 stores you'll find other top-of-the-line brands like Birks, Swarovski, Lacoste, and BCBG Maxazria.

MAP 12: 2452 blvd. Laurier, 418/653-4184, www.placestefoy.ca; Mon.-Wed. 9:30am-5:30pm, Thurs.-Fri. 9:30am-9pm, Sat. 9am-5pm, Sun. 10am-5pm

Hotels

Highlights

★ **Best Hostel:** One of the few hostels in the city center, **Auberge Internationale de Québec** is friendly, affordable, and couldn't be closer to the action (page 461).

★ **Most Romantic Hotel:** Situated in two of the most beautiful buildings in Vieux-Québec's Upper Town, **Auberge Place d'Armes** has a 17th-century meets 21st-century decor that makes it perfect for a getaway for two (page 461).

★ **Most Luxurious Hotel:** The **Fairmont Le Château Frontenac** is one of the most recognized hotels in the world. A stay here is nothing short of a fantasy (page 462).

★ **Best Location:** Tucked away on an unassuming side street near the old walls, **Hôtel Manoir Victoria** makes for an easy walk to just about anywhere in the city (page 465).

★ **Best Budget Hotel:** A charming bed-and-breakfast in Vieux-Québec's Upper Town, **La Marquise de Bassano** is both affordable, well located, and, above all, welcoming (page 465).

★ **Most Distinctive Building:** A former marine warehouse, **Auberge Saint-Antoine** has high ceilings, exposed beams, and stone floors that match perfectly with the minimal but opulent decor (page 466).

★ **Best Place to Bring the Gang:** Situated in the Old-Port and with modern suites at reasonable prices, **Hôtel Port-Royal** is ideal if you're traveling with the kids (page 467).

★ **Best Boutique Hotel:** With an accommodating staff and awesome views of the St-Lawrence River and Lower Town, chic **Hôtel 71** is a great home-away-from-home (page 467).

★ **Best Guesthouse:** Situated above the oldest grocery store in North America, **Auberge J.A. Moisan** is authentically Victorian without being stuffy (page 469).

★ **Hippest Hotel:** The modern, sleek interior, stunning views, and location in the heart of Saint-Roch make **Hôtel Pur** the ultimate hip hotel (page 471).

PRICE KEY

$ Less than CAN$150 per night

$$ CAN$150–250 per night

$$$ More than CAN$250 per night

Staying in Québec City can be expensive. Contrary to Montréal, there is a lack of choice when it comes to affordable accommodations, and it can sometimes feel as though hotels are taking advantage of a lucrative situation. The majority of the time, however, this isn't the case and service, at both moderately priced and more expensive hotels, couldn't be better. Like restaurants, hotels don't lack in numbers, and the highest concentration of hotels can be found in Vieux-Québec's Upper Town, where on about every little street you'll find a couple of smaller inns. It's here as well that the Château Frontenac is located, standing sentinel on the cliff and casting a shadow on some lesser-known but equally good hotels. Because of its proximity to sights such as the Château and the Citadelle, as well as a number of restaurants, Upper Town is the most sought-after area, but by extension it's also the most touristy.

If you're a fan of sleek, minimal boutique hotels, opt for something in Vieux-Québec's Lower Town or Vieux-Port, once the center of the city's financial district. Old banks, office buildings, and warehouses have been converted into some of the most exciting new hotels. Though it's just as much a tourist attraction as Upper Town, the area has a more relaxed vibe. And although you step out of your hotel into one of the oldest places in North America, it maintains a neighborhood feel that gives it a unique touch of authenticity.

One thing that stands out in Québec City's hotel landscape is the lack of major chains. The Delta and Hilton can be found in Upper Town on René-Lévesque just outside of the city walls, but they are just about the only ones. Most chain hotels are located outside of the city center, close to a collection of shopping malls in Sainte-Foy on the aptly named Avenue des Hôtels. Most of these hotels offer competitive rates and daily shuttles to downtown in the summer. In winter, this service doesn't necessarily apply, and though city buses are available they take much longer but aren't complicated. If you're traveling without a car, it might be more practical to spring for something closer to downtown.

If you want to be close to the action but also want to experience a bit of the city's hipper, younger side, check out hotels in the Saint-Roch and St-Jean Baptiste areas. Since they are not traditional tourist areas, the rates can be more competitive, and though you might not find yourself looking out onto the oldest square in North America, the history here is just as rich.

CHOOSING A HOTEL

When choosing a hotel in Québec City, one of the first things to consider is mobility and how you travel. Charles Dickens famously called it the "Gibraltar of America," and that's still a fitting description. Though it's possible to spend your entire trip in either Upper Town (on the hill) or Lower Town (below the hill), it is unlikely, and even then you'll encounter inclines and hills no matter where you go. Québec isn't a large city by any stretch, but, if you're limited in mobility or by the length of your stay, getting a hotel near the sights you most want to see makes sense. Upper and Lower Town are easily accessible by the funicular and Ecobuses, but if you like boutique hotels, for example, and only have a night, plan it all in the Vieux-Port and spend the next morning doing the rounds in Upper Town. Driving to the sights, especially in summer and unless they are far way, will be much more hassle than it's worth.

The competitive prices of Sainte-Foy hotels might be tempting, but if you're arriving by train or bus at the main station, you'll end up crossing the entire city just to get there. Instead, pick something more modest in the Vieux-Port or Saint-Roch neighborhoods that can be easily accessible when you arrive. Or make sure you get a ticket to the Sainte-Foy station instead.

As in Montréal, the majority of hotels have standard North American-style rooms and amenities like air-conditioning and coffee in the room. But since many of the hotels are also in historic buildings, the rooms in Québec City are usually more European in size. If you book a room in a quaint-looking Victorian house, avoid disappointment and expect it to be smaller than usual. Since they are old homes, it means some of them might not have elevators; it's worth inquiring before you book, though most will have a bellhop for those purposes.

Breakfasts also come in European sizes or not at all. Many hotels don't include breakfast as part of the room, or if they do, they are continental with fresh pastries, breads, cheeses, and fruit. In some cases it's wisest to skip the hotel breakfast altogether and head to one of the city's many bistros for a filling first meal instead.

Packages offer different options for guests when they book and can include breakfast as part of the deal as well as things like tours, museum entrances, and bottles of champagne. Parking, even at bigger hotels, can be hard to come by, but most paid parking lots are safe and relatively affordable. If you're staying near the Plains you might be lucky enough to find free street parking amid the upscale homes. Even if they don't provide parking themselves, the hotels are usually more than willing to help you find a spot or at the very least give you various options.

Vieux-Québec's Upper Town

Map 8

★ Auberge Internationale de Québec $

This hostel is a member of Hostelling International, and you won't find a more affordable place to stay in Vieux-Québec. Situated in what used to be a convent, this comfortable youth hostel has been providing sparse but spacious and spotless rooms for over 40 years. Along with dormitories—male, female, or mixed—they also offer private rooms available for 1-5 people, perfect if you're traveling with a group. Communal areas include a self-serve kitchen and a café bistro, a great place to relax and chat with fellow travelers. In summertime, you can enjoy breakfast in their charming little interior courtyard. The bilingual staff is warm and welcoming and offers a number of different activities, from tours outside the city to organized pub crawls.

MAP 8: 19 rue Ste-Ursule, 418/694-0755, www.aubergeinternationaledequebec.com

★ Auberge Place d'Armes $$

Spread throughout two buildings, one an old hotel and the other an old wax museum, Auberge Place d'Armes is one of the most beautiful hotels in the city, situated in the shadow of Fairmont Le Château Frontenac. Although walls date back to the 17th century, there is nothing old about this hotel; it's just charming. The rooms are all decorated in a mix of modern meets antiques, the most lavish of which is, appropriately, The Marie Antoinette Suite. With its eggshell-blue walls, ornate gold moldings, and rich fabrics, the room is kept light by the addition of pieces like a Plexiglas take on an baroque lamp and Philippe Stark-inspired Louis XIV chairs. Complimentary breakfast is served at Le Pain Béni, their on-site restaurant and one of the best in the city. Those traveling with pets can bring them here (for a small extra fee) but must request a specific room at time of booking.

MAP 8: 24 rue Ste-Anne, 418/694-9485, www.aubergeplacedarmes.com

Le Capitole de Québec $$

Blink and you might miss the sliver of a sign marking this discreet hotel. Tucked into an old building near the St-Jean Gate that includes restaurant Il Teatro and Le Capitole theater—special packages for all three are available—this small four-floor hotel with 45 rooms is in a great location. The interior is distinctly contemporary with bright colors and modern takes on classic furniture shapes. Rooms, however, can be quite small, and though they all boast en-suite bathrooms, some tubs are located next to the bed. It may be romantic, but it's not necessarily practical.

MAP 8: 972 rue St-Jean, 800/363-4040, www.lecapitole.com

Chez Hubert $

Tucked away on a quiet side street, this small three-room bed-and-breakfast is a good option for those looking for the Upper Town experience without the cost. This grand old Victorian townhouse has chandeliers in every room, stained-glass windows, and a beautiful curved staircase at the entrance. Owner Hubert is warm and amiable and offers guests a hearty buffet breakfast. Each of the rooms is decorated in soft hues, and one room looks out on the Château while another has a balcony. All three rooms, however, share bathroom facilities.

MAP 8: 66 rue Ste-Ursule, 418/692-0958, www.chezhubert.com

★ Fairmont Le Château Frontenac $$$

This is luxury at its finest. And having just undergone major renovations and refurbishing, this historic hotel and landmark is one of the chicest and most sought-after temporary addresses in the city. Just entering the sumptuously decorated lobby you feel as though you've stepped into a Victorian salon, with its rich wood paneled walls and ceilings, wall sconces in the shape of candelabras, and antique chandelier hung above the grand staircase. The decor of the 618 rooms and suites follows suit with high ceilings, classic fabrics, and Victorian-style wood furnishings. Like most fine hotels, it has all the amenities you'd expect: pool, spa, gym, and ballroom.

MAP 8: 1 rue des Carrières, 418/692-3861, www.fairmont.com

Chill Out at the Ice Hotel

Come winter, the **Hôtel de Glace** (www.hoteldeglace-canada.com) is one of the most magical places to lay your head. Started in 2001, it was the first ice hotel in North America and has since become one of the most extraordinary hotel experiences in the city. Open from January to March, and situated just outside of the city, the hotel takes roughly a month and a half and 60 workers to construct, with the ice built around a metal base that forms its foundations. Entirely redesigned and rebuilt every year, each incarnation is built around a different theme.

Though the design, theme, and architecture change, the materials don't. The interior is always decked out with ice furniture, sculptures, and touches of fur and animal hide to soften and warm up the space. Everything here, except for the heated bathrooms in a separate building, is made of ice, from the glasses at the bar, to the bar itself, the lobby chairs, the serving plates, and of course, the beds. Made of blocks of ice, the base of the bed is then layered with solid wood as well as a mattress, which is topped with an insulating bed sheet and pillow that are brought to your room just as you're getting ready for bed, along with an arctic sleeping bag. Though temperatures outside might dip to -25°C (13°F),

the four-foot thick walls keep the room between -3°C and -5°C (27°F and 23°F) no matter the temperature outside.

A typical night at the Ice Hotel starts at three in the afternoon with a check in at the Four Points by Sheraton, the base for the ice hotel; this is also where guests eat a hot breakfast the following morning. A free shuttle takes guests out to the hotel, where they can spend the afternoon and evening drinking in the ice bar, trying out the gigantic ice slide, or warming up in the outdoor hot tubs before heading to their rooms later in the night. Some rooms and suites even come with an optional fireplace or both a fireplace and private spa, perfect for a romantic getaway. The hotel even has its very own ice chapel for midwinter marriages. A night at the hotel will typically cost $400-500 per person, which includes a hotel room at the Four Points Sheraton as well as breakfast at Le Dijon, among other perks. Early-bird specials are available starting in the fall with prices hovering around $225 per person.

If you're not convinced sleeping in -3° weather is for you but feel oddly compelled to try out the **Nordic slide** (and who could blame you), tours are available daily between 10:30am and 4:30pm.

Hôtel Cap Diamant 🟢🟢

Located in a historic building on a small and quiet street not far from the walls of the Citadelle, Hôtel Cap Diamant is a charming bed-and-breakfast. Each of the 12 rooms is furnished with rich antiques, giving it a European charm. It's run by Mme. Guillot and her daughter, and the staff is warm, welcoming, and helpful. Guests are treated to a complimentary continental breakfast, which they're welcome to eat in the hidden backyard, full of flowers in the summer. Though there's an elevator for luggage, guests will have to climb the stairs to their rooms, some of which are on the fourth floor.

MAP 8: 39 ave. Ste-Geneviève, 418/694-0313, www.hotelcapdiamant.com

Hôtel Château Bellevue $$

Located in front of the Jardin des Gouveneurs just behind the Château Frontenac, this 48-room hotel offers great views of the St-Lawrence River and access to all the major sites on foot. Taking over four stately homes that were built at the turn of the 20th century, the rooms here are smaller than what you might be hoping for but are comfortably appointed with homey touches like throw pillows and antiques. The hotel offers a complimentary breakfast as well as free Internet and access to a fitness facility. Those up for the walk also have access to the saltwater pool and urban spa at the Château Laurier, the hotel's sister site, located about a 15-minute walk away.

MAP 8: 16 rue de la Porte, 418/692-2573 www.hotelchateaubellevue.com

Hôtel Clarendon $$

Built in 1858 and designed by Charles Baillairgé, this historic hotel is the oldest in Vieux-Québec. First a home, then offices, it became a hotel in 1870 and has remained one since. Originally a four-story building, it underwent two additions in the 20th century, one to include two floors and the mansard roof and the other a six-floor art deco extension, making it particularly striking. It's across the street from City Hall and next door to Édifice Price. Upon entering the Clarendon you're immediately hit with the art deco feel—wood beams feature on the ceiling and large mirrors are placed throughout. The rooms themselves are rather modest with simple decor, though some feature gorgeous circular windows.

MAP 8: 57 rue Ste-Anne, 418/692-2480, www.hotelclarendon.com

Hôtel Le Champlain $$

Eclectically decorated with bright modern furniture and subtly bold wallpaper, Hôtel Le Champlain is a welcoming boutique hotel. Surrounded by historic buildings, the hotel is distinctly modern, though the hardwood floors and exposed brick walls add a bit of European charm to the 49 rooms. Ideally located on a quiet street, it is close to everything but avoids the noise and bustle of streets like St-Jean and St-Louis. Guests are treated to a complimentary breakfast, as well as cappuccinos and espressos that are available throughout the day in the lobby.

MAP 8: 115 rue Ste-Anne, 418/694-0106, www.champlainhotel.com

Hôtel Le Clos Saint-Louis $$

If you're an old-fashioned romantic, you will swoon at Hôtel Le Clos St-Louis. Calling itself the "most romantic Victorian hotel in the city," it's fastidiously decorated with period antiques, including wardrobes, four-poster beds, and fainting couches. Its location close to the St-Louis gate makes sights both inside and outside the walls walkable. Catering to couples, this isn't a place for kids. They offer a variety of packages, including Engagement, Newlywed, and the **465** Babymoon package, for expectant mothers.

MAP 8: 69 rue St-Louis, 418/694-1311, www.clossaintlouis.com

★ Hôtel Manoir Victoria $\$$ $\$$

Though the building that now houses the Hôtel Manoir Victoria was built in 1904, the hotel's history dates back to the 1830s when Thomas Payne opened the city's most exclusive hotel across the street from its current location. Situated just off of St-Jean in Upper Town on a street that connects to Lower Town and the Saint-Roch area, Hôtel Manoir Victoria is sumptuously decorated with rich, embellished fabrics and classically comfortable furnishings. The rooms are modern but still traditional, and there's a homeyness to both the superior rooms and more luxurious suites. Though still beautiful, the hotel enjoyed its heyday in the 1920s, and no place is this more evident than with the pool. With its Grecian columns and small black-and-white tiles, it's like something out of The Great Gatsby. It's also connected to the Bistro Boréal, so you don't have to leave the premises to eat well.

MAP 8: 44 Côte du Palais, 418/692-1030, www.manoir-victoria.com

Hôtel Ste-Anne $\$$ $\$$

Chic and sophisticated is the best way to describe the feel of this 20-room hotel just across the square from Château Frontenac. Located on a busy cobblestone street, this historic building has been perfectly transformed into a sleek, boutique-style hotel. The stone walls, exposed ceiling beams, and Norman-style windows are the prefect complement to the simple, clean lines of the furnishings and the ultramodern bathrooms—black slate tiles, glass shower doors. The rooms can be quite small, however, so keep size in mind if you're choosing between a superior room and a junior suite.

MAP 8: 32 rue Ste-Anne, 418/694-1455, www.hotelste-anne.com

★ La Marquise de Bassano $\$$

Located on a quiet street lined with historic homes in Vieux-Québec's Upper Town, this charming bed-and-breakfast is steps away from Château Frontenac and Les Fortifications. It's run by a young, outgoing couple, and the five rooms of this gray-stone townhouse are uniquely decorated, and priced, with touches like a full bookshelf, writing desk, and vintage typewriter in the "library room," a claw-footed bathtub, or antique pieces. Only two rooms have their own bathrooms, however; the other three must share. Breakfast is served in the cold European style with meats, hard-boiled eggs, and various breads and pastries.

MAP 8: 12 rue des Grisons, 418/692-0316, www.marquisedebassano.com

Vieux-Québec's Lower Town

Map 9

★ Auberge Saint-Antoine $$$

Once a port-side warehouse, Auberge St-Antoine retained its high ceilings, exposed beams, and stone floors, all the things that make it one of the most inviting hotels in the city today. It was built on the archaeological site of Ilôt Hunt, an area full of wharfs and warehouses at the peak of Québec's port history, and artifacts that were found on this site have been incorporated into the hotel design. The rooms are sleek and modern with a touch of luxury: plush headboards with unique motifs and heated bathroom floors. Many also have balconies, terraces, or fireplaces, so request one when you book. Unique services include an archaeological tour, on-site cinema, and Wednesday drinks with the family of owners. One of the city's top restaurants, Panache, is also located here, in what was once the warehouse lobby.

MAP 9: 8 rue St-Antoine, 418/692-2211, www.saint-antoine.com

Auberge Saint-Pierre $$

The first of the boutique hotels to open in Québec City, Auberge Saint-Pierre has a charm all its own. Though it's been recently been remodeled with slightly sleeker furniture and a more minimalist decor, the Saint-Pierre still makes you feel as though you're staying with a close friend or family (but without the bickering). Brick walls and classic black and white photos are the backdrop for cozy white wooden furniture and pops of bright color. Each room comes with its own coffee maker, iron, and umbrella—now that's thinking ahead. The feeling of home continues in the main area with a complimentary gourmet breakfast in the relaxed dining room and a library with a roaring fireplace, perfect for relaxing with a nightcap.

MAP 9: 79 rue St-Pierre, 418/694-7981, www.auberge.qc.ca

Hôtel Belley $

Looking out over the marina and farmers market, Hôtel Belley is just a close walk to sights in both Upper and Lower Town and is a stone's throw from the cool Saint-Roch area. This tiny eight-room hotel has a definite laid-back atmosphere, perhaps helped in part by the historic tavern on the ground floor, which provides an excellent place to socialize and relax all year long. The rooms here are small and simply furnished, but the views, especially at night, are lovely. Come summer, *terrasses* are open in both the front and back of the building, attracting locals and tourists alike.

MAP 9: 249 rue St-Paul, 418/692-1694, www.quebecweb.com/hotelbelley

Hôtel Le Germain-Dominion ❸❸❸

With its grandiose neoclassical facade and modern, understated interior, you'd never guess that this chic boutique hotel started off as a fish warehouse. Located in the former financial district, this nine-floor hotel, the first of Le Germain's to open in North America, offers great views over both the St-Lawrence and Lower Town. The large, open lobby with big windows, comfy couches, and a laid-back atmosphere is immediately inviting. You'll want to spend all morning in the adjoining dining room, sinking back into your plush seat with a paper while you finish off breakfast. The rooms themselves are equally inviting, with big windows, simple, uncomplicated design, and a Nespresso machine making it the ultimate getaway.

MAP 9: 126 rue St-Pierre, 418/692-2222, www.germaindominion.com

Hôtel Le Priori ❸❸

At the base of Cap Diamant in the Vieux-Port on one of the oldest streets in North America, Hôtel Le Priori occupies the space that was once the home of architect Jean Baillairgé. In summer, its white-washed facade is punctuated with color from hanging flowers and vines that crown the entrance and its surrounding windows. Inside, a modern interior contrasts with the stone walls that date as far back as 1734. The hotel features 21 bedrooms and five suites. The emphasis is on minimalist chic but with a touch of art deco at this boutique hotel. Furniture in asymmetrical shapes and unusual colors like deep purple or bright red can be found in most rooms. Each suite, however, is uniquely decorated. Make sure to take advantage of the secluded outdoor *terrasse* or make reservations at the in-house restaurant Toast!

MAP 9: 15 rue du Sault-au-Matelot, 418/692-3992, www.hotellepriori.com

★ Hôtel Port-Royal ❸❸

This old storehouse with gray stone exterior in the center of the Vieux-Port has since been converted exclusively into suites. Offering three different types of suites (deluxe, superior, and executive), Hôtel Port-Royal provides a home away from home with each suite equipped with living room and kitchenette, a great option if you want to save costs by eating in. The decor throughout is simple and modern with wood floors, sandy-colored walls, and each suite decorated just so, whether with dramatic striped wallpaper or a colorful, floral couch. It's perfect if you're traveling with the family.

MAP 9: 144 rue St-Pierre, 418/692-2777, www.leportroyal.com

★ Hôtel 71 ❸❸❸

Located on a cobblestone street in what was once the city's financial district, Hôtel 71 is in a building that was once the National Bank's head office. The neoclassical facade of this boutique hotel

top: Fairmont Le Château Frontenac from the interior courtyard, Vieux-Québec's Upper Town; **bottom:** inside the Hôtel de Glace

is juxtaposed against the sleek, modern interior. Rooms are uncluttered, with earth-toned furniture with clean lines giving them an especially Zen feeling. The bathrooms, too, are relaxing, with gray slate tiles and geometric lines. Large windows in almost every room allow not only for natural light but also great views of the city and surrounding area. It's the choice of design lovers with a larger budget. Breakfast is served in the adjoining restaurant and offers a delicious cappuccino to wash down your hearty continental breakfast.

MAP 9: 71 rue St-Pierre, 418/692-1171, www.hotel71.ca

Parliament Hill and the Plains
Map 10

Hôtel Château Laurier $$

Set back from the Plains of Abraham and a two-minute walk to Vieux-Québec's Upper Town, Hôtel Château Laurier is ideally located. The newly renovated lobby is open and inviting with a blazing fire in the winter. Rooms here run the gamut from European-style rooms that are smaller than usual North American rooms and simply decorated to big, bright, newly renovated rooms with updated modern furniture and more of a Zen quality. No matter your room type, all guests are welcome to try the indoor saltwater pool.

MAP 10: 1220 Place Georges-V W., 418/-522-8108, www.oldquebec.com/en/laurier

Saint-Jean-Baptiste and Saint-Roch
Map 11

★ Auberge J.A. Moisan $$

This four-bedroom guesthouse invites you to be a part of history by sleeping above the oldest grocery store in North America. Charmingly decorated with impeccable moldings, antique furniture, homemade quilts, and Laura Ashley prints, it gives just a taste of what it was like to be a successful businessman in the 19th century. The beautifully restored Victorian house also boasts a living room, library, solarium, and *terrasse*, all of which guests have access to. Just to take things a little bit further, 4 o'clock tea is served.

MAP 11: 699 rue St-Jean, 418/529-9764, www.jamoisan.com/auberge

Auberge L'Autre Jardin 💰💰

If traveling gives you eco-anxiety, then staying at Auberge L'Autre Jardin will give you a clear conscience. This 28-room hotel is dedicated to sustainable and responsible tourism, with organic breakfasts made with fair-trade products and furnishings that come from sustainable sources. Owned by Carrefour Tiers-Monde, a Québec-based charity that raises awareness on issues in developing countries, the hotel is the money-making side of the business. The rooms are tastefully decorated and feel more like a friend's place, with classic but not swank bedding. They're decorated with art from Africa, Asia, and India. The hotel also has a fair-trade store selling coffee, jewelry, and different international art crafts and accessories.

MAP 11: 365 blvd. Charest E., 418/523-1790, www.autrejardin.com

Auberge Le Vincent 💰💰

The keyword here is "concierge." Every effort is put into making your stay nothing less than fantastic and tailor made. From the made-to-order breakfasts to in-house movie rentals (there are over 100 to choose from at the front desk), the staff evinces old-school charm, taking care of dinner reservations, walking tours, and more—you name it and they're on it. Of course they can handle it all because this is a small, 10-room hotel located in the trendy Saint-Roch area. It is impeccably designed. Each room is uniquely decorated, but all feature exposed brick walls, 400-thread-count sheets, and the most modern bathrooms, often separated by a crystal-clear glass window—with optional blind.

MAP 11: 295 rue St-Vallier E., 418/523-5000, www.aubergelevincent.com

Château des Tourelles 💰💰

Just across the street from Château du Faubourg is this light and airy bed-and-breakfast, marked by a turret that stands out on this strip of St-Jean, which is lined with neighborhood bistros and small boutiques. Climb a flight of stairs into this warm and welcoming place. Wood floors and exposed brick give the rooms a cozy and a little bit country feel, without being kitschy. A filling breakfast is served in the sunny dining room, and a roaring fire in the sitting room is great for guests in the winter, while the rooftop terrace offers views of (nearly) all of the sights in the city.

MAP 11: 212 rue St-Jean, 418/346-9136, www.chateaudestourelles.qc.ca

Le Château du Faubourg 💰

Set back from the road on busy rue St-Jean is a huge Second Empire-style chateau. Built by the rich Imperial Tobacco family in the 1800s, it retains its original grandeur and is one of the city's most impressive bed-and-breakfasts. A gilded staircase and chandelier greet you as you enter and set the tone for the rooms, which give off the air of an old manor house with rich antique furnishings, sumptuous fabrics, and, in the case of one room, an entire library as headboard. Each room has its own individual bathroom. Breakfast is served in a grand library, and though the owners are lovely and charming, their 12 pet birds get on the nerves of some.

MAP 11: 429 rue St-Jean, 418/524-2902, www.lechateaudufaubourg.com

★ Hôtel Pur $$

This chic, boutique-style hotel in the heart of Saint-Roch, one of the city's up-and-coming neighborhoods, couldn't be cooler. Standing 18 floors tall, it's the highest building in the area, so just about every room has a view from the floor-to-ceiling windows, looking out on to the city, the Laurentian mountains, or the newly refurbished Saint-Roch church. The sleek design and minimal color palette—gray, black, and white with bursts of orange—give it an uncluttered but still relaxed vibe. The slate-gray bathrooms give it an added touch of Zen, as do the Japanese-style baths and glass-door showers. Visitors can dine in the adjoining restaurant Table, which is equally as chic with long communal tables, comfy couches, and a menu that goes all day long.

MAP 11: 395 rue de la Couronne, 418/647-2611, www.hotelpur.com

Greater Québec City

Map 12

Château Bonne Entente $$

This large, sprawling hotel outside of the city offers an alternative to those who want the feel of a country getaway with a close proximity to the downtown. Just about every room in this cottage-style hotel with mansard roofs and soft-yellow clapboard is distinctly decorated, from the hardwood floors and country fabrics of the "Cocooning" room to the carpeted, sleek but comfortable decor of the "Business" room. With an on-site spa, large outdoor pool and hot tub, and golf course, relaxation is never far away.

MAP 12: 3400 chemin Ste-Foy, 418/653-5221, www.chateaubonneentente.com

Hôtel Sépia $$

Located outside of the city center and close to other hotels, the city's largest shopping malls, and the aquarium, Hôtel Sépia is a bit of urbania in suburbia. With its sleek modern design—rain shower heads, Barcelona chairs, and refinished wood floors—this boutique-style hotel will make you feel like you're in the middle of downtown even when you're not. It's approximately a 15-minute drive to downtown, and the hotel offers free shuttle services during the summer months; those traveling without a car, however, might find it impractical come winter. This hotel might not give you a great view of the Vieux-Port but it will give you a great view of the famous Québec Bridge.

MAP 12: 3135 chemin St-Louis, 418/653-4941, www.hotelsepia.ca

Excursions from Québec City

Highlights

★ **Best Historic Road:** One of the oldest roads in North America, **Route de la Nouvelle France** is lined with ancestral homes dating back hundreds of years (page 478).

★ **Best Waterfall:** Taller than Niagara Falls, **Chute Montmorency** is an impressive sight, especially when you're on the suspension bridge over the falls with 360-degree breathtaking views (page 479).

★ **Oldest Pilgrimage Site:** Built in honor of Sainte-Anne, the patron saint of shipwrecked sailors, the **Basilique Sainte-Anne-de-Beaupré** is one of the oldest pilgrimage sites in the world. The interior is lined with crutches as a testament to its healing powers (page 479).

★ **Best Place to Pick Your Own Fruits and Vegetables:** **Île d'Orléans** is an island in the middle of the St-Lawrence River. It has some of the oldest homes in the region and some of the best agriculture. Head to the island to pick your own fresh fruit and vegetables (page 480).

★ **Most Artistic Town:** The birthplace of Cirque du Soleil, **Baie-Saint-Paul** is full of galleries and folk art boutiques (page 485).

★ **Best Skiing:** Overlooking the St-Lawrence River and cutting through the boreal forest, the hills at **Le Massif** offer views just as stunning as the slopes themselves (page 488).

★ **Best Bike Excursion:** Only 11 kilometers long and 3 kilometers wide, the **Isle-aux-Coudres,** near Tadoussac, is filled with old churches, windmills, and other rarities, to be discovered by bike (page 489).

★ **Best Place to Play Blackjack:** Located in a long-established holiday town, the **Casino de Charlevoix** is the one place you should place your bets (page 493).

★ **Best Hiking:** The gorges and fjords of **Parc National des Hautes-Gorges-de-la-Rivière-Malbaie,** along with its unique mix of tundra and taiga, make it one of the most breathtaking sites to hike in the region (page 494).

★ **Best Whale-Watching:** At the confluence of the Saguenay and St-Lawrence Rivers, the shores surrounding the historic town of **Tadoussac** have one of the most diverse ecosystems in the world. This is the annual meeting place for 10 species of whales, from humpbacks to belugas (page 495).

Montréal and Québec City might give you a clear picture of the province's urban popula-tion, but if you really want to get to know the prov-ince and see the culture and nature that have shaped it, you have to go north.

Referred to as the *régions* (regions), the forests and the jagged cliffs of the St-Lawrence provide a real sense of the province and its rugged beauty. Barely a half-hour-drive from Québec you'll find yourself in the picturesque Côte-de-Beaupré, lined with quaint an-cestral homes—most continue to be residential homes. Not every historical event took place in and around the city; in fact, this area was where General Wolfe and his men camped before they laid siege to the city.

Once mostly farmland the area is now a large tourist destination thanks to the pilgrimages to the Basilique Sainte-Anne-de-Beaupré and Chute Montmorency. Across the water on the Île d'Orléans, however, things have stayed much the same as they have for hun-dreds of years. Île d'Orléans is full of vineyards and farms, and agri-tourism is a big part of the island; visitors should take full advantage by picking their own fruits and vegetables to take home.

Navigating the Côte-Nord (North Coast) couldn't be easier; two highways take you to the same destination, and it all depends on whether you want the scenic route, Route 362, or the faster route, Route 138. Truth be told, even the faster route could be described as scenic; the high cliffs, rolling hills, and patches of tundra land-scape as you head farther north are hard to ignore. Baie-Saint-Paul seems to emerge like a mirage, its church steeple sparkling on the shores of a low valley flanked by stone cliffs and the St-Lawrence. More picturesque than most of the other towns, it's worth a wander.

North again, La Malbaie sneaks up on you from the corners of the twisting turning road, and though the sites aren't much, the landscape is lovely. Once you're this far north you might as well continue to the jewel of Charlevoix and cross the majestic Saguenay by ferry to Tadoussac. The massive cliffs that plunge into the river make for breathtaking scenery, and if you're lucky enough to catch a view of the diverse whale life that thrives in these waters, you'll understand the atypical beauty that defines the region and the province.

PLANNING YOUR TIME

Some of these excursions can be done by day or even an afternoon by car. However, some places, including Tadoussac and the Saguenay Fjord are three hours (or sometimes more) away, so plan to spend at least a night in these locations. Of course, no matter how far afield you're willing to travel, if you have the time, it's always fun to stay a bit longer in order to really get to know a place. Though Québec is a big province and you could drive for hours without hitting on any sights, all the excursions in this section are easily reached, the longest taking at most three hours from the city.

Most of the sights are accessible by national highways, though in some places these highways slim down to two lanes. If you're driving in winter, the journey could take longer, especially if there are bad driving conditions. Snow tires are required by law December-March; if you don't have them on your car, avoid trips into the rocky and hilly Charlevoix, or rent a car with the right tires.

High season is May-October; those traveling north to Charlevoix later in the year should make sure to plan well ahead, or opt for a package deal at places like La Massif. Getting a hotel, dinner, and recreation in one deal will allow you to see the beauty of the area without worrying about whether there'll be restaurants open or not.

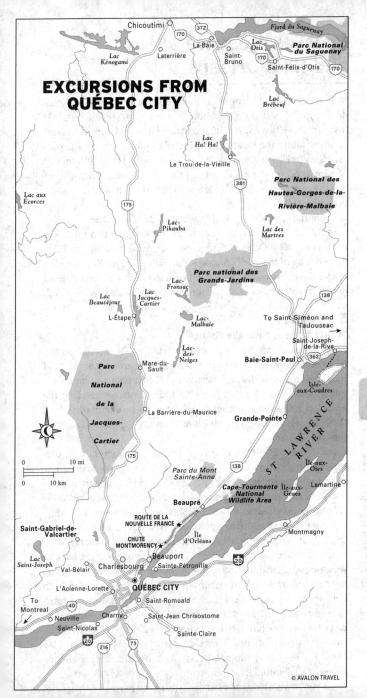

EXCURSIONS FROM QUÉBEC CITY

EXCURSIONS FROM QUÉBEC CITY

Chicoutimi
372
170
La Baie
Fjord du Saguenay
Lac Otis
Parc National du Saguenay
170
Laterrière
Saint-Bruno
Saint-Félix-d'Otis
170
Lac Kénogami

Lac Brébeuf

Lac Ha! Ha!
Le Trou-de-la-Vieille
381
Parc National des Hautes-Gorges-de-la-Rivière-Malbaie

Lac aux Écorces
175
Lac-Pikauba
Lac des Martres

Parc national des Grands-Jardins
138

Lac-Fronsac
Lac Beauséjour
Lac Jacques-Cartier
L-Étape
Lac-Malbaie
To Saint-Siméon and Tadoussac →
Saint-Joseph-de-la-Rive
362

Lac-des-Neiges
Baie-Saint-Paul

Mare-du-Sault
Isle-aux-Coudres

Parc National de la Jacques-Cartier
La Barrière-du-Maurice
Grande-Pointe

ST. LAWRENCE RIVER

175
Île-aux-Oies

0   10 mi
0   10 km

Parc du Mont Sainte-Anne
138
Île-aux-Grues
Lamartine

Cape-Tourmente National Wildlife Area

Saint-Gabriel-de-Valcartier
Beaupré
ROUTE DE LA NOUVELLE FRANCE ★
Île d'Orléans

CHUTE MONTMORENCY ★
Montmagny

Lac Saint-Joseph
Val-Bélair
Beauport
Charlesbourg
Sainte-Pétronille
20

L'Acienne-Lorette
QUÉBEC CITY
To Montreal →
40
Saint-Romuald
Neuville
Saint-Nicolas
Charny
Saint-Jean Chrisostome
216
73
Sainte-Claire
20

© AVALON TRAVEL

Côte-de-Beaupré and Île d'Orléans

Minutes outside of Québec on Route 138, you'll reach the Côte-de-Beaupré. Located on the banks of the St-Lawrence River, this historical area boasts ancient ancestral homes and open farmland running along the Route de la Nouvelle France, one of the oldest roads in North America. As you pass along the 50 kilometers of roadways, you'll pass through a number of small towns, all of which are between the high cliffs of the Laurentians and the shores of the river.

From the Côte-de-Beaupré you can see the Île d'Orléans, an island in the stream of the St-Lawrence. Linking the two historical areas is the Île d'Orléans Bridge, which can be used by car, bike, or foot. The island itself has one main road, Chemin Royal, which circles the entire island. It's dotted with towns, but much of the island is devoted to local agriculture and can be visited year-round.

SIGHTS

★ Route de la Nouvelle France

Leave Québec City heading northeast and you'll soon be on the **Route de la Nouvelle France** (www.routenouvelle-france.com), one of the oldest roads in North America. In 1626 Samuel de Champlain established a livestock farm on Cap Tourmente farther along the river, but it was Bishop Monsignor de Laval who originally traced the road, which brought provisions from the Côte-de-Beaupré to the city.

All along the 50-kilometer road are heritage homes, some dating as far back as the 1600s. Each is designed in its own particular style, indicative of early New France architecture. Though many of the homes are private residences, the public can visit **Maison Vézina** (171 rue des Grenadiers, 418/822-3183, www.maisonvezina.ca, May-late-Aug. Tues.-Sat. 10am-4pm, Sept.-Apr. Tues.-Sat. noon-4pm, free). Built in 1720, it's now an interpretation center and exhibition space. If you're looking to get in touch with your roots, **Centre de Généalogie** (277 rue du Couvent, 418/824-3079, www3.telebecinter-net.com/archives.chateau-richer, summer daily 9am-4pm, free) can help you with genealogical research, a popular Québécois pastime.

If you want a little history of the area, the **Centre d'Interprétation de la Côte-de-Beaupré** (7976 ave. Royale, 418/824-3677, www.his-toire-cotedebeaupre.org, May-Oct. daily 9:30am-4pm, Oct.-May Mon.-Fri. 9:30am-4:30pm, $6) has lots of documentation and exhibits and is housed in an old seminary.

As you travel along the road, you'll notice cavern-like structures built directly into the hillsides; these are root cellars, some of which date back more than 300 years. Also along the route is the **Moulin du Petit Pré** (7007 ave. Royale, 418/824-7007, www.moulin-petit-pre.com, mid-Apr.-mid-Oct. daily 9am-5pm, $5 adult, $3 child). Founded in 1695, it's the oldest operating flour mill in North America. Take a guided tour, then have lunch at the on-site café or get some bread for the road.

★ Chute Montmorency

Carry on along the Route de la Nouvelle France and you'll soon reach **Chute Montmorency** (4300 blvd. Ste-Anne, 800/665-6527, www.sepaq.com/ct/pcm) an 83-meter-high waterfall (even taller than Niagara Falls, as everyone will point out) that dominates the landscape between the cliffs of the Laurentians and the St-Lawrence. It's a stunning natural wonder in the middle of lush greenery, and visitors can discover the falls by foot or take a cable car ($12 adult, $6 child round-trip). There's access at either side of the falls year-round and a suspension bridge that allows you to cross along the top; it offers great views of Île d'Orleans and even looks onto Québec City.

★ Basilique Sainte-Anne-de-Beaupré

This is the oldest pilgrimage site in North America, and people have been coming to **Basilique Sainte-Anne-de-Beaupré** (10018 ave. Royale, 418/827-3781, www.shrinesaintanne.org, May daily 6am-7pm, June-late-Sept. daily 6am-9pm, Oct.-Apr. Mon.-Sat. 6am-6pm, Sun. 6am-5pm) since the 1660s. The first chapel was constructed on the site in 1658 as a place of worship for the area's new settlers and to house a statue of Sainte-Anne, Québec's patron saint. She's also the patron saint of shipwrecked sailors, and it was a group of Breton sailors caught in a storm that vowed to erect a chapel in Sainte-Anne's honor if they got safely back to land. While the chapel was being constructed, a man with rheumatism was said to have been cured after laying just three bricks, and a pilgrimage was born.

The first basilica was built in 1876 to accommodate the legions of pilgrims who visited the shrine. The structure that exists today, built in the shape of a Latin cross and featuring 214 stained-glass windows, was constructed in 1926 after the first church was destroyed by fire in 1922. One image that strikes you as you enter the church is the multitude of crutches, club shoes, and other pieces of ephemera that hang on the pillars from those who have been cured. A small museum in the church's parking lot exhibits some of the church's treasures as well as donations made by pilgrims.

Located five kilometers from downtown Québec City, Île d'Orléans is an island in the middle of the St-Lawrence and one of the oldest parts of New France to be colonized. It measures 34 kilometers long and 8 kilometers wide. Explorer Jacques Cartier first called it Île de Bacchus, because of the amount of wild grapes found growing on the island. Today, it's home to a number of small villages, but agriculture is still a large part of life on the island.

The first parish was founded here in 1661, and a visit to **Maison Drouin** (4700 chemin Royal, 418/829-0330, www.fondationfran-coislamy.org, mid-June-Aug. daily 10am-6pm, Sept. Sat.-Sun. 1pm-5pm, Oct.-May dates vary, $4) will give you an idea of what the early houses looked like. Built in 1730, it has been preserved in its original state.

Manoir Mauvide-Genest (1451 chemin Royal, 418/829-2630, www.manoirmauvidegenest.com, June-Aug. daily 10am-5pm, Sept.-Oct. Tues.-Sun. 10am-5pm, $6 adult, $5 senior and student, $4 child, children 5 and under free) offers a view of the seignorial home of the 18th century, with furniture, objects, and reenactments of daily life on view.

Agri-tourism is a big draw to the island; you can visit **Cassis Monna & Filles** (721 chemin Royal, 418/828-2525, www.cassismonna.com, May-Nov. daily 10am-6pm, free) and learn about how they make their black currant liqueur, or go for a tasting at **Vignoble de Sainte-Pétronille** (1A chemin du Bout-de-l'Île, 418/828-4554, www.vignobleorleans.com, May-Dec. daily 10am-5pm, free) and try their reds and whites as you look at the Chute Montmorency. Visitors are also welcome to pick their own fruits and vegetables at local farms, including **Ferme la Rosacée** (165 chemin Royal, 418/828-9662, June-mid-Oct. daily 8:30am-6:30pm, free), where you can pick everything from raspberries to seasonal vegetables and buy homemade products like jam, pickles, and ketchup.

RESTAURANTS

If you left Québec City early in the morning, stop in at **Patisserie Praline et Chocolat** (7874 ave. Royale, 418/978-0528, www.pralinechocolat.ca, mid-June-early Sept. daily 8am-6pm, early Sept-mid-June Thurs.-Sun. 8am-6pm, $10) for some mouthwatering pastries. They offer 10 different kinds of *viennoiseries* (baked goods) made fresh daily, as well as artisanal bread, jams, and other treats.

Whether you're looking for breakfast or dinner, **L'Aventure** (355 rue Dupont, 418/827-5748, www.laventure.ca, daily 11am-11pm, $30) in Beaupré has you covered with everything from grilled trout and filet mignon to eggs Benedict, all in a relaxed atmosphere. If you're in the mood for something less refined, **Casse Croute Chez**

clockwise from top left: Chute Montmorency, Cote-de-Beaupré and Île d'Orleans; explore the artistic town of Baie-Saint-Paul and spend the night at Hotel Le Ferme.; the sand dunes in Tadoussac, Charlevoix

Chantale (17 rue de l'Église, 418/827-7005, daily 8:30am-7:30pm, $10) has over 100 different kinds of poutine on the menu, including the house specialty, poutine with goose.

On Île d'Orléans, tuck into some traditional cuisine or take part in the *cabane à sucre* experience at **Le Relais des Pins** (3029 chemin Royal, 418/829-3455, www.lerelaisdespins.com, June-Sept. daily 11am-9pm, winter by reservation only, $15). Open year-round, this delightful log cabin has lots of natural light and a modern take on decor.

If you've got a sweet tooth, **Chocolaterie de Île d'Orléans** (150 chemin du Bout de Île, 418/828-2250, www.chocolaterieorleans.com, $10) will satisfy with rich chocolate desserts, homemade ice cream, and delicious coffees.

Treat yourself to fine dining overlooking the St-Lawrence at **La Goéliche** (22 chemin de Quai, 418/828-2248, www.goeliche.ca, daily 8am-8:30pm, $40), where breakfast includes dishes like French toast with custard, and dinner has choices like rack of lamb and boneless rib eye with shallots.

RECREATION
Bird-Watching and Hiking
Cap-Tourmente
The site of a livestock farm established by Samuel de Champlain in the early 1600s, **Cap-Tourmente** (570 chemin du Cap-Tourmente, 418/827-4591, www.captourmente.com, mid-Apr.-Nov. daily 8:30am-5pm, Jan.-Mar. daily 9am-5pm, $6) became a farm headed by Monsignor de Laval in 1664. It was an active farm well into the 20th century, and some of the early buildings still remain. Today the area is mostly a nature reserve; it's a great place to bird-watch and learn about the greater snow goose and American bulrush marshes. Interpretive guides and 20 kilometers of hiking trails are available.

Golf
Le Grand Vallon
One of the best courses in eastern Canada, **Le Grand Vallon** (100 rue Beau-Mont, Beaupré, 418/827-4561, www.legrandvallon.com, May-Nov. daily dawn-10pm, $45-95 for 18 holes), designed by Howard Watson, was once nicknamed the "minister's club" because of the number of high-level politicians that frequented the links. Along the 6,583-yard course there are four lakes and 42 white-sand bunkers, and the changing scenery moves from rolling tree-lined fairways to a large open plan at mid-course. Equipment rentals, driving range, and lessons are also available here and an electric cart and use of the practice range are included in the green fee.

Skiing, Snowboarding, and Snowshoeing
Mont-Sainte-Anne

The most popular ski station in the Québec City region, **Mont-Saint-Anne** (2000 blvd. Beau Pré, Beaupré, 888/827-4579 www.mont-sainte-anne.com, mid-Nov.-mid-Apr. Mon.-Fri. 9am-9pm, Sat.-Sun. 8:30am-9pm, $64 adult, $68 senior, $53 youth, $36 child 7-12) offers both day and night skiing, with the highest elevation of night skiing in the country. Officially opened in 1966, the history here goes back to 1947, when the Canadian Championships where held on these slopes. About an hour's drive north of the city, 66 trails cover both the north and south face of the mountain. It also has popular cross-country and snowshoeing trails.

HOTELS

Cozy but modern, the 31 rooms at **Auberge la Camarine** (10947 blvd. Ste-Anne, 800/567-3939, www.camarine.com, $100-250) in the Côte-de-Beaupré are often fitted with a warming gas fire, perfect after a long day outdoors.

On Île d'Orléans, grab a room with a view at **Auberge La Goéliche** (22 chemin de Quai, 418/828-2248, www.goeliche.ca, $104-144). Named after a small schooner, the white clapboard house has charm in spades; the views of the river and well-appointed rooms with country touches like handmade quilts make it an ideal choice.

Total country charm is the best way to describe **Auberge Le Canard Huppé** (2198 chemin Royal, 800/838-2292, www.canard-huppe.com, $150-250). The oversized wood furniture, pine paneling, and wood floors are welcoming, and the beautiful garden and seasonal regional cuisine on offer in the restaurant are the icing on the cake.

INFORMATION AND SERVICES

Before you go to the area, read up on the Côte-de-Beaupré area at **www.cotedebeaupre.com**, which offers the useful information on restaurants, hotels, grocery stores, and events. Once you're on the ground, the **Côte-de-Beaupré Tourist Office** (3 rue de la Seigneurie, Château-Richer, 866/932-9082, Mon.-Sat. 9am-5pm, Sun. 10am-4pm) can provide you with hands-on information.

The year-round **Île d'Orléans Tourist Office** (490 Côte du Pont, St-Pierre, 418/828-9411 or 866/941-9411, www.iledorleans.com, July-Aug. daily 8:30am-7:30pm, Sept.-June. daily 10am-5pm) has a wealth of information and tips on hand.

GETTING THERE AND AROUND
By Bus

Old Québec Tours, also known as **Tours Dupont** (800/267-8687, www.tourdupont.com, June-Oct. daily 9am and 1pm, Nov.-May daily 1pm, $50), offers different tours that essentially drop you off at the highlights along the Côte-de-Beaupré and pick you up later. They leave from three points throughout Québec City for your convenience, so check before you book.

Sainte-Anne-de-Beaupré can be reached by **Intercar** (320 Abraham Martin, 888/861-4592, www.intercar.qc.ca) coach, which leaves from Québec City's Gare du Palais bus terminal heading toward Baie Comeau three times a day Monday-Saturday and once on Sunday. A return ticket costs $16 and the journey takes 25 minutes.

By Bike

Bike path **Corridor du Littoral** will take you right from Québec's Vieux-Port all the way to Chute Montmorency and even along the **Route de la Nouvelle France.** Once you've made it onto the Île d'Orléans, bikes are available to rent from **Écolocyclo** (517 Chemin Royal, 418/828-0370, www.ecolocyclo.net, May-mid-June Sat.-Sun. 9am-6pm, mid-June-Sept. daily 9am-6pm). The Chemin Royal encircles the island and is a great way to sightsee by bike.

By Car

The simplest and quickest way to get around is to take Autoroute 440 east out of Québec City and watch for the signs; all of the sights are well marked out with the exits that accompany them. To get to Île d'Orléans, take the Pont Île d'Orléans to the island.

Charlevoix

Some of the most stunning views of the province can be found here. People come here to camp, hike, and to catch a glimpse of the whales.

Follow Route 138 north out of Québec City and you'll come across some of the most spectacular scenery you've ever seen. The impact of a meteorite 350 million years ago has shaped the face of the Charlevoix region and could be the cause of its mysterious seismic activity (rest assured—most temblors hit little more than 2.0 on the Richter scale).

One of the first vacation destinations in Canada thanks to a couple of enterprising Scottish soldiers, Charlevoix's landscape is distinct in its variety. At times pastoral and hilly, the region's high cliffs and breathtaking fjords are adorned with tundra, while nearby, steep sand dunes rise unexpectedly along the coastline. These manifold landscapes translate into an area rich in biodiversity, where moose and caribou thrive alongside an astounding range of sea life. Where else can you sit on a sandy beach waiting to catch a glimpse of a pod of white beluga whales?

Drive northwest out of Québec City and you'll soon come across Wendake, a First Nations reserve that is home to over 3,000 residents. The home of the Huron-Wendat tribe since 1697, this unique reserve offers both a historical and modern perspective on the tribe and its people. It's an active town, and many of the 19th-century buildings resemble those found back in the city—white-washed houses and clapboard churches—but look a little closer and you'll see something entirely different.

Shaped like an old Algonquin smokehouse, the **Huron-Wendat Museum** (15 Place de la Rencontre, 418/847-2260, www.museehuronwendat.com, mid-June-Oct. daily 9am-4pm, Nov.-mid-June Wed.-Sun. 9am-4pm, $14 adult, $7 child) conserves and promotes the tribe's heritage. The permanent exhibit—Territories, Memories, Knowledge—takes visitors from the creation myth to the forming of the Huron-Wendat people and events that shaped the tribe right up until today. The museum also offers tours of the numerous heritage sites throughout the town, including Notre-Dame-de-Lorette Church, the Kabir Kouba waterfall, and Tsawenhohi House.

Those who want to experience the past firsthand can head over to **Onhoüa Chetek8e** (575 Chef Stanislas-Koska St., 418/842-4308, www.huron-wendat.qc.ca), a traditional Huron site, where a tour guide will take you through typical buildings and rituals of the Huron First Nations people. Visitors will get to meet the Clan Mother, enter a traditional long house, learn about meat preservation at the smokehouse and the drying tent, and also how to make canoes. Native games, traditional cooking, and dances are part of the visit.

One of the latest additions to Wendake is the **Hôtel-Musée Premières Nations** (5 Place de la Rencontre, 866/551-9222, www.hotelpremieresnations.ca, $180-400), a beautiful hotel connected to the museum. Its 55 rooms seamlessly blend minimal contemporary design with natural accents, including tree trunks and stone. While you're here, have dinner at **La Traite Restaurant,** which takes inspiration from traditional Huron cooking to create dishes like grilled bison and pan-seared seal.

To orient yourself when you get here, head to the **Wendake Tourism Center** (100 blvd. Bastien, Wendake, 418/847-1835, www.tourismewendake.ca, mid-June-mid. Oct. Mon.-Fri. 8:30am-4:30pm, Sat.-Sun. 9am-5pm; mid-Oct.-mid-June Mon.-Fri. 8:30am-4:30pm) for useful maps and other information.

★ BAIE-SAINT-PAUL

One of the biggest towns in Charlevoix, Baie-Saint-Paul is known for its unique artist community, galleries, off-beat boutiques, and as the birth place of Cirque du Soleil. The home of roughly 7,000 full-time inhabitants, the downtown core is quaint, full of shops and cafés, and is a lovely place to spend the afternoon strolling the streets no matter the season.

Sights

Musée d'Art Contemporain Baie-Saint-Paul (23 rue Ambroise-Fafard, 418/435-3681, www.macbsp.com, summer Tues.-Sun. 11am-5pm, winter Tues.-Sun. noon-5pm, $6 adult) honors the area's artistic heritage with a collection and temporary exhibits dedicated to contemporary works. Founded in 1992, the museum is located in what was once an old cinema and is a definite must on any itinerary.

Born in Switzerland in 1895, artist René Richard moved to Canada with his family as a child and was working as a fur trapper in northern Alberta by the time he was 18. By the 1940s he'd settled in Baie-Saint-Paul, where he painted some of his best-known landscapes and hosted a number of revered Canadian artists, including members of the Group of Seven. His century-old house, **Maison René-Richard** (104 rue St-Jean-Baptiste, 418/435-5571, daily 10am-6pm, free), has remained unchanged and is located on the main street. Visitors get the chance to see both his home and his work in the adjoining gallery.

On the outskirts of town you'll find **Le Moulin de la Rémy** (235 Terrasse de la Rémy, 418/435-6579, www.moulindelaremy.com, summer Tues.-Sun. 10am-4pm, $5). Built in 1827, this is one of the few flour mills still active in Québec; tours and tastings are available throughout the summer and visitors are invited to explore the surrounding paths and countryside. Pick up a fresh loaf at the bakery, traditionally made with wheat grown in Charlevoix and ground on-site.

Sustainability is the focus of **Habitat 07** (212 rue Ste-Anne, 418/435-5514, www.habitat07.org, May-Aug. daily 10am-6pm, Sept.-mid-Oct. Sat.-Sun. 10am-6pm, $5 adult, $2 student), an eco-friendly house built to showcase the latest developments in new energy and recycling. Opened in 2007, the construction methods used were inspired by ancient practices and used local, sustainable materials. The best part of the house, though, is the amazing view of the St-Lawrence River.

Restaurants

Baie-Saint-Paul has the best range of restaurants in the region. Fans of a good microbrew shouldn't miss **Le Saint-Pub** (2 rue Racine, 418/240-2332, www.saint-pub.com, late May-Oct. daily 11:30am-10pm, Nov.-late May daily 11:30am-8pm, $25). This pub and bistro keeps things local and serves seasonal mussels, fresh fish, Charlevoix sausage, and deer steaks. They also offer more regular pub-style dishes like nachos and fries.

Relaxed dining can be found at **Vice-Café** (1 rue Ste-Anne, 418/435-0006, daily 11:30am-onward, $20), situated directly in front of the church. Their specialties include grilled salmon and crêpes. Head there for dinner on Friday night and stay for the local musical entertainment.

A French-born and trained chef puts his skills to work on local ingredients at the **Mouton Noir** (43 rue Ste-Anne, 418/240-3030, www.moutonnoirresto.com, daily 11:30am-3pm and 5pm-10pm,

Le Train Le Massif du Charlevoix

Take a leisurely trip up the St-Lawrence on Le Train Le Massif du Charlevoix.

If you want to travel through Charlevoix region in luxury forgo the convertible and grab a seat on **Le Train Le Massif du Charlevoix.** Inaugurated in 2012, the train chugs along a long-dormant track of railroad that follows the shore of the great St-Lawrence River all the way from Québec City to La Malbaie. The 140-kilometer-long train trip is an awe-inspiring journey and it's all thanks to Daniel Gauthier, co-founder and former president of the Cirque du Soleil, and his project to entice tourists to explore the region and the town of Baie-Saint-Paul, in particular.

Gauthier first started his project with Le Massif, a ski station just minutes away from the town that's quickly become one of the best in the country. For his second act, he's created a gourmet train journey that disposes travelers in front of one of the most modern and welcoming hotels ever built in the province. Hotel Le Ferme is a vision of what accommodations in this region should be like and it's a response to

the stuffy guesthouses and humdrum highway motels that have long ruled the area. Called a hotel "terroir," Le Ferme is integrated with the environment. A flock of 50 sheep graze near the grounds, vegetable gardens greet you as you come off the train, and the hotel is heated by geothermal heating.

Despite the hotel's charms, however, it's the train that's the real star of the show. With its high, arched ceilings, picture windows, and interactive displays, it immerses you in the surroundings. Trains for Baie-Saint-Paul ($175 per person) and La Malbaie ($275 per person) depart from the base of Chutes Montmorency, about a 20-minute drive outside of Québec City, 11 months out of the year (May-Oct. and Dec.-Apr.). Once on board, guests are treated to a gourmet breakfast and tapas, or an elaborate four-course meal on the return journey.

It's definitely not the most affordable way to get to your destination, but it is perhaps the most memorable.

$35). The emphasis here is on modern French cuisine and the menu includes everything from organic pork tongue to quail and beet ravioli. Book ahead, and expect a crowd and lively atmosphere.

When Hotel La Ferme opened its doors in 2012, it brought a new level of culinary excellence to its surroundings. Their in-house restaurant, **Les Labours** (50 rue de la Ferme, 418/240-4123, www. lemassif.com, Sun.-Wed. 11:30am-2pm and 6pm-9pm, Thurs.-Sat.

11:30am-2pm and 5pm-10pm, $25), serves up tasty, modern cuisine—wild mushroom salad, roasted arctic char, pan-seared veal liver—in a chic yet cozy atmosphere. Get a seat at the bar and watch as the chefs do their magic. This is a great way to experience the hotel, even if you're not staying here.

Hiking

Parc National des Grands-Jardins

Once you're in the area you might as well take advantage of the nature that's available to you. West of Baie-Saint-Paul is the **Parc National des Grands-Jardins** (800/665-6527, www.sepaq.com/pq/grj), open year-round. This gorgeous national park has some of the most interesting vegetation, with a mix of both taiga and tundra. The landscape is vaguely arctic, with thick layers of lichen and black spruce forest. Home to a large caribou population, it has many activities available, including 34 kilometers of hiking trails in the summer, as well as kayaking and canoeing. In winter, visitors can use the 55 kilometers of cross-country ski trails and try their hand at ice fishing.

Skiing

★ Le Massif

One of the best hills in the province, **Le Massif** (877/536-2774, www.lemassif.com, mid-Dec.-mid-Apr. daily 8:30am-4pm, $64 adult day pass) is the area's largest ski mountain. Many high-ranking skiers come to train here, but even if you're more comfortable on the bunny runs, the views alone are worth the fees. It's on a cliff that looks out over the St-Lawrence, and there are times on these runs when you're sure the bottom is going to be on the shores. With 49 different trails of varying levels, it has something for everyone.

Hotels

Daniel Gauthier, one of the founding members of Cirque de Soleil, opened **Hôtel La Ferme** (50 rue de la Ferme, 418/240-4100, www.le-massif.com, $150-400) as a way of giving back to the community, and as such, the hotel is more than just a place to rest your head. Located on a tract of landed facing the St-Lawrence and between two rolling hills, it has a concert hall, two restaurants, a café, a spa, a gym, and a mini-farm, as the name suggests. It also happens to be the final destination on the whistle-stop train, La Massif, which brings visitors to the region by way of a riverside journey. The hotel itself is well-appointed, with a modern rustic design—exposed ceiling beams, heavy gray felt blankets, all-white decor—and is made up of a cluster of four buildings. With 145 rooms on offer (including a few dorm options), they can accommodate just about any budget.

The stone-clad, 30-room inn **Maison Otis** (23 rue St-Jean-Baptiste,

418/435-2255, www.maisonotis.com, $120-260) in Baie-Saint-Paul has its own sort of cozy charm with wood furniture, floral bedding, and stone walls. Slightly more modern but still with that floral country vibe, **Auberge La Muse** (39 rue St-Jean-Baptiste, 800/841-6839, www.lamuse.com, $120-400) is ideally located on a tree-lined street in the center of town, and the rooms are tastefully decorated.

Information and Services

Baie-Saint-Paul Tourist Office (6 rue St-Jean-Baptiste, 800/677-2276, winter daily 9am-4pm, summer daily 9am-7pm) is just off the highway on a hill overlooking the city below; it's a great view, but the turnoff is sharp. The website **www.tourisme-charlevoix.com** is also a great online resource.

Getting There and Around

By Bus

Intercar (320 Abraham Martin, 888/861-4592, www.intercar.qc.ca) coaches leave from Québec City's Gare du Palais bus terminal heading toward Baie Comeau three times a day Monday-Saturday and once on Sunday. The same bus runs all along the Charlevoix coast. A round-trip ticket to Baie-Saint-Paul costs $39 and the ride takes one hour and 15 minutes and drop off is at the Baie-Saint-Paul Library (9 rue Forget) in the middle of the town. When heading out of town, the bus departs from a gas station at 909 boulevard Monseigneur-de-Laval, which can be reached by either a local bus system or a taxi (418/435-5000). Check with the bus company at the time of departure to be sure.

By Car

Take Autoroute 440 out of Québec City and continue past Côte-de-Beaupré on Route 138 all the way to Baie-Saint-Paul. Depending on traffic and weather conditions, the drive should take approximately an hour and 20 minutes.

By Train

The exclusive **Train Le Massif de Charlevoix** (877/536-2774, www.le-massif.com, Mar.-mid-Oct., $110-275) offers stunning views, great food, and a totally unique way to get from Québec City to Baie-Saint-Paul. The train departs Québec City twice daily from the base of the Chute Montmorency, once early in the morning and once at noon. The train pulls into the station at La Ferme, about a five-minute walk from Baie-Saint-Paul's downtown core.

★ ISLE-AUX-COUDRES

Off the shores of Baie-Saint-Paul is Isle-aux-Coudres, one of the most picturesque islands in the St-Lawrence. Hop on the free ferry

top: skiing at Le Massif, Charlevoix; **bottom:** the majestic Fairmont Le Manoir Richelieu in La Malbaie, Charlevoix

from St-Joseph-de-la-Rive just south of Baie-Saint-Paul and take the 15-minute ride out to the island.

Sights

Once on the island, it's easy to be transported to an earlier time. **Les Moulins de Ilse aux Coudres** (36 chemin du Moulin, 418/760-1065, www.lesmoulinsdelisleauxcoudres.com, mid-May-mid-Oct. daily 10am-5:30pm, $9 adult, $5 child), a watermill and windmill that were built in 1825 and 1838, respectively, are a visceral link to the past. Still in operation today, you can tour these working mills and learn how the buckwheat and wheat were once ground all over the region. Guided tours are available, but you're also welcome to explore all buildings and surroundings on your own.

With a parish that dates back to 1741, **Église Saint-Louis de Isle-aux-Coudres** is one of the oldest religious sites on the island, built in 1885. It boasts hand-painted frescoes and impressive stone work.

No matter the season, stop in at **Cidrerie et Verger Pedneault** (3384 chemin des Coudriers, 418/438-2365, www.vergerspedneault.com). Opened in 1918, this family-run apple orchard also creates their own apple cider (alcoholic and non), jams, syrups, and honey. They offer tours of their premises year-round and apple-picking come the fall.

Restaurants

On Isle-aux-Coudres, many restaurants are located in hotels. **La Marinière** (1933 chemin des Coudriers, 418/438-2208, daily 5pm-10pm, $25) is located in the interestingly named Hôtel Motel Les Voitures d'Eau (Hotel Motel for Water Vehicles) but offers a menu pre pared exclusively with local products, including Charlevoix meats and seafood. The food is so fresh here that the menu changes daily.

If you like a little entertainment with your meal, **Le Cabaretier** (1064 chemin des Coudriers, 418/438-1070, daily 10am-5pm, $25) does double duty as both a bistro and wine bar as well as a typical *boîte à chansons,* the perfect end to a day cycling around the island. Another great option for the hungry traveler is a stop at **Casse-Croûte Le Mouillage** (922 chemin des Coudriers, 418/438-2208), where specialties include hot dogs, poutine, club sandwiches, BLTs, and anything else that's greasy yet delicious.

The menu at **Hôtel du Captitane** (3031 chemin des Coudriers, 418/438-2242, daily 5pm-9pm, $25) meanwhile focuses on healthier local recipes and also has an extensive menu of crepes.

Recreation

Named Isle-aux-Coudres after the hazelnuts that Jacques Cartier found here, the 11-kilometer-long and 3-kilometer-wide island is

Parc National de la Jacques-Cartier

Less than a half-hour drive from downtown Québec City is **Parc National de la Jacques-Cartier** (700 blvd. Lebourgneuf, Stoneham, 418/848-3169 summer, 418/528-8787 winter, www.sepaq.com/pq/jac). Situated in a valley with the same name, this park boasts both calm waters and rapids. Home of a 26-kilometer-long river, this is the perfect place to learn basic maneuvers. Those who haven't had the opportunity to learn how to canoe or kayak can do so here. They also have a number of mini-rafts, inflatable canoes, and inner tubes to rent for more relaxed water fun. Though the park is open year-round, equipment rental (canoe $14 per hour, kayak $13 per hour, dinghy $11 per hour) is only available mid-May–mid-October. There are also a number of bike trails for those who want to do some off-roading.

easily explored by bike. **Vélo-Coudres** (2926 chemin des Coudriers, 418/432-2118, www.charlevoix.qc.ca/velocoudres, May-June and Sept. daily 9am-5pm, July-Aug. daily 8am-sunset, $7/hour) has different models available, including tandem, kids' bikes, and even quadricycles with room for a family of four.

Hotels

Located on the northern tip of the island, **L'Hôtel Cap-aux-Pierres** (444 chemin la Baleine, 888/222-3308, www.dufour.ca, $84-250) has 46 rooms, tastefully decorated with wood floors, antique-style furniture, and a country feel. Each room has classic views of both the river and the garden. The hotel also has an outdoor pool.

Hôtel du Capitaine (3031 chemin des Coudriers, 418/438-2242, www.hotelducapitaine.com, $90-150) is also located on the northern tip, but closer to where the mainland ferry docks. The rooms have a country feel with their floral bedspreads and wooden furniture; the views of the river, however, are stunning and you can opt to have a gourmet dinner included in the price. The breakfasts are complimentary.

Boating fans might want to opt for the **Hôtel Motel Les Voitures d'Eau** (1933 chemin des Coudriers, 418/438-2208, $90-200), since a stay here means you can check out their boating museum. The accommodations have a rustic feel reminiscent of a cottage getaway, though the exterior looks like just about any highway-side motel. In addition to the mini museum, they also offer bike rentals and have a saltwater pool.

Information and Services

Isle Aux Coudres Tourist Office (1024 chemin des Coudriers, 800/667-2276, mid-May–mid-Oct. daily 8am-noon and 1pm-4pm) can be found on the main road, just a short walk from the quay. Though it's open daily during the peak-months, it closes during the off-season (typically after Canadian Thanksgiving). Read up on the island at **www.tourismeisleauxcoudres.com** before packing your bags.

Getting There and Around
By Boat
The only way to get to the island is by ferry. The ferry departs from Saint-Joseph-de-la-Rive and arrives at Saint-Bernard-sur-Mer on the west coast of the island. The trip takes about 15 minutes. It can take approximately 367 passengers and 55 vehicles. The boats are run by a government agency **Traversiers** (877/787-7483, www.traversiers.com) and as such the service is free. Boats leave the mainland and the island about once an hour during peak-season, but travelers should contact the company directly before making concrete plans. Once on the island, visitors are welcome to drive or ride a bike.

LA MALBAIE
If you want to continue exploring the region of Charlevoix, stay on the mainland and continue north from Baie-Saint-Paul on Route 362 until you arrive at La Malbaie, one of the oldest tourist spots in the region. Originally called Murray Bay, the area was first made popular by two Scottish officers who saw the potential in the area's beauty and made it the top resort choice from the 19th century right up until the 1950s.

Sights
Musée de Charlevoix
Learn all you need to know about the region at **Musée de Charlevoix** (10 chemin du Havre, 418/665-4411, www.museedecharlevoix. qc.ca, June-mid-Oct. daily 9am-5pm, mid-Oct.-May Mon.-Fri. 10am-5pm, Sat.-Sun. 1pm-5pm, $7 adult, $5 senior). This charming museum offers exhibitions about the region's culture and history, including photographs of beluga whale-hunting, artifacts from Manoir Richelieu, and folk art from the 1930s and '40s.

★ Casino de Charlevoix
In more recent times, one of the biggest draws to the region has been the **Casino de Charlevoix** (183 ave. Richelieu, 800/665-2274, www.casino-de-charlevoix.com, Mon.-Thurs. and Sun. 11am-midnight, Fri.-Sat. 11am-3am, free). Opened in 1994, it has cherrywood paneling, granite floors, and is a step up from most casinos. Visitors must be 18 years old or over to enter.

Restaurants
Run by two head chefs, **Vices Versa** (216 St-Etienne, 418/665-6869, www.vicesversa.com, Tues.-Sat. 6pm-10pm, $65 for a table d'hôte) is a unique take on fine dining. Customers are presented with two

menus (one created by each chef) and must decide between the two. Choices include sautéed scallops vs. scallop cerviche, or duck breast with potatoes and fennel or duck confit with quinoa cake and goat cheese cream. At the restaurant, it's all about pleasing the diner and the chefs' friendly rivalry. Situated on a busier street, it has a relaxed elegance that perfectly suits the flavors flowing from the kitchen.

Sometimes a little comfort food is the only way to go. **Pizzaria Du Poste** (448 rue St-Étiennem, 418/665-4884, www.pizzariaduposte. ca, June-Aug. daily 11am-midnight, Sept.-May Sun.-Tues. 11am-10pm, Wed.-Sat. 11am-midnight, $20) serves up Italian favorites like spaghetti, lasagna, and pizza in a convivial and sometimes raucous atmosphere. The pizza is thin-crusted and topped with the usual suspects and some that are more unexpected (shrimp and crab, anyone?). What's best about this place is the low-key atmosphere and the outdoor patio in the summer.

Hiking

★ Parc National des Hautes-Gorges-de-la-Rivière-Malbaie

Named after a series of valleys, **Parc National des Hautes-Gorges-de-la-Rivière-Malbaie** (800/665-6527, www.sepaq.com/pq/hgo, late May-Oct. daily 24 hours) has steep sloping mountains that fall to meet Rivière Malbaie. With its unique mix of fauna, Hautes-Gorges is one of the most beautiful spots in eastern Canada. Not far west from La Malbaie, it offers a huge amount of outdoor activities, like boat cruises, rock climbing, cycling, and 33 kilometers of hiking. Swimming, canoeing, and kayaking can also be done here.

Golf

Murray Bay Golf Club (1013 chemin du Golf, 877/665-2494, www.golfmurraybay.com, $44) is one of the oldest courses in the country and the third oldest in North America. It first opened its links in 1876. Built high above the cliffs that look out over the St-Lawrence, it's a spectacular place to tee-up and a must for any golfer visiting the area.

Hotels

In La Malbaie, one of the area's biggest draws is the romantic **Fairmont Le Manoir Richelieu** (181 rue Richelieu, 866/540-4464, www.fairmont.com, $140-350). Built in 1899, in a similar style as the Château Frontenac, it sits atop the Pointe-au-Pic overlooking the St-Lawrence River. Destroyed by fire and rebuilt in 1929, the hotel today is a luxury resort with an adjoining 18-hole golf course and an on-site spa, as well as five different restaurants. The rooms are elegant and tastefully decorated and aim for a comfortable instead of sleek luxury.

If you're looking for a more intimate luxury, head to **La Pisonniere**

(124 rue St-Raphaël, 800/387-4431, www.lapinsonniere.com, $240-450), a family-run inn with incredible views and the stamp of approval from the Relais Château. Modern yet cozy, the rooms feature fireplaces, sumptuous linens, classic wingback chairs for reading, and private balconies. If you want to leave your abode, you have the option of heading to the indoor pool, their private beach, the in-house spa, or the wine cellar for a tasting.

Auberge des Peupliers (381 rue St-Raphael, 418/665-4423, www. aubergedespeupliers.com, $140-250) keeps things luxurious but at a more affordable price point. There's a contemporary edge to this hotel that others in the region lack, making it ideal for urbanites or those looking for a modern hotel in rustic settings.

Information and Services

La Malbaie Tourist Office (495 blvd. de Comporté, Route 362, 800/667-2276, daily 8:30am-4:30pm) is right on the water looking out over the river and has a nice park in front in which to take a break.

Getting There and Around

By Bus

If traveling by public transport, hop on the **Intercar** (320 Abraham Martin, 888/861-4592, www.intercar.qc.ca) coach which leaves from Québec City's Gare du Palais bus terminal heading toward Baie Comeau three times a day Monday-Saturday and once on Sunday. The trip will take about two hours from Québec City and you'll be dropped off and picked up at Dépanneur J. E. Otis (46 rue Ste-Catherine) in the middle of the town. A round-trip ticket costs $60.

By Car

Follow Autoroute 440 out of Québec City and continue north on Route 138 all the way to La Malbaie. Depending on traffic and weather conditions, the drive should take approximately two hours.

★ TADOUSSAC

Tadoussac is the meeting point of the Saguenay and St-Lawrence Rivers. Before you can get to Tadoussac, however, you have to take a ferry across the convergence of these two mighty waterways. A free ferry will take you the short trip across the water to the historic town, one of the oldest places in Québec. It was France's first trading post and was established in 1600. Today the area's main draw is the rich marine life that thrives here, thanks to the warm St-Lawrence saltwater and the freshwater of the Saguenay.

Sights

Though the town itself is quite small, it's completely charming, the

Saguenay Fjord

Before you arrive in Tadoussac, a charming town three hours north of Québec City, you come to a dead stop. It's here that the cliffs widen to reveal the banks of the Saguenay River and the majestic fjord beyond. It's a rare natural wonder, the fjord is one of the most southerly in the world and was created by the weight of a glacier turning a crevice into a wide, calm river approximately 200 million years ago.

Once a hotbed of activity for the logging industry, the region's forests were critically depleted by the 1920s. In order to preserve the fjord, the government began buying up land, even-tually turning it into a national park in the 1980s. The Parc national du Fjord-du-Saguenay has since become one of the most popular in the province with close to a million visitors in 2010. Activities in the park include everything from skiing to hiking and camping, but it's the kayaking adventures offered by the park, which allow you to explore the fjord firsthand, that are the most exciting.

In addition to the awesome cliffs that rise out of the water, the fjord is also home to a number of species, including four species of whales: the blue whale, the fin whale, the minke, and the beluga.

perfect place to stroll around. Visit **Chauvin Trading Post** (157 rue Bord De L'Eau, 418/235-4433, June 1-June 21 daily 10am-6pm, June 22-Sept. 20 daily 9:30am-7pm, Sept. 21-Oct. 13 daily 10am-noon and 3pm-6pm, $4 adult, $3 senior, $2.50 student and child). This may just be a reconstruction, but it's still cool to visit a reasonable facsimile of the first trading post in Québec, and the exhibitions, though brief, are informative.

About five kilometers northeast of the town are sand dunes, an incongruous natural phenomenon in the region. **La Maison des Dunes** (chemin du Moulin-à-Baude, 418/235-4238, free) is a restored house that's been turned into an interpretation center that explains exactly how the sand dunes came about.

After the French arrived in 1600, the Jesuit monks quickly fol-lowed. **La Petite Chapelle de Tadoussac** (rue Bord de L'Eau, 418/235-4324, June-Oct. daily, free) was constructed in 1747, and is the oldest wooden church still in existence in North America. In addition to offering great views of the river, it's also home to a number of religious artifacts. It's a bit of untouched history in the region.

Restaurants

In Tadoussac most of the restaurants are only open May-October, something to keep in mind if you're traveling north in winter. If you're visiting in summer, there's a lot more choice but it isn't always varied. One of your best bets for a light breakfast, lunch, or dinner is **Café Bohême** (239 rue des Pionniers, 418/235-1180, daily 8am-10pm, $15). Serving different types of fair-trade coffee, they also have a selection of desserts (try the brownie) and other treats as well as a range of soups, sandwiches, and salads. On the second floor, they also have a small book exchange library and you can pick up some gourmet Charlevoix products.

For something more upscale, there is the **Restaurant le William** (165 rue Bord-de-l'Eau, 418/235-4421, www.hoteltadoussac. com, daily 5pm-10pm, $70 tasting menu) in the Hotel Tadoussac, which offers a four-course tasting menu and views over the Bay of Tadoussac and the St-Lawrence.

Recreation

Between mid-May and mid-October tourists come from all over the world to see the whales that flock to the region; approximately 10 different species can be found every year, including humpback, finback, blue whales, and white belugas. The best places to catch a glimpse of these majestic creatures are the **Parc Marin du Saguenay-Saint-Laurent** (182 rue de l'Église, 888/773-8888, www.parcmarin. qc.ca) and **Parc du Saguenay** (91 rue Notre-Dame, Rivière-Éternité, 800/665-6527, www.sepaq.com/pq/sag). Both of these national parks offer a number of different ways to see the whales, including boat excursions and sea kayaking. Interpretation centers are open along the trails and they both offer stunning views of the fjords and the rivers.

Independent companies offer up-close and personal whale tours, including **Croisières AML** (Baie du Tadoussac, 866/856-6668, www. croisieresaml.com, May-Sept., $70) and **Group Dufour** (329 Hwy. 138, Baie-Sainte-Catherine, 800/463-5250, www.dufour.ca, May-Sept., $70), both of which offer tours of varying lengths. Most of the tours take place on larger boats with food facilities and naturalists who'll walk you through the action; tours on Zodiacs (sleek, low boats) let you get even closer to the animals. Passengers are given life jackets and waterproof overalls but will likely get wet anyhow as you bump along the waves. Departure times vary depending on the day of the week, the month, and the type of tour you'd like to take. However, there is typically only one tour of a certain type per day, so book and plan ahead.

For the brave and experienced, kayak trips are also available through **Mer et Monde Ecotours** (866/637-6663, www.meretmonde. qc.ca, May-Sept., $50), whose three-hour-long tours start at the bay of Tadoussac, just past the lawn of the Hotel Tadoussac.

Hotels

Sitting on the Baie de Tadoussac, **Hôtel Tadoussac** (165 rue Bord-de-l'Eau, 800/561-0718, www.hoteltadoussac.com, $150-250) stands out on the horizon with its red copper roof and white clapboard siding. Opened in 1864, it's one of the oldest hotels in the region and maintains its historic feel (it has no air-conditioning in summer, but then again you don't really need it). The rooms have recently been modernized and have a nice, airy quality about them. Tadoussac chapel is also on the property. Built by Jesuit missionaries, it is the oldest wooden church in North America and still has some of its original artifacts.

Information and Services

Before you go, check out the website **www.tourisme-charlevoix.com** for all the necessary tips and information.

The **Tadoussac Tourist Office** (197 rue des Pionniers, 866/235-4744, www.tadoussac.com, May-late Oct. Mon.-Sat. 9am-5pm and Sun. 10am-4pm) is in the center of town and hard to miss. It has loads of information on the region as well as a few historical exhibits to give you more of an idea about the place, its culture, and history.

Getting There and Around

By Bus

Intercar (320 Abraham Martin, 888/861-4592, www.intercar.qc.ca) coaches leave from Québec City's Gare du Palais bus terminal heading north three times a day Monday-Saturday and once on Sunday. The same bus runs all along the Charlevoix coast. A round-trip ticket to Tadoussac costs $90 and the ride takes 3.5 hours, depending on traffic and weather. The bus pick-up and drop-off is located at Accommodation JB (443 Bateau-Passeir) in the center of the town.

By Car

From Québec City take Autoroute 440 and then Route 138 all along the coast to Tadoussac. The drive should take a little over 3 hours depending on the weather and traffic conditions.

BACKGROUND
AND
ESSENTIALS

Background

The Land

GEOGRAPHY

Québec is Canada's largest province and covers an area of 1,540,681 square kilometers, basically the size of France, Germany, Belgium, Spain, Portugal, and a couple Switzerlands put together, all in all an enormous territory. For the most part, it is filled with boundless forests and innumerable lakes (some say more than 400,000), vestiges of the huge Sea of Champlain that flooded the area 10,000 years ago.

Québec's geography can be divided into three main regions. The Canadian Shield goes from the extreme north down to the plain of St-Lawrence River and includes the Laurentian mountains, said to be the oldest mountain range in the world. The Appalachians, at the south of that plain, turn the landscape into a green and hilly area characteristic of the Eastern Townships region and extend down to the United States. A rift valley between these two antediluvian geological formations, the St-Lawrence is a 1,200-kilometer-long river that takes its source from the Great Lakes and ends up in the world's largest estuary. Most of Québec's residents live along the banks of the river, and it's also the center of Québec's development. Looking out over the landscape from the window of a plane, along with the sprawling cities of Montréal and Québec, you can see the rural landscape divided into narrow rectangular tracts of land extending from the river: These patterns denote the seigneurial land system and date back to the settlement of 17th-century Nouvelle France (New France).

Montréal

The second largest and second most populated city in Canada (after Toronto) and the largest in Québec, Montréal has a population of almost four million. Standing at the confluence of the St-Lawrence and Ottawa Rivers, it is set on an island of 500 square kilometers, 50 kilometers long and 15 kilometers wide at its widest. North of the island is the suburb of Laval, and beyond that the Laurentian mountains; south of it, across the St-Lawrence, you'll find the south shore cities of Longueil and Brossard. Smaller islands surround Montréal, such as Île des Sœurs or Île Bizard; most of the islands are now suburban communities. South of the Vieux-Port, what used to be several little islands were consolidated into Île Sainte-Hélène for the Expo 67. Next to it, Île Notre-Dame was built from scratch with the 15 million tons of rocks excavated from the construction of the Métro in 1965.

The most prominent geographical feature of the island, from

Best Frenemies: Québec vs. Montréal

Québec City and Montréal have a long, friendly rivalry. Québec was the site of the first European settlement in the province, and for centuries the two cities were competing trading posts. Even as Montréal's population grew, Québec continued to be the center of economic and political power. Then in the 19th century, the tides changed and Montréal supplanted Québec as the province's economic center. Its location at the crossroads between Europe and North America turned it into one of the most cosmopolitan cities on the continent, and business boomed.

In the 20th century, Montréal hosted Expo 67 and the 1976 Olympics, solidifying its prominence on the world stage. Then in the 1990s, Québec City's NHL franchise, the beloved Québec Nordiques, was moved to Denver and the city spiraled into emotional depression, a state it's still

recovering from. All seemed lost for the province's capital city, until preparations began for its 400th anniversary in 2008.

Suddenly Québec City was changing, old working-class neighborhoods were being revitalized, the waterfront got a needed face-lift, and, perhaps most important, the mayor vowed to bring the NHL back to the city—an election promise that will be hard to make good on.

For the time being, the cities are on relatively equal footing, but that hasn't changed the way they view each other. Québec City still sees Montréal as a city of two solitudes, where the citizens feel like strangers in their own town, while Montréalers chide those in Québec for being from a "village" and having an inferiority complex. As with all healthy rivalries, it's this push and pull between the two cities that propels them forward.

which it takes its name, is the triple-peaked hill Mount Royal. Though locals like to call it a "mountain," its highest point is only 232 meters high. Except for the plateau surrounding the diminutive peak, the rest of the city is flatter than flat. The opening of the Lachine Canal in 1824 and its enlargement over the 19th century permitted ships to bypass the unnavigable Lachine Rapids, making Montréal a major port and linking the St-Lawrence to the Great Lakes, all of which turned the city into a booming economic center.

As in most North American cities, one of the biggest problems facing Montréal is traffic. The city's two main bridges off the island, Pont Jacques-Cartier and Pont Champlain, are chronically congested, a problem that worsens each year. The City of Montréal does not include all the boroughs located on the island. In fact, five boroughs, including Hamstead, Montréal West, and Westmount, refused to merge with the rest of the city at the beginning of the 21st century and remain politically independent. This can sometimes get in the way when dealing with topics like city infrastructure.

Québec City

Located 240 kilometers northeast of Montréal, Québec City, with a population of half a million, thrives on the north bank of the

St-Lawrence near its meeting point with the St-Charles River and not far from the foothills of the Laurentian mountains. Built on top and around the 98-meter-high Cap-Diamant, it overlooks the dramatic narrowing of the river that takes place in the St-Lawrence after Île d'Orléans. It's from this narrowing that the city gets its name, taken from the Algonquin word *kebec*, which means "where the river narrows."

It's this particular position that made it, in the mind of the colonizers, a logical commercial port as well as a strategic military point. The ramparts surrounding Vieux-Québec's Upper Town, the only fortified city left in North America, have made it an architectural jewel and helped the city earn the name the "Gibraltar of North America." Near the southern edge of Cap-Diamant, the Plains of Abraham (Québec's version of Central Park) extend along the cliffs. It was on these rolling hills that North America's fate was sealed in the haze of a battle between the British and the French in 1759.

One of the main physical features of the city is its two-level construction. Cap-Diamant and its cliffs break the urban landscape in two, prompting significant opposition between Haute-ville (Upper Town) and Basse-ville (Lower Town). This opposition is as significant sociologically as it is topographically. Thus, Upper Town (with the exception of Faubourg Saint-Jean-Baptiste) is historically the home of the ruling bourgeoisie, while Lower Town (Limoilou, Saint-Roch, Saint-Sauveur), which developed along the shores of the St-Lawrence and St-Charles Rivers, was the home of seamen, dock workers, and factory workers. This antagonism is in flux nowadays as exemplified by Nouvo Saint-Roch's gentrification. Motivated by the 400th anniversary's celebrations, much urban redevelopment has been done, particularly along the banks of the rivers, making Québec City one of the most likable cities in the world.

CLIMATE

"Mon pays ce n'est pas un pays, c'est l'hiver" (My country is not a country, it's winter) sang Québec's premier *chansonnier*, Gilles Vigneault. Truer words have never been spoken, especially regarding the six months during which winter takes over, changing the landscape and affecting the mood of its resigned inhabitants. Yes, wintertime temperatures have an average of -10°C in Montréal and can drop down to -30°C. In Québec City, it is usually 2-3 degrees colder. However, the winters aren't as harsh, cold, and snowy as they used to be, thanks to global warming. But the freezing wind, blowing *poudreuse* (drifting snow) everywhere like a tempest in the desert, is probably the toughest thing about being here in the winter. When the temperatures dip to bone-chilling proportions,

make sure to cover up everything from your nose to your toes or you could end up with frostbite.

Approximately three meters of snow fall every winter, but sometimes there's more. In December 2012, 45 centimeters of snow that fell on the city in less than 24 hours, causing major travel disruptions. Snowstorms are frequent and can last up to a day if not more. Snow removal can be interesting to watch if you're a tourist and have never seen it before. Every snowstorm costs the city of Montréal approximately $10 million in snow-removal operations. The sidewalk and road snowplows can also be deadly—they caused five deaths in the winter of 2010—so be careful, especially when walking at night.

Despite being harsh and long, winters in Québec are also sunny, with a bright luminosity that can sometimes be blinding. Because of the length of the season, stoical locals have adopted a "if you can't beat 'em join 'em" attitude in order to survive, and you'll be surprised to see just how active Quebeckers can be in winter, putting on their skates and snowshoes after every snowstorm, sometimes going to work on cross-country skis and pulling their kids in toboggans along the sidewalks. There is no need to say that winter has had a major cultural impact on this society; its influence is apparent in everything from the architecture to the invention of the Underground City.

Of course, Québec isn't just about winter, and people are often surprised to see just how hot and humid the summers are, with temperatures often reaching 35°C. After having complained about the cold all winter, locals curse the heat and turn their air-conditioning on full blast.

Autumn and spring are shorter in Québec, but in many ways they are the most impressive seasons. In spring, the snow melts away, revealing new blossoms, while autumn has a particular beauty as the trees change to a rainbow of colors before shedding their leaves.

Flora and Fauna

The best place to explore Québec's rich and diverse fauna and flora is in the national parks. National parks offer interpretive materials and guides to help you understand just exactly what it is you're surrounded by.

Since Montréal and Québec are cities, there's not much chance to run into a moose or a black bear while getting a pint of milk at the *dép* (corner store). But, these two cities both have parks with protected fauna and flora (Parc du Mont-Royal in Montréal and Parc des Plaines d'Abraham in Québec), where you might see animals that can be exotic for some: red and gray squirrels, chipmunks, and raccoons. If you're wandering through Mont-Royal, you might also glimpse a fox.

Both cities are remarkably green for their size, with trees lining just about every side street. Originally part of the Laurentian forest ecosystem, the vegetation has changed over time due to urbanization. A good example of this is Mont-Royal, originally made up exclusively of red oaks and sugar maples. The introduction in the 1960s and '70s of the Norway maple, which is more resistant to city pollution, has considerably changed the face of the beloved mountain. And today, they've overtaken much of the sugar maple; this is most visible in the fall when, instead of turning bright red the way sugar maples do, the Norway maples turn yellow.

History

EARLY INHABITANTS

Long before its European takeover, the North American continent was home to the indigenous people for thousands of years. Historians date the population back to 12,000 years ago, when hunting tribes crossed the Bering Strait in pursuit of game from Siberia. Those tribes then scattered all over the land, developing diverse ways of life as they adapted to different environments. At the time explorers arrived, the area that would eventually become known as the St-Lawrence valley was populated by the nomadic Algonquin and sedentary Iroquoian tribes who lived off game, fish, and crops, and were particularly well adapted to their environment.

EUROPEAN ARRIVAL

When it comes to the "discovery" of Canada, it's French explorer Jacques Cartier's name that usually pops up. But what's less known is that by the time he finally made it to Québec in 1534, Newfoundland's coastline was being periodically cruised by explorers and fishermen from different nations and that Vikings had sailed its coast and even put down a few roots 500 years before.

What Jacques Cartier did first, though, before other Europeans, was explore the interior of the river, a river that he named in honor of the saint on the calendar the day he reached it: St-Lawrence. Sent by the king of France, Francis I, with the mandate of finding gold and—the typical request of the day—a passage to Asia, the sailor explored the region thoroughly, visiting Iroquoian villages Stadacona (Québec) and, farther upstream, Hochelaga, which he rechristened Mont-Royal, in honor of the king. After many voyages, he found neither gold nor Asia, bringing home instead a bunch of made-up stories told by fabulist natives and a handful of rocks he thought were diamonds (a popular French saying of the time was "*faux comme un diamant du Canada*" (fake as a Canadian diamond). Deemed inhospitable and dull, the land of Canada would remain unvisited and almost forgotten by the French for half a century.

NOUVELLE FRANCE (NEW FRANCE)

Two things rekindled the French interest in this part of the world: the fur trade and an appetite for colonial expansion. In addition to these two motives, the Catholic Church saw an opportunity to spread the gospel to the Amerindian population and sent missionaries along on the expedition. Seeing promise in the new European fashion of fur hats and coats, trading companies quickly formed, including the Compagnie des Cent-Associés, which set up outposts around Québec where the Amerindians and French could trade.

In 1608, Samuel de Champlain set up the first permanent European trading post in an abandoned Iroquoian village that Jacques Cartier had visited 80 years before, building a wooden fort he called l'Abitation de Québec (*kebec* in Algonquin means "where the river narrows"). That first winter, most of the settlers died of scurvy and harsh weather, but the colony continued even though it faced numerous difficulties and was slow to grow. In 1635 (the year Samuel de Champlain, the Father of New France, died), the population was slightly more than 300 settlers, a fair number of them Catholic missionaries. Some of these missionaries organized the Société Notre-Dame de Montréal and, in 1642, decided to establish an evangelizing mission near the deserted village of Hochelaga. Called Ville-Marie, it would eventually become Montréal.

While colonists cleared forests and cultivated the land, the thriving fur trade attracted a different kind of young explorer, one daring enough to go farther and farther in to the continent seeking bearskins, mink furs, and, above all, the popular and coveted beaver pelts. Called *coureurs des bois* (wood runners, or woodsmen), these adventurers are legendary figures in Québec, since they represent a life of freedom and a particular connection with nature that characterized the colonization of the continent. These *coureurs* also paved the way for the explorers and voyageurs to whom we owe the exploration of the regions of the Great Lakes and the Mississippi Valley, much of which they claimed for the French. These explorers left their mark on places all over the United States, including Detroit, St. Louis, and Baton Rouge.

The commercial relations brought on by the trade helped the French secure alliances with the Hurons, who in exchange for the pelts received copper and iron utensils, alcohol, and rifles. This alliance put the French colony in the middle of a bloody war when the English-backed Iroquois Five Nations launched an offensive

Coming North: United Empire Loyalists

When things started looking really bad for the British during the American Revolution, a number of colonists who wanted to remain loyal to the British crown were offered free land and passage to other—non-rebelling—parts of the British colonies.

Called United Empire Loyalists because of their unyielding devotion to King George III, many chose to escape north, settling in the regions of southern Ontario and Québec. So many immigrated to the province, close to 50,000, that it sent the Québécois into a breeding frenzy and kicked off the *revanche des berceaux*, the "revenge of the cradle."

By 1791 so many loyalists had arrived in the country that the government signed the Constitutional Act, dividing the province in two: Upper Canada, which would eventually become Ontario, and Lower Canada, the province of Québec.

Though many Loyalists and descendants of Loyalists eventually moved out of the province, their influence can still be seen in the Eastern Townships, where covered bridges, clapboard houses, and Victorian gingerbread moldings are the norm.

campaign to wipe out the Hurons, their long-time enemies. The war lasted 25 years and seriously affected the young colony.

TOWARD DEFEAT

The conflicting commercial and political interests of the French and the English caused a succession of inter-colonial wars. In 1713, following a military defeat in Europe, the Treaty of Utrecht resulted in France relinquishing control of Newfoundland, Acadia, and the Hudson Bay, something that considerably hurt the fur trade and jeopardized the colony. This date marks the beginning of the end for New France, even if it took another 50 years for the British to secure power, a takeover that seemed inevitable considering the difference in population. Indeed, on the eve of the final battle, there were 60,000 French living in a huge territory, surrounded by two million British colonists living in the narrow strip of the 13 colonies.

The final showdown happened on September 13, 1759, on an open field by Cap-Diamant. After a two-month-long siege, the French Army, led by General Montcalm, was attacked by surprise early in the morning. General Wolfe and the British Army used a dried-up old creek to climb the cliff, something everyone thought was impossible. The Battle of the Plains of Abraham, which sealed the fate of French North America, was bloody, lasted barely 20 minutes, and cost the lives of both generals. One year after, Montréal capitulated and thus France lost all of its colonies in North America, leaving behind a small population of deeply rooted French Catholics in an ocean of British Protestants.

Though at first they tried to assimilate the French minority by imposing British Common Law and having them swear an oath to the British King, the victors decided that it was wiser to accommodate the French, wanting to secure their allegiance as social unrest and rebellion smoldered in the south. In order to cement the support of the French-Canadians, England wrote up the Act of Québec in 1774, recognizing both the French language and French civil law, and granting them freedom of religion. These concessions succeeded in preventing the French-Canadians from joining the rebels in the south who started the American Revolution a year later.

At the end of that war, in 1783, 50,000 United Empire Loyalists (British Loyalists) had fled the United States for the province of Québec, many of them settling into the Eastern Townships region. To accommodate these Loyalists, who were an English minority in a French-speaking majority, a new Constitutional Act was signed in 1791, dividing the province in two: Upper Canada (which would eventually become Ontario) and Lower Canada (the province of Québec). The names Upper and Lower Canada were given according to their location on the St. Lawrence River.

The 19th century was marked by the power struggles between the Francophones and the Anglophones in Lower Canada. The elected French-Canadian representatives were constantly at odds with the colonial British executive and legislative powers. Over the years, the nationalist and reformist Parti Canadien denounced the untenable situation, ending up in an armed insurrection. The Patriots War (Guerre des Patriotes) of 1837-1838 was immediately crushed and an emissary was sent from London to study the problems of this wayward colony. The solution proposed by Lord Durham was radical: make every effort to assimilate French-Canadians. This was the impetus behind the Union Act, laid down by the British government in 1840. Along with unifying Upper and Lower Canada and giving them an equal political power—despite the fact that Lower Canada was much more populated—it also made English the only official language, despite the fact that the vast majority were Francophone-speakers. These new laws and the constant arrival of English-speaking immigrants prompted a major exodus of Francophones, many of whom immigrated to the United States.

CONFEDERATION

The troubled politics of the subsequent years coupled with a dire economic situation prompted leaders of Upper and Lower Canada to unify. The British North America Act, signed in 1867, is the constitutional act that solidified Canada as an independent nation that would eventually stretch from the Atlantic to the Pacific.

It also created the two-level structure of government, in which power is split between the federal and provincial levels. Even though Québec's minority status was deepened by it, the new structure granted the province jurisdiction over certain aspects, like education, civil law, and culture. Québec maintained a central importance in the evolution of the country, and, before long, a French-Canadian, Wilfrid Laurier, became prime minister of Canada. Elected in 1896, he was the first of many Québécois, including Pierre Elliot Trudeau and Jean Chrétien, who would lead the country.

Faced with a prodigious period of economic growth at the beginning of the 20th century, Prime Minister Laurier declared it "Canada's century." The prediction fell short, though, when the Great Depression disrupted economic and social progress in Québec for many years. World War II finally put an end to the economic doldrums, and, in fact, Québec came out of the war economically stronger than ever before and ready for social change, as the anarchist manifest *Refus Global* (Total Refusal), signed by artists and writers, made clear.

Despite this exciting new energy and mind-set, the province would remain under the spell of Maurice Duplessis and his conservative party (Union Nationale) for another 15 years. In spite of its considerable economic growth, this period is often referred to as "La Grande Noirceur" (The Great Darkness), the last obstacle before real transformation.

A QUIET REVOLUTION AND CONTEMPORARY TIMES

After the death of Maurice Duplessis in 1959, Québec was ripe for change, and the Liberal Party government of Jean Lesage was elected the year after, kicking off what would be dubbed the Révolution Tranquille (Quiet Revolution), a wide range of bold economic and social reforms. The most important result of these reforms is the secularization of society, putting an end to the centuries-long overarching power of the church in every aspect of Québécois society. Education, health care, and social services were no longer under the control of the church as the state began to take over.

The most ambitious economic project of the time, the nationalization of the province's electric companies under Hydro Quebec is a powerful symbol of that new ambition. The Quiet Revolution also witnessed the rise of nationalism. Jean Lesage's Liberal government election slogan, *maîtres chez nous* (masters in our own home), meant to put a stop to the unbridled selling of the province's natural resources to foreign business interests.

Montréal hosted two major international events that still define its identity: the 1967 World's Fair (Exposition Universelle—Terre des Hommes) and the Summer Olympic Games in 1976. The sentiment of empowerment at the time exacerbated enthusiasm for the idea of a stronger autonomy within the Canadian federation, and more and more people became attracted by the idea of building a new country instead, some groups even falling into extremism. Thus, the Front de Liberation du Québec (FLQ), founded in 1963, used terrorist tactics against the Québec and national governments and businesses with the aim of establishing a socialist independent country.

In 1970, during the October crisis, when the FLQ kidnapped Québec Labour Minister Pierre Laporte and eventually killed him, Pierre Elliot Trudeau, then Canadian prime minister, launched the War Measures Act against Québec dissidents, putting the country under martial law to much public controversy. After that, the FLQ declined drastically and eventually disappeared.

Despite these radical actions and a certain support the FLQ gained with the public, the majority of pro-sovereigntists preferred moderate nationalism. In 1967, René Lévesque, a rising star of the Liberal government, quit the party and founded the Parti Québécois (PQ). Soon after, in 1976, a stunning and unexpected victory brought the PQ to power, putting the question of sovereignty at the forefront of political and social life of Québec society for decades. Bill 101 in 1977 made French the only official language of Québec. In 1980 Lévesque's government launched a referendum on the issue of independence, losing when the "no" side won with 60 percent of the vote. In time, the tensions with the federal government became aggravated, mostly over constitutional matters and Québec's refusal to ratify the repatriated Canadian constitution in 1982.

In 1995, a second referendum campaign was launched. This time the results were extremely close, and Canada held its breath: 49.4 percent of Québecers voted "yes" and 50.6 percent voted "no," underlining the deep division of the population over the issue.

However, the national question has faded in importance over the last 20 years, with public attention drifting toward other public matters like the environment and economy. In 2003, the PQ was ousted from power after 10 years, and the Québec Liberal Party, resolutely federalist, was elected. Led by Premier Jean Charest, they were voted in for a third term in 2009.

Thanks to political unrest related to the rising costs of tuition, the PQ regained political power with a minority government in the autumn 2012 election. Lead by Pauline Marois, the party is focused less on the question of sovereignty than during their previous term in power.

Government and Economy

POLITICS

Canada's political system is modeled after the British parliamentary system it historically inherited. Central in the government organization is the House of Commons, sitting in Ottawa, a democratically elected body consisting of 308 members known as Members of Parliament (MPs). Each MP in the House of Commons is elected by simple plurality in an electoral district, also known as a riding. Elections are called within four years of the previous election or when the government loses a confidence vote.

The leader of the party that won the most seats becomes the new prime minister and forms the new government. Canada being a federation, this political structure is reproduced for every province. Therefore, each of them has its own parliament. In Québec, it is called the Assemblée Nationale, and its 125 elected members sit in Québec City. The Canadian Constitution divides the power between federal and provincial governments. For example, defense, postal services, and international relations are under federal jurisdiction, while education, health, and natural resources are under provincial jurisdiction. Since the Constitution is not always clear about these divided powers, constitutional conflicts arise, a situation that has been particularly true between Québec and the federal government.

Canada is also a constitutional monarchy. People are often surprised to know that there is a queen in Canada: Queen Elizabeth II of England is the Canadian head of state. Actually, it is mostly a formal and symbolic title, although she does have a representative in Canada acting on her behalf: the governor general. She is represented by the lieutenant-governor in the provinces.

This type of governmental structure favors a two-party system, but in Canada's case, four parties make up the federal government: the right-leaning Conservative Party, centrist Liberal Party, left-leaning NDP (New Democratic Party), and the Bloc Québécois, the Québec sovereigntist party. In major political battles, the Conservatives and Liberals are always the front-runners, but the NDP and Bloc parties are instrumental to how government is run and what bills are passed in the House of Commons.

Since 2010, Prime Minister Stephen Harper of the Conservative party has been the head of the federal government, but the government only rules with a minority. The Conservatives have ruled with a minority government since their re-election in 2011. The province of Québec is largely responsible for the current political landscape, due to its overwhelming support for the left-leaning National

Democratic Party (NDP) during the 2011 election. The province's support for the NDP and its leader, Jack Layton, single-handedly shattered the Conservative's dream of a majority. Québec's political death knell was christened "Orange Crush."

On the provincial stage, two parties have been exchanging power for half a century: the centrist, federalist Québec Liberal Party, and the sovereigntist Parti Québécois founded by René Lévesque. In the 1980s and '90s, the Parti Québécois (PQ) became the center of international attention when it organized two referendums on Québec sovereignty, the outcome of which threatened to break up Canadian unity. The consecutive defeats of the PQ in these referendums and in recent elections has laid the sovereigntist question aside for the time being.

ECONOMY

Since the beginning, Québec's natural resources have been the major asset in the province's economy. Vast forests, mining resources, rich agricultural land, and a huge potential for hydroelectricity—because of all the lakes—make this province a gift from the gods. Historically everything began with the fur trade, kicking off the European colonization of the territory and sustaining it for over a century. In the 19th and most of the 20th centuries, wood, pulp, and paper industries took the lead and are still, along with the mining sector and hydroelectricity production, the most important sectors of Québec's economy.

The government plays an important role in the economy and is the largest employer in the province. Despite the trend toward more privatization, this strong state involvement reaches a certain consensus in the population and is considered essential due to the small size of its economy. Government-owned Hydro Québec, the world's leader in hydroelectricity, remains a national pride, and dams and development projects in the north are thoroughly followed by the population. Another economic national jewel is aerospace and railway maker Bombardier, a world-class company started 70 years ago by Joseph Bombardier, the inventor of the snowmobile.

Montréal

Once the undisputed economic center of Canada, Montréal lost its predominance to Toronto 40 years ago and now plays second fiddle to "the city that works." Even if most of Montréal's defenders would say this relative decline was caused by the massive fleeing of Anglophone businesses after the PQ reached power in 1976, you have to admit that the demographic and economic trends were already on track at the time. The last episode in this rivalry between the two cities was the acquisition of the Bourse de Montréal (Montréal Stock Exchange) by the Toronto Stock Exchange in 20

Despite this relative decline, however, Montréal thrives with high-class industries like aerospace (Bombardier, Pratt & Whitney, etc.) and information technology companies. In 1997, Ubisoft, a major French video game publisher, opened (with government funds) a subsidiary in Montréal, establishing itself in the new hip area Mile End. This studio, responsible for developing games like *Prince of Persia* and *Assassin's Creed*, is now one of the world's largest, with over 1,700 employees, making the city a central hub for that industry.

Québec City

Economically outpaced by its provincial counterpart in the middle of the 19th century, Québec City has nevertheless discreetly developed into a very successful city, with one of the lowest unemployment rates in Canada at 4.5 percent. Most jobs in Québec City are found in public administration, services, and tourism, with a large proportion of civil servants, because it is the seat of the entire provincial political apparatus.

The past few years have seen a particularly sound growth rate and many urban development projects, probably prompted by the enthusiasm occasioned by the city's 400th anniversary. The result of this growth meant that Québec City virtually averted the economic crisis of 2008 and has continued to grow since then.

People and Culture

FIRST NATIONS

Québec's first inhabitants were the Amerindians. Eleven different First Nations tribes, including the Inuit, called the province home before the early days of colonization. Today, they represent a small part of the population, and three-quarters of them live on reserves throughout the province: The Mohawk reserves Kahnawake and Kanesatake in the Montréal region and the Wendat-Huron reserve Wendake north of Québec City are some of the bigger ones in the province. Though some Amerindians live in areas where they can hunt and fish, many of them have lost their traditional way of life and endure social hardships.

One of the most important political events of the past 20 years was the Oka Crisis: For two months in the summer of 1990 Mohawks barricaded one of the main bridges into Montréal, protesting land claims and issues of self-government. The incident forced native issues to the forefront, and in recent years many agreements have granted Amerindians more autonomy.

FRANCOPHONES

The vast majority of the Québécois people are descendants of the settlers who arrived between 1608 and 1759. From the 60,000 French-Canadians in 1759 there are now seven million living in Canada. Part of the reason Québec has such a strong cultural and social heritage is because of the population's demographics. In the late 18th century with the arrival of the United Empire Loyalists, the French-Canadians became nervous at the idea of being over-populated by the English-speaking contingent. One response to this immigration was something that would later be called the *revanche des berceaux* (revenge of the cradle), which saw the families of French-Canadians growing larger by the year. Of course, the province's Catholic background helped, and throughout the years Québécois families were typically large and women had an average of 8 children (Celine Dion is from a family of 14 kids). In the 1970s, however, the birthrate dropped considerably, and it remains one of the lowest in the world.

Though today the province is experiencing a baby boom, it is a mere blip compared to the numbers in the mid-20th century. Much of the growth to the province's Francophone population now comes from immigration.

ANGLOPHONES

The first Anglophone immigrants arrived after the British conquest in 1759. Most of them were well-to-do Protestant merchants, for-ever forging the stereotype of the rich Anglophone. However, this wasn't always the case; one of the most important groups of im-migrants was the working-class Irish, who arrived in the province as early as the founding of New France. The biggest wave of Irish immigrants came 1815-1860, driven from Ireland by the potato famine. They came to the province by the boatload, disembarking at Grosse-Île, an island off the shores of Québec City that was set up as a reception center. During the summer of 1847, thousands died during a typhus epidemic, and the orphaned children were adopted by Québec families. It is estimated that a staggering 45 percent of Quebeckers have Irish ancestry, even if most of them don't know it. In Québec City many immigrant families were relegated to the slum-like dwellings in Petite Champlain, while in Montréal they congregated in places like Griffintown and Point-St-Charles closer to the banks of the river.

The arrival of the United Empire Loyalists between 1783 and the beginning of the 19th century shaped not only the Eastern Townships, where most of them settled, but also the future of the country. They fled the United States in such great numbers as to fa-cilitate the division of the province into Upper and Lower Canada. The 19th century also saw the largest number of immigrants fr the British Isles, many of whom would put down roots in Montréal and, in the case of the Scots, found McGill University.

In the 1970s, after the rise to power of the PQ and the October Crisis in particular, many English-speakers left Québec, many settling in Ontario. Nowadays, they make up only 10 percent of the total population of the province and live mostly in Montréal. The west end of the city has the most prominent English boroughs: Westmount, Notre-Dame-de-Grace (NDG), and Montréal-West. Of the English-speakers who did stay, some 60 percent of them are now bilingual.

QUEBECKERS OF OTHER ETHNIC ORIGINS

Immigration from countries other than Britain and France only started in the 20th century. This growing ethnic diversity is particularly obvious in Montréal, whose history has been defined by successive waves of immigrants. After World War II, the majority of immigrants arrived from Italy, Greece, and Portugal, communities that continue to have a stronghold in neighborhoods like the Mile End and Little Italy. For the most part, these immigrants aligned themselves with the Anglophone community, raising Québec's perennial concerns over French language subsistence. In 1977, the Parti Québécois passed Bill 101 as a solution to that perceived threat, forcing new arrivals into French schools. Immigration demographics began to change in the latter part of the century, and the 1970s and '80s saw exiles from Vietnam and Haiti join the ranks, followed more recently by North African, Chinese, and Central European immigrants.

Québec also has a large Jewish community, whose roots can be traced all the way back to the British conquest, while a large Hassidic community can be found in Outremont.

LGBT COMMUNITY

The first recorded gay establishment in North America, Moise Tellier's apples and cake shop, opened in Montréal in 1869. You can't get a better picture of the city's attitude toward the gay, lesbian, bi, and trans community than that. Like all LGBT communities, Montréal's has faced discrimination and hardships, one of the most crucial being a raid in October 1977, during which 144 men were arrested. Those arrests, however, led to a 2,000-person-strong protest the following day. It's this show of political support and acceptance that Montréal has become known for.

Though the Village is instrumental to gay life, there are queer establishments and events all over the city. There is also massive support both within the city and community for younger members

Jewish Québec

King Louis XIV of France might have banned Jews from entering the colony of Nouvelle France, but Québec's Jewish roots can still be traced for centuries.

The first Jewish people to settle in Québec were members of the British Army who arrived after the initial conquest. Several are thought to have been a part of General Jeffery Amherst's battalion, four of which were officers. Of those officers at least one, Aaron Hart, remained in Canada, settling in Trois-Rivières and eventually becoming a wealthy landowner. One of his sons, Ezekiel Hart, later became the first Jew to be elected to public office in the British Empire.

Though the Jewish community in Montréal numbered little more than 200, the Spanish and Portuguese Synagogue of Montréal opened its doors in 1768 and became the first non-Catholic house of worship in the province. In Québec City the first known Jewish inhabitant was Abraham Jacob Franks, who settled in the city in 1767, but it wasn't until 1892 that the Jewish population in Québec City had enough members to warrant a proper synagogue. In the interim, however, they had founded a number of institutions, including the Québec Hebrew Sick Benefit Association, the Québec Hebrew Relief Association for Immigrants, and the Québec Zionist Society. By 1905, Québec City's Jewish population numbered 350.

As anti-Semitism mounted in Europe, over 155,000 Jews resettled in Canada, many of them in Montréal, where they became storekeepers, tradespeople, and workers in the city's numerous garment factories. The history of one of the city's greatest streets, boulevard St-Laurent, can be traced back to the immigrant families who worked and lived along the Main or in the factories nearby. Jewish businesses left an indelible mark on the city, and many of Montéal's most recognizable symbols—the smoked-meat sandwich, the bagel—come from that strong Jewish lineage.

At the end of World War II approximately 40,000 Holocaust survivors came to Canada, and in 1947, the Workmen's Circle and Jewish Labour Committee started the Tailors Project, aimed at bringing Jewish refugees to Montréal in the needle trades. Jewish immigration continued to expand in Québec, especially in the 1950s when North African Jews fled the continent, settling in Québec City and Montréal where their French language would be an asset.

The community today is concentrated in Montréal, in areas such as Hamstead, Côte-St-Luc, and Outremont, with a large Hassidic community in the Mile End. Though Québec City still has a Jewish community, the majority of the province's Jewish population lives in Montréal, and in fact, many of the city's most recognizable citizens come from this community, including literary giants Irving Layton and Mordecai Richler, poet and musician Leonard Cohen, psychologist and linguist Steven Pinker, and even American Apparel founder Dov Charney.

of the LGBT community. The community is smaller and subtler in Québec City, but it's no less supported.

Divers/Cité and Celebrations de la Fierte Montréal (Montréal's Pride Celebrations) are the city's two pride festivals, which take place in the summer a few weeks apart. Montréal also hosts a number of dance parties throughout the year aimed at the gay community, including Black and Blue, a weekend-long party that's been going strong for over 20 years.

Québec City hosts its own annual pride celebration; decorations go up all over rue St-Jean, and Place d'Youville turns into a street party.

RELIGION

There is no denying the influence of the Catholic Church on the history of Québec, and almost every street corner features a three-story high cathedral, though today many of them have been converted into condos. Instrumental in the founding of the nation and throughout most of its history, the Catholic Church only really began to lose its prominence in the 1960s and '70s. For the most part, Francophones remain Catholic (though most are non-practicing) and Anglophones are Protestant, but there are also diverse religions encompassing Muslims, Jews, Hindus, and Sikhs.

LANGUAGE

The language issue is arguably the most important for Québécois Francophones since it's really what makes them both distinct and recognizable. They can be very touchy about how other people view their language, be it toward other Francophones who consider *joual* a mere dialect, or toward people who obstinately refuse to make any efforts to speak French. Don't be afraid, though; they're usually not hard to please, and using a mere *bonjour* (hello) or *merci* (thank you) is the safest way to gain their respect. They will often switch to English (even broken English) if they see you struggling.

In order to understand this somewhat intransigent stand on Québécois you have to understand the history. After the British conquest in 1759, even though language, religion, and other rights were granted to the French community, they were barred from political and economical power for a long time. This linguistic exclusionism, in which access to the upper levels of business and power was barred to the French-Canadians, lasted well into the 20th century. In fact, until the 1970s English-speakers were the minority that ran many of the businesses and held positions of power in the province.

The Quiet Revolution in the 1960s, however, helped to change all that as it fostered nationalist sentiment, which reached a peak when the Parti Québécois was elected in 1976. In 1977, Bill 101 was passed, asserting the primacy of French on public signs across the province, and apostrophes were removed from store fronts in the 1980s to comply with French usage. English is allowed on signage as long as it's half the size of the French lettering. Despite the debate that surrounded the bill when it was first implemented, many believe it has helped to preserve the language.

Anyone with a good ear will likely be able to tell that there's a big difference between the French spoken here and the French in France. The French here is said to be equivalent to the French spoken in the 17th and 18th centuries in France, preserved due to its geographical isolation. The language spoken in everyday life is very specific and somewhat entertaining, since it's full of funny expressions and syntax. Depending on where you are in the province, some accents are harder to understand than those in the cities.

Unlike in France where they've integrated English terms like "weekend" into regular usage, Québec is much more ardent about the preservation of the language. That's not to say English words aren't in common usage in Québec; there is simply a heightened awareness of them. The Office Québécoise de la Langue Française is an institution whose mandate is to translate new words, typically those related to IT or technology, into a French equivalent. For example, in Québec, email is *courriel*, the French contraction of electronic mail, and Québec's stop signs are also written in French, with the word *arrêt* at their center, though even in France the signs read "stop."

Montréal is the largest French-speaking city outside of Paris, and 57 percent of Montréalers speak both official languages. Young Montréalers are less concerned with language issues than past generations, and a large majority, especially those that come from immigrant families, speak more than two languages.

Festivals and Events

There's no helping Québec—it's simply a province that wants people to get together and have a good time. If you had to spend six months locked up indoors, you'd want to get out and celebrate too, which is why one of the biggest festivals of the year, Québec City's Carnaval de Québec, is held during the coldest months. Of course, when the warm weather finally arrives, Québec City throws it a big party too, in the form of the Festival d'Été de Québec.

MONTRÉAL
Winter
La Fête des Neiges
The biggest winter festival in Montréal, **La Fête des Neiges** (Parc Jean-Drapeau, www.parcjeandrapeau.com, free) takes place in Parc Jean-Drapeau during three consecutive weekends between January and February. It's a great festival for the kids. Bundle the whole family up for a day full of winter activities, including tubing, ice fishing, curling, hockey, and ice sculpture. It's hosted by Boule de

Neige (a.k.a. Snowball), and furry suits, face paint, kid-friendly tunes, and hot chocolate are on the agenda.

Igloofest

At its base, electronic music festival **Igloofest** (Jacques-Cartier Pier, www.igloofest.ca, from $10) is a large outdoor winter rave full of trippy beats, mesmerizing visuals, an enormous igloo, and audience members dancing around in snowsuits. It takes over Jacques-Cartier Pier for three weekends at the end of January—it takes a lot of dancing to get rid of the chill that blows in off the St-Lawrence. DJs pack their mittens and touques (hats) and come from all corners of the world to keep revelers moving.

Montréal en Lumière

Montréal en Lumière (various locations, www.montrealenlumiere.com, free), a 10-day cultural celebration of food, arts, and music, takes place in mid- to late February all over the city. It is hands-down the most anticipated of winter festivals, if only because of the closing-night festivities. The whole Highlights Festival culminates in Nuit Blanche, an all-night party where people take to the streets and trek from live shows to free museum exhibits well into the wee hours of the morning, refueling with flasks of hot chocolate and stronger stuff as they go.

Rencontres Internationales du Documentaire Montréal

Dedicated to documentary films, the 10-day **Rencontres Internationales du Documentaire Montréal** (various locations, 514/499-3676, www.ridm.qc.ca, $11/film adult, $10/film senior and student, $75 pass), which takes place in mid- to late November, was founded in 1998 by filmmakers who wanted to create a new platform for perspectives in the discipline. It now features the work of international and local documentary filmmakers with the aim of presenting the films in their original languages. Alongside the films, the festival includes a number of panel discussions, workshops, and master classes.

Rendez-vous du Cinéma Québécois

Québécois cinema is celebrated annually in mid- to late February during the **Rendez-vous du Cinéma Québécois** (various locations, 514/526-9635, www.rvcq.com, $10/film, $100 pass), which screens films made in the last 12 months. This 10-day festival is fascinating, whether or not you're familiar with Québécois movies. The range on view here is spectacular, everything from mediocre comedies to astounding documentaries full of emotion and surprise. Though the festival's name is in French, selections are not limited to the

French language; this is really dedicated to any and all films made in Québec, so there are English and First Nations selections as well.

Spring

Blue Metropolis Literary Festival

Internationally renowned authors converge on Montréal in late April to early May to take part in **Blue Metropolis Literary Festival** (777 ave. University, 514/790-1245, www.bluemetropolis.org, $10-15, $45 pass), the world's first multilingual literary festival. Writers of fiction, nonfiction, poetry, and journalism come to be a part of the panel discussions, interviews, question and answer periods, book signings and launches, and of course to read their work to a captive audience. Unique in its vision, each year's event has a specific theme, with the discussions and authors invited tying into that theme. Previous years have included James Frey, Yann Martel, Margaret Atwood, and A. L. Kennedy.

Elektra

Elektra (various locations, www.elektramontreal.ca, $12-20) is a cutting-edge digital arts festival that takes place in early May. It offers some of the most unusual experiences you're likely to come across at a festival. Internationally renowned and drawing artists from such diverse nations as Japan and Mexico, the exhibits here range from sound and light installations to live performances and interactive exhibits. The latest technologies and futuristic designs, like clothing with GPS tracking, are incorporated into almost every work, and there is an emphasis on new digital media, though the artists themselves come from varied backgrounds, like contemporary dance and musical composition.

Festival TransAmériques

Contemporary dance and theater are the focus of **Festival TransAmériques** (various locations, 514/842-0704, www.fta.qc.ca, $25-60), which runs late May-mid-June. Though it shares the stage with theater, this is the most important contemporary dance festival in the city, and the works on view here are usually standouts. Drawing talents from across Canada and the world, Festival TransAmériques is known for some audience participation in its works—a public dance performance, for example, or a play that invites the audience to join the cast, if only for a fleeting moment.

Mutek

Celebrating digital creativity and electronic music, **Mutek** (various locations, www.mutek.org, $10-35) is a generally sweaty four days of dancing and chilling out to the latest electronic sounds, while magical worlds are created on a screen behind a stage. Usually taking place in early June, it is presented by Mutek, a not-for-profit organization leading the way in digital sounds and visual arts. It draws talent from emerging and established international scenes and is a great festival for anyone drawn to the digital age and all that comes with it.

Suoni per il Popolo

As the name suggests, **Suoni per il Popolo** (various locations, 514/282-0122, ext. 222, www.suoniperilpopolo.org, $10-35, $225 festival pass), which takes place throughout June, is organized by the same people behind café/bar/venue Casa del Popolo and is aimed at underground and experimental music. Started in 2001, the festival has since grown and is now one of the foremost festivals of experimental music of all kinds. If weird and wonderful is your thing, Suoni per il Popolo is the place for you. Past editions have seen the likes of Jay Reatard, The Microphones, Vic Chesnut, and Jandek.

Summer
Divers/Cité

Divers/Cité (various locations, 514/285-4011, www.diverscite.org, free-$25) is a week-long celebration of gay pride in late July, and though it's not the only queer celebration in the city, Divers/Cité is the biggest, with free outdoor performances and art shows happening throughout the week. The mission of this festival is to focus on the art and culture of the LGBT community; the performances on view here range from modern dance to jazz, funk, and world music. It's recognized throughout the world, and members of the LGBT community flock to the city during this event.

Fantasia Film Festival

Running throughout the entire month of July, **Fantasia Film Festival** (various locations, www.fantasiafestival.com, $9/film, $80 for 10 films) is North America's premiere genre film festival. From the obscure to the grotesque, the Japanese to the Korean, it offers a wide range of films from all over the globe. Established in 1996, it has since grown to become the place where distributors come to scope out the best of the weird and the strange. Popular with moviegoers, it has become a destination festival for die-hard genre fans.

Festival International de Jazz de Montréal

One of the most recognizable festivals in the world, the **Festival International de Jazz de Montréal** (various locations, 514/840-3618, www.montrealjazzfest.com), free-$150) attracts thousands of tourists to the city each summer, running from the end of June to early July. Some of the biggest names in music have played here, including Tony Bennett, B. B. King, and Norah Jones. The 11-day festival offers nonstop music with big international acts playing for free in the middle of a shut-down rue Ste-Catherine. The outdoor atmosphere and huge crowds make it one of the most exciting festivals in the city.

Festival International Nuits d'Afrique

Fans of African music will rejoice at the **Festival International Nuits d'Afrique** (various locations, 514/499-9215, www.festivalnuitsdafrique.com, $10-35), which focuses on music with African roots. From Ethiopian jazz to Algerian *raï* and even sounds from Latin America, this festival has it all. Established in 1987, it has become the springboard for African music in North America and has helped introduce many international groups to Canadian audiences. Happening throughout July and August with free shows at Place Émilie-Gamelin, it is the city's premiere world music festival.

Festival Mondial de la Bière

Canada's largest beer festival, the **Festival Mondial de la Bière** (various locations, 514/722-9640, www.festivalmondialbiere.qc.ca, free entry, tasting $1-5), takes place every June. Local and international microbreweries share the stage with giants like Molson and Stella Artois. Brewers from all over the world converge, allowing visitors to taste hundreds of different types of beers. Entrance is free, but a full pint will set you back about $8. Tasting coupons are also available for a dollar a pop.

Festival St-Ambroise Fringe de Montréal

Though not as big as the Edinburgh Fringe, Montréal's version, the **Festival St-Ambroise Fringe de Montréal** (various locations, 514/849-3378, www.montrealfringe.ca, $10-25, $250 unlimited Fringe Pass) comes close, with over 55,000 attendees at the week-long festival. Running in early June, the festival takes over venues around the city with local and international Fringe performances that are randomly picked by lottery; if your play makes it to the stage, it is all about luck. Though the program is released a few days early, the best way to see if there's anything that tickles your fancy is to stop by the Fringe for All a few days before opening to see snippets from upcoming shows.

La Fête des Enfants de Montréal

La Fête des Enfants de Montréal (Parc Jean-Drapeau, www.parcjean-drapeau.com, free) takes place in Parc Jean-Drapeau for a weekend during the month of August. Kids 12 and under can participate in 100 different activities, including singing, dancing, games, live music shows, and creative and sports workshops. Characters in costume entertain the kids; there is also a specialty area for those with infants, offering changing tables, bottle warming, and stroller parking.

Les FrancoFolies de Montréal

Les FrancoFolies de Montréal (various locations, 514/876-8989, www. francofolies.com, free-$120) is a massive street festival in celebration of Francophone music that takes over downtown every June. A whole strip of rue Ste-Catherine is blocked off to make way for the throngs of fans who come out in force to check out emerging and established Francophone bands and musicians. Not all concerts are free, however; bigger names play to a more contained crowd in venues across the city. It's a great way to check out the latest in the Québécois and francophone music scenes.

Heavy MTL

Heavy MTL (Parc Jean-Drapeau, www.heavymtl.com, $130 weekend pass): The name says it all. This two-day festival, which takes place outdoors at Parc Jean-Drapeau, is all about heavy metal. Offering a mix of old time metalheads like Megadeath, Danzig, and Rob Zombie with new kids on the block like Mastadon, Avenged Sevenfold, and Baroness, it keeps fans from all generations pleased. No matter who's playing, you can guarantee it'll be loud.

Just for Laughs

What started as a two-day Francophone comedy event, **Juste pour Rire** (Just for Laughs, various locations, 514/845-4000, www. hahaha.com, $15-120), has since grown into one of the biggest comedy festivals in the world. During July, streets all over downtown are closed off to make room for the street performers stationed throughout the city. Each year a number of established comedians, including Bill Cosby, Louis CK, Jerry Seinfeld, and Flight of the Conchords, bring their own brand of stand-up to the city. The recently launched Zoofest, also part of Just for Laughs, has a younger take on funny and features more obscure (sometimes funnier) acts.

Montréal Pride

Montréal Pride (various locations, www.fiertemontrealpride.com, free-$35) is quite the celebration. Since taking over organization of the gay and lesbian pride parade from Divers/Cité in 2007, nonprofit Fierté Montréal has expanded the celebration to include a community day and five days worth of gay pride activities, including outdoor concerts and dance parties, drag races, and performances by interdisciplinary artists in early August.

clockwise from top left: one of the many churches that can be found throughout Québec City; typical architecture in St-Jean-Baptiste, Québec City; city hall, Québec City

Osheaga Music and Arts Festival

The three-day **Osheaga Music and Arts Festival** (Parc Jean-Drapeau, www.osheaga.com, $90/day, $235 weekend) is one of the biggest in Montréal, taking place off-island in the picturesque Parc Jean-Drapeau. Thousands of people of all ages and creeds spend the weekend checking out unknown emerging bands, musicians like Robyn and Hot Chip, and big-name acts like Arcade Fire, The Cure, and Snoop Dogg. Local art collectives set up installations in a designated area of the site and you can often check out the work as it is in process. Among leafy-green forests, it is a great way to spend the first weekend in August.

Fall

Festival du Monde Arabe

Established in 2000, the **Festival du Monde Arabe** (various locations, 514/747-0000, www.festivalarabe.com, $15-50), which takes place late October-mid-November, aims to develop a dialogue between Arab and Western cultures in the city. Featuring everything from dance to visual arts and music to movies, it attempts to present every aspect of the culture. Since many Arab cultures were once colonized by the French, many of the events are in French, though English events also exist; check the website for details.

Festival du Nouveau Cinéma

Founded in 1971, the **Festival du Nouveau Cinéma** (various locations, 514/282-0004, www.nouveaucinema.ca, $10/film adult, $8/film senior and student, $125 pass adult, $100 pass senior and student) is an independent film festival dedicated to showing independent films from the world over. Taking place over 10 days in October, it has become a huge draw for cinemaphiles, and is viewed as one of the most prestigious festivals for films of this kind. It is even a qualifying festival for the Academy Awards in the category of short film. Directors such as Kenneth Anger, Wim Wenders, and Atom Egoyan have attended the festival.

Image+Nation

Held at the end of October, **Image+Nation** (various locations, www.image-nation.org, $12/film adult, $9/film senior and student) is the preeminent gay and lesbian film festival in the city. With international titles and 11 days of screenings, and thanks to the collapse of independent film distribution, it has become one of the most important festivals of its kind. Titles by and for the LGBT community are on view here, and the films include animation and shorts.

Montréal World Film Festival

With the aim of supporting cultural diversity in cinema, the **Montréal World Film Festival** (various locations, 514/848-3883, www. ffm-montreal.org, $10/film, $100 pass) supports many emerging filmmakers. The public festival invites viewers to be the jury; and audience members participate in the process by voting for films in various categories—like the Oscars but without Hollywood. That's not to say bigger name directors don't show here; they do, but they rarely come from Hollywood. During the late August festival, free viewings of films are offered out under the stars in front of Place des Arts.

Pop Montréal

Pop Montréal (various locations, 514/842-1919, www.popmontreal. com, $10-35, $200 Pop Pass) is an annual five-day festival occurring late September-early October that features Francophone, Canadian, and international acts. It's one of the most highly anticipated festivals of the year, especially among fans of indie music. Emerging and underground artists might outnumber other bands on the schedule, but industry pioneers include Burt Bacharach, Swans, and Os Mutantes. Though primarily a music festival, it has grown to include offshoots like Puces Pop, Art Pop, Film Pop, Fashion Pop, and Kids Pop.

QUÉBEC CITY
Winter
Carnaval de Québec

The most iconic of all the festivals in the province, **Carnaval de Québec** (various locations, 418/626-3716, www.carnaval.qc.ca) has its roots in the early days of New France, when everyone got together in the weeks leading up to Lent to drink and let loose. Following tradition, the festival is held between the end of January and early February. The first big Carnaval took place in 1894 as a way of combating the winter blahs, and it's in this spirit that the festival has taken place every winter since 1955. Lead by Bonhomme, a life-size snowman with a floppy red hat and a *ceinture fléchée* (a traditional Québécois belt), the festival is all about fun in the outdoors. From parades to dog-sled races, tobogganing to ice canoeing, ice-skating to outdoor dance parties and snow sculpture competitions, there's always something going on. It's also the only festival to give adults full rights to wander the town in snowsuits without shame while sipping on something to keep them warm. An added bonus? Most events are free.

Mois Multi

The international festival **Mois Multi** (various locations, 418/524-7553, www.moismulti.org), founded in 2000, focuses on multidisciplinary and electronic arts. Artists from such diverse countries as Russia, Australia, and Mexico have exhibited here, bringing with them their various light and sound installations and multimedia performances that explore topics like synesthesia, sound-architecture, and light chaos. Throughout the month-long festival in February, visitors are invited to witness these man-made realms, making it more than just an event, it becomes an experience.

Red Bull Crashed Ice

If you think walking the icy streets of Québec City is tough, imagine skating down them. That's the challenge with the yearly **Red Bull Crashed Ice** (various locations, 877/643-8131, www.redbullcrashedice.ca), which takes place in March. Competitors from all over the world, kitted out in full hockey gear, take to the ice track laid out throughout the steep winding streets of Old Québec and attempt to skate their way to the bottom. Fans are free to line the 550-meter track and watch as both the men's and women's heats go by like a flash in this mash-up between downhill skiing, hockey, and boardercross.

Spring

Carrefour International de Théâtre de Québec

The city's preeminent theater festival, **Carrefour International de Théâtre de Québec** (various locations, 418/692-3131, www.carrefourtheatre.qc.ca) presents innovative theater work from Canada and beyond. Though established playwrights often present here, there's an eye on emerging playwrights and artists as well. Held from the end of May to early June, all the productions presented are premieres in the province—they do not accept pieces that have already been mounted in Québec. Since it is an international festival, there are often a few English or bilingual selections.

Festival de la Gastronomiede Québec

For gourmands interested in seeing and tasting the latest in cuisine, the **Festival de la Gastronomiede Québec** (Gastronomy Festival, Expo Cité, 418/683-4150, www.crq.ca, $12 adult) brings out the best in new merchandise. Over three days in mid-April, 200 exhibitors invite the public to taste their wares, from wineries to microbreweries, pastries to cheese, with over 60 percent of the products coming from Québec. Visitors are welcome to browse the aisles, pick up some cooking tips, and indulge in all kinds of different food. Restaurants from around the city are also here, cooking up new or classic dishes. A word of warning: With fees for entering, parking, and the occasional bite, it can add up to be an expensive day.

Manif d'Art

Simply put, **Manif d'Art** (various locations, 418/524-1917, www.manifdart.org) is the Québec City biennial, held in May and June. Every even-numbered year, the city and the world's established and up-and-coming artists present their works at what is the biggest contemporary art festival in Québec City. Events outside of the exhibitions are held as well, including colloquiums and forums, and satellite activities with other disciplines such as live performances and shows. A nominal fee allows visitors to see all the exhibitions and gives them access to guided tours, theme-related events, and creative workshops.

Summer

Expo Québec

The largest agricultural fair in Eastern Canada, **Expo Québec** (Expo Cité, 250 blvd. Wilfrid-Hamel, 888/866-3976, www.expoquebec.com, $30 adult, $20 senior, $12 child) was founded in 1911 and has been celebrating with a public exhibition every August since. The 10-day event is aimed at families, with attractions like candy, inflatable castles, mini-rollercoasters, educational exhibits on science and organic food production, and concerts for kids and adults alike. The real draw here, however, is the animals; with close to 2,000 animals on view, kids and adults have a chance to learn more about horses, ponies, cattle, sheep, goats, alpacas, and a host of other, smaller animals.

Festibière

It isn't summer without a beer festival. **Festibière** (100 Quai St-André, 418/948-1166, www.festibieredequebec.com, $12 adult) takes place along the waterfront for three days in August and couldn't be better located. In order to expand the tastebuds of beer lovers everywhere, various tents are dedicated to various beers with locations dedicated to both local and international brews. There's also a conference dedicated to the art of brewing where you can test your knowledge of hops against that of the experts. Legal drinking age in Québec is 18, so don't be surprised to find yourself surrounded by a few amateur, yet eager beavers.

Festival des Journées d'Afrique, Danses et Rythmes du Monde

Celebrating African dance and music, this two-week **Festival des Journées d'Afrique, Danses et Rythmes du Monde** (various locations, 418/640-4213, www.festivaljourneedafrique.com), which occurs late July–early August, sees artists from all over the world performing a diverse range of African-roots music. Everything is represented here, from soukous from the Congo to Trinidadian calypso, South African Afro-beat, and roots reggae from Québec. Dance troupes, drumming, and dance workshops are also part of the fest. Prices vary depending on venue with some events free.

Festival d'Été de Québec

One of the biggest events in the entire calendar year, **Festival d'Été de Québec** (Québec Summer Festival, various locations, 888/992-5200, www.infofestival.com, $80 adult pass) is essentially one 11-day-long concert. With literally hundreds of shows—some of them for free—happening during the beginning of July, this event gives the city the attitude of a nonstop party. Started in 1968, the focus was mainly on Francophone and world artists, but since 2000 the festival has presented some of the most interesting international acts in the world, including Ethiopiques, Andrew Bird, Caribou, Black Eyed Peas, and a number of emerging talents. The biggest outdoor shows take place on the Plains of Abraham and in the past have featured musicians like Iron Maiden, Arcade Fire, and Paul McCartney.

Fête Arc-en-Ciel de Québec

Taking place in early September, usually over Labor Day weekend, **Fête Arc-en-Ciel de Québec** (Rainbow Celebration, various locations, 418/809-3383, www.glbtquebec.org, $12 adult) is Québec's gay pride celebration. Each year, the three-day event is based on a different theme, usually one that can be loosely interpreted and allow for some great street decorations. Though the center of the celebrations is the gay pride parade, they include a number of free performances, concerts, and conferences that look at important topics like homophobia in high schools.

Fête Nationale St-Jean Baptiste

Fête Nationale St-Jean Baptiste (Plains of Abraham, 418/640-0799, www.snqc.qc.ca, free) is Québec's national holiday, which takes place on June 24. "Nationale" refers to the nation of Québec; this holiday isn't celebrated elsewhere in Canada. Though Saint-Jean-Baptiste Day has been celebrated in Québec since the first European settlers, it took a patriotic turn in 1834 after Ludger Duvernay, who would later found the Saint-Jean-Baptiste Society, was inspired by St. Patrick's Day celebrations in Montréal. In celebration of the province's national holiday, the people of Québec usually spend the afternoon with an aperitif before heading out to the free concert on the Plains of Abraham in the evening, featuring famous Québécois performers and stars.

Les Fêtes de la Nouvelle-France

For four days in August, the public is invited to step back in time during **Les Fêtes de la Nouvelle France** (various locations, 866/391-3383, www.nouvellefrance.qc.ca, $12 adult, children under 12 free) to experience Québec as it was during the French regime. Bringing to life over a dozen sites in the Vieux-Québec's Lower Town, each year is centered around a theme in order to give viewers a fuller picture of what life was like in New France. Past events have included the baptism of an Amerindian and a public blessing of women's pregnant bellies. Visitors are encouraged to dress up in period costumes, which are available to buy or rent. This is good family fun.

Le Grand Rire

The Québec City equivalent of Just for Laughs, **Le Grand Rire** (The Big Laugh, various locations, 877/441-7473, www.grandrire.com, $20 and up, children under 12 free) caters to a Francophone audience. Occasionally, however, they have some big-name English acts like Bill Cosby on the bill. It runs throughout the month of June and into early July, and with over 70 shows on the schedule, there are often a few offered in English. Shows take place at indoor and outdoor venues all over the city.

Québec City International Festival of Military Bands

For five days at the end of August, military bands and a few dancers from all over the world take to the stage and streets for the **Québec City International Festival of Military Bands** (various locations, 888/693-5757, www.fimmq.com). Bands from all over Canada, Germany, France, Italy, and the United States regularly participate, including surprising acts like the New York City Police Department's Jazz Band. Locals line the Grande-Allée during the opening parade, then head to the main stage near the Manège Militaire to catch a free show. Most events are free, but some shows require tickets, including the grand finale Tattoo.

Fall

Envol et Macadam

The alternative music festival **Envol et Macadam** (various locations, 418/522-1611, www.envoletmacadam.com) was founded in 1996, with the aim of both nurturing up-and-coming talent and bringing established artists to the city who wouldn't necessarily play here otherwise. Taking place in September, the festival has three main outdoor stages in the downtown core and takes over a number of indoor venues during the fest. Though "alternative" isn't as defining a moniker as it was in the 1990s, bands here are still outside of the mainstream, and have included acts like Bloc Party and

Metric as well as punk, hardcore, and metal bands like Mastadon, Pennywise, and Bad Religion.

Festival Antenne-A

Music, books, art, film, theater: It's all here at arts-focused **Festival Antenne-A** (various locations, www.antenne-a.com), which brings together emerging artists from all disciplines from late September to early October. Though the schedule is often heavy with bands and DJs from Québec, Canada, and the world, there is a focus on acts that go beyond just the musical aspects and delve into the realms of visual art and technology.

The festival also presents a number of group talks and conferences in both English and French around various themes, including emerging culture.

Festival de Jazz de Québec

The **Festival de Jazz de Québec** (various locations, www.jazzaquebec.ca) is for real jazz buffs only; you won't find any Top 40 artists here. The target audiences for this fest, running from the end of September to early October, are jazz aficionados. Montréal's International Jazz Festival might be known for huge, big-name performers like Stevie Wonder and Lionel Ritchie, but here you'll find entire sets dedicated to greats like Charles Mingus and John Coltrane. Local jazz musicians also take to the stage, including younger avant-garde artists.

Festival des Musiques Sacréesde Québec

The **Festival des Musiques Sacréesde Québec** (Québec Festival of Sacred Music, Église Saint-Roch, 590 rue St-Jean, 866/525-9777, www.imsq.ca) is just that: a three-week-long, October festival filled with compositions inspired by spirituality. Taking place at the Église Saint-Roch, where they are the proud owners of a (partly) Casavantes organ, programs include standards like Brahms's and Verdi's requiems, as well as occasional dance performances, gospel concerts, and compositions from lesser-known sources like sacred songs from Anatolia.

Journées de la Culture

The province-wide **Journées de la Culture** (various locations, 866/734-4441, www.journeesdelaculture.qc.ca, free) opens a number of cultural and artistic hubs to the public by inviting visitors into architecture offices, design studios, and local theaters for a behind-the-scenes look. Also called "Days of Culture," this free, three-day event runs at the end of September, with cities offering complimentary shuttle services to various sites and events, so there's no excuse to miss out. Various workshops and kid-specific events make it an adventure for the whole family.

Parade des Jouets

Held annually at the end of November, the **Parade des Jouets** (Children's Parade, various locations, 418/780-3006, www.parad-edesjouets.ca, free) has a long history. It was started at the end of World War II by fireman Marcel Bourassa. Firefighters of the city worked together to repair old toys and make new ones for the less-fortunate children in the city. The tradition continues today, and since 2004, 900 underprivileged children are the recipients of new and refurbished toys each year. This parade is run in celebration of that event and includes floats and marching bands.

The Arts

MUSIC

Without a doubt the province's best-known recording artist is Celine Dion. Born in the small town of Charlemagne 30 kilometers from Montréal, she was a mega-star in Québec and France when she was just a teenager and well before she started singing in English. Although she was criticized at first by her Francophone fan base for "selling out," her worldwide success is now a huge source of pride for the province, and fans now love (and buy) her English albums just as much as her French ones.

The province's second biggest export, music-wise, is Montréal's Arcade Fire, who took over the airwaves in 2004 with their infectious indie rock anthems and haven't looked back. Despite their rock star status—they've shared the stage with everyone from David Byrne to David Bowie—they remain active in the community, and many of the group's members play in other Montréal bands. Their success in the early 2000s was also part of a bigger Montréal indie rock explosion, with bands like The Dears, Wolfe Parade, and the Unicorns, among others. The scene has continued to grow since then and is constantly evolving. In recent years Francophone bands like Malajube, Radio Radio, and Karkwa—who won the 2010 Polaris Music Prize, Canada's largest for an "indie" band—have been gaining fans across the language divide.

Poet and singer/songwriter Leonard Cohen is one of the city's most-loved inhabitants, and many of his melancholy and soulful compositions were inspired by the city, including the song *So Long Maryanne*. Grammy Award-winning artist Rufus Wainwright is also from Montréal, though he now resides in New York. Mixing symphonic sounds with a pop mentality, his sweeping compositions are utterly unique and catchy. His sister, Martha Wainwright, also a musician, is somewhat less experimental in her style, but continues to push the boundaries of pop. On one of her more recent albums (*Sans Fusils, Ni Souliers, à Paris*) she sings the songs of Edith Piaf. Of course, it helps when you have good genes, and the Wainwrights have them in spades: Their father is American folk singer Loudon Wainwright III, and their mother is Kate McGarrigle; Kate and her sister Anna are two of the biggest folk singers in the province. Since the 1960s, the McGarrigle sisters have sung and written in both French and English.

It wasn't until the 1960s that modern music really started to hit its stride in the province. Québec held a festival of experimental music in 1961, and by the mid-1960s, the symphony was starting to attract a larger audience. It was also the heyday of folk singers or *chansonniers* like Félix Leclerc and Gilles Vigneault. Leclerc in particular had been singing and writing for a long time, even finding success in Paris, before returning to find the same success at home. Singing about themes like nature and celebrations has made him one of the most revered musicians in the province.

CINEMA

After being under religious censorship during the first half of the 20th century, Québec cinema really kicked off in the 1960s, when a generation of directors formed the National Film Board (NFB). This film board gave them a platform, and they started to make movies mostly about the Québécois identity. Part of the enthusiastic social transformations that were happening in arts in this period, they shot documentaries and features that gained international recognition, despite their local flavor. Experiments in documentary film led to the Direct Cinema genre, which included Pierre Perreault's *Pour la Suite du Monde*, a vivid documentary about the ancestral beluga hunt in Isle-aux-Coudres, and Michel Brault's *Les Orders*, a rendition of the October crisis of 1971.

In the 1970s, a number of feature films gained wide critical acclaim and today are seen as part of a golden age in Québec cinema. Among these are *La Vraie Vie de Bernadette* by Gilles Carle (1972), *J.A. Martin Photographe* by Jean Beaudin (1977), and Frank Mankiewicz's *Les Bons Débarras* (1979). Most important of all is Claude Jutra's 1971 movie *Mon Oncle Antoine*, a coming-of-age story set in the rural Québec of the 1940s, which is considered to be the greatest Canadian film.

The Québec film industry is seen as the strongest in the country, and Québec films regularly win top accolades at the Genie Awards, which are the Canadian film industry awards. Québec's French cinema has a stronger character than its English counterpart, which often struggles to differentiate itself from American cinema.

With movies like *Le Déclin de l'Empire Américain* (1986) and *Jésus de Montréal* (1988), Denys Arcand is probably the best-known Québécois director. *Les Invasions Barbares* (2003), a poignant critique of the aging generation of the Quiet Revolution, won the Oscar for Best Foreign Film and was Best Screenplay at Cannes. Other stand-out directors have been scooped up by Hollywood including Jean-Marc Vallée, whose most recent film was *Dallas Buyers Club*, and Denis Villeneuve, who directed *Prisoners*. Newcomer Xavier Dolan has won big at the Cannes Film Festival for his films *J'ai Tué Ma Mère, Les Amours Imaginaries, (Heartbeats)* and *Lawrence, Anyways*, and has set the course for a new generation of filmmakers.

LITERATURE

After Paris, Montréal has the most French-language writers in the world, many of whom have been translated into English. Playwright and author Michel Tremblay wrote *Chroniques du Plateau*, which has made him one of the most prolific and well-recognized authors in the province. His stories about working-class French-Canadians in the 1960s, written almost entirely in *joual*, defined the writing of his generation. Other writers include Hubert Aquin, Dany Laferrière, Marie-Claire Blais, and Anne Hébert, whose *Kamouraska* looks at treachery and love in 19th-century Québec. Gabrielle Roy's *The Tin Flute* tells the tale of a young woman in working-class Verdun during the Depression.

English-language Montréal literature has pretty much been defined, and reigned over, by the acerbic wit of Mordecai Richler, who continues to be one of the strongest voices in Anglophone literature, even after his death in 2001. His novels *The Apprenticeship of Duddy Kravitz, Son of a Smaller Hero,* and *St-Urbain's Horseman* defined not only the city's Jewish population but the city itself.

The witty and poignant novels and short stories of Mavis Gallant continue to weave their way through Montréal, despite the fact that she's long since immigrated to France.

New writers include Rawi Hage, who moved to Montréal in 2001 and whose 2006 novel *De Niro's Game* was nominated for the Scotiabank Giller Prize. His second novel, *Cockroach*, is an intimate look at an immigrant's experience in Montréal.

VISUAL ARTS

Early-Québec art can be divided into two subject matters: landscapes and religion. The province's first painters were Catholic missionaries who used paintings and engravings to convert the Amerindians. Since many of the works were by priests and nuns, they have a particularly naïve quality, a trend that continues in Québécois art. The first great Québécois painters emerged in the 19th century and included Théophile Hamel, known for

Montréal Writers

The 20th century saw a number of literary stars from many of the city's communities debut with unimaginable success. The most prominent of those is poet and musician **Leonard Cohen.** Born in Westmount, a well-to-do and predominantly English neighborhood, Cohen went on to study at McGill University before publishing his first book of poetry, *Let Us Compare Mythologies,* in 1956. In 1964 he published the novel *The Favourite Game,* a semi-autobiographical book about a boy growing up in Montréal. Tracing Cohen's adolescence from primary through high school and university, you'll find many recognizable places and streets that in some cases remain unchanged.

Another Jewish-Canadian writer who became known for his semi-autobiographical tales of Montréal is **Mordecai Richler.** Where Cohen grew up on the affluent side of the city, Richler was born on rue St-Urbain, a working-class, mostly Jewish neighborhood in the Mile End. One of his most well-known novels, *The Apprenticeship of Duddy Kravitz,* revolves around the neighborhood, and you can still visit many of the places mentioned in the book—and in some cases

shown in the movie (starring Richard Dreyfuss)— including the timeless St-Viateur Bagel. His last novel, **Barney's Version,** which became an acclaimed film of the same name in 2010, was set and filmed here.

Life in the French community of the Plateau is vividly brought to life in the work of novelist and playwright **Michel Tremblay,** the preeminent Québécois writer of his time and famous for his 1965 play *Les Belles-Soeurs.* Tremblay's creations perfectly evoke life in the working-class neighborhood in the 1950s and '60s, right down to his use of *joual,* colloquial speech.

Born in Winnipeg, Manitoba, to a French-Canadian family, **Gabrielle Roy** eventually settled in Montréal, where she published her novel *Bonheur d'Occasion* in 1945 to rave reviews and a prestigious prize. Published in English two years later as *The Tin Flute,* it tells the story of a young woman during World War II struggling with poverty and ignorance in the working-class neighborhood of St-Henri. Even today it remains one of the few novels to accurately describe the struggles of the neighborhood and its inhabitants.

portraits of explorers; Dutch-born Cornelius Krieghoff, who depicted settlers and images of the wilderness; and Ozias Leduc, whose portrait *Boy with Bread* is one of the defining images of Québécois art.

Work continued to be defined by snowy city-scapes and bucolic farmland until the modern era of Canadian painting was ushered in by Paul-Émile Bourduas, John Lyman, and Alfred Pellan in the 1940s. Bourduas was the most prolific and outspoken of all three and developed a radical style of surrealism that came to be identified with a group called the Automatistes.

In 1948 Bourduas published the manifesto *Refus Global* (Global Refusal), rejecting traditional social, artistic, and psychological norms of Québécois society and the religious and bucolic art that defined it. The manifesto called instead for an untamed liberation of creativity and championed abstract art.

Canadian art and Québec's artistic community were never the same again. Automatiste artist Jean-Paul Riopelle would soon emerge as the movement's newest driving force, and his abstract works, called "grand mosaics," would become world-renowned.

The 1960s and '70s were defined by artists like Claude Tousignant and Guido Molinari, whose abstract works used hypnotic geometric shapes and unusual color combinations to almost psychedelic proportions.

Some of Québec's biggest contemporary artists include David Altmejd, known for mixed-media pieces that incorporate various materials—everything from a decapitated werewolf head to shards of broken mirrors—into something cohesive and anthropomorphic. Valérie Blass also plays with a mix of materials and human yet non-human forms. Adnad Hannah's film and photographic works play with traditional art history. Two of the province's biggest artists are collectives: The work of BGL plays with conventional objects or pop culture icons in unconventional ways—a melted Darth Vader, or a motorcycle covered with snow in the middle of a gallery floor. Cooke et Sasseville play with similar ideas, and one of their works involves a giant flamingo laying its head down on train tracks.

DANCE AND THEATER

The established Québécois culture and the province's bohemian disposition help nurture a particularly diverse arts scene in both languages.

French theater is some of the best in the world, whether you're in Québec City or Montréal, while English theater struggles to keep the pace. The country's top performing arts educational institution, the National Theater School, is found in the Plateau, attracting Canada's most promising playwrights and stage actors in either language.

There is an innovative contemporary dance scene in the province that has fostered internationally recognized companies like La La La Human Steps, O Vertigo, and Fondation Jean-Pierre Perreault, as well as the careers of dancers and choreographers Margie Gillis, Marie Chouinard, and Benoît Lachambre. A number of Montréal institutions, like Agora de la Danse, Tangante, and Studio 301, are dedicated exclusively to emerging dance artists. Québec also supports two classical ballet companies, Les Grands Ballets Canadiens and Le Ballet de Québec.

Architecture in Québec

When settlers first arrived in Québec their main concern was with security; with that in mind all of the first towns started out as fortified enclosures. These were made of wood or stone and designed in the five-pointed Vauban style. By the end of the French regime, New France closely resembled provincial towns in the old country, with hospitals, convents, colleges, and churches whose steeples peeked out over the walls.

Early-1700s inhabitants had trouble adapting their homes to the cold weather, and many froze to death before the colony got it right. The design was altered and structures were made of rubble stone instead of wood, with small casement windows that were few and far between. The number of rooms in the house matched the number of chimneys. In 1721, wooden houses with mansard roofs were banned after a devastating fire, and stone firewalls and attic floors covered in terracotta tiles became the standard.

Although the British conquest took place in 1759, it wasn't until the 1780s that English influence could be seen in architecture around the province. A few high-ranking officials started building homes in the popular Palladian and Regency styles, with open-air porticoes and Italian columns. The Re-gency balconies and windows allowed for a perfect mix between inside and out, while also stopping the snow from blocking windows and doors in winter. Roofs became less slanted so the snow no longer fell directly on your head as you closed the door on your way out. All buildings during this period, commercial or residential, resembled country homes. You can still get a sense of this today on rue St-Jean in Québec City. Commercial buildings were set up to look like homes in part because the Catholic Church disapproved of the expansion of commerce.

The industrialization of the province led to an architectural style that would forever define Montréal: the duplexes and triplexes with circular exterior staircases. Built between 1900 and 1930, these economical structures were meant to accommodate large families. With outdoor staircases to save on heating and space, and balconies reminiscent of rural galleries, they also gave inhabitants the feel of a personal entrance. Covered in either limestone or brick, each had decorative touches like a cornice, Tuscan columns, or art nouveau-inspired windows. Over 100 years later, these unique staircases and multiple-family dwellings continue to thrive in the city and define its architectural identity.

THE CIRCUS

Cirque du Soleil is undoubtedly the most famous Québécois circus, founded in Baie-Saint-Paul in the early 1980s by a group of street performers. These stilt-walkers, jugglers, and fire-eaters banded together to create a performance platform, since the circus tradition didn't exist in the province at the time. In the years since then, they've become part of a rich circus culture they helped to create. There are now two schools dedicated to the circus arts: the National Circus School, established in 1981, and Tohu, established in 2004, are both located in Montréal.

Cirque d'Éloize, established in 1993, is another professional company situated in Montréal that is quickly following in the footsteps of Cirque du Soleil when it comes to pushing boundaries and innovation. They bring an edginess and dance sensibility to their shows, which can be seen throughout the world. This dedication to circus arts also means that the province has some of the best street performers in the world, who are especially visible during festival season.

Essentials

Getting There

MONTRÉAL
By Air

All international and in-country flights to Montréal arrive at **Pierre Trudeau International Airport** (514/394-7377, www.admtl.com) in Dorval.

The cheapest way to get from the airport to downtown is to take the 747 Express. The ride on this elongated city bus costs $9 and the ticket can then be used on other STM buses and Métros throughout the city. The bus takes passengers from the airport to nine downtown intersections, including Berri-UQÀM, the largest Métro station in the city. It runs 24 hours a day, 365 days a year, and takes approximately 40 minutes depending on traffic. During rush hour and bad weather, give yourself an extra 90 minutes leeway.

Airport shuttle **L'Aérobus** departs from the main bus terminal (Gare d'Autocars, 505 blvd. de Maisonneuve E., 514/842-2281, www.stationcentrale.com) and Montréal Trudeau every 30 minutes 9:30am-9pm, after which it runs once every hour, 24 hours a day. One-way tickets cost $16 and can be bought at electronic kiosks at the bus station, at a regular kiosk at the airport, or on the bus. The ride takes about 30 minutes depending on traffic and weather.

A taxi from the airport to downtown will cost you $35 before tip. All taxis charge the same rate for destinations inside the downtown perimeter.

By Rail

Montréal's train station, **Gare Centrale** (895 rue de la Gauchetière W., 514/989-2626), is located in the downtown core and is a major hub for Canada's **VIA Rail trains** (888/842-7245, www.viarail.ca). **Amtrak** (800/872-7245, www.amtrak.com) has a daily train heading to and from New York City, and though the ride is long—it clocks in at approximately 10 hours—it's a scenic one alongside the Hudson River.

By Bus

Montréal's central bus terminal, the **Gare d'Autocars** (1717 rue Berri, 514/842-2281, www.stationcentrale.com), is located in the Quartier Latin and has a restaurant, shops, an information booth, as well as electronic ticket dispensers, which are often faster than lining up at the ticket counter. It connects with the Berri-UQÀM Métro station, a major junction for the city's subway lines. Taxis are always lined up outside the exit on rue Berri.

By Car

Like most major Canadian cities, Montréal is accessible via the Trans-Canadian Highway, which crosses the island with two parallel routes. The southern part of the island can be traversed on Route 20 (Route 720 leads to downtown), the northern part of the island on Route 40; both have exits leading to downtown, including St-Laurent and St-Denis.

There are a number of ways to cross the border from the United States; from New York State, you can take I-87 or I-89 north. From Massachusetts via New Hampshire and Vermont, take Route 55. At the border, all travelers must present a valid passport and drivers must show the car's registration.

QUÉBEC CITY

By Air

A number of major airlines fly directly into Québec City's teeny-tiny **Aéroport International Jean-Lesage de Québec** (418/640-2600, www.aeroportdequebec.com). Most air traffic comes from Montréal, though there are a few direct flights from within Canada as well as some international flights, mostly from France and from a few major U.S. cities, including Detroit, Chicago, Newark, and Cleveland.

The airport is about 15 kilometers from downtown; there is no bus or shuttle service available, so the only way to get to downtown is by taxi, which will set you back about $35.

By Rail

Train passengers arrive at Québec City at the **Gare du Palais** (450 rue de la Gare-du-Palais, 418/525-3000) in Vieux-Québec's Lower Town. Depending on where you're staying and the amount of baggage you're carrying, it might be wise to take a taxi. City buses are also available just outside the terminal to Upper Town, including bus 800, which will take you through Saint-Jean-Baptiste and up to the Grande-Allée, Parliament, and the Plains area. A single ride costs $2.75.

By Bus

Buses to Québec arrive at the same place as the trains at **Gare du Palais** (320 rue Abraham-Martin, 418/525-3000), near the Vieux-Port; most hotels will be a short cab ride or uphill walk away.

By Car

Like Montréal, Québec City can be reached by Autoroute 20 in the south and Autoroute 40 in the north. The drive from Montréal will take approximately 2.5 hours, and though the drive along Route 40 is more scenic, it's also a little bit longer. From Toronto, Route

401 connects with Route 20, as do I-87 in New York and I-89 and I-91 in Vermont. Arriving on Route 20, follow the signs for Pont Pierre-Laporte, and once you've crossed the bridge, turn right onto boulevard Laurier, which becomes Grande-Allée. Route 40 turns into boulevard Charest as you approach the city.

TRAVELING BETWEEN MONTRÉAL AND QUÉBEC CITY

By Air

Short-haul 50-minute flights depart from both cities 12 times a day on **Air Canada** (800/247-2262, www.aircanada.com), though by the time you go to the airport, check in, and collect your baggage afterwards, it might be just as fast to drive.

By Rail

The train is a fast and fairly efficient way to travel, though the costs can sometimes be prohibitive. **VIA Rail** (888/842-7245, www.viarail.ca) runs the only service between the two cities and offers four daily departures from both **Montréal's Gare Centrale** (895 rue de la Gauchetière W., 514/989-2626) and **Québec City's Gare du Palais** (450 rue de la Gare-du-Palais, 418/525-3000). Train times run anywhere from 3 to 3.5 hours, and a regular one-way ticket costs $102 before taxes, though seat sales can bring the price as low as $60.

By Bus

Both cities are served by the **Orléans Express** (888/999-3977, www.orleansexpress.com), with hourly departures from both **Montréal's Gare d'Autocars** (505 blvd. de Maisonneuve E., 514/842-2281, www.stationcentrale.com) and **Québec's Gare du Palais** (320 rue Abraham-Martin, 418/525-3000). A round-trip ticket costs approximately $80 and the ride can take anywhere from three to five hours.

By Car

Driving between the two cities is often the quickest and easiest. The drive can last anywhere from 2.5 to 4 hours depending on traffic. Take Autoroute 20 or Route 40 out of either city and head in the direction of the opposite city. Arriving in Québec on Route 20, follow the signs for Pont Pierre-Laporte and then exit onto boulevard Laurier, which becomes Grande-Allée. If you're on Route 40, it will turn into boulevard Charest as you approach Québec.

Heading into Montréal on Route 20, follow the signs for Pont Jacques-Cartier, which will take you straight into the heart of the Plateau. From Route 40, exit on any number of southbound streets, including Papineau, St-Denis, and St-Laurent.

Taking the 40 instead of the 20 will add approximately 20 minutes onto your trip, but it's more scenic and you have the option of stopping off at Trois Trois-Rivières about halfway between the two cities.

There are also a couple of ride-share companies that can help save costs for both drivers and passengers: **Allo Stop** (www.allostop.com) and **Amigo Express** (www.amigoexpress.com).

Getting Around

PUBLIC TRANSPORTATION
Montréal

Montréal's Métro and bus system is run by the **STM** (Société de Transport de Montréal, 514/786-4656, www.stm.info). The **Métro** is quick, safe, and efficient and consists of five lines. It is easy to navigate. A single fare on both bus and Métro is $3, 10 tickets will set you back $24.50. If you're in town for a short stay and plan to take the Métro often in one day, get the unlimited weekend pass for $12. Sales are cash only at the ticket booth, but you can use both debit and credit cards at the newly installed automated machines.

Individual tickets also count as your transfer, so if you're planning on getting off the Métro and hopping onto a bus make sure you keep the card with you. The Métro runs 5am-1am.

Métro and bus tickets are interchangeable, but if you want to get on the bus and don't have a ticket, make sure you have exact change. Once you've paid for your bus ticket, make sure to take a transfer, which will look like a regular ticket, especially if you're heading to the Métro or want to take another bus. Buses run all night long on many major streets, including Sherbrooke, Mont-Royal, St-Laurent, St-Denis, and avenue du Parc, but the night-bus number is often different from the daytime number, so double-check with the driver before you hop on.

Québec City

Québec City buses (www.rtcquebec.ca) are fast and efficient, with three major bus lines, called **MétroBus,** that run frequently and cover all the major areas of the city—some will even take you as far out as Chute Montmorency. A single bus ticket costs $3 and also acts as a transfer if you're transferring lines; if you don't have a ticket the bus accepts exact change.

The city also has a few buses aimed at tourists. The **Navette Desjardins** runs from June to mid-October and carries passengers from Beauport and Domain des Maizrets, north of the city, through the Vieux-Port and Lower Town and out to the Aquarium du Quebec and Promenade de Samuel de Champlain. A ticket costs $3 for all-day unlimited use, and a child under 5 rides for free.

Carrying approximately 20 passengers at a time, the **Ecobus** costs $2 and takes you from Vieux-Québec Lower Town to Upper Town.

545

DRIVING

In Montréal it is illegal to make a right-hand turn on a red light. Once you're off-island, it is fair game, but not in the city. Full of one-way streets and busy boulevards, Montréal is an easy city to navigate by car. But traffic, especially during rush hour or during construction (most of the time), gets a little out of hand. Parking can also be a real pain in the city, especially on quiet residential streets where permits, usually for residents only, are required. Free parking downtown is especially hard to come by, but there are meters that start around $3 per hour. Most of the meters are now automated and each parking spot is given a specific number; you punch that number into the machine and then place the receipt on your dashboard. You can also pay online or through a new app, P$ Mobile Service—available for iPhone, Blackberry, and Android users—which allows you to extend your parking time or pay when you're in a rush. If you don't see a machine but see a number on the spot, you're not looking far enough; some machines can be half a block away.

For a city that gets such cold winters, underground parking lots are hard to find, though the majority of them exist downtown and offer reasonable day rates. Parking, underground or otherwise, isn't always included with the price of your hotel, so double-check before you book. Overall, driving in the city can be a time waster; it's best to use a car just for side trips and excursions.

Though you *can* make a right turn on a red in Québec City, driving is not ideal, especially if you're heading into Vieux-Québec's Upper and Lower Towns. The small, winding streets make them difficult to navigate, especially if you're not used to that type of driving. In the summer, many of the streets are blocked off to accommodate pedestrians, mainly during the day and into the night. In the winter, it's these same streets that are covered in ice and snow. Though there is less traffic in general in Québec City, parking is still a problem, especially on streets with slopes of 45 degrees. And much like Montréal, the city has very few underground parking lots.

The speed limit on Canadian highways is 100 kilometers per hour (kph), and it's 50 kph on city streets unless otherwise noted. U.S. citizens don't need an international license and neither do drivers from England or France. If your driver's license is in a language other than English or French, you need an International Driver's Permit; see the Québec government website (www.saaq.gouv.qc.ca) for more information. Members of AAA (American Automobile Association, www.aaa.com) are covered under the

Canadian equivalent CAA (www.caa.ca). Gasoline is more expensive than in the United States so fill up before crossing the border.

Rental Cars

Many of the large rental companies (Avis, Budget, Discount) are available in Montréal and Québec City. The minimum age to rent a vehicle is 25, and rates run the gamut from $34 per day to $60 depending on time of year. If you're renting from downtown to head out of the city on weekends, plan ahead; many Montréalers have the same idea.

TAXIS

ESSENTIALS
GETTING AROUND

Montréal and Québec City both have a ton of different taxi companies. **Taxi Champlain** (514/273-2435) and **Taxi Co-op** (514/725-9885) can be found in Montréal. Try **Taxi Coop Québec** (418/525-5191) in Québec City. The initial charge is $3.30, each kilometer adds $1.60, and each minute of waiting is $0.60. Tip is usually 10-15 percent. Some drivers know the city well, others not so much, so make sure you have your destination with the cross street written down to show the driver, especially if it's a word you're unsure how to pronounce.

BICYCLING

In Montréal between April and November **Bixi bikes** (www.bixi.com) are available around the city. These are one of the fastest ways to get around and are easy to use. Swipe your credit card to get a number code, then type that number code into the bike of your choice to unlock it, and you're ready to ride. When you get to your destination return the Bixi to a station and make sure it is locked in. A 24-hour rental will cost you $7 as long as you keep your individual trips under 45 minutes; after that, a charge of $1.50 to $6 for each subsequent 30-minute period will apply. A $32 per month plan is available through the website.

Unless you're an experienced biker and brought your own ride, biking in Québec City is not recommended; there are some seriously steep hills that aren't fun going up or down. That being said, if you're planning on staying exclusively, or at least mostly, in Lower Town or Upper Town, then renting a bike is a great way to get around, and will allow you to ride along the river and the Vieux-Port.

Visas and Officialdom

PASSPORTS AND VISAS

All visitors must have a valid passport or other accepted secure documents to enter the country, even those entering from the United States by road or train. Citizens of the United States, Australia, New Zealand, Israel, Japan, and most western European countries don't need visas to enter Canada for stays up to 180 days. U.S. permanent residents are also exempt. Travelers who travel regularly between Canada and the United States should consider getting a Nexus membership; details are available online (www.cdp.gov).

Nationals from South Africa, China, and about 150 other countries must apply for a temporary resident visa (TRV) in their home country. Full details can be found at **Citizen and Immigration Canada** (888/242-2100, www.cic.gc.ca). Single-entry visitor visas are valid for six months and cost $75; multiple-entry visas last for two years, as long as a single stay doesn't last for longer than six months, and cost $150. A separate visa is required if you intend to work in Canada.

CUSTOMS

Depending on how long your stay in Canada is, you're allowed to take various amounts of goods back home without paying any duty or import tax. There is a limit on the amount of tobacco and liquor you can bring back duty-free, and some countries have a limit on perfumes. For exact amounts, check with the customs department in your home country. Also check the **Canadian Border Services Agency** (505/636-5064, www.cbsa-asfa.gc.ca) for details on bringing in and taking home goods.

There are very strict rules on bringing plants, flowers, food, and other vegetation into the country, so it's not advisable to bring them. If you're 18 years or older, you're allowed to bring into the country 50 cigars or 200 grams of tobacco, as well as 1.14 liters of liquor, 1.5 liters of wine, or 24 cans or bottles of beer. If you bring more, you'll face a hefty fine. Those traveling with their pets will need a health certificate and a rabies vaccination certificate. The vaccination must be carried out 30 days before your departure. Nonresidents can be refunded for the GST (government sales tax) paid on purchases made in Canada. If you want a refund, however, keep your receipts; to be eligible, your receipts must add up to $200. Call 800/668-4748 for details.

Blasphemy the Québécois Way

In Québec, swearing is its own language. Instead of being derived from naughty sexual innuendo, however, swear words come from Catholicism and its practices. Originating in the early 19th century, many of the swear words or *sacres* developed out of a frustration at the church that seemingly controlled everything. The church is much less influential since the Quiet Revolution of the 1960s, and though the swear words are still in use, they are no longer as powerful and have become part of common language. Even English-speakers get into the habit, especially when talking with Québécois friends.

Among the most popular *sacres* and the ones you'll likely hear the most are *crisse* (Christ), *tabarnak* (from tabernacle), *ostie* (from host), and *sacrement* (from sacrement). Like all good swear words, however, they work best when used together, as in *criss d'ostie de tabarnak*, which defies translation.

Another word you might hear is *fucké*, which, weirdly enough, has nothing to do with the English pejorative; instead it means strange or bizarre, as in *"ce film était vraiment fucké,"* or "that film was really weird."

Conduct and Customs

MOVING DAY

While the rest of the country celebrates Canada Day, the nation's national holiday, on July 1, Quebeckers move. It is the unofficial moving day for renters across the province—this is the day most leases change hands—and it is usually a hot, sweaty day with cars, vans, trucks, SUVs, and even bikes loaded to the hilt and headed for new digs. It's also not uncommon to see people simply schlepping their belongings by foot.

Don't even think about renting a car on this day, as there likely won't be any left. A thrifter's paradise, the aftermath of the move leaves sidewalks and alleyways littered with discarded belongings and unwanted junk, which may turn out to be your treasure.

ALCOHOL

As in most Canadian provinces, if you're looking for wine, beer, or spirits, you have to get it at the **SAQ** (Société des Alcools de Québec, www.saq.ca), the store run by the provincial liquor board. Found all over the city, they carry a wide selection of wine and spirits and a small selection of imported beer. Québec differs from most other provinces in that beer and wine can also be purchased in your local grocery and corner stores.

The selection of wine and beer varies from store to store; if you're in an upscale neighborhood, the selection of wine at both the *dépanneur* (corner store) and the grocery store will likely be of a higher caliber than what you'd find elsewhere. (Montréalers commonly use the term "*dép* wine" to denote overpriced cheap-quality wine—though that's not always the case.) If you're looking for beer, a *dép* is your best bet. If you don't find the brand you're looking for, just step into the fridge yourself; it might look like just another display case but step through the camouflaged door and you're in beerville. Drinking age in Québec is 18, and stores stop selling alcohol at 11pm.

STRIP CLUBS

Montréal is known for its strip clubs, a long and proud tradition that's been part of the city's landscape since the early 20th century. They are as out in the open as you can get, with many of them slotted in between shops on rue Ste-Catherine. In fact, Super Sexe, one of the larger clubs in the city, is hard to miss since its facade is adorned with an illuminated mural of flying women in capes and bikinis.

There are over 40 strip clubs in the city, both full-contact and non-contact. Full-contact dances are legal in Québec, and popular. Dancers work on a freelance basis, which allows them to work at any club they'd like.

Montréal embraces its position as a sex-positive city. It's not unusual to see women in strip clubs, and one of the most popular clubs in town, for both men and women, is Café Cleopatra, which has a popular drag cabaret on the second floor. Québec City has far fewer strip clubs, but the same ethos applies (though you won't find them along a main shopping strip).

TIPPING

Tips and service charges aren't covered in the bill; instead a 15-percent tip should be added to the total bill at restaurants and bars at which you run a tab. When you order a drink at a bar, you're usually expected to pay when the drink is brought to you; a $1-2 tip for drinks is the standard. Tip the same for valet parking attendants, bellhops at the hotel, and coat-check attendants. Housekeeping staff should be tipped $3-5.

SMOKING

Since May 2006, smoking is illegal in bars, cafés, clubs, and restaurants and not permitted in enclosed public spaces. Outdoors on the sidewalk or on a restaurant's or bar's patio is fair game. Some hotels, however, still have smoking and non-smoking options, though it's becoming rarer. There are a few cigar bars, including Whisky Café in Montréal and Société Cigare in Québec City, where smoking indoors is allowed due to specialized ventilation systems. You must be 18 years or older to buy tobacco in Québec.

Tips for Travelers

TRAVELING WITH CHILDREN

There are a ton of kid-friendly activities in Montréal and Québec City, most of which will tucker any kid out by the end of the day. Top choices include ice-skating and tobogganing in winter, wading pools and bike rides along the canal in summer. Public parks with playgrounds can be found throughout both cities and are perfect for blowing off some steam. However, some of the sleeker, cooler boutique hotels might not be the most fun for the kids. Children are also given half-price or free entry to most museums and attractions; some venues offer family rates. Hotels will recommend babysitting services if none are available in-house.

WOMEN TRAVELERS

Montréal and Québec are relatively safe cities and women should feel at ease traveling alone in both. Still, the usual rules apply, women should avoid walking alone on quiet streets and dimly lit areas, such as Mont-Royal, late at night. Violence is far less prevalent here than in the States, but if you are attacked or sexually assaulted call 911 or the **Sexual Assault Center** (514/934-4504 in Montréal and 418/522-2120 in Québec City).

LGBT TRAVELERS

Québec is one of the top destinations for gay travelers. In 1977 Québec became the second political entity (after Holland) to include a non-discrimination clause on the basis of sexual orientation in its charter of rights. Gay marriage is legal in Québec, and attitudes toward homosexuality in the province are open and tolerant.

Of the two cities, Montréal is the queer capital, and **Tourisme Montréal** (www.tourisme-montreal.org) even has a gay and lesbian mini-site with suggestions for hotels, restaurants, meet-ups, and beyond. There's even the **Village Tourism Information Centre** (249 rue St-Jacques #302, 888/595-8110, summer Tues.-Thurs., winter Mon.-Fri.), which offers information on everything from restaurants to places to work out and is run by the **Québec Gay Chamber of Commerce** (www.ccgq.ca). **CAEO Québec** (www.caeoquebec.org) offers services for Montréal's English-speaking LGBT community and is behind **Gay Line** (888/505-1010), a help line that offers information on accommodations, services, and events.

Though there are a number of LGBT publications, monthly magazine *Fugues* (www.fugues.com) is the most comprehensive and has information on everything from hotels to saunas and upcoming gay events. It's available for free at racks around the city.

Most public buildings, including tourist offices, museums, and sights, are wheelchair accessible. Métro stations in Montréal, however, are not accessible; instead almost all major bus routes are serviced by NOVA LFS buses adapted for wheelchairs. See www.stm.info for full details about your journey.

Access to Travel (www.accesstotravel.gc.ca) is a guide to accessible transportation across the country.

Kéroul (514/252-3104, www.keroul.qc.ca) is an association that specializes in tourism for people with disabilities. It publishes *Québec Accessible,* which lists 1,000-plus hotels, restaurants, museums, and theaters that are accessible. For English speakers, there is *The Accessible Road,* which offers information on everything from the most accessible top sights to how to get a handicapped parking sticker. It can be downloaded for free from the website.

Health and Safety

HOSPITALS AND CLINICS

Canadians have free health care, but it's not free for visitors, so get travel insurance before you leave your home country. Montréal has a number of high-ranking hospitals, but the emergency room wait can be lengthy, and if you're not a Canadian citizen, the treatment could be pricey (though not compared to U.S. hospitals).

Emergency rooms can be found in Montréal at **Montréal General Hospital** (1650 ave. Cedar, 514/934-1934, ext. 42190) and **Royal Victoria Hospital** (ave. des Pins W., 514/934-1934, ext. 31557). There's also the **Montréal Children's Hospital** (2300 Tupper, 514/412-4400). In Québec City, head to the **Hôpital Laval** (2725 chemin Ste-Foy, 418/656-8711).

For minor maladies, visit walk-in clinic **CLSC** (514/527-2361, www.santemontreal.qc.ca); the one closest to downtown Montréal is at Guy-Concordia Métro station (1801 blvd. de Maisonneuve W., 514/934-0354), or call to find the closest one. In Québec City, the closest clinic can be found by calling 418/529-4777 or checking online at www.csssvc.qc.ca. Though the clinics will be glad to help you, you will have to pay cash to see a doctor; they don't take debit or credit.

If you're feeling unwell and just want some advice, call the health hotline (811) from any land line to speak with a nurse 24 hours a day.

Winter Essentials

If you want to fit in among the locals during winter's deep freeze you need two things: a parka and a pair of Sorel boots.

- **Parka:** When it comes to parkas, there are two schools: The younger generation goes for a selection from Canada Goose, while many mature Quebeckers opt for the Kanuk. Both are made in Canada and offer that important balance of warmth without the puffiness. When buying a parka the goal is to avoid the "Michelin Man" look; don't buy white and stay away from anything that has a ringed effect. Make sure it's got a fur-trimmed hood and covers your bum—good coverage is essential, especially when you want to take a crazy carpet down Mont-Royal.

- **Boots:** Made with a heavy insulated rubber sole and sturdy leather, Sorel winter boots have been a Canadian staple since 1959. Introduced to the market by Kaufman Footwear of Kitchener, Ontario, the boots were an instant hit. Originally they were made in Canada, but the company was bought by Columbia Sports in 2000. Though the boots are no longer Canadian owned and made, there is still a strong connection to their Canadian heritage. The ingenious construction of a thermal, waterproof sole paired with a more stylish upper is ideal for city life when 99.9 percent of the time you're walking through freezing gray slush.

- **Fur:** Another popular winter material in Québec is fur, and it's not unusual to see both men and women covered in fur from head to toe. If you find fur offensive, try to suppress your inner activist and instead take a deep breath—see that? Your nose is now completely frozen. Fur in Québec is less about style and more about survival and heritage, and many of the furs have been passed down through family members.

PHARMACIES

There are two big pharmacy chains in Montréal, Pharmaprix (www.pharmaprix.ca) and Jean Coutu (www.jeancoutu.com), both of which offer late-night services at various locations. **Pharmaprix** (1500 rue Ste-Catherine W., 514/933-4744, daily 8am-midnight) also has a 24-hour location north of Mont-Royal (5122 chemin de la Côte-des-Neiges, 514/738-8464). **Jean Coutu** (1675 rue Ste-Catherine W., 514/933-4221, Mon.-Sat. 8am-midnight, Sun. 9am-midnight) is another option.

In Québec City, the largest pharmacy is **Jean Coutu** (110 blvd. René-Lévesque, 418/522-1235, Mon.-Sat. 9am-9pm, Sun. 10am-9pm), near avenue Cartier.

EMERGENCY SERVICES

The fire department, police, and ambulance can all be reached by dialing **911.** When in doubt, you can reach the operator by dialing **0.** There's also the **Poison Center** (800/463-5060) if you're worried about something you've ingested.

CRIME AND HARASSMENT

Both Montréal and Québec City are relatively safe and violent crime is rare. Tourists are more likely to be the targets of thieves, like pickpockets at crowded bars, markets, and Métro stations. Cars with out-of-province license plates are also targets, so make sure not to leave anything of value in the car and remove your car registration and identification papers. Pedestrians in Montréal should be careful, especially late at night when drivers don't always heed stop signs.

Information and Services

MONEY

Prices quoted in this book are in Canadian dollars. Canadian coins come in 5-cent (nickel), 10-cent (dime), 25-cent (quarter), $1 (loonie), and $2 (toonie) pieces. Paper money comes in $5 (blue), $10 (purple), $20 (green), $50 (red), and $100 (brown). In 2013, the government phased out the penny, so most companies round up their prices to the closest 5-cents. Though the Canadian dollar's value was once much lower than the American dollar, it now trades at a few cents off par; www.xe.com has the most current rates.

ATMs

ATMs are all round the city, not just in banks. Though if you're getting money out from a foreign account, the safest way is to get it from a proper bank machine, to avoid fraud. Most banks charge you an additional fee when you withdraw a currency different from that of your home country as well as the original transaction fee. Check your daily withdrawal limit, so you don't get caught short.

Changing Money

Counters dedicated solely to exchanging money are becoming rarer and rarer. It's much simpler just to head to the bank; you'll find plenty in Montréal on rue Ste-Catherine, boulevard St-Laurent, and rue St-Denis. Foreign-exchange desks can also be found at the main tourist office and at the airport. In Montréal there's **Calforex** (1230 Peel, 514/392-9100), and in Québec City try **Transchange International** (43 rue de Baude, 418/694-6906).

Credit Cards

Major international credit cards are accepted at most stores, hotels, and restaurants. Carrying a credit card means you don't have the worry of carrying cash and it also gives you excellent exchange rates. Visa and MasterCard are the most widely accepted, though certain places also accept American Express and Diners Club.

MAPS AND TOURIST INFORMATION

Airports have information offices open year-round. Information for Montréal can be obtained from **Tourisme Montréal** (877/266-5687, www.tourism-montreal.org). For Québec province info about Montréal, Québec City, and environs, visit **Bonjour Québec** (www.bonjourquebec.com).

Montréal has two main tourist offices. **Centre Infotouriste** (1001 rue Square Dorchester, daily 9am-6pm) will help you rent boats or cars, plan a city tour, and even reserve a hotel room. Though not as big, **Old Montréal Tourist Office** (174 rue Notre-Dame E., June-Oct. daily 9am-7pm, Nov.-May daily 9am-5pm) is also helpful.

In Vieux-Québec's Upper Town there's **Centre Infotouriste** (12 rue Ste-Anne, 800/363-7777, late June-early Oct. daily 9am-7pm, early Oct.-late June daily 9am-5pm), and backing on to the Plains of Abraham is another **Centre Infotouriste** (835 ave. Wilfrid-Laurier, 800/266-5687, late June-late Aug. daily 9am-7pm, late Aug.-mid-June daily 9am-5pm).

COMMUNICATIONS AND MEDIA
Phones

Thanks to the massive popularity of cell phones, public pay phones are becoming almost impossible to find, but if you do manage to fine one, a single local call will set you back $0.50. Though many are coin operated, some also accept phone cards and credit cards. The main area code for Montréal is **514**, though some newer numbers have the **438** area code. Québec City's area code is **418**. When dialing local numbers, you must include the area code.

Toll-free numbers begin with **800, 866,** or **888** and must be preceded by a 1. Most of these numbers work in both Canada and the United States, but some may only work in a specified province. Dialing **0** for the operator or **911** for emergency services is free of charge from land lines and public phones, but calling **411** for directory assistance will cost you.

Cell Phones

Tribrand model cell phones working on GSM 1900 and other frequencies are the only foreign cell phones that will work in Canada. If your phone doesn't work, it might be worth picking up an inexpensive phone at an electronics store and getting a pay-as-you-go plan. Travelers from the United States will likely have service, though roaming charges will probably apply; check with your provider for details.

Mobile Apps **555**

Both cities have mobile apps that you can download for free for both Android and iPhone.

If you're using public transit to get around, the **STM** mobile app will help you navigate Montréal's buses and subway system. **DistrictMontreal** will clue you into what's happening and what events to catch on your visit.

Québec City's tourism board has created apps for both platforms, and their website is also mobile-friendly. Head to www.quebecregion.com to check them out before downloading from the appropriate app store.

Internet Services

A number of cafés offer free Wi-Fi; you can register for free at **Île Sans Fil** (www.ilesansfil.org) and find out where the 150-plus places are where you can get online with your laptop. Visit www.zapquebec.org for free Wi-Fi in Québec. If you left your computer at home and can't check your email at your hotel, your best bets are the local libraries.

In Québec City, a couple of libraries offer free Internet access to visitors. **Bibliothèque Saint-Jean-Baptiste** (755 rue St-Jean, 418/641-6798, Mon.-Tues. and Thurs. noon-5pm, Wed. noon-8pm, Fri. 10am-5:30pm, Sat. 1pm-5pm), in the Faubourg Saint-Jean-Baptiste, offers an hour of free access, and **Bibliothèque Gabrielle-Roy** (350 rue St-Joseph E., 418/641-6789, Mon.-Fri. 8:30am-9pm, Sat.-Sun. 10am-5pm) in Saint-Roch offers two hours of free access.

In Montréal, the **Grand Bibliothéque** (475 blvd. De Maisonneuve E., 514/873-1100, www.banq.qc.ca, Tues.-Thurs. 10am-10pm, Fri.-Sun. 10am-6pm) offers free Internet access as well as Wi-Fi. **Atwater Library** (1200 Atwater, 514/935-7344, www.atwaterlibrary.ca, Mon. and Wed. 10am-8pm, Tues., Thurs., and Fri. 10am-6pm, Sat. 10am-5pm) offers Internet services for $4 per hour as well as free Wi-Fi access.

Many hotels, though not all, offer free Wi-Fi access, and the majority also have public computers.

Mail Services

Montréal's main post office is at 1250 rue University, but there are a number of locations downtown and around. If you know the post code of where you're staying, you can look up the closest branch to you at www.canadapost.ca or call **Canada Post** (866/607-6301) for general information.

Québec City's main post office is at 5 rue du Fort in Upper Town and offers a number of services. Stamps can also be purchased at newsstands, convenience stores, and tourist shops. Standard first-class airmail postage for letters and postcards costs $0.65 to

Canadian destinations and $1.10 to the United States. Other destinations cost $1.85.

Newspapers and Periodicals

Montréal's only English-language daily paper is the *Gazette* (www.montrealgazette.com), which covers local and national news as well as arts and politics.

The Globe & Mail (www.globeandmail.com) and the *National Post* (www.nationalpost.com) are the country's two national papers, and while both cover national and international events as well as the arts, the *Globe* leans more to the center-left and the *Post* to the right.

For French readers there's the federalist *La Presse* and separatist-leaning *Le Devoir,* both of which cover the news and art of the entire province, not just the Francophone community (though that's a large part of it). There's also *Le Journal de Montréal,* a tabloid paper, that mainly covers local events. And in Québec there's *Le Soleil,* a great little paper with a focus on events in the capital. There's also the Francophone alternative weekly *Voir* (www.voir.ca), in both a Montréal and Québec version, great for getting the latest scoop on what's going on in town or for scoping out their restaurant reviews.

L'actualité is the Québec monthly news magazine, and *Maclean's* is Canada's only weekly news magazine.

Television

The main public-radio and television stations are run by the Canadian Broadcasting Corporation. The CBC is the English-language component and Radio-Canada is the French-language component; both are revered for their long broadcast history. The other major English-language network is the Canadian Television Network (CTV), which broadcasts both Canadian and U.S. programs as well as nightly newscasts.

For Francophone audiences there's Télé-Québec (TVA) and Télévision Quatre-Saison (TQS), both of which broadcast news programs, movies, and shows from France, as well as dubbed American sitcoms and dramas.

Radio

There are a number of Francophone and Anglophone radio stations in Montréal, but stations in Québec are mostly Francophone, with the exception of the English-language artists they play. Many young, English-speaking Montréalers are fans of CBC Montréal 1 (88.5 FM), sort of the area's version of NPR. It has educational and cultural programs, and CBF (95.1 FM) is its French counterpart. Fans of Led Zeppelin hear them on heavy rotation on CHOM (97.7 FM); though it also plays alternative music, it's primarily classic rock. CKUT (90.3 FM) is a nonprofit station that plays an eclectic mix of music and news stories. CISM (89.3 FM) is Université de Montréal's station, with a focus on indie and Francophone tunes. CJFM (95.9 FM) is Virgin Radio playing Top 40 hits all day long, and CKGM (990 AM) is your classic oldies station.

In Québec City, however, Anglophones can tune into CBC Québec 1 (104.7 FM streaming), the city's only English-language radio station for all their cultural, news, and educational programs. Tune into CHYZ (94.3 FM) to hear what the students at Université Laval are listening to. CHIK (98.9 FM) gives you top pop and Francophone hits, and Radio-Canada (106.3 FM) keeps you informed in French about news and culture.

WEIGHTS AND MEASURES
Electricity
Like the United States and Japan, Canada uses 110-volt, 60-cycle electrical power. Canadian electrical goods have a plug with two flat, vertical prongs and sometimes a third rounded prong. Travelers from outside North America should bring a plug adapter for small appliances.

Measurements
Canada uses the metric system of measurement. Distances are measured in kilometers, liquids in liters and milliliters, but height, strangely enough, is measured in feet.

Time
Montréal and Québec City are both on eastern standard time (EST/EDT), the same as New York and Toronto. Canada switches to daylight saving time (one hour later than standard time) from the second Sunday in March to the first Sunday in November. "Spring forward, fall back," is a simple way to remember how to set your clocks properly. In Québec the 24-hour clock is used for most schedules, including movies and trains.

Resources

Glossary

l'Abitation: the first settlement (habitation)

allongé: a long espresso coffee, the French name for an Italian *lungo*

Anglophone: a native English speaker

Bill 101: a Québec law that deals with French and English language issues

boîte à chansons: a place where you can hear singer/songwriters (*chansonniers*) play

boréal: the type of forest that is found in the province of Québec

branchée: plugged in, which translates to hip, or cool, in the French vernacular

brasserie: a brewery or pub

brioche: a type of sweet French bread

cabane à sucre: a sugar shack; this is where you go to see maple syrup tapped from trees and eat maple-drenched treats

café: where you buy coffee as well as the drink itself; usually refers to an espresso

calèche: a horse-drawn carriage

chansonnier: a folk singer/songwriter

côte: hill; if a street has *"côte"* in its name, it's on a hill

coureurs de bois: early fur hunters and adventurers who helped explore North America

dépanneur: meaning "to help out"; it's the name for convenience stores in Québec, which are commonly referred to as *"dép."*

First Nations: the name for Canada's Amerindian population

frites: French fries

joual: a popular form of slang

loonie: Canadian one-dollar coin

Nouvelle France: the name given to Québec by the French; it also means New France

pâté chinois: a meat, potato, and vegetable pie similar to shepherd's pie

patriotes: the name given to patriots who led an uprising against the government in 1837; it's used today to denote those who are against federal rule

pont: a bridge

poudreuse: blowing snow

quai: quay that juts out into the water

Quebecker: English name for all native citizens of the province of Québec

Québécois: the name for the Francophone population in the province as well as

Refus Global (Total Refusal): a manifesto of a group of Québec artists that radically changed the face of modern Québec art

sacres: the name for Québécois swear words

sandwicherie: a place that makes sandwiches

sloche: slush made from melted snow

sovereigntists: those who want Québec to separate from the rest of Canada

stimés: hot dog with a steamed bun

Sulpicians: society of Catholic priests founded in Paris in 1641 who were part of the founding of Québec

table d'hôte: a fixed-price meal

terrasse: an outdoor patio

terroir: food products that come from the area, as in "terroir" cooking

tire sur la neige: maple syrup that has been frozen on snow, a popular treat during the sugaring-off season

toastés: hot dog with a toasted bun

toonie: a Canadian two-dollar coin

tourtière: a meat pie made with everything from pork and beef to game

viennoiseries: pastries and sweet breads usually eaten at breakfast

French Phrasebook

If you're uncomfortable about breaking out your rusty 10th-grade French, relax. You might not even crease the spine of this phrasebook, since just about everyone in Montréal understands English, even if they're not adept at speaking it. In Québec City their English isn't as fluid, but those who work in tourism and hospitality speak it flawlessly. Even if you do feel confident with your French, the Québécois accent will take some getting used to, and the language you hear on the street won't have much to do with the words you read in this phrasebook. The Québécois also have a tendency to speak very fast, so don't be afraid to ask them to slow down if you're having trouble understanding.

As has been explained throughout the guide, language is a central issue in Québec, so a good rule of thumb is to be polite; the Québécois are especially receptive to people who are at least trying to speak a little French, and they're always encouraging. Throw in a few easy French words here and there like *bonjour* or *merci* and you'll soon earn a friend for life, or at least gain their respect.

PRONUNCIATION

French is known for being difficult to pronounce—and as payback for creating such a difficult language, French-speakers are unable to properly pronounce any other language. When it comes to phonetic pronunciation, French is as bad as English. Most of the spellings and the pronunciations don't have much in common, which can make learning French difficult. Here are a few guidelines to get you started.

Vowels

Vowels in French can be confusing for an English speaker: the "a" is **e,** the "e" is **i,** and the "u" is from outer space. Here is the secret:

a pronounced a, as in "cat"

i pronounced ee, as in "free"

y pronounced the same way as **i**

o pronounced ah, as in "dog," or oh, as in "bone"

u This vowel has always been a tough one for English-speakers. The closest you can get would be to put your lips and tongue in position to say "oh" and try to say "ee" instead. Something like the ew in "stew" is not that far off.

e pronounced uh, as in "about." Before two or more consonants, it is pronounced eh as in "set." At the end of a word, such as *chaise* (chair), **e** is silent, except in words of one syllable like *je* (I), where it is pronounced "uh."

Vowel Groups

To make things harder, French assembles certain letters to produce new sounds.

ai pronounced eh, as in "set," as well as **ei**

au pronounced oh, as in "bone," as well as **eau**

eu pronounced uh, as in "about." It is sometimes spelled **œu,** as in *œuf* or *sœur*

oi pronounced wa, as in "wagon"

ou pronounced oo, as in "foot"

Nasal Vowels

A typical aspect of French speech is nasal vowels, vowels pronounced through both the mouth and nose. They are as difficult for English-speakers to reproduce as the **u** and will require quite a bit of phonetic gymnastics before you get it right.

an, am pronounced ahn, as in "aunt"

en, em pronounced pretty close to ahn, combined with the on of "honk"

in where the a of "bag" is nasalized as in "anchor." You'll find more or less the same sound in many different spellings, such as **im, un, um, yn, ym, ain, aim, ein,** and **eim**

on, om pronounced on, as in "long"; a nasalized **o**

Accents

French has five different accents that stick to vowels and make French as exotic to read as it is to hear: In French they are called *accent aigu* ('), *accent* grave (`` ` ``), *accent circonflexe* (^), *accent tréma* (¨), and the *cédille* (ç), which is only used with the letter **c**.

The circumflex and grave accents appear as **è, à, ù, ê, â, û, î,** and **ô.** Except for **ê** and **è,** which are pronounced eh as in "set," and **ô,** which always sounds like oh as in "bone," the accents don't change the pronunciation of the letters; they are mere decoration.

The acute accent, as in **é,** is pronounced ay as in "day," but shorter. The cedilla makes **c** sound like **s.**

Last but not least, the dieresis (*tréma*) separates two vowel sounds, such as **ï** in *naïve,* which is not pronounced nev, but as two separate syllables, na-ive.

Consonants

Most French consonants are similar to their English equivalents, even if there are a few differences. For example, *some* final consonants are silent; rather than pronouncing *vous* as "vooz," you'd say "voo." In general the following consonants are usually silent: **b, d, g, m, n, p, t, x,** and **z. S** is always silent in plurals but often pronounced otherwise. Others are generally pronounced: **c, f,** and **l. R** is usually pronounced, except in the endings **er** and **ier.**

c pronounced k as in "kick" before **a, o,** or **u,** and s as in "set" before **e, i,** or **y.** Combine **c** and **h,** as in *chance* (luck), and it is pronounced like sh as in "ship"

g pronounced g as in "god," except when placed before **e, i,** or **y,** when it is pronounced zh as in "measure." Combine it with **n,** as in *vigne* (vine), and it is pronounced like ny in "canyon"

h always silent

j pronounced zh as in "measure"

ll pronounced y as in "yes," in words like *famille*

r emphasized more strongly than in English and comes from the far back of the throat

BASIC EXPRESSIONS

Hello *Bonjour*

Hi *Salut*

Good-bye *Au revoir/Salut*

Good morning/afternoon *Bonjour*

Good evening *Bonsoir*

Good night *Bonne nuit*

How are you? (courteous) *Allez-vous?*

How are you doing? (colloquial) *Ça va?/Vas-tu?*

Fine, thank you. *Ça va bien, merci.*

And you? *Et vous?*

See you later. *À plus tard/À bientôt.*

Nice to meet you. *Enchanté.*

Yes *Oui*

No *Non*

Please *S'il vous plaît*

Thank you *Merci*

You're welcome *Bienvenu/de rien*

Excuse me *Excusez-moi*

Sorry *Pardon/désolé*

What's your name? *Comment vous appelez-vous?*

My name is . . . *Je m'appelle...*

Where are you from? *D'où venez-vous?*

I'm from . . . *Je viens de...*

Do you speak English? *Parlez-vous anglais?*

I don't speak French. *Je ne parle pas français.*

I don't understand. *Je ne comprends pas.*

I don't know. *Je ne sais pas.*

Can you please repeat? *Pourriez-vous répéter?*

What's it called? *Ça s'appelle?*

Would you like . . . ? *Voulez-vous . . . ?*

TERMS OF ADDRESS

I *je*

you *tu*

he *il*

she *elle*

we *nous*

you (plural) *vous*

they *ils/elles*

Mr./Sir *monsieur*

Mrs./Madame *madame*

Miss *mademoiselle*

young man *jeune homme*

young woman *jeune fille*

child *enfant*

brother/sister *frère/sœur*

father/mother *père/mère*

son/daughter *fils/fille*

husband/wife *mari/femme*

friend *ami/amie*

boyfriend/girlfriend *copain/copine*

married *marié/mariée*

single *célibataire*

divorced *divorcé/divorcée*

QUESTIONS

When? *Quand?*

What? *Quoi?*

What is it? *Qu'est-ce que c'est?*

Who? *Qui?*

Why? *Pourquoi?*

How? *Comment?*
Where is …? *Où est…?*
What's it called? *Ça s'appelle?*
Would you like …? *Voulez-vous …?*

GETTING AROUND

Where is …? *Où est…?*
How far away is …? *À quelle distance est…?*
How can I get to …? *Puis-je aller à …?*
bus *bus*
car *voiture*
train *train*
bus station *la station d'autobus*
train station *la gare de trains*
airport *l'aéroport*
What time do we leave? *À quelle heure est le départ?*
What time do we arrive? *À quelle heure arrive-t-on?*
a one-way ticket *un aller simple*
a round-trip ticket? *un aller retour*
Can you take me to this address? *Pourriez-vous m'emmener à cette adresse?*
north *nord*
south *sud*
east *est*
west *ouest*
left/right *gauche/droite*
straight ahead *tout droit*
entrance *entrée*
exit *sortie*
first *premier*
last *dernier*
next *prochain*

ACCOMMODATIONS

Are there any rooms available? *Avez-vous des chambres disponibles?*
I'd like to make a reservation. *J'aimerais faire une réservation.*
I want a single room. *J'aimerais une chambre simple.*
Is there a double room? *Y a-t-il une chambre double?*
private bathroom *salle de bains privée*
key *clé*
one night *une nuit*
Can you change the sheets/towels? *Pourriez-vous changer les draps/les serviettes?*
Could you please wake me up? *Pourriez-vous me réveiller?*
Is breakfast included? *Est-ce que le petit déjeuner est inclus?*

FOOD

to eat *manger*

to drink *boire*

breakfast *déjeuner*

lunch *dîner*

dinner *souper*

Can I see the menu? *Puis-je voir le menu?*

We're ready to order. *Nous sommes prêts à commander.*

Can I have some more wine? *Puis-je avoir un peu plus de vin?*

Can you bring me the bill please? *Pourriez-vous apporter l'addition?*

Is the service/the tip included? *Est-ce que le service est compris?*

I'm a vegetarian. *Je suis végétarien.*

It was delicious. *C'était délicieux.*

hot *chaud*

cold *froid*

sweet *sucré*

salty *salé*

bread *pain*

rice *riz*

Enjoy! *Bon appétit!*

Meat and Fish

meat *viande*

beef *bœuf*

pork *porc*

lamb *agneau*

chicken *poulet*

ham *jambon*

fish *poisson*

salmon *saumon*

mussels *moules*

oysters *huîtres*

shrimp *crevette*

tuna *thon*

rare *saignant*

medium *à point*

well done *bien cuit*

roasted *rôti*

boiled *bouilli*

grilled *grillé*

fried *frit*

Eggs and Dairy

milk *lait*

cream *crème*

butter *beurre*

cheese *fromage*
ice cream *crème glacée*
egg *œuf*
hard-boiled egg *œuf dur*
scrambled eggs *œufs brouillés*
poached egg *œuf poché*

Vegetables and Fruits

vegetables *légumes*
carrot *carotte*
tomato *tomate*
potato *patate/pomme de terre*
cucumber *concombre*
pepper *poivron*
mushrooms *champignons*
eggplant *aubergine*
peas *petits pois*
cabbage *chou*
apple *pomme*
pear *poire*
banana *banane*
orange *orange*
lemon *citron*
grape *raisin*
strawberry *fraise*
blueberry *bleuet*
raspberry *framboise*

Seasoning and Spices

sugar *sucre*
salt *sel*
black pepper *poivre*
onion *oignon*
garlic *ail*
olive oil *huile d'olive*
vinegar *vinaigre*
cinnamon *cannelle*
basil *basilic*
parsley *persil*
mint *menthe*
ginger *gingembre*

Drinks

drinks *boissons*
beer *bière*
wine *vin*

wine list *la carte des vins*
cheers! *à votre santé!*
water *eau*
ice *glace*
juice *jus*
filtered coffee *café filtre*
coffee with milk *café au lait*
black coffee *café noir*

SHOPPING

money *argent*
ATM *guichet automatique*
credit card *carte de crédit*
to buy *acheter*
to shop *magasiner*
I don't have change. *Je n'ai pas de monnaie.*
more *plus*
less *moins*
a good price *un bon prix*
sales *soldes*
How much does it cost? *Combien ça coûte?*
That's too expensive. *C'est trop cher.*
discount *rabais*
Can I try it on? *Est-ce que je peux l'essayer?*
It's too tight. *C'est trop serré.*
It's too big. *C'est trop grand.*
Can I exchange it? *Est-ce que je peux l'échanger?*

HEALTH AND SAFETY

Can you help me? *Pouvez-vous m'aider?*
I don't feel well. *Je ne me sens pas bien.*
I'm sick. *Je suis malade.*
Is there a pharmacy close by? *Y a-t-il une pharmacie pas loin?*
Can you call a doctor? *Pouvez-vous appeler un docteur?*
I need to go to the hospital. *Je dois aller à l'hôpital.*
medicine *médicament*
condom *condom, préservatif*
Is this neighborhood safe? *Est-ce que ce quartier est sécuritaire?*
Help! *À l'aide!, Au secours!*
Call the police! *Appeler la police.*
thief *voleur*

COMMUNICATIONS

to talk, to speak *parler*
to hear, to listen *écouter, entendre*
to make a phone call *faire un appel téléphonique*

cell phone *cellulaire*
What's your phone number? *Quel est ton numéro de téléphone?*
What's your email address? *Quelle est ton adresse électronique?*
collect call *appel à frais virés*
Do you have Internet? *Avez-vous Internet ici?*
post office *bureau de poste*
letter *lettre*
stamp *timbre*
postcard *carte postale*

NUMBERS

0 *zéro*
1 *un*
2 *deux*
3 *trois*
4 *quatre*
5 *cinq*
6 *six*
7 *sept*
8 *huit*
9 *neuf*
10 *dix*
11 *onze*
12 *douze*
13 *treize*
14 *quatorze*
15 *quinze*
16 *seize*
17 *dix-sept*
18 *dix-huit*
19 *dix-neuf*
20 *vingt*
21 *vingt-et-un*
30 *trente*
40 *quarante*
50 *cinquante*
60 *soixante*
70 *soixante-dix*
80 *quatre-vingt*
90 *quatre-vingt dix*
100 *cent*
101 *cent un*
200 *deux cent*
500 *cinq cent*
1000 *mille*
2000 *deux mille*

TIME

What time is it? *Quelle heure est-il?*
It's 2 o'clock. *Il est deux heures.*
It's 2:15. *Il est deux heures et quart.*
It's 2:30. *Il est deux heures et demie.*
It's 2:45. *Il est deux heures quarante-cinq.*
in two hours *dans deux heures*
now *maintenant*
before *avant*
after *après*
late/early *tard/tôt*
When? *Quand?*

DAYS AND MONTHS

day *jour*
night *nuit*
morning *matin*
afternoon *après-midi*
yesterday *hier*
tomorrow *demain*
today *aujourd'hui*
week *semaine*
month *mois*
year *année*
Monday *lundi*
Tuesday *mardi*
Wednesday *mercredi*
Thursday *jeudi*
Friday *vendredi*
Saturday *samedi*
Sunday *dimanche*
January *janvier*
February *février*
March *mars*
April *avril*
May *mai*
June *juin*
July *juillet*
August *août*
September *septembre*
October *octobre*
November *novembre*
December *décembre*

SEASONS AND WEATHER

season *saison*

spring *printemps*
summer *été*
autumn *automne*
winter *hiver*
weather *temps/météo*
sun *soleil*
It's sunny. *Il fait soleil.*
rain *pluie*
It's raining. *Il pleut.*
snow *neige*
It's snowing. *Il neige.*
snowstorm *tempête de neige*
ice *glace/verglas*
It's hot. *Il fait chaud.*
It's cold. *Il fait froid.*

Suggested Reading

HISTORY AND GENERAL INFORMATION

Dickinson, John A., and Brian Young. *A Short History of Québec.* Montréal: McGill-Queen's University Press, 1993, revised 2008. Originally written in 1992, this book is now into its fourth edition and offers a comprehensive overview of the province's social and economic development from pre-European to modern times. This latest edition includes reflections on the Bouchard-Taylor Commission on Accommodation and Cultural Differences, which examined attitudes toward immigration and immigrants in the province.

Fox, Joanna. *Montréal's Best Terrasses.* Montréal: Véhicule Press, 2012. One of Montréal's greatest attributes is its outdoor dinning options. Restaurant reviewer and food industry insider Joanna Fox gives readers the low-down on 60 of the city's best patios, with a selection to suit all tastes and budgets.

Grescoe, Taras. *Sacré Blues: An Unsentimental Journey through Quebec.* Toronto: Macfarlane Walter & Ross, 2001. Montréal author Taras Grescoe's modern account of Québec explores the stranger side of the province's pop culture, takes readers to a Francophone country-and-western festival, meets up with UFO-obsessed followers of Raël, and, of course, deconstructs a Montréal Canadiens hockey game. The book won the Québec Writers' Federation First Book Award and the Mavis Gallant Prize for Nonfiction in 2001.

Jenish, D'Arcy. *The Montreal Canadiens: 100 Years of Glory.* Toronto: Doubleday Canada, 2008. Published to coincide with the hockey team's 100th anniversary, this is the definitive history of the team—from the days of their first Stanley Cup win to the return of former player Bob Gainey as general manager. Even if you're not a fan, this book provides an insider's look at one of the NHL's most storied teams.

Lacoursière, Jacques, and Robin Philpot. *A People's History of Québec.* Montréal: Baraka Books, 2009. First published in French, this concise book looks at the history of the province through the people that discovered, explored, and inhabited it. The focus is on day-to-day life and offers little-known details, like the despicable "mixed dancing" at times of celebration and early settlers' love of *charivari,* a loud, rambunctious party through the streets.

FICTION AND MEMOIRS

Carrier, Roch. *The Hockey Sweater.* Montréal: Tundra Books, 1979. This semi-autobiographical children's picture book is one of the most memorable Canadian stories. It tells the tale of a boy in small-town Québec who orders a Canadiens hockey sweater from the Eaton's catalogue only to receive a Toronto Maple-Leaf jersey. Full of subtle comments on Québec and the rest of Canada, it's a touching story that has been immortalized by an NFB film.

Cohen, Leonard. *The Favourite Game.* New York: Vintage, 1963. In this semi-autobiographical book, protagonist Lawrence Breavman wanders through the Montréal streets with his best friend and confidant, Krantz, reminisces about his years at summer camp, and tries to understand the death of his father.

Doucet, Julie. *365 Days: A Diary.* Montréal: Drawn & Quarterly, 2008. Born and raised in Montréal, comic artist Julie Doucet first gained recognition as an artist for her zine *Dirty Plotte,* a funny, demented take on her own life experiences. *365 Days* offers an intimate look at the artistic community Doucet surrounded herself with in her early days and the experience of an artist in Montréal.

Hage, Rawi. *Cockroach.* Toronto: House of Anansi Press, 2009. IMPAC-Dublin award-winner Rawi Hage's second effort, *Cockroach* tells the tale of a struggling immigrant living in Montréal's underbelly. Hage, who is originally from Lebanon, brings a unique perspective and an adept eye to the Montréal experience.

MacLennan, Hugh. *Two Solitudes.* Toronto: McClelland & Stewart, 1945. The title of this book has become emblematic of the country's French/English cultural and linguistic divide. Set between World War I and 1939, the book takes place in Saint-Marc-des-Érables, a small Québec town, and the booming, predominantly English city of Montréal. Centered on Paul Tallard, a Québécois at home with both languages, the book follows him on a quest to find his own identity and a way of defining the Canadian experience.

O'Neill, Heather. *Lullabies for Little Criminals.* Toronto: Harper Perennial, 2006. Heather O'Neill was born and (mostly) raised in Montréal, and her debut novel tells the story of Baby, a 12-year-old girl growing up in the seedy area of lower St-Laurent with her young, well-meaning junkie father. There is a touching humanity to O'Neill's writing, and her depiction of Montréal in all its real, gritty glory is fascinating.

Proulx, Monique. *Les Aurores Montréales.* Toronto: Douglas & McIntyre, 1997. Twenty-seven short stories make up this collection that takes place in pre- and post-referendum Québec. Weaving in and out of Montréal, the stories look at the lives of Quebeckers and how they are affected by the changing times.

Richler, Mordecai. *Son of a Smaller Hero.* Paris: André Deutsch, 1955. From Mile End's Jewish ghetto to the bed of a downtown non-Jewish woman, this book follows prodigal son Noah Adler as he searches to find his identity in the neighborhoods and communities that make up Montréal.

Tremblay, Michel. *Les Belles Sœurs.* Vancouver: Talonbooks, revised ed., 1992. Arguably the most important Québécois writer of his generation, Tremblay was only 23 years old when he wrote this play in 1965. First presented in 1968 at Théâtre du Rideau Vert, it ushered in a new era of Québécois theater. Written in *joual* (working-class slang), the play is set in the triplexes of Montréal's Plateau and follows the exploits of an extended family.

Internet Resources

An Endless Banquet
www.endlessbanquet.blogspot.com
This Montréal couple closely connected with the food scene—she's a chef at the FoodLab, he's a former restaurant critic—give readers the lowdown on restaurants and food happenings around the city. From the best late-night burger to the best place to blow $200 on a meal, they've got you covered.

Bonjour Québec
www.bonjourquebec.com

The province's official tourism website has comprehensive information on anything and everything to do with the province, from national parks to kid-friendly fun.

Cult Montréal
www.cultmontreal.com

This website and bi-monthly publication gives you the goods on the city's cultural happenings and covers everything from news stories to movies, music, art events, and restaurant reviews.

Foodie in Québec City
www.foodiequebec.com

This English language blog covers all aspects of the food and restaurant scene in Québec City and beyond.

Montréal Eater
www.montreal.eater.com

A website that covers the eating habits and news of cities all over North America has recently added a Montréal version. Expect everything from exclusive interviews with local chefs to review round-ups.

Québec T'aime
www.quebectaime.com

This Québec City-based blog run by the hippest writers in the city offers information on everything from the 10 Best Ice Cream Shops to the latest art openings.

Said the Gramophone
www.saidthegramophone.com

Though not exclusively Montréal-based (one of the writers lives in Toronto), this music blog offers an interesting insider take on the Québec and Montréal music scenes.

Tourism Montréal
www.tourisme-montreal.org

The official tourism site for the city also has a number of bloggers dedicated to specific aspects of the city—gay, nightlife, women's interests—that keep the site fresh and interesting.

Voir
www.voir.ca

The online component to the Francophone alternative weekly, Voir has event listings, restaurant reviews, and a weekly webcast that takes you behind the scenes of the weekly photo shoot and gives you a rundown of the week's biggest events.

Index

M

NO

P

Restaurants Index

Nightlife Index

Québec City

Shops Index

Québec City

Hotels Index

Photo Credits

MOON MONTRÉAL & QUÉBEC CITY

Avalon Travel
a member of the Perseus Books Group
1700 Fourth Street
Berkeley, CA 94710, USA
www.moon.com

Editor: Leah Gordon
Series Manager: Erin Raber
Copy Editor: Naomi Adler-Dancis
Graphics Coordinator: Darren Alessi
Production Coordinator: Darren Alessi
Interior design: Domini Dragoone
Cover design: Faceout Studios, Charles Brock
Moon logo: Tim McGrath
Map Editor: Albert Angulo
Cartographers: Albert Angulo, Stephanie Poulain

ISBN-13: 978-1-61238-748-2
ISSN: 1559-3479

Printing History
1st Edition – 2006
3rd Edition – May 2014
5 4 3 2 1

clockwise from top left: treat yourself to a night at the newly revamped Ritz Carlton, Vieux-Montréal; Place d'Armes Hôtel and Suites; Fairmont Queen Elizabeth, Centre-Ville

Métro station. The rooms themselves, which are your standard hotel fare, have been freshened up with a recent renovation. Some guests might find the rooms to be noisy in the summer due to the air-conditioners. Parking is available just around the corner and Wi-Fi is free for guests. Breakfast isn't included at the hotel, but since it's next to a number of cafès and restaurants, finding a good meal is hardly a problem.

MAP 4: 1254 rue St-Denis, 514/849-4526, www.hotel-st-denis.com

La Loggia $

Located on Amherst in the center of the Village, this charming bed-and-breakfast serves up both art and breakfast. Situated in a three-story early-20th-century townhouse, the five rooms are all uniquely decorated with antique chairs, modern art, and personal touches, like vibrant cushions or Persian rugs, all of which give it a homey vibe. Close to the Plateau and Berri Métro station, the hotel offers packages that include private yoga classes, personal trainer sessions, or a course in sculpture. Breakfast is made with local, fair-trade, and organic ingredients and is served on the terrace in the summer.

MAP 4: 1637 rue Amherst, 514/524-2493, www.laloggia.ca

★ Sir Montcalm $$

This ultra-chic bed-and-breakfast in the Village—think matte black walls, sleek white linens, and ambient lighting—may cater to the LGBT community, but anyone with an eye for design will be instantly smitten. It's a perfect blend of comfortable yet polished. Perks include a day pass to the local gym, access to the gorgeous patio in summer, and a filling four-course breakfast. Close to Vieux-Montréal and the Métro, it's an urban oasis that's sure to please.

MAP 4: 1453 rue Montcalm, 514/522-7747, www.sirmontcalm.com

Plateau Mont-Royal

Map 5

Anne Ma Soeur Anne $

Situated in the middle of the Plateau close to Parc LaFontaine and the restaurant-filled avenue Duluth, this hotel is a good option for those traveling on a budget or those looking to stay in the heart of the action. The no-frills, studio apartment-sized rooms are comfortable enough, and most come equipped with Murphy beds that you can fold into the wall when not in use. Since it's directly above a jazz club, the noise, especially on weekends, will keep some guests up at night. The small rooms also come equipped with a micro kitchen for some simple self-catering.

MAP 5: 4119 rue St-Denis, 514/281-3187, www.annemasoeuranne.com

Auberge de la Fontaine $

This turn-of-the-20th-century townhouse looks out onto Parc LaFontaine, one of the most pleasant spots in the city. Three floors of rooms offer an intimate place to stay in a residential, mainly Francophone area. Though parking can be a bit of a hassle—the hotel only has three spots, the rest are on the street—it is situated on a bike path and is perfect for anyone wanting to bike the city. A buffet breakfast and free Wi-Fi are available, and guests also have access to the kitchen after hours, where they can help themselves to tea, coffee, and various snacks.

MAP 5: 1301 rue Rachel E., 514/597-0166, www.aubergedelafontaine.com

Gingerbread Manor $

Just off of Carré St-Louis between St-Denis and St-Laurent and located in a Victorian three-story townhouse built in 1885, this charming bed-and-breakfast is a different way to see the city. With large bay windows, original molding (it's named after the period's "gingerbread" ornamental details), and an attached carriage house, it harkens back to a bygone golden age. All five rooms are fitted with either a king or queen bed, have hardwood floors, and are uniquely furnished. Only one, however, has a private bath. A hot breakfast includes croissants and fruit salad, and they also have bikes available to rent.

MAP 5: 3445 ave. Laval, 514/597-2804, www.gingerbreadmanor.com

L'Hôtel de l'Institut $

As this is the training ground for future hotel staff, you're unlikely to find better service in the city. A recent renovation has modernized this 35-year-old hotel to rival the sleek design of just about any hotel in Montréal. With only 42 rooms, it is relatively small, but each room has its own balcony, affording views of the city. Ideally located in the Plateau, it is within walking distance to downtown and is directly above a Sherbrooke Métro station. The sole drawback is the slightly overpriced parking, which isn't always available.

MAP 5: 3535 rue St-Denis, 514/282-5120, www.ithq.qc.ca

Pensione Popolo $

The owners of cafè and music venue Casa del Popolo have opened a small, European-inspired pensione above the cafè (look for the red door). Ideally located on the border of the

Plateau and Mile End, it's perfect for the self-sufficient traveler looking for a no-frills bed. Bathrooms and the kitchen are shared, but the cozy rooms and the location above one of the city's hottest bars is worth it. Guests also get free passes to see bands playing during their stay, and the location alone, near tons of affordable restaurants and within walking distance of the city's coolest addresses, sweetens the deal.

MAP 5: 4871 blvd. St-Laurent, 514/284-0122, www.casadelpopolo.com